Cost and Management Accounting

AN INTRODUCTION

FIFTH EDITION

Cost and Management Accounting

AN INTRODUCTION

Colin Drury

THOMSON

Australia • Canada • Mexico • Singapore • Japan • United Kingdom • United States

Cost and Management Accounting: An Introduction – Fifth Edition

Copyright © 1987, 1990, 1994, 1998, 2003 Colin Drury

The Thomson logo is a registered trademark used herein under licence.

For more information, contact Thomson Learning, High Holborn House, 50–51 Bedford Row, London WC1R 4LR or visit us on the World Wide Web at: http://www.thomsonlearning.co.uk

British Library Cataloguing-in-Publication Data
A catalogue record for this book is available from the British Library

ISBN 1-86152-905-8

First edition published as Costing: An Introduction by Chapman and Hall, 2–6 Boundary Row, London, SE1 8HN

First edition 1987
Reprinted 1988, 1989
Second edition 1990
Reprinted 1991 (twice), 1992, 1993
Third edition 1994
Reprinted 1995
Reprinted 1996 by International Thomson Publishing
Fourth edition 1998 by International Thomson Publishing
Reprinted 2000
Reprinted 2001 by Thomson Learning
This edition published as Cost and Management Accounting: An Introduction 2003 by Thomson Learning

Typeset by Techset Composition Ltd, Salisbury, Great Britain

Printed by Zrinski, Croatia

Abbreviated contents

v

Contents

Part Two
Cost Accumulation for Inventory Valuation and Profit Measurement 39

Part Three
Information for Decision-making 197

Part Four
Information for Planning, Control and Performance Measurement   309

Preface

The aim of the fifth edition of this book is to provide an introduction to the theory and practice of cost and management accounting. A cost accounting system is concerned with accumulating costs for inventory valuation to meet external financial accounting and internal monthly or quarterly profit measurement requirements. A management accounting system accumulates, classifies, summarizes and reports information that will assist employees within an organization in their decision-making, planning, control and performance measurement activities. This book is concerned with both cost and management accounting, with equal emphasis being placed on both systems.

Intended primarily for students who are pursuing a one-year cost and management accounting course, the book is ideal for those approaching this subject for the first time. The more advanced topics contained in the final stages of the cost and management accounting syllabuses of the professional accountancy bodies and final year degree courses are not included. These topics are included in the author's successful *Management and Cost Accounting*, the fifth edition of which is also published by Thomson Learning.

Feedback from teachers in a large number of universities indicated that they had found the content, structure and presentation of *Management and Cost Accounting* extremely satisfactory and most appropriate for students pursuing a two-year management accounting course at an *advanced* professional or degree level. They also indicated that there was a need for a book (based on *Management and Cost Accounting*) tailored to meet the requirements of a one-year introductory course in cost and management accounting. Many lecturers, in particular those running introductory courses, felt there was a need for an introductory text which covered the required ground in an academically sound manner and which was also appropriate for students on non-advanced courses. This book is aimed specifically at students who are pursuing a one year non-advanced cost and management accountancy course and is particularly suitable for the following courses:

- Foundation/intermediate professional accountancy (e.g. Chartered Association of Certified Accountants, Chartered Institute of Management Accountants and one year college foundation courses)
- Association of Accounting Technicians at NVQ Levels 2, 3 and 4
- Higher national certificate and diploma in business and finance
- A first-level course for undergraduate accounting and finance or business students.

An introductory course in financial accounting is not a prerequisite, although many students will have undertaken such a course. The flexibility provided by modular courses can result in introductory classes consisting of a group of students not studying management accounting beyond an intermediate level and a further group continuing their studies beyond the intermediate level. *Cost and Management Accounting: An Introduction* is appropriate for the former group and *Management and Cost Accounting* can be adopted by the latter. Because much of the content (and most of the examples and questions) in *Cost and Management Accounting: An Introduction* has been extracted from *Management and Cost Accounting*, lecturers can assign identical reading and questions and also recommend two separate books that are geared to the specific requirements of the students.

Structure and plan of the book

In writing this book I have adopted the same structure as that in *Management and Cost Accounting*. The major theme is that different financial information is required for different purposes. The framework is based on the principle that there are three ways of constructing accounting information. The first is cost accounting with its emphasis on producing product costs for allocating costs between cost of goods sold and inventories to meet external and internal financial accounting inventory valuation and profit measurement requirements. The second is the notion of decision relevant costs with the emphasis on providing information to help managers to make good decisions. The third is responsibility accounting and performance measurement which focuses on both financial and non-financial information, in particular the assignment of costs and revenues to responsibility centres.

This book has 15 chapters divided into four parts. The first part (Part One) consists of two chapters and provides an introduction to cost and management accounting and a framework for studying the remaining chapters. The following three parts reflect the three different ways of constructing accounting information. Part Two consists of six chapters and is entitled 'Cost Accumulation for Inventory Valuation and Profit Measurement'. This section focuses mainly on assigning costs to products to separate the costs incurred during a period between costs of goods sold and the closing inventory valuation for internal and external profit measurement. The extent to which product costs accumulated for inventory valuation and profit measurement should be adjusted for meeting decision-making, cost control and performance measurement requirements is also briefly considered. Part Three consists of four chapters and is entitled 'Information for Decision-making'. Here the focus is on measuring and identifying those costs which are relevant for different types of decisions. The title of Part Four is 'Information for Planning, Control and Performance Measurement'. It consists of three chapters and concentrates on the process of translating goals and objectives into specific activities and the resources that are required, via the short-term (budgeting) and long-term planning processes, to achieve the goals and objectives. In addition, the management control systems that organizations use are described and the role that management accounting control systems play within the overall control process is examined. The emphasis here is on the accounting process as a means of providing information to help managers control the activities for which they are responsible.

In devising a framework around the three methods of constructing financial information there is a risk that the student will not appreciate that the three categories use many common elements, that they overlap, and that they constitute a single overall management accounting system, rather than three independent systems. I have taken steps to minimize this risk in each section by emphasizing why financial information for one purpose should or should not be adjusted for another purpose. In short, each section of the book is not presented in isolation and an integrative approach has been taken.

Major changes in the content of the fifth edition

During the late 1980s and the 1990s the theory and practice of management accounting have been subject to enormous changes. Some of these changes were described in the fourth edition of this book, published in 1998, but they were presented as emerging management accounting issues. They were also presented as separate topics, rather than being integrated with the existing theories, concepts and techniques. It was unclear at the time of writing the fourth edition whether the proposed changes would become part of mainstream management accounting. In the intervening years these changes have become firmly established in the literature and adopted by innovative companies around the world.

One of the major objectives in writing the fifth edition has therefore been to integrate some of the recent developments in management accounting with the established conventional wisdom of the subject. This objective created a need to review the content of the fourth edition and, besides integrating some of the recent developments, the opportunity was taken to rewrite and improve the presentation of much of the existing material. The end result has been an extensive rewrite of the text but the existing structure has been maintained.

The notable alterations are:

1. Since the publication of the first edition of the book the later editions have incorporated an increasing amount of management accounting as well as retaining the cost accounting element. To reflect the change in emphasis the title of the book has been changed from *Costing: An Introduction* to *Cost and Management Accounting: An Introduction.*

2. A substantial number of new end-of-chapter review problems with solutions have been added to enable students to practise typical examination problems and compare their solutions with those provided by the author.

3. Chapter 17 (Past, current and future developments in management accounting) of the fourth edition has been deleted. As indicated above the current and future developments that were considered to be relevant to the content of this book have been integrated with the established conventional wisdom.

4. Extensive changes have been made to Chapter 2 (Cost and revenue classification). The content is now presented in a revised Chapter 2 and re-titled 'An introduction to cost terms and concepts'.

5. Chapter 3 (Accounting for materials and labour) of the fourth edition has been rewritten and restructured. The order of the presentation of the material has been reversed with accounting for labour being presented prior to the accounting for materials. In addition, the content of Chapter 16 (Quantitative models for the planning and control of stocks) of the fourth edition has been reduced and incorporated into Chapter 3 of the fifth edition. This has enabled aspects relating to the accounting and control of materials to be co-ordinated and presented within a single chapter.

6. Chapter 4 (Accounting for overhead expenditure) has been rewritten and retitled 'Cost assignment'. The new chapter emphasizes cost system design issues and explains why the optimal cost system is different for different organizations. The factors that determine the choice of an optimal cost system for an organization are also discussed.

7. Less extensive changes have been made to Chapters 5–9 of the fourth edition. The content of Chapter 6 (Process costing) remains similar to the chapter of the previous edition but substantial changes have been made to the presentation. The

more complex material relating to losses in process and equivalent production has been transferred to the appendix of the chapter. This has resulted in a simplified and more concise presentation of the core material. Chapter 8 has been retitled 'Income effects of alternative cost accumulation systems'. New material relating to a mathematical model of profit functions for absorption and variable costing has also been included in this chapter. The most notable change in Chapter 9 (Cost–Volume–Profit analysis) is the inclusion of new material relating to multi-product cost–volume–profit analysis.

8. Chapter 10 (Special studies: measuring relevant costs for decision-making) has been substantially rewritten and is now titled 'Measuring relevant costs and revenues for decision-making.'

9. The chapter relating to activity-based-costing (Chapter 11) has also been extensively revised. A substantial amount of new material has been added. The example of overhead cost assignment introduced in Chapter 4 for a traditional costing system is extended to incorporate activity-based costing. In addition, more emphasis is given to ABC in service organizations.

10. Chapter 14 of the fourth edition (Operational control, management control and performance evaluation) has been replaced by a new chapter titled 'Management control systems.' To fully understand the role that management accounting control systems play in the control process, it is necessary to be aware of how they relate to the entire array of control mechanisms used by organizations. Chapter 14 describes the different types of controls that are used by companies. The elements of management accounting control systems are described within the context of the overall control process.

11. The end-of-chapter questions have been reviewed and revised to reflect the questions set by the professional accountancy bodies subsequent to the previous edition.

12. The fifth edition now includes a dedicated website.

International focus

Previous editions of this book have presented the content mainly within a UK setting. The book has now become an established text in many different countries throughout the world. Because of this, the fifth edition has adopted a more international focus and regulatory requirements and taxation aspects have not been restricted to a UK setting. A new feature is the presentation of boxed exhibits of surveys relating to management accounting in many different countries, particularly the European mainland. To simplify the presentation, however, the UK pound monetary unit has been used throughout the book. Most of the assessment material has incorporated questions set within a UK context. These questions are, however, appropriate for worldwide use.

Assessment material

Throughout this book I have kept the illustrations simple. You can check your understanding of each chapter by answering the end-of-chapter review problems and comparing your answers with the solutions that are provided. Additional questions without answers are also provided in a separate section at the end of the book. Solutions to these questions are provided in either the *Students' Manual* or the *Instructors' Manual.*

The *Students' Manual* suggests answers to the questions which are asterisked here in the main text and an *Instructors' Manual* provides answers to the remaining questions. Students are strongly recommended to purchase the *Students' Manual,* which complements this book. It contains suggested answers to over 200 questions. Both the *Students' Manual* and the *Instructors' Manual* have been revised and extended. New answers have been added and the content of both manuals has been substantially revised.

Supplementary material

DEDICATED WEBSITE

The dedicated website can be found at **www.thomsonlearning.co.uk/drury-online**. The lecturer section is password protected and the password is available free to lecturers who confirm their adoption of the fifth edition – lecturers should complete the registration form on the website to apply for their password, which will then be sent to them by email.

The following range of material is available.

For students and lecturers (open access)

Case studies
Internationally focused case studies. (NB Teaching notes to accompany the cases are available in the password protected lecturer area of the site). Additional case studies will be added to the website during the life of the fifth edition.

Testbank (compiled by Wayne Fiddler of Huddersfield University)
Interactive multiple choice questions to accompany each chapter. The student takes the test online to check their grasp of the key points in each chapter. Detailed feedback is provided for each question if the student chooses the wrong answer.

Links to accounting and finance sites on the web
Including links to the main accounting firms, accounting magazines and journals and careers and job search pages.

IEBM definitions
Alphabetical list of accounting and finance definitions taken from the pocket edition of the *International Encyclopedia of Business and Management.*

For lecturers only (password protected)

Instructors' manual
Available to download free from the site in PDF (Portable Document Format), the manual includes answers to the end of book questions that are not available to students. (Please note: the *Instructors' Manual* is also available in print format, free to adopting lecturers, ISBN 1-86152-924-4.)

Teaching notes to the case studies

To accompany the case studies available in the student area of the website.

Spreadsheet exercises (compiled and designed by Alicia Gazely of Nottingham Trent University)

Created in Excel to accompany the review problem exercises in the book, the exercises can be saved by the lecturer to their own directories and distributed to students as each topic is covered. Each exercise explains a basic spreadsheet technique which illustrates, and allows the student to explore, examples in the main text.

Overhead transparencies

Available to download free from the site in PDF.

PowerPoint™ slides

PowerPoint presentations to accompany each chapter.

PRINTED SUPPLEMENTARY MATERIALS

For lecturers

Lecturers who adopt this text are provided with the following comprehensive package of additional materials to assist in the preparation and delivery of courses:

Students' Manual (ISBN 1-86152-923-6)*
Instructors' Manual (ISBN 1-86152-924-4)*

*If you already have a copy of the text please order these individually. If you require the entire package, which includes the main text, the *Student's Manual* and the *Instructors' Manual*, please use ISBN 1-86152-995-3) to order the comprehensive Lecturer's Pack.

To order additional material please contact the publisher on info@thomsonlearning.co.uk or telephone the Customer Services Department on 44 (0) 1264 342 932 (Fax to 44 (0) 1264 342 761).

For students

A *Students' Manual* to help you work through the text is available from all good bookshops. Order it by quoting ISBN 1-86152-923-6.

Acknowledgements

I am indebted to many individuals for their ideas and assistance in preparing this and previous editions of the book. In particular, I would like to thank Jonathan Rooks of South Bank University and Rona O'Brien of Sheffield Hallam University for their in-depth comments. I would also like to thank the following for their valuable feedback.

- Pieter Koortzen – Polytechnic of Namibia
- John MacKenzie – Napier University
- Lau Siok Hwa – Multimedia University, Malaysia

- Chong Chin Wei – Multimedia University, Malaysia
- Mark Pilkington – University of Westminster
- Darren Duxbury – Leeds University Business School.

I am also indebted to Patrick Bond at Thomson Learning for his valuable publishing advice, support and assistance; and to all of the staff at Thomson Learning who have worked on the book; in particular, Fiona Freel and Anna Herbert. My appreciation goes also to the Chartered Institute of Management Accountants, the Chartered Association of Certified Accountants, the Institute of Chartered Accountants in England and Wales, and the Association of Accounting Technicians for permission to reproduce examination questions. Questions from the Chartered Institute of Management Accountants' examinations are designated CIMA; questions from the Chartered Association of Certified Accountants are designated CACA or ACCA; questions from the Institute of Chartered Accountants in England and Wales are designated ICAEW; and questions from the Association of Accounting Technicians are designated AAT. The answers in the accompanying teachers' and students' guides to this book are my own and are in no way the approved solutions of the above professional bodies. Finally, and most importantly I would like to thank my wife, Bronwen, for converting the original manuscript of the earlier editions into final type-written form and for her continued help and support throughout the five editions of this book.

PART ONE

Introduction to Cost and Management Accounting

The objective of this section is to provide an introduction to management and cost accounting. In Chapter 1 we define accounting and distinguish between financial, management and cost accounting. This is followed by an examination of the role of management accounting in providing information to managers for decision-making, planning, control and performance measurement. In addition, the important changes that are taking place in the business environment are considered. Progression through the book will reveal how some of these changes are influencing management accounting systems. In Chapter 2 the basic cost terms and concepts that are used in the management accounting literature are described.

Introduction to management accounting

There are many definitions of accounting, but the one that captures the theme of this book is the definition formulated by the American Accounting Association. It describes accounting as

> the process of identifying, measuring and communicating economic information to permit informed judgements and decisions by users of the information.

In other words, accounting is concerned with providing both financial and non-financial information that will help decision-makers to make good decisions. An understanding of accounting therefore requires an understanding of the decision-making process and an awareness of the users of accounting information.

During the past decade many organizations in both the manufacturing and service sectors have faced dramatic changes in their business environment. Deregulation combined with extensive competition from overseas companies in domestic markets has resulted in a situation where most companies are now competing in a highly competitive global market. At the same time there has been a significant reduction in product life cycles arising from technological innovations and the need to meet increasingly discriminating customer demands. To compete successfully in today's highly competitive global environment companies are making customer satisfaction an overriding priority, adopting new management approaches, changing their manufacturing systems and investing in new technologies. These changes are having a significant influence on management accounting systems. Progression through the book will reveal how these changes are influencing management accounting systems, but first of all it is important that you have a good background knowledge of some of the important changes that are occurring in the business environment. This chapter aims to provide such knowledge.

The objective of this first chapter is to provide the background knowledge that will enable you to achieve a more meaningful insight into the issues and problems of management accounting

Learning objectives

After studying this chapter, you should be able to:

- differentiate between management accounting, cost accounting and financial accounting;
- list and describe each of the seven factors involved in the decision-making, planning and control process;
- justify the view that, broadly, firms seek to maximize the present value of future net cash inflows;
- explain the factors that have influenced the changes in the competitive environment;
- outline the key success factors that directly affect customer satisfaction;
- describe the functions of a management accounting system.

that are discussed in the book. We begin by looking at the users of accounting information and identifying their requirements. This is followed by a description of the decision-making process and the changing business and manufacturing environment. Finally, the different functions of management accounting are described.

The users of accounting information

Accounting is a language that communicates financial and non-financial information to people who have an interest in an organization – managers, shareholders and potential investors, employees, creditors and the government. Managers require information that will assist them in their decision-making and control activities; for example, information is needed on the estimated selling prices, costs, demand, competitive position and profitability of various products that are made by the organization. Shareholders require information on the value of their investment and the income that is derived from their shareholding. Employees require information on the ability of the firm to meet wage demands and avoid redundancies. Creditors and the providers of loan capital require information on a firm's ability to meets its financial obligations. Government agencies like the Central Statistical Office collect accounting information and require such information as the details of sales activity, profits, investments, stocks, dividends paid, the proportion of profits absorbed by taxation and so on. In addition, the tax authorities need information on the amount of profits that are subject to taxation. All this information is important for determining policies to manage a country's economy.

Accounting information is not confined to business organizations. Accounting information about individuals is also important and is used by other individuals; for example, credit will only be extended to an individual after the prospective borrower has furnished a reasonable accounting of his or her private financial affairs. Non-profit-making organizations such as churches, charitable organizations, clubs and government units such as local authorities, also require accounting information for decision-making, and for reporting the results of their activities. For example, a tennis club will require information on the cost of undertaking its various activities so that a decision can be made as to the amount of the annual subscription that it will charge to its members. Similarly, local authorities need information on the costs of undertaking specific activities so that decisions can be made as to which activities will be undertaken and the resources that must be raised to finance them.

The foregoing discussion has indicated that there are many users of accounting information who require information for decision-making. The objective of accounting is to provide sufficient information to meet the needs of the various users at the lowest possible cost. Obviously, the benefit derived from using an information system for decision-making must be greater than the cost of operating the system.

An examination of the various users of accounting information indicates that they can be divided into two categories:

1. internal parties within the organization;
2. external parties such as shareholders, creditors and regulatory agencies, outside the organization.

It is possible to distinguish between two branches of accounting, that reflect the internal and external users of accounting information. **Management accounting** is concerned with the provision of information to people within the organization to help them make better decisions and improve the efficiency and effectiveness of existing operations, whereas **financial accounting** is concerned with the provision of information to external parties outside the organization. Thus, management accounting could be called internal accounting and financial accounting could be called external accounting. This book concentrates on management accounting.

Differences between management accounting and financial accounting

The major differences between these two branches of accounting are:

- *Legal requirements.* There is a statutory requirement for public limited companies to produce annual financial accounts regardless of whether or not management regards this information as useful. Management accounting, by contrast, is entirely optional and information should be produced only if it is considered that the benefits from the use of the information by management exceed the cost of collecting it.

- *Focus on individual parts or segments of the business.* Financial accounting reports describe the whole of the business whereas management accounting focuses on small parts of the organization, for example the cost and profitability of products, services, customers and activities. In addition, management accounting information measures the economic performance of decentralized operating units, such as divisions and departments.

- *Generally accepted accounting principles.* Financial accounting statements must be prepared to conform with the legal requirements and the generally accepted accounting principles established by the regulatory bodies such as the Financial Accounting Standards Board (FASB) in the USA and the Accounting Standards Board (ASB) in the UK. These requirements are essential to ensure the uniformity and consistency that is needed for external financial statements. Outside users need assurance that external statements are prepared in accordance with generally accepted accounting principles so that inter-company and historical comparisons are possible. In contrast, management accountants are not required to adhere to generally accepted accounting principles when providing managerial information for internal purposes. Instead, the focus is on serving management's needs and providing information that is useful to managers relating to their decision-making, planning and control functions.

- *Time dimension.* Financial accounting reports what has happened in the past in an organization, whereas management accounting is concerned with *future* information as well as past information. Decisions are concerned with *future* events and management therefore requires details of expected *future* costs and revenues.

- *Report frequency.* A detailed set of financial accounts is published annually and less detailed accounts are published semi-annually. Management requires information quickly if it is to act on it. Consequently management accounting reports on various activities may be prepared at daily, weekly or monthly intervals.

The decision-making process

Because information produced by management accountants must be judged in the light of its ultimate effect on the outcome of decisions, a necessary precedent to an understanding of management accounting is an understanding of the *decision-making process*.

FIGURE 1.1 *The decision-making, planning and control process.*

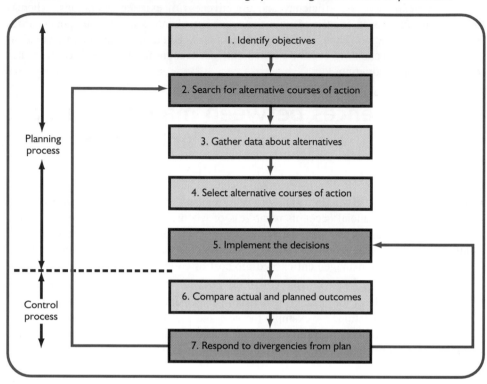

Figure 1.1 presents a diagram of a decision-making model. The first five stages represent the decision-making or the planning process. **Planning** involves making choices between alternatives and is primarily a decision-making activity. The final two stages represent the *control process*, which is the process of measuring and correcting actual performance to ensure that the alternatives that are chosen and the plans for implementing them are carried out. Let us now consider each of the elements of the decision-making and control process.

IDENTIFYING OBJECTIVES

Before good decisions can be made there must be some guiding aim or direction that will enable the decision-makers to assess the desirability of favouring one course of action over another. Hence, the first stage in the decision-making process should be to specify the **goals** or **objectives of the organization**.

Considerable controversy exists as to what the objectives of firms are or should be. Economic theory normally assumes that firms seek to maximize profits for the owners of the firm (the ordinary shareholders in a limited company) or, more precisely, the maximization of shareholders' wealth. Various arguments have been used to support the profit maximization objective. There is the legal argument that the ordinary shareholders are the owners of the firm, which therefore should be run for their benefit by trustee managers. Another argument supporting the profit objective is that profit maximization leads to the maximization of overall economic welfare. That is, by doing the best for yourself, you are unconsciously doing the best for society. Moreover, it seems a reasonable belief that the interests of firms will be better served by a larger profit than by a smaller profit, so that maximization is at least a useful approximation.

Some writers (e.g. Simon, 1959) believe that businessmen are content to find a plan that provides satisfactory profits rather than to maximize profits. Because people have limited powers of understanding and can deal with only a limited amount of information at a time (Simon uses the term **bounded rationality** to describe these constraints), they tend to search for solutions only until the first acceptable solution is found. No further attempt is made to find an even better solution or to continue the search until the best solution is discovered. Such behaviour, where the search is terminated on finding a satisfactory, rather than optimal solution, is known as **satisficing**.

Cyert and March (1969) have argued that the firm is a coalition of various different groups – shareholders, employees, customers, suppliers and the government – each of whom must be paid a minimum to participate in the coalition. Any excess benefits after meeting these minimum constraints are seen as being the object of bargaining between the various groups. In addition, a firm is subject to constraints of a societal nature. Maintaining a clean environment, employing disabled workers and providing social and recreation facilities are all examples of social goals that a firm may pursue.

Clearly it is too simplistic to say that the only objective of a business firm is to maximize profits. Some managers seek to establish a power base and build an empire; another goal is security; the removal of uncertainty regarding the future may override the pure profit motive. Nevertheless, the view adopted in this book is that, broadly, firms seek to maximize the value of future net cash inflows (that is, future cash receipts less cash payments) or to be more precise the present value of future net cash inflows.[1] This is equivalent to maximizing shareholder value. (The concept of present value is explained in Chapter 12.) The reasons for choosing this objective are as follows:

1. It is unlikely that any other objective is as widely applicable in measuring the ability of the organization to survive in the future.

2. It is unlikely that maximizing the present value of future cash flows can be realized in practice, but by establishing the principles necessary to achieve this objective you will learn how to increase the present value of future cash flows.

3. It enables shareholders as a group in the bargaining coalition to know how much the pursuit of other goals is costing them by indicating the amount of cash distributed among the members of the coalition.

THE SEARCH FOR ALTERNATIVE COURSES OF ACTION

The second stage in the decision-making model is a search for a range of possible courses of action (or **strategies**) that might enable the objectives to be achieved. If the management of a company concentrates entirely on its present product range and markets, and market shares and cash flows are allowed to decline, there is a danger that the company will be unable to generate sufficient cash flows to survive in the future. To maximize future cash flows, it is essential that management identifies potential opportunities and threats in its current environment and takes specific steps immediately so that the organization will not be taken by surprise by any developments which may occur in the future. In particular, the company should consider one or more of the following courses of action:

1. developing *new* products for sale in *existing* markets;
2. developing *new* products for *new* markets;
3. developing *new* markets for *existing* products.

The search for alternative courses of action involves the acquisition of information concerning future opportunities and environments; it is the most difficult and important stage of the decision-making process. Ideally, firms should consider all alternative courses of action, but, in practice they consider only a few alternatives, with the search process being localized initially. If this type of routine search activity fails to produce satisfactory solutions, the search will become more widespread (Cyert and March, 1969).

GATHER DATA ABOUT ALTERNATIVES

When potential areas of activity are identified, management should assess the potential growth rate of the activities, the ability of the company to establish adequate market shares, and the cash flows for each alternative activity for various **states of nature**. Because decision problems exist in an uncertain environment, it is necessary to consider certain factors that are outside the decision-maker's control, which may occur for each alternative course of action. These uncontrollable factors are called states of nature. Some examples of possible states of nature are economic boom, high inflation, recession, the strength of competition and so on.

The course of action selected by a firm using the information presented above will commit its resources for a lengthy period of time, and show how the overall place of the firm will be affected within its environment – that is, the products it makes, the markets it operates in and its ability to meet future changes. Such decisions dictate the firm's long-run possibilities and hence the type of decisions it can make in the future. These decisions are normally referred to as **long-run** or **strategic decisions**. Strategic decisions have a profound effect on the firm's future position, and it is therefore essential that adequate data are gathered about the firm's capabilities and the environment in which it operates. Because of their importance, strategic decisions should be the concern of top management.

Besides strategic or long-term decisions, management must also make decisions that do not commit the firm's resources for a lengthy period of time. Such decisions are known as **short-term** or **operating decisions** and are normally the concern of lower-level managers. Short-term decisions are based on the environment of today, and the physical, human and financial resources presently available to the firm. These are, to a considerable extent, determined by the quality of the firm's long-term decisions. Examples of short-term decisions include the following.

1. What selling prices should be set for the firm's products?
2. How many units should be produced of each product?
3. What media should we use for advertising the firm's products?
4. What level of service should we offer customers in terms of the number of days required to deliver an order and the after-sales service?

Data must also be gathered for short-term decisions; for example, data on the selling prices of competitors' products, estimated demand at alternative selling prices, and predicted costs for different activity levels must be assembled for pricing and output decisions. When the data have been gathered, management must decide which courses of action to take.

SELECT APPROPRIATE ALTERNATIVE COURSES OF ACTION

In practice, decision-making involves choosing between competing alternative courses of action and selecting the alternative that best satisfies the objectives of an organization. Assuming that our objective is to maximize future net cash inflows, the alternative selected should be based on a comparison of the differences between the cash flows. Consequently, an incremental analysis of the net cash benefits for each alternative should be applied. The alternatives are ranked in terms of net cash benefits, and those showing the greatest benefits are chosen subject to taking into account any qualitative factors. We shall discuss how incremental cash flows are measured for short-term and long-term decisions and the impact of qualitative factors in Chapters 9–12.

IMPLEMENTATION OF THE DECISIONS

Once alternative courses of action have been selected, they should be implemented as part of the budgeting process. The **budget** is a financial plan for implementing the various decisions that management has made. The budgets for all of the various decisions are expressed in terms of cash inflows and outflows, and sales revenues and expenses. These budgets are merged together into a single unifying statement of the organization's expectations for future periods. This statement is known as a **master budget**. The master budget consists of a budgeted profit and loss account, cash flow statement and balance sheet. The budgeting process communicates to everyone in the organization the part that they are expected to play in implementing management's decisions. Chapter 13 focuses on the budgeting process.

COMPARING ACTUAL AND PLANNED OUTCOMES AND RESPONDING TO DIVERGENCIES FROM PLAN

The final stages in the process outlined in Figure 1.1 of comparing actual and planned outcomes and responses to divergencies from plan represent the firm's control process. The managerial function of **control** consists of the measurement, reporting and subsequent correction of performance in an attempt to ensure that the firm's objectives and plans are achieved. In other words, the objective of the control process is to ensure that the work is done so as to fulfil the original intentions.

To monitor performance, the accountant produces **performance reports** and presents them to the appropriate managers who are responsible for implementing the various decisions. Performance reports consisting of a comparison of actual outcomes (actual costs and revenues) and planned outcomes (budgeted costs and revenues) should be issued at regular intervals. Performance reports provide **feedback** information by comparing planned and actual outcomes. Such reports should highlight those activities that do not conform to plans, so that managers can devote their scarce time to focusing on these items. This process represents the application of **management by exception**. Effective control requires that corrective action is taken so that actual outcomes conform to planned outcomes. Alternatively, the plans may require modification if the comparisons indicate that the plans are no longer attainable.

The process of taking corrective action so that actual outcomes conform to planned outcomes, or the modification of the plans if the comparisons indicate that actual outcomes do not conform to planned outcomes, is indicated by the arrowed lines in Figure 1.1 linking stages 7 and 5 and 7 and 2. These arrowed lines represent '**feedback loops**'. They signify that the process is dynamic and stress the interdependencies between the various stages in the process. The feedback loop between stages 7 and 2 indicates that the plans should be regularly reviewed, and if they are no longer attainable then alternative courses of action must be considered for achieving the organization's objectives. The second loop stresses the corrective action taken so that actual outcomes conform to planned outcomes. Chapters 13–15 focus on the planning and control process.

Changing competitive environment

Prior to the 1980s many organizations in Western countries operated in a protected competitive environment. Barriers of communication and geographical distance, and sometimes protected markets, limited the ability of overseas companies to compete in domestic markets. There was little incentive for firms to maximize efficiency and improve management practices, or to minimize costs, as cost increases could often be passed on to customers. During the 1980s, however, manufacturing organizations began to encounter severe competition from overseas competitors that offered high-quality products at low prices. By establishing global networks for acquiring raw materials and distributing goods overseas, competitors were able to gain access to domestic markets throughout the world. To be successful companies now have to compete not only against domestic competitors but also against the best companies in the world.

Virtually all types of service organization have also faced major changes in their competitive environment. Before the 1980s many service organizations, such as those operating in the airlines, utilities and financial service industries, were either government-owned monopolies or operated in a highly regulated, protected and non-competitive environment. These organizations were not subject to any great pressure to improve the quality and efficiency of their operations or to improve profitability by eliminating services or products that were making losses. Furthermore, more efficient competitors were often prevented from entering the markets in which the regulated companies operated. Prices were set to cover operating costs and provide a predetermined return on capital. Hence cost increases could often be absorbed by increasing the prices of the services. Little attention was therefore given to developing cost systems that accurately measured the costs and profitability of individual services.

Privatization of government-controlled companies and deregulation in the 1980s completely changed the competitive environment in which service companies operated. Pricing and competitive restrictions have been virtually eliminated. Deregulation, intensive competition and an expanding product range created the need for service organizations to focus on cost management and develop management accounting information systems that enabled them to understand their cost base and determine the sources of profitability for their products, customers and markets. Many service organizations have only recently turned their attention to management accounting.

Focus on customer satisfaction and new management approaches

In order to compete in today's competitive environment companies are having to become more 'customer-driven' and make customer satisfaction an overriding priority. Customers are demanding ever-improving levels of service in cost, quality, reliability, delivery, and the choice of innovative new products. Figure 1.2 illustrates this focus on customer satisfaction as the overriding priority. In order to provide customer satisfaction organizations must concentrate on those key success factors that directly affect it. Figure 1.2 identifies cost efficiency, quality, time and innovation as the key success factors. In addition to concentrating on these factors organizations are adopting new management approaches in their quest to achieve customer satisfaction. These new approaches are illustrated in

FIGURE 1.2 *Focus on customer satisfaction.*

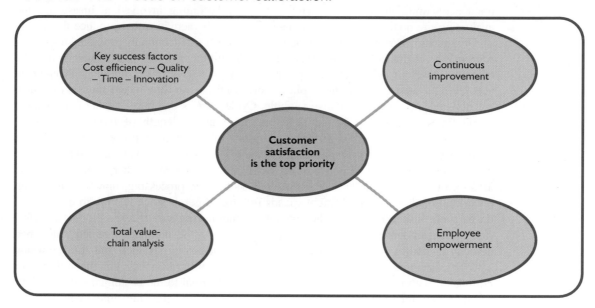

Figure 1.2. They are continuous improvement, employee empowerment and total value-chain analysis. Let us now examine each of the items shown in Figure 1.2 in more detail.

Since customers will buy the product with the lowest price, all other things being equal, keeping costs low and being **cost efficient** provides an organization with a strong competitive advantage. Increased competition has also made decision errors due to poor cost information more probable and more costly. If the cost system results in distorted product costs being reported, then overcosted products will lead to higher bid prices and business lost to those competitors who are able to quote lower prices purely because their cost systems produce more accurate cost information. Alternatively, there is a danger that undercosted products will result in the acceptance of unprofitable business.

These developments have made many companies aware of the need to improve their cost systems so that they can produce more accurate cost information to determine the cost of their products, pinpoint loss-making activities and analyse profits by products, sales outlets, customers and markets.

In addition to demanding low cost products, customers are demanding high quality products and services. Most companies are responding to this by focusing on **total quality management** (TQM). The goal of TQM is customer satisfaction. TQM is a term used to describe a situation where *all* business functions are involved in a process of continuous quality improvement. TQM has broadened from its early concentration on the statistical monitoring of manufacturing processes, to a customer-oriented process of continuous improvement that focuses on delivering products or services of consistently high quality in a timely fashion.

Most European and American companies had always considered quality an additional cost of manufacturing, but by the end of the 1980s they began to realize that quality saved money. The philosophy had been to emphasize production volume over quality; but this resulted in high levels of stocks at each production stage in order to protect against shortages caused by inferior quality at previous stages and excessive expenditure on inspection, rework, scrap and warranty repairs. Companies discovered that it was cheaper to produce the items correctly the first time rather than to waste resources making substandard items that had to be detected, reworked, scrapped or returned by customers. In other words, the emphasis in TQM is to design and build quality in rather than trying to inspect and repair it. The emphasis on TQM has created fresh demands on the management accounting function to expand its role by becoming involved in measuring and evaluating the quality of products and services and the activities that produce them.

Organizations are also seeking to increase customer satisfaction by providing a speedier response to customer requests, ensuring 100% on-time delivery and reducing the time taken to develop and bring new products to market. For these reasons management accounting systems are starting to place more emphasis on **time-based measures**, which are now an important competitive variable. **Cycle time** is one measure that management accounting systems have begun to focus on. It is the length of time from start to completion of a product or service. It consists of the sum of processing time, move time, wait time and inspection time. Move time is the amount of time it takes to transfer the product during the production process from one location to another. Wait time is the amount of time that the product sits around waiting for processing, moving, inspecting, reworking or the amount of time it spends in finished goods stock waiting to be sold and despatched. Inspection time is the amount of time making sure that the product is defect free or the amount of time actually spent reworking the product to remedy identified defects in quality. Only processing time adds value to the product, and the remaining

activities are **non-value added activities** in the sense that they can be reduced or eliminated without altering the product's service potential to the customer. Organizations are therefore focusing on minimizing cycle time by reducing the time spent on such activities. The management accounting system has an important role to play in this process by identifying and reporting on the time devoted to value added and non-value added activities.

The final key success factor shown in Figure 1.2 relates to **innovation**. To be successful companies must develop a steady stream of innovative new products and services and have the capability to adapt to changing customer requirements. It has already been stressed earlier in this chapter that being later to the market than competitors can have a dramatic effect on product profitability. Companies have therefore begun to incorporate performance measures that focus on flexibility and innovation in their management accounting

systems. Flexibility relates to the responsiveness in meeting customer requirements. Flexibility measures include the total launch time for new products, the length of development cycles and the ability to change the production mix quickly. Innovation measures include an assessment of the key characteristics of new products relative to those of competitors, feedback on customer satisfaction with the new features and characteristics of newly introduced products, and the number of new products launched and their launch time.

You can see by referring to Figure 1.2 that organizations are attempting to achieve customer satisfaction by adopting a philosophy of **continuous improvement**. Traditionally, organizations have sought to study activities and establish standard operating procedures and materials requirements based on observing and establishing optimum input/output relationships. Operators were expected to follow the standard procedures and management accountants developed systems and measurements that compared actual results with predetermined standards. This process created a climate whereby the predetermined standards represented a target to be achieved and maintained rather than a policy of continuous improvement. In today's competitive environment performance against static historical standards is no longer appropriate. To compete successfully companies must adopt a philosophy of continuous improvement, an ongoing process that involves a continuous search to reduce costs, eliminate waste and improve the quality and performance of activities that increase customer value or satisfaction.

Benchmarking is a technique that is increasingly being adopted as a mechanism for achieving continuous improvement. It is a continuous process of measuring a firm's products, services or activities against the other best performing organizations, either internal or external to the firm. The objective is to ascertain how the processes and activities can be improved. Ideally, benchmarking should involve an external focus on the latest developments, best practice and model examples that can be incorporated within various operations of business organizations. It therefore represents the ideal way of moving forward and achieving high competitive standards.

In their quest for the continuous improvement of organizational activities managers have found that they have had to rely more on the people closest to the operating processes and customers to develop new approaches to performing activities. This has led to employees being provided with relevant information to enable them to make continuous improvements to the output of processes. Allowing employees to take such actions without the authorization of superiors has come to be known as **employee empowerment**. It is argued that by empowering employees and giving them relevant information they will be able to respond faster to customers, increase process flexibility, reduce cycle time and improve morale. Management accounting is therefore moving from its traditional emphasis on providing information to managers to monitor the activities of employees to providing information to employees to empower them to focus on the continuous improvement of activities.

Increasing attention is now being given to **value-chain analysis** as a means of increasing customer satisfaction and managing costs more effectively. The value chain is illustrated in Figure 1.3. It is the linked set of value-creating activities all the way from basic raw material sources for component suppliers through to the ultimate end-use product or service delivered to the customer. Coordinating the individual parts of the value chain together to work as a team creates the conditions to improve customer satisfaction, particularly in terms of cost efficiency, quality and delivery. It is also appropriate to view the value chain from the customer's perspective, with each link being seen as the customer of the previous link. If each link in the value chain is designed to meet the needs of its customers, then end-customer satisfaction should ensue. Furthermore, by viewing each link in the value chain as a supplier–customer relationship, the opinions of the customers can be used to provide useful feedback information on assessing the quality of service provided by the supplier. Opportunities are thus identified for improving activities throughout the entire value chain.

Finally, there is one aspect of customer satisfaction that is not specified in Figure 1.2 – namely, **social responsibility** and **corporate ethics**. Customers are no longer satisfied if companies simply comply with the legal requirements of undertaking their activities. They expect company managers to be more proactive in terms of their social responsibility. Company stakeholders are now giving high priority to social responsibility, safety and environmental issues, besides corporate ethics. In response to these pressures many companies are now introducing a code of ethics as an essential part of their corporate culture. In addition, professional accounting organizations play an important role in promoting a high standard of ethical behaviour by their members. Both of the professional bodies representing management accountants in the UK (Chartered Institute of Management Accountants) and the USA (Institute of Management Accountants) have issued a code of ethical guidelines for their members.

The impact of the changing environment of management accounting systems

All of the changes in the business environment that have been described in this chapter are having a significant influence on management accounting systems. Most organizations

FIGURE 1.3 *The value chain.*

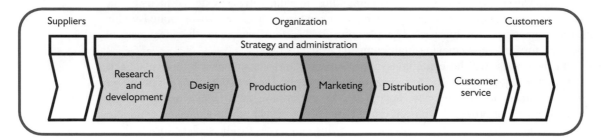

have faced changing cost structures with a growth in those costs which do not change directly with changes in output, and which are difficult to trace accurately to products or services. This change in cost structure has created a need for organizations to review their existing management accounting systems and consider implementing new systems that have emerged during the late 1980s and early 1990s.

In today's world-wide competitive environment we have noted that companies are competing in terms of product (or service) quality, delivery, reliability, after-sales service and customer satisfaction. Until recently management accounting systems have not reported on these variables, despite the fact that they represent key competitive variables. Traditionally management accounting systems have focused mainly on reporting financial measures. However, in response to the changing environment, management accounting systems have begun to place greater emphasis on collecting and reporting non-financial quantitative and qualitative information on those key variables that are necessary to compete effectively and which also support the strategies of an organization. There has been a shift from treating financial figures as the foundation of the management accounting system to treating them as part of a broader set of measures.

Functions of management accounting

A cost and management accounting system should generate information to meet the following requirements. It should:

1. allocate costs between cost of goods sold and inventories for internal and external profit reporting;
2. provide relevant information to help managers make better decisions;
3. provide information for planning, control and performance measurement.

Financial accounting rules require that we match costs with revenues to calculate profit. Consequently any unsold finished goods stock or partly completed stock (work in progress) will *not* be included in the cost of goods sold, which is matched against sales revenue during a given period. In an organization that produces a wide range of different products it will be necessary, for stock (inventory) valuation purposes, to charge the costs to each individual product. The total value of the stocks of completed products and work in progress plus any unused raw materials forms the basis for determining the inventory valuation to be deducted from the current period's costs when calculating profit. This total is also the basis for determining the stock valuation for inclusion in the balance sheet. Costs are therefore traced to each individual job or product for financial accounting requirements in order to allocate the costs incurred during a period between cost of goods sold and inventories. This information is required for meeting external financial accounting requirements, but most organizations also produce *internal* profit reports at monthly intervals. Thus product costs are also required for periodic internal profit reporting. Many service organizations, however, do not carry any stocks and product costs are therefore not required by these organizations for valuing inventories.

The second requirement of a cost and management accounting system is to provide relevant financial information to managers to help them make better decisions. This involves both routine and non-routine reporting. Routine information is required relating to the profitability of various segments of the business such as products, services, customers and distribution channels in order to ensure that only profitable activities are undertaken. Information is also required for making resource allocation and product mix and discontinuation decisions. In some situations cost information extracted from the costing system also plays a crucial role in determining selling prices, particularly in markets where customized products and services are provided that do not have readily available market prices. Non-routine information is required for strategic decisions. These decisions are made at infrequent intervals and include decisions relating to the development and introduction of new products and services, investment in new plant and equipment and the negotiation of long-term contracts with customers and suppliers.

Accurate cost information is required in decision-making for distinguishing between profitable and unprofitable activities. If the cost system does not capture accurately enough the consumption of resources by products, the reported product (or service) costs will be distorted, and there is a danger that managers may drop profitable products or continue the production of unprofitable products. Where cost information is used to determine selling prices the undercosting of products can result in the acceptance of unprofitable business whereas overcosting can result in bids being rejected and the loss of profitable business.

Management accounting systems should also provide information for planning, control and performance measurement. Planning involves translating goals and objectives into the specific activities and resources that are required to achieve the goals and objectives. Companies develop both long-term and short-term plans and the management accounting function plays a critical role in this process. Short-term plans, in the form of the budgeting process, are prepared in more detail than the longer-term plans and are one of the mechanisms used by managers as a basis for control and performance evaluation. Control is the process of ensuring that the actual outcomes conform with the planned outcomes. The control process involves the setting of targets or standards (often derived from the budgeting process) against which actual results are measured. Performance is then measured and compared with the targets on a periodic basis. The management accountant's role is to provide managers with feedback information in the form of periodic reports, suitably analysed, to enable them to determine if operations are proceeding according to plan and identify those activities where corrective action is necessary. In particular, the management accounting function should provide economic feedback to managers to assist them in controlling costs and improving the efficiency and effectiveness of operations.

It is appropriate at this point to distinguish between cost accounting and management accounting. **Cost accounting** is concerned with cost accumulation for inventory valuation to meet the requirements of external reporting and internal profit measurement, whereas **management accounting** relates to the provision of appropriate information for decision-making, planning, control and performance evaluation. It is apparent from an examination of the literature that the distinction between cost accounting and management accounting is extremely vague with some writers referring to the decision-making aspects in terms of 'cost accounting' and other writers using the term 'management accounting'; the two terms are often used synonymously. In this book no attempt will be made to distinguish between these two terms.

You should now be aware from the above discussion that a management accounting system serves multiple purposes. The emphasis throughout the book is that costs must be assembled in different ways for different purposes. A firm can choose to have multiple accounting systems (i.e. a separate system for each purpose) or one basic accounting system and set of accounts that serve inventory valuation and profit measurement, decision-making and performance evaluation requirements. Most firms choose, on the basis of costs versus benefits criteria, to operate a single accounting system. A single database is maintained with costs appropriately coded and classified so that relevant cost information can be extracted to meet each of the above requirements. Where future cost information is required the database may be maintained at target (standard) costs, or if actual costs are recorded, they are adjusted for anticipated price changes. We shall examine in the next chapter how relevant cost information can be extracted from a single database and adjusted to meet different user requirements.

Summary of the contents of this book

This book is divided into four parts. The first part (Part One) consists of two chapters and provides an introduction to cost and management accounting and a framework for studying the remaining chapters. Part Two consists of six chapters and is entitled 'Cost Accumulation for Inventory Valuation and Profit Measurement'. This section focuses mainly on cost accounting. It is concerned with assigning costs to products to separate costs incurred during a period between costs of goods sold and the closing inventory valuation. The extent to which product costs accumulated for inventory valuation and profit measurement should be adjusted for meeting decision-making, cost control and performance measurement requirements is also briefly considered. Part Three consists of four chapters and is entitled 'Information for Decision-making'. Here the focus is on measuring and identifying those costs which are relevant for different types of decisions.

The title of Part Four is 'Information for Planning, Control and Performance Measurement'. It consists of three chapters and concentrates on the process of translating goals and objectives into specific activities and the resources that are required, via the short-term (budgeting) and long-term planning processes, to achieve the goals and objectives. In addition, the management control systems that organizations use are described and the role that management accounting control systems play within the overall control process is examined. The emphasis here is on the accounting process as a means of providing information to help managers control the activities for which they are responsible.

Summary

Accounting is defined as the process of identifying, measuring and communicating financial and non-financial information to permit informed judgements and decisions by users of the information. We have distinguished between internal users (management accounting) and external users (financial accounting), and have considered a decision-making, planning and control model.

This chapter has also described some of the major changes in the business environment which organizations have faced over the past decade. Intensive competition from overseas companies has resulted in a situation where most companies are now having to operate in a highly competitive global market. Technical innovation and customer demands for a constant stream of innovative products have also resulted in a significant reduction in product life cycles. To compete successfully in today's highly competitive environment companies are finding that it is in their best interests to make customer satisfaction a top priority.

In order to provide customer satisfaction organizations must concentrate on four key success factors: cost efficiency, quality, time and innovation. Companies must manage their costs effectively if they are to become low cost suppliers and compete on the basis of selling price. Total quality management is a customer-oriented process that focuses on delivering products or services of consistent high quality in a timely fashion. Customers also value a prompt service and a speedy response to their request for products or services. Organizations have therefore begun to concentrate on time-based measures that focus on the length of time it takes to complete various activities. Finally, there is now an increasing awareness that a continuous flow of innovative products is essential to an organization's continued success. In addition to concentrating on key success factors, organizations are adopting new management approaches such as continuous improvement and employee empowerment.

Conventional management accounting systems were designed for use in an environment which is very different from that of today. It is therefore important that, where necessary, management accounting systems are modified to meet the requirements of today's manufacturing and global competitive environment.

Finally, three different objectives of a management accounting system were described. They are:

1. to allocate costs between cost of goods sold and inventories for internal and external profit reporting;
2. to provide relevant information to help managers make better decisions;
3. to provide information for planning, operational control and performance measurement.

Notes

1 The Statement of Standard Accounting Practice on Stocks and Work in Progress (SSAP 9) requires that all manufacturing costs be regarded as product costs.

Key Terms and Concepts

Each chapter includes a section like this. You should make sure that you understand each of the terms listed below before you proceed to the next chapter. Their meanings are explained on the page numbers indicated.

benchmarking (p. 12)
bounded rationality (p. 7)
budget (p. 9)
continuous improvement (p. 12)
control (p. 9)
corporate ethics (p. 13)
cost accounting (p. 15)
cost efficient (p. 11)
cycle time (p. 12)
employee empowerment (p. 13)
feedback (p. 9)

feedback loops (p. 9)
financial accounting (pp. 5, 14)
goals of the organization (p. 6)
innovation (p. 12)
long-run decisions (p. 8)
management accounting (pp. 4, 15)
management by exception (p. 9)
master budget (p. 9)
non-value added activities (p. 12)
objectives of the organization (p. 6)
operating decisions (p. 8)

performance reports (p. 9)
planning (p. 6)
satisficing (p. 7)
short-term decisions (p. 8)
social responsibility (p. 13)
states of nature (p. 8)
strategic decisions (p. 8)
strategies (p. 7)
time-based measures (p. 12)
total quality management (p. 11)
value-chain analysis (p. 13)

Key Examination Points

Chapter 1 has provided an introduction to the scope of management accounting. It is unlikely that examination questions will be set that refer to the content of an introductory chapter. However, questions are sometimes set requiring you to outline how a costing system can assist the management of an organization. Note that the examiner may not distinguish between cost accounting and management accounting. Cost accounting is often used to also embrace management accounting. Your discussion of a cost accounting system should therefore include a description (with illustrations) of how the system provides information for decision-making, planning and control. Make sure that you draw off your experience from the whole of a first-year course and not just this introductory chapter.

An introduction to cost terms and concepts

In Chapter 1 it was pointed out that accounting systems measure costs which are used for profit measurement and inventory valuation, decision-making, performance measurement and controlling the behaviour of people. The term cost is a frequently used word that reflects a monetary measure of the resources sacrificed or forgone to achieve a specific objective, such as acquiring a good or service. However, the term must be defined more precisely before 'the cost' can be determined. You will find that the word *cost* is rarely used without a preceding adjective to specify the type of cost being considered.

To understand how accounting systems calculate costs and to communicate accounting information effectively to others requires a thorough understanding of what cost means. Unfortunately, the term has multiple meanings and different types of costs are used in different situations. Therefore a preceding term must be added to clarify the assumptions that underlie a cost measurement. A large terminology has emerged to indicate more clearly which cost meaning is being conveyed. Examples include variable cost, fixed cost, opportunity cost and sunk cost. The aim of this chapter is to provide you with an understanding of the basic cost terms and concepts that are used in the management accounting literature.

Learning objectives

After studying this chapter, you should be able to:

- define and illustrate a cost object;
- explain the meaning of each of the key terms listed at the end of this chapter;
- describe the three purposes for which cost information is required;
- distinguish between job costing and process costing;
- explain why in the short term some costs and revenues are not relevant for decision-making.

Cost objects

A **cost object** is any activity for which a separate measurement of costs is desired. In other words, if the users of accounting information want to know the cost of something, this something is called a cost object. Examples of cost objects include the cost of a product, the cost of rendering a service to a bank customer or hospital patient, the cost of operating a particular department or sales territory, or indeed anything for which one wants to measure the cost of resources used.

We shall see that the cost collection system typically accounts for costs in two broad stages:

1. It accumulates costs by classifying them into certain categories such as labour, materials and overhead costs (or by cost behaviour such as fixed and variable).
2. It then assigns these costs to cost objects.

In this chapter we shall focus on the following cost terms and concepts:

- direct and indirect costs;
- period and product costs;
- cost behaviour in relation to volume of activity;
- relevant and irrelevant costs;
- avoidable and unavoidable costs;
- sunk costs;
- opportunity costs;
- incremental and marginal costs.

Direct and indirect costs

Costs that are assigned to cost objects can be divided into two categories: direct costs and indirect costs. **Direct costs** are those costs that can be specifically and exclusively identified with a particular cost object. In contrast, **indirect costs** cannot be identified specifically and exclusively with a given cost object. Let us assume that our cost object is a product, or to be more specific a particular type of desk that is manufactured by an organization. In this situation the wood that is used to manufacture the desk can be specifically and exclusively identified with a particular desk and can thus be classified as a direct cost. Similarly, the wages of operatives whose time can be traced to the specific desk are a direct cost. In contrast, the salaries of factory supervisors or the rent of the factory cannot be specifically and exclusively traced to a particular desk and these costs are therefore classified as indirect.

Sometimes, however, direct costs are treated as indirect because tracing costs directly to the cost object is not cost effective. For example, the nails used to manufacture a particular desk can be identified specifically with the desk, but, because the cost is likely to be insignificant, the expense of tracing such items does not justify the possible benefits from calculating more accurate product costs.

Direct costs can be accurately traced because they can be physically identified with a particular object whereas indirect costs cannot. An estimate must be made of resources consumed by cost objects for indirect costs. Therefore, the more direct costs that can be traced to a cost object, the more accurate is the cost assignment.

The distinction between direct and indirect costs also depends on the cost object. A cost can be treated as direct for one cost object but indirect in respect of another. If the cost object is the cost of using different distribution channels, then the rental of warehouses and the salaries of storekeepers will be regarded as direct for each distribution channel. Also consider a supervisor's salary in a maintenance department of a manufacturing company. If the cost object is the maintenance department, then the salary is a direct cost. However, if the cost object is the product, both the warehouse rental and the salaries of the storekeepers and the supervisor will be an indirect cost because these costs cannot be specifically identified with the product.

CATEGORIES OF MANUFACTURING COSTS

In manufacturing organizations products are frequently the cost object. Traditionally, cost accounting systems in manufacturing organizations have reflected the need to assign costs to products to value stocks and measure profits based on imposed external financial accounting requirements. Traditional cost accounting systems accumulate product costs as follows:

Direct materials	xxx
Direct labour	xxx
Prime cost	xxx
Manufacturing overhead	xxx
Total manufacturing cost	xxx

Direct materials consist of all those materials that can be identified with a specific product. For example, wood that is used to manufacture a desk can easily be identified as part of the product, and can thus be classified as direct materials. Alternatively, materials used for the repair of a machine that is used for the manufacture of many different desks are classified as **indirect materials**. These items of materials cannot be identified with any one product, because they are used for the benefit of all products rather than for any one specific product. Note that indirect materials form part of the manufacturing overhead cost.

  Direct labour consists of those labour costs that can be specifically traced to or identified with a particular product. Examples of direct labour costs include the wages of operatives who assemble parts into the finished product, or machine operatives engaged in the production process. By contrast, the salaries of factory supervisors or the wages paid to the staff in the stores department cannot be specifically identified with the product, and thus form part of the **indirect labour** costs. The wages of all employees who do not work on the product itself but who assist in the manufacturing operation are thus classified as part of the indirect labour costs. As with indirect materials, indirect labour is classified as part of the manufacturing overhead cost.

  Prime cost refers to the direct costs of the product and consists of direct labour costs plus direct material costs plus any direct expenses. The cost of hiring a machine for producing a specific product is an example of a direct expense.

  Manufacturing overhead consists of all manufacturing costs other than direct labour, direct materials and direct expenses. It therefore includes all indirect manufacturing labour and materials costs plus indirect manufacturing expenses. Examples of indirect manufacturing expenses in a multi-product company include rent of the factory and depreciation of machinery.

  To ascertain the total manufacturing cost of a product, all that is required for the direct cost items is to record the amount of resources used on the appropriate documents. The specific product or order (i.e. the cost object) to which the costs should be assigned should be entered on the document. For example, the units of materials used in making a particular product are recorded on a stores requisition, and the hours of direct labour used are recorded on job cards. Having obtained the quantity of resources used for the direct items, it is necessary to ascertain the price paid for these resources. The total of the resources used multiplied by the price paid per unit of resources used provides us with the total of the direct costs or the prime cost for a product.

  Manufacturing overheads cannot be directly traced to products. Instead they are assigned to products using **cost allocations**. A cost allocation is the process of estimating the cost of resources consumed by products that involves the use of surrogate, rather than direct measures. The process of assigning indirect costs (overheads) to cost objects will be explained in Chapter 4.

Period and product costs

External financial accounting rules in most countries require that for inventory valuation, only manufacturing costs should be included in the calculation of product costs (see United Kingdom Statement of Standard Accounting Practice (SSAP 9), published by the Accounting Standards Committee). Accountants therefore classify costs as product costs and period costs. **Product costs** are those costs that are identified with goods purchased or produced for resale. In a manufacturing organization they are costs that the accountant attaches to the product and that are included in the inventory valuation for finished goods, or for partly completed goods (work in progress), until they are sold; they are then recorded as expenses and matched against sales for calculating profit. **Period costs** are those costs that are not included in the inventory valuation and as a result are treated as expenses in the period in which they are incurred. *Hence no attempt is made to attach period costs to products for inventory valuation purposes.*

In a manufacturing organization all manufacturing costs are regarded as product costs and non-manufacturing costs are regarded as period costs. Companies operating in the merchandising sector, such as retailing or wholesaling organizations, purchase goods for resale without changing their basic form. The cost of the goods purchased is regarded as a product cost and all other costs such as administration and selling and distribution expenses are considered to be period costs. The treatment of period and product costs for a manufacturing organization is illustrated in Figure 2.1. You will see that both product and period costs are eventually classified as expenses. The major difference is the point in time at which they are so classified.

Why are non-manufacturing costs treated as period costs and not included in the inventory valuation? There are two reasons. First, inventories are assets (unsold production) and assets represent resources that have been acquired that are expected to contribute to future revenue. Manufacturing costs incurred in making a product can be expected to generate future revenues to cover the cost of production. There is no guarantee, however, that non-manufacturing costs will generate future revenue, because they do not represent value added to any specific product. Therefore, they are not included in the inventory valuation. Second, many non-manufacturing costs (e.g. distribution costs) are not incurred when the product is being stored. Hence it is inappropriate to include such costs within the inventory valuation.

An illustration of the accounting treatment of period and product costs for income (profit) measurement purposes is presented in Example 2.1.

Cost behaviour

A knowledge of how costs and revenues will vary with different levels of activity (or volume) is essential for decision-making. Activity or volume may be measured in terms of units of production or sales, hours worked, miles travelled, patients seen, students enrolled or any other appropriate measure of the activity of an organization. Examples of decisions that require information on how costs and revenues vary with different levels of activity include the following:

1. What should the planned level of activity be for the next year?
2. Should we reduce the selling price to sell more units?
3. Would it be wiser to pay our sales staff by a straight commission, a straight salary or by some combination of the two?
4. How do the costs and revenues of a hospital change if one more patient is admitted for a seven-day stay?

EXAMPLE 2.1

The Flanders company produces 100 000 identical units of a product during period 1. The costs for the period are as follows:

	(£)	(£)
Manufacturing costs:		
Direct labour	400 000	
Direct materials	200 000	
Manufacturing overheads	200 000	800 000
Non-manufacturing costs		300 000

During period 1, the company sold 50 000 units for £750 000, and the remaining 50 000 units were unsold at the end of the period. There was no opening stock at the start of the period. The profit and loss account for period 1 will be as follows:

	(£)	(£)
Sales (50 000)		750 000
Manufacturing costs (*product costs*):		
Direct labour	400 000	
Direct materials	200 000	
Manufacturing overheads	200 000	
	800 000	
Less closing stock (50% or 50 000 units)	400 000	
Cost of goods sold (50% or 50 000 units)		400 000
Gross profit		350 000
Less non-manufacturing costs (*period costs*)		300 000
Net profit		50 000

Fifty per cent of the production was sold during the period and the remaining 50% was produced for inventories. Half of the product costs are therefore identified as an expense for the period and the remainder are included in the closing inventory valuation. If we assume that the closing inventory is sold in the next accounting period, the remaining 50% of the product costs will become expenses in the next accounting period. However, all the period costs became an expense in this accounting period, because this is the period to which they relate. Note that only product costs form the basis for the calculation of cost of goods sold, and that period costs do not form part of this calculation.

5. How do the costs and revenues of a hotel change if a room and meals are provided for two guests for a seven-day stay?

For each of the above decisions management requires estimates of costs and revenues at different levels of activity for the alternative courses of action.

The terms 'variable', 'fixed', 'semi-variable' and 'semi-fixed' have been traditionally used in the management accounting literature to describe how a cost reacts to changes in

FIGURE 2.1 *Treatment of period and product costs.*

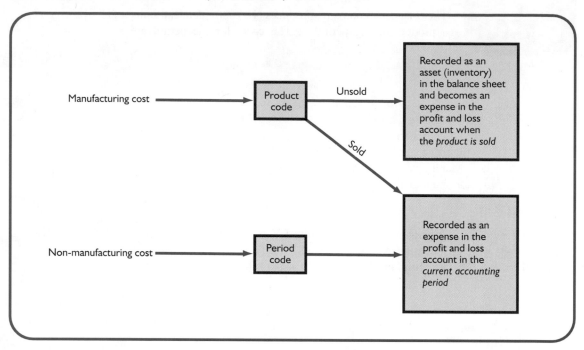

activity. Short-term **variable costs** vary in direct proportion to the volume of activity; that is, doubling the level of activity will double the total variable cost. Consequently, *total* variable costs are linear and *unit* variable cost is constant. Figure 2.2 illustrates a variable cost where the variable cost per unit of activity is £10. It is unlikely that variable cost per unit will be constant for all levels of activity. We shall discuss the reasons why accountants normally assume that variable costs are constant per unit of activity in Chapter 9. Examples of short-term variable manufacturing costs include piecework labour, direct materials and energy to operate the machines. These costs are assumed to fluctuate directly in proportion to operating activity within a certain range of activity. Examples of non-manufacturing variable costs include sales commissions, which fluctuate with sales value, and petrol, which fluctuates with the number of miles travelled.

Fixed costs remain constant over wide ranges of activity for a specified time period. Examples of fixed costs include depreciation of the factory building, supervisors' salaries and leasing charges for cars used by the salesforce. Figure 2.3 illustrates fixed costs.

You will see that the *total* fixed costs are constant for all levels of activity whereas *unit* fixed costs decrease proportionally with the level of activity. For example, if the total of the fixed costs is £5000 for a month the fixed costs per unit will be as follows:

Units produced	Fixed cost per unit (£)
1	5000
10	500
100	50
1000	5

Because unit fixed costs are not constant per unit they must be interpreted with caution. For decision-making, it is better to work with total fixed costs rather than unit costs.

FIGURE 2.2 *Variable costs: (a) total; (b) unit.*

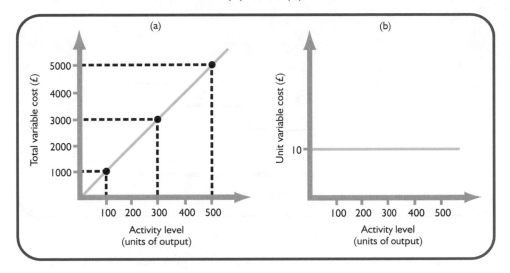

FIGURE 2.3 *Fixed costs: (a) total; (b) unit.*

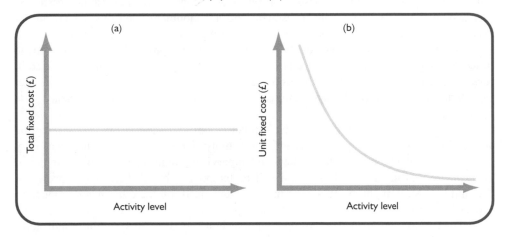

In practice it is unlikely that fixed costs will be constant over the full range of activity. They may increase in steps in the manner depicted in Figure 2.4. We shall discuss the justification for assuming that fixed costs are constant over a wide range of activity in Chapter 9.

The distinction between fixed and variable costs must be made relative to the time period under consideration. Over a sufficiently long time period of several years, virtually all costs are variable. During such a long period of time, contraction in demand will be accompanied by reductions in virtually all categories of costs. For example, senior managers can be released, machinery need not be replaced and even buildings and land can be sold. Similarly, large expansions in activity will eventually cause all categories of costs to increase.

Within shorter time periods, costs will be fixed or variable in relation to changes in activity. The shorter the time period, the greater the probability that a particular cost will be fixed. Consider a time period of one year. The costs of providing the firm's operating

FIGURE 2.4 *Step fixed costs.*

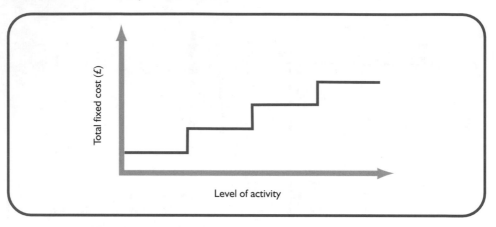

capacity such as depreciation and the salaries of senior plant managers are likely to be fixed in relation to changes in activity. Decisions on the firm's intended future potential level of operating capacity will determine the amount of capacity costs to be incurred. These decisions will have been made previously as part of the capital budgeting and long-term planning process. Once these decisions have been made, they cannot easily be reversed in the short term. Plant investment and abandonment decisions should not be based on short-term fluctuations in demand within a particular year. Instead, they should be reviewed periodically as part of the long-term planning process and decisions made based on long-run demand over several years. Thus capacity costs will tend to be fixed in relation to changes of activity within short-term periods such as one year. However, over long-term periods of several years, significant changes in demand will cause capacity costs to change.

Spending on some fixed costs, such as direct labour and supervisory salaries, can be adjusted in the short term to reflect changes in activity. For example, if production activity declines significantly then direct workers and supervisors might continue to be employed in the hope that the decline in demand will be temporary; but if there is no upsurge in demand then staff might eventually be made redundant. If, on the other hand, production capacity expands to some critical level, additional workers might be employed, but the process of recruiting such workers may take several months. Thus within a short-term period, such as one year, labour costs can change in response to changes in demand in a manner similar to that depicted in Figure 2.4. Costs that behave in this manner are described as **semi-fixed** or **step fixed costs**. The distinguishing feature of step fixed costs is that within a given time period they are fixed within specified activity levels, but they eventually increase or decrease by a constant amount at various critical activity levels as illustrated in Figure 2.4.

Our discussion so far has assumed a one-year time period. Consider a shorter time period such as one month and the circumstances outlined in the previous paragraph where it takes several months to respond to changes in activity and alter spending levels. Over very short-term periods such as one month, spending on direct labour and supervisory salaries will be fixed in relation to changes in activity.

You should now understand that over a given short-term period, such as one year, costs will be variable, fixed or semi-fixed. Over longer-term time periods of several years, all costs will tend to change in response to large changes in activity (or to changes in the range and variety of products or services marketed), and fixed costs will become semi-fixed and change in the manner depicted in Figure 2.4. Because fixed costs do not remain fixed in the long-term, some writers prefer to describe them as **long-term variable costs**, but we shall continue to use the term 'fixed costs' since this is the term most widely used in the literature.

Note, however, that in the short term, even though fixed costs are normally assumed to remain unchanged in response to changes in the level of activity, they may change in response to other factors. For example, if price levels increase then some fixed costs such as management salaries will increase.

Before concluding our discussion of cost behaviour in relation to volume of activity, we must consider **semi-variable costs**. These include both a fixed and a variable component. The cost of maintenance is a semi-variable cost consisting of planned maintenance that is undertaken whatever the level of activity, and a variable element that is directly related to the level of activity. A further example of semi-variable costs is where sales representatives are paid a fixed salary plus a commission on sales.

Relevant and irrelevant costs and revenues

For decision-making, costs and revenues can be classified according to whether they are relevant to a particular decision. **Relevant costs and revenues** are those *future* costs and revenues that will be changed by a decision, whereas **irrelevant costs and revenues** are those that will not be affected by the decision. For example, if you are faced with a choice of making a journey using your own car or by public transport, the car tax and insurance costs are irrelevant, since they will remain the same whatever alternative is chosen. However, petrol costs for the car will differ depending on which alternative is chosen, and this cost will be relevant for decision-making.

Let us now consider a further illustration of the classification of relevant and irrelevant costs. Assume a company purchased raw materials a few years ago for £100 and that there appears to be no possibility of selling these materials or using them in future production apart from in connection with an enquiry from a former customer. This customer is prepared to purchase a product that will require the use of all these materials, but he is not prepared to pay more than £250 per unit. The additional costs of converting these materials into the required product are £200. Should the company accept the order for £250? It appears that the cost of the order is £300, consisting of £100 material cost and £200 conversion cost, but this is incorrect because the £100 material cost will remain the same whether the order is accepted or rejected. The material cost is therefore irrelevant for the decision, but if the order is accepted the conversion costs will change by £200, and this conversion cost is a relevant cost. If we compare the revenue of £250 with the relevant cost for the order of £200, it means that the order should be accepted, assuming of course that no higher-priced orders can be obtained elsewhere. The following calculation shows that this is the correct decision.

	Do not accept order (£)	Accept order (£)
Materials	100	100
Conversion costs	—	200
Revenue	—	(250)
Net costs	100	50

The net costs of the company are £50 less, or alternatively the company is £50 better off as a result of accepting the order. This agrees with the £50 advantage which was suggested by the relevant cost method.

We have now established an important principle regarding the classification of cost and revenues for decision-making; namely, that in the short-term not all costs and revenues are relevant for decision-making.

Avoidable and unavoidable costs

Sometimes the terms **avoidable** and **unavoidable costs** are used instead of relevant and irrelevant cost. Avoidable costs are those costs that may be saved by not adopting a given alternative, whereas unavoidable costs cannot be saved. Therefore, only avoidable costs are relevant for decision-making purposes. Consider the example that we used to illustrate relevant and irrelevant costs. The material costs of £100 are unavoidable and irrelevant, but the conversion costs of £200 are avoidable and hence relevant. The decision rule is to accept those alternatives that generate revenues in excess of the avoidable costs.

Sunk costs

These costs are the cost of resources already acquired where the total will be unaffected by the choice between various alternatives. They are costs that have been created by a decision made in the past and that cannot be changed by any decision that will be made in the future. The expenditure of £100 on materials that were no longer required, referred to in the preceding section, is an example of a **sunk cost**. Similarly, the written down values of assets previously purchased are sunk costs. For example, if a machine was purchased four years ago for £100 000 with an expected life of five years and nil scrap value then the written down value will be £20 000 if straight line depreciation is used. This written down value will have to be written off, no matter what possible alternative future action might be chosen. If the machine was scrapped, the £20 000 would be written off; if the machine was used for productive purposes, the £20 000 would still have to be written off. This cost cannot be changed by any future decision and is therefore classified as a sunk cost.

Sunk costs are irrelevant for decision-making, but they are distinguished from irrelevant costs because not all irrelevant costs are sunk costs. For example, a comparison of two alternative production methods may result in identical direct material expenditure for both alternatives, so the direct material cost is irrelevant because it will remain the same whichever alternative is chosen, but the material cost is not a sunk cost since it will be incurred in the future.

Opportunity costs

Some costs for decision-making cannot normally be collected within the accounting system. Costs that are collected within the accounting system are based on past payments or commitments to pay at some time in the future. Sometimes it is necessary for decision-making to impute costs that will not require cash outlays, and these imputed costs are called opportunity costs. An **opportunity cost** is a cost that measures the opportunity that is lost or sacrificed when the choice of one course of action requires that an alternative course of action be given up. Consider the information presented in Example 2.2.

It is important to note that opportunity costs only apply to the use of scarce resources. Where resources are not scarce, no sacrifice exists from using these resources. In Example 2.2 if machine X was operating at 80% of its potential capacity then the decision to accept the contract would not have resulted in reduced production of product A. Consequently, there would have been no loss of revenue, and the opportunity cost would be zero.

You should now be aware that opportunity costs are of vital importance for decision-making. If no alternative use of resources exist then the opportunity cost is zero, but if resources have an alternative use, and are scarce, then an opportunity cost does exist.

EXAMPLE 2.2

A company has an opportunity to obtain a contract for the production of a special component. This component will require 100 hours of processing on machine X. Machine X is working at full capacity on the production of product A, and the only way in which the contract can be fulfilled is by reducing the output of product A. This will result in a lost profit contribution of £200. The contract will also result in *additional* variable costs of £1000.

If the company takes on the contract, it will sacrifice a profit contribution of £200 from the lost output of product A. This represents an opportunity cost, and should be included as part of the cost when negotiating for the contract. The contract price should at least cover the additional costs of £1000 plus the £200 opportunity cost to ensure that the company will be better off in the short term by accepting the contract.

Incremental and marginal costs

Incremental (also called **differential**) **costs** and revenues are the difference between costs and revenues for the corresponding items under each alternative being considered. For example, the incremental costs of increasing output from 1000 to 1100 units per week are the additional costs of producing an extra 100 units per week. Incremental costs may or may not include fixed costs. If fixed costs change as a result of a decision, the increase in costs represents an incremental cost. If fixed costs do not change as a result of a decision, the incremental costs will be zero.

Incremental costs and revenues are similar in principle to the economist's concept of **marginal cost** and **marginal revenue**. The main difference is that marginal cost/revenue represents the additional cost/revenue of one extra unit of output whereas incremental cost/revenue represents the additional cost/revenue resulting from a group of additional units of output. The economist normally represents the theoretical relationship between cost/revenue and output in terms of the marginal cost/revenue of single additional units of output. We shall see that the accountant is normally more interested in the incremental cost/revenue of increasing production and sales to whatever extent is contemplated, and this is most unlikely to be a single unit of output.

Job costing and process costing systems

There are two basic types of systems that companies can adopt – job costing and process costing systems. **Job costing** relates to a costing system that is required in organizations where each unit or batch of output of a product or service is unique. This creates the need for the cost of each unit to be calculated separately. The term 'job' thus relates to each unique unit or batch of output. Job costing systems are used in industries that provide customized products or services. For example, accounting firms provide customized services to clients with each client requiring services that consume different quantities of resources. Engineering companies often make machines to meet individual customer specifications. The contracts undertaken by construction and civil engineering companies differ greatly for each customer. In all of these organizations costs must be traced to each individual customer's order.

In contrast, **process costing** relates to those situations where masses of identical units are produced and it is unnecessary to assign costs to individual units of output. Products are produced in the same manner and consume the same amount of direct costs and overheads. It is therefore unnecessary to assign costs to individual units of output. Instead, the average cost per unit of output is calculated by dividing the total costs assigned to a product or service for a period by the number of units of output for that period. Industries where process costing is widely used include chemical processing, oil refining, food processing and brewing.

In practice these two costing systems represent extreme ends of a continuum. The output of many organizations requires a combination of the elements of both job costing and process costing.

Maintaining a cost database

In the previous chapter we noted that a cost and management accounting system should generate information to meet the following requirements:

1. to allocate costs between cost of goods sold and inventories for internal and external profit measurement and inventory valuation;
2. to provide relevant information to help managers make better decisions;
3. to provide information for planning, control and performance measurement.

A database should be maintained, with costs appropriately coded and classified, so that relevant cost information can be extracted to meet each of the above requirements.

A suitable coding system enables costs to be accumulated by the required cost objects (such as products or services, departments, responsibility centres, distribution channels, etc.) and also to be classified by appropriate categories. Typical cost classifications, within the database, are by categories of expense (direct materials, direct labour and overheads) and by cost behaviour (fixed and variable). In practice, direct materials will be accumulated by each individual type of material, direct labour by different grades of labour and overhead costs by different categories of indirect expenses (e.g. rent, depreciation, supervision, etc.).

For *inventory valuation* the costs of all partly completed products (work in progress) and unsold finished products can be extracted from the database to ascertain the total cost assigned to inventories. The cost of goods sold that is deducted from sales revenues to compute the profit for the period can also be extracted by summing the manufacturing costs of all those products that have been sold during the period.

The allocation of costs to products is inappropriate for *cost control and performance measurement*, as the manufacture of the product may consist of several different operations, all of which are the responsibility of different individuals. To overcome this problem, costs and revenues must be traced to the individuals who are responsible for incurring them. This system is known as **responsibility accounting**.

Responsibility accounting involves the creation of responsibility centres. A **responsibility centre** may be defined as an organization unit for whose performance a manager is held accountable. Responsibility accounting enables accountability for financial results and outcomes to be allocated to individuals throughout the organization. The objective of responsibility accounting is to measure the results of each responsibility centre. It involves accumulating costs and revenues for each responsibility centre so that deviations from a performance target (typically the budget) can be attributed to the individual who is accountable for the responsibility centre.

For *cost control and performance measurement* the accountant produces performance reports at regular intervals for each responsibility centre. The reports are generated by extracting from the database costs analysed by responsibility centres and categories of expenses. Actual costs for each item of expense listed on the performance report should be compared with budgeted costs so that those costs that do not conform to plan can be pinpointed and investigated.

Future costs, rather than past costs, are required for *decision-making*. Therefore costs extracted from the database should be adjusted for anticipated price changes. We have noted that classification of costs by cost behaviour is important for evaluating the financial impact of expansion or contraction decisions. Costs, however, are not classified as relevant or irrelevant within the database because relevance depends on the circumstances. Consider a situation where a company is negotiating a contract for the sale of one of its products with a customer in an overseas country which is not part of its normal market. If the company has temporary excess capacity and the contract is for 100 units for one month only, then the direct labour cost will remain the same irrespective of whether or not the contract is undertaken. The direct labour cost will therefore be irrelevant. Let us now assume that the contract is for 100 units per month for three years and the company has excess capacity. For long-term decisions direct labour will be a relevant cost because if the contract is not undertaken direct labour can be redeployed or made redundant. Undertaking the contract will result in additional direct labour costs.

The above example shows that the classification of costs as relevant or irrelevant depends on the circumstances. In one situation a cost may be relevant, but in another the same cost may not be relevant. Costs can only be classified as relevant or irrelevant when the circumstances have been identified relating to a particular decision.

Where a company sells many products or services their profitability should be monitored at regular intervals so that potentially unprofitable products can be highlighted for a more detailed study of their future viability. This information is extracted from the database with costs reported by categories of expenses and divided into their fixed and variable elements. In Chapter 10 we shall focus in more detail on product/segmented profitability analysis. Finally, you should note that when the activities of an organization consist of a series of common or repetitive operations, targets or standard product costs, rather than actual costs, may be recorded in the database. Standard costs are predetermined costs; they are target costs that should be incurred under efficient operating conditions. They should be reviewed and updated at periodic intervals. If product standard costs are recorded in the database there is no need continuously to trace costs to products and therefore a considerable amount of data processing time can be saved. Actual costs, however, will still be traced to responsibility centres for cost control and performance evaluation.

Summary

The term cost has multiple meanings and different types of costs are used in different situations. Therefore a preceding term must be added to clarify the assumptions that underlie a cost measurement. A large terminology has emerged to indicate more clearly which cost meaning is being conveyed. This chapter has described the following basic cost terms that are used in the management accounting literature:

1. direct and indirect costs;
2. period and product costs;
3. cost behavior in relation to volume of activity;
4. relevant and irrelevant costs;
5. avoidable and unavoidable costs;
6. sunk costs;
7. opportunity costs;
8. incremental and marginal costs.

A cost and management accounting system should generate information to meet the following requirements:

1. to allocate costs between cost of goods sold and inventories for internal and external reporting;
2. to provide relevant information to help managers make better decisions;
3. to provide information for planning, control and performance measurement.

A database should be maintained with costs appropriately coded or classified, so that relevant cost information can be extracted to meet each of the above requirements.

Key Terms and Concepts

avoidable costs (p. 28)
cost allocations (p. 21)
cost object (p. 19)
differential costs (p. 29)
direct costs (p. 20)
direct labour (p. 21)
direct materials (p. 21)
fixed costs (p. 24)
incremental costs (p. 29)
indirect cost (p. 20)
indirect labour (p. 21)
indirect materials (p. 21)
irrelevant costs and revenues (p. 27)
job costing (p. 30)
long-term variable costs (p. 27)
manufacturing overhead (p. 21)

marginal cost/revenue (p. 29)
opportunity cost (p. 29)
period costs (p. 22)
prime cost (p. 21)
process costing (p. 30)
product costs (p. 22)
relevant costs and revenues (p. 27)
responsibility accounting (p. 31)
responsibility centre (p. 31)
semi-fixed costs (p. 26)
semi-variable costs (p. 27)
step fixed costs (p. 26)
sunk cost (p. 28)
unavoidable costs (p. 28)
variable costs (p. 24)

Key Examination Points

First year management accounting course examinations frequently involve short essay questions requiring you to describe various cost terms or to discuss the concept that different costs are required for different purposes (see Questions 2.2–2.9 for examples). It is therefore important that you understand all of the cost terms that have been described in this chapter. In particular, you should be able to explain the context within which a cost term is normally used. For example, a cost such as wages paid to casual labourers will be classified as indirect for inventory valuation purposes but as a direct charge to a responsibility centre or department for cost control purposes. A common error is for students to produce a very short answer, but you must be prepared to expand your answer and to include various situations within which the use of a cost term is appropriate. Always make sure your answer includes illustrations of cost terms. Multiple choice questions are also often set on topics included in this chapter. The first seven questions within the following section containing the review problems are typical examples of such questions. You should now attempt these questions and compare your answers within the solutions.

Review problems

(For additional problems without answers relating to the content of this chapter you should refer to pages 416–419.)

1 Classify each of the following as being usually fixed (F), variable (V), semi-fixed (SF) or semi-variable (SV):
   (a) direct labour;
   (b) depreciation on machinery;
   (c) factory rental;
   (d) supplies and other indirect materials;
   (e) advertising;
   (f) maintenance of machinery;
   (g) factory manager's salary;
   (h) supervisory personnel;
   (i) royalty payments.

2 Which of the following costs are likely to be controllable by the head of the production department?
   (a) price paid for materials;
   (b) charge for floor space;
   (c) raw materials used;
   (d) electricity used for machinery;
   (e) machinery depreciation;
   (f) direct labour;
   (g) insurance on machinery;
   (h) share of cost of industrial relations department.

3 If actual output is lower than budgeted output, which of the following costs would you expect to be lower than the original budget?
   A   Total variable costs
   B   Total fixed costs
   C   Variable costs per unit
   D   Fixed costs per unit
   ACCA Foundation Paper 3

4 The following data relate to two output levels of a department:

Machine hours	17 000	18 500
Overheads	£246 500	£251 750

The variable overhead rate per hour is £3.50. The amount of fixed overheads is:
   A   £5250
   B   £59 500
   C   £187 000
   D   £246 500
   CIMA Stage 1

5 Prime cost is:
   A   all costs incurred in manufacturing a product;
   B   the total of direct costs;
   C   the material cost of a product;
   D   the cost of operating a department.
   CIMA Stage 1

6 A direct cost is a cost which:
   A   is incurred as a direct consequence of a decision;
   B   can be economically identified with the item being costed;
   C   cannot be economically identified with the item being costed;
   D   is immediately controllable;
   E   is the responsibility of the board of directors.
   CIMA Stage 2

7 Which of the following would be classed as indirect labour?
   A   assembly workers in a company manufacturing televisions;
   B   a stores assistant in a factory store;
   C   plasterers in a construction company;
   D   an audit clerk in a firm of auditors.
   CIMA Stage 1 Cost Accounting

8 **Data** (£)

Cost of motor car	5500
Trade-in price after 2 years or 60 000 miles is expected to be	1500
Maintenance – 6-monthly service costing	60
Spares/replacement parts, per 1000 miles	20
Vehicle licence, per annum	80
Insurance, per annum	150
Tyre replacements after 25 000 miles, four at £37.50 each	
Petrol, per gallon	1.90
Average mileage from one gallon is 25 miles.	

(a) From the above data you are required:
  (i) to prepare a schedule to be presented to management showing for the mileages of 5000, 10 000, 15 000 and 30 000 miles per annum:
    (1) total variable cost
    (2) total fixed cost
    (3) total cost
    (4) variable cost per mile (in pence to nearest penny)
    (5) fixed cost per mile (in pence to nearest penny)
    (6) total cost per mile (in pence to nearest penny)
    If, in classifying the costs, you consider that some can be treated as either variable or fixed, state the assumption(s) on which your answer is based together with brief supporting reason(s).
  (ii) on graph paper plot the information given in your answer to (i) above for the costs listed against (1), (2), (3) and (6).
  (iii) to read off from your graph(s) in (ii) and state the approximate total costs applicable to 18 000 miles and 25 000 miles and the total cost per mile at these two mileages.
(b) 'The more miles you travel, the cheaper it becomes.' Comment briefly on this statement.

(25 marks)
CIMA Cost Accounting 1

Solutions to Review Problems

SOLUTION 1

(a) SV (or variable if direct labour can be matched exactly to output)
(b) F
(c) F
(d) V
(e) F (Advertising is a discretionary cost. See Chapter 10 for an explanation of this cost.)
(f) SV
(g) F
(h) SF
(i) V

SOLUTION 2

Controllable (c), (d), (f)
Non-controllable (a), (b), (e), (g), (h)

SOLUTION 3

Item (B) will be constant within the relevant range of output.

Item (C) will be constant per unit.
If output declines fixed cost per unit will decrease.
Total variable cost will fall in line with a decline in output and therefore item A is the correct answer.

SOLUTION 4

Total variable overheads = 17 000 × £3.50 = £59 500.
Total variable overhead (£59 500) + Total fixed overhead = Total overhead (£246 500).
Total fixed overhead = £246 500 − £59 500 = £187 000.
Answer = C

SOLUTION 5

Answer = B

SOLUTION 6

Answer = B

SOLUTION 7

Answer = B

SOLUTION 8

(a) (i) *Schedule of annual mileage costs*

	5000 miles (£)	10 000 miles (£)	15 000 miles (£)	30 000 miles (£)
Variable costs:				
Spares	100	200	300	600
Petrol	380	760	1140	2280
Total variable cost	480	960	1440	2880
Variable cost per mile	0.096	0.096	0.096	0.096
Fixed costs				
Depreciation[a]	2000	2000	2000	2000
Maintenance	120	120	120	120
Vehicle licence	80	80	80	80
Insurance	150	150	150	150
Tyres[b]	—	—	75	150
	2350	2350	2425	2500
Fixed cost per mile	0.47	0.235	0.162	0.083
Total cost	2830	3310	3865	5380
Total cost per mile	0.566	0.331	0.258	0.179

Notes

[a] Annual depreciation

$$= \frac{£5500 \text{ (cost)} - £1500 \text{ (trade-in price)}}{2 \text{ years}} = £2000$$

[b] At 15 000 miles per annum tyres will be replaced once during the two-year period at a cost of £150.

The average cost per year is £75. At 30 000 miles per annum tyres will be replaced once each year.

Comments

Tyres are a semi-fixed cost. In the above calculations they have been regarded as a step fixed cost. An alternative approach would be to regard the semi-fixed cost as a variable cost by dividing £150 tyre replacement by 25 000 miles. This results in a variable cost per mile of £0.006.

Depreciation and maintenance cost have been classified as fixed costs. They are likely to be semi-variable costs, but in the absence of any additional information they have been classified as fixed costs.

(ii) See Figure 1.

(iii) The respective costs can be obtained from the vertical dashed lines in the graph (Figure 1).

(b) The *cost per mile* declines as activity increases. This is because the majority of costs are fixed and do not increase when mileage increases. However, *total cost* will increase with increases in mileage.

FIGURE 1   *The step increase in fixed cost is assumed to occur at an annual mileage of 12 500 miles and 25 000 miles, because tyres are assumed to be replaced at this mileage.*

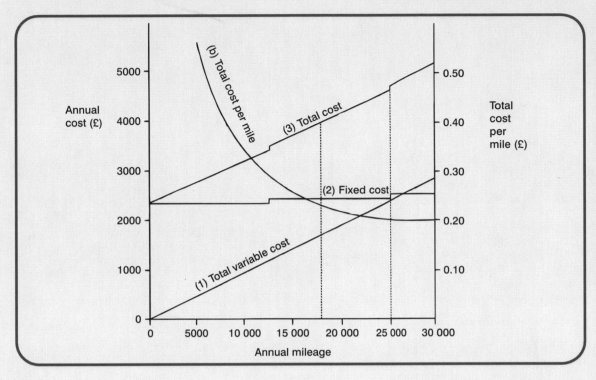

PART TWO

Cost Accumulation for Inventory Valuation and Profit Measurement

This section consisting of six chapters focuses mainly on assigning costs to products to separate costs incurred during a period between costs of goods sold and the closing inventory valuation. The extent to which product costs accumulated for inventory valuation and profit measurement should be adjusted for meeting decision-making, cost control and performance measurement requirements is also briefly considered.

Chapter 3 is concerned with the recording procedures for labour and materials. This chapter also focuses on the materials control procedure, methods of establishing optimal stock levels and alternative approaches to scheduling materials requirements. The aim of Chapter 4 is to provide you with an understanding of how indirect costs are assigned to cost objects. In particular the chapter focuses on the assignment of indirect costs using traditional costing systems. In Chapter 5 the emphasis is on the accounting entries necessary to record transactions within a job costing system. The issues relating to a cost accumulation procedure for a process costing system are described in Chapter 6. This is a system that is applicable to industries that produce many units of the same product during a particular period. In Chapter 7 the problems associated with calculating product costs in those industries that produce joint and by-products are discussed. The final chapter in this section is concerned with the alternative accounting methods of assigning fixed manufacturing overheads to products and their implications for profit measurement and inventory valuation.

3

Accounting for labour and materials

In the previous chapter it was pointed out that labour and material costs can be categorized as either direct or indirect costs. You should be able to recall that direct costs are those costs that can be specifically and exclusively identified with a particular cost object whereas indirect costs cannot be identified with a particular cost object. In this, and the next five chapters, we shall assume products, services or customers' orders are the cost objects.

You will see in this chapter that the assignment of direct labour and materials to cost objects merely involves the implementation of suitable clerical/computer procedures to identify the quantity and prices of the resources consumed. At several stages throughout the chapter it will be pointed out that indirect labour and material costs are classified as overheads and the costs are assigned to an overhead accounts classified by the type and location of expense. For example, where workers are unoccupied for short periods of time it will be recommended that the costs should be charged to an idle time overhead account for each department. In some situations, indirect labour and materials costs may not be easily identifiable with a particular department and the costs will be assigned to an appropriate overhead account for the business unit as a whole. For example, you will see that materials handling expenses are charged to a material handling expenses overhead account for the whole business unit since it is not possible to identify the costs with a particular department.

Indirect labour and material costs are assigned to overhead accounts classified by type and location of expense for cost control purposes so that management can monitor such costs and prioritize areas for cost reduction. In addition, manufacturing indirect labour and material costs must be assigned to products for inventory valuation purposes. At this stage you should note that the processes of accumulating indirect costs described in this chapter enables the costs to be more accurately allocated to products. However, the mechanisms that can be used to allocate the indirect costs from overhead accounts to products will not be explained until the next chapter.

The emphasis throughout this chapter is on how labour and materials costs that have already been incurred should be accu-

Learning objectives

After studying this chapter, you should be able to:

- distinguish between payroll and labour cost accounting;
- describe the materials recording procedure;
- explain the accounting treatment of holiday pay, overtime premiums, employment costs, idle time, stores losses and delivery and materials handling costs;
- calculate the cost of stores issues and closing stock values using FIFO, LIFO and average cost methods of stores pricing;
- explain the arguments for and against using FIFO, LIFO and average cost methods of stores pricing;
- justify which costs are relevant and should be included in the calculation of the economic order quantity (EOQ);
- calculate the EOQ using the formula and tabulation methods;
- describe the ABC classification method;
- describe materials requirement planning (MRP) systems;

mulated for allocating costs between costs of goods sold and inventories for internal and external profit reporting purposes. For decision-making the emphasis is on using future costs rather than past costs, so the accumulation of past costs is generally not relevant for decision-making. For example, many companies obtain customers' orders by submitting bids or quotations, which, if accepted become the agreed selling prices. The assignment of actual costs incurred may provide useful feedback information on the accuracy of the bids, and help to improve the accuracy of future bids, but past costs are normally not directly used for decision-making. Exceptions do exist, however, such as garages that charge for repairs on the basis of actual costs incurred. In these circumstances, the approaches described in this chapter can represent a direct input for determining the selling prices.

An understanding of the process of accounting for labour and materials requires a knowledge of the appropriate recording procedures and documentation. To simplify the presentation, and help you understand the recording procedures, manual clerical procedures are described. You should note, however, that in most organizations the recording procedures are computerized. Nevertheless, the basic principles described in this chapter still apply.

Finally, besides focusing on accounting for labour and materials this chapter also describes the materials control procedure, methods of establishing optimal stock levels and alternative approaches to scheduling materials requirements.

- explain just-in-time (JIT) production and purchasing and list the benefits arising from adopting JIT concepts.

Accounting for labour costs

Accounting for labour costs can be divided into the following two distinct phases:

1. Computations of gross pay for each employee and calculation of payments to be made to employees, government, pension funds etc. (i.e. **payroll accounting**).
2. Allocation of labour costs to cost objects such as products or services, individual customers' orders and overhead accounts (i.e. **labour cost accounting**).

PAYROLL ACCOUNTING

Payroll accounting requires the provision of information relating to an employee's attendance time, details of absenteeism, hourly rates of pay, and details of various deductions such as tax and National Insurance. **Clock cards** or absenteeism reports provide the basic information for the calculation of attendance time, and the employee's personal record card provides details of the various deductions. Where incentive payment systems are in operation, **piecework tickets** contain details of the number of items produced by each employee, and this is multiplied by the rate per item to give the total weekly wage. Where **bonus schemes** are in operation, the total payment will be based on an attendance time (the time rate wage) plus a bonus. The time rate wage is obtained from

ACCOUNTING FOR LABOUR COSTS** 43**

the clock card and the bonus details from the job card. Under a bonus scheme, a set time is allowed for each operation and a bonus is paid based on the proportion of time that is saved. An illustration of a bonus system is given in Example 3.1.

In the situation described in Example 3.1 the time allowed will previously have been recorded on the job card, and the actual time taken will be entered on the card when the operation is completed. The bonus can then be calculated and recorded on the employee's record card, which becomes the basis for determining the total weekly bonus to be included on the payroll. In most organizations the payroll accounting function will be computerized.

You should note that the objective of an incentive scheme is to benefit both the employer and employee. Consider a situation where an employee is paid £8 per hour and in one hour produces 10 units. The average labour cost per unit will be £0.80. To stimulate production, a piecework system is introduced where workers are paid £0.70 per unit produced. Assuming that this results in an increase in productivity to 12 units per hour, the hourly rate would increase to £8.40 (12 × £0.70). The overall effect is that there is an increase in the hourly rate of the employee and a reduction in the labour cost per unit produced for the employer (from £0.80 to £0.70).

EXAMPLE 3.1

The time allowed for a specific operation is 20 hours and the actual time taken by an employee was 16 hours. A bonus scheme is in operation where employees receive a bonus of 50% of the time saved. The hourly wage rate is £8 per hour.

The employee, having worked for 16 hours, will receive a time rate wage of £128 (16 hours at £8) plus a bonus of £16 (50% of 4 hours saved at £8 per hour).

LABOUR COST ACCOUNTING

The objective of labour cost accounting is to record the amount of time that employees have taken on various activities. The time spent on providing a service to a specific customer, or manufacturing a specific product, is recorded on source documents, such as **time sheets** or **job cards**. Details of the customer's account number, job number or the product's code are also entered on these documents. The employee's hourly rate of pay is then entered so that the direct labour cost for the employee can be assigned to the appropriate cost object. For indirect labour costs the same procedure applies with the overhead account number to which the costs should be assigned being entered on the source documents.

Sometimes productive workers will be unoccupied for short periods and **idle time cards** are used to record the amount of idle or waiting time incurred. The amount of idle time is costed at the hourly wage rate and charged to an idle time overhead account for each department. An entry should be made on the card indicating the reasons for the idle time. Periodically, a report should be compiled for each department, showing a breakdown of the idle time and the proportion that it represents of recorded direct labour hours.

In many organizations the recording procedures for accounting for labour will be computerized and the source documents will only exist in the form of computer records.

Some categories of labour, such as general labourers or supervision, may be engaged on numerous activities and it would not be feasible to record minute amounts of time on each activity. The labour costs of these employees should be derived from payroll details and charged to departmental overhead accounts for supervision or general labour. The procedure for accounting for overheads is explained in the next chapter.

Accounting treatment of various labour cost items

HOLIDAY PAY, OVERTIME AND SHIFT PREMIUMS

Holiday pay received by employees whose labour cost is normally regarded as direct should be charged to activities by means of an inflated hourly rate. For example, if the employee is normally paid £8 per hour for a 40-hour week and is entitled to six weeks annual holiday he or she will receive a total of £1920 holiday pay (six weeks at £320 per week). Assuming that the employee works the remaining 46 weeks, the attendance time will amount to 1840 hours (46 weeks at 40 hours per week). Dividing £1920 by 1840 hours gives an addition of approximately £1.04 per hour to the employee's hourly wage rate to ensure that the holiday pay is recovered. The advantage of this approach is that holiday pay is treated as a direct labour cost.

Overtime premiums and **shift-work premiums** are included as part of overheads. If overtime premiums are charged directly to products/services or customers' orders undertaken during the overtime or night-shift period, they will bear higher costs than those produced during a regular working week. Overtime and night-shift work is usually necessitated by a generally high level of activity, not by specific products or customers. It is therefore inappropriate to record activities undertaken during overtime or night hours as being more costly than their counterparts undertaken during, say, a regular eight-hour day. If, however, the overtime or shift premiums are a direct result of a customer's urgent request for the completion of the order and not due to the general pressure of work, then the overtime or shift premiums should be charged directly to the customer. It is important that overtime and shift premiums are also analysed by departments for cost control purposes.

Let us now examine the comments made in the preceding paragraph with the aid of a simple illustration. Consider a situation where an employee is paid time and a half for weekly hours worked in excess of 40 hours. Assume that the employee works for 50 hours and that the 10 hours of overtime were spent on a particular activity. The hourly wage rate is £8. The employee's weekly wage will be calculated as follows:

Normal time rate wage: 50 hours at £8	£400
Overtime premium (1/2 × 10 hours at £8)	£40
	£440

The normal time rate wage will be allocated to the activities on which the employee was engaged during the period, but if the overtime was a result of demand exceeding productive capacity, it would be unreasonable to charge the overtime premium to the particular activity merely because it was scheduled to be produced during the overtime period. In such circumstances it would be preferable to charge the overtime premium to the appropriate overhead account, the total of which would be apportioned to all activities worked on during the period.

PIECEWORK AND BONUS PAYMENTS

Let us now consider the accounting problems associated with incentive payment schemes. The earnings of an employee on **piecework** are computed for each payroll period by multiplying the agreed rate per piece by the number of good units produced. There will usually also be a specified minimum weekly wage, so that if an employee's production falls below the weekly minimum, he or she will be paid at the time rate rather than the piecework rate for that period. For example, if an individual is paid on the basis of £0.45 per piece with a £8 per hour guaranteed wage rate and works 38 hours during the week, the minimum wage for the week is £304 (38 × £8) even though the week's output might only be 600 pieces, which would entitle him or her to only £270 on a piecework basis. The difference between the guaranteed minimum wage of £304 and the piecework earnings of £270 will normally be charged to an overhead account established for this purpose.

EMPLOYMENT COSTS

In addition to the wage and salary payments to employees, the employer will incur a number of other costs that are incidental to their employment. These costs include such items as the employer's share of National Insurance contributions and pension fund contributions. Employment costs are frequently recorded as overheads, but it is preferable to calculate an average hourly rate for employment costs and add this to the hourly wage rate paid to the employees. For example, the employer may be responsible for employment costs of £40 for an operative who is paid £8 per hour for a 40-hour week. Here we can establish that the employment costs are £1 per hour and this cost can be added to the hourly wage rate of £8 per hour, giving a total rate of £9 per hour. This approach is conceptually preferable to the alternative of charging the £40 to an overhead account, since employment costs are a fundamental part of acquiring labour services.

Materials recording procedure

According to a survey by Drury and Tayles (2000) of 176 UK organizations the cost of direct materials represented the dominant costs in manufacturing organizations, averaging 51% of total costs for the responding organizations within the manufacturing sector. The accounting and control of materials is therefore of vital importance in manufacturing organizations. In the remainder of this chapter the mechanisms for recording and controlling materials are explained. Because of the importance to the manufacturing sector the focus is mainly on manufacturing organizations but the materials recording procedure that is described is also applicable to non-manufacturing organizations. The materials recording procedure involves the following stages:

- storage of materials;
- purchase of materials;
- receipt of materials;
- issue of materials;
- assigning the cost of materials to cost objects.

To simplify the presentation, and help you understand the recording procedures, the following sections describe the clerical procedures for each of the above stages. You should note, however, that in most organizations the recording procedure is computerized using bar coding and other forms of on-line information recording. The source documents that are described and illustrated are likely to exist only in the form of computer records.

STORAGE OF MATERIALS

In a manufacturing organization the stores department will be responsible for ensuring that optimal stock levels are maintained for each item of material in stock. Thus, to control the quantity of stocks held, adequate records must be maintained for each stores item. When items of materials have reached their re-order point a **purchase requisition** is initiated requesting the purchase department to obtain the re-order quantity from an appropriate supplier. Methods that are used for establishing optimum stock levels, re-order points and re-order quantities will be explained later in this chapter.

PURCHASE OF MATERIALS

Upon the receipt of a purchase requisition, purchasing department staff will select an appropriate supplier based on their expert knowledge, and then complete a **purchase order** requesting that the supplier supply the materials listed on the order. A copy of the purchase order is sent to the receiving section within the stores department for checking with the goods when they arrive.

RECEIPT OF MATERIALS

When the goods are received by the receiving section they are inspected and checked with the supplier's delivery note and a copy of the purchase order. The receiving section then lists the materials received on a **goods received note** (GRN) and forwards copies of the GRN to the purchasing and accounting departments. The purchasing department will record that the order has been completed, and the accounting department will check the GRN with the supplier's invoice to ensure that payment is made only in respect of goods actually received. The department will also use the invoice to price each of the items listed on the GRN. The GRN is the source document for entering details of the items received in the receipts column of the appropriate **stores ledger account**. An illustration of a stores ledger account is provided in Exhibit 3.1. This document is merely a record of the quantity and value of each individual item of material stored by the organization.

EXHIBIT 3.1

A stores ledger account

		Receipts			Issues				Stock		
Date	GRN no.	Quantity	Unit price (£)	Amount (£)	Stores req. no.	Quantity	Unit price (£)	Amount (£)	Quantity	Unit price (£)	Amount (£)

Stores ledger account

Material: .... Code: ....   Maximum quantity: ....
Minimum quantity: ....

ISSUE OF MATERIALS

The formal authorization for the issue of materials is a **stores requisition**. The type and quantity of materials issued are listed on the requisition. This document also contains details of either the customer's order number, product/service code or overhead account for which the materials are required. Exhibit 3.2 provides an illustration of a typical stores requisition. Each of the items listed on the materials requisition are priced from the information recorded in the receipts column of the appropriate stores ledger account. The information for each of the items listed on the stores requisition is then recorded in the issues column of the appropriate stores ledger account and a balance of the quantity and value is calculated for each item of material.

EXHIBIT 3.2

A stores requisition

			Stores requisition			No.	
Material required for: (Product code or overhead account) Department:						Date:	
[Quantity]	Description	Code no.	Weight	Rate	£	[Notes]	
Departmental Head							

ASSIGNING THE COST OF MATERIALS TO COST OBJECTS

The total cost of the items of material listed on the stores requisition is assigned to the appropriate customer's account number, overhead account or product or service code. The details on the material requisition thus represent the source information for assigning the cost of the materials to the appropriate cost object. Thus the accounting entries required for an issue of materials involve:

1. Reducing the value of raw materials stocks by recording the values issued in the issues column of the appropriate stores ledger account.
2. Assigning the cost of the issues to the appropriate customer's order number, product/service code or overhead account.

Pricing the issues of materials

A difficulty that arises with material issues is the cost to associate with each issue. This is because the same type of material may have been purchased at several different prices.

Actual cost can take on several different values, and some method of pricing material issues must be selected. Consider the situation presented in Example 3.2.

EXAMPLE 3.2

On 5th March Nordic purchased 5000 units of materials at £1 each. A further 5000 units were purchased on 30 March at £1.20 each. During April, 5000 units were issued to job Z. No further issues were made during April and you are now preparing the monthly accounts for April.

There are three alternative methods that you might consider for calculating the cost of materials issued to job Z which will impact on both the cost of sales and the inventory valuation that is incorporated in the April monthly profit statement and balance sheet. First, you can assume that the first item received was the first item to be issued, that is **first in, first out (FIFO)**. In the example the 5000 units issued to job Z would be priced at £1 and the closing inventory would be valued at £6000 (5000 units at £1.20 per unit).

Secondly, you could assume that the last item to be received was the first item to be issued, that is, **last in, first out (LIFO)**. Here a material cost of £6000 (5000 units at £1.20 per unit) would be recorded against the cost of job Z and the closing inventory would be valued at £5000 (5000 units at £1 per unit).

Thirdly there may be a strong case for issuing the items at the **average cost** of the materials in stock (i.e. £1.10 per unit). With an average cost system the job cost would be recorded at £5500 and the closing inventory would also be valued at £5500. The following is a summary of the three different materials pricing methods relating to Example 3.2:

	Cost of sales (i.e. charge to job Z) £	Closing inventory £	Total costs £
First in, first out (FIFO)	5000 (5000 × £1)	6000 (5000 × £1.20)	11 000
Last in, first out (LIFO)	6000 (5000 × £1.20)	5000 (5000 × £1)	11 000
Average cost	5500 (5000 × £1.10)	5500 (5000 × £1.10)	11 000

FIFO appears to be the most logical method in the sense that it makes the same assumption as the physical flow of materials through an organization; that is, it is assumed that items received first will be issued first. During periods of inflation, the earliest materials that have the lowest purchase price will be issued first. This assumption leads to a lower cost of sales calculation, and therefore a higher profit than would be obtained by using either of the other methods. Note also that the closing inventory will be at the latest and therefore higher prices. With the LIFO method the latest and higher prices are assigned to the cost of sales and therefore lower profits will be reported compared with using either FIFO or average cost. The value of the closing inventory will be at the earliest and therefore lower prices. Under the average cost method, the cost of sales and the closing inventory will fall somewhere between the values recorded for the FIFO and LIFO methods.

LIFO is not an acceptable method of pricing for taxation purposes in the UK, although this does not preclude its use provided that the accounts are adjusted for taxation purposes. The UK Statement of Standard Accounting Practice on stocks and Work in Progress (SSAP 9), however, states that LIFO does not bear a reasonable relationship to actual costs obtained during the period, and implies that this method is inappropriate for external reporting. In view of these comments, the FIFO or the average cost method should be used for external financial accounting purposes. Instead of using FIFO or average cost for inventory valuation and profit measurement many organizations maintain their inventories at standard prices using a standard costing system. With a standard costing system the process of pricing material issues is considerably simplified. We shall look at standard costing in detail in Chapter 15.

The above discussion relates to pricing the issue of materials for internal and external profit measurement and inventory valuation. For decision-making the focus is on future costs, rather than the allocation of past costs, and therefore the different methods of pricing materials is not normally an issue.

The aim so far in this section has been to provide you with a simplistic example, in the form of Example 3.2, to provide you with an understanding of the implications of the three different methods of stores pricing. In practice pricing stores issues is likely to be more complex than the situation presented in Example 3.2. To ensure that you can price stores issues in more complex situations you should now refer to Example 3.3 and then examine each of the entries in stores ledger accounts for the three different pricing methods that are presented in Exhibit 3.3. Do remember, however, that in practice computer programs exist for pricing stores issues by the chosen method so it is most unlikely that the process will be carried out manually.

EXAMPLE 3.3

The purchase and issue of a raw material by the Midshire Water Authority for a five month period were as follows:

1 July	Received	2000 units at £10 per unit
9 July	Received	520 units at £10.50 per unit
18 July	Issued	1400 units
5 August	Received	800 units at £11.50 per unit
22 August	Received	600 units at £12.50 per unit
15 September	Issued	1240 units
14 October	Issued	480 units
8 November	Received	1000 units at £11 per unit
24 November	Issued	760 units

There was no opening stock of the raw material. You are required to prepare the stores ledger accounts when issues are priced, respectively, according to the FIFO, LIFO and average cost methods. Please refer to Exhibit 3.3 for the answer.

You should note in Exhibit 3.3 that with the FIFO method the issue of 1240 units on 15 September is at three different purchase prices. This is because 1400 units out of the earliest purchase of 2000 units have already been issued The remaining 600 units are therefore the first items to be issued out of the 1240 units on 15 September. The next earliest purchase of 520 units is now issued, leaving a balance of 120 units to be issued from the purchase of 5 August. The closing stock consists of the final purchase for the period of 1000 units plus 40 units from the 22 August purchase that have not yet been issued.

Now refer to the LIFO method in Exhibit 3.3 and look at the issue of 480 units on 14 October. This issue includes the 160 units at the 5 August purchase price of £11.50 because all of the units from the latest purchase on 22 August have previously been issued, together with 640 units from the next latest purchase of 5 August. Only 160 units from the 5 August purchase are available for issue. The balance of 320 units issued is at £10 as all

EXHIBIT 3.3

Pricing stores issues for the Midshire Water Authority

Stores ledger account – FIFO method

Material: .... Code: .... Maximum quantity: ....
Minimum quantity: ....

Date	GRN no.	Receipts Quantity	Unit price (£)	Amount (£)	Issues Quantity	Unit price (£)	Amount (£)	Stock Quantity	Unit price (£)	Amount (£)
July 1		2000	10.00	20 000				2000		20 000
9		520	10.50	5 460				2520		25 460
18					1400	10.00	14 000	1120		11 460
Aug 5		800	11.50	9 200				1920		20 660
Aug 22		600	12.50	7 500				2520		28 160
Sept 15					600	10.00				
					520	10.50				
					120 1240	11.50	12 840	1280		15 320
Oct 14					480	11.50	5 520	800		9 800
Nov 8		1000	11.00	11 000	200	11.50		1800		20 800
Nov 24					560 760	12.50	9 300	1040		11 500

The closing stock represents:

$$\begin{aligned}
40 \text{ units at £12.50 per unit} &= £500 \\
1000 \text{ units at £11.00 per unit} &= £11\,000 \\
&\underline{£11\,500}
\end{aligned}$$

Stores ledger account – LIFO method

Material: .... Code: .... Maximum quantity: ....
Minimum quantity: ....

Date	GRN no.	Receipts Quantity	Unit price (£)	Amount (£)	Issues Quantity	Unit price (£)	Amount (£)	Stock Quantity	Unit price (£)	Amount (£)
July 1		2000	10.00	20 000				2000		20 000
9		520	10.50	5 460				2520		25 460
18					520	10.50				
					880 1400	10.00	14 260	1120		11 200
Aug 5		800	11.50	9 200				1920		20 400
Aug 22		600	12.50	7 500				2520		27 900
Sept 15					600	12.50				
					640 1240	11.50	14 860	1280		13 040
Oct 14					160	11.50				
					320 480	10.00	5 040	800		8 000
Nov 8		1000	11.00	11 000				1800		19 000
Nov 24					760	11.00	8 360	1040		10 640

The closing stock represents:

$$\begin{aligned}
800 \text{ units at £10.00 per unit} &= £8\,000 \\
240 \text{ units at £11.00 per unit} &= £2\,640 \\
&\underline{£10\,640}
\end{aligned}$$

		Stores ledger account – **average-cost method**									
Material:			Code:		Maximum quantity:						
					Minimum quantity:						

| Date | Receipts | | | | Issues | | | | Stock | | |
	GRN no.	Quantity	Unit price (£)	Amount (£)	Stores req.	Quantity	Unit price (£)	Amount (£)	Quantity	Unit price (£)	Amount (£)
July 1		2000	10.00	20 000					2000	10.00	20 000
9		520	10.50	5 460					2520	10.1032	25 460
18						1400	10.1032	14 144	1120		11 316
Aug 5		800	11.50	9 200					1920	10.6854	20 516
Aug 22		600	12.50	7 500					2520	11.1175	28 016
Sept 15						1240	11.1175	13 785	1280		14 231
Oct 14						480	11.1175	5 536	800		8 895
Nov 8		1000	11.00	11 000					1800	11.0528	19 895
Nov 24						760	11.0528	8 400	1040		11 495

$$9 \text{ July} = \frac{£25\,460}{2520 \text{ units}} = £10.1032$$

$$22 \text{ August} = \frac{£28\,016}{2520 \text{ units}} = £11.1175$$

the previous later purchases have already been issued. Hence LIFO does not always ensure that the issues are at the latest purchase price. The closing stock consists of 240 units at the latest purchase price of £11 plus 800 units at the earliest purchase price of £10.

Finally, with the average cost method shown in the third section of Exhibit 3.3 you should note that each of the items are issued at the average cost per unit. This is calculated by dividing the total value of the material in stock by the total quantity in stock; after each new purchase. An illustration of the average unit cost calculations for the 9 July and 22 August purchases is shown in the third section of Exhibit 3.3. An important point to note with the average cost method is that each item is issued at the latest average price and this average price changes only when a new purchase is received.

Issues relating to accounting for materials

In this section three issues that relate to accounting for materials are examined. The issues relate to the treatment of:

1. stores losses;
2. materials delivery costs; and
3. materials handling costs.

TREATMENT OF STORES LOSSES

To achieve accurate profit measurement, the clerical or computer record in respect of each item of materials in stock must be in agreement with the actual stock held. This means that the actual stock must be physically counted and compared with the clerical or computer record. For this to be done effectively, there must be either a **complete periodic**

stockcount or some form of continuous stocktaking. The former refers to a situation where all the stores items are counted at one point in time, whereas the latter involves a sample of stores items being counted regularly on, say, a daily basis. If there is **continuous stocktaking** production is unlikely to be disrupted.

Sometimes it may be found that the actual stock level is different from the clerical or computer records. The reasons for this may be:

1. an entry having been made in the wrong stores ledger account;
2. the items having been placed in the wrong physical location;
3. arithmetical errors made when calculating the stores balance on the stores ledger when a manual system is operated;
4. theft of stock.

When a discrepancy arises the individual stores ledger accounts must be adjusted so that they are in agreement with the actual stock. Assume, for example, that the actual stock is less than the clerical or computer record. The quantity and value of the appropriate stores ledger account must be reduced and the difference charged to an overhead account for stores losses. The total amount charged to the stores losses overhead account should be allocated to cost objects based on the overhead procedure described in the next chapter.

TREATMENT OF MATERIALS DELIVERY COSTS

Ideally, delivery charges made by suppliers should be included as part of the purchase price of the materials so that these costs can be charged as direct costs. Wherever possible, materials should be charged directly to cost objects rather than being grouped as indirect costs and apportioned to cost objects. The delivery charge will normally be shown separately on the invoice for the consignment of materials delivered. When the invoice is for one kind of material only, there is no problem in accounting for the materials, since the delivery charge merely needs to be added to the cost of the materials and the resulting total entered as a receipt for the appropriate item of material. When the delivery charge refers to several different types of material, the charge must be apportioned to each type of material delivered. Such an apportionment could be made according to either the value or the weight of the materials. Alternatively, the clerical work could be simplified by charging delivery costs to an overhead account and apportioning these costs as part of the overhead procedure described in the next chapter.

TREATMENT OF MATERIALS HANDLING COSTS

The term 'materials handling costs' refers to the expenses involved in receiving, storing, issuing and handling materials. Various approaches can be used to account for materials handling costs. They involve charging the costs to a materials handling overhead account and allocating these costs to cost objects based on the approaches described for traditional costing systems in the next chapter or those for activity-based costing systems described in Chapter 11. You can therefore defer studying accounting for materials handling costs to the next chapter. However, it is appropriate at this stage that you should be aware that some companies establish a separate **materials handling rate**. Consider, for example, a situation where the materials handling costs for a period were £1 million and the direct materials issued during the period were valued at £5 million. In this situation the materials handling cost could be allocated to cost objects (i.e. products, services or customers) at a materials handling rate of 20% of the cost of direct materials issued (£1 million/£5 million) thus resulting in the £1 million materials handling cost being charged to cost objects.

Quantitative models for the planning and control of stocks

Investment in stocks represents a major asset of most industrial and commercial organizations, and it is essential that stocks be managed efficiently so that such investments do not become unnecessarily large. A firm should determine its optimum level of investment in stocks – and, to do this, two conflicting requirements must be met. First, it must ensure that stocks are sufficient to meet the requirements of production and sales; and, secondly, it must avoid holding surplus stocks that are unnecessary and that increase the risk of obsolescence. The optimal stock level lies somewhere between these two extremes. Our objective in the following sections is to consider how economic order quantities and the levels at which stocks should be replenished can be derived.

Relevant costs for quantitative models under conditions of certainty

The relevant costs that should be considered when determining optimal stock levels consist of holding costs and ordering costs. **Holding costs** usually consist of the following:

1. opportunity cost of investment in stocks;
2. incremental insurance costs;
3. incremental warehouse and storage costs;
4. incremental material handling costs;
5. cost of obsolescence and deterioration of stocks.

The relevant holding costs for use in quantitative models should include only those items that will vary with the levels of stocks. Costs that will not be affected by changes in stock levels are not relevant costs. For example, in the case of warehousing and storage only those costs should be included that will vary with changes in the number of units ordered. Salaries of storekeepers, depreciation of equipment and fixed rental of equipment and buildings are often irrelevant because they are unaffected by changes in stock levels.

To the extent that funds are invested in stocks, there is an opportunity cost of holding them. This opportunity cost is reflected by the required return that is lost from investing in stocks rather than some alternative investment. The opportunity cost should be applied only to those costs that vary with the number of units purchased. The relevant holding costs for other items such as material handling, obsolescence and deterioration are difficult to estimate, but we shall see that these costs are unlikely to be critical to the investment decision. Normally, holding costs are expressed as a percentage rate per pound of average investment.

Ordering costs usually consist of the clerical costs of preparing a purchase order, receiving deliveries and paying invoices. Ordering costs that are common to all stock decisions are not relevant, and only the incremental costs of placing an order are used in formulating the quantitative models.

The costs of acquiring stocks through buying or manufacturing are not a relevant cost to be included in the quantitative models, since the acquisition costs remain unchanged, irrespective of the order size or stock levels, unless quantity discounts are available. (For a discussion of how quantity discounts should be incorporated you should refer to Drury, 2000; ch. 25.) For example, it does not matter in terms of acquisition cost whether total annual requirements of 1000 units at £10 each are purchased in one 1000-unit batch, ten 100-unit batches or one hundred 10-unit batches; the acquisition cost of £10 000 will remain unchanged. The acquisition cost is not therefore a relevant cost, but the ordering and holding costs will change in relation to the order size, and these will be relevant for decision-making models.

Determining the economic order quantity

If we assume certainty, the optimum order will be determined by those costs that are affected by either the quantity of stocks held or the number of orders placed. If more units are ordered at one time, fewer orders will be required per year. This will mean a reduction in the ordering costs. However, when fewer orders are placed, larger average stocks must be maintained, which leads to an increase in holding costs. The problem is therefore one of trading off the costs of carrying large stocks against the costs of placing more orders. The optimum order size is the order quantity that will result in the total amount of the ordering and holding costs being minimized. This optimum order size is known as the **economic order quantity (EOQ)**; it can be determined by tabulating the total costs for various order quantities, by a graphical presentation or by using a formula. All three methods are illustrated using the information given in Example 3.4.

TABULATION METHOD

The annual relevant costs for various order quantities are set out in Exhibit 3.4.

You will see that the economic order quantity is 400 units. At this point the total annual relevant costs are at a minimum.

EXAMPLE 3.4

A company purchases a raw material from an outside supplier at a cost of £9 per unit. The total annual demand for this product is 40 000 units, and the following additional information is available.

	(£)	(£)
Required annual return on investment in stocks (10% × £9)	0.90	
Other holding costs per unit	0.10	
Holding costs per unit		1.00
Cost per purchase order:		
Clerical costs, stationery, postage, telephone etc.		2.00

You are required to determine the optimal order quantity.

EXHIBIT 3.4

*Relevant costs
for various
order quantities*

Order quantity	100	200	300	400	500	600	800	10 000
Average stock in units[a]	50	100	150	200	250	300	400	5 000
Number of purchase orders[b]	400	200	133	100	80	67	50	4
Annual holding costs[c]	£50	£100	£150	£200	£250	£300	£400	£5 000
Annual ordering cost	£800	£400	£266	£200	£160	£134	£100	£8
Total relevant cost	£850	£500	£416	£400	£410	£434	£500	£5 008

[a]If there are no stocks when the order is received and the units received are used at a constant rate, the average stock will be one-half of the quantity ordered. Even if a minimum safety stock is held, the average stock relevant to the decision will still be one-half of the quantity ordered, because the minimum stock will remain unchanged for each alternative order quantity.
[b]The number of purchase orders is ascertained by dividing the total annual demand of 40 000 units by the order quantity.
[c]The annual holding cost is ascertained by multiplying the average stock by the holding cost of £1 per unit.

GRAPHICAL METHOD

The information tabulated in Exhibit 3.4 is presented in graphical form in Figure 3.1 for every order size up to 800 units. The vertical axis represents the relevant annual costs for the investment in stocks, and the horizontal axis can be used to represent either the various order quantities or the average stock levels; two scales are actually shown on the horizontal axis so that both items can be incorporated. You will see from the graph that as the average stock level or the order quantity increases, the holding cost also increases. Alternatively, the ordering costs decline as stock levels and order quantities are increased. The total cost line represents the summation of both the holding and the ordering costs.

Note that the total cost line is at a minimum for an order quantity of 400 units and occurs at the point where the ordering cost and holding cost curves intersect. That is, the economic order quantity is found at the point where the holding costs equal the ordering costs. It is also interesting to note from the graph (see also Exhibit 3.4) that the total relevant costs are not particularly sensitive to changes in the order quantity. For example, if you refer to Exhibit 3.4 you will see that a 25% change in the order quantity from 400 units to either 300 or 500 units leads to an increase in annual costs from £400 to £410 or £416, an increase of 2.5% or 4%. Alternatively, an increase of 50% in the order quantity from 400 units to 600 units leads to an increase in annual costs from £400 to £434 or 8.5%.

FORMULA METHOD

The economic order quantity can be found by applying a formula that incorporates the basic relationships between holding and ordering costs and order quantities. These relationships can be stated as follows: the number of orders for a period is the total

FIGURE 3.1 *Economic order quantity graph.*

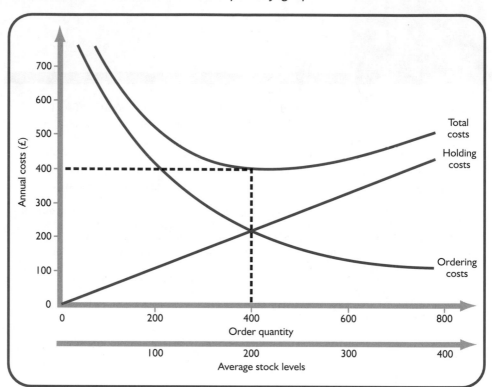

demand for that item of stock for the period (denoted by *D*) divided by the quantity ordered in units (denoted by *Q*). The total ordering cost is obtained by multiplying the number of orders for a period by the ordering cost per order (denoted by *O*), and is given by the formula

$$\frac{\text{total demand for period}}{\text{quantity ordered}} \times \text{ordering cost per order} = \frac{DO}{Q}$$

Assuming that holding costs are constant per unit, the total holding cost for a period will be equal to the average stock for the period, which is represented by the quantity ordered divided by two (*Q*/2), multiplied by the holding cost per unit (denoted by *H*); it is therefore given by

$$\frac{\text{quantity ordered}}{2} \times \text{holding cost per unit} = \frac{QH}{2}$$

The total relevant cost (TC) for any order quantity can now be expressed as

$$\text{TC} = \frac{DO}{Q} + \frac{QH}{2}$$

We can determine a minimum for this total cost function by differentiating the above formula with respect to *Q* and setting the derivative equal to zero.[1] We then get the economic order quantity *Q*:

$$Q = \sqrt{\left(\frac{2\,DO}{H}\right)}$$

or

$$Q = \sqrt{\left(\frac{2 \times \text{total demand for period} \times \text{cost per order}}{\text{holding cost per unit}}\right)}$$

If we apply this formula to Example 3.4, we have

$$Q = \sqrt{\left(\frac{2 \times 40\,000 \times 2}{1}\right)} = 400 \text{ units}$$

Assumptions of the EOQ formula

The calculations obtained by using the EOQ model should be interpreted with care, since the model is based on a number of important assumptions. One of these is that the holding cost per unit will be constant. While this assumption might be correct for items such as the funds invested in stocks, other costs might increase on a step basis as stock levels increase. For example, additional storekeepers might be hired as stock levels reach certain levels. Alternatively, if stocks decline, it may be that casual stores labour may be released once stocks fall to a certain critical level.

Another assumption that we made in calculating the total holding cost is that the average balance in stock was equal to one-half of the order quantity. If a constant amount of stock is not used per day, this assumption will be violated; there is a distinct possibility that seasonal and cyclical factors will produce an uneven usage over time. Despite the fact that much of the data used in the model represents rough approximations, calculation of the EOQ is still likely to be useful. If you examine Figure 3.1, you will see that the total cost curve tends to flatten out, so that total cost may not be significantly affected if some of the underlying assumptions are violated or if there are minor variations in the cost of predictions.

Determining when to place the order

To determine the point at which the order should be placed to obtain additional stocks (i.e. the **re-order point**), we must ascertain the time that will elapse between placing the order and the actual delivery of the stocks. This time period is referred to as the **lead time**. In a world of certainty the re-order point will be the number of days/weeks lead time multiplied by the daily/weekly usage during the period. For materials, components and supplies the re-order point is the point in time when the purchase requisition is initiated and the order is sent to the supplier. For the finished goods stock of a manufacturer the re-order point is the level of finished goods stock at which the production order should be issued.

If we assume that an annual usage of a raw material is 6000 units and the weekly usage is constant then if there are 50 working weeks in a year, the weekly usage will be 120 units. If the lead time is two weeks, the order should be placed when stocks fall to 240 units. The economic order quantity can indicate how frequently the stocks should be purchased. For example, if the EOQ is 600 then, with an annual demand of 6000 units, ten orders will be placed every five weeks. However, with a lead time of two weeks, the firm will place an order three weeks after the first delivery when the stock will have fallen to 240 units (600 units EOQ less three weeks usage at 120 units per week). The order will then be repeated at five-weekly intervals. The EOQ model can therefore under certain circumstances be

FIGURE 3.2 *Fluctuations in stock levels under conditions of certainty.*

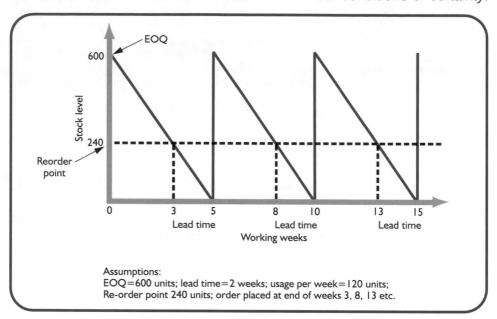

Assumptions:
EOQ=600 units; lead time=2 weeks; usage per week=120 units;
Re-order point 240 units; order placed at end of weeks 3, 8, 13 etc.

used to indicate when to replenish stocks and the amount to replenish. This process is illustrated in Figure 3.2.

Control of stocks through classification

In large firms it is quite possible for tens of thousands of different items to be stored. It is clearly impossible to apply the techniques outlined in this chapter to all of these. It is therefore essential that stocks be classified into categories of importance so that a firm can apply the most elaborate procedures of controlling stocks only to the most important items. The commonest procedure is known as the **ABC classification method**. This is illustrated in Exhibit 3.5.

The ABC method requires that an estimate be made of the total purchase cost for each item of stock for the period. The sales forecast is the basis used for estimating the quantities of each item of stock to be purchased during the period. Each item is then grouped in decreasing order of annual purchase cost. The top 10% of items in stock in terms of annual purchase cost are categorized as A items, the next 20% as B items and the final 70% as C items. If we assume there are 10 000 stock items then the top 1000 items in terms of annual purchase costs will be classified as A items, and so on. In practice, it will be unnecessary to estimate the value of many of the 7000 C items, since their annual purchase cost will be so small it will be obvious that they will fall into the C category.

You will see from Exhibit 3.5 that 10% of all stock items (i.e. the A items) represents 73% of the total cost; 20% of the items (B items) represent 19% of the total cost; and 70% of the items (C items) represent 8% of the total cost. It follows that the greatest degree of control should be exerted over the A items, which account for the high investment costs, and it is the A category items that are most appropriate for the application of the quantitative techniques discussed in this chapter. For these items an attempt should be made to maintain low safety stocks consistent with avoiding high stockout costs. Larger orders and safety stocks are likely to be a feature of the C-category items. Normally, re-order points for these items will be determined on a subjective basis rather than using quantitative methods, the objective being to minimize the expense in

Stage 1. For each item in stock multiply the estimated usage for a period by the estimated unit price to obtain the total purchase cost:

Item	Estimated usage	Unit price (£)	Total purchase cost (£)
1	60 000	1.00	60 000
2	20 000	0.05	1 000
3	1 000	0.10	100
4	10 000	0.02	200
5	100 000	0.01	1 000
6	80 000	2.00	160 000

(This list is continued until all items in stock are included.)

Stage 2. Group all the above items in descending order of purchase price and then divide into class A (top 10%), class B (next 20%) and then class C (bottom 70%). The analysis might be as follows:

	Number of items in stock		Total cost	
	No	%	Amount (£)	%
Class A	1 000	10	730 000	73
Class B	2 000	20	190 000	19
Class C	7 000	70	80 000	8
	10 000	100	1 000 000	100

controlling these items. The control of B-category items is likely to be based on quantitative methods, but they are unlikely to be as sophisticated as for the A-category items.

The percentage value of total cost for the A, B and C categories in Exhibit 3.5 is typical of most manufacturing companies. In practice, it is normal for between 10 and 15% of the items in stock to account for between 70 and 80% of the total value of purchases. At the other extreme, between 70 and 80% of the items in stock account for approximately 10% of the total value. The control of stock levels is eased considerably if it is concentrated on that small proportion of stock items that account for most of the total cost.

Materials requirement planning

The discussion so far in this chapter has assumed that the replenishment of stocks and the determination of re-order points and order quantities (i.e. the EOQ) for each item of material occurs independently of other activities. However, in complex manufacturing environments the demand for material purchases is dependent on the volume of the planned output of components and sub-components which include the raw materials that must be purchased. **Materials requirement planning (MRP)** originated in the early 1960s as a computerized approach for coordinating the planning of materials acquisition and production. The major feature of MRP is that it first involves an estimation of the quantity and timing of finished goods demanded and then uses this to determine the requirements for components/sub-components at each of the prior stages of production. This provides the basis for determining the quantity and timing of purchased materials and any bought-in components.

Figure 3.3 provides an overview of the approach. You can see that the top-level items represent three finished goods items (FG1, FG2 and FG3). The MRP system determines the requirements for each product into its components (or sub-components) and these are further separated into second, third and so on levels of sub-components, until at the lowest level of the hierarchy only purchased items (i.e. direct materials, DM) exist. For both FG1 and FG2 purchased raw materials are used to produce components before production of the end finished product. You should also note that in Figure 3.3 both FG1 and FG2 require the same sub-component (SC1), which in turn require the same direct materials (DM1).

The operation of an MRP system involves the following:

1. A *master production schedule*: This schedule is the starting point for MRP. It specifies both the timing, and quantity demanded of each of the top-level finished goods items.

2. A *bill of materials file*, which specifies the components/sub-components and materials required for each finished product.

3. A *master parts file* containing planned lead times of all items to be purchased and internally produced components.

4. An *inventory file* for each item of material and component/sub-component containing details of the current balance available, scheduled orders and items allocated to production but not yet drawn from stocks.

The aim of MRP is to generate a planned coordinated schedule of materials requirements for a specified time period for each item of material after taking into account scheduled receipts, projected target stock levels and items already allocated to production but not yet drawn from stocks. The EOQ model can be used within MRP systems to determine economic quantity sizes to be purchased provided that the major assumption of the EOQ model of constant demand broadly applies.

Finally, you should note that after its introduction in the 1960s, materials requirement planning was later extended to the management of all manufacturing resources. In particular, it focuses on machine capacity planning and labour scheduling as well as materials requirement planning. This extended system is known as **manufacturing resource planning** or MRP II. The term MRP I is used to describe materials requirement planning.

Just-in-time systems

The success of Japanese firms in international markets in the 1980s generated interest among many Western companies as to how this success was achieved. The implementation of **just-in-time (JIT) methods** was considered to be one of the major factors contributing to this success. A JIT approach is best described as a philosophy of management dedicated to the elimination of **non-value-added activities**. A non-value added activity is defined as an activity where there is an opportunity for cost reduction without reducing the customer's

FIGURE 3.3 *An overview of the structure of an MRP system.*

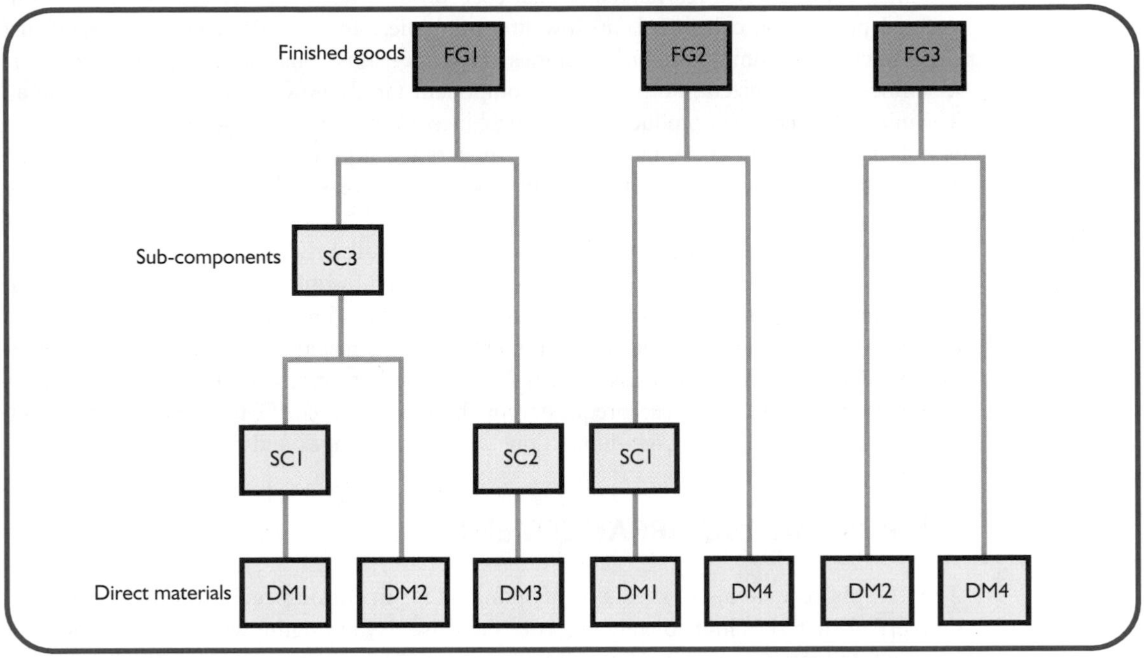

perceived usefulness of a product or service. In contrast, a **value-added activity** is an activity that customers perceive as adding usefulness to the product or service they purchase. The lead or cycle time involved in manufacturing and selling a product consists of process time, inspection time, move time, queue time and storage time. Of these five steps, only process time actually adds value to the product. All the other activities add cost but no value to the product, and are thus deemed non-value added processes within the JIT philosophy. According to Berliner and Brimson (1988), process time is less than 10% of total manufacturing lead time in many organizations in the USA. Therefore 90% of the manufacturing lead time associated with a product adds costs, but no value, to the product. By adopting a JIT philosophy and focusing on reducing lead times, it is claimed that total costs can be significantly reduced. The ultimate goal of JIT is to convert raw materials to finished products with lead times equal to processing times, thus eliminating all non-value added activities.

REARRANGEMENT OF THE PRODUCTION PROCESS

The first stage in implementing JIT manufacturing techniques is to rearrange the production process away from a **batch production functional layout** towards a product layout using flow lines. With a functional plant layout products pass through a number of specialist departments that normally contain a group of similar machines. Products are processed in large batches so as to minimize the set-up times when machine settings are changed between processing batches of different products. Batches move via different and complex routes through the various departments before they are completed. Each process normally involves a considerable amount of waiting time. The consequences of this complex routing process are high work in progress stock levels and long manufacturing cycle times.

The JIT solution is to reorganize the production process by dividing the many different products that an organization makes into families of similar products or components. All of the products in a particular group will have similar production requirements and routings. Production is rearranged so that each product family is manufactured in a well-defined production cell based on flow line principles. In a **product flow line** specialist departments containing *similar* machines no longer exist. Instead groups of *dissimilar* machines are organized into product or component family flow lines that function like an assembly line. For each product line the machines are placed close together in the order in which they are required by the group of products to be processed. Items in each product family can now move, one at a time, from process to process more easily, thereby reducing work in progress stocks and lead times.

JIT manufacturing aims to produce the right parts at the right time, only when they are needed, and only in the quantity needed. This philosophy has resulted in a **pull manufacturing system**, which means that parts move through the production system based on end-unit demand, focusing on maintaining a constant flow of components rather than batches of work-in-progress (WIP). With the pull system, work on components does not commence until specifically requested by the next process. JIT techniques aim to keep the materials moving in a continuous flow with no stoppages and no storage.

JIT PURCHASING ARRANGEMENTS

The JIT philosophy also extends to adopting **JIT purchasing techniques**, whereby the delivery of materials immediately precedes their use. By arranging with suppliers for more frequent deliveries, stocks can be cut to a minimum. JIT purchasing also normally requires suppliers to inspect materials before their delivery and guarantee their quality. This can result in considerable savings in material handling expenses. This improved service is obtained by giving more business to fewer suppliers and placing long-term purchase orders. Therefore the supplier has an assurance of long-term sales, and can plan to meet this demand. For JIT purchasing to be successful close cooperation with suppliers, including providing them with planned production schedules, is essential.

Companies that have implemented JIT purchasing techniques claim to have substantially reduced their investment in raw materials and work in progress stocks. Other advantages include significant quantity discounts, savings in time from negotiating with fewer suppliers and a reduction in clerical work from issuing long-term orders to a few suppliers rather than individual purchase orders to many suppliers.

Finally, you should note that the aim of JIT production and purchasing techniques is for production and purchases to immediately precede customer required delivery dates. By seeking to ensure that production and purchases are timed to coincide with demand, the determination of economic order quantities and re-order points is no longer required.

Summary

This chapter has described how labour and material costs that have already been incurred should be accumulated for allocating costs between cost of goods sold and inventories for internal and external reporting purposes. It was pointed out that for decision-making the focus should be on future costs rather than past costs.

Two distinct phases of accounting for labour were explained. The first was payroll accounting relating to the computations of gross pay for each employee and the calculation of payments to be made to employees, government, pension funds, etc. The second was labour cost accounting where the focus was on the assignment of different types of labour costs to cost objects such as products or services, individual customers' orders and overhead accounts.

The recording procedures and documentation required for accounting for materials were explained. To simplify the presentation, the manual clerical procedures were described but it was emphasized that in most organizations the recording procedure and documentation are computerized. Nevertheless, the basic principles described in this chapter still apply to both noncomputerized and computerized procedures.

Because the same type of materials may have been purchased at several different prices actual cost can take on several different values, and some method of pricing material issues must be selected. Three different methods of pricing, and their respective merits, were described – first in, first out (FIFO); last in, first out (LIFO); and average cost.

One of the major objectives of stock control is to establish and maintain the optimum level of investment in stocks. This requires that economic order quantities and re-order points are established. Mechanisms for determining economic order quantities and re-order points were described. These mechanisms assume that demand is constant and can be predicted with certainty. More complex approaches exist that can incorporate uncertainty and fluctuations in demand but they are beyond the scope of this book. For a description of approaches that deal with uncertainty you should refer to Drury (2000, ch. 25).

Finally, alternative methods of scheduling production and purchasing requirements that may be more applicable to large organizations were explained. First, a computerized approach for coordinating the planning of materials acquisitions in a complex production environment known as materials requirement planning (MRP) was described. It was pointed out that the EOQ model can be used within MRP systems to determine economic quantity sizes to be purchased provided that the major assumption of the EOQ model of constant demand broadly applies. Second, JIT production and purchasing techniques were described. The JIT approach aims for production and purchases to immediately precede customer required delivery dates. By seeking to ensure that production and purchases are timed to coincide with demand the determination of economic order quantities and re-order points become unnecessary.

Notes

1 The steps are as follows:

$$TC = \frac{DO}{Q} + \frac{QH}{2}$$

$$\frac{dTC}{dQ} = \frac{-DO}{Q^2} + \frac{H}{2}$$

set

$$\frac{dTC}{dQ} = 0 : \quad \frac{H}{2} - \frac{DO}{Q^2} = 0$$

$$HQ^2 = 2DO = 0$$

$$Q^2 = \frac{2DO}{H}$$

Therefore $\quad Q = \sqrt{\left(\frac{2DO}{H}\right)}$

Key Terms and Concepts

ABC classification method (p. 58)
average cost (p. 48)
batch production functional layout (p. 61)
bonus scheme (p. 42)
clock card (p. 42)
complete periodic stockcount (p. 51)
continuous stocktaking (p. 52)
economic order quantity (EOQ) (p. 54)
first in, first out (FIFO) (p. 48)
goods received note (p. 46)
holding costs (p. 53)
holiday pay (p. 44)
idle time card (p. 43)
job card (p. 43)
just-in-time (JIT) methods (p. 60)
just-in-time (JIT) purchasing techniques (p. 62)
labour cost accounting (p. 42)
last in, first out (LIFO) (p. 48)
lead time (p. 57)

manufacturing resource planning (p. 60)
materials handling rate (p. 52)
materials requirement planning (MRP) (p. 60)
non-value added activity (p. 60)
ordering costs (p. 53)
overtime premium (p. 44)
payroll accounting (p. 42)
piecework (p. 44)
piecework tickets (p. 42)
product flow line (p. 62)
pull manufacturing system (p. 62)
purchase order (p. 46)
purchase requisition (p. 46)
re-order point (p. 57)
shift-work premium (p. 44)
stores ledger account (p. 46)
stores requisition (p. 47)
time sheet (p. 43)
value-added activity (p. 61)

Key Examination Points

Typical examination questions relating to the content of this chapter include questions on incentive schemes (including the calculation of bonuses), stores pricing and computations of the economic order, maximum, minimum and re-order quantities. Also essay questions (see questions 3.1–3.4 for examples) are sometimes set. The second and third review problems are examples of typical examination questions relating to incentive schemes. Questions on stores pricing often require you to calculate the amount charged to products/ production, to determine the stock valuation and discuss arguments for and against using each method. For a typical stores pricing examination question you should refer to the fourth review problem and questions 3.5–3.9. Question 6 of the review problems is concerned with most aspects covered in the chapter relating to the computation of the economic order quantity and is typical of the type of examination questions set on this topic. A common mistake that students make in computing

the EOQ is to unitize fixed holding and ordering costs. The EOQ should be calculated using only variable costs. Also note that the purchase cost of materials should not be included in EOQ calculations. When the purchase cost per unit varies with the quantity ordered you should prepare a schedule of relevant costs for different order quantities. For an illustration of this approach, see Exhibit 3.4 in Chapter 3. Sometimes examination questions (see, for example, the fifth review problem and questions 3.8 and 3.19) require you to calculate maximum, minimum and re-order levels. You should use the following formulae:

Re-order level = Maximum usage × maximum lead time
Maximum stock level = Re-order level − average usage during average lead time
Maximum stock level = Re-order level + EOQ − minimum usage for the minimum lead time

Review problems

(For additional problems without answers relating to the content of this chapter you should refer to pages 419–428.)

1 Using the first in, first out (FIFO) system for pricing stock issues means that when prices are rising:

A product costs are overstated and profits understated;

B product costs are kept in line with price changes;

C product costs are understated and profits understated;

D   product costs are understated and profits overstated.   *CIMA Stage 1*

2 (a) A company is proposing to introduce an incentive scheme into its factory.
Required:
Three advantages and three disadvantages of individual incentive schemes.   *6 marks*

(b) The company is undecided on what kind of scheme to introduce.
Required:
From the following information calculate for each employee his earnings, using:
(i)   guaranteed hourly rates only (basic pay);
(ii) piecework, but with earnings guaranteed at 75% of basic pay where the employee fails to earn this amount;
(iii) premium bonus, in which the employee receives two-thirds of time saved in addition to hourly pay.

	Employees			
	A	**B**	**C**	**D**
Actual hours worked	38	36	40	34
Hourly rate of pay	£3	£2	£2.50	£3.60
Output (units) X	42	120	—	120
Y	72	76	—	270
Z	92	—	50	—

Standard time allowed (per unit):
X: 6 minutes; Y: 9 minutes; Z: 15 minutes

Each minute earned is valued at £0.05 for piecework calculation.
16 marks
Total 22 marks
AAT

3 You have been approached for your advice on the proposed introduction of an incentive scheme for the direct operatives in the final production department of a factory producing one standard product. This department, the Finishing Shop, employs 30 direct operatives, all of whom are paid £8 per hour for a basic 40-hour week, with a guaranteed wage of £320 per week. When necessary, overtime is worked up to a maximum of 15 hours per week per operative and is paid at time rate plus one-half. It is the opinion of the personnel manager that no more direct operatives could be recruited for this department.

An analysis of recent production returns from the Finishing Shop indicates that the current average output is approximately 6 units of the standard product per productive man-hour. The work study manager has conducted an appraisal of the working methods in the Finishing Shop and suggests that it would be reasonable to expect operatives to process 8 units of the product per man-hour and that a piecework scheme be introduced in which the direct operatives are paid £1.40 for each unit processed. It is anticipated that, when necessary, operatives would continue to work overtime up to the previous specified limit, although as the operatives would be on piecework no premium would be paid.

Next year's budgeted production for the factory varies from a minimum of 7000 units per week to a maximum of 12 000 units per week, with the most frequent budgeted weekly output being 9600 units. The expected selling price of the product next year is £11 per unit and the budgeted variable production cost of the incomplete product passed into the Finishing Shop amounts to £8 per unit. Variable production overheads in the Finishing Shop, excluding the overtime premium of the direct operatives, are budgeted to be £0.48 per direct labour hour worked, and it is considered that variable overheads do vary directly with productive hours worked. Direct material costs are not incurred by the Finishing Shop. The fixed overheads incurred by the factory amount in total to £9000 per week.

Stocks of work in progress and finished goods are not carried.

Required:
(i)   Calculate the effect on the company's budgeted weekly profits of the proposed incentive scheme in the Finishing Shop. (Calculation should be to the nearest £.)
15 marks
(ii) Explain the reasons for the changes in the weekly budgeted profits caused by the proposed incentive scheme.
7 marks
ACCA Level 1 Costing

4 On 1 January Mr G started a small business buying and selling a special yarn. He invested his savings of £40 000 in the business, and

during the next six months the following transactions occurred:

Date of receipt	Yarn purchases quantity (box)	Total cost (£)	Date of despatch	Yarn sales quantity (box)	Total value (£)
13 Jan	200	7 200	10 Feb	500	25 000
8 Feb	400	15 200			
11 Mar	600	24 000	20 Apr	600	27 000
12 Apr	400	14 000			
15 June	500	14 000	25 June	400	15 200

The yarn is stored in premises Mr G has rented, and the closing stock of yarn, counted on 30 June, was 500 boxes.

Other expenses incurred, and paid in cash, during the six-month period amounted to £2300.

Required:
(a) Calculate the value of the material issues during the six-month period, and the value of the closing stock at the end of June, using the following methods of pricing:
   (i)   first in, first out;
   (ii) last in, first out;
   (iii) weighted average (calculations to two decimal places only).   *10 marks*
(b) Calculate and discuss the effect each of the three methods of material pricing will have on the reported profit of the business, and examine the performance of the business during the first six-month period.

12 marks
Total 22 marks
ACCA Level 1 Costing

5 (a) Write short notes to explain each of the following in the context of materials control:
   (i)   Continuous stocktaking.
   (ii) Perpetual inventory system.
   (iii) ABC inventory analysis.   *9 marks*
(b) State the factors that should influence the decision regarding economic order quantities of raw materials.   *7 marks*
(c) Calculate three normal control levels, which may be used in stock control systems, from the following information for a particular raw material:
   Economic order quantity, 12 000 kilos
   Lead time, 10 to 14 working days
   Average usage, 600 kilos per day
   Minimum usage, 400 kilos per day
   Maximum usage, 800 kilos per day

9 marks
Total 25 marks
ACCA Level 1 Costing

6 A large local government authority places orders for various stationery items at quarterly intervals.

In respect of an item of stock coded A32, data are:

   annual usage quantity   5000 boxes
   minimum order quantity   500 boxes
   cost per box   £2

Usage of material is on a regular basis and on average, half of the amount purchased is held in inventory. The cost of storage is considered to be 25% of the inventory value. The average cost of placing an order is estimated at £12.50.

The chief executive of the authority has asked you to review the present situation and to consider possible ways of effecting cost savings. You are required to:
(a) tabulate the costs of storage and ordering item A32 for each level of orders from four to twelve placed per year;
(b) ascertain from the tabulation the number of orders which should be placed in a year to minimize these costs;
(c) produce a formula to calculate the order level which would minimize these costs – your answer should explain each constituent part of the formula and their relationships;
(d) give an example of the use of the formula to confirm the calculation in (b) above;
(e) calculate the percentage saving on the annual cost which could be made by using the economic order quantity system;
(f) suggest *two* other approaches which could be introduced in order to reduce the present cost of storage and ordering of stationery.

25 marks
CIMA Cost Accounting 2

Solutions to Review Problems

SOLUTION 1

Answer $= D$

SOLUTION 2

(a) *Advantages:*
  (i) Both the firm and the employee should benefit from the introduction of an incentive scheme. Employees should receive an increase in wages arising from the increased production. The firm should benefit from a reduction in the fixed overhead per unit and an increase in sales volume.
  (ii) The opportunity to earn higher wages may encourage efficient workers to join the company.
  (iii) Morale may be improved if extra effort is rewarded.

Disadvantages:
  (i) Incentive schemes can be complex and difficult to administer.
  (ii) Establishing performance levels leads to frequent and continuing disputes.
  (iii) The quality of the output may decline.

(b)
  (i) Hourly rate
    Employee A $38 \times £3.00 = £114.00$
    B $36 \times £2.00 = £72.00$
    C $40 \times £2.50 = £100.00$
    D $34 \times £3.60 = £122.40$
  (ii) Piecework
    Employee A $(42 \times £0.30) + (72 \times £0.45) + (92 \times £0.75) = £114$
    B $(120 \times £0.30) + (76 \times £0.45)$ $= £70.20$
    C $(50 \times £0.75)$ $= £37.50$
    D $(120 \times £0.30) + (270 \times £0.45)$ $= £157.50$

Note that with the piecework system the employees are paid an agreed rate per unit produced. The piece rates are £0.30 per unit for X (6 minutes $\times$ £0.05), £0.45 for Y ($9 \times$ £0.05) and £0.75 for Z ($15 \times$ £0.05). Only employee C earns less than 75% of basic pay. Therefore C will receive a gross wage of £75. The piece-rate wages should be charged directly to the products and the difference between the guaranteed minimum wage of £75 and the piecework wage of £37.50 for employee C should be charged to an appropriate overhead account.

With a bonus scheme a set time is allowed for each job and a bonus is paid based on the proportion of time saved. The calculations for each employee are:

	Time allowed (hours)	Time saved (hours)	Bonus (£)	Total wages (£)
A	$\dfrac{42 \times 6}{60} + \dfrac{72 \times 9}{60}$ $+ \dfrac{92 \times 15}{60} = 38$	0	0	114
B	$\dfrac{120 \times 6}{60} + \dfrac{76 \times 9}{60} = 23.4$	0	0	72
C	$\dfrac{50 \times 15}{60} = 12.5$	0	0	100
D	$\dfrac{120 \times 6}{60} + \dfrac{270 \times 9}{60} = 52.5$	18.5	$\tfrac{2}{3} \times 18.5$ $\times £3.60$ $= £44.40$	£122.40 $+ £44.40$

Employees A, B and C do not earn a bonus because the time taken is in excess of time allowed.

SOLUTION 3

(i) Current average maximum production $=$
30×55 hrs $\times 6$ units $= 9900$ units.
Proposed maximum production $=$
30×55 hrs $\times 8$ units $= 13\,200$ units

Existing payment system:

Output level (units)	7 000	9 600	9 900
	£	£	£
Sales value (£11 per unit)	77 000	105 600	108 900
Pre-finishing VC	56 000	76 800	79 200
Direct labour:			
Guaranteed	9 600	9 600	9 600
Overtime ($W1$)	—	4 800	5 400
Variable overhead ($W2$)	560	768	792
Fixed overhead	9 000	9 000	9 000
Total cost	75 160	100 968	103 992
Profit	1 840	4 632	4 908

Proposed scheme:

Output level (units)	7 000	9 600	9 900	12 000
	£	£	£	£
Sales value	77 000	105 600	108 900	132 000
Pre-finishing VC	56 000	76 800	79 200	96 000
Direct labour at £1.40 per unit	9 800	13 440	13 860	16 800
Variable overhead ($W3$)	420	576	594	720
Fixed overhead	9 000	9 000	9 000	9 000
Total cost	75 220	99 816	102 654	122 520
Profit	1 780	5 784	6 246	9 480

Working:

(*W*1) 9600 units requires 1600 hrs (9600/6)
∴ Overtime = 400 hrs × £12
9900 units requires 1650 hrs (9900/6)
∴ Overtime = 450 hrs × £12
Basic hours = 1200 hrs

(*W*2) 7000 units = 7000/6 × £0.48
9600 units = 9600/6 × £0.48
9900 units = 9900/6 × £0.48

(*W*3) 7000 units = 7000/8 × £0.48
9600 units = 9600/8 × £0.48
9900 units = 9900/8 × £0.48
12 000 units = 12 000/8 × £0.48

(ii) At low output levels the average wage rate per unit is £1.33 (£8/6 units), compared with £1.40 with the incentive scheme. However, once overtime is worked, the wage rate per unit of output exceeds £1.40 per unit under the incentive scheme. For example, at an output level of 9600 units the wage rate per unit of output is £1.50 (£14 400/9600).

Variable overheads vary with productive hours. Therefore variable overhead per unit will be £0.08 (£0.48/6) under the old scheme and £0.06 per unit under the new scheme (£0.48/8).

The proposed incentive scheme will also enable the maximum output level to be achieved, thus enabling maximum sales demand to be achieved.

SOLUTION 4

(a) (i) *FIFO:* 2100 boxes were purchased and 1500 boxes were issued to production, leaving a balance of 600 boxes. Actual closing stock is 500 boxes, resulting in a stock loss of 100 boxes. The closing stock will be valued at the latest purchase price: £28 per unit (£14 000/500).
Closing stock valuation = £14 000
(500 × £28)
Cost of sales (including stock loss) = £60 400 (Total purchase cost (74 400) − (14 000))

(ii) *LIFO:*

Date	Issue	Cost (£)
10/2	400 units	15 200
	100 units at £7200/200	3 600
		18 800
20/4	400 units	14 000
	200 units at £24 000/600	8 000
		22 000
25/6	400 units at £14 000/500	11 200
30/6	100 units (stock loss) at	
	£14 000/500	2 800
	Total cost of issues	54 800

Closing stock = Purchase cost (£74 000)
− Issue cost (£54 800)
= £19 600

Note:

(1) If the question does not require you to prepare a stores ledger account, you are recommended for the FIFO method to follow the approach shown in this answer. First calculate the closing stock in units. With the FIFO method the closing stock will be valued at the latest purchase prices. You can calculate the cost of sales as follows:

Cost of sales = Opening stock + Purchases
− Closing stock

(iii)

Weighted average method

	Receipts			Issues		Closing balance		
								Weighted average issue price
		Total cost			Total cost			
	Quantity	cost		Quantity	cost	Quantity	Cost	
Date	(boxes)	(£)	Date	(boxes)	(£)	(boxes)	(£)	(£)
13/1	200	7 200				200	7 200	36.00
8/2	400	15 200				600	22 400	37.33
			10/2	500 at £37.33	18 665	100	3 735	37.33
11/3	600	24 000				700	27 735	39.62
12/4	400	14 000				1 100	41 735	37.94
			20/4	600 at £37.94	22 764	500	18 971	37.94
15/6	500	14 000				1 000	32 971	32.97
			25/6	400 at £32.97	13 188	600	19 783	32.97
			30/6	100 at £32.97	3 297	500	16 486	32.97
					57 914			

(b) Profit calculations

	FIFO (£)	LIFO (£)	Weighted average (£)
Sales	67 200	67 200	67 200
Cost of sales and stock loss	(60 400)	(54 800)	(57 914)
Other expenses	(2 300)	(2 300)	(2 300)
Profit	4 500	10 100	6 986

The purchase cost per box is £36 (Jan.), £38 (Feb.), £40 (March), £35 (April) and £28 (June).

The use of FIFO results in the lowest profit because prices are falling and the higher earlier prices are charged to production, whereas with LIFO the later and lower prices are charged to production. The use of the weighted average method results in a profit calculation between these two extremes. There are two items of concern regarding the performance of the business:

(i) There was a large purchase at the highest purchase price in March. This purchase could have been delayed until April so as to take advantage of the lower price.

(ii) The stock loss has cost over £3000. This should be investigated. A materials control procedure should be implemented.

SOLUTION 5

(a) (i) Continuous stocktaking refers to a situation where a sample of store items are counted regularly on, say, a daily basis. Sufficient items should be checked each day so that during a year all items are checked at least once. The alternative system of stocktaking is a complete physical stockcount where all the stock items are counted at one point in time. Continuous stocktaking is preferable because production is not disrupted and any discrepancies and losses are revealed earlier.

(ii) A perpetual inventory system is a stock recording system whereby the balance is shown for a stock item after each receipt or issue. In a non-computerized system the records are maintained on bin cards or stores ledger cards. A separate record is maintained for each item of materials in stores. Therefore the stock balance for each stores item is available at any point in time.

(iii) For an explanation of ABC inventory analysis see the section on control of stocks through classification in Chapter 3.

(b) For the answer to this question you should refer to Chapter 3 (sections on relevant costs for quantitative models under conditions of certainty and determining the economic order quantity).

(c) Normal control levels are the re-order level, minimum level and maximum level explained in the 'Key Examination Points' section.

$$\text{Reorder level} = \text{Maximum usage} \times \text{Maximum lead time}$$
$$= 800 \text{ kg} \times 14 \text{ days}$$
$$= 11\,200 \text{ kg}$$

$$\text{Minimum level} = \text{Re-order level} - \text{Average usage in average lead time}$$
$$= 11\,200 \text{ kg} - (600 \text{ kg} \times 12 \text{ days})$$
$$= 4000 \text{ kg}$$

$$\text{Maximum level} = \text{Re-order level} + \text{EOQ} - \text{Minimum usage in minimum lead time}$$
$$= 11\,200 \text{ kg} + 12\,000 \text{ kg} - (400 \text{ kg} \times 10 \text{ days})$$
$$= 19\,200 \text{ kg}$$

SOLUTION 6

(a) *Item A32: storage and ordering cost schedule*

No. of orders per year	4	5	6	7	8	9	10	11	12
Order size (boxes)	1250	1000	833	714	625	556	500	455	417
Average stock (boxes)	625	500	417	357	313	278	250	228	208
	(£)	(£)	(£)	(£)	(£)	(£)	(£)	(£)	(£)
Storage costs (average stock × 25% of £2)	312.5	250.0	208.5	178.5	156.5	139.0	125.0	114.0	104.0
Ordering costs (£12.5 per order)	50.0	62.5	75.0	87.5	100.0	112.5	125.0	137.5	150.0
Total cost	£362.5	£312.5	£283.5	£266.0	£256.5	£251.5	£250.0	£251.5	£254.0

(b) The number of orders which should be placed in a year to minimize costs is 10.

(c)

$$EOQ = \sqrt{\left(\frac{2DO}{H}\right)}$$

where D = total demand for period, O = ordering cost per order, H = holding cost per unit.

(d)

$$EOQ = \sqrt{\left(\frac{2 \times 5000 \times 12.5}{0.5}\right)}$$

$$= 500 \text{ units}$$

(e) The maximum saving that could be made if the authority process four orders per year would be:

$$\frac{£362.50 - £250}{£362.50} = 31\%$$

(f) (i) Reducing the number of stock items by eliminating slow moving and obsolete stocks.

(ii) Standardization of stock items thus reducing the total number of items in stock.

Cost assignment

In Chapters 1 and 2 it was pointed out that companies need cost and management accounting systems to perform a number of different functions. In this chapter we are going to concentrate on two of these functions – they are (i) allocating costs between cost of goods sold and inventories for internal and external profit reporting and (ii) providing relevant decision-making information for distinguishing between profitable and unprofitable activities.

In order to perform the above functions a cost accumulation system is required that assigns costs to cost objects. The aim of this chapter is to provide you with an understanding of how costs are accumulated and assigned to cost objects. You should have remembered from Chapter 2 that a cost object is anything for which a separate measurement of cost is desired. Typical cost objects include products, services, customers and locations. In this chapter we shall either use the term cost object as a generic term or assume that products are the cost object. However, the same cost assignment principles can be applied to all cost objects.

We begin by explaining how the cost assignment process differs for direct and indirect costs.

Learning objectives

After studying this chapter, you should be able to:

- distinguish between cause-and-effect and arbitrary cost allocations;

- explain why different cost information is required for different purposes;

- describe how cost systems differ in terms of their level of sophistication;

- understand the factors influencing the choice of optimal cost system;

- explain why departmental overhead rates should be used in preference to a single blanket overhead rate;

- construct an overhead analysis sheet and calculate cost centre allocation rates;

- justify why budgeted overhead rates should be used in preference to actual overhead rates;

- calculate and explain the accounting treatment of the under/over recovery of overheads;

- record inter-service department transfers using one of the methods described in Appendix 4.1.

Assignment of direct and indirect costs

Costs that are assigned to cost objects can be divided into two categories – direct costs and indirect costs. Sometimes the term **overheads** is used instead of indirect costs. Direct costs can be accurately traced to cost objects because they can be specifically and exclusively traced to a particular cost object whereas indirect costs cannot. Where a cost can be directly assigned to a cost object the term **cost tracing** is used. In contrast, indirect costs cannot be traced directly to a cost object because they are usually common to several cost objects. Indirect costs are therefore assigned to cost objects using cost allocations.

A **cost allocation** is the process of assigning costs when a direct measure docs not exist for the quantity of resources consumed by a particular cost object. Cost allocations involve the use of surrogate rather than direct measures. For example, consider an activity such as receiving incoming materials. Assuming that the cost of receiving materials is strongly influenced by the number of receipts then costs can be allocated to products (i.e. the cost object) based on the number of material receipts each product requires. The basis that is used to allocate costs to cost objects (i.e. the number of material receipts in our example) is called an **allocation base** or **cost driver**. If 20% of the total number of receipts for a period were required for a particular product then 20% of the total costs of receiving incoming materials would be allocated to that product. Assuming that the product was discontinued, and not replaced, we would expect action to be taken to reduce the resources required for receiving materials by 20%.

In the above illustration the allocation base is assumed to be a significant determinant of the cost of receiving incoming materials. Where allocation bases are significant determinants of the costs we shall describe them as **cause-and-effect allocations**. Where a cost allocation base is used that is not a significant determinant of its cost the term **arbitrary allocation** will be used. An example of an arbitrary allocation would be if direct labour hours were used as the allocation base to allocate the costs of materials receiving. If a labour intensive product required a large proportion of direct labour hours (say 30%) but few material receipts it would be allocated with a large proportion of the costs of material receiving. The allocation would be an inaccurate assignment of the resources consumed by the product. Furthermore, if the product were discontinued, and not replaced, the cost of the material receiving activity would not decline by 30% because the allocation base is not a significant determinant of the costs of the materials receiving activity. Arbitrary allocations are therefore likely to result in inaccurate allocations of indirect costs to cost objects.

Figure 4.1 provides a summary of the assignment process. You can see that direct costs are assigned to cost objects using cost tracing whereas indirect costs are assigned using cost allocations. For accurate assignment of indirect costs to cost objects cause-and-effect allocations should be used. Two types of systems can be used to assign indirect costs to cost objects. They are **traditional costing systems** and **activity-based-costing (ABC) systems**. Traditional costing systems were developed in the early 1900s and are still widely used today. They rely extensively on arbitrary cost allocations. ABC systems only emerged in the late 1980s. One of the major aims of ABC systems is to use only cause-and-effect cost allocations. In this chapter we shall concentrate on traditional costing systems and ABC systems will be examined in Chapter 11.

Different costs for different purposes

Manufacturing organizations assign costs to products for two purposes: first, for internal profit measurement and external financial accounting requirements in order to allocate the manufacturing costs incurred during a period between cost of goods sold and inventories;

FIGURE 4.1 *Cost allocations and cost tracing.*

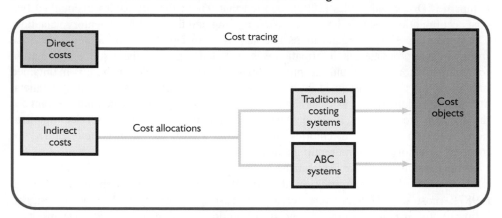

secondly, to provide useful information for managerial decision-making requirements. In order to meet financial accounting requirements, it may not be necessary to accurately trace costs to *individual* products. Consider a situation where a firm produces 1000 different products and the costs incurred during a period are £10 million. A well-designed product costing system should accurately analyse the £10 million costs incurred between cost of sales and inventories. Let us assume the true figures are £7 million and £3 million. Approximate but inaccurate *individual* product costs may provide a reasonable approximation of how much of the £10 million should be attributed to cost of sales and inventories. Some product costs may be overstated and others may be understated, but this would not matter for financial accounting purposes as long as the *total* of the individual product costs assigned to cost of sales and inventories was approximately £7 million and £3 million.

For decision-making purposes, however, more accurate product costs are required so that we can distinguish between profitable and unprofitable products. By more accurately measuring the resources consumed by products, or other cost objects, a firm can identify its sources of profits and losses. If the cost system does not capture sufficiently accurately the consumption of resources by products, the reported product costs will be distorted, and there is a danger that managers may drop profitable products or continue production of unprofitable products.

Besides different levels of accuracy, different cost information is required for different purposes. For meeting external financial accounting requirements, financial accounting regulations and legal requirements in most countries require that inventories should be valued at manufacturing cost. Therefore only manufacturing costs are assigned to products for meeting external financial accounting requirements. For decision-making non-manufacturing costs must be taken into account and assigned to products. Not all costs, however, may be relevant for decision-making. For example, depreciation of plant and machinery will not be affected by a decision to discontinue a product. Such costs were described in Chapter 2 as irrelevant and sunk for decision-making. Thus depreciation of plant must be assigned to products for inventory valuation but it should not be assigned for discontinuation decisions.

MAINTAINING A SINGLE OR SEPARATE DATABASES

Because different costs and different levels of accuracy are required for different purposes some organizations maintain two separate costing systems, one for decision-making and the other for inventory valuation and profit measurement. In a survey of 187 UK companies Drury and Tayles (2000) reported that 9% of the companies maintained two cost accumulation systems, one for decision-making and the other for inventory valuation. The remaining 91% of organizations maintained a costing system on a single database from which appropriate cost information was extracted to provide the required information for both decision-making and inventory valuation. When a single database is maintained only costs that must be assigned for inventory valuation are extracted for meeting financial accounting requirements, whereas for decision-making only costs which are relevant for the decision are extracted. Inventory valuation is not an issue for many service organizations. They do not carry inventories and therefore a costing system is not required for meeting inventory valuation requirements.

Where a single database is maintained cost assignments cannot be at different levels of accuracy for different purposes. In the late 1980s, according to Johnson and Kaplan (1987), most organizations were relying on costing systems that had been designed primarily for meeting external financial accounting requirements. These systems were designed decades ago when information processing costs were high and precluded the use of more sophisticated methods of assigning indirect costs to products. Such systems are still widely used today. They rely extensively on arbitrary cost allocations which may be sufficiently accurate for meeting external financial accounting requirements but not for meeting decision-making requirements. Johnson and Kaplan concluded that management accounting practices have followed and become subservient to meeting financial accounting requirements.

Cost–benefit issues and cost systems design

These criticisms resulted in the emergence of ABC in the late 1980s. Surveys in many countries suggest that between 20 and 30% of the surveyed organizations have implemented ABC systems. The majority of organizations therefore continue to operate traditional systems. Both traditional and ABC systems vary in their level of sophistication but, as a general rule, traditional systems tend to be simplistic whereas ABC systems tend to be sophisticated. What determines the chosen level of sophistication of a costing system? The answer is that the choice should be made on costs versus benefits criteria. Simplistic systems are inexpensive to operate, but they are likely to result in inaccurate cost assignments and the reporting of inaccurate costs. Managers using cost information extracted from simplistic systems are more likely to make important mistakes arising from using inaccurate cost information. The end result may be a high cost of errors. Conversely, sophisticated systems are more expensive to operate but they minimize the cost of errors. However, the aim should not be to have the most accurate cost system. Improvements should be made in the level of sophistication of the costing system up to the point where the marginal cost of improvement equals the marginal benefit from the improvement.

Figure 4.2 illustrates the above points with costing systems ranging from simplistic to sophisticated. Highly simplistic systems are located on the extreme left. Common features of such systems are that they are inexpensive to operate, make extensive use of arbitrary allocations of indirect costs and normally result in low levels of accuracy and a high cost of errors. On the extreme right are highly sophisticated systems. These systems use only cause-and-effect allocations, are more expensive to operate, have high levels of accuracy and minimize the cost of errors. Cost systems in most organizations are not located at either of these extreme points. Instead, they are located at different points within the range shown in Figure 4.2.

FIGURE 4.2 *Cost systems — varying levels of sophistication for cost assignment.*

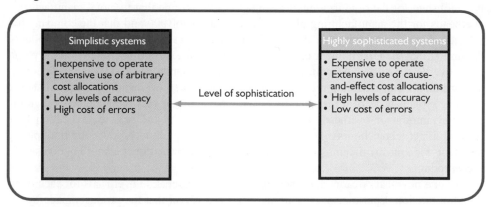

The optimal cost system is different for different organizations. For example, the optimal costing system will be located towards the extreme left for an organization whose indirect costs are a low percentage of total costs. In these circumstances simplistic systems may not result in the reporting of inaccurate costs. In contrast, the optimal costing system for organizations with a high proportion of indirect costs, will be located towards the extreme right. More sophisticated costing systems are required to accurately assign the high level of indirect costs to different cost objects.

Assigning direct costs to objects

Both simplistic and sophisticated systems accurately assign direct costs to cost objects. Cost assignment merely involves the implementation of suitable clerical procedures to identify and record the resources consumed by cost objects. It was pointed out in the previous chapter that the time spent on providing a service to a specific customer, or manufacturing a specific product, is recorded on source documents, such as **time sheets** or **job cards**. Details of the customer's account number, job number or the product's code are also entered on these documents. The employee's hourly rate of pay is then entered so that the direct labour cost for the employee can be assigned to the appropriate cost object.

For direct materials the source document is a **materials requisition**. Details of the materials issued for manufacturing a product, or providing a specific service, are recorded on the materials requisition. The customer's account number, job number or product code is also entered and the items listed on the requisition are priced at their cost of acquisition. The details on the material requisition thus represent the source information for assigning the cost of the materials to the appropriate cost object. Because direct costs can be accurately assigned to cost objects whereas indirect costs cannot, the remainder of this chapter will focus on indirect cost assignment.

In many organizations the recording procedure for direct costs is computerized using bar coding and other forms of on-line information recording. The source documents only exist in the form of computer records.

Plant-wide (blanket) overhead rates

The most simplistic traditional costing system assigns indirect costs to cost objects using a single overhead rate for the organization as a whole. You will recall at the start of this chapter that it was pointed out that indirect costs are also called overheads. The terms **blanket overhead rate** or **plant-wide rate** are used to describe a single overhead rate that is established for the organization as a whole. Let us assume that the total manufacturing overheads for the manufacturing plant of Arcadia are £900 000 and that the company has selected direct labour hours as the allocation base for assigning overheads to products. Assuming that the total number of direct labour hours are 60 000 for the period the plant-wide overhead rate for Arcadia is £15 per direct labour hour (£900 000/60 000 direct labour hours). This calculation consists of two stages. First, overheads are accumulated in one single plant-wide pool for a period. Second, a plant-wide rate is computed by dividing the total amount of overheads accumulated (£900 000) by the selected allocation base (60 000 direct labour hours). The overhead costs are assigned to products by multiplying the plant-wide rate by the units of the selected allocation base (direct labour hours) used by each product.

Assume now that Arcadia is considering establishing separate overheads for each of its three production departments. Further investigations reveal that the products made by the company require different operations and some products do not pass through all three departments. These investigations also indicate that the £900 000 total manufacturing overheads and 60 000 direct labour hours can be analysed as follows:

	Department A	Department B	Department C	Total
Overheads	£200 000	£600 000	£100 000	£900 000
Direct labour hours	20 000	20 000	20 000	60 000
Overhead rate per direct labour hour	£10	£30	£5	£15

Consider now a situation where product Z requires 20 direct labour hours in department C but does not pass through departments A and B. If a plant-wide overhead rate is used then overheads of £300 (20 hours at £15 per hour) will be allocated to product Z. On the other hand, if a departmental overhead rate is used, only £100 (20 hours at £5 per hour) would be allocated to product Z. Which method should be used? The logical answer must be to establish separate departmental overhead rates, since product Z only consumes overheads in department C. If the plant-wide overhead rate were applied, all the factory overhead rates would be averaged out and product Z would be indirectly allocated with some of the overheads of department B. This would not be satisfactory, since product Z does not consume any of the resources and this department incurs a large amount of the overhead expenditure.

Where some departments are more 'overhead-intensive' than others, products spending more time in the overhead-intensive departments should be assigned more overhead costs than those spending less time. Departmental rates capture these possible effects but plant-wide rates do not, because of the averaging process. We can conclude that a plant-wide rate will generally result in the reporting of inaccurate product costs. A plant-wide rate can only be justified when all products consume departmental overheads in approximately the same proportions. In the above illustration each department accounts for one-third of the total direct labour hours. If all products spend approximately one-third of their time in each department, a plant-wide overhead rate can be used. Consider a situation where product X spends one hour in each department and product Y spends five hours in each department. Overheads of £45 and £225 respectively would be allocated to products X and Y using either a plant-wide rate (3 hours at £15 and 15 hours at £15) or separate departmental overhead rates. If a diverse product range is produced with products spending different proportions of time in each department, separate departmental overhead rates should be established.

However, significant usage of plant-wide overhead rates have been reported in survey undertaken in many different countries. For example, the percentage usages vary from 20–30% in UK (Drury and Tayles, 1994), USA (Emore and Ness, 1991), Australian (Joye and Blayney, 1990; 1991) and Indian (Joshi, 1998) surveys. In contrast, in Scandinavia only 5% of the Finnish companies (Lukka and Granlund, 1996), one Norwegian company (Bjornenak, 1997b) and none of the Swedish companies sampled (Ask *et al.*, 1996) used a single plant-wide rate. Zero usage of plant-wide rates was also reported from a survey of Greek companies (Ballas and Venieris, 1996). In a more recent study of UK organizations Drury and Tayles (2000) reported that a plant-wide rate was used by 3% of surveyed organizations possibly suggesting a move towards more sophisticated costing systems.

The two-stage allocation process

A framework, known as the two-stage allocation process, can be used to summarize the different approaches we have looked at for Arcadia to assign overhead costs to products. The process applies to assigning costs to other cost objects, besides products, and is applicable to all organizations that assign indirect costs to cost objects. The framework applies to both traditional and ABC systems.

The framework is illustrated in Figure 4.3. You can see that in the first stage overheads are assigned to cost centres (also called cost pools). The terms **cost centres** or **cost pools** are used to describe a location to which overhead costs are initially assigned. Normally cost centres consist of departments, but in some cases they consist of smaller segments such as groups of machines. In the second stage the costs accumulated in the cost centres are allocated to cost objects using selected allocation bases (you should remember from our discussion earlier that allocation bases are also called cost drivers). Traditional costing systems tend to use a small number of second stage allocation bases, typically direct labour hours or machine hours. In other words, traditional systems assume that direct labour or machine hours have a significant influence in the long term on the level of overhead expenditure. Other allocation bases used to a lesser extent by traditional systems are direct labour cost, direct materials cost and units of output. These methods are illustrated in Appendix 4.2 at the end of this chapter. Exhibit 4.1 (Section C) shows details of the extent to which different second stage allocation bases are used in different countries. You will see that direct labour and machine hours are the dominant methods.

Let us now apply the framework to our discussion in the previous stage relating to Arcadia. The plant-wide rate overheads (£900 000) are collected in a single cost pool for the plant, or the whole organization if non-manufacturing overheads are to be incorporated in the overhead rate. In the second stage a single plant-wide overhead rate (£15 per hour) is allocated to products based on the number of direct labour hours used by each product.

We concluded that, because some departments were more 'overhead intensive' than others, it is preferable to establish separate cost centre overhead rates based on departments. With this approach the total overheads of £900 000 were assigned to the three production departments in the first stage. Separate departmental overhead rates were computed for each department in the second stage (i.e. £10 per direct labour hour department A, £30 for B and £5 for C). Finally, departmental overheads were assigned to products by multiplying the hours spent by a product in each department by the hourly overhead rate. The total overhead assigned to a product is simply the sum of the amounts applied in each department.

How many cost centres should a firm establish? If only a small number of cost centres are established it is likely that activities within a cost centre will not be homogeneous and, if the consumption of the activities by products/services within the cost centres varies,

FIGURE 4.3 *The two-stage allocation process for a traditional costing system.*

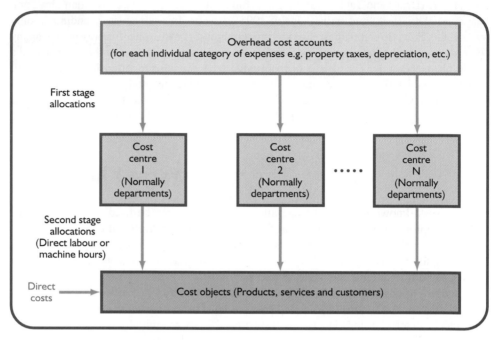

activity resource consumption will not be accurately measured. Therefore, in most situations, increasing the number of cost centres increases the accuracy of measuring the indirect costs consumed by cost objects. The choice of the number of cost centres should be based on cost–benefit criteria using the principles described on pages 74–75. Exhibit 4.1 (Section A) shows the number of cost centres and second stage cost allocation bases reported by Drury *et al.* (1993) in a survey of 187 UK organizations. It can be seen that 35% of the organizations used less than 11 cost centres whereas 23% used more than 30 cost centres. In terms of the number of different second stage cost drivers/allocation bases 69% of the responding organizations used less than four.

An illustration of the two-stage process for a traditional costing system

We shall now use Example 4.1 to provide a more detailed illustration of the two-stage allocation process for a traditional costing system. To keep the illustration manageable it is assumed that the company has only five cost centres – machine departments X and Y, an assembly department and materials handling and general factory support cost centres. The illustration focuses on manufacturing costs but we shall look at non-manufacturing costs later in the chapter. Applying the two-stage allocation process requires the following four steps:

1. assigning all manufacturing overheads to production and service cost centres;
2. reallocating the costs assigned to service cost centres to production cost centres;
3. computing separate overhead rates for each production cost centre;
4. assigning cost centre overheads to products or other chosen cost objects.

EXHIBIT   4.1

*Surveys of
practice*

(a) Cost centres used in the first stage of the two-stage allocation process

- A survey of Australian organizations by Joye and Blayney (1990):
  36% of the responding organizations used a single plant-wide rate
  24% used overhead rates for groups of work centres
  31% used overhead rates for each work centre
  9% used overhead rates for each machine

- A survey of Swedish organizations by Ask and Ax (1992)[a]:
  70% indicated that cost centres consisted of departments
  32% consisted of work cells
  22% consisted of groups of machines
  15% consisted of single machines

- A Norwegian study by Bjornenak (1997b) reported an average of 38.3 cost centres used by the respondents

- A survey of UK organizations by Drury and Tayles (2000):
  14% used less than 6 cost centres
  21% used 6–10 cost centres
  29% used 11–20 cost centres
  36% used more than 20 cost centres

(b) Number of different second stage allocation bases/cost drivers used

- A survey of UK organizations by Drury and Tayles (2000):
  34% used 1 cost driver
  25% used 2 drivers
  10% used 3 drivers
  21% used 3–10 drivers
  10% used more than 10 drivers

- A Norwegian study by Bjornenak (1997a) reported an average usage of 1.79 cost drivers

(c) Second stage cost allocation bases/cost drivers used[a]

	Norway[b]	Holland[c]	Ireland[d]	Australia[e]	Japan[e]	UK[f]	UK[f]
Direct labour hours/cost	65%	20%	52%	57%	57%	68%	73%
Machine hours	29	9	19	19	12	49	26
Direct materials costs	26	6	10	12	11	30	19
Units of output	40	30	28	20	16	42	31
Prime cost				1	21		
Other	23	35	9				
ABC cost drivers						9	7

A survey of Finnish companies by Lukka and Granlund (1996) reported that direct labour costs, direct labour hours, machine hours, materials use and production quantity were the most widely used allocation bases. Usage rates were not reported.

Notes

[a] The reported percentages exceed 100% because many companies used more than one type of cost centre or allocation base.
[b] Bjornenak (1997b).
[c] Boons *et al*. (1994).
[d] Clarke (1995).
[e] Blayney and Yokoyama (1991).
[f] Drury *et al*. (1993) – The first column relates to the responses for automated and the second to non-automated production centres.

Steps 1 and 2 comprise stage one and steps 3 and 4 relate to the second stage of the two-stage allocation process. Let us now consider each of these steps in detail.

STEP 1 – ASSIGNING ALL MANUFACTURING OVERHEADS TO PRODUCTION AND SERVICE COST CENTRES

Using the information given in Example 4.1 our initial objective is to assign all manufacturing overheads to production and service cost centres. To do this requires the preparation of an **overhead analysis sheet**. This document is shown in Exhibit 4.2. In many organizations it will consist only in computer form.

If you look at Example 4.1 you will see that the indirect labour and indirect material costs have been directly traced to cost centres. Although these items cannot be directly assigned to products they can be directly assigned to the cost centres. In other words, they are indirect costs when products are the cost objects and direct costs when cost centres are the cost object. Therefore they are traced directly to the cost centres shown in the overhead analysis sheet in Exhibit 4.2. The remaining costs shown in Example 4.1 cannot be traced directly to the cost centres and must be allocated to the cost centre using appropriate allocation bases. The term **first stage allocation bases** is used to describe allocations at this point. The following list summarizes commonly used first stage allocation bases:

Cost	Basis of allocation
Property taxes, lighting and heating	Area
Employee-related expenditure:	
works management, works canteen, payroll office	Number of employees
Depreciation and insurance of plant and machinery	Value of items of plant and machinery

Applying the allocation bases to the data given in respect of the Enterprise Company in Example 4.1 it is assumed that property taxes, lighting and heating, and insurance of buildings are related to the total floor area of the buildings, and the benefit obtained by each cost centre can therefore be ascertained according to the proportion of floor area which it occupies. The total floor area of the factory shown in Example 4.1 is 50 000 square metres; machine centre X occupies 20% of this and machine centre Y a further 10%. Therefore, if you refer to the overhead analysis sheet in Exhibit 4.2 you will see that

EXAMPLE 4.1

The annual overhead costs for the Enterprise Company which has three production centres (two machine centres and one assembly centre) and two service centres (materials procurement and general factory support) are as follows:

	(£)	(£)
Indirect wages and supervision		
Machine centres: X	1 000 000	
Y	1 000 000	
Assembly	1 500 000	
Materials procurement	1 100 000	
General factory support	1 480 000	6 080 000
Indirect materials		
Machine centres: X	500 000	
Y	805 000	
Assembly	105 000	
Materials procurement	0	
General factory support	10 000	1 420 000
Lighting and heating	500 000	
Property taxes	1 000 000	
Insurance of machinery	150 000	
Depreciation of machinery	1 500 000	
Insurance of buildings	250 000	
Salaries of works management	800 000	4 200 000
		11 700 000

The following information is also available:

	Book value of machinery (£)	Area occupied (sq. metres)	Number of employees	Direct labour hours	Machine hours
Machine shop: X	8 000 000	10 000	300	1 000 000	2 000 000
Y	5 000 000	5 000	200	1 000 000	1 000 000
Assembly	1 000 000	15 000	300	2 000 000	
Stores	500 000	15 000	100		
Maintenance	500 000	5 000	100		
	15 000 000	50 000	1000		

Details of total materials issues (i.e. direct and indirect materials) to the production centres are as follows:

	£
Machine shop X	4 000 000
Machine shop Y	3 000 000
Assembly	1 000 000
	8 000 000

To allocate the overheads listed above to the production and service centres we must prepare an overhead analysis sheet, as shown in Exhibit 4.2.

EXHIBIT 4.2

Overhead analysis sheet

Item of expenditure	Basis of allocation	Total (£)	Production centres			Service centres	
			Machine centre X (£)	Machine centre Y (£)	Assembly (£)	Materials procurement (£)	General factory support (£)
Indirect wage and supervision	Direct	6 080 000	1 000 000	1 000 000	1 500 000	1 100 000	1 480 000
Indirect materials	Direct	1 420 000	500 000	805 000	105 000		10 000
Lighting and heating	Area	500 000	100 000	50 000	150 000	150 000	50 000
Property taxes	Area	1 000 000	200 000	100 000	300 000	300 000	100 000
Insurance of machinery	Book value of machinery	150 000	80 000	50 000	10 000	5 000	5 000
Depreciation of machinery	Book value of machinery	1 500 000	800 000	500 000	100 000	50 000	50 000
Insurance of buildings	Area	250 000	50 000	25 000	75 000	75 000	25 000
Salaries of works management	Number of employees	800 000	240 000	160 000	240 000	80 000	80 000
	(1)	11 700 000	2 970 000	2 690 000	2 480 000	1 760 000	1 800 000
Reallocation of service centre costs							
Materials procurement	Value of materials issued	—	880 000	660 000	220 000	1 760 000	
General factory support	Direct labour hours	—	450 000	450 000	900 000		1 800 000
	(2)	11 700 000	4 300 000	3 800 000	3 600 000	—	—
Machine hours and direct labour hours			2 000 000	1 000 000	2 000 000		
Machine hour overhead rate			£2.15	£3.80			
Direct labour hour overhead rate					£1.80		

20% of property taxes, lighting and heating and insurance of buildings are allocated to machine centre X, and 10% are allocated to machine centre Y.

The insurance premium paid and depreciation of machinery are generally regarded as being related to the book value of the machinery. Because the book value of machinery for machine centre X is 8/15 of the total book value and machine centre Y is 5/15 of the total book value then 8/15 and 5/15 of the insurance and depreciation of machinery is allocated to machine centres X and Y.

It is assumed that the amount of time that works management devotes to each cost centre is related to the number of employees in each centre; since 30% of the total employees are employed in machine centre X, 30% of the salaries of works management will be allocated to this centre.

If you now look at the overhead analysis sheet shown in Exhibit 4.2, you will see in the row labelled '(1)' that all manufacturing overheads for the Enterprise Company have been assigned to the three production and two service cost centres.

STEP 2 – REALLOCATING THE COSTS ASSIGNED TO SERVICE COST CENTRES TO PRODUCTION COST CENTRES

The next step is to reallocate the costs that have been assigned to service cost centres to production cost centres. **Service departments** (i.e. service cost centres) are those departments that exist to provide services of various kinds to other units within the organization. They are sometimes called **support departments**. The Enterprise Company has two service centres. They are materials procurement and general factory support which includes activities such as production scheduling and machine maintenance. These service centres render essential services that support the production process, but they do not deal directly with the products. Therefore it is not possible to allocate service centre costs to products passing through these centres. To assign costs to products traditional costing systems reallocate service centre costs to production centres that actually work on the product. The method that is chosen to allocate service centre costs to production centres should be related to the benefits that the production centres derive from the service rendered.

We shall assume that the value of materials issued (shown in Example 4.1) provides a suitable approximation of the benefit that each of the production centres receives from materials procurement. Therefore 50% of the value of materials is issued to machine centre X, resulting in 50% of the total costs of materials procurement being allocated to this centre. If you refer to Exhibit 4.2 you will see that £880 000 (50% of material procurement costs of £1 760 000) has been reallocated to machine centre X. It is also assumed that direct labour hours provides an approximation of the benefits received by the production centres from general factory support resulting in the total costs for this centre being reallocated to the production centres proportionate to direct labour hours. Therefore since machine centre X consumes 25% of the direct labour hours £450 000 (25% of the total costs of £1 800 000 assigned to general factory support) has been reallocated to machine centre X. You will see in the row labelled '(2)' in Exhibit 4.2 that all manufacturing costs have now been assigned to the three production centres. This completes the first stage of the two-stage allocation process.

STEP 3 – COMPUTING SEPARATE OVERHEAD RATES FOR EACH PRODUCTION COST CENTRE

The second stage of the two-stage process is to allocate overheads of each production centre to overheads passing through that centre. The most frequently used allocation bases used by traditional costing systems are based on the amount of time products spend in each production centre – normally direct labour hours and machine hours. In respect of non-machine centres, direct labour hours is the most frequently used allocation base. This implies that the overheads incurred by a production centre are closely related to direct labour hours worked. In the case of machine centres a machine hour overhead rate is preferable since most of the overheads (e.g. depreciation) are likely to be more closely related to machine hours. We shall assume that the Enterprise Company uses a **machine hour rate** for the machine production centres and a **direct labour hour rate** for the assembly centre. The overhead rates are calculated by applying the following formula:

$$\frac{\text{cost centre overheads}}{\text{cost centre direct labour hours or machine hours}}$$

The calculations using the information given in Example 4.1 are as follows:

$$\text{Machine centre X} = \frac{£4\,300\,000}{2\,000\,000 \text{ machine hours}} = £2.15 \text{ per machine hour}$$

$$\text{Machine centre Y} = \frac{£3\,800\,000}{1\,000\,000 \text{ machine hours}} = £3.80 \text{ per machine hour}$$

$$\text{Assembly department} = \frac{£3\,600\,000}{2\,000\,000 \text{ direct labour hours}} = £1.80 \text{ per direct labour hour}$$

STEP 4 – ASSIGNING COST CENTRE OVERHEADS TO PRODUCTS OR OTHER CHOSEN COST OBJECTS

The final step is to allocate the overheads to products passing through the production centres. Therefore if a product spends 10 hours in machine cost centre A overheads of £21.50 (10 × £2.15) will be allocated to the product. We shall compute the manufacturing costs of two products. Product A is a low sales volume product with direct costs of £100. It is manufactured in batches of 100 units and each unit requires 5 hours in machine centre A, 10 hours in machine centre B and 10 hours in the assembly centre. Product B is a high sales volume product thus enabling it to be manufactured in larger batches. It is manufactured in batches of 200 units and each unit requires 10 hours in machine centre A, 20 hours in machine centre B and 20 hours in the assembly centre. Direct costs of £200 have been assigned to product B. The calculations of the manufacturing costs assigned to the products are as follows:

Product A	**£**
Direct costs (100 units × £100)	10 000
Overhead allocations	
Machine centre A (100 units × 5 machine hours × £2.15)	1 075
Machine centre B (100 units × 10 machine hours × £3.80)	3 800
Assembly (100 units × 10 direct labour hours × £1.80)	1 800
Total cost	16 675
Cost per unit (£16 675/100 units) = £166.75	

Product B	**£**
Direct costs (200 units × £200)	40 000
Overhead allocations	
Machine centre A (200 units × 10 machine hours × £2.15)	4 300
Machine centre B (200 units × 20 machine hours × £3.80)	15 200
Assembly (200 units × 20 direct labour hours × £1.80)	7 200
Total cost	66 700
Cost per unit (£66 700/200 units) = £333.50	

The overhead allocation procedure is more complicated where service cost centres serve each other. In Example 4.1 it was assumed that materials procurement does not provide any services for general factory support and that general factory support does not provide any services for materials procurement. An understanding of situations where service cost centres do serve each other is not, however, necessary for a general understanding of the overhead procedure, and the problem of service centre reciprocal cost allocations is therefore dealt with in Appendix 4.1.

Extracting relevant costs for decision-making

The cost computations relating to the Enterprise Company for products A and B represent the costs that should be generated for meeting stock valuation and profit measurement requirements. For decision-making, non-manufacturing costs should also be taken into account. In addition, some of the costs that have been assigned to the products may not be relevant for certain decisions. For example, if you look at the overhead analysis sheet in Exhibit 4.2 you will see that property taxes, depreciation of machinery and insurance of buildings and machinery have been assigned to cost centres, and thus included in the costs assigned to products. If these cost are unaffected by a decision to discontinue a product they should not be assigned to products when undertaking product discontinuation reviews. However, if cost information is used to determine selling prices such costs may need to be assigned to products to ensure that the selling price of a customer's order covers a fair share of all organizational costs. It is therefore necessary to ensure that the costs incorporated in the overhead analysis are suitably coded so that different overhead rates can be extracted for different combinations of costs. This will enable relevant cost information to be extracted from the database for meeting different requirements. For an illustration of this approach you should refer to the answer to the sixth review problem shown at the end of this chapter.

Our objective in this chapter has not been to focus on the cost information that should be extracted from the costing system for meeting decision-making requirements. Instead, it is to provide you with an understanding of how cost systems assign costs to cost objects. In Chapter 10 we shall concentrate on the cost information that should be extracted for decision-making.

Budgeted overhead rates

Our discussion in this chapter has assumed that the *actual* overheads for an accounting period have been allocated to the products. However, the calculation of overhead rates based on the *actual* overheads incurred during an accounting period causes a number of problems. First, the product cost calculations have to be delayed until the end of the accounting period, since the overhead rate calculations cannot be obtained before this date, but information on product costs is required quickly if it is to be used for monthly profit calculations and inventory valuations or as a basis for setting selling prices. Secondly, one may argue that the timing problem can be resolved by calculating actual overhead rates at more frequent intervals, say on a monthly basis, but the objection to this proposal is that a large amount of overhead expenditure is fixed in the short term whereas activity will vary from month to month, giving large fluctuations in the overhead rates. Consider Example 4.2.

Such fluctuating overhead rates are not representative of typical, normal production conditions. Management has committed itself to a specific level of fixed costs in the light of foreseeable needs for beyond one month. Thus, where production fluctuates, monthly overhead rates may be volatile. Furthermore, some costs such as repairs, maintenance and heating are not incurred evenly throughout the year. Therefore, if monthly overhead rates are used, these costs will not be allocated fairly to units of output. For example, heating costs would be charged only to winter production so that products produced in winter would be more expensive than those produced in summer.

An average, annualized rate based on the relationship of total annual overhead to total annual activity is more representative of typical relationships between total costs and

EXAMPLE 4.2

The fixed overheads for Euro are £24 000 000 per annum, and monthly production varies from 400 000 to 1 000 000 hours. The monthly overhead rate for fixed overhead will therefore fluctuate as follows:

Monthly overhead	£2 000 000	£2 000 000
Monthly production	400 000 hours	1 000 000 hours
Monthly overhead rate	£5 per hour	£2 per hour

Overhead expenditure that is fixed in the short term remains constant each month, but monthly production fluctuates because of holiday periods and seasonal variations in demand. Consequently the overhead rate varies from £2 to £5 per hour. It would be unreasonable for a product worked on in one month to be allocated overheads at a rate of £5 per hour and an identical product worked on in another month allocated at a rate of only £2 per hour.

volume than a monthly rate. What is required is a normal product cost based on average long-term production rather than an actual product cost, which is affected by month-to-month fluctuations in production volume. Taking these factors into consideration, it is preferable to establish a **budgeted overhead rate** based on annual *estimated* overhead expenditure and activity. Consequently the procedure outlined in the previous sections for calculating cost centre overhead rates should be based on *standard* activity levels and not *actual* activity levels. Surveys of product costing practices indicate that most organizations use annual budgeted activity as a measure of standard activity.

Under- and over-recovery of overheads

The effect of calculating overhead rates based on budgeted annual overhead expenditure and activity is that it will be most unlikely that the overhead allocated to products manufactured during the period will be the same as the actual overhead incurred. Consider a situation where the estimated annual fixed overheads are £2 000 000 and the estimated annual activity is 1 000 000 direct labour hours. The estimated fixed overhead rate will be £2 per hour. Assume that actual overheads are £2 000 000 and are therefore identical with the estimate, but that actual activity is 900 000 direct labour hours instead of the estimated 1 000 000 hours. In this situation only £1 800 000 will be charged to production. This calculation is based on 900 000 direct labour hours at £2 per hour, giving an under-recovery of overheads of £200 000.

Consider an alternative situation where the actual overheads are £1 950 000 instead of the estimated £2 000 000, and actual activity is 1 000 000 direct labour hours, which is identical to the original estimate. In this situation 1 000 000 direct labour hours at £2 per hour will be charged to production giving an over-recovery of £50 000. This example illustrates that there will be an **under- or over-recovery of overheads** whenever actual activity or overhead expenditure is different from the budgeted overheads and activity used to estimate the budgeted overhead rate. This under- or over-recovery of fixed overheads is also called a **volume variance**.

Accounting regulations in most countries recommend that the under- or over-recovery of overheads should be regarded as a period cost adjustment. For example, the UK Statement of Standard Accounting Practice on Stocks and Work in Progress (SSAP 9)

FIGURE 4.4 *Illustration of under-recovery of factory overheads.*

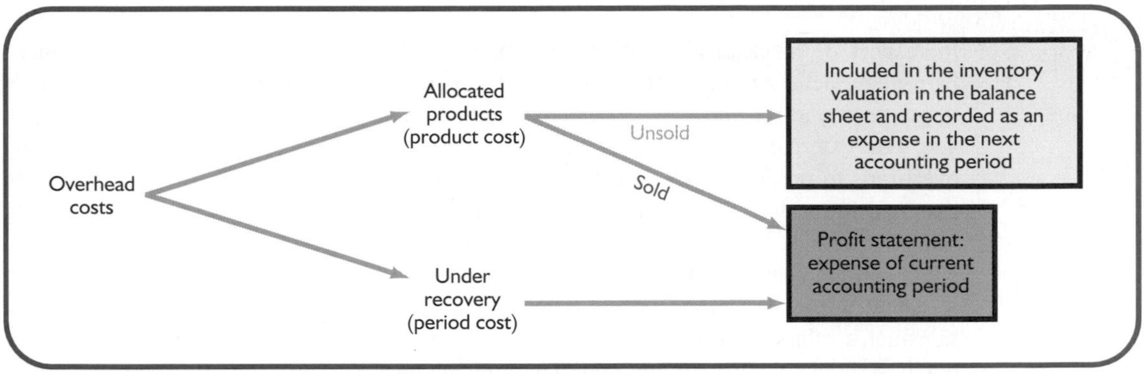

recommends the allocation of overheads in the valuation of inventories and work in progress needs to be based on the company's normal level of activity and that any under- or over-recovery should be written off in the current year. This procedure is illustrated in Figure 4.4. Note that any under- or over-recovery of overheads is not allocated to products. Also note that the under-recovery is recorded as an expense in the current accounting period whereas an over-recovery is recorded as a reduction in the expenses for the period. Finally you should note that our discussion here is concerned with how to treat any under- or over-recovery for the purpose of financial accounting and its impact on inventory valuation and profit measurement.

Maintaining the database at standard costs

Most organizations whose activities consist of a series of common or repetitive operations maintain their database at standard, rather than actual cost, for both traditional and ABC systems. **Standard costs** are pre-determined target costs that should be incurred under efficient operating conditions. For example, assume that the standard direct labour cost for performing a particular operation is £40 (consisting of 5 hours at £8 per hour) and the standard cost of a purchased component (say component Z) is £50. The direct costs for a product requiring only this operation and the purchased component Z would be recorded in the database at a standard cost of £90. Assuming that the product only passed through a single cost centre with a budgeted overhead rate of £20 per direct labour hour the overhead cost for the product would be recorded in the database at £100 standard cost (5 standard direct labour hours at £20 per hour). Instead of a product being recorded in the database at its standard *unit* cost the database may consist of the standard costs of a batch of output, such as normal batch sizes of say 100 or 200 units output of the product.

When a standard costing system is used the database is maintained at standard cost and actual output is costed at the standard cost. Actual costs are recorded, but not at the individual product level, and an adjustment is made at the end of the accounting period by recording as a period cost the difference between standard cost and actual cost for the actual output. This adjustment ensures that the standard costs are converted to actual costs in the profit statement for meeting external financial accounting reporting requirements.

It is not important at this point that you have a detailed understanding of a standard costing system. However, it is important that you are aware that a database may consist of standard (estimated) costs rather than actual costs. We shall look at standard costing in detail in Chapter 15.

Non-manufacturing overheads

In respect of financial accounting, only manufacturing costs are allocated to products. Non-manufacturing overheads are regarded as period costs and are disposed of in exactly the same way as the under- or over-recovery of manufacturing overheads outlined in Figure 4.4. For external reporting it is therefore unnecessary to allocate non-manufacturing overheads to products. However, for decision-making non-manufacturing costs should be assigned to products. For example, in many organizations it is not uncommon for selling prices to be based on estimates of total cost or even actual cost. Housing contractors and garages often charge for their services by adding a percentage profit margin to actual cost.

Some non-manufacturing costs may be a direct cost of the product. Delivery costs, salesmen's salaries and travelling expenses may be directly identifiable with the product, but it is likely that many non-manufacturing overheads cannot be allocated directly to specific products. On what basis should we allocate non-manufacturing overheads? The answer is that we should select an allocation base/cost driver that corresponds most closely to non-manufacturing overheads. The problem is that allocation bases that are widely used by traditional costing systems, such as direct labour hours, machine hours and direct labour cost are not necessarily those that are closely related to non-manufacturing overheads. Therefore traditional systems tend to use arbitrary, rather than cause-and-effect allocation bases, to allocate non-manufacturing overheads to products. The most widely used approach (see Exhibit 4.3) is to allocate non-manufacturing overheads on the ability of the products to bear such costs. This approach can be implemented by allocating non-manufacturing costs to products on the basis of their manufacturing costs. This procedure is illustrated in Example 4.3.

Because of the arbitrary nature of the cost allocations, some organizations that use traditional costing systems as a basis for setting selling prices do not allocate non-manufacturing overheads to products. Instead, they add a percentage profit margin to each product so that it provides a profit contribution and a contribution to non-manufacturing overheads. Recent developments in ABC have provided a mechanism for more accurately assigning non-manufacturing overheads to products. These developments will be explained in Chapter 11 when ABC is examined in more depth.

EXHIBIT 4.3

Methods used by UK organizations to allocate non-manufacturing overheads to products

	(%)
Allocation as a percentage of total manufacturing cost	32
Direct labour hours/cost methods	25
Percentage of total selling price	12
Non-manufacturing overheads not traced to products	23
Other method	8
	100

SOURCE: Drury *et al.* (1993).

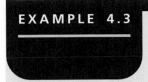

EXAMPLE 4.3

The estimated non-manufacturing and manufacturing costs of a company for the year ending 31 December are £500 000 and £1 million respectively. The non-manufacturing overhead absorption rate is calculated as follows:

$$\frac{\text{estimated non-manufacturing overhead}}{\text{estimated manufacturing cost}}$$

In percentage terms each product will be allocated with non-manufacturing overheads at a rate of 50% of its total manufacturing cost.

Summary

The aim of this chapter has been to provide you with an understanding of how costs are assigned to cost objects. Direct costs can be accurately traced to cost objects whereas indirect costs cannot. Therefore indirect costs must be assigned using cost allocation bases. Allocation bases which are significant determinants of costs that are being allocated are described as cause-and-effect allocations whereas arbitrary allocations refer to allocation bases that are not the significant determinant of the costs. To accurately measure the cost of resources used by cost objects cause-and-effect allocations should be used.

Most organizations accumulate costs within a single database and different categories of costs are extracted for meeting different purposes. The sophistication and accuracy of costing systems vary and cost–benefit criteria should determine the optimal costing system for an organization. The range of the sophistication of costing systems varies from simplistic traditional to sophisticated ABC systems. Simplistic traditional systems make significant use of arbitrary cost allocations whereas ABC systems aim to use only cause-and-effect cost allocations.

Both systems use the two-stage allocation process. In the first stage overheads are assigned to cost centres, while the second stage allocates cost centre overheads to products. Some companies use only a single plant-wide overhead rate, but it has been shown that this approach can only be justified where products spend approximately equal proportions of time in each production cost centre. The two-stage procedure involves the following steps:

1. the allocation of overheads to production and service centres or departments;
2. the apportionment of service department overhead to production departments;
3. the calculation of appropriate departmental overhead rates;
4. the allocation of overheads to products passing through each department.

These steps were illustrated with Example 4.1 for a traditional costing system. The allocation bases that are most frequently used in the second stage by traditional costing systems are the direct labour hour method for non-machine departments and the machine hour rate for machine departments. Other methods of allocating overheads such as the direct wages percentage, units of output, direct materials and prime cost percentage methods are discussed in Appendix 4.2, but they can only be recommended in certain circumstances.

As the use of actual overhead rates causes a delay in the calculation of product costs, and the use of monthly overhead rates causes fluctuations in monthly overhead rates, it has been suggested that budgeted annual overhead rates should be used. However, the use of annual budgeted overhead rates gives an under- or over-recovery of overhead whenever actual overhead expenditure or activity is different from budget. Any under- or over-recovery of overhead is generally regarded as a period cost adjustment and written off to the profit and loss account, although some writers argue that the under- or over-recovery should be apportioned between the cost of sales and closing stocks.

For meeting financial accounting requirements non-manufacturing overheads are not assigned to products. Instead, they are treated as period costs.

For decision-making non-manufacturing costs must be considered but traditional costing systems allocate them using arbitrary allocations that result in the reporting of distorted product costs. Recent developments in ABC have provided a mechanism for more accurately assigning non-manufacturing overheads to products.

Finally, you should note that the allocation of service department overheads when service departments serve each other and the use of alternative second stage allocation bases, other than direct labour and machine hours, are presented in Appendices 4.1 and 4.2. These topics tend to be included in the syllabus requirements of the examinations set by professional accountancy bodies but may not represent part of the curriculum for other courses. You should therefore check if these topics are included in your course curriculum. You can omit reading Appendices 4.1 and 4.2 if the topics are not part of your course curriculum.

Appendix 4.1: Inter-service department reallocations

Service departments provide services for other service departments as well as for production departments. For example, a personnel department provides services for other service departments such as the power generating plant, maintenance department and stores. The power generating department also provides heat and light for other service departments, including the personnel department, and so on. When such interactions occur, the allocation process can become complicated. Difficulties arise because each service department begins to accumulate charges from other service departments from which it receives services, and these must be reallocated back to the user department. Once it has begun, this allocation and reallocation process can continue for a long time before a solution is found. The problem is illustrated in Example 4A.1. We shall use the example to illustrate four different methods of allocating the service department costs:

1. **repeated distribution method;**
2. **simultaneous equation method;**
3. **specified order of closing method;**
4. **direct allocation method.**

1. REPEATED DISTRIBUTION METHOD

Where this method is adopted, the service department costs are repeatedly allocated in the specified percentages until the figures become too small to be significant. You can see from line 2 of Exhibit 4A.1 that the overheads of service department 1 are allocated according to

---

EXAMPLE 4A.1

A company has three production departments and two service departments. The overhead analysis sheet provides the following totals of the overheads analysed to production and service departments:

		(£)
Production department	X	48 000
	Y	42 000
	Z	30 000
Service department	1	14 040
	2	18 000
		152 040

The expenses of the service departments are apportioned as follows:

	Production departments			**Service departments**	
	X	**Y**	**Z**	**1**	**2**
Service department 1	20%	40%	30%	—	10%
Service department 2	40%	20%	20%	20%	—

the prescribed percentages. As a result, some of the overheads of service department 1 are transferred to service department 2. In line 3 the overheads of service department 2 are allocated, which means that service department 1 receives some further costs. The costs of service department 1 are again allocated, and service department 2 receives some further costs. This process continues until line 7, by which time the costs have become so small that any further detailed apportionments are unnecessary. As a result, the total overheads in line 8 of £152 040 are allocated to production departments only.

EXHIBIT 4A.1

Repeated distribution method

Line	Production departments			Service departments		Total
	X	Y	Z	1	2	
1. Allocation as per overhead analysis	48 000	42 000	30 000	14 040	18 000	152 040
2. Allocation of service department 1	2 808 (20%)	5 616 (40%)	4 212 (30%)	(14 040)	1 404 (10%) 19 404	
3. Allocation of service department 2	7 762 (40%)	3 881 (20%)	3 880 (20%)	3 881 (20%)	(19 404)	
4. Allocation of service department 1	776 (20%)	1 552 (40%)	1 165 (30%)	(3 881)	388 (10%)	
5. Allocation of service department 2	154 (40%)	78 (20%)	78 (20%)	78 (20%)	(388)	
6. Allocation of service department 1	16 (20%)	31 (40%)	23 (30%)	(78)	8 (10%)	
7. Allocation of service department 2	4 (40%)	2 (20%)	2 (20%)	—	(8)	
8. Total overheads	59 520	53 160	39 360	—	—	152 040

2. SIMULTANEOUS EQUATION METHOD

When this method is used simultaneous equations are initially established as follows: Let

$$x = \text{total overhead of service department 1}$$
$$y = \text{total overhead of service department 2}$$

The total overhead transferred into service departments 1 and 2 can be expressed as

$$x = 14\,040 + 0.2y$$
$$y = 18\,000 + 0.1x$$

Rearranging the above equations:

$$x - 0.2y = 14\,040 \qquad (1)$$
$$-0.1x + y = 18\,000 \qquad (2)$$

We can now multiply equation (1) by 5 and equation (2) by 1, giving

$$5x - y = 70\,200$$
$$-0.1x + y = 18\,000$$

Adding the above equations together we have

$$4.9x = 88\,200$$

Therefore $\qquad\qquad\qquad x = 18\,000\ (= 88\,200/4.9)$

Substituting this value for x in equation (1), we have

$$18\,000 - 0.2y = 14\,040$$

Therefore $\qquad\qquad\qquad -0.2y = -3\,960$

Therefore $\qquad\qquad\qquad y = 19\,800$

We now apportion the values for x and y to the production departments in the agreed percentages.

Line	X	Y	Z	Total
1. Allocation as per overhead analysis	48 000	42 000	30 000	120 000
2. Allocation of service department 1	3 600 (20%)	7 200 (40%)	5 400 (30%)	16 200
3. Allocation of service department 2	7 920 (40%)	3 960 (20%)	3 960 (20%)	15 840
4.	59 520	53 160	39 360	152 040

You will see from line 2 that the value for X (service department 1) of £18 000 is allocated in the specified percentages. Similarly, in line 3 the value for Y (service department 2) of £19 800 is apportioned in the specified percentages. As a result the totals in line 4 are in agreement with the totals in line 8 of the repeated distribution method (Exhibit 4A.1).

3. SPECIFIED ORDER OF CLOSING

If this method is used the service departments' overheads are allocated to the production departments in a certain order. The service department that does the largest proportion of work for other service departments is closed first; the service department that does the second largest proportion of work for other service departments is closed second; and so on. Return charges are not made to service departments whose costs have previously been

EXHIBIT 4A.2

Specified order of closing method

allocated. Let us now apply this method to the information contained in Example 4A.1. The results are given in Exhibit 4A.2.

	Production departments			Service departments		
Line	X	Y	Z	1	2	Total
1. Allocation as per overhead analysis	48 000	42 000	30 000	14 040	18 000	152 040
2. Allocate service department 2	7 200 (40%)	3 600 (20%)	3 600 (20%)	3 600 (20%)	(18 000)	
3. Allocate service department 1	3 920 (2/9)	7 840 (4/9)	5 880 (3/9)	(17 640)	—	
4.	59 120	53 440	39 480	—	—	152 040

The costs of service department 2 are allocated first (line 2) because 20% of its work is related to service department 1, whereas only 10% of the work of service department 1 is related to service department 2. In line 3 we allocate the costs of service department 1, but the return charges are not made to department 2. This means that the proportions allocated have changed as 10% of the costs of service department 1 have not been allocated to service department 2. Therefore 20% out of a 90% total or 2/9 of the costs of service department 1 are allocated to department X.

You will see that the totals allocated in line 4 do not agree with the totals allocated under the repeated distribution or simultaneous equation methods. This is because the specified order of closing method sacrifices accuracy for clerical convenience. However, if this method provides a close approximation to an alternative accurate calculation then there are strong arguments for its use.

4. DIRECT ALLOCATION METHOD

This method is illustrated in Exhibit 4A.3. It ignores inter-service department service reallocations. Therefore service department costs are reallocated only to production departments. This means that the proportions allocated have changed as 10% of the costs of service department 1 have not been allocated to service department 2. Therefore 20% out of a 90% total, or 2/9 of the costs of service department 1, are allocated to department X, 4/9 are allocated to department Y and 3/9 are allocated to department Z. Similarly the proportions allocated for service department 2 have changed with 4/8 (40% out of 80%) of the costs of service department 2 being allocated department X, 2/8 to

	Production departments			Service departments		
Line	X	Y	Z	1	2	Total
1. Allocation as per overhead analysis	48 000	42 000	30 000	14 040	18 000	152 040
2. Allocate service department 1	3 120 (2/9)	6 240 (4/9)	4 680 (3/9)	(14 040)		
3. Allocate service department 2	9 000 (4/8)	4 500 (2/8)	4 500 (2/8)	—	(18 000)	
4	60 120	52 740	39 180	—	—	152 040

department Y and 2/8 to department Z. The only justification for using the direct allocation method is its simplicity. The method is recommended when inter-service reallocations are relatively insignificant.

Appendix 4.2: Other allocation bases used by traditional systems

In the main body of this chapter it was pointed out that traditional costing systems tend to rely on using two second stage allocation bases – namely, direct labour hours and machine hours. Example 4.1 was used to illustrate the application of these allocation bases. With traditional systems it is generally assumed that overhead expenditure is related to output measured by either direct labour hours or machine hours required for a given volume. Products with a high direct labour or machine hour content are therefore assumed to consume a greater proportion of overheads. In addition, to direct labour and machine hours, the following allocation bases are also sometimes used by traditional costing systems:

1. **direct wages percentage method**;
2. **units of output method**;
3. **direct materials percentage method**;
4. **prime cost percentage method**.

Each of these methods is illustrated using the information given in Example 4A.2.

EXAMPLE 4A.2

The budgeted overheads for a department for the next accounting period are £200 000. In addition, the following information is available for the period:

Estimated direct wages	£250 000
Estimated direct materials	£100 000
Estimated output	10 000 units

1. DIRECT WAGES PERCENTAGE METHOD

The direct wages percentage overhead rate is calculated as follows:

$$\frac{\text{estimated departmental overheads} \times 100}{\text{estimated direct wages}}$$

Using information given in Example 4A.2,

$$\frac{£200\,000}{£250\,000} \times 100 = 80\% \text{ of direct wages}$$

If we assume that the direct wages cost for a product is £20 then overheads of £16 (80% × £20) will be allocated to the product.

The direct wages percentage method is suitable only where uniform wage rates apply within a cost centre or department. In such a situation this method will yield exactly the same results as the direct labour hour method. However, consider a situation where wage rates are not uniform. Products X and Y spend 20 hours in the same production department, but product X requires skilled labour and product Y requires unskilled labour, with direct wages costs respectively of £200 and £100. If we apply the direct wages percentage overhead rate of 80% we should allocate overheads of £160 to product X and £80 to product Y. If both products spend the same amount of time in the department, are such apportioned amounts fair? The answer would appear to be negative, and the direct wages percentage method should therefore only be recommended when similar wage rates are paid to direct employees in a production department.

2. UNITS OF OUTPUT METHOD

If this method is used, the overhead rate is calculated as follows:

$$\frac{\text{estimated departmental overhead}}{\text{estimated output}}$$

Using the information given in Example 4A.2, this would give an overhead rate of £20 per unit produced. The units of output method is only suitable where all units produced within a department are identical. In other words, it is best suited to a process costing system, and it is not recommended for a job costing system where all jobs or products spend a different amount of time in each production department. If, for example, two of the units produced in Example 4A.2 required 100 hours and 2 hours respectively then they would both be allocated £20. Such an allocation would not be logical.

3. DIRECT MATERIALS PERCENTAGE METHOD

The direct materials percentage overhead rate is calculated as follows:

$$\frac{\text{estimated departmental overhead}}{\text{estimated direct materials}}$$

Using the information given in Example 4A.2,

$$\frac{£200\,000}{£100\,000} = 200\% \text{ of direct materials}$$

If we assume that the direct material cost incurred by a product in the department is £50 then the product will be allocated with £100 for a share of the overheads of the department.

If the direct materials percentage overhead rate is used, the overheads allocated to products will bear little relationship to the amount of time that products spend in each department. Consequently, this method of recovery cannot normally be recommended, unless the majority of overheads incurred in a department are related to materials rather than time. In particular, the method is appropriate for allocating materials handling expenses to products. With this approach, a cost centre is created for material handling expenses and the expenses are allocated to products using a materials handling overhead rate (normally the direct materials percentage allocation method). Companies that use a materials handling overhead rate allocate the remaining factory overheads to products using one or more of the allocation bases described in this chapter.

4. PRIME COST PERCENTAGE METHOD

The prime cost percentage overhead rate is calculated as follows:

$$\frac{\text{estimated departmental overheads}}{\text{estimated prime cost}} \times 100$$

Using the information given in Example 4A.2, you will see that the estimated prime cost is £350 000, which consists of direct wages of £250 000 plus direct materials of £100 000. The calculation of the overhead rate is

$$\frac{£200\,000}{£350\,000} \times 100 = 57.14\%$$

A product that incurs £100 prime cost in the department will be allocated £57.14 for the departmental overheads.

As prime cost consists of direct wages and direct materials, the disadvantages that apply to the direct materials and direct wages percentage methods also apply to the prime cost percentage method of overhead recovery. Consequently, the prime cost method is not recommended.

Key Terms and Concepts

activity-based-costing (ABC) system (p. 72)
allocation base (p. 72)
arbitrary allocation (p. 72)
blanket overhead rate (p. 76)
budgeted overhead rate (p. 86)
cause-and-effect allocations (p. 72)
cost allocation (p. 72)
cost centre (p. 77)

cost driver (p. 72)
cost pool (p. 77)
cost tracing (p. 72)
direct allocation method (p. 92)
direct labour hour rate (p. 83)
direct materials percentage method (p. 96)
direct wages percentage method (p. 96)
first stage allocation bases (p. 80)

Key Examination Points

A typical question (e.g. Review Problem 4) will require you to analyse overheads by departments and calculate appropriate overhead allocation rates. These questions require a large number of calculations, and it is possible that you will make calculation errors. Do make sure that your answer is clearly presented, since marks tend to be allocated according to whether you have adopted the correct method. You are recommended to present your answer in a format similar to Exhibit 4.2. For a traditional costing system you should normally recommend a direct labour hour rate if a department is non-mechanized and a machine hour rate if machine hours are the dominant activity. You should only recommend the direct wages percentage method when the wage rates within a non-mechanized department are uniform.

Where a question requires you to present information for decision-making, do not include apportioned fixed overheads in the calculations. Remember the total manufacturing costs should be calculated for stock valuation, but incremental manufacturing costs should be calculated for decision-making purposes (see answer to Review Problem 6).

Finally, ensure that you can calculate under- or over-recoveries of overheads and deal with reciprocal cost allocations. To check your understanding of these topics you should refer to the solutions of Review Problems 5 and 7. Normally questions on reciprocal cost allocations do not specify which allocation method should be adopted. You should therefore use either the simultaneous equation method or the repeated distribution method.

Review Problems

(For additional problems without answers relating to the content of this chapter you should refer to pages 428–439.)

1 A company uses a predetermined overhead recovery rate based on machine hours. Budgeted factory overhead for a year amounted to £720 000, but actual factory overhead incurred was £738 000. During the year, the company absorbed £714 000 of factory overhead on 119 000 actual machine hours.

What was the company's budgeted level of machine hours for the year?
A 116 098
B 119 000
C 120 000
D 123 000

ACCA Foundation Paper 3

2 A company absorbs overheads on machine hours which were budgeted at 11 250 with overheads of £258 750. Actual results were 10 980 hours with overheads of £254 692.
Overheads were:
A under-absorbed by £2152
B over-absorbed by £4058
C under-absorbed by £4058
D over-absorbed by £2152

CIMA Stage 1

3 The following data are to be used for sub-questions (i) and (ii) below:

Budgeted labour hours	8 500
Budgeted overheads	£148 750
Actual labour hours	7 928
Actual overheads	£146 200

(i) Based on the data given above, what is the labour hour overhead absorption rate?

A   £17.50 per hour
B   £17.20 per hour
C   £18.44 per hour
D   £18.76 per hour

(ii) Based on the data given above, what is the amount of overhead under/over-absorbed?

A   £2550 under-absorbed
B   £2529 over-absorbed
C   £2550 over-absorbed
D   £7460 under-absorbed

CIMA Stage 1

4 A company manufactures and sells two products, X and Y, whose selling prices are £100 and £300, respectively, and each product passes through two manufacturing processes, A and B. In process A, product X takes 2 hours per unit and product Y takes 4 hours. In process B, product X takes 1 hour per unit, and product Y takes 3 hours. Labour in process A is paid £4 per hour, and in process B £5 per hour.

The two products are made out of materials P, Q and R, and the quantities of each material used in making one unit of each product are:

	Product X	Product Y
Material P	37 lbs	93 lbs
Material Q	10	240
Material R	20 sq. feet	75 sq. feet

Material prices are £1 per lb for P, £2.40 per dozen for Q and £0.20 per square foot for R.

Salesmen are paid a commission of 5% of sales. The packing materials are £1 for X and £4 for Y. Costs of transporting the goods to the customer are £2 for X and £5 for Y.

Other annual costs are:

		£	£
Indirect wages:	Process A	25 000	
	Process B	40 000	
	Stores	20 000	
	Canteen	10 000	
			95 000
Indirect materials:	Process A	51 510	
	Process B	58 505	
	Stores	1 310	
	Canteen	8 425	
			119 750
Rent and rates			450 000
Depreciation of plant and machinery			140 000

	£
Power	50 000
Insurance: Fire on buildings	3 750
Workmen's compensation @ 2% of wages	12 000
Heating and lighting	4 500
Advertising	90 000

A royalty of £1 per unit is payable on product X. The annual quantities sold are 15 000 units of X and 10 000 units of Y.

Other relevant information is:

Cost centre	Area in square feet	Book value of plant and machinery (£)	Horsepower machinery (%)	Direct labour hours	Number of employees	Number of stores issue notes
Process A	100 000	1 000 000	80	70 000	40	10 000
Process B	50 000	200 000	20	45 000	30	5 000
Stores	100 000	150 000			10	
Canteen	50 000	50 000			5	
	300 000	1 400 000	100	115 000	85	15 000

You are required to:

(a) prepare a production overhead analysis and apportionment sheet, showing clearly the bases of apportionment used; *(10 marks)*
(b) calculate appropriate rates of overhead recovery for processes A and B; *(2 marks)*
(c) calculate the total cost of making and selling one unit of each product; *(6 marks)*
(d) calculate the unit profit or loss for each product. *(2 marks)*

(Total 20 marks)
CIMA Stage 1

5 A factory with three departments uses a single production overhead absorption rate, expressed as a percentage of direct wages cost. It has been suggested that departmental overhead absorption rates would result in more accurate job costs. Set out below are budgeted and actual data for the previous period, together with information relating to job no. 657.

		Direct wages (£000s)	Direct labour hours	Machine hours	Production overheads (£000s)
Budget:					
Department:	A	25	10 000	40 000	120
	B	100	50 000	10 000	30
	C	25	25 000	—	75
Total:		150	85 000	50 000	225
Actual:					
Department:	A	30	12 000	45 000	130
	B	80	45 000	14 000	28
	C	30	30 000	—	80
Total:		140	87 000	59 000	238

During this period job no. 657 incurred the actual costs and actual times in the departments as shown below:

Department:	Direct material (£)	Direct wages (£)	Direct labour hours	Machine hours
A	120	100	20 000	40 000
B	60	60	40 000	10 000
C	10	10	10 000	—

After adding production overhead to prime cost, one-third is added to production cost for gross profit. This assumes that a reasonable profit is earned after deducting administration, selling and distribution costs. You are required to:

(a) calculate the current overhead absorption rate;

(b) using the rate obtained in (a) above, calculate the production overhead charged to job no. 657, and state the production cost and expected gross profit on this job;

(c) (i) comment on the suggestion that departmental overhead absorption rates would result in more accurate job costs; and
   (ii) compute such rates, briefly explaining your reason for each rate;

(d) using the rates calculated in (c) (ii) above, show the overhead, by department and in total, that would apply to job no. 657;

(e) show the over-/under-absorption, by department and in total, for the period, using:
   (i) the current rate in your answer to (a) above; and
   (ii) your suggested rates in your answers to (c) (ii) above. (*20 marks*)
   CIMA Cost Accounting 1

6 Shown below is next year's budget for the forming and finishing departments of Tooton Ltd. The departments manufacture three different types of component, which are incorporated into the output of the firm's finished products.

	Component		
	A	B	C
Production (units)	14 000	10 000	6000
Prime cost (£ per unit):			
Direct materials			
Forming dept	8	7	9
Direct labour			
Forming dept	6	9	12
Finishing dept	10	15	8
	24	31	29

Manufacturing times (hours per unit):

Machining			
Forming dept	4	3	2
Direct labour			
Forming dept	2	3	4
Finishing dept	3	10	2

	Forming department (£)	Finishing department (£)
Variable overheads	200 900	115 500
Fixed overheads	401 800	231 000
	£602 700	£346 500

Machine time required and available	98 000 hours	—
Labour hours required and available	82 000 hours	154 000 hours

The forming department is mechanized and employs only one grade of labour, the finishing department employs several grades of labour with differing hourly rates of pay.

Required:

(a) Calculate suitable overhead absorption rates for the forming and finishing departments for next year and include a brief explanation for your choice of rates. (*6 marks*)

(b) Another firm has offered to supply next year's budgeted quantities of the above components at the following prices:

Component A £30 Component B £65
Component C £60

Advise management whether it would be more economical to purchase any of the above components from the outside supplier. You must show your workings and, considering cost criteria only, clearly state any assumptions made or any aspects that may require further investigation. (*8 marks*)

(c) Critically consider the purpose of calculating production overheads absorption rates. (*8 marks*)
(*Total 22 marks*)
ACCA Foundation Costing

7 A company reapportions the costs incurred by two service cost centres, materials handling and inspection, to the three production cost centres of machining, finishing and assembly.

The following are the overhead costs which have been allocated and apportioned to the five cost centres:

	(£000)
Machining	400
Finishing	200
Assembly	100
Materials handling	100
Inspection	50

Estimates of the benefits received by each cost centre are as follows:

	Machining %	Finishing %	Assembly %	Materials handling %	Inspection %
Materials handling	30	25	35	—	10
Inspection	20	30	45	5	—

You are required to:

(a) calculate the charge for overhead to *each* of the *three* production cost centres, including the amounts reapportioned from the two service centres, using:
   (i) the continuous allotment (or repeated distribution) method;
   (ii) an algebraic method;   (*15 marks*)

(b) comment on whether reapportioning service cost centre costs is generally worthwhile and suggest an alternative treatment for such costs;

(c) discuss the following statement: 'Some writers advocate that an under- or over-absorption of overhead should be apportioned between the cost of goods sold in the period to which it relates and to closing stocks. However, the United Kingdom practice is to treat under- or over-absorption of overhead as a period cost.'   (*6 marks*)
     (*Total 25 marks*)
     CIMA Stage 2 Cost Accounting 3

Answers to Review Problems

SOLUTION 1

Overhead absorbed (£714 000)
$\quad$ = Actual hours (119 000)
$\quad\quad$ × Pre-determined overhead rate.
Pre-determined overhead rate
$\quad$ = £714 000/119 000 = £6.
Budgeted overheads (£720 000)
$\quad$ = Budgeted machine hours × Budgeted overhead rate (£6).
Budgeted machine hours
$\quad$ = £720 000/£6 = 120 000 hours.
Answer = C

SOLUTION 2

Budgeted overhead rate = £258 750/11 250 hours
= £23 per machine hour.
Overheads absorbed = £23 × 10 980 Actual hours
= £252 540.
Overheads incurred = £254 692
Overheads absorbed = £252 540
Under-absorbed overheads = £2152
Answer = A

SOLUTION 3

(i) Budgeted overhead rates and not actual overhead rates should be used as indicated in Chapter 4.

Overhead rate = £148 750/8500 hours
= £17.50 per hour.
Answer = A

(ii) Actual overheads incurred = £146 200
Overheads absorbed (7928 × £17.50)
= £138 740
Under-absorbed overheads = £7460
Answer = D

SOLUTION 4

(a) Production overhead analysis and apportionment sheet:

Overhead	Bases of apportionment	Total cost (£)	Production processes A (£)	B (£)	Service departments Stores (£)	Canteen (£)
Indirect wages	Direct	95 000	25 000	40 000	20 000	10 000
Indirect materials	Direct	119 750	51 510	58 505	1 310	8 425
Rent and rates	Area	450 000	150 000	75 000	150 000	75 000
Depreciation, plant	Book value, plant	140 000	100 000	20 000	15 000	5 000
Power	HP of plant	50 000	40 000	10 000		
Fire insurance	Area	3 750	1 250	625	1 250	625
WC insurance	2% of wages	12 000	6 100	5 300	400	200
Heat and light	Area	4 500	1 500	750	1 500	750
		875 000	375 360	210 180	189 460	100 000
Canteen	No. of employees	—	50 000	37 500	12 500	(100 000)
Stores	No. of stores issues	—	134 640	67 320	(201 960)	
		875 000	560 000	315 000	—	—

Note that the workmen's compensation (WC) insurance premium is based on a charge of 2%

of wages. Consequently an insurance charge of 2% of the total wages should be allocated to each department. The calculations are:

	Process A (£)		Process B (£)		Stores (£)	Canteen (£)
Direct wages	280 000	(1)	225 000	(2)	—	—
Indirect wages	25 000		40 000		20 000	10 000
Total wages	305 000		265 000		20 000	10 000
Allocation at 2% of total wages	6 100		5 300		400	200

Notes:

(1) Product X (15 000 units × 2 hours × £4)

$$= £120\,000,$$

Product Y (10 000 units × 4 hours × £4)

$$= £160\,000,$$
$$\underline{\underline{£280\,000}}.$$

(2) Product X (15 000 units × 1 hour × £5)

$$= £75\,000,$$

Product Y (10 000 units × 3 hours × £5)

$$= £150\,000,$$
$$\underline{\underline{£225\,000}}.$$

(b)

	Process A	Process B
Direct labour hours	70 000	45 000
Production overhead	£560 000	£315 000
Overhead rate per direct labour hour	£8	£7

(c) **Product costs**

		X (£)	Y (£)
Direct materials: P	37		93	
Q	2		48	
R	4	43	15	156
Direct wages: Process A	8		16	
Process B	5	13	15	31
Production overhead (3): Process A	16		32	
Process B	7	23	21	53
Royalty		1		—
Absorption (manufacturing) cost		80		240
Commission		5		15
Packing materials		1		4
Transport		2		5
Advertising (4)		2		6
Total cost		90		270

Notes:

(3) The overhead absorption rates are £8 per hour for process A and £7 per hour for process B. Product X spends 2 hours in process A and 1 hour in process B. The production overhead charge is thus £23 for product X. Product Y takes 4 hours in process A and 3 hours in process B.

Consequently £32 production overhead is charged in respect of process A and £21 in respect of process B.

(4) Advertising is apportioned on the basis of total sales revenue. Total sales revenue is £4 500 000, consisting of 15 000 units of X at £100 and 10 000 units of Y at £300. Advertising is 2% of sales (£90 000/£4 500 000). Therefore advertising is allocated to products at the rate of 2% of the selling price.

(d)

	X (£)	Y (£)
Unit selling price	100	300
Unit total cost	90	270
Profit	10	30

SOLUTION 5

(a) Overhead rate $= \dfrac{\text{Budgeted overhead}}{\text{Budgeted direct wages}} \times 100$

$$= \frac{£225\,000}{£150\,000} \times 100$$
$$= \underline{150\%}$$

(b)

	(£)
Direct materials	190
Direct wages	170
Production overhead (150% × £170)	255
Production cost	615
Gross profit ($\frac{1}{3}$ × £615)	205
	820

(c) (i) Each department incurs different overhead costs. For example, the overhead costs of department A are considerably higher than those of the other departments. A blanket overhead rate is only appropriate where jobs spend the same proportion of time in each department. See the section on blanket overhead rates in Chapter 4 for an explanation of why departmental overhead rates are preferable.

(ii) *Department A machine-hour overhead rate:*

$$\frac{£120\,000}{40\,000 \text{ machine hours}}$$
$$= £3 \text{ per machine hour}$$

A machine-hour rate is preferable because machine hours appear to be the dominant activity. Also, most of the overheads incurred are likely to be related to machine hours rather than direct labour hours. Possibly one worker operates four machines since the ratio is 40 000 machine hours to 10 000 direct labour hours. If some jobs do not involve machinery but others do, then two separate cost centres should be established (one related to machinery and the other related to jobs which involve direct labour hours only).

Department B direct labour hour overhead rate:

$$\frac{£30\,000}{50\,000 \text{ direct labour hours}} = £0.60 \text{ per labour hour}$$

Because direct labour hours are five times greater than machine hours a direct labour hour overhead rate is recommended. A comparison of direct labour hours and direct wages for budget, actual and job 657 for department B suggests that wage rate are not equal throughout the department. Therefore the direct wages percentage method is inappropriate.

Department C direct labour hour overhead rate:

$$\frac{£75\,000}{25\,000 \text{ direct labour hours}} = £3 \text{ per direct labour hour}$$

This method is chosen because it is related to time and machine hours are ruled out. A comparison of budgeted direct wages and labour hours for budget, actual and job 657 for department C suggests that wage rates are equal at £1 per hour throughout the department. Therefore direct labour hours or direct wages percentage methods will produce the same results.

(d) Department A (40 machine hours × £3) 120

B (40 labour hours × £0.60) 24

C (10 labour hours × £3) 30

174

(e) (i) *Current rate (actual wages × 150%):*

	Absorbed	Actual	Over/(under)-absorbed
	(£000s)	(£000s)	(£000s)
Department A	45	130	(85)
B	120	28	92
C	45	80	(35)
	210	238	(28)

(ii) *Proposed rates:*

	Absorbed	Actual	Over/(under)-absorbed
	(£000s)	(£000s)	(£000s)
Department A	135	130	5
B	27	28	(1)
C	90	80	10
	252	238	14

SOLUTION 6

(a) The calculation of the overhead absorption rates are as follows:

Forming department machine hour rate = £6.15 per machine hour (£602 700/98 000 hours)
Finishing department labour hour rate = £2.25 per labour hour (£346 500/154 000 hours)

The forming department is mechanized, and it is likely that a significant proportion of overheads will be incurred as a consequence of employing and running the machines. Therefore a machine hour rate has been used. In the finishing department several grades of labour are used. Consequently the direct wages percentage method is inappropriate, and the direct labour hour method should be used.

(b) The decision should be based on a comparison of the incremental costs with the purchase price of an outside supplier if spare capacity exists. If no spare capacity exists then the lost contribution on displaced work must be considered. The calculation of incremental costs requires that the variable element of the total overhead absorption rate must be calculated. The calculation is:

Forming department variable machine hour rate = £2.05 (£200 900/98 000 hours)
Finishing department variable direct labour hour rate = £0.75 (£115 500/154 000 hours)

The calculation of the variable costs per unit of each component is:

	A (£)	B (£)	C (£)
Prime cost	24.00	31.00	29.00
Variable overheads: Forming	8.20	6.15	4.10
Finishing	2.25	7.50	1.50
Variable unit manufacturing cost	34.45	44.65	34.60
Purchase price	£30	£65	£60

On the basis of the above information, component A should be purchased and components B and C manufactured. This decision is based on the following assumptions:

(i) Variable overheads vary in proportion to machine hours (forming department) and direct labour hours (finishing department).

(ii) Fixed overheads remain unaffected by any changes in activity.

(iii) Spare capacity exists.

For a discussion of make-or-buy decisions see Chapter 10.

(c) Production overhead absorption rates are calculated in order to ascertain costs per unit of output for stock valuation and profit measurement purposes. Such costs are inappropriate for decision-making and cost control. For an explanation of this see the section in Chapter 4 titled 'Different costs for different purposes'.

SOLUTION 7

(a) (i)

	Machining (£)	Finishing (£)	Assembly (£)	Materials handling (£)	Inspection (£)
Initial cost	400 000	200 000	100 000	100 000	50 000
Reapportion:					
Materials handling	30 000	25 000	35 000	(100 000)	10 000
	430 000	225 000	135 000	—	60 000
Inspection	12 000 (20%)	18 000 (30%)	27 000 (45%)	3 000 (5%)	(60 000)
	442 000	243 000	162 000	3 000	—
Materials handling	900 (30%)	750 (25%)	1 050 (45%)	(3 000)	300 (10%)
	442 900	243 750	163 050	—	300
Inspection	60 (20%)	90 (30%)	135 (45%)	15 (5%)	(300)
	442 960	243 840	163 185	(15)	
	5	4	6	(15)	
	442 965	243 844	163 191		

(ii) Let

$$x = \text{material handling}$$
$$y = \text{inspection}$$
$$x = 100\,000 + 0.05y$$
$$y = 50\,000 + 0.1x$$

Rearranging the above equations:

$$x - 0.05y = 100\,000 \qquad (1)$$
$$-0.1x + y = 50\,000 \qquad (2)$$

Multiply equation (1) by 1 and equation (2) by 10:

$$x - 0.05y = 100\,000$$
$$-x + 10y = 500\,000$$

Adding the above equations:

$$9.95y = 600\,000$$
$$y = 60\,301$$

Substituting for y in equation (1):

$$x - 0.05 \times 60\,301 = 100\,000$$
$$x = 103\,015$$

Apportioning the values of x and y to the production departments in the agreed percentages:

		Machining (£)	Finishing (£)	Assembly (£)
Initial cost		400 000	200 000	100 000
(x) Materials handling	(0.3)	30 905 (0.25)	25 754 (0.35)	36 055
(y) Inspection	(0.2)	12 060 (0.3)	18 090 (0.45)	27 136
		442 965	243 844	163 191

(b) Reapportioning production service department costs is necessary to compute product costs for stock valuation purposes in order to meet the requirements of SSAP 9. However, it is questionable whether arbitrary apportionments of fixed overhead costs provides useful information for decision-making. Such apportionments are made to meet stock valuation requirements, and they are inappropriate for decision-making, cost control and performance reporting.

An alternative treatment would be to adopt a variable costing system and treat fixed overheads as period costs. This would eliminate the need to reapportion service department fixed costs. A more recent suggestion is to trace support/service department costs to products using an activity-based costing system (ABCS). For a description of ABCS you should refer to Chapter 11.

(c) For the answer to this question see 'Under- and over-recovery of overheads' (Chapter 4, p. 86).

Accounting entries for a job costing system

This chapter is concerned with the accounting entries necessary to record transactions within a job costing system. In Chapter 2 it was pointed out that job costing relates to a costing system that is required in organizations where each unit or batch of output of a product or service is unique. This creates the need for the cost of each unit to be calculated separately. The term 'job' thus relates to each unique unit or batch of output. In contrast, process costing relates to those situations where masses of identical units are produced and it is unnecessary to assign costs to individual units of output. Instead, the cost of a single unit of output can be obtained by merely dividing the total costs assigned to the cost object for a period by the units of output for that period. In practice these two costing systems represent extreme ends of a continuum. The output of many organizations requires a combination of the elements of both job costing and process costing. However, the accounting methods described in this chapter can be applied to all types of costing systems ranging from purely job to process, or a combination of both. In the next chapter we shall look at process costing in detail.

The accounting system on which we shall concentrate our attention is one in which the cost and financial accounts are combined in one set of accounts; this is known as an **integrated cost accounting system**. An alternative system, where the cost and financial accounts are maintained independently, is known as an **interlocking cost accounting system**. The integrated cost accounting system is generally considered to be preferable to the interlocking system, since the latter involves a duplication of accounting entries.

Learning objectives

After studying this chapter, you should be able to:

- distinguish between an integrated and interlocking accounting system;
- explain the distinguishing features of contract costing;
- prepare contract accounts and calculate attributable profit.

Control accounts

The recording system is based on a system of control accounts. A **control account** is a summary account, where entries are made from *totals* of transactions for a period. For example, the balance in the stores ledger control account will be supported by a voluminous file of stores ledger accounts, which will add up to agree with the total in the stores ledger control account. Assuming 1000 items of materials were received for a period that totalled £200 000, an entry of the total of £200 000 would be recorded on the debit (receipts side) of the stores ledger *control* account. This will be supported by 1000 separate entries in each of the individual stores ledger accounts. The total of all these *individual* entries will add up to £200 000. A system of control accounts enables one to check the accuracy of the various accounting entries, since the total of all the *individual* entries in the various stores ledger accounts should agree with the control account, which will have received the *totals* of the various transactions. The file of all the individual accounts (for example the individual stores ledger accounts) supporting the total control account is called the subsidiary ledger.

We shall now examine the accounting entries necessary to record the transaction outlined in Example 5.1. A manual system is described so that the accounting entries can

EXAMPLE 5.1

The following are the transactions of AB Ltd for the month of April.

1. Raw materials of £182 000 were purchases on credit.
2. Raw materials of £2000 were returned to the supplier because of defects.
3. The total of stores requisitions for direct materials issued for the period was £165 000.
4. The total issues for indirect materials for the period was £10 000.
5. Gross wages of £185 000 were incurred during the period

consisting of wages paid to employees	£105 000
Tax deductions payable to the Government (i.e. Inland Revenue)	£60 000
National Insurance contributions due	£20 000

6. All the amounts due in transaction 5 were settled by cash during the period.
7. The allocation of the gross wages for the period was as follows:

Direct wages	£145 000
Indirect wages	£40 000

8. The employer's contribution for National Insurance deductions was £25 000.
9. Indirect factory expenses of £41 000 were incurred during the period.
10. Depreciation of factory machinery was £30 000.
11. Overhead expenses allocated to jobs by means of overhead allocation rates was £140 000 for the period.
12. Non-manufacturing overhead incurred during the period was £40 000.
13. The cost of jobs completed and transferred to finished goods stock was £300 000.
14. The sales value of goods withdrawn from stock and delivered to customers was £400 000 for the period.
15. The cost of goods withdrawn from stock and delivered to customers was £240 000 for the period.

be followed, but the normal practice is now for these accounts to be maintained on a computer. You will find a summary of the accounting entries set out in Exhibit 5.1, where each transaction is prefixed by the appropriate number to give a clearer understanding of the necessary entries relating to each transaction. In addition, the appropriate journal entry is shown for each transaction together with a supporting explanation.

Recording the purchase of raw materials

The entry to record the purchase of materials in transaction 1 is

> Dr Stores ledger control account   182 000
>   Cr Creditors control account   182 000

This accounting entry reflects the fact that the company has incurred a short-term liability to acquire a current asset consisting of raw material stock. Each purchase is also entered in the receipts column of an individual stores ledger account (a separate record is used for each item of materials purchases) for the quantity received, a unit price and amount. In addition, a separate credit entry is made in each individual creditor's account. Note that the entries in the control accounts form part of the system of double entry, whereas the separate entries in the individual accounts are detailed subsidiary records, which do not form part of the double entry system.

The entry for transaction 2 for materials returned to suppliers is

> Dr Creditors control account   2000
>   Cr Stores ledger control account   2000

An entry for the returned materials is also made in the appropriate stores ledger records and in the individual creditors' accounts.

Recording the issue of materials

The storekeeper issues materials from store in exchange for a duly authorized stores requisition. For direct materials the job number will be recorded on the stores requisition, while for indirect materials the overhead account number will be entered on the requisition. The issue of direct materials involves a transfer of the materials from stores to production. For transaction 3, material requisitions will have been summarized and the resulting totals will be recorded as follows:

> Dr Work in progress account   165 000
>   Cr Stores ledger control account   165 000

This accounting entry reflects the fact that raw material stock is being converted into work in progress (WIP) stock. In addition to the above entries in the control accounts, the individual jobs will be charged with the cost of the material issued so that job costs can be calculated. Each issue is also entered in the issues column on the appropriate stores ledger record.

EXHIBIT 5.1

Summary of accounting transactions for AB Ltd

Stores ledger control account

1. Creditors a/c	182 000	2. Creditors a/c		2 000
		3. Work in progress a/c		165 000
		4. Factory overhead a/c		10 000
		Balance c/d		5 000
	182 000			182 000
Balance b/d	5 000			

Factory overhead control account

4. Stores ledger a/c	10 000	11. Work in progress a/c	140 000
7. Wages control a/c	40 000	Balance – under recovery	
8. National Insurance	25 000	transferred to costing P&L a/c	6 000
contributions a/c			
9. Expense creditors a/c	41 000		
10. Provision for depreciation a/c	30 000		
	146 000		146 000

Non-manufacturing overhead control account

12. Expense creditor a/c	40 000	Transferred to costing P&L a/c	40 000

Creditors account

2. Stores ledger a/c	2 000	1. Stores ledger a/c	182 000

Wages accrued account

6. Cash/bank	105 000	5. Wages control a/c	105 000

Tax payable account

6. Cash/bank	60 000	5. Wages control a/c	60 000

National Insurance contributions account

6. Cash/bank	20 000	5. Wages control a/c	20 000
8. Cash/bank	25 000	8. Factory overhead a/c	25 000
	45 000		45 000

Expense creditors account

		9. Factory overhead a/c	41 000
		12. Non-manufacturing overhead	40 000

Work in progress control account

3. Stores ledger a/c	165 000	13. Finished goods	
7. Wages control a/c	145 000	stock a/c	300 000
11. Factory overhead a/c	140 000	Balance c/d	150 000
	450 000		450 000
Balanced b/d	150 000		

Finished goods stock account

13. Work in progress a/c	300 000	15. Cost of sales a/c	240 000
		Balance c/d	60 000
	300 000		300 000
Balance b/d	60 000		

Cost of sales account

15. Finished goods stock a/c	240 000	Transferred to costing P&L a/c	240 000

Provision for depreciation account

		10. Factory overhead	30 000

Wages control account

5. Wages accrued a/c	105 000	7. Work in progress a/c	145 000
5. Tax payable a/c	60 000	7. Factory overhead a/c	40 000
5. National Insurance a/c	20 000		
	185 000		185 000

Sales account

Transferred to costing P&L	400 000	14. Debtors	400 000

Debtors account

14. Sales a/c	400 000		

Costing profit and loss account

Sales a/c		400 000
Less cost of sales a/c		240 000
Gross profit		160 000
Less under recovery of factory overhead	6 000	
Non-manufacturing overhead	40 000	46 000
Net profit		114 000

The entry for transaction 4 for the issue of indirect materials is

Dr Factory overhead control account	10 000	
Cr Stores ledger control account		10 000

In addition to the entry in the factory overhead account, the cost of material issued will be entered in the individual overhead accounts. These separate overhead accounts will normally consist of individual indirect material accounts for each responsibility centre. Periodically, the totals of each responsibility centre account for indirect materials will be entered in performance reports for comparison with the budgeted indirect material cost.

After transactions 1–4 have been recorded, the stores ledger control account would look like this:

Stores ledger control account

1. Creditors a/c	182 000	2. Creditors a/c	2 000
		3. Work in progress a/c	165 000
		4. Factory overhead a/c	10 000
		Balance c/d	5 000
	182 000		182 000
Balance b/d	5 000		

Accounting procedure for labour costs

In Chapter 3 it was pointed out that accounting for labour costs can be divided into the following two distinct phases:

1. Computations of the gross pay for each employee and calculation of payments to be made to employees, government, pension funds, etc. (**payroll accounting**).

2. Allocation of labour costs to jobs, overhead account and capital accounts (**labour cost accounting**).

An employee's gross pay is computed from information on the employee's personal record, and attendance or production records. For each employee a separate record is kept, showing the employee's employment history with the company, current rate of pay and authorized deductions such as National Insurance, pension plans, savings plans, union dues, and so on. The clock card contains details of attendance time; job cards provide details of bonuses due to employees; and if a piecework system is in operation, the piecework tickets will be analysed by employees and totalled to determine the gross wage. The gross wages are calculated from these documents, and an entry is then made in the payroll for each employee, showing the gross pay, tax deductions and other authorized deductions. The gross pay less the deductions gives the net pay, and this is the amount of cash paid to each employee.

The payroll gives details of the total amount of cash due to employees and the amounts due to the Government (i.e. Inland Revenue), Pension Funds and Savings Funds, etc. To keep the illustration simple at this stage, transaction 5 includes only deductions in respect of taxes and National Insurance. The accounting entries for transaction 5 are

Dr Wages control account	185 000	
Cr Tax payable account		60 000
Cr National Insurance contributions account		20 000
Cr Wages accrued account		105 000

The credit entries in transaction 5 will be cleared by a payment of cash. The payment of wages will involve an immediate cash payment, but some slight delay may occur with the payment of tax and National Insurance since the final date for payment of these items is normally a few weeks after the payment of wages. The entries for the cash payments for these items (transaction 6) are

Dr Tax payable account	60 000	
Dr National Insurance contributions account	20 000	
Dr Wages accrued account	105 000	
Cr Cash/bank		185 000

Note that the credit entries for transaction 5 merely represent the recording of amounts due for future payments. The wages control account, however, represents the gross wages for the period, and it is the amount in this account that must be allocated to the job, overhead and capital accounts. Transaction 7 gives details of the allocation of the gross wages. The accounting entries are

Dr Work in progress control account	145 000	
Dr Factory overhead control account	40 000	
Cr Wages control account		185 000

In addition to the total entry in the work in progress control account, the labour cost will be charged to the individual job accounts. Similarly, the total entry in the factory overhead control account will be supported by an entry in each individual overhead account for the indirect labour cost incurred.

Transaction 8 represents the employer's contribution for National Insurance payments. The National Insurance deductions in transaction 5 represent the employees' contributions where the company acts merely as an agent, paying these contributions on behalf of the employee. The employer is also responsible for making a contribution in respect of each employee. To keep the accounting entries simple here, the employer's contributions will be charged to the factory overhead account. The accounting entry for transaction 8 is therefore:

Dr Factory overhead control account	25 000	
Cr National Insurance contributions account		25 000

The National Insurance contributions account will be closed with the following entry when the cash payment is made:

Dr National Insurance contributions account	25 000	
Cr Cash/bank		25 000

After recording these transactions, the wages control account would look like this:

Wages control account

5. Wages accrued a/c	105 000	7.	Work in progress a/c	145 000
5. Tax payable a/c	60 000	7.	Factory overhead a/c	40 000
5. National Insurance a/c	20 000			
	185 000			185 000

Accounting procedure for manufacturing overheads

Accounting for manufacturing overheads involves entering details of the actual amount of manufacturing overhead incurred on the debit side of the factory overhead control account.

The total amount of overheads charged to production is recorded on the credit side of the factory overhead account. In the previous chapter we established that manufacturing overheads are charged to production using budgeted overhead rates. It is most unlikely, however, that the actual amount of overhead incurred, which is recorded on the debit side of the account, will be in agreement with the amount of overhead allocated to jobs, which is recorded on the credit side of the account. The difference represents the under- or over-recovery of factory overheads, which is transferred to the profit and loss account, in accordance with the requirements of the UK Statement of Standard Accounting Practice on Stocks and Work in Progress (SSAP 9).

Transaction 9 represents various indirect expenses that have been incurred and that will eventually have to be paid in cash, for example property taxes and lighting and heating. Transaction 10 includes other indirect expenses that do not involve a cash commitment. For simplicity it is assumed that depreciation of factory machinery is the only item that falls into this category. The accounting entries for transactions 9 and 10 are

Dr Factory overhead control account	71 000	
Cr Expense creditors control account		41 000
Cr Provision of depreciation account		30 000

In addition, subsidiary entries, not forming part of the double entry system, will be made in individual overhead accounts. These accounts will be headed by the title of the cost centre followed by the object of expenditure. For example, it may be possible to assign indirect materials directly to specific cost centres, and separate records can then be kept of the indirect materials charge for each centre. It will not, however, be possible to allocate property taxes, lighting and heating directly to cost centres, and entries should be made in individual overhead accounts for these items. Such expenses could, if so requested by management, be apportioned to resonsibility cost centres according to, say, floor area, but note that they should be regarded as non-controllable by the cost centre managers.

Transaction 11 refers to the total overheads that have been charged to jobs using the estimated overhead absorption rates. The accounting entry in the control accounts for allocating overheads to jobs is

Dr Work in progress control account	140 000	
Cr Factory overhead control account		140 000

In addition to this entry, the individual jobs are charged so that job costs can be calculated. When these entries have been made the factory overhead control account would look like this:

Factory overhead control account

4. Stores ledger control a/c	10 000	11. Work in progress		
7. Wages control a/c	40 000	control a/c		140 000
8. Employer's National		Balance – Under-recovery		
Insurance contributions a/c	25 000	of overhead transferred to		
		costing profit and loss a/c		6 000
9. Expense creditors a/c	41 000			
10. Provision for depreciation a/c	30 000			
	146 000			146 000

The debit side of this account indicates that £146 000 overhead has been incurred, but examination of the credit side indicates that only £140 000 has been allocated to jobs via overhead allocation rates. The balance of £6000 represents an under-recovery of factory overhead, which is regarded as a period cost to be charged to the costing profit and loss account in the current accounting period. The reasons for this were explained in the previous chapter.

Non-manufacturing overheads

You will have noted in the previous chapter that non-manufacturing overhead costs are regarded as period costs and not product costs, and non-manufacturing overheads are not therefore charged to the work in progress control account. The accounting entry for transaction 12 is

Dr Non-manufacturing overheads account	40 000	
Cr Expense creditors account		40 000

At the end of the period the non-manufacturing overheads will be transferred to the profit and loss account as a period cost by means of the following accounting entry:

Dr Profit and loss account	40 000	
Cr Non-manufacturing overheads account		40 000

In practice, separate control accounts are maintained for administrative, marketing and financial overheads, but, to simplify this example, all the non-manufacturing overheads are included in one control account. In addition, subsidiary records will be kept that analyse the total non-manufacturing overheads by individual accounts, for example office stationery account, sales person's travelling expenses account, etc.

Note that these accounts do not form part of the double entry system, but represent a detailed breakdown of the total entries included in the non-manufacturing overhead control account.

Accounting procedures for jobs completed and products sold

When jobs have been completed, they are transferred from the factory floor to the finished goods store. The total of the job accounts for the completed jobs for the period is recorded as a transfer from the work in progress control account to the finished goods stock account. The accounting entry for transaction 13 is

Dr Finished goods stock account	300 000	
Cr Work in progress control account		300 000

When the goods are removed from the finished goods stock and delivered to the customers, the revenue is recognized. It is a fundamental principle of financial accounting that only costs associated with earning the revenue are included as expenses. The cost of those goods that have been delivered to customers must therefore be matched against the revenue due from delivery of the goods so that the gross profit can be calculated. Any goods that have not been delivered to customers will be included as part of the finished stock valuation. The accounting entries to reflect these transactions are:

Transaction 14		
Dr Debtors control account	400 000	
Cr Sales account		400 000
Transaction 15		
Dr Cost of sales account	240 000	
Cr Finished goods stock account		240 000

Costing profit and loss account

At frequent intervals management may wish to ascertain the profit to date for the particular period. The accounting procedure outlined in this chapter provides a data base from which a costing profit and loss account may easily be prepared. The costing profit and loss account for AB Ltd based on the information given in Example 5.1 is set out in Exhibit 5.1 shown on pages 110–111. As cost control procedures should exist at cost (responsibility) centre levels, management may find the final profit calculation sufficient when it is combined with a summary of the various performance reports. Alternatively, management may prefer the profit statement to be presented in a format similar to that which is necessary for external reporting. Such information can easily be extracted from the subsidiary records. For example, the factory and non-manufacturing overhead control accounts are supported by detailed individual accounts such as factory depreciation, factory lighting and heating, office salaries and so on. The items in the costing profit and loss account can therefore be easily replaced with those items normally presented in the financial accounts by extracting from the subsidiary records the appropriate information. The accounting procedure outlined in Exhibit 5.1, however, provides the data base for ascertaining the job costs and stock valuations that are essential to external reporting. In addition, information in the subsidiary records provides the data from which the accountant can extract relevant decision-making and control information to suit the needs of the various users of accounting information.

Interlocking accounting

Interlocking accounting is a system where the cost and financial accounts are maintained independently of each other, and in the cost accounts no attempt is made to keep a separate record of the financial accounting transactions. Examples of financial accounting transactions include entries in the various creditors, debtors and capital accounts. To maintain the double entry records, an account must be maintained in the cost accounts to record the corresponding entry that, in an integrated accounting system, would normally be made in one of the financial accounts (creditors, debtors accounts, etc.). This account is called a cost control or general ledger adjustment account.

Using an interlocking accounting system to record the transactions listed in Example 5.1, the entries in the creditors, wages accrued, taxation payable, National Insurance contributions, expense creditors, provision for depreciation and debtors accounts would be replaced by the following entries in the cost control account:

Cost control account

2. Stores ledger control a/c	2 000	1. Stores ledger control a/c	182 000
14. Sales a/c	400 000	5. Wages control a/c	185 000
Balance c/d	215 000	8. Factory overhead control a/c	25 000
		9. Expense creditors a/c	41 000
		12. Non-manufacturing overhead a/c	40 000
		10. Factory overhead a/c	30 000
		Profit and loss a/c	
		(profit for period)	114 000
	617 000		617 000
		Balance b/d	215 000

The entries in the remaining accounts will be unchanged.

For a detailed answer to an interlocking accounts question you should refer to the solution to the fourth review problem at the end of this chapter. Sometimes examination questions are set that require you to reconcile the profit that has been calculated in the cost accounts with the profits calculated in the financial accounts. Most firms use an integrated accounting system, and hence there is no need to reconcile a separate set of cost and financial accounts. The reconciliation of cost and financial accounts is not therefore dealt with in this chapter. For an explanation of the reconciliation procedure you should refer to the solution to the sixth review problem at the end of this chapter.

Contract costing

Contract costing is a system of job costing that is applied to relatively large cost units, which normally take a considerable length of time to complete. Building and construction work, civil engineering and shipbuilding are some examples of industries where large contract work is undertaken, and where contract costing is appropriate.

A contract account is maintained for each contract. All the direct costs of the contract are debited to the specific contract and overheads are apportioned in the manner prescribed in Chapter 4. The contract price is credited to the contract account, and each contract account therefore becomes a small profit and loss account.

Because of the considerable length of time that is taken to complete a contract, it is necessary to determine the profit to be attributed to each accounting period. Financial accounting normally recognizes revenue when the goods are delivered, but such an approach is inappropriate for long-term contracts, since profits on large contracts would not be reported until they were completed. The profit and loss account would not reflect a fair view of the profitability of the company during the year but would show only the results of contracts that had been completed before the year end. To overcome this problem, it is preferable to take credit for profit while contracts are in progress.

The UK Statement of Standard Accounting Practice on Stocks and Work in Progress (SSAP 9) provides the following guidance on the attributable profit to be taken up for a particular period:

> Where the business carries out long-term contracts and it is considered that their outcome can be assessed with reasonable certainty before their conclusion, the attributable profit should be calculated on a prudent basis and included in the accounts for the period under review. The profit taken up needs to reflect the proportion of the work carried out at the accounting date and to take into account any known inequalities of profitability in the various stages of a contract. The procedure to recognize profit is to include an appropriate proportion of total contract value as turnover in the profit and loss account as the contract activity progresses. The costs incurred in reaching that stage of completion are matched with this turnover, resulting in the reporting of results that can be attributed to the proportion of work completed.
>
> Where the outcome of long-term contracts cannot be assessed with reasonable certainty before the conclusion of the contract, no profit should be reflected in the profit and loss account in respect of those contracts although, in such circumstances, if no loss is expected it may be appropriate to show as turnover a proportion of the total contract value using a zero estimate of profit.
>
> If it is expected that there will be a loss on a contract as a whole, all of the loss should be recognized as soon as it is foreseen (in accordance with the prudence concept).

Let us now prepare some contract accounts and determine the attributable profit to be taken up for an accounting period. Consider Example 5.2.

Before we compile the accounts, some of the terms used in Example 5.2 require an explanation. A customer is likely to be required under the terms of the contract to make **progress payments** to the contractor throughout the course of the work. The amount of the payments will be based on the sales value of the work carried out, as assessed by the architect or surveyor in the **architect's certificate**. A certificate provides confirmation that work to a certain sales value has been completed, and that some payment to the contractor is now due. The amount of the progress payment will consist of:

1. the sales value of work carried out and certified by the architect; less
2. a retention; less
3. the payments made to date.

So if the architect's certificates assess the value of work carried out to be £300 000 and if the retention is 10%, and if £230 000 has already been paid in progress payments, the current payment will be

$$£300\,000 - £30\,000\,\text{retention} - £230\,000\,\text{previous payment} = £40\,000$$

There is frequently a contract clause which entitles the customer to withhold payment of **retention money** for a proportion of the value of work certified for a specified period after the end of the contract. During this period, the contractor must make good all contractual defects. When the defects have been satisfactorily completed the customer will release the retention money.

Let us now prepare the cost accounts from the information contained in Example 5.2 for contracts A, B and C:

You will see that the contract accounts are divided into three sections. The objective of the first section is to determine the costs that should be included in the cost of sales for the purposes of calculating the profit taken up for the period. The balance shown in the first

EXAMPLE 5.2

A construction company is currently undertaking three separate contracts and information relating to these contracts for the previous year, together with other relevant data, are shown below:

	Contract A (£000)	Contract B (£000)	Contract C (£000)
Contract price	1760	1485	2420
Balances b/fwd at beginning of year:			
Material on site	—	20	30
Written-down value of plant and machinery	—	77	374
Wages accrued	—	5	10
Transactions during previous year:			
Profit previously transferred to profit and loss a/c	—	—	35
Cost of work certified (cost of sales)	—	418	814
Transactions during current year:			
Materials delivered to sites	88	220	396
Wages paid	45	100	220
Salaries and other costs	15	40	50
Written-down value of plant issued to sites	190	35	—
Head office expenses apportioned during the year	10	20	50
Balances c/fwd at the end of year:			
Material on site	20	—	—
Written-down value of plant and machinery	150	20	230
Wages accrued	5	10	15
Value of work certified at end of year	200	860	2100
Cost of work not certified at end of year	—	—	55

The agreed retention rate is 10% of the value of work certified by the contractee's architects. Contract C is scheduled for handing over to the contractee in the near future, and the site engineer estimates that the extra costs required to complete the contract, in addition to those tabulated above, will total £305 000. This amount includes an allowance for plant depreciation, construction services and for contingencies.

You are required to prepare a cost account for each of the three contracts and recommend how much profit or loss should be taken up for the year.

Contract accounts

	A (£000)	B (£000)	C (£000)		A (£000)	B (£000)	C (£000)
				Wages accrued b/fwd		5	10
Materials on site b/fwd		20	30	Materials on site c/fwd	20		
Plant on site b/fwd		77	374	Plant on site c/fwd	150	20	230
Materials control a/c	88	220	396	Cost of work not certified c/fwd			55

Contract accounts (continued)

	A (£000)	B (£000)	C (£000)		A (£000)	B (£000)	C (£000)
Wages control a/c	45	100	220	Cost of sales – current			
Salaries	15	40	50	period (balance)			
Plant control a/c	190	35		c/fwd	183	497	840
Apportionment of head office expenses	10	20	50				
Wages accrued c/fwd	5	10	15				
	353	522	1135		353	522	1135
Cost of sales b/fwd	183	497	840	Attributable sales revenue (current period)[a]	183	442	1122
Profit taken this period			282	Loss taken		55	
	183	497	1122		183	497	1122
Cost of work not certified b/fwd			55	Wages accrued b/fwd	5	10	15
Materials on site b/fwd	20						
Plant on site b/fwd	150	20	230				

[a] Profit taken plus cost of sales for the current period or cost of sales less loss to date.

section of the contract accounts represents the **cost of sales** (also known as **cost of work certified**) attributable to each of the contracts.

You should note that unexpired costs such as the cost of work not certified and the written-down balance of the plant at the end of the period are carried forward to the third section of the contract accounts. This section represents the unexpired costs of the current period which will become an expired cost in future periods. The third section of the account should therefore be regarded as a future cost section.

In the second section of the contract accounts the period cost of sales is compared with the sales revenue that is estimated to be attributable to the contracts. The sales revenues attributable to the contracts for each period are estimated by adding the attributable profit taken up for the current period to the cost of sales for the current period (or cost of sales less the loss where a contract is currently running at a loss). The profits/losses on the three contracts to date are calculated by deducting the cost of sales (consisting of the sum of the cost of sales for the current and previous periods) from the value of work certified:

	(£000)	
Contract A	17	(£200–£183)
Contract B	(55)	(£860–£915)
Contract C	446	(£2100–£1654)

However, these profits/(losses) do not necessarily represent the profits/(losses) taken up on the contracts. According to SSAP 9, the concept of prudence should be applied when determining the profits/(losses) taken up on contracts. You are recommended to adopt the following guidelines:

1. If the contract is in its early stages, no profit should be taken. Profit should only be taken when the outcome of the contract can be assessed with reasonable certainty. You will see from Example 5.2 that the contract price for Contract A is £1 760 000, but the value of work certified is only £200 000. The contract is therefore approximately one-eighth complete, and it is unlikely that the outcome of the contract can be foreseen with reasonable certainty. Despite the fact that the profit to date is £17 000, it is recommended that no profit be taken.

2. If a loss is incurred, the prudence concept should be applied, and the total loss should be recognized in the period in which it is incurred. Consequently, the loss of £55 000 on Contract B is recognized in the current accounting period. Where further additional future losses are anticipated, all of the loss should be recognized as soon as it is foreseen and added to the cost of sales. In addition, the foreseeable loss should be shown in the balance sheet under the heading 'Provision/accrual for foreseeable losses'.

3. If the contract is nearing completion, the size of the eventual profit should be foreseen with reasonable certainty, and there is less need to be excessively prudent in determining the amount of profit to be recorded in the profit and loss account. With regard to Contract C, the value of work certified is approximately 87% of the contract price, and the **anticipated profit** is calculated as follows:

	(£000)
Cost of work certified (cost of sales to date $= 814 + 840$)	1654
Cost of work not certified	55
Estimated costs to complete	305
Estimated cost of contract	2014
Contract price	2420
Anticipated profit	406

The profit taken is calculated using the following formula:

$$\text{cash received to date } \frac{(0.90 \times £2100)}{\text{contract price } (£2420)}$$
$$\times \text{ estimated profit from the contract } (£406) \simeq £317\,000$$

You should note that other more prudent approaches are sometimes used to determine the profit earned to date. The profit for the current period consists of the profit to date (£317 000) less the profit of £35 000 previously transferred to the profit and loss account. The profit taken to the profit and loss account for the current period is therefore £282 000.

4. Where substantial costs have been incurred on a contract, and it is not nearing completion (say it is in the region of 35–85% complete), the following formula is often used to determine the attributable profit to date:

$$\text{profit taken} = 2/3 \times \text{notional profit} \times \frac{\text{cash received}}{\text{value of work certified}}$$

This formula is one of several approaches that can be used to apply the prudence concept. Estimates of anticipated profit are likely to be inaccurate when contracts are not near to completion. To overcome this problem, **notional profit** should be used instead of anticipated profit. Notional profit is the value of work certified to date less the cost of work certified (that is, cost of sales) to date less a provision for any anticipated unforeseen eventualities.

Note than for Contract C £35 000 profit was recognized in the previous period and cost of sales of £814 000 was recorded. Therefore attributable sales revenue of £849 000 (£814 000 + £35 000) would have been recorded in the contract account for the *previous* period. For Contract B, no profits were recognized in the *previous period* and attributable sales for the period will thus be identical to the cost of sales (£418 000). Contract A commenced in the current period and so no transactions will have been recorded in the previous period. The debit side of the debtors accounts will be as follows:

	Contract A (£000)	Contract B (£000)	Contract C (£000)
Previous period – attributable sales	—	418	849
Current period – attributable sales	183	442	1122
Total to date	183	860	1971

Work in progress valuation and amounts recoverable on contracts

The UK Statement of Standard Accounting Practice on Stocks on Work in Progress (SSAP 9) requires that the proportion of the total contract value appropriate to the stage of completion reached at balance sheet date be recognized as sales revenue. The costs relating to that completed work are included in the cost of sales. Any further costs that are attributable to the contract but that have not been included in the cost of sales are included at cost in the balance sheet and separately disclosed as 'Long-term contract balances' under the balance sheet heading 'Stocks'.

The associated balance sheet item for the contract value that is recorded as sales is debtors. The debtors balance is calculated by deducting progress payments received on account from the amount recognized as sales. This balance is included as a separate item within debtors and described as 'Amounts recoverable on contracts'. The balance sheet entries for Example 5.2 are as follows:

	Contract A (£000)	Contract B (£000)	Contract C (£000)	
Stocks:				
Total costs incurred to date	183	860	1709	(814 + 840 + 55)
Included in cost of sales	183	860	1654	
Included in long-term contract balances	0	0	55	
Debtors				
Cumulative sales turnover	183	860	1971	
Less cumulative progress payments	180	774	1890	
Amounts recoverable on contracts	3	86	81	

For Contract B, the total costs incurred to date are £915 000 (£418 000 + £497 000) but £55 000 of these costs have been recognized as a loss in the current period, so that cumulative cost of sales to be matched against cumulative sales is £860 000 (£915 000 − £55 000). Note also that the cumulative progress payments are 90% of the value of work certified and that the loss on Contract B has been charged to the current period. Other balance sheet entries will include the following:

	(£000)
Materials on site	20
Plant on site	400
Accruals	30

Summary

In this chapter we have examined the accounting entries necessary to record transactions within a job costing system. Discussion has been concentrated on an integrated accounting system and the accounting transactions have been illustrated with a comprehensive example. A major feature of the system is the use of control accounts. A summary of the accounting entries, where all purchases and expenses are settled in cash, is shown diagrammatically in Figure 5.1. We have also examined a system of contract costing, which is the name given to a system of job costing that is applied to relatively large cost units, which normally take a considerable length of time to complete.

FIGURE 5.1 *Flow of accounting entries in an integrated accounting system.*

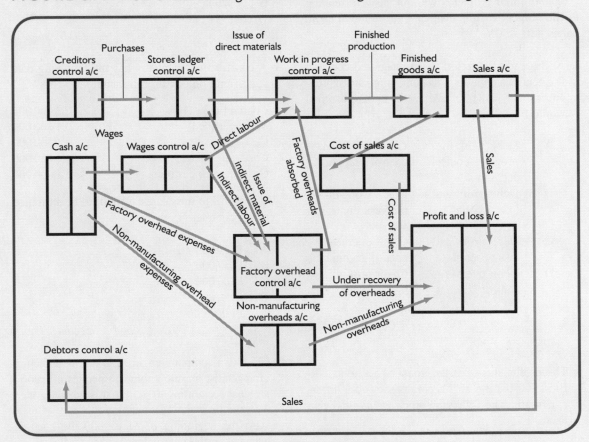

Key Terms and Concepts

anticipated profit (p. 121)
architect's certificate (p. 118)
contract costing (p. 117)
control account (p. 108)
cost of sales (p. 120)
cost of work certified (p. 120)
integrated cost accounting system (p. 107)

interlocking cost accounting system (pp. 107, 116)
labour cost accounting (p. 112)
notional profit (p. 121)
payroll accounting (p. 112)
progress payments (p. 118)
retention money (p. 118)

Key Examination Points

Examination questions require the preparation of accounts for both integrated and interlocking systems (see Review Problems 4 and 5 for examples). You may also be required to reconcile the cost and financial accounts. For an illustration of the approach see the answer to the sixth review problem. However, the reconciliation of cost and financial accounts is a topic that tends to be examined only on rare occasions.

Students often experience difficulty in recommending the amount of profit to be taken during a period for long-term contracts. Make sure you are familiar with the four recommendations listed on pp. 120–121 and that you can apply these recommendations to the final review problem and questions 5.17–5.20.

Review Problems

(For additional problems without answers relating to the content of this chapter you should refer to pages 440–450.)

1 At the end of a period, in an integrated cost and financial accounting system, the accounting entries for £18 000 overheads under-absorbed would be

A	Debit work-in-progress control account	Credit overhead control account
B	Debit profit and loss account	Credit work-in-progress control account
C	Debit profit and loss account	Credit overhead control account
D	Debit overhead control account	Credit profit and loss account

CIMA Stage 1 Cost Accounting

2 The profits shown in the financial accounts was £158 500 but the cost accounts showed a different figure. The following stock valuations were used:

Stock valuations	Cost accounts	Financial accounts
	(£)	(£)
Opening stock	35 260	41 735
Closing stock	68 490	57 336

What was the profit in the cost accounts?
A £163 179
B £140 871
C £176 129
D £153 821

CIMA Stage 1

3 A construction company has the following data concerning one of its contracts:

Contract price	£2 000 000
Value certified	£1 300 000
Cash received	£1 200 000
Costs incurred	£1 050 000
Cost of work certified	£1 000 000

The profit (to the nearest £1000) to be attributed to the contract is

A £250 000
B £277 000
C £300 000
D £950 000
E £1 000 000

CIMA Stage 2 Specimen Paper

4 CD Ltd, a company engaged in the manufacture of specialist marine engines, operates a historic job cost accounting system that is not integrated with the financial accounts.

At the beginning of May 2000 the opening balances in the cost ledger were as follows:

	(£)
Stores ledger control account	85 400
Work in progress control account	167 350
Finished goods control account	49 250
Cost ledger control account	302 000

During the month, the following transactions took place:

	(£)
Materials:	
Purchases	42 700
Issues to production	63 400
to general maintenance	1 450
to construction of manufacturing equipment	7 650
Factory wages:	
Total gross wages paid	124 000

£12 500 of the above gross wages were incurred on the construction of manufacturing equipment, £35 750 were indirect wages and the balance was direct.

Production overheads: the actual amount incurred, excluding items shown above, was £152 350; £30 000 was absorbed by the manufacturing equipment under construction and under absorbed overhead written off at the end of the month amounted to £7550.

Royalty payments: one of the engines produced is manufactured under licence. £2150 is the amount that will be paid to the inventor for the month's production of that particular engine.

Selling overheads: £22 000.

Sales: £410 000.

The company's gross profit margin is 25% on factory cost.

At the end of May stocks of work in progress had increased by £12 000. The manufacturing equipment under construction was completed within the month, and transferred out of the cost ledger at the end of the month.

Required:
Prepare the relevant control accounts, costing profit and loss account, and any other accounts you consider necessary to record the above transactions in the cost ledger for May 2000.

(22 marks)
ACCA Foundation Costing

5 In the absence of the accountant you have been asked to prepare a month's cost accounts for a company which operates a batch costing system fully integrated with the financial accounts. The cost clerk has provided you with the following information, which he thinks is relevant:

	(£)
Balances at beginning of month:	
Stores ledger control account	24 175
Work in progress control account	19 210

	(£)
Finished Goods control account	34 164
Prepayments of production overheads brought forward from previous month	2 100

	(£)
Transactions during the month:	
Materials purchased	76 150
Materials issued: to production	26 350
for factory maintenance	3 280
Materials transferred between batches	1 450

	Direct workers (£)	**Indirect workers (£)**
Total wages paid:		
Net	17 646	3 342
Employees deductions	4 364	890
Direct wages charged to batches from work tickets	15 236	
Recorded non-productive time of direct workers	5 230	
Direct wages incurred on production of capital equipment, for use in the factory	2 670	
Selling and distribution overheads incurred	5 240	
Other production overheads incurred	12 200	
Sales	75 400	
Cost of finished goods sold	59 830	
Cost of goods completed and transferred into finished goods store during the month	62 130	
Physical stock value of work in progress at end of month	24 360	

The production overhead absorption rate is 150% of direct wages, and it is the policy of the company to include a share of production overheads in the cost of capital equipment constructed in the factory.

Required:
(a) Prepare the following accounts for the month:
   stores ledger control account
   wages control account
   work in progress control account
   finished goods control account
   production overhead control account
   profit/loss account.   *(12 marks)*

(b) Identify any aspects of the accounts which you consider should be investigated.

(*4 marks*)

(c) Explain why it is necessary to value a company's stocks at the end of each period and also why, in a manufacturing company, expense items such as factory rent, wages of direct operatives, power costs, etc. are included in the value of work in progress and finished goods stocks. (*6 marks*)

(*Total 22 marks*)

ACCA Level 1 Costing

6 K Limited operates separate cost accounting and financial accounting systems. The following manufacturing and trading statement has been prepared from the financial accounts for the *quarter* ended 31 March:

	(£)	(£)
Raw materials:		
Opening stock	48 800	
Purchases	108 000	
	156 800	
Closing stock	52 000	
Raw materials consumed		104 800
Direct wages		40 200
Production overhead		60 900
Production cost incurred		205 900
Work in progress:		
Opening stock	64 000	
Closing stock	58 000	6 000
Cost of goods produced		211 900
Sales		440 000
Finishing goods:		
Opening stock	120 000	
Cost of goods produced	211 900	
	331 900	
Closing stock	121 900	
Cost of goods sold		210 000
Gross profit		230 000

From the cost accounts, the following information has been extracted:

Control account balances at 1 January	(£)
Raw material stores	49 500
Work in progress	60 100
Finished goods	115 400

Transactions for the quarter:	(£)
Raw materials issued	104 800
Cost of goods produced	222 500
Cost of goods sold	212 100
Loss of materials damaged by flood (insurance claim pending)	2 400

A notional rent of £4000 *per month* has been charged in the cost accounts. Production overhead was absorbed at the rate of 185% of direct wages.

You are required to:

(a) prepare the following control accounts in the cost ledger:

   raw materials stores;

   work in process;

   finished goods;

   production overhead; (*10 marks*)

(b) prepare a statement reconciling the gross profits as per the cost accounts and the financial accounts; (*11 marks*)

(c) comment on the possible accounting treatment(s) of the under or over absorption of production overhead, assuming that the financial year of the company is 1 January to 31 December. (*4 marks*)

(*Total 25 marks*)

CIMA Cost Accounting 1

7 HR Construction plc makes up its accounts to 31 March each year. The following details have been extracted in relation to two of its contracts:

	Contract A	Contract B
Commencement date	1 April 1999	1 December 1999
Target completion date	31 May 2000	30 June 2000
Retention%	4	3

	£000	£000
Contract price	2000	550
Materials sent to site	700	150
Materials returned to stores	80	30
Plant sent to site	1000	150
Materials transferred	(40)	40
Materials on site 31 March 2000	75	15
Plant hire charges	200	30
Labour cost incurred	300	270
Central overhead cost	75	18
Direct expenses incurred	25	4
Value certified	1500	500

Cost of work not certified	160	20
Cash received from client	1440	460
Estimated cost of completion	135	110

Depreciation is charged on plant using the straight line method at the rate of 12% per annum.

Required:

(a) Prepare contract accounts, in columnar format, for EACH of the contracts A and B, showing clearly the amounts to be trans-ferred to profit and loss in respect of each contract. (*20 marks*)

(b) Show balance sheet extracts in respect of EACH contract for fixed assets, debtors and work in progress. (*4 marks*)

(c) Distinguish between job, batch and contract costing. Explain clearly the reasons why these methods are different. (*6 marks*)

(*Total 30 marks*)

CIMA Stage 2 Operational Cost Accounting

Answers to Review Problems

SOLUTION 1

Answer = C

SOLUTION 2

	Cost accounts	Financial accounts	Difference
Stock increase	£33 230	£15 601	£17 629

The stock increase shown in the cost accounts is £17 629 more than the increase shown in the financial accounts. Closing stocks represent expenses to be deferred to future accounting periods. Therefore the profit shown in the cost accounts will be £176 129 (£158 500 + £17 629).

Answer = C

SOLUTION 3

Where substantial costs have been incurred on a contract and it is nearing completion the following formula is often used to determine the attributable profit to date:

$$2/3 \times \text{Notional profit} \times \frac{\text{cash received}}{\text{value of work certified}}$$

$$= 2/3 \times (£1.3\,\text{m} - £1\,\text{m}) \times £1.2\,\text{m}/£1.3\,\text{m}$$

$$= £276\,923$$

Answer = B

SOLUTION 4

The company's cost accounts are not integrated with the financial accounts. For a description of a non-integrated accounting system see 'Interlocking accounts' in Chapter 5. The following accounting entries are necessary:

Cost ledger control account

	(£)			(£)
Sales a/c	410 000	1.5.00	Balance b/f	302 000
Capital under			Stores ledger a/c –	
construction a/c	50 150		Purchases	42 700
Balance c/f	237 500		Wages control a/c	124 000
			Production overhead a/c	152 350
			WIP a/c – Royalty	2 150
			Selling overhead a/c	22 000
			Profit	52 450
	£697 650			£697 650

Stores ledger control account

		(£)		(£)
1.5.00	Balance b/f	85 400	WIP a/c	63 400
	Cost ledger control a/c –		Production overhead a/c	1 450
	Purchases	42 700	Capital a/c	7 650
			31.5.00 Balance c/f	55 600
		£128 100		£128 100

Wages control account

	(£)		(£)
Cost ledger control a/c	124 000	Capital a/c	12 500
		Production	35 750
		WIP a/c	7 550
	£124 000		£124 000

Production overhead control account

	(£)		(£)
Stores ledger a/c	1 450	Capital a/c	30 000
Wages control a/c	35 750	WIP a/c – Absorption	152 000
Cost ledger control a/c	152 350	(balancing figure)	
		Costing P/L a/c (under absorption)	7 550
	£189 550		£189 550

Work in progress control account

		(£)		(£)
1.5.00	Balance b/f	167 350	Finished goods	281 300
	Stores ledger a/c –		control a/c	
	Issues	63 400	(balancing figure)	
	Wages control a/c	75 750	31.5.00 Balance c/f[a]	179 350

	(£)		(£)
Production overhead absorbed	152 000		
Cost ledger control a/c – Royalty	2 150		
	460 650		£460 650

Finished goods control account

		(£)			(£)
1.5.00	Balance b/f	49 250		Cost sales a/c[b]	328 000
	WIP a/c	281 300	31.5.00	Balance c/f	2 550
		£330 550			£330 550

Capital under construction account

	(£)		(£)
Stores ledger a/c	7 650	Cost ledger control a/c	50 150
Wages control a/c	12 500		
Production overhead absorbed	30 000		
	£50 150		£50 150

Sales account

	(£)		(£)
Costing P/L a/c	£410 000	Cost ledger control a/c	£410 000

Cost of sales account

	(£)		(£)
Finished goods a/c[b]	£328 000	Cost P/L a/c	£328 000

Selling overhead account

	(£)		(£)
Cost ledger control a/c	£22 000	Costing P/L a/c	£22 000

Costing profit and loss account

	(£)		(£)
Selling overhead a/c	22 000	Sales a/c	410 000
Production overhead (under absorbed)	7 550		
Cost of sales a/c	328 000		
Profit – Cost ledger control a/c	52 450		
	£410 000		£410 000

Notes

[a] Closing balance of work in progress = £167 350 (opening balance)

£12 000 (increase per question)

£179 350

[b] Transfer from finished goods stock to cost of sales account: £410 000 sales × (100/125) = £328 000

SOLUTION 5

(a)

Stores ledger control account

	(£)		(£)
Opening balances b/f	24 175	Materials issued:	
Creditors – materials purchased	76 150	Work in progress control	26 350
		Production overhead control	3 280
		Closing stock c/f	70 695
	£100 325		£100 325

Wages control account

	(£)		(£)
Direct wages:		WIP	15 236
Wages accrued a/c	17 646	Capital equipment a/c	2 670
Employees' contributions a/c	4 364	Factory overhead (idle time)	5 230
Indirect wages:		Factory overhead (indirect wages)	4 232
Wages accrued a/c	3 342		
Employees' contributions a/c	890		
Balances (Wages accrued a/c)	1 126		
	27 368		27 368

Work in progress control account

	(£)		(£)
Opening balance b/f	19 210	Finished goods control – cost of goods transferred	62 130
Stores ledger – materials issued	26 350		
Wages control direct wages	15 236	Closing stock c/f	24 360
Production overhead control: overhead absorbed (15 236 × 150%)	22 854		
Profit and loss a/c: stock gain[a]	2 840		
	£86 490		£86 490

Finished goods control account

	(£)		(£)
Opening balance b/f	34 164	Profit and loss a/c: cost of sales	59 830
Working in progress: cost of goods sold	62 130	Closing stock c/f (difference)	36 464
	£96 294		£92 294

Production overhead control account

	(£)		(£)
Prepayments b/f	2 100	Work in progress: overheads absorbed (15 236 × 150%)	22 854
Stores ledger: materials issued for repairs	3 280	Capital under construction a/c: overheads absorbed (2670 × 150%)	4 005
Wages control: idle time of direct workers	5 230		
Wages control: indirect workers' wages (3342 + 890)	4 232	Profit and loss a/c: underabsorbed overhead balance	183
Cash/creditors: other overheads incurred	12 200		
	£27 042		£27 042

Profit and loss account

	(£)		(£)
Cost of goods sold	59 830	Sales	75 400
Gross profit c/f	15 570		
	£75 400		£75 400
Selling and distribution overheads	5 240	Gross profit b/f	15 570
Production overhead control: underabsorbed overhead	183	Stock gain[a]: WIP control	2 840
Net profit c/f	12 987		
	£18 410		£18 410

Note

[a] The stock gain represents a balancing figure. It is assumed that the stock gain arises from the physical count of closing stocks at the end of the period.

Note that value of materials transferred between batches will be recorded in the subsidiary records, but will not affect the control (total) accounts.

(b) (i) Large increase in raw material stocks. Is this due to maintaining uneconomic stock levels or is it due to an anticipated increase in production to meet future demand?

(ii) WIP stock gain.

(iii) Idle time, which is nearly 25% of the total direct wages cost.

(iv) The gross direct wages are £22 010 (£17 646 + £4364), but the allocation amounts to £23 136 (£15 236 + £5230 + £2670).

(c) Stocks are valued at the end of the period because they represent unexpired costs, which should not be matched against sales for the purpose of calculating profits. Stocks represent unexpired costs, which must be valued for inclusion in the balance sheet. Manufacturing expense items such as factory rent are included in the stock valuations because they represent resources incurred in transforming the materials into a more valuable finished product. SSAP 9 states 'costs of stocks (and WIP) should comprise those costs which have been incurred in bringing the product to its present location and condition, including all related production overheads.'

SOLUTION 6

Raw materials stores account

	(£)		(£)
Balance b/d	49 500	Work in progress	104 800
Purchases	108 800	Loss due to flood to P&L a/c	2 400
		Balance c/d	51 100
	£158 300		£158 300
Balance b/d	51 100		

Work in progress control account

	(£)		(£)
Balance b/d	60 100	Finished goods	222 500
Raw materials	104 800	Balance c/d	56 970
Direct wages	40 200		
Production overhead	74 370		
	£279 470		£279 470
Balance b/d	56 970		

Finished goods control account

	(£)		(£)
Balance b/d	115 400	Cost of sales	212 100
Work in progress	222 500	Balance c/d	125 800
	£337 900		£337 900
Balance b/d	125 800		

Production overhead

	(£)		(£)
General ledger control	60 900	Work in progress	
Notional rent (3 × £4000)	12 000	(185% × £40 200)	74 370
Overhead over absorbed	1 470		
	£74 370		£74 370

General ledger control account

	(£)		(£)
Sales	440 000	Balance b/d	
Balance c/d	233 870	(49 500 +	
		60 100 + 115 400)	225 000
		Purchases	108 800
		Direct wages	40 200
		Production overhead	60 900
		Notional rent	12 000
		P & L a/c	226 970
		(profit for period: see (b))	
	£673 870		£673 870

(b) *Calculation of profit in cost accounts*

	(£)	(£)
Sales		440 000
Cost of sales	212 100	
Loss of stores	2 400	
	214 500	
Less overhead over absorbed	1 470	213 030
Profit		226 970

Reconciliation statement[a]

	(£)	(£)	(£)
Profit as per cost accounts			226 970
Differences in stock values:			
Raw materials opening stock	1 500		
Raw materials closing stock	900		
WIP closing stock	1 030	3 430	
WIP opening stock	3 900		
Finished goods opening stock	4 600		
Finished goods closing stock	3 900	(12 400)	(8 970)
Add items not included in financial accounts:			
Notional rent			12 000
Profit as per financial accounts			230 000

Note

[a] Stock valuations in the financial accounts may differ from the valuation in the cost accounts. For example, raw materials may be valued on a LIFO basis in the cost accounts, whereas FIFO or weighted average may be used in the financial accounts. WIP and finished stock may be valued on a marginal (variable costing) basis in the cost accounts, but the valuation may be based on an absorption costing basis in the financial accounts. To reconcile the profits, you should start with the profit from the cost accounts and consider what the impact would be on the profit calculation if the financial accounting stock valuations were used. If the opening stock valuation in the financial accounts exceeds the valuation in the cost accounts then adopting the financial accounting stock valuation will reduce the profits. If the closing stock valuation in the

financial accounts exceeds the valuation in the cost accounts then adopting the financial accounting stock valuation will increase profits. Note that the notional rent is not included in the financial accounts and should therefore be deducted from the costing profit in the reconciliation statement.

(c) The over recovery of overhead could be apportioned between costs of goods sold for the current period and closing stocks. The justification for this is based on the assumption that the under/over recovery is due to incorrect estimates of activity and overhead expenditure, which leads to incorrect allocations being made to the cost of sales and closing stock accounts. The proposed adjustment is an attempt to rectify this incorrect allocation.

The alternative treatment is for the full amount of the under/over recovery to be written off to the cost accounting profit and loss account in the current period as a period cost. This is the treatment recommended by SSAP 9.

SOLUTION 7

(a)

HR Construction plc – Contract Accounts

	A (£000)	B (£000)		A (£000)	B (£000)
Stores	700	150	Stores returns	80	30
Plant	1000	150	Transfers to B	40	—
Transfers from A	—	40	Materials c/fwd	75	15
Plant hire	200	30	Plant c/fwd[a]	880	144
Labour	300	270	Cost of work not		
			certified c/fwd	160	20
Overhead	75	18	Balance – Cost of work		
Direct expenses	25	4	certified c/fwd	1065	453
	2300	662		2300	662
Cost of work certified b/fwd	1065	453	Attributable sales		
			revenue[c]	1545	420
Profit recognized this period[b]	480		Loss recognized this		
			period[b]		33
	1545	453		1545	453
Cost of work not certified					
c/fwd	160	20			
Plant b/fwd	880	144			
Materials b/fwd	75	15			

Notes

[a] Value at the start of the year less one year's depreciation for Contract A and 3 months' depreciation for Contract B.

[b] The profits/(losses) recognized for the period are calculated as follows:

	Contract A (£000)	Contract B (£000)
Cost of work certified	1065	453
Cost of work not certified	160	20
Estimated costs to complete	135	110
Estimated cost of the contracts	1360	583
Contract price	2000	550
Estimated profit/(loss)	640	(33)

Profit recognized (Value certified (1500)/ Contract price (£2000) × £640 = £480 000 for Contract A.

An alternative more prudent approach would have been to multiply the estimated profit by cash received/contract price.

Applying the prudence concept the full anticipated loss is recognized in the current period.

[c] Profit recognized plus cost of work certified for A; Cost of work certified less loss recognized for B.

(b) *Balance sheet extracts*

	Contract A (£000)	Contract B (£000)
Fixed assets		
Plant at cost	1000	150
Depreciation	120	6
Written down value	880	144
Debtors		
Attributable sales	1545	420
Less cash received	1440	460
	105	(40)
Work-in-progress		
Total costs incurred to date	1225	473
Included in cost of sales	1065	453
	160	20

The loss of £33 000 for Contract A will be shown as a deduction from the total company profits. Alternatively, the loss can be deducted from the total costs incurred to date thus reflecting the fact that £33 000 of the total losses have been recognized during the current period.

(c) See 'Job costing systems and process costing systems' in Chapter 2 and 'Contract costing' in Chapter 5 for the answer to this question.

Process costing

A process costing system is used in those industries where masses of similar products or services are produced. Products are produced in the same manner and consume the same amount of direct costs and overheads. It is therefore unnecessary to assign costs to individual units of output. Instead, the average cost per unit of output is calculated by dividing the total costs assigned to a product or service for a period by the number of units of output for that period. Industries where process costing is widely used include chemical processing, oil refining, food processing and brewing. In contrast, job costing relates to a costing system where each unit or batch of output is unique. This creates the need for the cost of each unit to be calculated separately.

Our objective in this chapter is to examine the cost accumulation procedure that is required for inventory valuation and profit measurement for a process costing system. We shall also discuss briefly at the end of the chapter how cost information should be accumulated and extracted for decision-making and cost control. We begin with a description of the flow of production and costs in a process costing environment. We shall then focus on the cost accumulation system. To provide a structured presentation three different scenarios will be presented. First, all output is fully complete. Second, ending work in progress exists, but no beginning work in progress, and some of the units started during the period are incomplete at the end of the period. Our third scenario is the existence of both beginning and ending work in progress of uncompleted units. Finally, we shall turn our attention to decision-making and cost control. One of the most complex areas in process costing is accounting for losses when units within the process are both fully and partially complete. Because some courses omit this topic it will be discussed in Appendix 6.1.

Learning objectives

After studying this chapter you should be able to:

- distinguish between process and job costing;
- explain the accounting treatment for normal and abnormal losses;
- prepare process, normal loss, abnormal loss and abnormal gain accounts when there is no ending work in progress;
- compute the value of work in progress and completed production using the weighted average and first in, first out methods of valuing work in progress;
- differentiate between the different cost per unit calculations which are necessary for inventory valuation, decision-making and performance reporting for cost control;
- compute the value of normal and abnormal losses when there is ending work in progress.

Flow of production and costs in a process costing system

The flow of production and costs in a process costing system is illustrated in Exhibit 6.1. The major differences between process and job costing are also highlighted. You will see that production moves from one process (or department) to the next until final completion occurs. Each production department performs some part of the total operation and transfers its completed production to the next department, where it becomes the input for further processing. The completed production of the last department is transferred to the finished goods inventory.

The cost accumulation procedure follows this production flow. Control accounts are established for each process (or department) and direct and indirect costs are assigned to each process. A process costing system is easier to operate than a job costing system because the detailed work of allocating costs to many individual cost units is unnecessary. Also, many of the costs that are indirect in a job costing system may be regarded as direct in a process costing system. For example, supervision and depreciation that is confined to one department would be treated as part of the direct costs of that department in a process costing system, since these costs are directly attributable to the cost object (i.e. the department or process). However, such costs are normally regarded as indirect in a job costing system because they are not directly attributable to a specific job.

EXHIBIT 6.1

A comparison of job and process costing

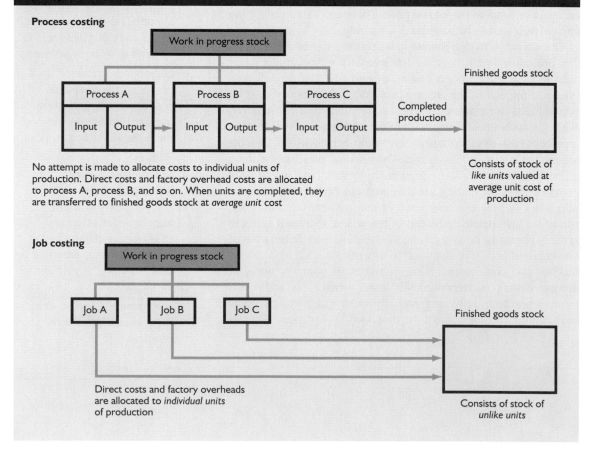

Process costing

Work in progress stock

Process A — Input | Output

Process B — Input | Output

Process C — Input | Output

Completed production

Finished goods stock

No attempt is made to allocate costs to individual units of production. Direct costs and factory overhead costs are allocated to process A, process B, and so on. When units are completed, they are transferred to finished goods stock at *average unit* cost

Consists of stock of *like units* valued at average unit cost of production

Job costing

Work in progress stock

Job A   Job B   Job C

Finished goods stock

Direct costs and factory overheads are allocated to *individual units* of production

Consists of stock of *unlike units*

As production moves from process to process costs are transferred with it. For example, in Exhibit 6.1 the costs of process A would be transferred to process B; process B costs would then be added to this cost and the resulting total cost transferred to process C; process C costs would then be added to this cost. Therefore the cost becomes cumulative as production proceeds and the addition of the costs from the last department's cost determines the total cost. The cost per unit of the completed product thus consists of the total cost accumulated in process C for the period divided by the output for that period.

Process costing when all output is fully complete

Throughout this section it is assumed that all output within each process is fully complete. We shall examine the following situations:

1. no losses within a process;
2. normal losses with no scrap value;
3. abnormal losses with no scrap value;
4. normal losses with a scrap value;
5. abnormal losses with a scrap value;
6. abnormal gains with no scrap value;
7. abnormal gains with a scrap value.

You should now look at Example 6.1. The information shown in this example will be used to illustrate the accounting entries. To simplify the presentation it is assumed that the product is produced within a single process.

EXAMPLE 6.1

Dartmouth Company produces a liquid fertilizer within a single production process. During the month of May the input into the process was 12 000 litres at a cost of £120 000. There were no opening or closing inventories and all output was fully complete. We shall prepare the process account and calculate the cost per litre of output for the single process for each of the following seven cases:

Case	Input (litres)	Output (litres)	Normal loss (litres)	Abnormal loss (litres)	Abnormal gain (litres)	Scrap value of spoilt output (£ per litre)
1	12 000	12 000	0	0	0	0
2	12 000	10 000	2000 (1/6)	0	0	0
3	12 000	9 000	2000 (1/6)	1000	0	0
4	12 000	10 000	2000 (1/6)	0	0	5
5	12 000	9 000	2000 (1/6)	1000	0	5
6	12 000	11 000	2000 (1/6)	0	1000	0
7	12 000	11 000	2000 (1/6)	0	1000	5

No losses within the process

To calculate the cost per unit (i.e. litre) of output for case 1 in Example 6.1 we merely divide the total cost incurred for the period of £120 000 by the output for the period (12 000 litres). The cost per unit of output is £10. In practice the cost per unit is analysed by the different cost categories such as direct materials and **conversion cost** which consists of the sum of direct labour and overhead costs.

Normal losses in process with no scrap value

Certain losses are inherent in the production process and cannot be eliminated. For example, liquids may evaporate, part of the cloth required to make a suit may be lost and losses occur in cutting wood to make furniture. These losses occur under efficient operating conditions and are unavoidable. They are referred to as **normal or uncontrollable losses**. Because they are an inherent part of the production process normal losses are absorbed by the good production. Where normal losses apply the cost per unit of output is calculated by dividing the costs incurred for a period by the *expected* output from the actual input for that period. Looking at case 2 in Example 6.1 you will see that the normal loss is one sixth of the input. Therefore for an input of 12 000 litres the *expected* output is 10 000 litres so that the cost per unit of output is £12 (£120 000/10 000 litres). Actual output is equal to expected output so there is neither an abnormal loss nor gain. Compared with case 1 the unit cost has increased by £2 per unit because the cost of the normal loss has been absorbed by the good production. Our objective is to calculate the cost of normal production under normal efficient operating conditions.

Abnormal losses in process with no scrap value

In addition to losses that cannot be avoided, there are some losses that are not expected to occur under efficient operating conditions, for example the improper mixing of ingredients, the use of inferior materials and the incorrect cutting of cloth. These losses are not an inherent part of the production process, and are referred to as **abnormal or controllable losses**. Because they are not an inherent part of the production process and arise from inefficiencies they are not included in the process costs. Instead, they are removed from the appropriate process account and reported separately as an abnormal loss. The abnormal loss is treated as a period cost and written off in the profit statement at the end of the accounting period. This ensures that abnormal losses are not incorporated in any inventory valuations.

For case 3 in Example 6.1 the expected output is 10 000 litres but the actual output was 9000 litres, resulting in an abnormal loss of 1000 litres. Our objective is the same as that for normal losses. That is to calculate the cost per litre of the *expected* output (i.e. normal production), which is:

$$\frac{\text{input cost } (£120\,000)}{\text{expected output } (10\,000 \text{ litres})} = £12$$

Note that the unit cost is the same for an output of 10 000 or 9000 litres since our objective is to calculate the cost per unit of normal output. The distribution of the input costs is as follows:

	(£)
Completed production transferred to the next process (or finished goods inventory) 9000 litres at £12	108 000
Abnormal loss: 1000 litres at £12	12 000
	120 000

The abnormal loss is valued at the cost per unit of normal production. Abnormal losses can only be controlled in the future by establishing the cause of the abnormal loss and taking appropriate remedial action to ensure that it does not reoccur. The entries in the process account will look like this:

Process account

	Litres	Unit cost (£)	(£)		Litres	Unit cost (£)	(£)
Input cost	12 000	10	120 000	Normal loss	2000	—	—
				Output to finished goods inventory	9000	12	108 000
				Abnormal loss	1000	12	12 000
			120 000				120 000

Process accounts represent work in progress (WIP) accounts. For example, if a second process were required and the 9000 litres had remained from the first process at the end of the accounting period the £108 000 would have represented the work in progress valuation in the process. In our example all of the work in progress has been completed and transferred to the finished goods inventory. Input costs are debited to the process account and the output from the process is entered on the credit side.

You will see from the process account that no entry is made in the account for the normal loss (except for an entry made in the units column). The transfer to the finished goods inventory (or the next process) is at the cost of normal production. The abnormal loss is removed from the process costs and reported separately as a loss in the abnormal loss account. This draws the attention of management to those losses that may be controllable. At the end of the accounting period the abnormal loss account is written off in the profit statement as a period cost. The inventory valuation will not therefore include any abnormal expenses. The overall effect is that the abnormal losses are correctly allocated to the period in which they arise and are not carried forward as a future expense in the closing inventory valuation.

NORMAL LOSSES IN PROCESS WITH A SCRAP VALUE

In case 4 actual output is equal to the expected output of 10 000 litres so there is neither an abnormal gain nor loss. All of the units lost represent a normal loss in process. However, the units lost now have a scrap value of £5 per litre. The sales value of the spoiled units should be offset against the costs of the appropriate process where the loss occurred. Therefore the sales value of the normal loss is credited to the process account and a corresponding debit entry will be made in the cash or accounts receivable (debtors) account. The calculation of the cost per unit of output is as follows:

$$\frac{\text{Input cost less scrap value of normal loss}}{\text{Expected output}} = \frac{£120\,000 - (2000 \times £5)}{10\,000\,\text{litres}} = £11$$

Compared with cases 3 and 4 the cost per unit has declined from £12 per litre to £11 per litre to reflect the fact that the normal spoilage has a scrap value which has been offset against the process costs.

The entries in the process account will look like this:

Process account

	Litres	Unit cost (£)	(£)		Litres	Unit cost (£)	(£)
Input cost	12 000	10	120 000	Normal loss	2 000	—	10 000
				Output to finished goods inventory	10 000	11	110 000
			120 000				120 000

Note that the scrap value of the normal loss is credited against the normal loss entry in the process account.

ABNORMAL LOSSES IN PROCESS WITH A SCRAP VALUE

In case 5 expected output is 10 000 litres for an input of 12 000 litres and actual output is 9000 litres resulting in a normal loss of 2000 litres and an abnormal loss of 1000 litres. The lost units have a scrap value of £5 per litre. Since our objective is to calculate the cost per unit for the expected (normal) output only the scrap value of the normal loss of 2000 litres should be deducted in ascertaining the cost per unit. Therefore the cost per unit calculation is the same as that for case 4 (i.e. £11). The sales value of the additional 1000 litres lost represents revenue of an abnormal nature and should not be used to reduce the process unit cost. This revenue is offset against the cost of the abnormal loss which is of interest to management. The net cost incurred in the process is £105 000 (£120 000 input cost less 3000 litres lost with a scrap value of £5 per litre), and the distribution of this cost is:

	(£)	(£)
Completed production transferred to the next process (or finished goods inventory) (9000 litres at £11 per litre)		99 000
Abnormal loss:		
1000 litres at £11 per litre	11 000	
Less scrap value (1000 litres at £5)	5 000	6 000
		105 000

The entries in the process account will be as follows:

Process account

	Litres	Unit cost (£)	(£)		Litres	Unit cost (£)	(£)
Input cost	12 000	10	120 000	Normal loss	2000	—	10 000
				Output to finished goods inventory	9000	11	99 000
				Abnormal loss	1000	11	11 000
			120 000				120 000

Abnormal loss account

	(£)		(£)
Process account	11 000	Cash sale for units scrapped	5 000
		Balance transferred to profit statement	6 000
	11 000		11 000

ABNORMAL GAINS WITH NO SCRAP VALUE

On occasions the actual loss in process may be less than expected, in which case an **abnormal gain** results. In case 6 the expected output is 10 000 litres for an input of 12 000 litres but the actual output is 11 000 litres resulting in an abnormal gain of 1000 litres. We are assuming for this case that the normal loss does not have a scrap value. As in the previous cases our objective is to calculate the cost per unit of expected (normal) output. The calculation of the cost per unit of normal output is the same as that for cases 2 and 3, which is:

$$\frac{\text{input cost (£120 000)}}{\text{expected output (10 000 litres)}} = £12$$

and the distribution of the input cost is as follows:

	(£)
Completed production transferred to the next process	
(or finished goods inventory) 11 000 litres at £12	132 000
Less: Abnormal gain: 1000 litres at £12	12 000
	120 000

The value of the gain is calculated in the same way as the abnormal loss and removed from the process account by debiting the account and crediting the abnormal gain account. The entries in the process account will be as follows:

Process account

	Litres	Unit cost (£)	(£)		Litres	Unit cost (£)	(£)
Input cost	12 000	10	120 000	Normal loss	2 000	—	—
Abnormal gain	1 000	12	12 000	Output to finished			
				goods inventory	11 000	12	132 000
			132 000				132 000

You will see in the process account that 11 000 litres are passed to the next process at the cost per unit of *normal* output. The gain is credited to the abnormal gain account and transferred to the credit of the profit and loss statement at the end of the period. This procedure ensures that the inventory valuation is not understated by gains of an abnormal nature.

ABNORMAL GAINS WITH A SCRAP VALUE

The only difference between cases 7 and 6 is that any losses have a scrap value of £5 per litre. As in the previous cases we start by calculating the cost per unit of normal output. For normal output our assumptions are the same as those for cases 4 and 5 (i.e. a normal loss of one sixth and a scrap value of £5 per litre) so the cost per unit of output is the same (i.e. £11 per litre). The calculation is as follows:

$$\frac{\text{Input cost less scrap value of normal loss}}{\text{Expected output}} = \frac{£120\,000 - (2000 \times £5)}{10\,000\ \text{litres}} = £11$$

The net cost incurred in the process is £115 000 (£120 000 input cost less 1000 litres spoilt with a sales value of £5 per litre), and the distribution of this cost is as follows:

		(£)
Transferred to finished goods inventory		
(11 000 litres at £11 per litre)		121 000
Less abnormal gain (1000 litres at £11 per litre)	11 000	
lost sales of spoiled units (1000 litres at £5 per litre)	5 000	6 000
		115 000

Note that the cost per unit is based on the normal production cost per unit and is not affected by the fact that an abnormal gain occurred or that sales of the spoiled units with a sales value of £5000 did not materialize. Our objective is to produce a cost per unit based on normal operating efficiency.

The accounting entries are as follows:

Process account

	Litres	Unit cost (£)	(£)		Litres	Unit cost (£)	(£)
Input cost	12 000	10	120 000	Normal loss	2 000	—	10 000
Abnormal gain	1 000	11	11 000	Output to finished			
				goods inventory	11 000	11	121 000
			131 000				131 000

Abnormal gain account

	(£)		(£)
Normal loss account	5 000	Process account	11 000
Profit and loss statement (Balance)	6 000		
	11 000		11 000

Income due from normal losses

	(£)		(£)
Process account	10 000	Abnormal gain account	5 000
		Cash from spoiled units	
		(1000 litres at £5)	5 000
	10 000		10 000

You will see that the abnormal gain has been removed from the process account and that it is valued at the cost per unit of normal production. However, as 1000 litres were gained, there was a loss of sales revenue of £5000, and this lost revenue is offset against the abnormal gain. The net gain is therefore £6000, and this is the amount that should be credited to the profit statement.

The process account is credited with the expected sales revenue from the normal loss (2000 litres at £5), since the objective is to record in the process account normal net costs of production. Because the normal loss of 2000 litres does not occur, the company will not obtain the sales value of £10 000 from the expected lost output. This problem is resolved by making a corresponding debit entry in a normal loss account, which represents the amount due from the sale proceeds from the expected normal loss. The amount due (£10 000) is then reduced by £5000 to reflect the fact that only 1000 litres were lost. This is achieved by crediting the normal loss account (income due) and debiting the abnormal gain account with £5000, so that the balance of the normal loss account shows the actual amount of cash received for the income due from the spoiled units (i.e. £5000, which consists of 1000 litres at £5 per litre).

Process costing with ending work in progress partially complete

So far we have assumed that all output within a process is fully complete. We shall now consider situations where output started during a period is partially complete at the end of the period. In other words, ending work in progress exists within a process. When some of the output started during a period is partially complete at the end of the period, unit costs cannot be computed by simply dividing the total costs for a period by the output for that period. For example, if 8000 units were started and completed during a period and another 2000 units were partly completed then these two items cannot be added together to ascertain their unit cost. We must convert the work in progress into finished equivalents (also referred to as **equivalent production**) so that the unit cost can be obtained.

To do this we must estimate the percentage degree of completion of the work in progress and multiply this by the number of units in progress at the end of the accounting period. If the 2000 partly completed units were 50% complete, we could express this as an equivalent production of 1000 fully completed units. This would then be added to the completed production of 8000 units to give a total equivalent production of 9000 units. The cost per unit would then be calculated in the normal way. For example, if the costs for the period were £180 000 then the cost per unit completed would be £20 (£180 000/9000 units) and the distribution of this cost would be as follows:

	(£)
Completed units transferred to the next process (8000 units at £20)	160 000
Work in progress (1000 equivalent units at £20)	20 000
	180 000

ELEMENTS OF COSTS WITH DIFFERENT DEGREES OF COMPLETION

A complication that may arise concerning equivalent units is that in any given stock of work in progress not all of the elements that make up the total cost may have reached the same degree of completion. For example, materials may be added at the start of the process, and are thus fully complete, whereas labour and manufacturing overhead (i.e. the conversion costs) may be added uniformly throughout the process. Hence, the ending work in progress may consist of materials that are 100% complete and conversion costs that are only partially complete. Where this situation arises, separate equivalent production calculations must be made for each element of cost. The calculation of unit costs and the allocation of costs to work in progress and completed production when different elements of costs are subject to different degrees of completion will now be illustrated using the data given in Example 6.2.

EXAMPLE 6.2

The Fontenbleau Company manufactures a product that passes through two processes. The following information relates to the two processes:

	Process A	Process B
Opening work in progress	—	—
Units introduced into the process	14 000	10 000
Units completed and transferred to the next process or finished goods inventory	10 000	9 000
Closing work in progress	4 000	1 000
Costs of production transferred from process A[a]		£270 000
Material costs added	£210 000	£108 000
Conversion costs	£144 000	£171 000

Materials are added at the start of process A and at the end of process B and conversion costs are added uniformly throughout both processes. The closing work in progress is estimated to be 50% complete for both processes.

Note
[a] This information is derived from the preparation of process A accounts.

The following statement shows the calculation of the cost per unit for process A:

Calculation of cost per unit for process A

Cost element	Total cost (£)	Completed units	WIP equivalent units	Total equivalent units	Cost per unit (£)
Materials	210 000	10 000	4000	14 000	15.00
Conversion cost	144 000	10 000	2000	12 000	12.00
	354 000				27.00

	(£)	(£)
Value of work in progress:		
Materials (4000 units at £15)	60 000	
Conversion cost (2000 units at £12)	24 000	84 000
Completed units (10 000) units at £27)		270 000
		354 000

The process account will look like this:

Process A account

Materials	210 000	Completed units transferred to process B	270 000
Conversion cost	144 000	Closing WIP c/fwd	84 000
	354 000		354 000
Opening WIP b/fwd	84 000		

You will see from the statement on the previous page that details are collected relating to the equivalent production for completed units and work in progress by materials and conversion costs. This information is required to calculate the cost per unit of equivalent production for each element of cost. The work in progress of 4000 units is considered to be fully complete regarding materials. As materials are issued at the start of the process any partly completed units in ending work in progress must be fully complete as far as materials are concerned. Therefore an entry of 4000 units is made in the work in progress equivalent units column in the above statement for materials. Regarding conversion cost, the 4000 units in progress are only 50% complete and therefore the entry in the work in progress column for this element of cost is 2000 units. To compute the value of work in progress, the unit costs are multiplied separately by the materials and conversion cost work in progress equivalent production figures. Only one calculation is required to ascertain the value of completed production. This is obtained by multiplying the total cost per unit of £27 by the completed production. Note that the cost of the output of £354 000 in the above statement is in agreement with the cost of input of £354 000.

PREVIOUS PROCESS COST

As production moves through processing, the output of one process becomes the input of the next process. The next process will carry out additional conversion work, and may add further materials. It is important to distinguish between these different cost items; this is achieved by labelling the transferred cost from the previous process 'previous process cost'. Note that this element of cost will always be fully complete as far as closing work in progress is concerned. Let us now calculate the unit costs and the value of work in progress and completed production for process B. To do this we prepare a statement similar to the one we prepared for process A.

Calculation of cost per unit for process B

Cost element	Total cost (£)	Completed units	WIP equivalent units	Total equivalent units	Cost per unit (£)
Previous process cost	270 000	9000	1000	10 000	27.00
Materials	108 000	9000	—	9 000	12.00
Conversion cost	171 000	9000	500	9 500	18.00
	549 000				57.00

		(£)	(£)
Value of work in progress:			
Previous process cost (1000 units at £27)		27 000	
Materials		—	
Conversion cost (500 units at £18)		9 000	36 000
Completed units (9000 units at £57)			513 000
			549 000 ←

Process B account

Previous process cost	270 000	Completed production	
Materials	108 000	transferred to finished stock	513 000
Conversions cost	171 000	Closing work in progress c/fwd	36 000
	549 000		549 000
Opening WIP b/fwd	36 000		

You will see that the previous process cost is treated as a separate process cost, and, since this element of cost will not be added to in process B, the closing work in progress must be fully complete as far as previous process cost is concerned. Note that, after the first process, materials may be issued at different stages of production. In process B materials are not issued until the end of the process, and the closing work in progress will not have reached this point; the equivalent production for the closing work in progress will therefore be zero for materials.

Normally, material costs are introduced at one stage in the process and not uniformly throughout the process. If the work in progress has passed the point at which the materials are added then the materials will be 100% complete. If this point has not been reached then the equivalent production for materials will be zero.

Beginning and ending work in progress of uncompleted units

When opening stocks of work in progress exist, an assumption must be made regarding the allocation of this opening stock to the current accounting period to determine the unit cost for the period. Two alternative assumptions are possible. First, one may assume that opening work in progress is inextricably merged with the units introduced in the current period and can no longer be identified separately – the **weighted average method** Secondly, one may assume that the opening work in progress is the first group of units to be processed and completed during the current month – the **first in, first out method**. Let us now compare these methods using the information contained in Example 6.3.

For more complex problems it is always a good idea to start by calculating the number of units completed during the period. The calculations are as follows:

	Process X	Process Y
Opening work in progress	6 000	2 000
Units introduced during period	16 000	18 000
Total input for period	22 000	20 000
Less closing work in progress	4 000	8 000
Balance – completed production	18 000	12 000

WEIGHTED AVERAGE METHOD

The calculation of the unit cost for process X using the weighted average method is as follows:

EXAMPLE 6.3

The Baltic Company has two processes, X and Y. Material is introduced at the start of process X, and additional material is added to process Y when the process is 70% complete. Conversion costs are applied uniformly throughout both processes. The completed units of process X are immediately transferred to process Y, and the completed production of process Y is transferred to finished goods stock. Data for the period include the following:

	Process X	Process Y
Opening work in progress	6000 units 60% converted, consisting of materials £72 000 and conversion cost £45 900	2000 units 80% converted, consisting of previous process cost of £91 800, materials £12 000 and conversion costs £38 400
Units started during the period	16 000 units	18 000 units
Closing work in progress	4000 units 3/4 complete	8000 units 1/2 complete
Material costs added during the period	£192 000	£60 000
Conversion costs added during the period	£225 000	£259 200

Process X – weighted average method

Cost element	Opening WIP (£)	Current cost (£)	Total cost (£)	Completed units	WIP equiv. units	Total equiv. units	Cost per [unit] (£)
Materials	72 000	192 000	264 000	18 000	4000	22 000	12.00
Conversion cost	45 900	225 000	270 900	18 000	3000	21 000	12.90
	117 900		534 900				24.90

	(£)	(£)
Work in progress:		
Materials (4000 units at £12)	48 000	
Conversion (3000 units at £12.90)	38 700	86 700
Completed units (18 000 units at £24.90)		448 200
		534 900

Process X account

Opening work in progress b/fwd	117 900	Completed production transferred to process Y	448 200
Materials	192 000	Closing work in progress c/fwd	86 700

Conversion cost	225 000	
	534 900	534 900
Opening work in progress b/fwd	86 700	

You can see from the statement of unit cost calculations that the opening work in progress is assumed to be completed in the current period. The current period's costs will include the cost of finishing off the opening work in progress, and the cost of the work in progress will be included in the total cost figure. The completed units will include the 6000 units in progress that will have been completed during the period. The statement therefore includes all the costs of the opening work in progress and the resulting units, fully completed. In other words, we have assumed that the opening work in progress is intermingled with the production of the current period to form one homogeneous batch of production. The equivalent number of units for this batch of production is divided into the costs of the current period, plus the value of the opening work in progress, to calculate the cost per unit.

Let us now calculate the unit cost for process Y using the weighted average method. From the calculation of the unit costs you can see the previous process cost is fully complete as far as the closing work in progress is concerned. Note that materials are added when the process is 70% complete, but the closing work in progress is only 50% complete. At the stage in question no materials will have been added to the closing work in progress, and the equivalent production will be zero. As with process X, it is necessary to add the opening work in progress cost to the current cost. The equivalent production of opening work in progress is ignored since this is included as being fully complete in the completed units column. Note also that the completed production cost of process X is included in the current cost column for 'the previous process cost' in the unit cost calculation for process Y.

Process Y – Weighted average method

Cost element	Opening WIP value (£)	Current period cost (£)	Total cost (£)	Completed units	WIP equiv. units	Total equiv. units	Cost per unit (£)
Previous process cost	91 800	448 200	540 000	12 000	8000	20 000	27.00
Materials	12 000	60 000	72 000	12 000	—	12 000	6.00
Conversion cost	38 400	259 200	297 600	12 000	4000	16 000	18.60
	142 200		909 600				51.60

	(£)	(£)
Value of work in progress:		
Previous process cost (8000 units at £27)	216 000	
Materials	—	
Conversion cost (4000 units at £18.60)	74 400	290 400
Completed units (12 000 units at £51.60)		619 200
		909 600 ←

Process Y account

Opening work in progress	142 200	Completed production		
Transferred from process X	448 200	transferred to finished stock	619 200	
Materials	60 000	Closing work in progress c/fwd	290 400	
Conversion cost	259 200			
	909 600		909 600	
Opening work in progress b/fwd	290 400			

FIRST IN FIRST OUT (FIFO) METHOD

The FIFO method of process costing assumes that the opening work in progress is the first group of units to be processed and completed during the current period. The opening work in progress is charged separately to completed production, and the cost per unit is based only on the *current period* costs and production for the current period. The closing work in progress is assumed to come from the new units started during the period. Let us now use Example 6.3 to illustrate the FIFO method for process X and Y.

Process X – FIFO method

Cost element	Current period costs (£)	Completed units less opening WIP equiv. units	Closing WIP equiv. units	Current total equiv. units	Cost per unit (£)
Materials	192 000	12 000 (18 000 − 6000)	4000	16 000	12.00
Conversion cost	225 000	14 400 (18 000 − 3600)	3000	17 400	12.93
	417 000				24.93

	(£)	(£)
Completed production:		
Opening WIP	117 900	
Materials (12 000 units at £12)	144 000	
Conversion cost (14 400 units at £12.93)	186 207	448 107
Closing work in progress:		
Materials (4000 units at £12)	48 000	
Conversion cost (3000 units at £12.93)	38 793	86 793
		534 900

From this calculation you can see that the average cost per unit is based on current period costs divided by the current total equivalent units for the period. The latter figure excludes the equivalent production for opening work in progress since this was performed in the previous period. Note that the closing work in progress is multiplied by the current period average cost per unit. The closing work in progress includes only the current costs and does not include any of the opening work in progress, which is carried forward from the previous period. The objective is to ensure that the opening work in progress is kept separate and is identified as part of the cost of the completed production. The opening work in progress of £117 900 is not therefore included in the unit cost calculations, but is added directly to the completed production.

Let us now calculate the units costs for process Y:

Process Y – FIFO method

Cost element	Current costs (£)	Completed units less opening WIP equiv. units	Closing WIP equiv. units	Current total equiv. units	Cost per unit (£)
Previous process cost	448 107	10 000 (12 000 − 2000)	8000	18 000	24.8948
Materials	60 000	10 000 (12 000 − 2000)	—	10 000	6.0
Conversion cost	259 200	10 400 (12 000 − 1600)	4000	14 400	18.0
	767 307				48.8948

	(£)	(£)
Cost of completed production:		
Opening WIP	142 200	
Previous process cost (10 000 units at £24.8948)	248 948	
Materials (10 000 units at £6)	60 000	
Conversion cost (10 400 units at £18)	187 200	638 348
Cost of closing work in progress:		
Previous process cost (8000 units at £24.8948)	199 159	
Materials	—	
Conversion cost (4000 units at £18)	72 000	271 159
		909 507

Note that in this calculation the *opening* work in progress is 80% completed, and that the materials are added when the process is 70% complete. Hence, they will be fully complete. Remember also that previous process cost is always 100% complete. Therefore in the third column of the above statement 2000 units opening work in progress is deducted for these two elements of cost from the 12 000 units of completed production. Conversion cost will be 80% complete so 1600 equivalent units are deducted from the completed production. Our objective in the third column is to extract the equivalent completed units that were derived from the units started during the current period. You should also note that the previous process cost of £448 107 represents the cost of completed production of process X, which has been transferred to process Y.

The closing work in progress valuations and the charges to completed production are fairly similar for both methods. The difference in the calculations between FIFO and the weighted average method is likely to be insignificant where the quantity of inventories and the input prices do not fluctuate significantly from month to month. Both methods are acceptable for product costing, but it appears that the FIFO method is not widely used in practice (Horngren, 1967).

Partially completed output and losses in process

Earlier in this chapter we looked at how to deal with losses in process when all of the output in a process was fully complete. We also need to look at the treatment of losses when all of the output is not fully complete. When this situation occurs the computations can become complex. Accounting for losses when all of the output is not fully complete does not form part of the curriculum for many courses. However, most professional management accounting courses do require you to have a knowledge of this topic. Because of these different requirements this topic is dealt with in Appendix 6.1. You should therefore check the requirements of your curriculum to ascertain whether you can omit Appendix 6.1.

Process costing for decision-making and control

The detailed calculations that we have made in this chapter are necessary for calculating profit and valuing stocks. For example, the process work in progress forms part of the balance sheet inventory valuations, and the transfers to succeeding processes become part of the work in progress of these processes or form part of the finished goods inventory. If the inventory is sold, these costs become part of the cost of goods sold for profit calculations. The calculations of unit costs, process work in progress valuations and the completed units valuation transferred to the next process are therefore necessary to determine the balance sheet inventory valuation and the cost of goods sold figure.

It is most unlikely that this same information will be appropriate for decision-making and cost control. In particular, process total unit costs will not be relevant for decision-making. What is required is an analysis of costs into their incremental and non-incremental elements for each process. A detailed discussion of those costs that are relevant for decision-making will be deferred to Chapter 10, but it is important that you should note at this point that the costs for decision-making purposes should be assembled in a different way.

COST CONTROL

In respect of cost control, we must ensure that the actual costs that are included on a performance report are the costs incurred for the *current period only* and do not include any costs that have been carried forward from previous periods. This principle can be illustrated using the information given in Example 6.3 for process X.

The unit cost statement for product X, using the weighted average method, shown on page 143 was as follows:

Cost element	Opening WIP value (£)	Current cost (£)	Total cost (£)	Completed units	WIP equiv. units	Total equiv. units	Cost per unit (£)
Materials	72 000	192 000	264 000	18 000	4000	22 000	12.00
Conversion cost	45 900	225 000	270 900	18 000	3000	21 000	12.90

This statement is not appropriate for cost control, since it includes the value of work in progress brought forward from the previous period. Also, the total equivalent units includes the opening work in progress equivalent units partly processed in the previous period. The inclusion of previous period costs and production is appropriate for inventory valuation and profit measurement, since the objective is to match costs (irrespective of when they were incurred) with revenues, but it is not appropriate to include previous costs for cost control. The objective of cost control is to compare the actual costs of the *current* period with the budgeted cost for the equivalent units produced during the *current* period. We wish to measure a manager's performance for the current period and to avoid this measure being distorted by carrying forward costs that were incurred in the previous period. We must therefore calculate the equivalent units produced during the current period by deducting the equivalent units produced during the previous period from the total number of equivalent units. The calculation is as follows:

	Total equivalent units	Opening WIP equiv. units	Equiv. units produced during period
Materials	22 000	6000	16 000
Conversion cost	21 000	3600 (60% × 6000)	17 400

Note that materials are introduced at the start of the process, and the 6000 units opening work in progress will have been fully completed in the previous period as far as materials are concerned. Assuming that the budgeted costs for the period are £11.40 for materials and £12 for conversion costs we can now present the following cost control performance report:

Performance report

	Budgeted cost (£)	Current period actual cost (£)	Difference (£)
Materials	182 400 (16 000 units at £11.40)	192 000	9 600 adverse
Conversion cost	208 800 (17 400 units at £12)	225 000	16 200 adverse

From this report you will see that we are comparing like with like; that is, both the budgeted costs and the actual costs refer to the equivalent units produced during the *current* period.

Note that information required for cost control must be analysed in far more detail than that presented in the performance report here. For example, the different types of materials and conversion costs must be listed and presented under separate headings for controllable and non-controllable expenses. The essential point to note, however, is that current period actual costs must be compared with the budgeted cost for the current period's production.

Batch/operating costing

It is not always possible to classify cost accumulation systems into job costing and process costing systems. Where manufactured goods have some common characteristics and also some individual characteristics, the cost accumulation system may be a combination of both the job costing and process costing systems. For example, the production of footwear,

EXHIBIT   6.2

*A batch
costing system*

Product	\multicolumn{5}{c	}{Operations}	Product cost

Product	1	2	3	4	5	Product cost
A	✓	✓	✓			A = cost of operations 1, 2, 3
B	✓			✓	✓	B = cost of operations 1, 4, 5
C	✓	✓		✓		C = cost of operations 1, 2, 4
D	✓		✓		✓	D = cost of operations 1, 3, 5
E	✓	✓			✓	E = cost of operations 1, 2, 5

clothing and furniture often involves the production of batches, which are variations of a single design and require a sequence of standardized operations. Let us consider a company that makes kitchen units. Each unit may have the same basic frame, and require the same operation, but the remaining operations may differ: some frames may require sinks, others may require to be fitted with work tops; different types of doors may be fitted to each unit, some may be low-quality doors while others may be of a higher quality. The cost of a kitchen unit will therefore consist of the basic frame plus the conversion costs of the appropriate operations. The principles of the cost accumulation system are illustrated in Exhibit 6.2.

The cost of each product consists of the cost of operation 1 plus a combination of the conversion costs for operations 2–5. The cost per unit produced for a particular operation consists of the average unit cost of each batch produced for each operation. It may well be that some products may be subject to a final operation that is unique to the product. The production cost will then consist of the average cost of a combination of operations 1–5 plus the specific cost of the final unique operation. The cost of the final operation will be traced specifically to the product using a job costing system. The final product cost therefore consists of a combination of process costing techniques and job costing techniques. This system of costing is referred to as **operation costing** or **batch costing**.

Surveys of practice

Little information is available on the extent to which process or job costing systems are used in practice. However, surveys of US (Schwarzbach, 1985), Finnish (Lukka and Granlund, 1996) and Australian (Joye and Blayney, 1990) companies report the following usage rates:

	USA %	Finland %	Australia %
Process costing	36	32	63
Job costing	28	30	40
No process or job costing		38	
Process and job combined	10		
Operation costing	18		

Presumably the Australian survey adopted a wider definition of process and job costing resulting in the respondents choosing one of the two categories whereas the Finnish study may have adopted a narrower definition. This may account for the fact that 38% of the organizations indicated that they adopted neither purely job nor process costing systems. These companies are likely to combine elements of both job and process costing.

Summary

In this chapter we have examined the cost accumulation procedure necessary for a process costing system for inventory valuation and profit measurement. A process costing system is an average cost system that is appropriate for those industries where the units of final output are identical. The cost of an individual order for a single unit can be obtained by merely dividing the costs of production for the period by the units produced for that period. Examples of industries where a system of process costing is appropriate include chemical, cement, oil, paint and textile industries.

The accounting treatment for normal and abnormal losses has been explained and illustrated. Normal losses are inherent in the production process, and cannot be eliminated; their cost should be borne by the good production. Abnormal losses are avoidable, and the cost of these losses should not be assigned to products but reported separately as an abnormal loss and written off as a period cost in the profit and loss statement. Scrap sales (if any) that result from the losses should be allocated to the appropriate process account (for normal losses) and the abnormal loss account (for abnormal losses).

We have established that where stocks of work in progress are in existence, it is necessary in order to create homogeneous units of output to convert the work in progress into finished equivalent units of production. Since materials are normally introduced at the start or end of the process and conversion costs are added uniformly throughout the process, it is necessary to keep a separate record of these items of cost. When materials are added at the start of the process, the materials element of the WIP is 100% complete. Alternatively, if materials are added at the end of the process, they are zero complete. Costs transferred from previous processes are recorded separately for unit cost calculations, since they are always regarded as 100% complete.

We have discussed and examined two alternative methods of allocating the opening work in progress costs to production: the weighted average and the first in, first out methods. If the weighted average method is used, both the units and the value of the opening work in progress are merged with the current period and production to calculate the average cost per unit. Using the first in, first out method, the opening work in progress is assumed to be the first group of units to be processed and completed during the current month. The opening work in progress is therefore assigned separately to completed production and the cost per unit is based only on current costs and production for the period. The closing work in progress is assumed to come from the new units that have been started during the period.

The differing ways in which cost information should be accumulated for decision-making and cost control was highlighted. In respect of decision-making, we are interested in the additional future costs and revenue resulting from a decision, and only incremental costs may be relevant for short-term decisions. In respect of cost control, it is only current costs and production that should be included in performance reports, since we are interested in a manager's performance in the current period and wish to avoid distorting the report with costs carried forward from the previous period.

Finally, you should note that because accounting for losses when all of the output is not fully complete is a complex topic and does not form part of the curriculum for many courses, this topic is dealt with in Appendix 6.1. You should check your course curriculum to ascertain if you need to read Appendix 6.1.

Appendix 6.1: Losses in process and partially completed units

NORMAL LOSSES

Earlier in this chapter, we established that normal losses should be considered as part of the cost of the good production. We need to know, however, at what stage in the process the loss occurs so that we can determine whether the whole loss should be allocated to completed production or whether some of the loss should also be allocated to the closing work in progress. If the loss occurs near the end of the process, or is discovered at the point of inspection, only the units which have reached the inspection point should be allocated with the cost of the loss. Alternatively, the loss could be assumed to occur at a specific point, earlier in the process.

Generally, it is assumed that normal losses take place at the stage of completion where inspection occurs. Where such an assumption is made, the normal loss will not be allocated to the closing work in progress, since the loss is related only to units that have reached the inspection point. Consider Example 6A.1.

To calculate the value of the normal loss, we prepare the normal unit cost statement, but with a separate column for the number of units lost:

Element of cost	Total cost (£)	Completed units	Normal loss	WIP equiv. units	Total equiv. units	Cost per unit (£)
Materials	5000	600	100	300	1000	5.0
Conversion cost	3400	600	100	150	850	4.0
	8400					9.0

	(£)	(£)
Value of work in progress:		
Materials (300 units at £5)	1500	
Conversion cost (150 units at £4)	600	2100
Completed units (600 units at £9)	5400	
Normal loss (100 units at £9)	900	6300
		8400 ←

Note here that all of the cost of the normal loss is added to the completed production, since it is detected at the completion stage. The closing work in progress will not have reached this stage, and therefore does not bear any of the loss. The cost per unit completed after the allocation of the normal loss is £10.50 (£6300/600 units).

Some writers suggest that if the equivalent units computation for normal losses is ignored, the cost of the normal loss will be automatically apportioned to the good production. However, the results from adopting this short-cut are not as accurate. The calculations adopting this short-cut approach are as follows:

EXAMPLE 6A.1

A department with no opening work in progress introduces 1000 units into the process; 600 are completed, 300 are half-completed and 100 units are lost (all normal). *Losses are detected upon completion.* Material costs are £5000 (all introduced at the start of the process) and conversion costs are £3400.

	Total cost (£)	Completed units	WIP equiv. units	Total equiv. units	Cost per unit (£)	WIP (£)
Materials	5000	600	300	900	5.5555	1666.65
Conversion cost	3400	600	150	750	4.5333	680.00
					10.0888	2346.65
				Completed units (600 × £10.0888)		6053.35
						8400.00

You can see that ignoring equivalent units for the normal loss decreased equivalent units and thus increases the cost per unit. The values of work in progress and completed production using each approach are as follows:

	Normal loss charged to good production (£)	Short-cut method (£)	Difference (£)
Work in progress	2100	2347	+247
Completed units	6300	6053	−247

If the short-cut approach is used, the work in progress valuation includes £247 normal loss that is not attributable to these units because they have not reached the inspection point. The £247 should be charged only to completed units that have reached the inspection point. It is therefore recommended that the cost of the normal loss is calculated and charged only to those units that have reached the inspection point.

Let us now assume for Example 6A.1 that the loss is detected when the process has reached the 50% stage of completion. The revised cost per unit will be as follows:

Element of cost	Total cost (£)	Completed units	Normal loss	WIP equiv. units	Total equiv. units	Cost per unit
Materials	5000	600	100	300	1000	5.00
Conversion cost	3400	600	50	150	800	4.25
	8400					9.25

The 100 lost units will not be processed any further once the loss is detected at the 50% completion stage. Therefore 50 units equivalent production (100 units × 50%) is entered in the normal loss column for conversion cost equivalent production. Note that materials are introduced at the start of the process and are fully complete when the loss is detected. The cost of the normal loss is

	(£)
Materials (100 × £5)	500.00
Conversion cost (50 × £4.25)	212.50
	712.50

When losses are assumed to occur at a specific point in the production process, you should allocate the normal loss over all units that have reached this point. In our example the loss is detected at the 50% stage of completion, and the work in progress has reached this point. Therefore the loss should be allocated between completed production and work in progress. If the losses were detected at the 60% stage, all of the normal loss would be allocated to completed production. Alternatively, if losses were detected before the 50% stage, the normal loss would be allocated to completed production and work in progress.

The question is: how should we allocate the normal loss between completed production and work in progress? Several different approaches are advocated, but the most common approach is to apportion the normal loss in the ratio of completed units and WIP equivalent units as follows:

Completed units		**WIP**	
	(£)		(£)
Materials 600/900 × £500	333.33	300/900 × £500	166.67
Conversion cost 600/750 × £212.50	170.00	150/750 × £212.50	42.50
	503.33		209.17

The cost of completed units and WIP is:

	(£)	(£)
Completed units:		
(600 × £9.25)	5550.00	
Share of normal loss	503.33	6053.33
WIP:		
Materials (300 × £5)	1500.00	
Conversion cost (150 × £4.25)	637.50	
Share of normal loss	209.17	2346.67
		8400.00

When the lost units have a scrap value the sales value should be deducted from the normal loss and the net cost apportioned between WIP and completed units.

You should note that where the normal loss is to be apportioned between completed production and WIP an alternative and simpler approach is to use the short-cut method described earlier, whereby the normal loss is not included in the unit cost statement. Using the short-cut method calculation (see page 153) you will see that the allocation of costs to completed units and WIP are identical (apart from small rounding differences) to the above calculation.

ABNORMAL LOSSES

Where abnormal losses are incurred, the correct procedure is to produce the normal unit cost statement, but with the addition of two separate columns for the units lost; one for normal losses and one for abnormal losses. Consider Example 6A.2.

EXAMPLE 6A.2

A department with no opening work in progress introduced 1000 units into the process; 600 are completed, 250 are 20% complete, and 150 units are lost consisting of 100 units of normal loss and 50 units of abnormal loss. Losses are detected *upon completion*. Material costs are £8000 (all introduced at the start of the process) and conversion costs are £4000.

The unit cost calculations are as follows:

Element of cost	Total cost (£)	Completed units	Normal loss	Abnormal loss	WIP equiv. units	Total equiv. units	Cost per unit (£)
Materials	8 000	600	100	50	250	1000	8
Conversion cost	4 000	600	100	50	50	800	5
	12 000						13

	(£)	(£)
Value of work in progress:		
Materials (250 units at £8)	2000	
Conversion cost (50 units at £5)	250	2 250
Completed units (600 units at £13)	7800	
Add normal loss (100 units at £13)	1300	9 100
Abnormal loss (50 units at £13)		650
		12 000

You can see that the normal loss has been charged to completed units only. The abnormal loss is charged to a separate account and written off as a period cost to the profit and loss account. The entries in the process account will be as follows:

Process account

Materials	8 000	Transfer to next process	9 100
Conversion cost	4 000	Abnormal loss written off to profit and loss account	650
		Closing work in progress c/fwd	2 250
	12 000		12 000

Note that there is an argument for allocating the normal loss of £1300 between the completed units and the abnormal loss. If the normal loss is of a significant value then there are strong arguments for doing this, since the normal loss is part of the cost of production. The abnormal loss should therefore be valued at the cost per unit of *normal output*. In the unit cost statement for Example 6A.2 you will see that the completed production is 600 units and the abnormal loss is 50 units. The normal loss of £1300 is therefore apportioned pro rata to completed production and the abnormal loss. The calculations are as follows:

$$\text{completed units } (600/650 \times £1300) = 1200$$
$$\text{abnormal loss } \quad (50/650 \times £1300) = 100$$

The revised value for completed production would then be £9000 (£7800 + £1200), while for the abnormal loss the value would be £750 (£650 + £100). For most examination questions it is unlikely that you will be expected to allocate the normal loss between completed units and the abnormal loss.

Key Terms and Concepts

abnormal gain (p. 137)
abnormal or controllable losses (p. 134)
batch costing (p. 149)
conversion cost (p. 134)
equivalent production (p. 139)

first in, first out method (p. 142)
normal or uncontrollable losses (p. 134)
operation costing (p. 149)
previous process cost (p. 141)
weighted average method (p. 142)

Key Examination Points

Process costing questions require many calculations and there is a possibility that you will make calculation errors. Make sure that your answer is clearly presented so that the examiner can ascertain whether or not you are using correct methods to calculate the cost per unit. Questions can generally be classified by three categories. First, all output is fully complete and the problem of equivalent production does not arise (see the fourth review question for an example). Second, work in progress (WIP) output is partially complete and there are no losses in process. Third, losses in process apply when WIP is partially complete. The fifth and sixth review problems fall within the second category

with the former assuming the weighted average and the latter FIFO method of stack valuation. The final review problem involves equivalent production and losses in process. Sometimes examination questions do not indicate the stage in the process that losses occur. In this situation you are recommended to assume that the loss occurs at the end of the process and allocate the normal loss to completed production. Do not forget to state this assumption in your answer. The short-cut method should not be used if the loss occurs at the end of the process because this method assumes that the loss is to be shared between WIP and completed units.

Review Problems

(For additional problems without answers relating to the content of this chapter you should refer to pages 450–458.)

1 AK Chemicals produces high-quality plastic sheeting in a continuous manufacturing operation. All materials are input at the beginning of the process. Conversion costs are incurred

evenly throughout the process. A quality control inspection occurs 75% through the manufacturing process, when some units are separated out as inferior quality. The following data are available for December.

Materials costs	£90 000
Conversion costs	£70 200

Units started	40 000
Units completed	36 000

There is no opening or closing work in progress. Past experience indicates that approximately 7.5% of the units started are found to be defective on inspection by quality control.

What is the cost of abnormal loss for December

A   £3600
B   £4050
C   £4680
D   £10 800

ACCA Paper 3

2 KL Processing Limited has identified that an abnormal gain of 160 litres occurred in its refining process last week. Normal losses are expected and have a scrap value of £2.00 per litre. All losses are 100% complete as to material cost and 75% complete as to conversion costs.

The company uses the weighted average method of valuation and last week's output was valued using the following costs per equivalent unit:

Materials	£9.40
Conversion costs	£11.20

The effect on the profit and loss account of last week's abnormal gain is

A   Debit £2528
B   Debit £2828
C   Credit £2528
D   Credit £2848
E   Credit £3168

CIMA Stage 2

3 The following details relate to the main process of W Limited, a chemical manufacturer:

Opening work in progress	2000 litres, fully complete as to materials and 40% complete as to conversion
Material input	24 000 litres
Normal loss is 10% of input	
Output to process 2	19 500 litres

Closing work in progress	3000 litres, fully complete as to materials and 45% complete as to conversion

The number of equivalent units to be included in W Limited's calculation of the cost per equivalent unit using a FIFO basis of valuation are:

	Materials	Conversion
A	19 400	18 950
B	20 500	20 050
C	21 600	21 150
D	23 600	20 750
E	23 600	21 950

CIMA Stage 2

4 'No Friction' is an industrial lubricant, which is formed by subjecting certain crude chemicals to two successive processes. The output of process 1 is passed to process 2, where it is blended with other chemicals. The process costs for period 3 were as follows:

Process 1
   Material: 3000 kg @ £0.25 per kg
   Labour: £120
   Process plant time: 12 hours @ £20 per hour

Process 2
   Material: 2000 kg @ £0.40 per kg
   Labour: £84
   Process plant time: 20 hours @ £13.50 per hour

General overhead for period 3 amounted to £357 and is absorbed into process costs on a process labour basis.

The normal output of process 1 is 80% of input, while that of process 2 is 90% of input.

Waste matter from process 1 is sold for £0.20 per kg, while that from process 2 is sold for £0.30 per kg.

The output for period 3 was as follows:
   Process 1   2300 kg
   Process 2   4000 kg

There was no stock or work in process at either the beginning or the end of the period, and it may be assumed that all available waste matter had been sold at the prices indicated.

You are required to show how the above data would be recorded in a system of cost accounts.

5 A cleansing agent is manufactured from the input of three ingredients. At 1 December there was no work in progress. During December the ingredients were put into the process in the following quantities:

A   2000 kg at £0.80 per kg
B   3000 kg at £0.50 per kg
C   6000 kg at £0.40 per kg

Additionally, labour working 941 hours and being paid £4 per hour was incurred, and overheads recovered on the basis of 50% of labour cost. There was no loss in the process. Output was 8600 kg.

The remaining items in work in progress were assessed by the company's works manager as follows:

Complete so far as materials were concerned:
One quarter of the items were 60% complete for labour and overheads;
Three-quarters were 25% complete for labour and overheads.

Required:
(a) A cleansing agent process account, showing clearly the cost of the output and work in progress carried forward.   (16 marks)
(b) Define the following terms, give examples and explain how they would be accounted for in process costing:
     (i)   By-products   (6 marks)
     (ii) Abnormal gain   (3 marks)
     (iii) Equivalent units   (3 marks)
                              (Total 28 marks)
                                         AAT

6 A company operates a manufacturing process where six people work as a team and are paid a weekly group bonus based upon the actual output of the team compared with output expected.

A basic 37 hour week is worked during which the expected output from the process is 4000 equivalent units of product. Basic pay is £5.00 per hour and the bonus for the group, shared equally, is £0.80 per unit in excess of expected output.

In the week just ended, basic hours were worked on the process. The following additional information is provided for the week:

Opening work in process (1000 units):
   Materials £540 (100% complete)

Labour and overheads £355 (50% complete).
During the week:
   Materials used £2255
   Overheads incurred £1748
   Completed production 3800 units
Closing work in process (1300 units)
   Materials (100% complete)
   Labour and overheads (75% complete).
There are no process losses.
The FIFO method is used to apportion costs.

Required:
(a) Prepare the process account for the week just ended.   (10 marks)
(b) Explain the purpose of the following documents which are used in the control of, and accounting for, the materials used in the process described in part (a)
     (i)   purchase requisition
     (ii) materials (stores) requisition.
                                 (4 marks)
                            (Total 14 marks)
           ACCA Foundation Stage Paper 3

7 A concentrated liquid fertilizer is manufactured by passing chemicals through two consecutive processes. Stores record cards for the chemical ingredients used exclusively by the first process show the following data for May 2000:

Opening stock	4 000 litres	£10 800
Closing stock	8 000 litres	£24 200
Receipts into store	20 000 litres	£61 000

Other process data for May is tabulated below:

	Process 1	Process 2
Direct labour	£4880	£6000
Direct expenses	£4270	—
Overhead absorption rates	250% of direct labour	100% of direct labour
Output	8000 litres	7500 litres
Opening stock of work in process	—	—
Closing stock of work in process	5600 litres	—
Normal yield	85% of input	90% of input
Scrap value of loss	—	—

In process 1 the closing stock of work in process has just passed through inspection, which is at the stage where materials and conversion costs are 100% and 75% completed respectively.

In process 2 inspection is the final operation. Required:

(a) Prepare the relevant accounts to show the results of the processes for May 2000 and present a detailed working paper showing your calculations and any assumptions in arriving at the data shown in those accounts. *(18 marks)*

(b) If supplies of the required chemicals are severely restricted and all production can be sold immediately, briefly explain how you would calculate the total loss to the company if, at the beginning of June, 100 litres of the correct mix of chemicals were spilt on issue to process 1.

(4 marks)
(Total 22 marks)
ACCA Foundation Costing

Solutions to Review Problems

SOLUTION 1

	Cost (£)	Units completed	Normal loss equiv. units	Abnormal loss equiv. units	Total equiv. units	Cost per unit (£)
Materials	90 000	36 000	3000 (100%)	1000 (100%)	40 000	2.25
Conversion cost	70 200	36 000	2250 (75%)	750 (75%)	39 000	1.80
						4.05

Cost of abnormal loss:
Materials	$1000 \times £2.25 = £2250$
Conversion cost	$750 \times £1.80 = £1350$
	£3600

Answer = A

SOLUTION 2

Abnormal gain debited to process account and credited to abnormal gain account:

	(£)	(£)
Materials (160 × £9.40)	1504	
Conversion cost (160 × 0.75 × £11.20)	1344	
		2848
Lost sales of scrap (180 × £2)		(360)
Net cost credited to profit and loss account		2528

Answer = C

SOLUTION 3

Input = Opening WIP (2000 units) +
Material input (24 000) = 26 000
Output = Completed units (19 500) +
Closing WIP (3000) + Normal Loss
(2400) = 24 900
Abnormal Loss = 1100 units (Balance of
26 000 − 24 900)

Equivalent units (FIFO)

	Completed units less Opening WIP equiv. units	Closing WIP equiv. units	Abnormal loss equiv. units	Total equiv. units
Materials	17 500 (19 500 − 2000)	3000 (100%)	1100 (100%)	21 600
Conversion	18 700 (19 500 − 800)	1350 (45%)	1100 (100%)	21 150

It is assumed that losses are detected at the end of the process and that the answer should adopt the short-cut method and ignore the normal loss in the cost per unit calculations.

Answer = C

SOLUTION 4

Process 1 account

	(kg)	(£)		(kg)	(£)
Material	3000	750	Normal loss (20%)	600	120
Labour		120	Transfer to process 2	2300	1150
Process plant time		240	Abnormal loss	100	50
General overhead					
(£120/£204 × £357)		210			
	3000	1320		3000	1320

$$\text{cost per unit} = \frac{\text{cost of production less scrap value of normal loss}}{\text{expected output}}$$

$$= \frac{£1320 - £120}{2400 \text{ kg}} = £0.50$$

Process 2 account

	(kg)	(£)		(kg)	(£)
Previous process cost	2300	1150	Normal loss	430	129
Materials	2000	800	Transfer to finished stock	4000	2400
Labour		84			
General overhead		147			
(£84/£204 × £357)					
Process plant time		270			
		2451			
Abnormal gain (130 kg at £0.60)	130	78			
	4430	2529		4430	2529

$$\text{cost per unit} = \frac{£2451 - £129}{3870 \text{ kg}} = £0.60$$

Finished stock account

	(£)	
Process 2	2400	

Normal loss account (income due)

	(£)		(£)
Process 1 normal loss	120	Abnormal gain account	39
Process 2 normal loss	129	Balance or cash received	230
Abnormal loss account	20		
	269		269

Abnormal loss account

	(£)		(£)
Process 1	50	Normal loss account	20
		(100 × £0.20)	
		Profit and loss account	30
	50		50

Abnormal gain account

	(£)		(£)
Normal loss account	39	Process 2	78
(Loss of income			
130 × £0.30)			
Profit and loss account	39		
	78		78

SOLUTION 5

(a)

Cleansing agent process account

	(kg)	(£)		(kg)	(£)
Ingredient A	2 000	1 600	Completed production	8 600	9 460
B	3 000	1 500	WIP c/fwd (1170 + 516)	2 400	1 686
C	6 000	2 400			
Wages		3 764			
Overheads		1 882			
	11 000	11 146		11 000	11 146

Calculation of cost per unit

	Total cost (£)	Completed units	Equivalent WIP(1)	Equivalent WIP(2)	Total equivalent units	Cost per unit (£)
Materials	5 500	8600	600	1800	11 000	0.50
Labour	3 764	8600	360	450	9 410	0.40
Overheads	1 882	8600	360	450	9 410	0.20
	11 146					1.10

				(£)
WIP(1):		Materials	600 × £0.50 = 300	
		Labour	360 × £0.40 = 144	
		Overheads	360 × £0.20 = 72	516
WIP(2):		Materials	1800 × £0.50 = 900	
		Labour	450 × £0.40 = 180	
		Overheads	450 × £0.20 = 90	1 170

	(£)
Completed units: 8600 × £1.10	9 460
	11 146

Note that 11 000 kg were put into the process and 8600 kg were completed. Therefore the WIP is 2400 kg consisting of two batches – one of 600 units 60% complete and the second of 1800 units 25% complete.

(b) See Chapter 6 for definitions and an explanation of the accounting treatment of abnormal gains and equivalent units. See Chapter 7 for a definition of by-products. Note that income from by-products should be credited to the process account from which the by-product emerges.

SOLUTION 6

(a)

Cost element	Current period costs (£)	Completed units less opening WIP equiv. units	Closing WIP equiv. units	Current total equiv. units	Cost per unit (£)
Materials	2255	2800	1300	4100	0.55
Conversion costs[a]	3078	3300	975	4275	0.72
	5333				

		(£)		(£)
Completed production:				
Opening WIP (£540 + £355)		895		
Materials (2800 × £0.55)		1540		
Conversion cost (3300 × £0.72)		2376		
				4811
Closing work in progress:				
Materials (1300 × £0.55)		715		
Conversion cost (975 × £0.72)		702		
				1417
				6228

Note
[a]Bonus = Current total equivalent units (4275) − Expected output (4000) = 275 units × £0.80 = £220
Labour cost = 6 men × 37 hours × £5 = £1110 + Bonus (£220) = £1330
Conversion cost = £1748 overhead + £1330 labour = £3078

Process account

	(£)		(£)
Opening WIP	895	Completed output	4811
Materials	2255	Closing WIP	1417
Labour and overhead	3078		
	6228		6228

(b) (i) In most organizations the purchasing function is centralized and all goods are purchased by the purchasing department. To purchase goods, user departments complete a purchase requisition. This is a document requesting the purchasing department to purchase the goods listed on the document.

(ii) See 'Materials recording procedure' in Chapter 3 for the answer to this question.

SOLUTION 7

(a) Calculation of input for process 1

	(litres)	(£)
Opening stock	4 000	10 800
Receipts	20 000	61 000
Less closing stock	(8 000)	(24 200)
Process input	16 000	47 600
Output		(litres)
Completed units		8 000
Closing WIP		5 600
Normal loss (15% of input)		2 400
		16 000

Because input is equal to output, there are no abnormal gains or losses.

Calculation of cost per unit (Process 1)
It is assumed that the loss occurs at the point of inspection. Because WIP has passed the inspection point, the normal loss should be allocated to both completed units and WIP.

(1) Element of cost	(2) (£)	(3) Completed units	(4) Normal loss	(5) Closing WIP	(6) Total equiv. units	(7) Cost per unit	(8) = (5) × (7) WIP
Materials	47 600	8000	2400	5600	16 000	£2.975	£16 600
Conversion cost[a]	21 350	8000	1800	4200	14 000	£1.525	£6 405
	68 950					£4.50	£23 065

Note
[a] Conversion cost = direct labour (£4880) + direct expenses (£4270) + overhead (250% + £4880)

Cost of normal loss	(£)
Materials	2400 × £2.975 = 7140
Conversion cost	1800 × £1.525 = 2745
	9885

The apportionment of normal loss to completed units and WIP is as follows:

	Completed units	WIP
Materials	(8000/13 600) × £7140 = £4200	(5600/13 600) × £7140 = £2940
Conversion	(8000/12 200) × £2745 = £1800	(4200/12 200) × £2745 = £945
	£6000	£3885

The cost of completed units and WIP is as follows:

		(£)	(£)
Completed units:	8000 units × £4.50	36 000	
	Share of normal loss	6 000	42 000
WIP:	Original allocation	23 065	
	Share of normal loss	3 885	26 950
			68 950

For an explanation of the above procedure see Appendix 6.1.

Where the normal loss is apportioned to WIP and completed units, a simple (but less accurate) approach is to use the short-cut approach and not to include the normal loss in the unit cost statement. The calculation is as follows:

Element of cost	(£)	Completed units	Closing WIP	Total equiv. units	Cost per unit (£)	WIP (£)
Materials	47 600	8000	5600	13 600	3.50	19 600
Conversion cost	21 350	8000	4200	12 200	1.75	7 350
					£5.25	£26 950

Completed units 8000 × £5.25 = £42 000

Process 1 account – May 2000

	(litres)	(£)		(litres)	(£)
Materials	16 000	47 600	Transfers to process 2	8 000	42 000
Labour		4 880	Normal loss	2 400	—
Direct expenses		4 270	Closing stock c/f	5 600	26 950
Overheads absorbed		12 200			
	16 000	68 950		16 000	68 950

With process 2, there is no closing WIP. Therefore it is unnecessary to express output in equivalent units. The cost per unit is calculated as follows:

$$\frac{\text{cost of production less scrap value of normal loss}}{\text{expected output}}$$

$$= \frac{54\,000^a}{(90\% \times 8000)} = 7.50$$

Note
[a] Cost of production = transferred in cost from process 1 (42 000) + labour (£6000) + overhead (£6000).

Process 2 account – May 2000

	Litres	(£)		Litres	(£)
Transferred from			Finished goods		
Process 1	8 000	42 000	store[b]	7 500	56 250
Labour		6 000	Normal loss	800	
Overheads absorbed		6 000	Closing stock	—	—
Abnormal gain[a]	300	2 250			
	8 300	56 250		8 300	56 250

Finished goods account

	Litres	(£)
Ex Process 2	7 500	56 250

Abnormal gain account

	(£)		Litres	(£)
Profit and loss account	2 250	Process 2 account	300	2 250

Notes
[a] Input = 8000 litres. Normal output = 90% × 8000 litres = 7200 litres. Actual output = 7500 litres. Abnormal gain = 300 litres × £7.50 per litre = £2250.
[b] 7500 litres at £7.50 per litre.

(b) If the materials can be replaced then the loss to the company will consist of the replacement cost of materials. If the materials cannot be replaced then the loss will consist of the lost sales revenue less the costs not incurred as a result of not processing and selling 100 litres.

Joint and by-product costing

A distinguishing feature of the production of joint and by-products is that the products are not identifiable as different products until a specific point in the production process is reached. Before this point joint costs are incurred on the production of all products emerging from the joint production process. It is therefore not possible to trace joint costs to individual products.

To meet internal and external profit measurement and inventory valuation requirements, it is necessary to assign all product-related costs (including joint costs) to products so that costs can be allocated to inventories and cost of goods sold. The assignment of joint costs, however, is of little use for decision-making. We shall begin by distinguishing between joint and by-products. This will be followed by an examination of the different methods that can be used to allocate joint costs to products for inventory valuation. We shall then go on to discuss which costs are relevant for decision-making.

Learning objectives

After studying this chapter, you should be able to:

- distinguish between joint products and by-products;
- explain and identify the split-off point in a joint-cost situation;
- explain the alternative methods of allocating joint costs to products;
- discuss the arguments for and against each of the methods of allocating joint costs to products;
- present relevant financial information for a decision as to whether a product should be sold at a particular stage or further processed;
- describe the accounting treatment of by-products.

Distinguishing between joint products and by-products

Joint products and by-products arise in situations where the production of one product makes inevitable the production of other products. When a group of individual products is simultaneously produced, and each product has a significant relative sales value, the outputs are usually called **joint products**. Those products that are part of the simultaneous

FIGURE 7.1 *Production process for joint and by-products.*

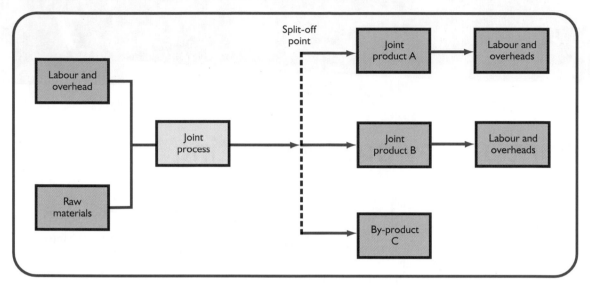

production process and have a minor sales value when compared with the joint products are called **by-products**.

As their name implies, by-products are those products that result incidentally from the main joint products. By-products may have a considerable absolute value, but the crucial classification test is that the sales value is small when compared with the values of the joint products. Joint products are crucial to the commercial viability of an organization, whereas by-products are incidental. In other words, by-products do not usually influence the decision as to whether or not to produce the main product, and they normally have little effect on the prices set for the main (joint) products. Examples of industries that produce both joint and by-products include chemicals, oil refining, mining, flour milling and gas manufacturing.

A distinguishing feature of the production of joint and by-products, is that the products are not identifiable as different individual products until a specific point in the production process is reached, known as the **split-off point**. All products may separate at one time, or different products may emerge at intervals. Before the split-off point, costs cannot be traced to particular products. For example, it is not possible to determine what part of the cost of processing a barrel of crude oil should be allocated to petrol, kerosene or paraffin. After the split-off point, joint products may be sold or subjected to further processing. If the latter is the case, any **further processing costs** can easily be traced to the specific products involved.

Figure 7.1 illustrates a simplified production process for joint and by-products. You will notice from this illustration that, at the split-off point, joint products A and B and by-product C all emerge, and that it is not possible to allocate costs of the joint process directly to the joint products or by-products. After the split-off point, further processing costs are added to the joint products before sale, and these costs can be specifically attributed to the joint products. By-product C in this instance is sold at the split-off point without further processing, although sometimes by-products may be further processed after the split-off point before they are sold on the outside market.

Methods of allocating joint costs

If all the production for a particular period was sold, the problem of allocating joint costs to products would not exist. Inventory valuations would not be necessary, and the calculation of profit would merely require the deduction of total cost from total sales. However, if inventories are in existence at the end of the period, cost allocation to products are necessary. As any such allocations are bound to be subjective and arbitrary, this area will involve the accountant in making decisions which are among the most difficult to defend. All one can do is to attempt to choose an allocation method that seems to provide a rational and reasonable method of cost distribution. The most frequently used methods that are used to allocate joint costs up to split-off point can be divided into the following two categories:

1. Methods based on physical measures such as weight, volume, etc.
2. Methods assumed to measure the ability to absorb joint costs based on allocating joint costs relative to the market values of the products.

We shall now look at four methods that are used for allocating joint costs using the information given in Example 7.1. In Example 7.1 products X, Y and Z all become finished products at the split-off point. The problem arises as to how much of the £600 000 joint costs should be allocated to each individual product? The £600 000 cannot be specifically identified with any of the individual products, since the products themselves were not separated before the split-off point, but some method must be used to split the £600 000 among the three products so that inventories can be valued and the profit for the period calculated. The first method we shall look at is called the **physical measures method**

PHYSICAL MEASURES METHOD

Using this method, the cost allocation is a simple allocation of joint costs in proportion to volume. Each product is assumed to receive similar benefits from the joint cost, and is therefore charged with its proportionate share of the total cost. The cost allocations using this method are as follows:

Product	Units produced	Proportion to total	Joint costs allocated (£)	Cost per unit (£)
X	40 000	$\frac{1}{3}$	200 000	5
Y	20 000	$\frac{1}{6}$	100 000	5
Z	60 000	$\frac{1}{2}$	300 000	5
	120 000		600 000	

Note that this method assumes that the cost per unit is the same for each of the products. Therefore an alternative method of allocating joint costs is as follows:

$$\text{cost per unit} = £5 \ (£600\,000/120\,000)$$

EXAMPLE 7.1

During the month of July the Van Nostrand Company processes a basic raw material through a manufacturing process that yields three products – products X, Y and Z. There were no opening inventories and the products are sold at the split-off point without further processing. We shall initially assume that all of the output is sold during the period. Details of the production process and the sales revenues are given in the following diagram.

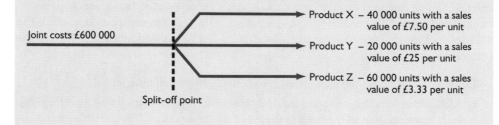

Thus the joint cost allocations are:

$$\text{Product X:} \quad 40\,000 \times £5 = £200\,000$$
$$\text{Product Y:} \quad 20\,000 \times £5 = £100\,000$$
$$\text{Product Z:} \quad 60\,000 \times £5 = £300\,000$$

Where market prices of the joint products differ, the assumptions of identical costs per unit for each joint product will result in some products showing high profits while others may show losses. This can give misleading profit calculations. Let us look at the product profit calculations using the information given in Example 7.1.

Product	Sales revenue (£)	Total cost (£)	Profit (loss) (£)	Profit/sales (%)
X	300 000	200 000	100 000	$33\frac{1}{3}$
Y	500 000	100 000	400 000	80
Z	200 000	300 000	(100 000)	(50)
	1 000 000	600 000	400 000	40

You will see from these figures that the allocation of the joint costs bears no relationship to the revenue-producing power of the individual products. Product Z is allocated with the largest share of the joint costs but has the lowest total sales revenue; product Y is allocated with the lowest share of the joint costs but has the highest total sales revenue. The physical measures method is not therefore very satisfactory, and its weakness can be further highlighted if we assume that 80% of the production X, Y and Z were sold during the period. The appropriate inventory valuations and corresponding sales value of each product would be as follows:

Product	Inventory valuations cost[a] (£)	Sales values[a] (£)
X	40 000	60 000
Y	20 000	100 000
Z	60 000	40 000
	120 000	200 000

[a] 20% of total cost and sales revenue.

It appears inappropriate to value the stock of product Z at a price higher than its market value and at a valuation three times higher than that of product Y, when in fact product Y is more valuable in terms of potential sales revenue. A further problem is that the joint products must be measurable by the same unit of measurement. Difficult measurement problems arise in respect of products emerging from the joint process consisting of solids, liquids and gases, and it is necessary to find some common base. For example, in the case of coke, allocations can be made on the basis of theoretical yields extracted from a ton of coke.

The main advantage of using the physical measures method is simplicity, but this is outweighed by its many disadvantages.

SALES VALUE AT SPLIT-OFF POINT METHOD

When the **sales value at split-off point method** is used, joint costs are allocated to joint products in proportion to the estimated sales value of production on the assumption that higher selling prices indicate higher costs. To a certain extent, this method could better be described as a means of apportioning profits or losses, according to sales value, rather than a method for allocating costs. Using the information in Example 7.1, the allocations under the sales value method would be as follows:

Product	Units produced	Sales value (£)	Proportion of sales value to total (%)	Joint costs allocated (£)
X	40 000	300 000	30	180 000
Y	20 000	500 000	50	300 000
Z	60 000	200 000	20	120 000
		1 000 000		600 000

The revised product profit calculations would be as follows:

Product	Sales revenue (£)	Total cost (£)	Profit (loss) (£)	Profit/sales (%)
X	300 000	180 000	120 000	40
Y	500 000	300 000	200 000	40
Z	200 000	120 000	80 000	40
	1 000 000	600 000	400 000	

If we assume that 80% of the production is sold, the stock valuations would be as follows:

Inventory valuations

Product	Cost^a £	Sales values^a £
X	36 000	60 000
Y	60 000	100 000
Z	24 000	40 000
	120 000	200 000

^{a}20% of total cost and sales revenue.

The sales value method ensures that the inventory valuation does not exceed the net realizable value, but can itself be criticized since it is based on the assumption that sales revenue determines prior costs. For example, an unprofitable product with low sales revenue will be allocated with a small share of joint cost, thus giving the impression that it is generating profits.

In our discussion so far, relating to inventory valuations, we have assumed that inventories represented 20% of total production for each product. Therefore the total inventory valuation was £120 000 for both the physical measures and sales value at split-off methods of allocating joint costs. However, significant differences in the allocation of joint costs to inventories and cost of sales can occur between the two allocation methods. Consider a situation where the proportions of output for each product shown in Example 7.1 is as follows:

	Proportion of joint output sold (%)	Proportion of joint output included in the closing inventory (%)
Product X	90	10
Product Y	70	30
Product Z	90	10

Using the joint-cost allocations that we have already computed the allocations to inventories and cost of goods sold are as follows:

	Physical measures method			Sales value at split-off point method		
	Total joint costs allocated (£)	Allocated to inventories (£)	Allocated to cost of goods sold (£)	Total joint costs allocated (£)	Allocated to inventories (£)	Allocated to cost of goods sold (£)
Product X	200 000	20 000 (10%)	180 000 (90%)	180 000	18 000 (10%)	162 000 (90%)
Product Y	100 000	30 000 (30%)	70 000 (70%)	300 000	90 000 (30%)	210 000 (70%)
Product Z	300 000	30 000 (10%)	270 000 (90%)	120 000	12 000 (10%)	108 000 (90%)
Total	600 000	80 000	520 000	600 000	120 000	480 000

There is a difference of £40 000 between the two methods in the costs allocated to inventories and cost of goods sold. Hence, reported profits will also differ by £40 000. The method chosen to allocate joint costs to products thus has a significant effect both on profit measurement and inventory valuation.

NET REALIZABLE METHOD

In Example 7.1 we have assumed that all products are sold at the split-off point and that no additional costs are incurred beyond that point. In practice, however, it is likely that joint products will be processed individually beyond the split-off point, and market values may not exist for the products at this stage. To estimate the sales value at the split-off point, it is therefore necessary to use the estimated sales value at the point of sale and work backwards. This method is called the **net realizable value method**. The net realizable value at split-off point can be estimated by deducting the further processing costs at the point of sale. This approach is illustrated with the data given in Example 7.2 which is the same as Example 7.1 except that further processing costs beyond split-off point are now assumed to exist. You should now refer to Example 7.2.

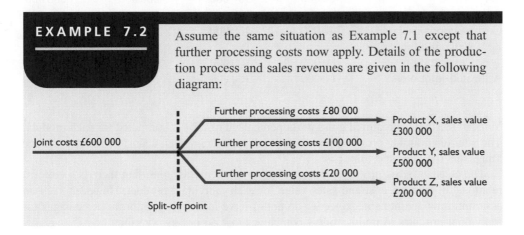

EXAMPLE 7.2 Assume the same situation as Example 7.1 except that further processing costs now apply. Details of the production process and sales revenues are given in the following diagram:

Further processing costs £80 000 → Product X, sales value £300 000
Joint costs £600 000
Further processing costs £100 000 → Product Y, sales value £500 000
Further processing costs £20 000 → Product Z, sales value £200 000
Split-off point

The calculation of the net realizable value and the allocation of joint costs using this method is as follows:

Product	Sales value (£)	Costs beyond split-off point (£)	Estimated net realizable value at split-off point (£)	Proportion to total (%)	Joint costs allocated (£)	Profit (£)	Gross profit (%)
X	300 000	80 000	220 000	27.5	165 000	55 000	18.33
Y	500 000	100 000	400 000	50.0	300 000	100 000	20.00
Z	200 000	20 000	180 000	22.5	135 000	45 000	22.50
	1 000 000	200 000	800 000		600 000	200 000	20.00

Note that the joint costs are allocated in proportion to each product's net realizable value at split-off point.

CONSTANT GROSS PROFIT PERCENTAGE METHOD

When the products are subject to further processing after split-off point and the net realizable method is used, the gross profit percentages are different for each product. In the above illustration they are 18.33% for product X, 20% for Y and 22.5% for Z. It could be argued that, since the three products arise from a single productive process, they should earn identical gross profit percentages. The **constant gross profit percentage method** allocates joint costs so that the overall gross profit percentage is identical for each individual product. From the information contained in Example 7.2 the joint costs would be allocated in such a way that the resulting gross profit percentage for each of the three products is equal to the overall gross profit percentage of 20%. Note that the gross profit percentage is calculated by deducting the *total* costs of the three products (£800 000) from the *total* sales (£1 000 000) and expressing the profit (£200 000) as a percentage of sales. The calculations are as follows:

	Product X (£)	Product Y (£)	Product Z (£)	Total (£)
Sales value	300 000	500 000	200 000	1 000 000
Gross profit (20%)	60 000	100 000	40 000	200 000
Cost of goods sold	240 000	400 000	160 000	800 000
Less separable further processing costs	80 000	100 000	20 000	200 000
Allocated joint costs	160 000	300 000	140 000	600 000

You can see that the required gross profit percentage of 20% is computed for each product. The additional further processing costs for each product are then deducted, and the balance represents the allocated joint costs.

The constant gross profit percentage method implicitly assumes that there is a uniform relationship between cost and sales value for each individual product. However, such an assumption is questionable, since we do not observe identical gross profit percentages for individual products in multi-product companies that do not involve joint costs.

COMPARISON OF METHODS

What factors should be considered in selecting the most appropriate method of allocating joint costs? The cause-and-effect criterion, described in Chapter 4, cannot be used because there is no cause-and-effect relationship between the *individual* products and the incurrence of joint costs. Joint costs are caused by *all* products and not by individual products. Where cause-and-effect relationships cannot be established allocations ought to based on the benefits received criterion. If benefits received cannot be measured costs should be allocated based on the principle of equity or fairness. The net realizable method or the sales value at split-off point are the methods that best meet the benefits received criterion. The latter also has the added advantage of simplicity if sales values at the split-off point exist. It is also difficult to estimate the net realizable value in industries where there are numerous subsequent further processing stages and multiple split-off points. Similar measurement problems can also apply with the physical measures methods. In some industries a common denominator for physical measures for each product does not exist. For example, the output of the joint process may consist of a combination of solids, liquids and gases.

The purpose for which joint-cost allocations are used is also important. Besides being required for inventory valuation and profit measurement joint-cost allocations may be used as a mechanism for setting selling prices. For example, some utilities recharge their customers for usage of joint facilities. If market prices do not exist selling prices are likely to be determined by adding a suitable profit margin to the costs allocated to the products. The method used to allocate joint costs will therefore influence product costs, and in turn, the selling price. If external market prices do not exist it is illogical to use sales value methods to allocate joint costs. This would involve what is called circular reasoning because cost allocations determine selling prices, which in turn affect cost allocations, which will also lead to further changes in selling prices and sales revenues. For pricing purposes a physical measures method should be used if external market prices do not exist. What methods do companies actually use? Little empirical evidence exists apart from a UK survey by Slater and Wootton (1984). Their survey findings are presented in Exhibit 7.1. You will see that a physical measures method is most widely used. In practice firms are likely to use a method where the output from the joint

EXHIBIT 7.1

Surveys of company practice

A survey of UK chemical and oil refining companies by Slater and Wootton (1984) reported the following methods of allocating joint costs:

	%
Physical measures method	76
Sales value method	5
Negotiated basis	19
Other	14

Note
The percentages add up to more than 100% because some companies used more than one method.

The analysis by industry indicated that the following methods were used:

Type of company	Predominant cost allocation method used
Petrochemicals	Sales value at split-off point or estimated net realizable method
Coal processing	Physical measures method
Coal chemicals	Physical measures method
Oil refining	No allocation of joint costs

The authors of the survey noted that it was considered by the majority of oil refineries that the complex nature of the process involved, and the vast number of joint product outputs, made it impossible to establish any meaningful cost allocation between products.

process can be measured without too much difficulty. Establishing a common output measure is extremely difficult in some organizations. To overcome this problem they value inventories at their estimated net realizable value minus a normal profit margin.

Irrelevance of joint cost allocations for decision-making

Our previous discussion has concentrated on the allocation of joint costs for inventory valuation and profit measurement. Joint product costs that have been computed for inventory valuation are entirely inappropriate for decision-making. For decision-making relevant costs should be used – these represent the incremental costs relating to a decision. Therefore costs that will be unaffected by a decision are classed as irrelevant. Joint-cost allocations are thus irrelevant for decision-making. Consider the information presented in Example 7.3.

EXAMPLE 7.3

The Adriatic Company incurs joint product costs of £1 000 000 for the production of two joint products, X and Y. Both products can be sold at split-off point. However, if additional costs of £60 000 are incurred on product Y then it can be converted into product Z and sold for £10 per unit. The joint costs and the sales revenue at split-off point are illustrated in the following diagram:

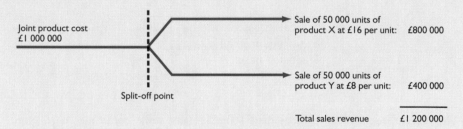

You are requested to advise management whether or not product Y should be converted into product Z.

The joint cost of £1 000 000 will be incurred irrespective of which decision is taken, and is not relevant for this decision. The information which is required for the decision is a comparison of the additional costs with the additional revenues from converting product Y into product Z. The following information should therefore be provided:

Additional revenue and costs from converting product Y into product Z	**(£)**
Additional revenues (50 000 × £2)	100 000
Additional conversion costs	60 000
Additional profit from conversion	40 000

The proof that profits will increase by £40 000 if conversion takes place is as follows:

	Convert to product Z (£)	**Do not convert (£)**
Sales	1 300 000	1 200 000
Total costs	1 060 000	1 000 000
Profits	240 000	200 000

The general rule is that it will be profitable to extend the processing of a joint product so long as the additional revenues exceed the additional costs, but note that the variable portion of the joint costs will be relevant for some decisions.

Accounting for by-products

By-products are products that have a minor sales value and that emerge incidentally from the production of the major product. As the major objective of the company is to produce the joint products, it can justifiably be argued that the joint costs should be allocated only to the joint products and that the by-products should not be allocated with any portion of the joint cost that are incurred before the split-off point. Any costs that are incurred in producing by-products after the split-off point can justifiably be charged to the by-product, since such costs are incurred for the benefit of the by-product only.

By-product revenues or by-product net revenues (the sales revenue of the by-product less the additional further processing costs after the split-off point) should be deducted from the cost of the joint products or the main product from which it emerges. Consider Example 7.4

EXAMPLE 7.4

The Neopolitan Company operates a manufacturing process which produces joint products A and B and by-product C. The joint costs of the manufacturing process are £3 020 000, incurred in the manufacture of:

Product A	30 000 kg
Product B	50 000 kg
Product C	5 000 kg

By-product C requires further processing at a cost of £1 per kg, after which it can be sold at £5 per kg.

None of the joint costs shown in Example 7.4 is allocated to the by-product but the further processing costs of £5000 (5000 kg × £1) are charged to the by-product. The net revenues from the by-product of £20 000 (sales revenue of £25 000 less further processing costs of £5000) are deducted from the costs of the joint process (£3 020 000). Thus joint costs of £3 000 000 will be allocated to joint products A and B using one of the allocation methods described in this chapter. The accounting entries for the by-product will be as follows:

Dr By-product stock (5000 × £4)	20 000	
Cr Joint process WIP acount		20 000

With the net revenue due from the production of the by-product:

Dr By-product stock	5000	
Cr Cash		5000

With the separable manufacturing costs incurred:

Dr Cash	25 000	
Cr By-product stock		25 000

With the value of by-products sales for the period.

By-products, scrap and waste

The terms 'by-products', 'scrap' and 'waste' are used to refer to outputs with little or no value. Because different people use these different terms to refer to the same thing, we shall briefly discuss the distinction between them.

Waste is a term used to describe material that has no value, or even negative value if it has to be disposed of at some cost. Examples include gases, sawdust, smoke and other unsaleable residues from the manufacturing process. Waste presents no accounting problems because it has no sales value, and therefore it is not included in the stock valuation.

By-products, as we have already seen, are those products that have a minor sales value and that emerge incidentally from the production of the major products.

Scrap also emerges as a consequence of the joint production process, but it is distinct from by-products in the sense that it is the leftover part of raw materials, whereas by-products are different from the material that went into the production process. The term 'scrap' is usually limited to material that has some minor sales value. Metal shavings with a minor sales value would normally be classified as scrap. When a product of minor sales value is processed beyond the split-off point, it should be considered as a by-product and not scrap, although the fact that a product will not be processed beyond the split-off point does not necessarily mean that it should be considered as scrap. The major distinguishing feature is that by-products are different from the materials that went into the production process.

The accounting procedures for scrap and by-products are fairly similar, and the accounting treatment which has already been outlined for by-products can also be applied to scrap.

Summary

The distinguishing feature of joint products and by-products is that they are not separately identifiable as different products before the split-off point. To meet the requirements of financial accounting, it is necessary to trace all product-related costs to products so that costs can be allocated to inventories and to the cost of goods sold. Consequently, joint costs need to be allocated to products. The allocation methods that we have considered are based on physical volume, sales value and gross profit. We have seen that the physical units method can lead to a situation where the recorded joint product cost inventory valuation is in excess of net realizable value, and this method of allocation is not recommended.

We have established that the allocation of joint cost for decision-making is unacceptable. Such decisions should be based on a comparison of the incremental costs with the incremental revenues. This principle was examined in the light of whether to sell products at the split-off point or to process further.

We have also considered accounting for by-products and noted that by-product net revenues should be deducted from the cost of the joint production process prior to allocating the costs to the individual joint products.

Finally, since the terms 'by-products', 'scrap' and 'waste' are subject to different interpretations, we have considered briefly the distinguishing features of these items.

Key Terms and Concepts

by-products (p. 164, 173, 174)
constant gross profit percentage method (p. 170)
further processing costs (p. 164)
joint products (p. 163)
net realizable value method (p. 169)

physical measures method (p. 165)
sales value at split-off point method (p. 167)
scrap (p. 174)
split-off point (p. 164)
waste (p. 174)

Key Examination Points

It is necessary to apportion joint costs to joint products for inventory valuation and profit measurement purposes. Remember that costs calculated for inventory valuation purposes should not be used for decision-making purposes. Examination questions normally require joint product profit calculations and the presentation of information as to whether a product should be sold at the split-off point or further processed. (See review problems 3 and 4 for an example of typical questions.) A common mistake with the latter requirement is to include joint cost apportionments. You should compare incremental revenues with incremental costs and indicate that in the short term joint costs are not relevant to the decision to sell at the split-off point or process further.

Review Problems

(For additional problems without answers relating to the content of this chapter you should refer to pages 458–466.)

1 A company operates a process which produces three joint products – K, P and Z. The costs of operating this process during September amounted to £117 000. During the month the output of the three products was:

K	2000 litres
P	4500 litres
Z	3250 litres

P is further processed at a cost of £9.00 per litre. The actual loss of the second process was 10% of the input which was normal. Products K and Z are sold without further processing.

The final selling prices of each of the products are:

K	£20.00 per litre
P	£25.00 per litre
Z	£18.00 per litre

Joint costs are attributed to products on the basis of output volume.

The profit attributed to product P was:

A £ 6 750
B £12 150
C £13 500
D £16 200
E £18 000

CIMA Stage 2

2 (a) Distinguish between the cost accounting treatment of joint products and of by-products. (*3 marks*)

(b) A company operates a manufacturing process which produces joint products A and B and by-product C.

Manufacturing costs for a period total £272 926, incurred in the manufacture of:

Product A 16 000 kg (selling price £6.10/kg)
Product B 53 200 kg (selling price £7.50/kg)
Product C 2 770 kg (selling price £0.80/kg)

Required:
Calculate the cost per kg (to three decimal places of a pound £) of products A and B in the period, using market values to apportion joint costs. (*5 marks*)

(c) In another of the company's processes, product X is manufactured using raw materials P and T, which are mixed in the proportions 1 : 2.

Material purchase prices are:

P £5.00 per kg
T £1.60 per kg

Normal weight loss 5% is expected during the process.

In the period just ended 9130 kg of Product X were manufactured from 9660 kg of raw materials. Conversion costs in the period were £23 796. There was no work in progress at the beginning or end of the period.

Required:
Prepare the product X process account for the period. (*6 marks*)
(*Total 14 marks*)
ACCA Foundation Paper 3

3 The marketing director of your company has expressed concern about product X, which for some time has shown a loss, and has stated that some action will have to be taken.

Product X is produced from material A which is one of two raw materials jointly produced by passing chemicals through a process.

Representative data for the process is as follows:

Output (kg):	
Material A	10 000
Material B	30 000
Process B (£):	
Raw material	83 600
Conversion costs	58 000

Joint costs are apportioned to the two raw materials according to the weight of output.

Production costs incurred in converting material A into product X are £1.80 per kg of material A used. A yield of 90% is achieved. Product X is sold for £5.60 per kg. Material B is sold without further processing for £6.00 per kg.

Required:
(a) Calculate the profit/loss per kg of product X and material B, respectively. (*7 marks*)
(b) Comment upon the marketing director's concern, advising him whether you consider any action should be taken. (*7 marks*)
(c) Demonstrate an alternative joint cost apportionment for product X and comment briefly upon this alternative method of apportionment. (*8 marks*)
(*Total 22 marks*)
ACCA Level 1 Costing

4 A process costing £200 000 produces 3 products – A, B and C. Output details are as follows:

Product A	6 000 litres
Product B	10 000 litres
Product C	20 000 tonnes

Each product may be sold at the completion of the process as follows:

**Sales value at the
end of the first process**

Product A	£10 per litre
Product B	£4 per litre
Product C	£10 per tonne

Alternatively, further processing of each individual product can be undertaken to produce an enhanced product thus:

	Subsequent processing costs	Sales value after final process
Enhanced Product A	£14 per litre	£20 per litre
Enhanced Product B	£2 per litre	£8 per litre
Enhanced Product C	£6 per tonne	£16 per tonne

Required:
(a) Explain the following terms:
    (i) normal process loss;
    (ii) joint product;
    (iii) by-product;
    and state the appropriate costing treatments for normal process loss and for by-products.   *(10 marks)*
(b) Calculate the apportionment of joint process costs to products A, B and C above.
                                      (8 marks)
(c) Explain whether the initial process should be undertaken and which, if any, of the enhanced products should be produced.
                                      (7 marks)
                             (Total 25 marks)
                                          AAT

Solutions to Review Problems

SOLUTION 1

	(£)
Joint costs apportioned to P $(4500/9750 \times £117\,000) =$	54 000
Further processing costs $(4500 \times £9) =$	40 500
Total cost	94 500
Sales revenues $(4050 \times £25)$	101 250
Profit	6 750

Answer $= A$

SOLUTION 2

(a) Joint products and by-products arise in situations where the production of one product makes inevitable the production of other products. When a group of individual products is simultaneously produced, and each product has a significant relative sales value, the outputs are usually called joint products. Those products that are part of the simultaneous processes and that have a *minor* sales value when compared to the joint products are called by-products.

   Because by-products are of relatively *minor* sales value their net revenues are deducted from the joint processing costs before they are allocated to the joint products.

(b) Costs to apportion to joint products: Joint process costs (£272 926) − Revenues from by-product C $(2770 \times £0.80) = £270\,710$.

Market value of output:	(£)
Joint product A $(16\,000\,\text{kg} \times £6.10) =$	97 600
Joint product B $(53\,200\,\text{kg} \times £7.50) =$	399 000
	496 600

Apportionment of joint costs:	
Product A $(£97\,600/£496\,600 \times £270\,710) =$	£53 204
Product B $(£399\,000/£496\,600 \times £270\,710) =$	£217 506
	£270 710

Cost per kg:
Product A $= £53\,204/16\,000 = £3.325$
Product B $= £217\,506/53\,200 = £4.088$

(c) Production costs:

		(£)
Material P:	3220 kg at £5 per kg $=$	16 100
Material T:	6440 kg at £1.60 per kg $=$	10 304
	9660	26 404
Conversion costs		23 796
		50 200

Analysis of output:	(kg)
Completed production	9130
Normal loss $(5\% \times 9660)$	483
Abnormal loss (Balance)	47
Total input	9660

Cost per kg $=$

$$\frac{\text{Cost of production (£50\,200)}}{\text{Expected output (9660 kg} - 483 \text{ kg)}} = £5.47$$

Process account

	(Units)	(£)		(Units)	(£)
Materials	9660	26 404	Normal loss	483	—
Conversion cost		23 796	Abnormal loss (1)	47	257
			Output (2)	9130	49 943
		50 200			50 200

Notes:

(1) 47 kg × £5.47 = £257

(2) 9130 kg × £5.47 = £49 943

SOLUTION 3

(a)

	Product X (£)	Material B (£)
Apportionment of joint costs (W1)	35 400	106 200
Further processing costs	18 000	—
	53 400	106 200
Sales (W2)	50 400	180 000
Profit/(loss)	(3 000)	73 800
Profit/(loss) per kg (W3)	(0.33)	2.46

Workings:

(W1) X = (£141 600/40 000 kg) × 10 000 kg
 B = (£141 600/40 000 kg) × 30 000 kg

(W2) X = 9000 kg at £5.60, B = 30 000 × £6

(W3) X = £3000/9000 kg, B = £73 800/30 000 kg

(b) The answer should stress that a joint product's costs cannot be considered in isolation from those of other joint products. If product X was abandoned the joint costs apportioned to X would still continue and would have to be absorbed by material B. Therefore no action should be taken on product X without also considering the implications for material B. Note that the process as a whole is profitable. The decision to discontinue product X should be based on a comparison of those costs which would be avoidable if X were discontinued with the lost sales revenue from product X. Joint costs apportionments are appropriate for stock valuation purposes but not for decision-making purposes.

(c) An alternative method is to apportion joint costs on the basis of net realizable value at split-off point. The calculations are as follows:

	Sales value	Costs beyond split-off point	Net-realizable value at split-off point	Joint cost apportionment
Product X	50 400	18 000	32 400	21 600 (W1)
Material A	180 000	—	180 000	120 000 (W2)
			212 400	141 600

Workings:

(W1) (£32 400/£212 400) × £141 600

(W2) (£180 000/£212 400) × £141 600

The revised profit calculation for product X is:

		(£)
Sales		50 400
Less Joint costs	21 600	
Processing costs	18 000	39 600
Profit		10 800
Profit per kg		£1.20 (£10 800/9000 kg)

Apportionment methods based on sales value normally ensure that if the process as a whole is profitable, then each of the joint products will be shown to be making a profit. Consequently it is less likely that incorrect decisions will be made.

SOLUTION 4

(a) See Chapters 6 and 7 for an explanation of the meaning of each of these terms.

(b) No specific apportionment method is asked for in this problem. It is recommended that the joint costs should be apportioned (see Chapter 7) according to the sales value at split-off point:

Product	Sales value (£)	Proportion to total (%)	Joint costs apportioned (£)
A	60 000	20	40 000
B	40 000	13.33	26 660
C	200 000	66.67	133 340
	300 000	100.00	200 000

(c) Assuming all of the output given in the problem can be sold, the initial process is profitable – the sales revenue is £300 000 and the joint costs are £200 000. To determine whether further processing is profitable the additional revenues should be compared with the additional relevant costs:

	A (£)	B (£)	C (£)
Additional relevant revenues	10 (20 − 10)	4 (8 − 4)	6 (16 − 10)
Additional relevant costs	14	2	6
Excess of relevant revenue over costs	(4)	2	=

Product B should be processed further, product A should not be processed further, and if product C is processed further, then profits will remain unchanged.

Income effects of alternative cost accumulation systems

In the previous chapters we looked at the procedures necessary to ascertain product or job costs for inventory valuation to meet the requirements of external reporting. The approach that we adopted was to allocate all manufacturing cost to products, and to value unsold stocks at their total cost of manufacture. Non-manufacturing costs were not allocated to the products but were charged directly to the profit statement and excluded from the inventory valuation. A costing system based on these principles is known as an **absorption** or **full costing system**.

In this chapter we are going to look at an alternative costing system known as **variable costing**, **marginal costing** or **direct costing**. Under this alternative system, only variable manufacturing costs are assigned to products and included in the inventory valuation. Fixed manufacturing costs are not allocated to the product, but are considered as period costs and charged directly to the profit statement. Both absorption costing and variable costing systems are in complete agreement regarding the treatment of non-manufacturing costs as period costs. The disagreement between the proponents of absorption costing and the proponents of variable costing is concerned with whether or not manufacturing fixed overhead should be regarded as a period cost or a product cost. An illustration of the different treatment of fixed manufacturing overhead for both absorption and variable costing systems is shown in Exhibit 8.1.

Learning objectives

After studying this chapter, you should be able to:

- explain the differences between an absorption costing and a variable costing system;
- prepare profit statements based on a variable costing and absorption costing system;
- explain the difference in profits between variable and absorption costing profit calculations;
- explain the arguments for and against variable and absorption costing.

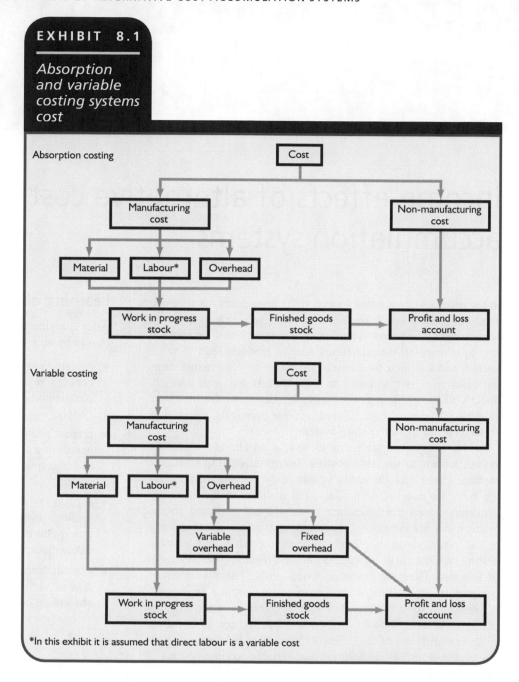

EXHIBIT 8.1

Absorption and variable costing systems cost

*In this exhibit it is assumed that direct labour is a variable cost

External and internal reporting

Many writers have argued the cases for and against variable costing for inventory valuation for external reporting. One important requirement for external reporting is consistency. It would be unacceptable if companies changed their methods of inventory valuation from year to year. In addition, inter-company comparison would be difficult if some companies valued their stocks on an absorption cost basis while others did so on a variable cost basis. Furthermore, the users of external accounting reports need reassurance that the published financial statements have been prepared in accordance with generally accepted standards of good accounting practice. Therefore there is a strong case for the acceptance of one method of stock valuation for external reporting. In the UK a Statement of Standard Accounting Practice on Stocks and Work in Progress was published by the Accounting Standards Committee (SSAP 9). This states:

> In order to match costs and revenue, cost of stocks and work in progress should comprise that expenditure which has been incurred in the normal course of business in bringing the product or service to its present location and condition. Such costs will include all related production overheads, even though these may accrue on a time basis.

The effect of this statement in SSAP 9 was to require absorption costing for external reporting and for non-manufacturing costs to be treated as period costs. The external financial reporting regulations in most other countries (see Exhibit 8.4 shown on page 189) also require that companies adopt absorption costing.

In spite of the fact that absorption costing is required for external reporting, the variable costing versus absorption costing debate is still of considerable importance for internal reporting. Management normally require profit statements at monthly or quarterly intervals, and will no doubt wish to receive separate profit statements for each major product group or segment of the business. This information is particularly useful in evaluating the performance of divisional managers. Management must therefore decide whether absorption costing or variable costing provides the more meaningful information in assessing the economic and managerial performance of the different segments of the business.

However, before discussing the arguments for and against absorption and variable costing, let us look at a simple illustration of both methods using Example 8.1. To keep things simple we shall assume that the company in this example produces only one product using a single overhead rate for the company as a whole, with units of output being used as the allocation base. These assumptions are very simplistic. As indicated in Chapter 4, most companies are multi-product companies and they do not use a single company or plant-wide overhead rate. Instead, many cost centres are established, each with their own allocation base. Nevertheless, the same general principles apply to both simplistic and complex product settings relating to the impact that variable and absorption costing have on profit measurement and inventory valuation. A more complex example would not enhance your understanding of the issues involved. You should now refer to Example 8.1.

Variable costing

The variable costing profit statements are shown in Exhibit 8.2. You will see that when a system of variable costing is used, the product cost is £6 per unit, and includes variable costs since only variable costs are assigned to the product. In period 1 production is 150 000 units at a variable cost of £6 per unit. The total fixed costs are then added separately to produce a total manufacturing cost of £1 200 000. Note that the fixed costs of £300 000 are assigned to the period in which they are incurred.

In period 2, 150 000 units are produced but only 120 000 are sold. Therefore 30 000 units remain in stock at the end of the period. In order to match costs with revenues, the sales of 120 000 units should be matched with costs for 120 000. As 150 000 units were produced, we need to value the 30 000 units in stock and deduct this sum from the production cost. Using the variable costing system, the 30 000 units in stock are valued at £6 per unit. A closing inventory of £180 000 will then be deducted from the production costs, giving a cost of sales figure of £720 000. Note that the closing inventory valuation does not include any fixed overheads.

EXAMPLE 8.1

The following information is available for periods 1–6 for the Samuelson Company:

	(£)
Unit selling price	10
Unit variable cost	6
Fixed costs per each period	300 000

The company produces only one product. Budgeted activity is expected to average 150 000 units per period, and production and sales for each period are as follows:

	Period 1	Period 2	Period 3	Period 4	Period 5	Period 6
Units sold (000's)	150	120	180	150	140	160
Units produced (000's)	150	150	150	150	170	140

There were no opening stocks at the start of period 1, and the actual manufacturing fixed overhead incurred was £300 000 per period. We shall also assume that non-manufacturing overheads are £100 000 per period.

The 30 000 units of closing inventory in period 2 becomes the opening inventory for period 3 and therefore an expense for this period. The production cost for the 150 000 units made in period 3 is added to this opening inventory valuation. The overall effect is that costs for 180 000 units are matched against sales for 180 000 units. The profits for periods 4–6 are calculated in the same way.

Absorption costing

Let us now consider in Exhibit 8.3 the profit calculations when closing stocks are valued on an absorption costing basis. With the absorption costing method, a share of the fixed production overheads are allocated to individual products and are included in the products' production cost. Fixed overheads are assigned to products by establishing overhead absorption rates as described in Chapter 4. To establish the overhead rate we must divide the fixed overheads of £300 000 for the period by an appropriate denominator level. Most companies use an annual budgeted activity measure of the overhead allocation base as the denominator level. Our allocation base in Example 8.1 is units of output and we shall assume that the annual budgeted output is 1 800 000 units giving an average for each monthly period of 150 000 units. Therefore the budgeted fixed overhead rate is £2 per unit (£300 000/150 000 units). The product cost now consists of a variable cost (£6) plus a fixed manufacturing cost (£2), making a total of £8 per unit. Hence, the production cost for period 1 is £1 200 000 (150 000 units at £8).

Now compare the absorption costing statement (Exhibit 8.3) with the variable costing statement (Exhibit 8.2) for period 1. With absorption costing, the fixed cost is included in the production cost figure, whereas with variable costing only the variable cost is included. With variable costing, the fixed cost is allocated separately and is not included in the cost of sales figure. Note also that the closing inventory of 30 000 units for period 2 is valued at £8 per unit in the absorption costing statement, whereas the closing inventory is valued at only £6 in the variable costing statement.

<table>
<tr>
<td rowspan="2" style="background:black;color:white">

EXHIBIT 8.2

Variable costing statements
</td>
<td>In calculating profits, the matching principle that has been applied in the absorption costing statement is the same way as that described for variable costing. However, complications arise in periods 5 and 6; in period 5, 170 000 units were</td>
</tr>
</table>

	Period 1 (£000's)	Period 2 (£000's)	Period 3 (£000's)	Period 4 (£000's)	Period 5 (£000's)	Period 6 (£000's)
Opening stock	—	—	180	—	—	180
Production cost	900	900	900	900	1020	840
Closing stock	—	(180)	—	—	(180)	(60)
Cost of sales	900	720	1080	900	840	960
Fixed costs	300	300	300	300	300	300
Total costs	1200	1020	1380	1200	1140	1260
Sales	1500	1200	1800	1500	1400	1600
Gross profit	300	180	420	300	260	340
Less non-manufacturing costs	100	100	100	100	100	100
Net profit	200	80	320	200	160	240

produced, so the production cost of £1 360 000 includes fixed overheads of £340 000 (170 000 units at £2). The total fixed overheads incurred for the period are only £300 000, so £40 000 too much has been allocated. This over-recovery of fixed overhead is recorded as a **period cost adjustment**. (A full explanation of under- and over-recoveries of overheads and the reasons for period cost adjustments was presented in Chapter 4; if you are unsure of this concept, please refer back now to the section headed 'Under- and over-recovery of overheads'.) Note also that the under- or over-recovery of fixed overheads is also called **volume variance**.

In period 6, 140 000 units were produced at a cost of £1 120 000, which included only £280 000 (140 000 units at £2) for fixed overheads. As a result, there is an under-recovery of £20 000, which is written off as a period cost. You can see that an under- or over-recovery of fixed overhead occurs whenever actual production differs from the budgeted average level of activity of 150 000 units, since the calculation of the fixed overhead rate of £2 per unit was based on the assumption that actual production would be 150 000 units per period. Note that both variable and absorption costing systems do not assign non-manufacturing costs to products for stock valuation.

Variable costing and absorption costing: a comparison of their impact on profit

A comparison of the variable costing and absorption costing statements produced from the information contained in Example 8.1 reveals the following differences in profit calculations:

	Period 1 (£000's)	Period 2 (£000's)	Period 3 (£000's)	Period 4 (£000's)	Period 5 (£000's)	Period 6 (£000's)
Opening stock	—	—	240	—	—	240
Production cost	1200	1200	1200	1200	1360	1120
Closing stock	—	(240)	—	—	(240)	(80)
Cost of sales	1200	960	1440	1200	1120	1280
Adjustments for under-/(over-) recovery of overhead	—	—	—	—	(40)	20
Total costs	1200	960	1440	1200	1080	1300
Sales	1500	1200	1800	1500	1400	1600
Gross profit	300	240	360	300	320	300
Less non-manufacturing costs	100	100	100	100	100	100
Net profit	200	140	260	200	220	200

(a) The profits calculated under the absorption costing and variable costing systems are identical for periods 1 and 4.

(b) The absorption costing profits are higher than the variable costing profits in periods 2 and 5.

(c) The variable costing profits are higher than the absorption costing profits in periods 3 and 6.

Let us now consider each of these in a little more detail.

PRODUCTION EQUALS SALES

In periods 1 and 4 the profits are the same for both methods of costing; in both periods production is equal to sales, and inventories will neither increase nor decrease. Therefore if opening inventories exist, the same amount of fixed overhead will be carried forward as an expense to be included in the current period in the opening inventory valuation as will be deducted in the closing inventory valuation from the production cost figure. The overall effect is that, with an absorption costing system, the only fixed overhead that will be included as an expense for the period will be the amount of fixed overhead that is incurred for the period. Thus, whenever sales are equal to production the profits will be the same for both the absorption costing and variable costing systems.

Production exceeds sales

In periods 2 and 5 the absorption costing system produces higher profits; in both periods production exceeds sales. Profits are higher for absorption costing when production is in excess of sales, because inventories are increasing. The effect of this is that a greater amount of fixed overheads in the closing inventory is being deducted from the expenses of the period than is being brought forward in the opening inventory for the period. For example, in period 2 the opening inventory is zero and no fixed overheads are brought forward from the previous period. However, a closing inventory of 30 000 units means that a £60 000 fixed overhead has to be deducted from the production cost for the period. In other words, only £240 000 is being allocated for fixed overhead with the absorption costing system, whereas the variable costing system allocates the £300 000 fixed overhead incurred for the period. The effect of this is that profits are £60 000 greater with the absorption costing system. As a general rule, if production is in excess of sales, the absorption costing system will show a higher profit than the variable costing system.

Sales exceed production

In periods 3 and 6 the variable costing system produces higher profits; in both periods sales exceed production. When this situation occurs, inventories decline and a greater amount of fixed overheads will need to be brought forward as an expense in the opening inventory than is being deducted in the closing inventory adjustment. For example, with the absorption costing system, in period 6, 30 000 units of opening inventory are brought forward, so that fixed costs of £60 000 are included in the inventory valuation. However, a closing inventory of 10 000 units requires a deduction of £20 000 fixed overheads from the production costs. The overall effect is that an additional £40 000 fixed overheads is included as an expense within the stock movements, and a total of £340 000 fixed overheads is allocated for the period. The variable costing system, on the other hand, would allocate fixed overheads for the period of only £300 000. As a result, profits are £40 000 greater with the variable costing system. As a general rule, if sales are in excess of production, the variable costing system will show a higher profit than the absorption costing system.

Impact of sales fluctuations

The profit calculations for an absorption costing system can produce some strange results. For example, in period 6 the sales volume has increased but profits have declined, in spite of the fact that both the selling price and the cost structure have remained unchanged. A manager whose performance is being judged in period 6 is likely to have little confidence in an accounting system that shows a decline in profits when sales volume has increased and the cost structure and selling price have not changed. The opposite occurs in period 5. In this period the sales volume declines but profit increases. The situations in periods 5 and 6 arise because the under- or over-recovery of fixed overhead is treated as a period cost, and such adjustments can at times give a misleading picture of profits.

In contrast, the variable costing profit calculations show that when sales volume increases profit also increases. Alternatively, when sales volume decreases, profit also decreases. These relationships continue as long as the selling price and cost structure remain unchanged. Looking again at the variable costing profit calculations, you will note that profit declines in period 5 when the sales volume declines, and increases in period 6 when the sales volume also increases. The reasons for these changes are that, with a system of variable costing, profit is a function of sales volume only, when the selling price and cost structure remain unchanged. However, with absorption costing, profit is a function of both sales volume and production volume.

A mathematical model of the profit functions

In Appendix 8.1 the following formula is developed to model the profit function for an absorption costing system when unit costs remain unchanged throughout the period:

$$\text{OPBT}_{AC} = (\text{ucm} - \text{ufmc})Q_s + (\text{ufmc} \times Q_p) - \text{FC} \qquad (8.1)$$

where

$\text{ucm} = $ Contribution margin per unit (i.e. selling price per unit $-$ variable cost per unit)
$\text{ufmc} = $ Pre-determined fixed manufacturing overhead per unit of output
$Q_p = $ Number of units produced
$Q_s = $ Number of units sold
$\text{FC} = $ Total fixed costs (manufacturing and non-manufacturing)
$\text{OPBT}_{AC} = $ Operating profit before taxes for the period (Absorption costing)
$(\text{OPBT}_{VC}) = $ Operating profit before taxes for the period (Variable costing)

Applying formula 8.1 to the data given in Example 8.1 gives the following profit function:

$$(\pounds 4 - \pounds 2)Q_s + (\pounds 2 \times Q_p) - \pounds 400\,000 = \pounds 2Q_s + \pounds 2Q_p - \pounds 400\,000$$

Applying the above profit function to periods 4–6 we get:

Period 4 $= \pounds 2(150\,000) + \pounds 2(150\,000) - \pounds 400\,000 = \pounds 200\,000$
Period 5 $= \pounds 2(140\,000) + \pounds 2(170\,000) - \pounds 400\,000 = \pounds 220\,000$
Period 6 $= \pounds 2(160\,000) + \pounds 2(140\,000) - \pounds 400\,000 = \pounds 200\,000$

When production equals sales identical profits with an absorption and variable costing system are reported. Therefore formula 8.1 converts to the following variable costing profit function if we let $Q_s = Q_p$:

$$\text{Variable costing operating profit } (\text{OPBT}_{VC}) = \text{ucm} \cdot Q_s - \text{FC} \qquad (8.2)$$

Using the data given in Example 8.1 the profit function is:

$$\pounds 4Q_s - \pounds 400\,000$$

Applying the above profit function to periods 4–6 we get:

Period 4 $= \pounds 4(150\,000) - \pounds 400\,000 = \pounds 200\,000$
Period 5 $= \pounds 4(140\,000) - \pounds 400\,000 = \pounds 160\,000$
Period 6 $= \pounds 4(160\,000) - \pounds 400\,000 = \pounds 240\,000$

The difference between the reported operating profits for an absorption costing and a variable costing system can be derived by deducting formulae 8.2 from 8.1 giving:

$$\text{ufmc}(Q_p - Q_s) \qquad (8.3)$$

If you look closely at the above term you will see that it represents the inventory change (in units) multiplied by the fixed manufacturing overhead rate. Applying formula 8.3 to period 5 the inventory change $(Q_p - Q_s)$ is 30 000 units (positive) so that absorption costing profits exceed variable costing profits by £60 000 (30 000 units at £2 overhead rate). For an explanation of how formulae (8.1) and (8.2) are derived you should refer to Appendix 8.1.

Some arguments in support of variable costing

VARIABLE COSTING PROVIDES MORE USEFUL INFORMATION FOR DECISION-MAKING

The separation of fixed and variable costs helps to provide relevant information about costs for making decisions. Relevant costs are required for a variety of short-term decisions, for example whether to make a component internally or to purchase externally, as well as problems relating to product-mix. These decisions will be discussed in Chapter 10. In addition, the estimation of costs for different levels of activities requires that costs be split into their fixed and variable elements. The assumption is that only with a variable costing system will such an analysis of costs be available. It is therefore assumed that projection of future costs and revenues for different activity levels, and the use of relevant cost decision-making techniques, are possible only if a variable costing system is adopted. There is no reason, however, why an absorption costing system cannot be used for profit measurement and inventory valuation and costs can be analysed into their fixed and variable elements for decision-making. The advantage of variable costing is that the analysis of variable and fixed costs is highlighted. (Such an analysis is not a required feature of an absorption costing system.)

VARIABLE COSTING REMOVES FROM PROFIT THE EFFECT OF INVENTORY CHANGES

We have seen that, with variable costing, profit is a function of sales volume, whereas, with absorption costing, profit is a function of both sales and production. We have also learned, using absorption costing principles, that it is possible for profit to decline when sales volumes increase. Where stock levels are likely to fluctuate significantly, profits may be distorted when they are calculated on an absorption costing basis, since the stock changes will significantly affect the amount of fixed overheads allocated to an accounting period.

Fluctuating stock levels are less likely to occur when one measures profits on an annual basis, but on a monthly or quarterly basis seasonal variations in sales may cause significant fluctuations. As profits are likely to be distorted by an absorption costing system, there are strong arguments for using variable costing methods when profits are measured at frequent intervals. Because frequent profit statements are presented only for management, the argument for variable costing is stronger for management accounting. A survey by Drury *et al.* (1993) relating to 300 UK companies reported that 97% of the companies prepared profit statements at monthly intervals. Financial accounts are presented for public release annually or at half-yearly intervals; because significant changes in stock levels are less likely on an annual basis, the argument for the use of variable costing in financial accounting is not as strong.

A further argument for using variable costing for internal reporting is that the internal profit statements may be used as a basis for measuring managerial performance. Managers may deliberately alter their inventory levels to influence profit when an absorption costing system is used; for example, it is possible for a manager to defer deliberately some of the fixed overhead allocation by unnecessarily increasing stocks over successive periods.

There is a limit to how long managers can continue to increase stocks, and eventually the situation will arise when it is necessary to reduce them, and the deferred fixed overheads will eventually be allocated to the periods when the inventories are reduced. Nevertheless, there is likely to remain some scope for manipulating profits in the short term. Also senior management can implement control performance measures to guard against such behaviour. For example, the reporting of performance measures that monitor changes in inventory volumes will highlight those situations where managers are manipulating profits by unnecessarily increasing inventory levels.

VARIABLE COSTING AVOIDS FIXED OVERHEADS BEING CAPITALIZED IN UNSALEABLE STOCKS

In a period when sales demand decreases, a company can end up with surplus stocks on hand. With an absorption costing system, only a portion of the fixed overheads incurred during the period will be allocated as an expense because the remainder of the fixed overhead will be included in the valuation of the surplus stocks. If these surplus stocks cannot be disposed of, the profit calculation for the current period will be misleading, since fixed overheads will have been deferred to later accounting periods. However, there may be some delay before management concludes that the stocks cannot be sold without a very large reduction in the selling price. The stocks will therefore be over-valued, and a stock write-off will be necessary in a later accounting period. The overall effect may be that the current period's profits will be overstated.

Some arguments in support of absorption costing

ABSORPTION COSTING DOES NOT UNDERSTATE THE IMPORTANCE OF FIXED COSTS

Some people argue that decisions based on a variable costing system may concentrate only on sales revenues and variable costs and ignore the fact that fixed costs must be met in the long run. For example, if a pricing decision is based on variable costs only, then sales revenue may be insufficient to cover all the costs. It is also argued that the use of an absorption costing system, by allocating fixed costs to a product, ensures that fixed costs will be covered. These arguments are incorrect. Absorption costing will not ensure that fixed costs will be recovered if actual sales volume is less than the estimate used to calculate the fixed overhead rate. For example, consider a situation where fixed costs are £100 000 and an estimated normal activity of 10 000 units is used to calculate the overhead rate. Fixed costs are recovered at £10 per unit. Assume that variable cost is £5 per unit and selling price is set at £20 (total cost plus one-third). If actual sales volume is 5000 units then total sales revenue will be £100 000 and total costs will be £125 000. Total costs therefore exceed total sales revenue. The argument that a variable costing system will cause managers to ignore fixed costs is based on the assumption that such managers are not very bright! A failure to consider fixed costs is due to faulty management and not to a faulty accounting system. Furthermore, using variable costing for inventory valuation and profit measurement still enables full cost information to be extracted for pricing decisions.

ABSORPTION COSTING AVOIDS FICTITIOUS LOSSES BEING REPORTED

In a business that relies on seasonal sales and in which production is built up outside the sales season to meet demand the full amount of fixed overheads incurred will be charged, in a variable costing system, against sales. However, in those periods where production is being built up for sales in a later season, sales revenue will be low but fixed costs will be recorded as an expense. The result is that losses will be reported during out-of-season periods, and large profits will be reported in the periods when the goods are sold.

By contrast, in an absorption costing system fixed overheads will be deferred and included in the closing inventory valuation, and will be recorded as an expense only in the period in which the goods are sold. Losses are therefore unlikely to be reported in the periods when stocks are being built up. In these circumstances absorption costing appears to provide the more logical profit calculation.

FIXED OVERHEADS ARE ESSENTIAL FOR PRODUCTION

The proponents of absorption costing argue that the production of goods is not possible if fixed manufacturing costs are not incurred. Consequently, fixed manufacturing overheads should be allocated to units produced and included in the inventory valuation.

CONSISTENCY WITH EXTERNAL REPORTING

Top management may prefer their internal profit reporting systems to be consistent with the external financial accounting absorption costing systems so that they will be congruent with the measures used by financial markets to appraise overall company performance. In a pilot study of six UK companies Hopper *et al*. (1992) observed that senior managers are primarily interested in financial accounting information because it is perceived as having a major influence on how financial markets evaluate companies and their management. If top management believe that financial accounting information does influence share prices then they are likely to use the same rules and procedures for both internal and external profit measurement and inventory valuation so that managers will focus on the same measures as those used by financial markets. Also the fact that managerial rewards are often linked to external financial measures provides a further motivation to ensure that internal accounting systems do not conflict with external financial accounting reporting requirements.

Surveys of company practice

Surveys have been undertaken in many countries relating to the use of variable costs and absorption costs. However, these surveys tend to focus on the information that is extracted from the costing system for decision-making rather than the costs that are used for inventory valuation and profit measurement. Many organizations accumulate and use absorption costs for inventory valuation but extract variable costs from the cost system for decision-making. Thus, the use of variable costs for decision-making does not imply that such costs are used for inventory valuation. Surveys that do not clearly indicate the costing method that is used for inventory valuation are therefore not included in the results reported below.

A UK study by Drury *et al.* (1993) indicated the following usage rates for internal profit measurement:

	(%)
Variable costing	13
Absorption costing	84
Other	3

A review of surveys of German organizations undertaken by Scherrer (1996) concluded that full costing is the most important system with only 12% of the responding organizations using only a variable costing system.

Similar results were observed in Spain by Saez-Torrecilla *et al.* (1996) who reported a 26% usage rate for variable costing.

In contrast, Virtanen *et al.* (1996) report that variable costing is widely used in Finland mainly because external financial accounting reporting regulations have not forced companies to use absorption costing for external reporting.

Summary

In this chapter we have examined and compared absorption costing systems and variable costing systems. With an absorption costing system, fixed manufacturing overheads are allocated to the products, and these are included in the inventory valuation. With a variable costing system, only variable manufacturing costs are assigned to the product; fixed manufacturing costs are regarded as period costs and written off to the profit and loss account. Both variable and absorption costing systems treat non-manufacturing overheads as period costs.

Illustrations of the inventory valuations and profit calculations for both systems have been presented, and we noted that when production is equal to sales, both systems yield identical profits. However, when production exceeds sales, absorption costing shows the higher profits. Variable costing yields the higher profits when sales exceed production. Nevertheless, total profits over the life of the business will be the same for both systems. Differences arise merely in the profits attributed to each accounting period.

The proponents of variable costing claim that it provides more useful information for decision-making but it has been argued that similar relevant cost information can easily be provided with an absorption costing system. The major advantage of variable costing is that profit is reflected as a function of sales, whereas in an absorption costing system profit is a function of both sales and production. For example, we have established that, with absorption costing, when all other factors remain unchanged, sales can increase but profit may decline. By contrast, with a variable costing system, when sales increase, profits also increase. A further advantage of variable costing is that fixed overheads are not capitalized in unsaleable stocks.

The arguments that we have considered in support of absorption costing include the following:

1. Absorption costing does not underestimate the importance of fixed costs.
2. Absorption costing avoids fictitious losses being reported.
3. Fixed overheads are essential to production.
4. Internal profit measurement is consistent with external reporting.

Appendix 8.1: Derivation of the profit function for an absorption costing system

Using the formulae listed in Exhibit 8A.1 the variable costing profit function can be expressed in equation form as follows:

$$\text{OPBT}_{\text{VC}} = \text{Sales} - \text{Variable manufacturing costs of goods sold}$$
$$- \text{non-manufacturing variable costs} - \text{All fixed costs}$$
$$= \text{usp.Q}_s - \text{uvmc.Q}_s - \text{uvnmc.Q}_s - \text{FC}$$
$$= \text{ucm.Q}_s - \text{FC (Note that the term contribution margin is used to}$$
$$\text{describe unit selling price less unit variable cost)} \qquad (8.\text{A1})$$

The distinguishable feature between absorption costing and variable costing relates to the timing of the recognition of fixed manufacturing overheads (FC_m) as an expense. Variable costing expenses fixed manufacturing overheads in the period that they are incurred, whereas absorption costing assigns fixed manufacturing overheads to the units produced, thus recording them as an expense in the period in which the units are sold. The only difference between the two methods is that absorption costing incorporates some of the

EXHIBIT 8.A1

Summary of notation used

ucm = Contribution margin per unit (i.e. selling price per unit − variable cost per unit)

usp = Selling price per unit

uvmc = Variable manufacturing cost per unit

uvnmc = Variable non-manufacturing cost per unit

ufmc = Pre-determined fixed manufacturing overhead per unit of output

Q_p = Number of units produced

Q_s = Number of units sold

FC = Total fixed costs (manufacturing and non-manufacturing)

FC_m = Total fixed manufacturing costs

FC_{nmc} = Total fixed manufacturing costs

$OPBT_{AC}$ = Operating profit before taxes for the period (Absorption costing)

$OPBT_{VC}$ = Operating profit before taxes for the period (Variable costing)

manufacturing fixed overheads in inventory. Therefore variable and absorption costing reported profits will differ by the amount of fixed manufacturing overheads that are included in the change in opening and closing inventories. This is equivalent to the difference between production and sales volumes multiplied by the manufacturing fixed overhead absorption rate.

We can therefore use equation (8.A1) as the basis for establishing the equation for the absorption costing profit function:

$$
\begin{aligned}
OPBT_{AC} &= ucm.Q_s - FC + (Q_p - Q_s)ufmc \\
&= ucm.Q_s - FC + (Q_p \times ufmc) - (Q_s \times ufmc) \\
&= (ucm - ufmc)Q_s + (ufmc \times Q_p) - FC \qquad (8.A2)
\end{aligned}
$$

Key Terms and Concepts

absorption costing (p. 179)
direct costing (p. 179)
full costing (p. 179)
marginal costing (p. 179)

period cost adjustment (p. 183)
variable costing (p. 179)
volume variance (p. 183)

Key Examination Points

A common mistake is for students to calculate *actual* overhead rates when preparing absorption costing profit statements. Normal or budgeted activity should be used to calculate overhead absorption rates, and this rate should be used to calculate the

production overhead cost for all periods given in the question. Do not calculate different actual overhead rates for each accounting period.

Remember not to include non-manufacturing overheads in the inventory valuations for both variable and absorption costing. Also note that variable selling overheads will vary with sales and not production. Another common mistake is not to include an adjustment for under-/over-recovery of fixed overheads when actual production deviates from the normal or budgeted production. You should note that under-/over-recovery of overhead arises only with fixed overheads and when an absorption costing system is used.

Review Problems

(For additional problems without answers relating to the content of this chapter you should refer to pages 466–471.)

1 Z Limited manufactures a single product, the budgeted selling price and variable cost details of which are as follows:

	(£)
Selling price	15.00
Variable costs per unit:	
Direct materials	3.50
Direct labour	4.00
Variable overhead	2.00

Budgeted fixed overhead costs are £60 000 per annum, charged at a constant rate each month. Budgeted production is 30 000 units per annum.

In a month when actual production was 2400 units and exceeded sales by 180 units the profit reported under absorption costing was

A   £6660
B   £7570
C   £7770
D   £8200
E   £8400

CIMA Stage 2

2 A company made 17 500 units at a total cost of £16 each. Three-quarters of the costs were variable and one-quarter fixed. 15 000 units were sold at £25 each. There were no opening stocks.

By how much will the profit calculated using absorption costing principles differ from the profit if marginal costing principles had been used?

A   The absorption costing profit would be £22 500 less.
B   The absorption costing profit would be £10 000 greater.
C   The absorption costing profit would be £135 000 greater.

D   The absorption costing profit would be £10 000 less.

CIMA Stage 1

3 A firm had opening stocks and purchases totalling 12 400 kg and closing stocks of 9600 kg. Profits using marginal costing were £76 456 and using absorption costing were £61 056.

What was the fixed overhead absorption rate per kilogram (to the nearest penny)?
A   £1.60
B   £5.50
C   £6.17
D   £6.36

CIMA Stage 1 Cost Accounting

4 Exe Limited makes a single product whose total cost per unit is budgeted to be £45. This includes fixed cost of £8 per unit based on a volume of 10 000 units per period. In a period, sales volume was 9000 units, and production volume was 11 500 units. The actual profit for the same period, calculated using absorption costing, was £42 000.

If the profit statement were prepared using marginal costing, the profit for the period
A   would be £10 000
B   would be £22 000
C   would be £50 000
D   would be £62 000
E   cannot be calculated without more information

CIMA Stage 1 Operational Cost Accounting

5 In a period, opening stocks were 12 600 units and closing stocks 14 100 units. The profit based on marginal costing was £50 400 and profit using absorption costing was £60 150. The fixed overhead absorption rate per unit (to the nearest penny) is
A   £4.00
B   £4.27

C   £4.77
D   £6.50

CIMA Stage 1 Cost Accounting

6 The unit cost of production for a firm which produces a single product is:

	(£)
Direct materials	2.60
Direct labour	3.00
Variable overhead	0.40
Fixed overhead	1.00
	7.00

The fixed overhead calculation is based on a budgeted level of activity of 150 000 units and budgeted manufacturing fixed overheads of £150 000 for each quarter. The budgeted selling and administration overheads are £100 000 per quarter (all fixed). The selling price for the product is £10 per unit. The production and sales for each quarter were:

	Quarter 1	Quarter 2	Quarter 3	Quarter 4
Production (units)	150 000	170 000	140 000	150 000
Sales (units)	150 000	140 000	160 000	160 000

There was no opening stock in Quarter 1 and you should assume that actual costs were identical to estimated costs.

You are required to:

(a) produce in columnar form absorption costing and variable costing statements;

(b) comment on the results for each quarter and the year as a whole.

7 The following data have been extracted from the budgets and standard costs of ABC Limited, a company which manufactures and sells a single product.

	£ per unit
Selling price	45.00
Direct materials cost	10.00
Direct wages cost	4.00
Variable overhead cost	2.50

Fixed production overhead costs are budgeted at £400 000 per annum. Normal production levels are thought to be 320 000 units per annum.

Budgeted selling and distribution costs are as follows:

Variable	£1.50 per unit sold
Fixed	£80 000 per annum

Budgeted administration costs are £120 000 per annum.

The following pattern of sales and production is expected during the first six months of the year:

	January–March	April–June
Sales (units)	60 000	90 000
Production (units)	70 000	100 000

There is to be no stock on 1 January.

You are required

(a) to prepare profit statements for each of the two quarters, in a columnar format, using
   (i) marginal costing, and
   (ii) absorption costing;   *(12 marks)*

(b) to reconcile the profits reported for the quarter January–March in your answer to (a) above;   *(3 marks)*

(c) to write up the production overhead control account for the quarter to 31 March, using absorption costing principles. Assume that the production overhead costs incurred amounted to £102 400 and the actual production was 74 000 units;   *(3 marks)*

(d) to state and explain briefly the benefits of using marginal costing as the basis of management reporting.   *(5 marks)*

(Total 23 marks)

CIMA Stage 1 Accounting

Solutions to Review Problems

SOLUTION 1

Fixed overhead = £2 per unit (£60 000/30 000 units)

Because production exceeded sales by 180 units a sum of £360 (180 × £2) is included in the stock valuation and not charged as an expense of the current period. Fixed overheads of £4640 (£5000 monthly cost − £360) are therefore charged as an expense for the period.

	(£)
Contribution (12 210 units sales × £5.50)	12 220
Fixed overheads charged as an expense	4 640
Profit	7 570

Answer = B

SOLUTION 2

Closing stock = 2500 units (17 500 − 15 000)

With absorption costing fixed overheads of £10 000 (2500 units × £4) are deferred as a future expense whereas marginal costing treats fixed overheads as a period expense. Therefore absorption costing will be £10 000 greater.

Answer = B

SOLUTION 3

The profit difference is due to the fixed overheads being incorporated in the stock movements with the absorption costing system.

Profit difference = £15 400 (£76 456 − £61 056)
Fixed overheads in stock movement = £15 400
Physical stock movement = 2800 kgs
Fixed overhead rate per kg = £15 400/2800 kg = £5.50 per kg

Answer = B

SOLUTION 4

Stocks have increased by 2500 units thus resulting in fixed overheads of £20 000 (2500 units at £8) being absorbed in the stock movements with the absorption costing system. Therefore the absorption costing system will record £20 000 less than the fixed overheads incurred for the period. In other words, the marginal costing system will record

£20 000 more fixed costs resulting in profit of £22 000 being reported.

Answer = B

SOLUTION 5

The profit difference is due to the fixed overheads being incorporated in the stock movements with the absorption costing system.

Profit difference = £9750 (£60 150 − £50 400)
Fixed overheads in stock movement = £9750
Physical stock movement = 1500 units
Fixed overhead rate per unit = £9750/1500 units = £6.50

Answer = D

SOLUTION 6

(a) *Variable costing profit statements:*

	Q1 (£)	Q2 (£)	Q3 (£)	Q4 (£)
Opening stock	—	—	180 000	60 000
Production at £6 per unit	900 000	1 020 000	840 000	900 000
Less closing stock (1)	—	180 000	60 000	—
Cost of sales	900 000	840 000	960 000	960 000
Sales at £10 per unit	1 500 000	1 400 000	1 600 000	1 600 000
Contribution	600 000	560 000	640 000	640 000
Fixed factory overheads	150 000	150 000	150 000	150 000
Fixed selling and administration overheads	100 000	100 000	100 000	100 000
Net profit	350 000	310 000	390 000	390 000
Total profits	£1 440 000			

Absorption costing profit statements:

	Q1 (£)	Q2 (£)	Q3 (£)	Q4 (£)
Opening stock	—	—	210 000	70 000
Production at £7 per unit	1 050 000	1 190 000	980 000	1 050 000
	1 050 000	1 190 000	1 190 000	1 120 000
Under-/(over)-recovery (2)	—	(20 000)	10 000	—
	1 050 000	1 170 000	1 200 000	1 120 000
Less closing stock (3)	—	210 000	70 000	—
Cost of sales	1 050 000	960 000	1 130 000	1 120 000
Sales	1 500 000	1 400 000	1 600 000	1 600 000
Gross profit	450 000	440 000	470 000	480 000
Selling and administration overheads	100 000	100 000	100 000	100 000
Net profit	350 000	340 000	370 000	380 000
Total profits	£1 440 000			

Notes:

(1) Quarter 2 = 30 000 units at £6 and quarter 3 = 10 000 units at £6.

(2) 20 000 units in excess of normal activity were produced in quarter 2, resulting in an

over-recovery of £20 000. In quarter 3 output was 10 000 units less than normal activity, resulting in an under-recovery of £10 000.

(3) Quarter 2 = 30 000 units at £7 and quarter 3 = 10 000 units at £7.

(b) *Comments*

(i) Both systems yield the same profits (quarter 1) when production equals sales.

(ii) When production volume is in excess of sales volume (quarter 2) absorption costing yields the higher profits.

(iii) When sales volume is in excess of production volume (quarters 3 and 4) variable costing yields the higher profits.

(iv) Sales volume remains unchanged in quarters 3 and 4, but with the absorption costing system changes in profit occur. Profit does not change with the variable costing system.

(v) Both systems yield identical profits over the four quarters.

SOLUTION 7

(a) *Calculation of unit costs*

Direct material cost	10.00
Direct wages cost	4.00
Variable overhead cost	2.50
Variable manufacturing cost	16.50
Fixed manufacturing overhead (£400 000/320 000 units)	1.25
Total manufacturing cost	17.75

Profit statements

(i) Marginal costing	January–March (£000)		April–June (£000)	
Opening stock	Nil		165	
Production costs:				
variable	1155	(70 000 × £16.50)	1650	(100 000 × £16.50)
Closing stock	(165)	(10 000 × £16.50)	(330)	(20 000 × £16.50)
	990		1485	
Selling and distribution				
costs: variable	90		135	
	1080		1620	
Revenue from sales	2700		4050	
Contribution	1620		2430	
Fixed production costs	(100)		(100)	
Fixed selling and				
distribution costs	(20)		(20)	
Fixed administration				
costs	(30)		(30)	
Budgeted profit	1470		2280	

(ii) Absorption costing	(£000)		(£000)	
Opening stock	Nil		177.5	
Total production costs	1242.5	(70 000 × £17.75)	1775.0	(100 000 × £17.75)
	1242.5		1952.5	
Closing stock	(177.5)	(10 000 × £17.75)	(355.0)	(20 000 × £17.75)
	1065.0		1597.5	
Add under-absorption of production overhead (10 000 × 1.25)	12.5		—	
Less over-absorption of production overhead (20 000 × 1.25)	—		(25.0)	
Total selling and distribution costs	110.0		155.0	
Administration costs	30.0		30.0	
	1217.5		1757.5	
Revenue from sales	2700.0		4050.0	
Budgeted profit	1482.5		2292.5	

(b) The difference in profits of £12 500 is due to the fact that part of the fixed production overheads (10 000 units at £1.25 per unit) are included in the closing stock valuation and not recorded as an expense during the current period. With the marginal costing system all of the fixed manufacturing costs incurred during a period are recorded as an expense of the current period.

(c) It is assumed that the question requires the production overhead account to be written up only in respect of fixed production overhead.

Fixed production overhead control account

	(£)		(£)
Actual expenditure	102 400	WIP a/c (74 000 × £1.25)	92 500
		Under-absorption transferred to P & L a/c	9 900
	102 400		102 400

(d) See 'Some arguments in support of variable costing' in Chapter 8 for the answer to this question.

PART THREE

Information for Decision-making

The objective of this Part, which contains four chapters, is to consider the provision of financial information that will help managers to make better decisions. Chapters 9–11 are concerned mainly with short-term decisions based on the environment of today, and the physical, human and financial resources that are presently available to a firm; these decisions are determined to a considerable extent by the quality of the firm's long-term decisions. An important distinction between the long-term and short-term decisions is that the former cannot easily be reversed whereas the latter can often be changed. The actions that follow short-term decisions are frequently repeated, and it is possible for different actions to be taken in the future. For example, the setting of a particular selling price or product mix can often be changed fairly quickly. With regard to long-term decisions, such as capital investment, which involves, for example, the purchase of new plant and machinery, it is not easy to change a decision in the short term. Resources may only be available for major investments in plant and machinery at lengthy intervals, and it is unlikely that plant replacement decisions will be repeated in the short term.

Chapters 9–11 concentrate mainly on how accounting information can be applied to different forms of short-term decisions. Chapter 9 focuses on what will happen to the financial results if a specific level of activity or volume fluctuates. This information is required for making short-term output decisions. Chapter 10 examines how costs and revenues should be measured for a range of non-routine short-term and long-term decisions. Chapter 11 focuses on an alternative approach for measuring resources consumed by cost objects. This approach is called activity-based costing. The final chapter in this part is concerned with long-term decisions. Chapter 12 looks at the techniques that are used for evaluating capital investment decisions, and introduces the concept of the time value of money.

9

Cost–volume–profit analysis

In the previous chapters we have considered how costs should be accumulated for inventory valuation and profit measurement, and we have stressed that costs should be accumulated in a different way for decision-making and cost control. In the next four chapters we shall look at the presentation of financial information for decision-making. We begin by considering how the management accounting information can be of assistance in providing answers to questions about the consequences of following particular courses of action. Such questions might include 'How many units must be sold to break-even?' 'What would be the effect on profits if we reduce our selling price and sell more units?' 'What sales volume is required to meet the additional fixed charges arising from an advertising campaign?' 'Should we pay our sales people on the basis of a salary only, or on the basis of a commission only, or by a combination of the two?' These and other questions can be answered using cost–volume–profit (CVP) analysis.

This is a systematic method of examining the relationship between changes in activity (i.e. output) and changes in total sales revenue, expenses and net profit. As a model of these relationships CVP analysis simplifies the real-world conditions that a firm will face. Like most models, which are abstractions from reality, CVP analysis is subject to a number of underlying assumptions and limitations, which will be discussed later in this chapter; nevertheless, it is a powerful tool for decision-making in certain situations.

This objective of CVP analysis is to establish what will happen to the financial results if a specified level of activity or volume fluctuates. This information is vital to management, since one of the most important variables influencing total sales revenue, total costs and profits is output or volume. For this reason output is given special attention, since knowledge of this relationship will enable management to identify the critical output levels, such as the level at which neither a profit nor a loss will occur (i.e. the break-even point).

CVP analysis is based on the relationship between volume and sales revenue, costs and profit in the short run, the short run normally being a period of one year, or less, in which the output of

Learning objectives

After studying this chapter, you should be able to:

- describe the differences between the accountant's and the economist's model of cost–volume–profit analysis;

- justify the use of linear cost and revenue functions in the accountant's model;

- apply the mathematical approach to answer questions similar to those listed in Example 9.1;

- construct break-even, contribution and profit–volume graphs;

- identify and explain the assumptions on which cost–volume–profit analysis is based;

- calculate break-even points for multi-product situations.

a firm is restricted to that available from the current operating capacity. In the short run, some inputs can be increased, but others cannot. For example, additional supplies of materials and unskilled labour may be obtained at short notice, but it takes time to expand the capacity of plant and machinery. Thus output is limited in the short run because plant facilities cannot be expanded. It also takes time to reduce capacity, and therefore in the short run a firm must operate on a relatively constant stock of production resources. Furthermore, most of the costs and prices of a firm's products will have already been determined, and the major area of uncertainty will be sales volume. Short-run profitability will therefore be most sensitive to sales volume. CVP analysis thus highlights the effects of changes in sales volume on the level of profits in the short run.

The theoretical relationship between total sales revenue, costs and profits with volume has been developed by economists. In order to provide a theoretical basis for comparing the accountant's approach to CVP analysis this chapter begins by describing the economist's model of CVP analysis.

The economist's model

An economist's model of CVP behaviour is presented in Figure 9.1. You will see that the total-revenue line is assumed to be curvilinear, which indicates that the firm is only able to sell increasing quantities of output by reducing the selling price per unit; thus the total revenue line does not increase proportionately with output. To increase the quantity of sales, it is necessary to reduce the unit selling price, which results in the total revenue line rising less steeply, and eventually beginning to decline. This is because the adverse effect of price reductions outweighs the benefits of increased sales volume.

The total cost line AD shows that, between points A and B, total costs rise steeply at first as the firm operates at the lower levels of the volume range. This reflects the difficulties of efficiently operating a plant designed for much larger volume levels. Between points B and C, the total cost line begins to level out and rise less steeply because the firm is now able to operate the plant within the efficient operating range and can take advantage of specialization of labour, and smooth production schedules. In the upper portion of the volume range the total cost line between points C and D rises more and more steeply as the cost per unit increases. This is because the output per direct labour hour declines when the plant is operated beyond the activity level for which it was designed: bottlenecks develop, production schedules become more complex, and plant breakdowns begin to occur. The overall effect is that the cost per unit of output increases and causes the total cost line to rise steeply.

The dashed horizontal line from point A represents the cost of providing the basic operating capacity, and is the economist's interpretation of the total fixed costs of the firm. Note also from Figure 9.1 that the shape of the total revenue line is such that it crosses the total cost line at two points. In other words, there are two output levels at which the total costs are equal to the total revenues; or more simply, there are two break-even points.

It is the shape of the variable cost function in the economist's model that has the most significant influence on the total cost function; this is illustrated in Figure 9.2. The

FIGURE 9.1 *Economist's cost–volume graph.*

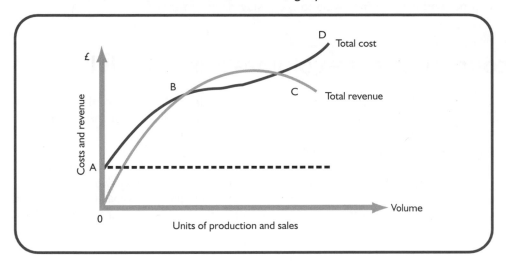

FIGURE 9.2 *Economist's variable cost function.*

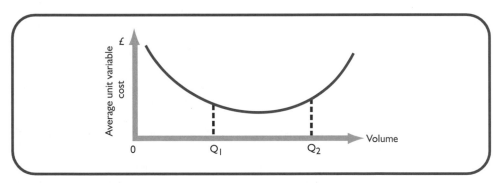

economist assumes that the average *unit* variable cost declines initially, reflecting the fact that, as output expands, a firm is able to obtain bulk discounts on the purchase of raw materials and can benefit from the division of labour; this results in the labour cost per unit being reduced. The economist refers to this situation as **increasing returns to scale**. The fact that *unit* variable cost is higher at lower levels of activity causes the total cost line between points A and B in Figure 9.1 to rise steeply. From Figure 9.2 you can see that the *unit* variable cost levels out between output levels Q_1 and Q_2 and then gradually begins to rise. This is because the firm is operating at its most efficient output level, and further economies of scale are not possible in the short term. However, beyond output level Q_2, the plant is being operated at a higher level than that for which it was intended, and bottlenecks and plant breakdowns occur. The effect of this is that output per direct labour hour declines, and causes the variable cost per unit to increase. The economist describes this situation as **decreasing returns to scale**.

It is also the shape of the variable cost function that causes the total cost line to behave in the manner indicated in Figure 9.1. Between points B and C, the total cost line rises less steeply, indicating that the firm is operating in the range where unit variable cost is at its lowest. Between points C and D, the total cost line rises more steeply, since the variable cost per unit is increasing owing to decreasing returns to scale.

The accountant's cost–volume–profit model

The diagram for the accountant's model is presented in Figure 9.3. Note that the dashed line represents the economist's total cost function, which enables a comparison to be made with the accountant's total cost function. The accountant's diagram assumes a variable cost and a selling price that are constant per unit; this results in a linear relationship (i.e. a straight line) for total revenue and total cost as volume changes. The effect is that there is only one **break-even point** in the diagram, and the profit area widens as volume increases. The most profitable output is therefore at maximum practical capacity. Clearly, the economist's model appears to be more realistic, since it assumes that the total cost curve is non-linear.

RELEVANT RANGE

How can we justify the accountant's assumption of linear cost and linear revenue functions? The answer is that the accountants' diagram is not intended to provide an accurate representation of total cost and total revenue throughout all ranges of output. The objective is to represent the behaviour of total cost and revenue over the range of output at which a firm expects to be operating within a short-term planning horizon. This range of output is represented by the output range between points X and Y in Figure 9.3. The term **relevant range** is used to refer to the output range at which the firm expects to be operating within a short-term planning horizon. This relevant range also broadly represents the output levels which the firm has had experience of operating in the past and for which cost information is available.

You can see from Figure 9.3 that, between points X and Y, the shape of the accountant's total cost line is very similar to that of the economist's. This is because the total cost line is only intended to provide a good approximation within the relevant range. Within this range, the accountant assumes that the variable cost per unit is the same throughout the entire range of output, and the total cost line is therefore linear. Note that the cost function is likely to be approximately linear within this range. It would be unwise, however, to make this assumption for production levels outside the relevant range. It would be more appropriate if the accountant's total cost line was presented for the relevant range of output only, and not extended to the vertical axis or to the output levels beyond Y in Figure 9.3.

FIXED COST FUNCTION

Note also that the accountant's fixed cost function in Figure 9.3 meets the vertical axis at a different point to that at which the economist's total cost line meets the vertical axis. The reason for this can be explained from Figure 9.4. The fixed cost level of 0A may be applicable to, say, activity level Q_2 to Q_3, but if there were to be a prolonged economic recession then output might fall below Q_1, and this could result in redundancies and shutdowns. Therefore fixed costs may be reduced to 0B if there is a prolonged and a significant decline in sales demand. Alternatively, additional fixed costs will be incurred if long-term sales volume is expected to be greater than Q_3. Over a longer-term time horizon,

FIGURE 9.3 *Accountant's cost–volume–profit diagram.*

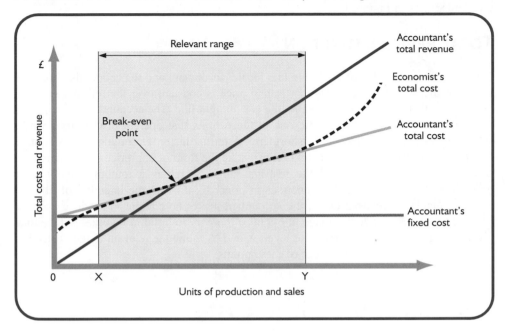

FIGURE 9.4 *Accountant's fixed costs.*

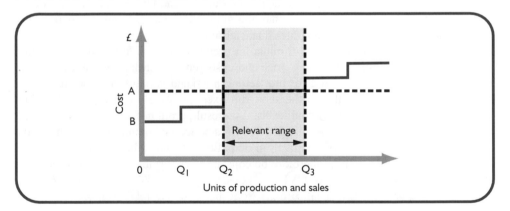

the fixed cost line will consist of a series of step functions rather than the horizontal straight line depicted in Figure 9.3. However, since within its short-term planning horizon the firm expects to be operating between output levels Q_2 and Q_3, it will be committed, in the short term, to fixed costs of 0A; but you should remember that if there was a prolonged economic recession then in the longer term fixed costs may be reduced to 0B.

The fixed cost line for output levels below Q_1 (i.e. 0B) represents the cost of providing the basic operating capacity, and this line is the equivalent to the point where the economist's total cost line meets the vertical axis in Figure 9.3. Because the accountant assumes that in the short term the firm will operate in the relevant range between Q_2 and Q_3, the accountant's fixed cost line 0A in Figure 9.4 represents the fixed costs for the relevant output range only, which the firm is committed to in the current period and does not represent the fixed costs that would be incurred at the extreme levels of output beyond the shaded area in Figure 9.4.

TOTAL REVENUE FUNCTION

Let us now compare the total revenue line for the accountant and the economist. We have seen that the accountant assumes that selling price is constant over the relevant range of output, and therefore the total revenue line is a straight line. The accountant's assumption about the revenue line is a realistic one in those firms that operate in industries where selling prices tend to be fixed in the short term. A further factor reinforcing the assumption of a fixed selling pricc is that competition may take the form of non-price rather than price competition. Moreover, beyond the relevant range, increases in output may only be possible by offering substantial reductions in price. As it is not the intention of firms to operate outside the relevant range, the accountant makes no attempt to produce accurate revenue functions outside this range. It might be more meaningful in Figure 9.3 if the total revenue line was presented for output levels X and Y within the relevant range, instead of being extended to the left and right of these points.

A mathematical approach to cost–volume–profit analysis

Instead of using a diagram to present CVP information, we can use mathematical relationships. The mathematical approach is a quicker and more flexible method of producing the appropriate information than the graphical approach, and is a particularly appropriate form of input to a computer financial model.

When developing a mathematical formula for producing CVP information, you should note that one is assuming that selling price and costs remain constant per unit of output. Such an assumption may be valid for unit selling price and variable cost, but remember that in Chapter 2 we noted that in the short run fixed costs are a constant *total* amount whereas *unit* cost changes with output levels. As a result, profit per *unit* also changes with volume. For example, if fixed costs are £10 000 for a period and output is 10 000 units, the fixed cost will be £1 per unit. Alternatively, if output is 5000 units, the fixed cost will be £2 per unit. Profit per unit will not therefore be constant over varying output levels and it is incorrect to unitize fixed costs for CVP decisions.

We can develop a mathematical formula from the following relationship:

net profit = (units sold × unit selling price)

− [(units sold × unit variable cost) + total fixed costs]

The following symbols can be used to represent the various items in the above equation:

NP = net profit

x = units sold

P = selling price

b = unit variable cost

a = total fixed costs

The equation can now be expressed in mathematical terms as

$$NP = Px - (a + bx) \qquad (9.1)$$

EXAMPLE 9.1

Norvik Enterprises operate in the leisure and entertainment industry and one of its activities is to promote concerts at locations throughout Europe. The company is examining the viability of a concert in Stockholm. Estimated fixed costs are £60 000. These include the fees paid to performers, the hire of the venue and advertising costs. Variable costs consist of the cost of a pre-packed buffet which will be provided by a firm of caterers at a price, which is currently being negotiated, but it is likely to be in the region of £10 per ticket sold. The proposed price for the sale of a ticket is £20. The management of Norvic have requested the following information:

1. The number of tickets that must be sold to break-even (that is, the point at which there is neither a profit or loss).
2. How many tickets must be sold to earn £30 000 target profit?
3. What profit would result if 8000 tickets were sold?
4. What selling price would have to be charged to give a profit of £30 000 on sales of 8000 tickets, fixed costs of £60 000 and variable costs of £10 per ticket?
5. How many additional tickets must be sold to cover the extra cost of television advertising of £8000?

You should now refer to Example 9.1. This example will be used to illustrate the application of the mathematical approach to CVP analysis.

Let us now provide the information requested in Example 9.1.

1. BREAK-EVEN POINT IN UNITS (I.E. NUMBER OF TICKETS SOLD)

Since $NP = Px - (a + bx)$, the break-even point is at a level of output (x) where

$$a + bx = Px - NP$$

Substituting the information in Example 9.1, we have

$$60\,000 + 10x = 20x - 0$$
$$60\,000 = 10x$$

and so $x = 6000$ tickets (or £120 000 total sales at £20 per ticket).

An alternative method, called the **contribution margin** approach, can also be used. Contribution margin is equal to sales minus variable expenses. Because the variable cost per unit and the selling price per unit are assumed to be constant the contribution margin per unit is also assumed to be constant. In Example 9.1 note that each ticket sold generates a contribution of £10, which is available to cover fixed costs and, after they are covered, to contribute to profit. When we have obtained sufficient total contribution to cover fixed costs, the break-even point is achieved, and the alternative formula is

$$\text{break-even point in units} = \frac{\text{fixed costs}}{\text{contribution per unit}}$$

The contribution margin approach can be related to the mathematical formula approach. Consider the penultimate line of the formula approach; it reads

$$£60\,000 = 10x$$

and so

$$x = \frac{£60\,000}{£10}$$

giving the contribution margin formula

$$\frac{\text{fixed costs}}{\text{contribution per unit}}$$

The contribution margin approach is therefore a restatement of the mathematical formula, and either technique can be used; it is a matter of personal preference.

2. UNITS TO BE SOLD TO OBTAIN A £30 000 TARGET PROFIT

Using the equation $NP = Px - (a + bx)$ and substituting the information in Example 9.1, we have

$$£30\,000 = £20x - (£60\,000 + £10x)$$
$$£90\,000 = £10x$$

and so

$$x = 9000 \text{ tickets}$$

If we apply the contribution margin approach and wish to achieve the desired profit, we must obtain sufficient contribution to cover the fixed costs (i.e. the break-even point) plus a further contribution to cover the target profit. Hence we simply add the target profit to the fixed costs so that the equation using the contribution margin approach is

$$\text{units sold for desired profit} = \frac{\text{fixed costs + desired profit}}{\text{contribution per unit}}$$

This is merely a restatement of the penultimate line of the mathematical formula, which reads

$$£90\,000 = £10x$$

and so

$$x = \frac{£90\,000}{£10}$$

3. PROFIT FROM THE SALE OF 8000 TICKETS

Substituting in the equation $NP = Px - (a + bx)$, we have

$$NP = £20 \times 8000 - (£60\,000 + £10 \times 8000)$$
$$= £160\,000 - (£60\,000 + £80\,000)$$

and so

$$NP = £20\,000$$

Let us now assume that we wish to ascertain the impact on profit if a further 1000 tickets are sold so that sales volume increases from 8000 to 9000 tickets. Assuming that fixed costs remain unchanged, the impact on a firm's profits resulting from a change in the number of units sold can be determined by multiplying the unit contribution margin by the change in units sold. Therefore the increase in profits will be £10 000 (1000 units times a unit contribution margin of £10).

4. SELLING PRICE TO BE CHARGED TO SHOW A PROFIT OF £30 000 ON SALES OF 8000 UNITS

Applying the formula for net profit (i.e. Equation 9.1)

$$£30\,000 = 8000P - (£60\,000 + (£10 \times 8000))$$
$$= 8000P - £140\,000$$

giving
$$8000P = £170\,000$$

and
$$P = £21.25 \text{ (i.e. an increase of £1.25 per ticket)}$$

5. ADDITIONAL SALES VOLUME TO MEET £8000 ADDITIONAL FIXED ADVERTISING CHARGES

The contribution per unit is £10 and fixed costs will increase by £8000. Therefore an extra 800 tickets must be sold to cover the additional fixed costs of £8000.

THE PROFIT–VOLUME RATIO

The **profit–volume ratio** (also known as the **contribution margin ratio**) is the contribution divided by sales. It represents the proportion of each £1 sales available to cover fixed costs and provide for profit. In Example 9.1 the contribution is £10 per unit and the selling price is £20 per unit; the profit–volume ratio is 0.5. This means that for each £1 sale a contribution of £0.50 is earned. Because we assume that selling price and contribution per unit are constant, the profit–volume ratio is also assumed to be constant. Therefore the profit–volume ratio can be computed using either unit figures or total figures. Given an estimate of total sales revenue, it is possible to use the profit–volume ratio to estimate total contribution. For example, if total sales revenue is estimated to be £200 000, the total contribution will be £100 000 (£200 000 × 0.5). To calculate the profit, we deduct fixed costs of £60 000; thus a profit of £40 000 will be obtained from total sales revenue of £200 000.

Expressing the above computations in mathematical terms:

$$NP = (\text{Sales revenue} \times PV \text{ ratio}) - \text{Fixed costs}$$
$$NP + \text{Fixed costs} = \text{Sales revenue} \times PV \text{ ratio}$$

Therefore the break-even sales revenue (where $NP = 0$) = Fixed costs/PV ratio.

RELEVANT RANGE

It is vital to remember that, as with the mathematical approach, the formulae method can only be used for decisions that result in outcomes within the relevant range. Outside this range the unit selling price and the variable cost are no longer deemed to be constant per unit, and any results obtained from the formulae that fall outside the relevant range will be incorrect. The concept of the relevant range is more appropriate for production settings but it can apply within non-production settings. Returning to Norvic Enterprises in Example 9.1, let us assume that the caterers' charges will be higher if ticket sales are below 4000 but lower if sales exceed 12 000 tickets. Thus, the £10 variable cost relates only to a sales volume within a range of 4000–12 000 tickets. Outside this range other costs apply. Also the number of seats made available at the venue is flexible and the hire cost will be reduced for sales of less than 4000 tickets and increased for sales beyond 12 000 tickets. In other words, we will assume that the relevant range is a sales volume of 4000–12 000 tickets and outside this range the results of our CVP analysis do not apply.

Margin of safety

The **margin of safety** indicates by how much sales may decrease before a loss occurs. Using Example 9.1, where unit selling price and variable cost were £20 and £10 respectively and fixed costs were £60 000, we noted that the break-even point was 6000 tickets or £120 000 sales value. If sales are expected to be 8000 tickets or £160 000, the margin of safety will be 2000 tickets or £40 000. Alternatively, we can express the margin of safety in a percentage form based on the following ratio:

$$\text{percentage margin of safety} = \frac{\text{expected sales} - \text{break-even sales}}{\text{expected sales}}$$
$$= \frac{£160\,000 - £120\,000}{£160\,000} = 25\%$$

Constructing the break-even chart

Managers may obtain a clearer understanding of CVP behaviour if the information is presented in graphical format. Using the data in Example 9.1, we can construct the **break-even chart** for Norvik Enterprises (Figure 9.5). In constructing the graph, the fixed costs are plotted as a single horizontal line at the £60 000 level. Variable costs at the rate of £10 per unit of volume are added to the fixed costs to enable the total cost line to be plotted. Two points are required to insert the total cost line. At zero sales volume total cost will be equal to the fixed costs of £60 000. At 12 000 units sales volume total costs will be £180 000 consisting of £120 000 variable cost plus £60 000 fixed costs. The total revenue line is plotted at the rate of £20 per unit of volume. The constraints of the relevant range consisting of two vertical lines are then added to the graph: beyond these lines we have little assurance that the CVP relationships are valid.

The point at which the total sales revenue line cuts the total cost line is the point where the concert makes neither a profit nor a loss. This is the break-even point and is 6000 tickets or £120 000 total sales revenue. The distance between the total sales revenue line and the total cost line at a volume below the break-even point represents losses that will occur for various sales levels below 6000 tickets. Similarly, if the company operates at a sales volume above the break-even point, the difference between the total revenue and the total cost lines represents the profit that results from sales levels above 6000 tickets.

Alternative presentation of cost–volume–profit analysis

CONTRIBUTION GRAPH

In Figure 9.5 the fixed cost line is drawn parallel to the horizontal axis, and the variable cost is the difference between the total cost line and the fixed cost line. An alternative to Figure 9.5 for the data contained in Example 9.1 is illustrated in Figure 9.6. This

FIGURE 9.5 *Break-even chart for Example 9.1.*

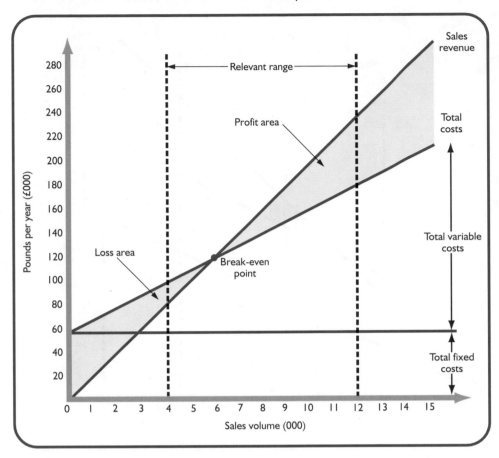

alternative presentation is called a **contribution graph**. In Figure 9.6 the variable cost line is drawn first at £10 per unit of volume. The fixed costs are represented by the difference between the total cost line and the variable cost line. Because fixed costs are assumed to be a constant sum throughout the entire output range, a constant sum of £60 000 for fixed costs is added to the variable cost line, which results in the total cost line being drawn parallel to the variable cost line. The advantage of this form of presentation is that the total contribution is emphasized in the graph, and is represented by the difference between the total sales revenue line and the total variable cost line.

PROFIT–VOLUME GRAPH

The break-even and contribution charts do not highlight the profit or loss at different volume levels. To ascertain the profit or loss figures from a break-even chart, it is necessary to determine the difference between the total-cost and total-revenue lines. The **profit–volume graph** is a more convenient method of showing the impact of changes in volume on profit. Such a graph is illustrated in Figure 9.7. The horizontal axis represents the various levels of sales volume, and the profits and losses for the period are recorded on the vertical scale. You will see from Figure 9.7 that profits or losses are plotted for each of the various sales levels, and these points are connected by a profit line. Two points are

FIGURE 9.6 *Contribution chart for Example 9.1.*

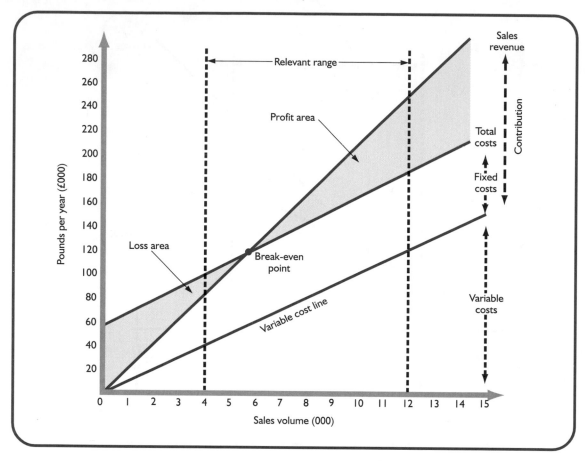

required to plot the profit line. When units sold are zero a loss equal to the amount of fixed costs (£60 000) will be reported. At the break-even point (zero profits) sales volume is 6000 units. Therefore the break-even point is plotted at the point where the profit line intersects the horizontal line at a sales volume of 6000 tickets. The profit line is drawn between the two points. With each unit sold, a contribution of £10 is obtained towards the fixed costs, and the break-even point is at 6000 tickets, when the total contribution exactly equals the total of the fixed costs. With each additional unit sold beyond 6000 tickets, a surplus of £10 per ticket is obtained. If 10 000 tickets are sold, the profit will be £40 000 (4000 tickets at £10 contribution). You can see this relationship between sales and profit at 10 000 tickets from the dotted lines in Figure 9.7.

Multi-product cost–volume–profit analysis

Our analysis so far has assumed a single-product setting. However, most firms produce and sell many products or services. In this section we shall consider how we can adapt the analysis used for a single-product setting to a multi-product setting. Consider the situation presented in Example 9.2. You will see that the company sells two products so that there are two unit contribution margins. We can apply the same approach as that used for a single product if all of the fixed costs are directly attributable to products (i.e. there are no common fixed costs) or our analysis focuses only on the contribution to common fixed

FIGURE 9.7 *Profit–volume graph for Example 9.1.*

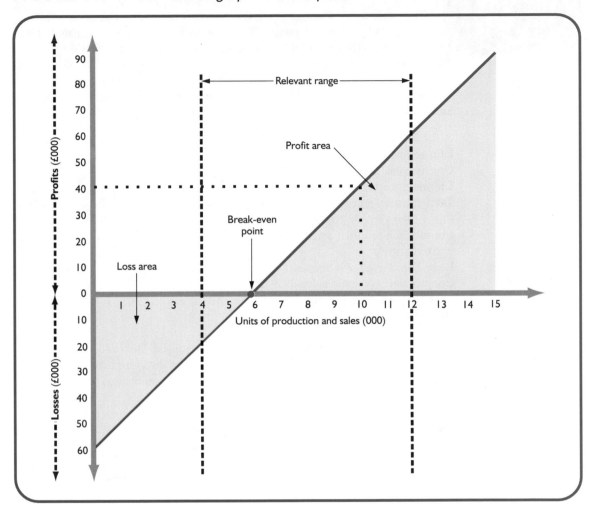

costs, rather than operating profit. We simply apply the analysis separately to each product as follows:

> De-luxe washing machine break-even point
>> = Direct fixed costs (£90 000)/Unit contribution (£150)
>> = 600 units

> Standard washing machine break-even point
>> = Direct fixed costs (£27 000)/Unit contribution (£90)
>> = 300 units

However, selling 600 de-luxe and 300 standard washing machines will generate a contribution that only covers direct fixed costs; the common fixed costs will not be covered. A loss equal to the common fixed costs will be reported. The break-even point for the firm as a whole has not been ascertained.

You may think that the break-even point for the firm as a whole can be derived if we allocate the common fixed costs to each individual product but this approach is

EXAMPLE 9.2

The Super Bright Company sells two types of washing machines – a de-luxe model and a standard model. The financial controller has prepared the following information based on the sales forecast for the period:

Sales volume (units)	De-luxe machine 1200	Standard machine 600	Total
	(£)	(£)	(£)
Unit selling price	300	200	
Unit variable cost	150	110	
Unit contribution	150	90	
Total sales revenues	360 000	120 000	480 000
Less: Total variable cost	180 000	66 000	246 000
Contribution to direct and common fixed costs[a]	180 000	54 000	234 000
Less: Direct avoidable fixed costs	90 000	27 000	117 000
Contribution to common fixed costs[a]	90 000	27 000	117 000
Less common (indirect) fixed costs			39 000
Operating profit			78 000

The common fixed costs relate to the costs of common facilities and can only be avoided if neither of the products is sold. The managing director is concerned that sales may be less than forecast and has requested information relating to the break-even point for the activities for the period.

Note
[a]Contribution was defined earlier in this chapter as sales less variable costs. Where fixed costs are divided into direct and common (indirect) fixed costs it is possible to identify two separate contribution categories. The first is described as contribution to direct and common fixed costs and this is identical to the conventional definition, being equivalent to sales less variable costs. The second is after a further deduction of direct fixed costs and is described as 'Contribution to common or indirect fixed costs'.

inappropriate because the allocation will be arbitrary. The common fixed costs cannot be specifically identified with either of the products since they can only be avoided if *both* products are not sold. The solution to our problem is to convert the sales volume measure of the individual products into standard batches of products based on the planned sales mix. You will from see from Example 9.2 that Super Bright plans to sell 1200 de-luxe and 600 standard machines giving a sales mix of 1200 : 600. Reducing this sales mix to the smallest whole number gives a mix of 2 : 1. In other words, for the sale of every two deluxe machines one standard machine is expected to be sold. We therefore define our standard batch of products as comprising two de-luxe and one standard machine giving a contribution of £390 per batch (two de-luxe machines at a contribution of £150 per unit sold plus and one standard machine at a contribution of £90).

The break-even point in standard batches can be calculated by using the same break-even equation that we used for a single product so that:

Break-even number of batches = Total fixed costs (£156 000)/Contribution margin per batch (£390)

= 400 batches

The sales mix used to define a standard batch $(2:1)$ can be now be used to convert the break-even point (measured in standard batches) into a break-even point expressed in terms of the required combination of individual products sold. Thus, 800 de-luxe machines (2×400) and 400 (1×400) standard machines must be sold to break-even. The following profit statement verifies this outcome:

Units sold	De-luxe machine 800 (£)	Standard machine 400 (£)	Total (£)
Unit contribution margin	150	90	
Contribution to direct and common fixed costs	120 000	36 000	156 000
Less: Direct fixed costs	90 000	27 000	117 000
Contribution to common fixed costs	30 000	9 000	39 000
Less: Common fixed costs			39 000
Operating profit			0

Let us now assume that the actual sales volume for the period was 1200 units, the same total volume as the break-even volume, but consisting of a sales mix of 600 units of each machine. Thus, the actual sales mix is $1:1$ compared with a planned sales mix of $2:1$. The total contribution to direct and common fixed costs will be £144 000 $([£150 \times 600] + [£90 \times 600])$ and a loss of £12 000 (£144 000 contribution − £156 000 total fixed costs) will occur. It should now be apparent to you that the break-even point (or the sales volumes required to achieve a target profit) is not a unique number: it varies depending upon the composition of the sales mix. Because the actual sales mix differs from the planned sales mix, the sales mix used to define a standard batch has changed from $2:1$ to $1:1$ so that the contribution per batch changes from £390 to £240 $([1 \times £150] + [1 \times £90])$. Therefore the revised break-even point will be 650 batches (£156 000 total fixed costs/£240 contribution per batch) which converts to a sales volume of 650 units of each machine based on a $1:1$ sales mix. Generally, an increase in the proportion of sales of higher contribution margin products will decrease the break-even point whereas increases in sales of the lower margin products will increase the break-even point.

Cost–volume–profit analysis assumptions

It is essential that anyone preparing or interpreting CVP information is aware of the underlying assumptions on which the information has been prepared. If these assumptions are not recognized, serious errors may result and incorrect conclusions may be drawn from the analysis. We shall now consider these important assumptions. They are as follows:

1. All other variables remain constant.
2. A single product or constant sales mix.
3. Total costs and total revenue are linear functions of output.
4. The analysis applies to the relevant range only.
5. Costs can be accurately divided into their fixed and variable elements.
6. The analysis applies only to a short-term time horizon.
7. Complexity-related fixed costs do not change.

1. ALL OTHER VARIABLES REMAIN CONSTANT

It has been assumed that all variables other than the particular one under consideration have remained constant throughout the analysis. In other words, it is assumed that volume is the only factor that will cause costs and revenues to change. However, changes in other variables such as production efficiency, sales mix, price levels and production methods can have an important influence on sales revenue and costs. If significant changes in these other variables occur the CVP analysis presentation will be incorrect.

2. SINGLE PRODUCT OR CONSTANT SALES MIX

CVP analysis assumes that either a single product is sold or, if a range of products is sold, that sales will be in accordance with a predetermined sales mix. When a predetermined sales mix is used, it can be depicted in the CVP analysis by measuring sales volume using standard batch sizes based on a planned sales mix. Any CVP analysis must be interpreted carefully if the initial product mix assumptions do not hold.

3. TOTAL COSTS AND TOTAL REVENUE ARE LINEAR FUNCTIONS OF OUTPUT

The analysis assumes that unit variable cost and selling price are constant. This assumption is only likely to be valid within the relevant range of production described on page 202.

4. ANALYSIS APPLIES TO RELEVANT RANGE ONLY

Earlier in this chapter we noted that CVP analysis is appropriate only for decisions taken within the relevant production range, and that it is incorrect to project cost and revenue figures beyond the relevant range.

5. COSTS CAN BE ACCURATELY DIVIDED INTO THEIR FIXED AND VARIABLE ELEMENTS

CVP analysis assumes that costs can be accurately analysed into their fixed and variable elements. The separation of semi-variable costs into their fixed and variable elements is extremely difficult in practice. Nevertheless a reasonably accurate analysis is necessary if CVP analysis is to provide relevant information for decision-making.

6. THE ANALYSIS APPLIES ONLY TO A SHORT-TERM TIME HORIZON

At the beginning of this chapter we noted that CVP analysis is based on the relationship between volume and sales revenue, costs and profits in the short-term, the short-term being typically a period of one year. In the short-term the costs of providing a firm's operating capacity, such as property taxes and the salaries of senior managers, are likely to be fixed in relation to changes in activity. Decisions on the firm's intended future potential level of operating capacity will determine the amount of capacity costs to be incurred. These decisions will have been made previously as part of the long-term planning process. Once these decisions have been made, they cannot easily be reversed in the short-term. It takes time to significantly expand the capacity of plant and machinery or reduce capacity. Furthermore, plant investment and abandonment decisions should not be based on short-term fluctuations in demand within a particular year. Instead, they should be reviewed periodically as part of the long-term planning process and decisions based on predictions of long-run demand over several years. Thus capacity costs will tend to be fixed in relation to changes of activity within short-term periods such as one year. However, over long-term periods significant changes in volume or product complexity will cause fixed costs to change.

It is therefore assumed that in the short term some costs will be fixed and unaffected by changes in volume whereas other (variable) costs will vary with changes in volume. In the short-run volume is the most important variable influencing total revenue, costs and profit. For this reason volume is given special attention in the form of CVP analysis. You should note, however, that in the long-term other variables, besides volume, will cause costs to change. Therefore, the long-term analysis should incorporate other variables, besides volume, and recognize that fixed costs will increase or decrease in steps in response to changes in the explanatory variables.

7. COMPLEXITY-RELATED FIXED COSTS DO NOT CHANGE

CVP analysis assumes that **complexity-related costs** will remain unchanged. Cooper and Kaplan (1987) illustrate how complexity-related fixed costs can increase as a result of changes in the range of items produced, even though volume remains unchanged. They illustrate the relationship with an example of two identical plants. One plant produces one million units of product A. The second plant produces 100 000 units of A and 900 000 similar units of 199 similar products. The first plant has a simple production environment and requires limited manufacturing support facilities. Set-ups, expediting, inventory movements and schedule activities are minimal. The other plant has a much more complex production management environment. The 200 products must be scheduled through the plant, and this requires frequent set-ups, inventory movements, purchase receipts and inspections. To handle this complexity, the support departments' fixed costs must be larger.

Cooper and Kaplan use the above example to illustrate that many so-called fixed costs vary not with the volume of items manufactured but with the range of items produced (i.e. the complexity of the production process). Complexity-related costs do not normally vary significantly in the short-term with the volume of production. If a change in volume does not alter the range of products then it is likely that complexity-related fixed costs will not alter, but if volume stays constant and the range of items produced changes then support department fixed costs will eventually change because of the increase or decrease to product complexity.

CVP analysis assumptions will be violated if a firm seeks to enhance profitability by product proliferation: that is, by introducing new variants of products based on short-term contribution margins. The CVP analysis will show that profits will increase as sales volume increases and fixed costs remain constant in the short-term. The increased product diversity, however, will cause complexity-related fixed costs to increase in future periods, and there is a danger that long-term profits may decline as a result of product proliferation. The CVP analysis incorporates the fixed costs required to handle the diversity and complexity within the current product range, but the costs will remain fixed only if diversity and complexity are not increased further. Thus CVP analysis will not capture the changes in complexity-related costs arising from changes in the range of items produced.

Cost–volume–profit analysis and computer applications

The output from a CVP model is only as good as the input. The analysis will include assumptions about sales mix, production efficiency, price levels, total fixed costs, variable costs and selling price per unit. Obviously, estimates regarding these variables will be subject to varying degrees of uncertainty.

Sensitivity analysis is one approach for coping with changes in the values of the variables. Sensitivity analysis focuses on how a result will be changed if the original estimates or the underlying assumptions change. With regard to CVP analysis, sensitivity analysis answers questions such as the following:

1. What will the profit be if the sales mix changes from that originally predicted?

2. What will the profit be if fixed costs increase by 10% and variable costs decline by 5%?

The widespread use of spreadsheet packages has enabled management accountants to develop CVP computerized models. Managers can now consider alternative plans by keying the information into a computer, which can quickly show changes both graphically and numerically. Thus managers can study various combinations of changes in selling prices, fixed costs, variable costs and product mix, and can react quickly without waiting for formal reports from the management accountant.

Separation of semi-variable costs

CVP analysis assumes that costs can be accurately analysed into their fixed and variable elements. Direct material is generally presumed to be a variable cost, whereas depreciation, which is related to time and not usage, is a fixed cost. Semi-variable costs, however, include both a fixed and variable component. The cost of maintenance is a semi-variable cost consisting of planned maintenance which is undertaken whatever the level of activity, and a variable element which is directly related to activity. The separation of semi-variable costs into their fixed and variable elements is extremely difficult in practice, but an accurate analysis is necessary for CVP analysis.

Mathematical techniques should be used to separate costs accurately into fixed and variable elements. For a discussion of these techniques you should refer to Chapter 24 of Drury (2000). First-year cost and management accounting examinations sometimes require you to separate fixed and variable costs using a non-mathematical technique called the **high–low method**.

The high–low method consists of examining past costs and activity, selecting the highest and lowest activity levels and comparing the changes in costs which result from the two levels. Assume that the following activity levels and costs are extracted:

	Volume of production (units)	Indirect costs (£)
Lowest activity	5 000	22 000
Highest activity	10 000	32 000

If variable costs are constant per unit and the fixed costs remain unchanged the increase in costs will be due entirely to an increase in variable costs. The variable cost per unit is therefore calculated as follows:

$$\frac{\text{Difference in cost}}{\text{Difference in activity}} = \frac{£10\,000}{5000\ \text{units}}$$

$$= £2\ \text{variable cost per unit of activity}$$

The fixed cost can be estimated at any level of activity by subtracting the variable cost portion from the total cost. At an activity level of 5000 units the total cost is £22 000 and the total variable cost is £10 000 (5000 units at £2 per unit). The balance of £12 000 is assumed to represent the fixed cost.

Summary

CVP analysis has been a core topic in the management accounting education process for over 50 years. It would also appear to be widely used in practice with a recent survey indicating that 86% of Australian firms had adopted the technique (Chenhall and Langfield-Smith, 1998).

CVP analysis is concerned with examining the relationship between changes in volume and changes in total revenue and costs in the short term. In this chapter we have compared the economist's and accountant's models of CVP behaviour. The major differences are that the total cost and total revenue functions are curvilinear in the economist's model, whereas the accountant's model assumes linear relationships. However, we have noted that the accountant's model was intended to predict CVP behaviour only within the relevant range, where a firm is likely to be operating on constant returns to sale. A comparison of the two models suggested that, within the relevant production range, the total costs and revenue functions are fairly similar.

We have seen that for decision-making a numerical presentation provides more precise information than a graphical one. Given that the cost and revenue functions will already have been determined at the decision-making stage, the major area of uncertainty relates to the actual level of output. The graphical approach provides a useful representation of how costs, revenues and profits will behave for the many possible output levels that may actually materialize.

It is essential when interpreting CVP information that you are aware of the following important assumptions on which the analysis is based:

1. All other variables remain constant.
2. The analysis is based on a single product or constant sales mix.
3. Total costs and revenues are a linear function of output.
4. The analysis applies to the relevant range only.
5. Costs can be accurately divided into their fixed and variable elements.
6. The analysis applies only to a short-term time horizon.
7. Complexity-related costs do not change.

Key Terms and Concepts

break-even chart (p. 208)
break-even point (p. 202)
complexity-related costs (p. 215)
contribution graph (p. 209)
contribution margin (p. 205)
contribution margin ratio (p. 207)
decreasing returns to scale (p. 201)

high-low method (p. 216)
increasing returns to scale (p. 201)
margin of safety (p. 208)
profit–volume graph (p. 209)
profit–volume ratio (p. 207)
relevant range (p. 202)
sensitivity analysis (p. 216)

Key Examination Points

Students tend to experience little difficulty in preparing break-even charts, but many cannot construct profit–volume charts. Remember that the horizontal axis represents the level of activity, while profit/losses are shown on the vertical axis. The maximum loss is at zero activity, and is equal to fixed costs. For practice on preparing a profit–volume chart you should attempt the sixth review problem and compare your answer with the solution. Students also experience difficulty with the following:

1. coping with multi-product situations;
2. calculating the break-even point when total sales and costs are given but no information is given on the unit costs;
3. explaining the assumptions of CVP analysis.

For multi-product situations you should base your answer on the average contribution per unit, using the approach shown in Example 9.2. Review problem 8 requires the computation of a break-even point in a multi-product setting. When unit costs are not given the break-even point in sales value can be calculated as follows:

$$\text{Fixed costs} \times \frac{\text{total estimated sales}}{\text{total estimated contribution}}$$

or

$$\frac{\text{Fixed costs}}{\text{profit–volume ratio}}$$

Review Problems

(For additional problems without answers relating to the content of this chapter you should refer to pages 471–484.)

1 A company manufactures and sells two products, X and Y. Forecast data for a year are:

	Product X	Product Y
Sales (units)	80 000	20 000
Sales price (per unit)	£12	£8
Variable cost (per unit)	£8	£3

Annual fixed costs are estimated at £273 000.

What is the break-even point in sales revenue with the current sales mix?
A £570 000
B £606 667
C £679 467
D £728 000
ACCA Foundation Paper 3 Sample Question

2 H Limited manufactures and sells two products, J and K. Annual sales are expected to be in the ratio of J : 1, K : 3. Total annual sales are planned to be £420 000. Product J has a contribution to sales ratio of 40%, whereas that of product K is 50%. Annual fixed costs are estimated to be £120 000.
The budgeted break-even sales value (to the nearest £1000):

A £196 000
B £200 000
C £253 000
D £255 000
E cannot be determined from the above data.
CIMA Stage 2

3 The following details relate to product R:

Level of activity (units)	1000 (£/unit)	2000 (£/unit)
Direct materials	4.00	4.00
Direct labour	3.00	3.00
Production overhead	3.50	2.50
Selling overhead	1.00	0.50
	11.50	10.00

The total fixed cost and variable cost per unit are:

	Total fixed cost (£)	Variable cost per unit (£)
A	2000	1.50
B	2000	7.00
C	2000	8.50
D	3000	7.00
E	3000	8.50

CIMA Stage 2

4 Z plc makes a single product which it sells for £16 per unit. Fixed costs are £76 800 per month and the product has a contribution to sales ratio of 40%.

In a period when actual sales were £224 000, Z plc's margin of safety, in units, was

A   2000
B   6000
C   8000
D   12 000
E   14 000

CIMA Stage 2

5 A break-even chart is shown below for Windhurst Ltd.

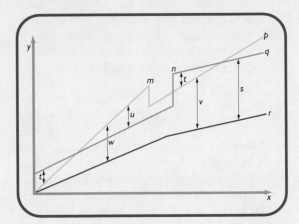

You are required:
(i)   to identify the components of the break-even chart labelled $p, q, r, s, t, u, v, w, x$ and y;   (*5 marks*)
(ii) to suggest what events are represented at the values of x that are labelled m and n on the chart;   (*3 marks*)
(iii) to assess the usefulness of break-even analysis to senior management of a small company.   (*7 marks*)

ICAEW Management Accounting

6 ZED plc manufactures one standard product, which sells at £10. You are required to:
(a) prepare from the data given below, a graph showing the results for the six months ending 30 April and to determine:
   (i)   the fixed costs;
   (ii) the variable cost per unit;

(iii) the profit–volume ratio;
(iv) the break-even point;
(v)   the margin of safety;

Month	Sales (units)	Profit/(loss) (£)
November	30 000	40 000
December	35 000	60 000
January	15 000	(20 000)
February	24 000	16 000
March	26 000	24 000
April	18 000	(8 000)

(b) discuss the limitations of such a graph;
(c) explain the use of the relevant range in such a graph.   (*20 marks*)
CIMA Cost Accounting 2

7 Z plc operates a single retail outlet selling direct to the public. Profit statements for August and September are as follows:

	August	September
Sales	80 000	90 000
Cost of sales	50 000	55 000
Gross profit	30 000	35 000
Less:		
Selling and distribution	8 000	9 000
Administration	15 000	15 000
Net profit	7 000	11 000

Required:
(a) Use the high- and low-points technique to identify the behaviour of:
   (i)   cost of sales;
   (ii) selling and distribution costs;
   (iii) administration costs.   (*4 marks*)
(b) Draw a contribution break-even chart and identify the monthly break-even sales value and area of contribution.   (*10 marks*)
(c) Assuming a margin of safety equal to 30% of the break-even value, calculate Z plc's annual profit.   (*2 marks*)
(d) Z plc is now considering opening another retail outlet selling the same products. Z plc plans to use the same profit margins in both outlets and has estimated that the specific

fixed costs of the second outlet will be £100 000 per annum.

Z plc also expects that 10% of its annual sales from its existing outlet would transfer to this second outlet if it were to be opened.

Calculate the annual value of sales required from the new outlet in order to achieve the same annual profit as previously obtained from the single outlet.

(5 marks)

(e) Briefly describe the cost accounting requirements of organizations of this type.

(4 marks)

(Total 25 marks)

Chartered Institute of Management Accountants
Operational Cost Accounting Stage 2

8 XYZ Ltd produces two products and the following budget applies for 20 × 2:

	Product X (£)	Product Y (£)
Selling price	6	12
Variable costs	2	4
Contribution margin	4	8
Fixed costs apportioned	£100 000	£200 000
Units sold	70 000	30 000

You are required to calculate the break-even points for each product and the company as a whole and comment on your findings.

9 The summarized profit and loss statement for Exewye plc for the last year is as follows:

	(£000)	(£000)
Sales (50 000 units)		1000
Direct materials	350	
Direct wages	200	
Fixed production overhead	200	
Variable production overhead	50	
Administration overhead	180	
Selling and distribution overhead	120	
		1100
Profit/(loss)		(100)

At a recent board meeting the directors discussed the year's results, following which the chairman asked for suggestions to improve the situation.

You are required as management accountant, to evaluate the following alternative proposals and to comment briefly on each:

(a) Pay salesmen a commission of 10% of sales and thus increase sales to achieve break-even point. *(5 marks)*

(b) Reduce selling price by 10%, which it is estimated would increase sales volume by 30%. *(3 marks)*

(c) Increase direct wage rates from £4 to £5 per hour, as part of a productivity/pay deal. It is hoped that this would increase production and sales by 20%, but advertising costs would increase by £50 000. *(4 marks)*

(d) Increase sales by additional advertising of £300 000, with an increased selling price of 20%, setting a profit margin of 10%.

(8 marks)

(Total 20 marks)

CIMA P1 Cost Accounting

10 Tweed Ltd is a company engaged solely in the manufacture of jumpers, which are bought mainly for sporting activities. Present sales are direct to retailers, but in recent years there has been a steady decline in output because of increased foreign competition. In the last trading year (2001) the accounting report indicated that the company produced the lowest profit for 10 years. The forecast for 2002 indicates that the present deterioration in profits is likely to continue. The company considers that a profit of £80 000 should be achieved to provide an adequate return on capital. The managing director has asked that a review be made of the present pricing and marketing policies. The marketing director has completed this review, and passes the proposals on to you for evaluation and recommendation, together with the profit and loss account for year ending 31 December 2001.

Tweed Ltd profit and loss account for year ending 31 December 2001

	(£)	(£)	(£)
Sales revenue			
(100 000 jumpers at £10)			1 000 000
Factory cost of goods sold:			
Direct materials		100 000	

Direct labour	350 000	
Variable factory overheads	60 000	
Fixed factory overheads	220 000	730 000
Administration overhead		140 000
Selling and distribution overhead		
Sales commission (2% of sales)	20 000	
Delivery costs (variable per unit sold)	50 000	
Fixed costs	40 000	110 000	980 000
Profit		20 000

The information to be submitted to the managing director includes the following three proposals:

(i) To proceed on the basis of analyses of market research studies which indicate that the demand for the jumpers is such that 10% reduction in selling price would increase demand by 40%.

(ii) To proceed with an enquiry that the marketing director has had from a mail order company about the possibility of purchasing 50 000 units annually if the selling price is right. The mail order company would transport the jumpers from Tweed Ltd to its own warehouse, and no sales commission would be paid on these sales by Tweed Ltd. However, if an acceptable price can be negotiated, Tweed Ltd would be expected to contribute £60 000 per annum towards the cost of producing the mail order catalogue. It would also be necessary for Tweed Ltd to provide special additional packaging at a cost of £0.50 per jumper. The marketing director considers that in 2002 the sales from existing business would remain unchanged at 100 000 units, based on a selling price of £10 if the mail order contract is undertaken.

(iii) To proceed on the basis of a view by the marketing director that a 10% price reduction, together with a national advertising campaign costing £30 000 may increase sales to the maximum capacity of 160 000 jumpers.

Required:

(a) The calculation of break-even sales value based on the 2001 accounts.

(b) A financial evaluation of proposal (i) and a calculation of the number of units Tweed Ltd would require to sell at £9 each to earn the target profit of £80 000.

(c) A calculation of the minimum prices that would have to be quoted to the mail order company, first, to ensure that Tweed Ltd would, at least, break even on the mail order contract, secondly, to ensure that the same overall profit is earned as proposal (i) and, thirdly, to ensure that the overall target profit is earned.

(d) A financial evaluation of proposal (iii).

Solutions to Review Problems

SOLUTION 1

	Product X	Product Y	Total
Budgeted sales volume (units)	80 000	20 000	
Budgeted contribution per unit	£4	£5	
Budgeted total contribution	£320 000	£100 000	£420 000
Budgeted sales revenue	£960 000	£160 000	£1 120 000

Average contribution per unit = £420 000/100 000 units = £4.20

Break-even point

$$= \frac{\text{Fixed costs (£273 000)}}{\text{Average contribution per unit (£4.20)}}$$

= 65 000 units

Average selling price per unit = £1 120 000/100 000 units = £11.20

Break-even point in sales revenue = 65 000 units × £11.20 = £728 000

Answer = D

SOLUTION 2

Average contribution to sales ratio

$$= \frac{(40\% \times 1) + (50\% \times 3)}{4} = 47.5\%$$

Break-even point is at the point where 47.5% of the sales equal the fixed costs (i.e. £120 000/0.475 = £252 632).

In other words, the break-even point $= \dfrac{\text{Fixed costs}}{\text{PV ratio}}$

Answer = C

SOLUTION 3

	Total cost (1000 units) (£)	Total cost (2000 units) (£)
Production overhead	3500 (£3.50 × 1000)	5 000 (£2.50 × 2000)
Selling overhead	1000 (£1 × 1000)	1 000 (£0.5 × 2000)

$$\text{Variable cost per unit} = \frac{\text{Change in cost}}{\text{Change in activity}}$$

Production overhead $= £1500/1000$ units $= £1.50$
Selling overhead $=$ Fixed cost since total costs remain unchanged.
The unit costs of direct materials are constant at both activity levels and are therefore variable.

Production overheads fixed cost element

$$= \text{Total cost } (£3500) - \text{Variable cost}$$
$$(1000 \times £1.50) = £2000$$

Total fixed cost $= £2000 + £1000 = £3000$
Unit variable cost $£4 + £3 + £1.50 = £8.50$

Answer $= E$

SOLUTION 4

Break-even point in sales value $=$ Fixed costs
$(£76\,800)$/Profit–volume ratio
(i.e. contribution/sales ratio)
$= £76\,800/(0.40)$
$= £192\,000$

Actual sales	$= £224\,000$
Margin of safety	$= £32\,000$ (in sales revenues)
Margin of safety in units	$= 2000\ (£32\,000/£16)$

Answer $= A$

SOLUTION 5

(i) $p =$ total sales revenue
$q =$ total cost (fixed cost + variable cost)
$r =$ total variable cost
$s =$ fixed costs at the specific level of activity
$t =$ total loss at the specific level of activity
$u =$ total profit at that level of activity
$v =$ total contribution at the specific level of activity
$w =$ total contribution at a lower level of activity
$x =$ level of activity of output sales
$y =$ monetary value of cost and revenue function for level of activity

(ii) At event m the selling price per *unit* decreases, but it remains constant. Note that p is a straight line, but with a lower gradient above m compared with below m.

At event n there is an increase in fixed costs equal to the dotted line. This is probably due to an increase in capital expenditure in order to expand output beyond this point. Also note that at this point the variable cost per unit declines as reflected by the gradient of the variable cost line. This might be due to more efficient production methods associated with increased investment in capital equipment.

(iii) Break-even analysis is less useful in a multi-product company, but the analysis can be a very useful aid to the management of a small single product company. The following are some of the main benefits:

(a) Break-even analysis forces management to consider the functional relationship between costs, revenue and activity, and gives an insight into how costs and revenue change with changes in the level of activity.

(b) Break-even analysis forces management to consider the fixed costs at various levels of activity and the selling price that will be required to achieve various levels of output.

You should refer to Chapter 9 for a discussion of more specific issues of break-even analysis. Break-even analysis can be a useful tool, but it is subject to a number of assumptions that restrict its usefulness (see, especially, 'Cost–volume–profit analysis assumptions').

SOLUTION 6

Preliminary calculations:

	Sales (units)	Profit/(loss)
November	30 000	£40 000
December	35 000	£60 000
Increase	5 000	£20 000

An increase in sales of 5000 units increases contribution (profits) by £20 000. Therefore contribution is £4 per unit. Selling price is £10 per unit (given) and variable cost per unit will be £6.

At 30 000 unit sales:

Contribution	minus Fixed costs	= Profit
£120 000	minus ?	= £40 000

∴ Fixed costs $= £80\,000$

The above information can now be plotted on a graph. A break-even chart or a profit–volume graph could be constructed. A profit–volume graph avoids the need to calculate the profits since the information can be read directly from the graph. (See Figure 1 for a break-even chart and Figure 2 for a profit–volume graph.)

(a) (i) Fixed costs = £80 000.

(ii) Variable cost per unit = £6.

(iii) Profit–volume ratio =

$$\frac{\text{Contribution per unit (£4)}}{\text{Selling price per unit (£10)}} \times 100 = 40\%$$

FIGURE 1 *Break-even chart.*

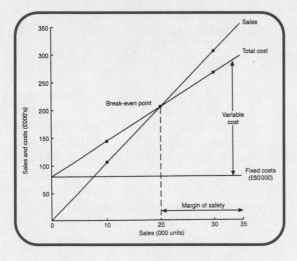

FIGURE 2 *Profit–volume graph.*

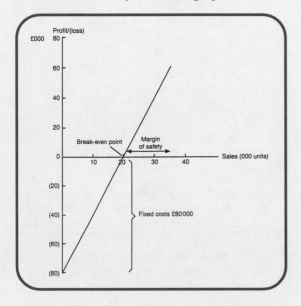

(iv) Break-even point = 20 000 units.

(v) The margin of safety represents the difference between actual or expected sales volume and the break-even point. Therefore the margin of safety will be different for each month's sales. For example, the margin of safety in November is 10 000 units (30 000 units − 20 000 units). The margin of safety can be read from Figure 2 for various sales levels.

(b) and (c) See the sections on 'The accountants' cost–volume–profit model' and 'Cost–volume–profit analysis assumptions' in Chapter 9 for the answers.

SOLUTION 7

(a)

	August (£)	September (£)	Change (£)
Sales	80 000	90 000	10 000
Cost of sales	50 000	55 000	5 000
Selling and distribution	8 000	9 000	1 000
Administration	15 000	15 000	Nil

The only activity measure that is given is sales revenue. An increase in sales of £10 000 results in an increase in cost of sales of £5000 and an increase in selling and distribution costs of £1000. It is therefore assumed that the increase is attributable to variable costs and variable cost of sales is 50% of sales and variable selling and distribution costs are 10% of sales.

Fixed costs are derived by deducting variable costs from total costs for either month. The figures for August are used in the calculations below:

	Total cost (£)	Variable cost (£)	Fixed cost (Balance) (£)
Cost of sales	50 000	40 000	10 000
Selling and distribution	8 000	8 000	Nil
Administration	15 000	Nil	15 000
			25 000

Total cost = £25 000 fixed costs + variable costs (60% of sales)

(b) The following items are plotted on the graph (Figure 3):

	Variable cost	Total cost
Zero sales	Nil	£25 000 fixed cost
£80 000 sales	£48 000 (60%)	£73 000
£90 000 sales	£54 000 (60%)	£79 000
£50 000 sales	£30 000 (60%)	£55 000
£100 000 sales	£60 000	£85 000

Break-even point

$$= \frac{\text{Fixed costs (£25 000)}}{\text{Contribution to sales ratio (0.40)}} = £62\,500 \text{ sales}$$

FIGURE 3 *Contribution break-even graph.*

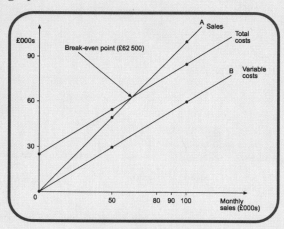

Area of contribution = Area AOB

(c)

		(£)
Actual sales = 1.3 × Break-even sales (£62 500)	=	81 250
Contribution (40% of sales)	=	32 500
Fixed costs	=	25 000
Monthly profit	=	7 500
Annual profit	=	90 000

(d)

		(£)
Annual contribution from single outlet (£32 500 × 12)	=	390 000
Contribution to cover lost sales (10%)	=	39 000
Specific fixed costs	=	100 000
Total contribution required		529 000

Required sales = £529 000/0.4 = £1 322 500

(e) The answer should draw attention to the need for establishing a sound system of budgeting and performance reporting for each of the different outlets working in close conjunction with central office. The budgets should be merged together to establish a master budget for the whole company.

SOLUTION 8

$$\text{Break-even point} = \frac{\text{Fixed costs}}{\text{Contribution per unit}}$$

Product X	25 000 units (£100 000/£4)
Product Y	25 000 units (£200 000/£8)
Company as a whole	57 692 units (£300 000/£5.20[a])

Note:

[a]Average contribution per unit

$$= \frac{(70\,000 \times £4) + (30\,000 \times £8)}{100\,000 \text{ units}}$$

$$= £5.20$$

The sum of the product break-even points is less than the break-even point for the company as a whole. It is incorrect to add the product break-even points because the sales mix will be different from the planned sales mix. The sum of the product break-even points assumes a sales mix of 50% to X and 50% to Y. The break-even point for the company as a whole assumes a planned sales mix of 70% to X and 30% to Y. CVP analysis will yield correct results only if the planned sales mix is equal to the actual sales mix.

SOLUTION 9

Workings:	(£000)
Sales	1000
Variable costs	600
Contribution	400
Fixed costs	500
Profit/(loss)	(100)

Unit selling price	= £20	(£1 m/50 000)
Unit variable cost	= £12	(£600 000/50 000)
Unit contribution	= £ 8	

(a) Sales commission will be £2 per unit, thus reducing the contribution per unit to £6. The break-even point will be 83 333 units (£500 000/£6) or £1 666 666 sales value. This requires an increase of 67% on previous sales and the company must assess whether or not sales can be increased by such a high percentage.

(b) A 10% decrease in selling price will decrease the selling price by £2 per unit and the revised unit contribution will be £6:

	(£)
Revised total contribution	390 000
(65 000 × £6)	
Less fixed costs	500 000
Profit/(loss)	(110 000)

The estimated loss is worse than last year and the proposal is therefore not recommended.

(c) Wages will increase by 25% – that is, from £200 000 to £250 000 – causing output to increase by 20%.

	(£)	(£)
Sales		1 200 000
Direct materials and variable overheads	480 000	
Direct wages	250 000	730 000
Contribution		470 000
Less fixed costs		550 000
Profit/(loss)		(80 000)

This represents an improvement of £20 000 on last year's loss of £100 000.

(d) Revised selling price = £24

Let X = Revised sales volume
∴ sales revenue less (variable costs + fixed costs) = Profit
$$24X \text{ less } (12X + 800\,000) = 0.1\,(24X)$$
$$\therefore 9.6X = 800\,000$$
$$\therefore X = 83\,333 \text{ units}$$

Clearly this proposal is preferable since it is the only proposal to yield a profit. However, the probability of increasing sales volume by approximately 67% plus the risk involved from increasing fixed costs by £300 000 must be considered.

SOLUTION 10

(a)

$$\text{BEP} = \frac{400\,000 \text{ (fixed costs)} \times £1\,000\,000 \text{ (sales)}}{£420\,000 \text{ (contribution)}}$$

$$= 952\,380$$

(b) (i)

	(£)	(£)
Revised selling price		9.00
Less variable costs:		
Direct materials	1.00	
Direct labour	3.50	
Variable overhead	0.60	
Delivery expenses	0.50	
Sales commission	0.18	
(2% of selling price)		5.78
Contribution per unit		3.22

Number of units sold	140 000
Total contributioin (140 000 × 3.22)	450 800
Fixed costs	400 000
Profit from proposal (i)	50 800

(ii)

Desired contribution	= 480 000
Contribution per unit for present proposal	= 3.22
Required units to earn large profit	= 149 068

(c) (i) The variable cost of selling to the mail order firm is:

	(£)
Direct material	1.00
Direct labour	3.50
Variable overhead	0.60
Delivery expenses	nil
Sales commission	nil
Additional package cost	0.50
	5.60

To break even, a contribution of £1.20 is required (60 000 fixed cost/50 000 units sold). Therefore selling price to break even is £6.80 (£5.60 + £1.20).

(ii) To earn £50 800 profit, a contribution of £110 800 (£60 000 + £50 800) is required.
That is, a contribution of £2.22 per unit is required. Therefore required selling price is £7.82 (£5.60 + £2.22).

(iii) To earn the target profit of £80 000, a contribution of £140 000 is required. That is, £2.80 per unit. Therefore required selling price = £8.40 (£5.60 + £2.80).

(d) Contribution per unit is £3.22 per (B)

Unit sold	160 000
Total contribution	£515 200
Fixed costs	£430 000
Profit	£ 85 200

Measuring relevant costs and revenues for decision-making

In this chapter we are going to focus on measuring costs and benefits for non-routine decisions. The term **'special studies'** is sometimes used to refer to decisions that are not routinely made at frequent intervals. In other words, special studies are undertaken whenever a decision needs to be taken; such as discontinuing a product or a channel of distribution, making a component within the company or buying from an outside supplier, introducing a new product and replacing existing equipment. Special studies require only those costs and revenues that are relevant to the specific alternative courses of action to be reported. The term **'decision-relevant approach'** is used to describe the specific costs and benefits that should be reported for special studies. We shall assume that the objective when examining alternative courses of action is to maximize the present value of future net cash inflows. The calculations of present values will be explained in Chapter 12.

It is important that you note at this stage that a decision-relevant approach adopts whichever planning time horizon the decision maker considers appropriate for a given situation. However, it is important not to focus excessively on the short term, since the objective is to maximize long-term net cash inflows.

The aim of this chapter is to provide you with an understanding of the principles that should be used to identify relevant costs and revenues. It is assumed that relevant costs can be easily measured but, in reality, some indirect relevant costs can be difficult to measure. The measurement of indirect relevant costs for decision-making using activity-based-costing techniques will be examined in the next chapter.

We begin by introducing the concept of relevant cost and applying this principle to special studies relating to the following:

1. special selling price decisions;
2. product-mix decisions when capacity constraints exist;

Learning objectives

After studying this chapter, you should be able to:

● define relevant and irrelevant costs and revenues;

● explain the importance of qualitative factors;

● distinguish between the relevant and irrelevant costs and revenues for the five decision-making problems described;

● explain why the book value of equipment is irrelevant when making equipment replacement decisions;

● describe the opportunity cost concept.

3. decisions on replacement of equipment;
4. outsourcing (make or buy) decisions;
5. discontinuation decisions.

The meaning of relevance

The **relevant costs** and benefits required for decision-making are only those that will be affected by the decision. Costs and benefits that are independent of a decision are obviously not relevant and need not be considered when making that decision. The relevant financial inputs for decision-making purposes are therefore *future* cash flows, which will differ between the various alternatives being considered. In other words, only **differential (or incremental) cash flows** should be taken into account, and cash flows that will be the same for all alternatives are irrelevant. Since decision-making is concerned with choosing between future alternative courses of action, and nothing can be done to alter the past, then past costs (also known as sunk costs) are not relevant for decision-making. Consider a situation where an individual is uncertain as to whether he or she should purchase a monthly rail ticket to travel to work or use their car. Assuming that the individual will keep the car, whether or not he or she travels to work by train, the cost of the road fund licence and insurance will be irrelevant, since these costs remain the same irrespective of the mode of travel. The cost of petrol will, however, be relevant, since this cost will vary depending on which method of transport is chosen.

You will see that both depreciation and the allocation of common fixed costs are irrelevant for decision-making. Both are sunk costs. Depreciation represents the allocation of past costs to future periods. The original cost is unavoidable and common to all alternatives. Therefore it is irrelevant. Similarly, any allocation of common fixed costs will be irrelevant for decision-making since the choice of allocation method does not affect the level of cost to the company. It merely results in a redistribution of the same sunk cost between cost objects (e.g. products or locations within the organization).

Importance of qualitative factors

In many situations it is difficult to quantify in monetary terms all the important elements of a decision. Those factors that cannot be expressed in monetary terms are classified as **qualitative factors**. A decline in employee morale that results from redundancies arising from a closure decision is an example of a qualitative factor. It is essential that qualitative factors be brought to the attention of management during the decision-making process, since otherwise there may be a danger that a wrong decision will be made. For example, the cost of manufacturing a component internally may be more expensive than purchasing from an outside supplier. However, the decision to purchase from an outside supplier could result in the closing down of the company's facilities for manufacturing the component. The effect of such a decision might lead to redundancies and a decline in employees' morale, which could affect future output. In addition, the company will now be at the mercy of the supplier who might seek to increase prices on subsequent contracts and/or may not always deliver on time. The company may not then be in a position to meet customers' requirements. In turn, this could result in a loss of customer goodwill and a decline in future sales.

It may not be possible to quantify in monetary terms the effect of a decline in employees' morale or loss of customer goodwill, but the accountant in such circumstances should present the relevant quantifiable financial information and draw attention to those qualitative items that may have an impact on future profitability. In circumstances such as those given in the above example management must estimate the likelihood of the supplier failing to meet the company's demand for future supplies and the likely effect on customer goodwill if there is a delay in meeting orders. If the component can be obtained from many suppliers and repeat orders for the company's products are unlikely then the company may give little weighting to these qualitative factors. Alternatively, if the component can be obtained from only one supplier and the company relies heavily on repeat sales to existing customers then the qualitative factors will be of considerable importance. In the latter situation the company may consider that the quantifiable cost savings from purchasing the component from an outside supplier are insufficient to cover the risk of the qualitative factors occurring.

If it is possible qualitative factors should be expressed in quantitative non-financial terms. For example, the increase in percentage of on-time deliveries from a new production process, the reduction in customer waiting time from a decision to invest in additional cash dispensing machines and the reduction in the number of units of defective output delivered to customers arising from an investment in quality inspection are all examples of qualitative factors that can be expressed in non-financial numerical terms.

Let us now move on to apply the relevant cost approach to a variety of decision-making problems. We shall concentrate on measuring the financial outcomes but do remember that they do not always provide the full story. Qualitative factors should also be taken into account in the decision-making process.

Special pricing decisions

Special pricing decisions relate to pricing decisions outside the main market. Typically they involve one-time only orders or orders at a price below the prevailing market price. Consider the information presented in Example 10.1.

At first glance it looks as if the order should be rejected since the proposed selling price is less than the total cost of £33. A study of the cost estimates, however, indicates that during the next quarter, the direct labour, manufacturing (i.e. non-variable) fixed overheads and the marketing and distribution costs will remain the same irrespective of whether or not the order is accepted. These costs are therefore irrelevant for this decision. The direct material costs, variable manufacturing overheads and the cost of adding the leisure company's logo will be different if the order is accepted. Hence they are relevant for making the decision. The financial information required for the decision is shown in Exhibit 10.1.

You can see from Exhibit 10.1 that different approaches can be used for presenting relevant cost and revenue information. Cost information can be presented that includes both relevant and irrelevant costs or revenues for all alternatives under consideration. If this approach is adopted the *same* amount for the irrelevant items (i.e. those items that remain unchanged as a result of the decision which are direct labour, manufacturing non-variable overheads and the marketing and distribution costs in our example) are included for all alternatives, thus making them irrelevant to the decision. This information is presented in columns (1) and (2) in Exhibit 10.1. Alternatively, you can present cost information in columns (1) and (2) that excludes the irrelevant costs and revenues because

EXAMPLE 10.1

The Caledonian Company is a manufacturer of clothing that sells its output directly to clothing retailers. One of its departments manufactures jumpers. The department has a production capacity of 50 000 jumpers per month. Because of the liquidation of one of its major customers the company has excess capacity. For the next quarter current monthly production and sales volume is expected to be 35 000 jumpers at a selling price of £40 per jumper. Expected costs and revenues for the next month at an activity level of 35 000 jumpers are as follows:

	(£)	(£)
Direct labour	420 000	12
Direct materials	280 000	8
Variable manufacturing overheads	70 000	2
Manufacturing non-variable overheads	280 000	8
Marketing and distribution costs	105 000	3
Total costs	1 155 000	33
Sales	1 400 000	40
Profit	245 000	7

Caledonian is expecting an upsurge in demand and considers that the excess capacity is temporary. A company in the leisure industry has offered to buy for its staff 3000 jumpers each month for the next three months at a price of £20 per jumper. The company would collect the jumpers from Caledonian's factory and thus no marketing and distribution costs will be incurred. No subsequent sales to this customer are anticipated. The company would require its company logo inserting on the jumper and Caledonian has predicted that this will cost £1 per jumper. Should Caledonian accept the offer from the company?

they are identical for both alternatives. A third alternative is to present only the relevant (differential) costs. This approach is shown in column (3) of Exhibit 10.1. Note that column (3) represents the difference between columns (1) and (2). All of the methods show that the company is better off by £27 000 *per month* if the order is accepted.

Four important factors must be considered before recommending acceptance of the order. Most of these relate to the assumption that there are no long-run implications from accepting the offer at a selling price of £20 per jumper. First, it is assumed that the future selling price will not be affected by selling some of the output at a price below the going market price. If this assumption is incorrect then competitors may engage in similar practices of reducing their selling prices in an attempt to unload spare capacity. This may lead to a fall in the market price, which in turn would lead to a fall in profits from future sales. The loss of future profits may be greater than the short-term gain obtained from accepting special orders at prices below the existing market price. Given that Caledonian has found a customer in a different market from its normal market it is unlikely that the market price would be affected. However, if the customer had been within Caledonian's normal retail market there would be a real danger that the market price would be affected. Secondly, the decision to accept the order prevents the company from accepting other orders that may be obtained during the period at the going price. In other words, it is assumed that no better opportunities will present themselves during the period. Thirdly, it is assumed that the company has unused resources that have no alternative uses that will yield a contribution to profits in excess of £27 000 *per month*. Finally, it is assumed that the

EXHIBIT 10.1

Evaluation of three month order from the company in the leisure industry

fixed costs are unavoidable for the period under consideration. In other words, we assume that the direct labour force and the fixed overheads cannot be reduced in the short term, or that they are to be retained for an upsurge in demand, which is expected to occur in the longer term.

	(1) Do not accept order (£ per month)	(2) Accept order (£ per month)	(3) Difference (relevant costs) (£ per month)
Direct labour	420 000	420 000	
Direct materials	280 000	304 000	24 000
Variable manufacturing overheads	70 000	76 000	6 000
Manufacturing non-variable overheads	280 000	280 000	
Inserting company logo		3 000	3 000
Marketing and distribution costs	105 000	105 000	
Total costs	1 155 000	1 188 000	33 000
Sales	1 400 000	1 460 000	60 000
Profit per month	245 000	272 000	27 000

It is important that great care is taken in presenting financial information for decision-making. For stock valuation, external financial regulations require that jumpers must be valued at their manufacturing cost of £30. Using this cost would lead to the incorrect decision being taken. For decision-making purposes only future costs that will be relevant to the decisions should be included. Costs that have been computed for meeting stock valuation requirements must not therefore be used for decision-making purposes.

When you are trying to establish which costs are relevant to a particular decision you may find that some costs will be relevant in one situation but irrelevant in another. In Example 10.1 we assumed that direct labour was not a relevant cost. The company wishes to retain the direct labour for an expected upsurge in demand and therefore the direct labour cost will be same whether or not the offer is accepted. Alternatively, Caledonian may have had an agreement with its workforce that entitled them to at least three months notice in the event of any redundancies. Therefore, even if Caledonian was not expecting an upsurge in demand direct labour would have been a fixed cost within the three month time horizon. But now let us consider what the relevant cost would be if direct labour consisted of casual labour who are hired on a daily basis. In this situation direct labour will be a relevant cost, since the labour costs will not be incurred if the order is not accepted.

The identification of relevant costs depends on the circumstances. In one situation a cost may be relevant, but in another the same cost may not be relevant. It is not therefore possible to provide a list of costs that would be relevant in particular situations. In each situation you should follow the principle that the relevant costs are future costs that differ among alternatives. The important question to ask when determining the relevant cost is: What difference will it make? The accountant must be aware of all the issues relating to a decision and ascertain full details of the changes that will result, and then proceed to select the relevant financial information to present to management.

EVALUATION OF A LONGER-TERM ORDER

In Example 10.1 we focused on a short-term time horizon of three months. Capacity cannot easily be altered in the short term and therefore direct labour and fixed costs are likely to be irrelevant costs with respect to short-term decisions. In the longer-term, however, it may be possible to reduce capacity and spending on fixed costs and direct labour. Let us now assume that for Example 10.1 that Caledonian's assumption about an expected upsurge in the market proved to be incorrect and that it estimates that demand in the foreseeable future will remain at 35 000 jumpers *per month*. Given that it has a productive capacity of 50 000 jumpers it has sought to develop a long-term market for the unutilized capacity of 15 000 jumpers. As a result of its experience with the one-time special order with the company in the leisure industry, Caledonian has sought to develop a market with other companies operating in the leisure industry. Assume that this process has resulted in potential customers that are prepared to enter into a contractual agreement for a three year period for a supply of 15 000 jumpers *per month* at an agreed price of £25 per jumper. The cost of inserting the insignia required by each customer would remain unchanged at £1 per jumper. No marketing and distribution costs would be incurred with any of the orders. Caledonian considers that it has investigated all other possibilities to develop a market for the excess capacity. Should it enter into contractual agreements with the suppliers at £25 per jumper?

If Caledonian does not enter into contractual agreement with the suppliers the direct labour required will be made redundant. No redundancy costs will be involved. Further investigations indicate that manufacturing non-variable costs of £70 000 *per month* could be saved if a decision was made to reduce capacity by 15 000 jumpers per month. For example, the rental contracts for some of the machinery will not be renewed. Also some savings will be made in supervisory labour and support costs. Savings in marketing and distribution costs would be £20 000 *per month*. Assume also that if the capacity was reduced factory rearrangements would result in part of the facilities being rented out at £25 000 *per month*. Note that because variable costs vary directly with changes in volume direct materials and variable manufacturing overheads will decline by 30% if capacity is reduced by 30% from 50 000 to 35 000 jumpers.

We are now faced with a longer-term decision where some of the costs that were fixed in the short term can be changed in the longer term. The appropriate financial data for the analysis is shown in Exhibit 10.2. Note that in Exhibit 10.2 the information for an activity of 35 000 jumpers incorporates the changes arising from the capacity reduction whereas the information presented for the same activity level in Exhibit 10.1 is based on the assumption that capacity will be maintained at 50 000 jumpers. Therefore the direct labour cost in Exhibit 10.1 is £420 000 because it represents the labour required to meet demand at full capacity. If capacity is permanently reduced from 50 000 to 35 000 jumpers (i.e. a 30% reduction) it is assumed that direct labour costs will be reduced by 30% from £420 000 to £294 000. This is the amount shown in Exhibit 10.2.

A comparison of the monthly outcomes reported in columns (1) and (2) of Exhibit 10.2 indicates that the company is better off by £31 000 *per month* if it reduces capacity to 35 000 jumpers, assuming that there are no qualitative factors. Instead of presenting the data in columns (1) and (2) you can present only the differential (relevant) costs and revenues shown in column (3). This approach also indicates that the company is better off by £31 000 per month. Note that the entry in column (3) of £25 000 is the lost revenues from the rent of the unutilized capacity if the company accepts the orders. This represents

<table>
<tr><td rowspan="2" style="background:black;color:white">**EXHIBIT 10.2**

Evaluation of orders for the unutilized capacity over a three year time horizon</td><td>the opportunity cost of accepting the orders. Where the choice of one course of action requires that an alternative course of action is given up, the financial benefits that are forgone or sacrificed are known as **opportunity costs**. In other words, opportunity costs represent the lost contribution to profits arising from the best use of the alternative forgone. Opportu-</td></tr>
</table>

Monthly sales and production in units	(1) Do not accept orders 35 000 (£)	(2) Accept the orders 50 000 (£)	(3) Difference (relevant costs) 15 000 (£)
Direct labour	294 000[a]	420 000	126 000
Direct materials	280 000[a]	400 000	120 000
Variable manufacturing overheads	70 000[a]	100 000	30 000
Manufacturing non-variable overheads	210 000	280 000	70 000
Inserting company logo		15 000	15 000
Marketing and distribution costs	85 000	105 000	20 000
Total costs	939 000	1 320 000	381 000
Revenues from rental of facilities	25 000		25 000
Sales revenues	1 400 000	1 775 000	(375 000)
Profit per month	486 000	455 000	31 000

Note
[a]Variable costs derived from 70% of the costs listed in column 2.

nity costs only arise when resources are scarce and have alternative uses. Thus, in our illustration the capacity allocated to producing 15 000 jumpers results in an opportunity cost (i.e. the lost revenues from the rent of the capacity) of £25 000 per month.

In Exhibit 10.2 all of the costs and revenues are relevant to the decision because some of the costs that were fixed in the short term could be changed in the longer term. Therefore whether or not a cost is relevant often depends on the time horizon under consideration. Thus it is important that the information presented for decision-making relates to the appropriate time horizon. If inappropriate time horizons are selected there is a danger that misleading information will be presented. Remember that our aim should always be to maximize *long-term* net cash inflows.

Product-mix decisions when capacity constraints exist

In the short-term sales demand may be in excess of current productivity capacity. For example, output may be restricted by a shortage of skilled labour, materials, equipment or space. When sales demand is in excess of a company's productive capacity, the resources responsible for limiting the output should be identified. These scarce resources are known as **limiting factors**. Within a short-term time period it is unlikely that production constraints can be removed and additional resources acquired. Where limiting factors apply, profit is maximized when the greatest possible contribution to profit is obtained each time the scarce or limiting factor is used. Consider Example 10.2.

In this situation the company's ability to increase its output and profits/net cash inflows is limited in the short term by the availability of machine capacity. You may think, when first looking at the available information, that the company should give top priority to producing component X, since this yields the highest contribution per unit sold, but this assumption would be incorrect. To produce each unit of component X, six scarce machine hours are required, whereas components Y and Z use only two hours and one hour respectively of scarce machine hours. By concentrating on producing components Y and Z, the company can sell 2000 units of each component and still have some machine capacity left to make component X. If the company concentrates on producing component X it will only be able to meet the maximum sales demand of component X, and will have no machine capacity left to make components Y or Z. The way in which you should determine the optimum production plan is to calculate the contribution per limiting factor for each component and then to rank the components in order of profitability based on this calculation.

Using the figures in the present example the result would be as follows:

	Component X	Component Y	Component Z
Contribution per unit	£12	£10	£6
Machine hours required	6 hours	2 hours	1 hour
Contribution per machine hour	£2	£5	£6
Ranking	3	2	1

The company can now allocate the 12 000 scarce machine hours in accordance with the above rankings. The first choice should be to produce as much as possible of component Z. The maximum sales are 2000 units, and production of this quantity will result in the use of 2000 machine hours, thus leaving 10 000 unused hours. The second choice should be to produce as much of component Y as possible. The maximum sales of 2000 units will result in the use of 4000 machine hours. Production of both components Z and Y require 6000 machine hours, leaving a balance of 6000 hours for the production of component X, which will enable 1000 units of component X to be produced.

We can now summarize the allocation of the scarce machine hours:

Production	Machine hours used	Balance of machine hours available
2000 units of Z	2000	10 000
2000 units of Y	4000	6 000
1000 units of X	6000	—

This production programme results in the following total contribution:

	(£)
2000 units of Z at £6 per unit contribution	12 000
2000 units of Y at £10 per unit contribution	20 000
1000 units of X at £12 per unit contribution	12 000
Total contribution	44 000

EXAMPLE 10.2

Rhine Autos is a major European producer of automobiles. A department within one of its divisions supplies component parts to firms operating within the automobile industry. The following information is provided relating to the anticipated demand and the productive capacity for the next quarter in respect of three components that are manufactured within the department:

	Component X	Component Y	Component Z
Contribution per unit of output	£12	£10	£6
Machine hours required per unit of output	6 hours	2 hours	1 hour
Estimated sales demand	2 000 units	2000 units	2000 units
Required machine hours for the quarter	12 000 hours	4000 hours	2000 hours

Because of the breakdown of one of its special purpose machines capacity is limited to 12 000 machine hours for the period, and this is insufficient to meet total sales demand. You have been asked to advise on the mix of products that should be produced during the period.

Always remember that it is necessary to consider other qualitative factors before the production programme is determined. For example, customer goodwill may be lost causing a fall in future sales if the company is unable to supply all three products to, say, 150 of its regular customers. Difficulties may arise in applying this procedure when there is more than one scarce resource. It could not be applied if, for example, labour hours were also scarce and the contribution per labour hour resulted in component Y being ranked first, followed by components X and Z. In this type of situation, where more than one resource is scarce, it is necessary to resort to linear programming methods in order to determine the optimal production programme. For an explanation of how linear programming can be applied to decision-making, when there are several scarce resources, you should refer to Drury (2000, Ch. 26).

The approach described above can also be applied in non-manufacturing organizations. For example, in a major UK retail store display space is the limiting factor. The store maximizes its short-term profits by allocating shelving space on the basis of contribution per metre of shelving space.

Finally, it is important that you remember that the approach outlined in this section applies only to those situations where capacity constraints cannot be removed in the short term. In the longer term additional resources should be acquired if the contribution from the extra capacity exceeds the cost of acquisition.

Replacement of equipment – the irrelevance of past costs

Replacement of equipment is a capital investment or long-term decision that requires the use of discounted cash flow procedures. These procedures are discussed in detail in

Chapter 12, but one aspect of asset replacement decisions which we will consider at this stage is how to deal with the book value (i.e. the **written-down value**) of old equipment. This is a problem that has been known to cause difficulty, but the correct approach is to apply relevant cost principles (i.e. past or sunk costs are irrelevant for decision-making). We shall now use Example 10.3 to illustrate the irrelevance of the book value of old equipment in a replacement decision. To avoid any possible confusion, it will be assumed here that £1 of cash inflow or outflow in year 1 is equivalent to £1 of cash inflow or outflow in, say, year 3. Such an assumption would in reality be incorrect and you will see why this is so in Chapter 12, but by adopting this assumption at this stage, the replacement problem can be simplified and we can focus our attention on the treatment of the book value of the old equipment in the replacement decision.

From an examination of Example 10.3 it can be seen that the total costs over a period of three years for each of the alternatives are as follows:

	(1) Retain present machine (£)	(2) Buy replacement machine (£)	(3) Difference (relevant costs/ revenues) (£)
Variable/incremental operating costs:			
20 000 units at £3 per unit for 3 years	180 000		
20 000 units at £2 per unit for 3 years		120 000	(60 000)
Old machine book value:			
3-year annual depreciation charge	90 000		
Lump sum write-off		90 000	
Old machine disposal value		(40 000)	(40 000)
Initial purchase price of new machine		70 000	70 000
Total cost	270 000	240 000	30 000

You can see from the above analysis that the £90 000 book value of the old machine is irrelevant to the decision. Book values are not relevant costs because they are past or sunk costs and are therefore the same for all potential courses of action. If the present machine is retained, three years' depreciation at £30 000 per annum will be written off annually whereas if the new machine is purchased the £90 000 will be written off as a lump sum if it is replaced. Note that depreciation charges for the new machine are not included in the analysis since the cost of purchasing the machine is already included in the analysis. The sum of the annual depreciation charges are equivalent to the purchase cost. Thus, including both items would amount to double counting.

The above analysis shows that the costs of operating the replacement machine are £30 000 less than the costs of operating the existing machine over the three-year period. Again there are several different methods of presenting the information. They all show a £30 000 advantage in favour of replacing the machine. You can present the information shown in columns (1) and (2) above, as long as you ensure that the same amount for the irrelevant items is included for all alternatives. Instead, you can present columns (1) and (2) with the irrelevant item (i.e. the £90 000) omitted or you can present the differential items listed in column (3). However, if you adopt the latter approach you will probably find it more meaningful to restate column (3) as follows:

EXAMPLE 10.3

A division within Rhine Autos purchased a machine three years ago for £180 000. Depreciation using the straight line basis, assuming a life of six years and with no salvage value, has been recorded each year in the financial accounts. The present written-down value of the equipment is £90 000 and it has a remaining life of three years. Management is considering replacing this machine with a new machine that will reduce the variable operating costs. The new machine will cost £70 000 and will have an expected life of three years with no scrap value. The variable operating costs are £3 per unit of output for the old machine and £2 per unit for the new machine. It is expected that both machines will be operated at a capacity of 20 000 units per annum. The sales revenues from the output of both machines will therefore be identical. The current disposal or sale value of the old machine is £40 000 and it will be zero in three years time.

	(£)
Savings on variable operating costs (3 years)	60 000
Sale proceeds of existing machine	40 000
	100 000
Less purchase cost of replacement machine	70 000
Savings on purchasing replacement machine	30 000

Outsourcing and make or buy decisions

Outsourcing is the process of obtaining goods or services from outside suppliers instead of producing the same goods or providing the same services within the organization. Decisions on whether to produce components or provide services within the organization or to acquire them from outside suppliers are called outsourcing or make or buy decisions. Many organizations outsource some of their activities such as their payroll and purchasing functions or the purchase of speciality components. Increasingly municipal local services such as waste disposal, highways and property maintenance are being outsourced. Consider the information presented in Example 10.4 (Case A).

At first glance it appears that the component should be outsourced since the purchase price of £30 is less than the current total unit cost of manufacturing. However, the unit costs include some costs that will be unchanged whether or not the components are outsourced. These costs are therefore not relevant to the decision. Assume also that there are no alternative uses of the released capacity if the components are outsourced. The appropriate cost information is presented in Exhibit 10.3 (Section A). Alternative approaches to presenting relevant cost and revenue information are presented. In columns (1) and (2) of Exhibit 10.3 cost information is presented that includes both relevant and irrelevant costs for both alternatives under consideration. The same amount for non-manufacturing overheads, which are irrelevant, is included for both alternatives. By including the same amount in both columns the cost is made irrelevant. Alternatively, you can present cost information in columns (1) and (2) that excludes any irrelevant costs and revenues because they are identical for both alternatives. Adopting either approach will result in a difference of £60 000 in favour of making component A.

The third approach is to list only the relevant costs, cost savings and any relevant revenues. This approach is shown in column (3) of Exhibit 10.3. This column represents

EXAMPLE 10.4

CASE A

One of the divisions within Rhine Autos is currently negotiating with another supplier regarding outsourcing component A that it manufactures. The division currently manufactures 10 000 units per annum of the component. The costs currently assigned to the components are as follows:

	Total costs of producing 10 000 components (£)	Unit cost (£)
Direct materials	120 000	12
Direct labour	100 000	10
Variable manufacturing overhead costs (power and utilities)	10 000	1
Fixed manufacturing overhead costs	80 000	8
Share of non-manufacturing overheads	50 000	5
Total costs	360 000	36

The above costs are expected to remain unchanged in the foreseeable future if the Rhine Autos division continues to manufacture the components. The supplier has offered to supply 10 000 components per annum at a price of £30 per unit guaranteed for a minimum of three years. If Rhine Autos outsources component A the direct labour force currently employed in producing the components will be made redundant. No redundancy costs will be incurred. Direct materials and variable overheads are avoidable if component A is outsourced. Fixed manufacturing overhead costs would be reduced by £10 000 per annum but non-manufacturing costs would remain unchanged. Assume initially that the capacity that is required for component A has no alternative use. Should the Division of Rhine Autos make or buy the component?

CASE B

Assume now that the extra capacity that will be made available from outsourcing component A can be used to manufacture and sell 10 000 units of part B at a price of £34 per unit. All of the labour force required to manufacture component A would be used to make part B. The variable manufacturing overheads, the fixed manufacturing overheads and non-manufacturing overheads would be the same as the costs incurred for manufacturing component A. The materials required to manufacture component A would not be required but additional materials required for making part B would cost £13 per unit. Should Rhine Autos outsource component A?

the differential costs or revenues and it is derived from the differences between columns (1) and (2). In column (3) only the information that is relevant to the decision is presented. You will see that this approach compares the relevant costs of making directly against outsourcing. It indicates that the additional costs of making component A are £240 000 but this enables purchasing costs of £300 000 to be saved. Therefore the company makes a net saving of £60 000 from making the components compared with outsourcing.

However, you will probably find column (3) easier to interpret if it is restated as two separate alternatives as shown in Exhibit 10.3. All of the approaches described in this and the preceding paragraph yield identical results. You can adopt any of them. It is a matter of personal preference.

Let us now re-examine the situation when the extra capacity created from not producing component A has an alternative use. Consider the information presented in Example 10.4 (Case B). The management of Rhine Autos now have three alternatives. They are:

1. Make component A and do not make part B.
2. Outsource component A and do not make part B.
3. Outsource component A and make and sell part B.

EXHIBIT 10.3

Evaluating a make or buy decision

Section A – Assuming there is no alternative use of the released capacity

	Total cost of continuing to make 10 000 components (1) (£ per annum)	Total cost of buying 10 000 components (2) (£ per annum)	Difference (relevant) (cost) (3) (£ per annum)
Direct materials	120 000		120 000
Direct labour	100 000		100 000
Variable manufacturing overhead costs (power and utilities)	10 000		10 000
Fixed manufacturing overhead costs	80 000	70 000	10 000
Non-manufacturing overheads	50 000	50 000	
Outside purchase cost incurred/(saved)		300 000	(300 000)
Total costs incurred/(saved) per annum	360 000	420 000	(60 000)

Column 3 is easier to interpret if it is restated as two separate alternatives as follows:

	Relevant cost of making component A (£ per annum)	Relevant cost of outsourcing component A (£ per annum)
Direct materials	120 000	
Direct labour	100 000	
Variable manufacturing overhead costs	10 000	
Fixed manufacturing overhead costs	10 000	
Outside purchase cost incurred		300 000
	240 000	300 000

(Exhibit 10.3 continued)

Section B – Assuming the released capacity has alternative uses

	(1) Make component A and do not make part B (£ per annum)	(2) Buy component A and do not make part B (£ per annum)	(3) Buy component A and make part B (£ per annum)
Direct materials	120 000		130 000
Direct labour	100 000		100 000
Variable manufacturing overhead costs	10 000		10 000
Fixed manufacturing overhead costs	80 000	70 000	80 000
Non-manufacturing overheads	50 000	50 000	50 000
Outside purchase cost incurred		300 000	300 000
Revenues from sales of part B			(340 000)
Total net costs	360 000	420 000	330 000

It is assumed there is insufficient capacity to make both component A and part B. The appropriate financial information is presented in Exhibit 10.3 (Section B). You will see that, with the exception of non-manufacturing costs, all of the items differ between the alternatives and are therefore relevant to the decision. Again we can omit the non-manufacturing costs from the analysis or include the same amount for all alternatives. Either approach makes them irrelevant. The first two alternatives that do not involve making and selling part B are identical to the alternatives considered in Case A so the information presented in columns (1) and (2) in Sections A and B of Exhibit 10.3 are identical. In column 3 of Section B the costs incurred in making part B in respect of direct labour, variable and fixed manufacturing overheads and non-manufacturing overheads are identical to the costs incurred in making component A. Therefore the same costs for these items are entered in column 3. However, different materials are required to make part B and the cost of these (10 000 units at £13) are entered in column 3. In addition, the revenues from the sales of part B are entered in column 3. Comparing the three columns in Section B of Exhibit 10.3 indicates that buying component A and using the extra capacity that is created to make part B is the preferred alternative.

The incremental costs of outsourcing are £60 000 more than making component B (see Section A of Exhibit 10.3) but the extra capacity released from outsourcing component A enables Rhine Autos to obtain a profit contribution of £90 000 (£340 000 incremental sales from part B less £250 000 incremental/relevant costs of making part B). The overall outcome is a £30 000 net benefit from outsourcing. Note that the relevant costs of making part B are the same as those of making component A, apart from direct materials, which cost £130 000. In other words, the relevant (incremental) costs of making part B are as follows:

	(£)
Direct materials	130 000
Direct labour	100 000
Variable manufacturing overhead costs	10 000
Fixed manufacturing overhead costs	10 000
	250 000

Discontinuation decisions

Most organizations periodically analyse profits by one or more cost objects, such as products or services, customers and locations. Periodic profitability analysis provides attention-directing information that highlights those unprofitable activities that require a more detailed appraisal (sometimes referred to as a special study) to ascertain whether or not they should be discontinued. In this section we shall illustrate how the principle of relevant costs can be applied to discontinuation decisions. Consider Example 10.5. You will see that it focuses on a decision whether to discontinue operating a sales territory, but the same principles can also be applied to discontinuing products, services or customers.

In Example 10.5 Euro Company analyses profits by locations. Profits are analysed by regions which are then further analysed by sales territories within each region. It is apparent from Example 10.5 that the Scandinavian region is profitable but the profitability analysis suggests that the Helsinki sales territory is unprofitable. A more detailed study is required to ascertain whether it should be discontinued. Let us assume that this study indicates that:

1. Discontinuing the Helsinki sales territory will eliminate cost of goods sold, salespersons salaries, sales office rent and regional and headquarters expenses arising from cause-and-effect cost allocations.

EXAMPLE 10.5

The Euro Company is a wholesaler who sells its products to retailers throughout Europe. Euro's headquarters is in Brussels. The company has adopted a regional structure with each region consisting of 3–5 sales territories. Each region has its own regional office and a warehouse which distributes the goods directly to the customers. Each sales territory also has an office where the marketing staff are located. The Scandinavian region consists of three sales territories with offices located in Stockholm, Oslo and Helsinki. The budgeted results for the next quarter are as follows:

	Stockholm (£000's)	Oslo (£000's)	Helsinki (£000's)	Total (£000's)
Cost of goods sold	800	850	1000	2650
Salespersons salaries	160	200	240	600
Sales office rent	60	90	120	270
Depreciation of sales office equipment	20	30	40	90
Apportionment of warehouse rent	24	24	24	72
Depreciation of warehouse equipment	20	16	22	58
Regional and headquarters costs				
Cause-and-effect allocations	120	152	186	458
Arbitrary apportionments	360	400	340	1100
Total costs assigned to each location	1564	1762	1972	5298
Reported profit/(loss)	236	238	(272)	202
Sales	1800	2000	1700	5500

Assuming that the above results are likely to be typical of future quarterly performance should the Helsinki territory be discontinued?

2. Discontinuing the Helsinki sales territory will have no effect on depreciation of sales of office equipment, warehouse rent, depreciation of warehouse equipment and regional and headquarters expenses arising from arbitrary cost allocations. The same costs will be incurred by the company for all of these items even if the sales territory is discontinued.

Note that in the event of discontinuation the sales office will not be required and the rental will be eliminated whereas the warehouse rent relates to the warehouse for the region as a whole and, unless the company moves to a smaller warehouse, the rental will remain unchanged. It is therefore not a relevant cost. Discontinuation will result in the creation of additional space and if the extra space remains unused there are no financial consequences to take into account. However, if the additional space can be sub-let to generate rental income the income would be incorporated as an opportunity cost for the alternative of keeping the Helsinki territory.

Exhibit 10.4 shows the relevant cost computations. Column (1) shows the costs incurred by the company if the sales territory is kept open and column (2) shows the costs that would be incurred if a decision was taken to drop the sales territory. Therefore in column (2) only those costs that would be eliminated (i.e. those items listed in item (1) above) are deducted from column (1). You can see that the company will continue to incur some of the costs (i.e. those items listed in item (2) above) even if the Helsinki territory is closed and these costs are therefore irrelevant to the decision. Again you can either include, or exclude, the irrelevant costs in columns (1) and (2) as long as you ensure that the same amount of irrelevant costs is included for both alternatives if you adopt the first approach. Both approaches will show that future profits will decline by £154 000 if the Helsinki territory is closed. Alternatively, you can present just the relevant costs and

EXHIBIT 10.4

Relevant cost analysis relating to the discontinuation of the Helsinki territory

	Total costs and revenues to be assigned		
	(1) Keep Helsinki territory open (£000's)	(2) Discontinue Helsinki territory (£000's)	(3) Difference incremental costs and revenues (£000's)
Cost of goods sold	2650	1650	1000
Salespersons salaries	600	360	240
Sales office rent	270	150	120
Depreciation of sales office equipment	90	90	
Apportionment of warehouse rent	72	72	
Depreciation of warehouse equipment	58	58	
Regional and headquarters costs			
Cause-and-effect allocations	458	272	186
Arbitrary apportionments	1100	1100	
Total costs to be assigned	5298	3752	1546
Reported profit	202	48	154
Sales	5500	3800	1700

revenues shown in column (3). This approach indicates that keeping the sales territory open results in additional sales revenues of £1 700 000 but additional costs of £1 546 000 are incurred giving a contribution of £154 000 towards fixed costs and profits.

You will have noted that we have assumed that the regional and headquarters costs assigned to the sales territories on the basis of cause-and-effect allocations can be eliminated if the Helsinki territory is discontinued. These are indirect costs that fluctuate in the longer-term according to the demand for them and it is assumed that the selected allocation base, or cost driver, provides a reasonably accurate measure of resources consumed by the sales territories. Cause-and-effect allocation bases assume that if the cause is eliminated or reduced, the effect (i.e. the costs) will be eliminated or reduced. If cost drivers are selected that result in allocations that are inaccurate measures of resources consumed by cost objects (i.e. sales territories) the relevant costs derived from these allocations will be incorrect and incorrect decisions may be made. We shall explore this issue in some detail in the next chapter when we look at activity-based costing.

Determining the relevant costs of direct materials

So far in this chapter we have assumed, when considering various decisions, that any materials required would not be taken from existing stocks but would be purchased at a later date, and so the estimated purchase price would be the relevant material cost. Where materials are taken from existing stock do remember that the original purchase price represents a past or sunk cost and is therefore irrelevant for decision-making. If the materials are to be replaced then using the materials for a particular activity will necessitate their replacement. Thus, the decision to use the materials on an activity will result in additional acquisition costs compared with the situation if the materials were not used on that particular activity. Therefore the future **replacement cost** represents the relevant cost of the materials.

Consider now the situation where the materials have no further use apart from being used on a particular activity. If the materials have some realizable value, the use of the materials will result in lost sales revenues, and this lost sales revenue will represent an opportunity cost that must be assigned to the activity. Alternatively, if the materials have no realizable value the relevant cost of the materials will be zero.

Determining the relevant costs of direct labour

Determining the direct labour costs that are relevant to short-term decisions depends on the circumstances. Where a company has temporary spare capacity and the labour force is to be maintained in the short term, the direct labour cost incurred will remain the same for all alternative decisions. The direct labour cost will therefore be irrelevant for short-term decision-making purposes. Consider now a situation where casual labour is used and where workers can be hired on a daily basis; a company may then adjust the employment of labour to exactly the amount required to meet the production requirements. The labour cost will increase if the company accepts additional work, and will decrease if production is reduced. In this situation the labour cost will be a relevant cost for decision-making purposes.

In a situation where full capacity exists and additional labour supplies are unavailable in the short term, and where no further overtime working is possible, the only way that labour resources could then be obtained for a specific order would be to reduce existing production. This would release labour for the order, but the reduced production would result in a lost contribution, and this lost contribution must be taken into account when ascertaining the relevant cost for the specific order. The relevant labour cost per hour where full capacity exists is therefore the hourly labour rate plus an opportunity cost consisting of the contribution per hour that is lost by accepting the order.

Summary

In this chapter we have focused on special studies and described the principles involved in determining the relevant cost of alternative courses of action. We have found that a particular cost can be relevant in one situation but irrelevant in another. The important point to note is that relevant costs represent those future costs that will be changed by a particular decision, while irrelevant costs are those that will not be affected by that decision. In the short-term total profits will be increased (or total losses decreased) if a course of action is chosen where relevant revenues are in excess of relevant costs. We noted that not all of the important inputs relevant to a decision can always be easily quantified, but that it is essential that any qualitative factors relevant to the decision should be taken into account in the decision-making process.

We have considered a variety of decision-making problems in the form of Examples 10.1–10.5. The important point that you should remember from these examples is that the decision-relevant approach adopts whatever time horizon the decision-maker considers relevant for a given situation. In the short-term some costs cannot be avoided, and are therefore irrelevant for decision-making purposes. In the longer term, however, many costs are avoidable, and it is therefore important that decision-makers do not focus excessively on the short-term. In the long-term revenues must be sufficient to cover all costs.

Key Terms and Concepts

decision-relevant approach (p. 229)
differential cash flow (p. 230)
incremental cash flow (p. 230)
limiting factor (p. 235)
opportunity cost (p. 235)
outsourcing (p. 239)

qualitative factors (p. 230)
relevant cost (p. 230)
replacement cost (p. 245)
special studies (p. 229)
written-down value (p. 238)

Key Examination Points

A common mistake that students make when presenting information for decision-making is to compare *unit* costs. With this approach, there is a danger that fixed costs will be unitized and treated as variable costs. In most cases you should compare total amounts of costs and revenues rather than unit amounts. Many students do not present the information clearly and concisely. There are many alternative ways of presenting the information, but the simplest way is normally to list the future costs and revenues for each alternative in a format similar to Exhibit 10.1. You should exclude irrelevant items or ensure that the same amount for irrelevant items is included for each alternative. To determine the amount to be entered for each alternative, you should ask yourself what difference it makes if the alternative is selected.

Never allocate common fixed costs to the alternatives. The focus should be on how the choice of each alternative will affect future cash flows of the organization. Changes in the apportionment of fixed costs will not alter future cash flows of the company. Remember that if a resource is scarce, the analysis should recommend the alternative that yields the largest contribution per limiting factor. You should now attempt the review problems and compare your answers with the solutions that are provided. These problems will test your understanding of a variety of decision problems that have been covered in Chapter 10.

Review Problems

(For additional problems without answers relating to the content of this chapter you should refer to pages 484–498.)

1 Z Limited manufactures three products, the selling price and cost details of which are given below:

	Product X (£)	Product Y (£)	Product Z (£)
Selling price per unit	75	95	95
Costs per unit:			
Direct materials (£5/kg)	10	5	15
Direct labour (£4/hour)	16	24	20
Variable overhead	8	12	10
Fixed overhead	24	36	30

In a period when direct materials are restricted in supply, the most and the least profitable uses of direct materials are

	Most profitable	Least profitable
A	X	Z
B	Y	Z
C	X	Y
D	Z	Y
E	Y	X

CIMA Stage 2

2 Your company regularly uses material X and currently has in stock 600 kg, for which it paid £1500 two weeks ago. If this were to be sold as raw material it could be sold today for £2.00 per kg. You are aware that the material can be bought on the open market for £3.25 per kg, but it must be purchased in quantities of 1000 kg.

You have been asked to determine the relevant cost of 600 kg of material X to be used in a job for a customer. The relevant cost of the 600 kg is:
(a) £1200
(b) £1325
(c) £1825
(d) £1950
(e) £3250

CIMA Stage 2

3 BB Limited makes three components: S, T and U. The following costs have been recorded:

	Component S Unit cost (£)	Component T Unit cost (£)	Component U Unit cost (£)
Variable cost	2.50	8.00	5.00
Fixed cost	2.00	8.30	3.75
Total cost	4.50	16.30	8.75

Another company has offered to supply the components to BB Limited at the following prices:

	Component S	Component T	Component U
Price each	£4	£7	£5.50

Which component(s), if any, should BB Limited consider buying in?
(a) Buy in all three components.
(b) Do not buy any.
(c) Buy in S and U.
(d) Buy in T only.

CIMA Stage 1

4 A company is considering accepting a one-year contract which will require four skilled employees. The four skilled employees could be recruited on a one-year contract at a cost of £40 000 per employee. The employees would be supervised by an existing manager who earns £60 000 per annum. It is expected that supervision of the contract would take 10% of the manager's time.

Instead of recruiting new employees, the company could retrain some existing employees who currently earn £30 000 per year. The training would cost £15 000 in total. If these employees were used they would need to be replaced at a total cost of £100 000.

The relevant labour cost of the contract is:
A   £100 000
B   £115 000

C   £135 000
D   £141 000
E   £166 000

CIMA Stage 2

5 Two decision-making problems are faced by a company which produces a range of products and absorbs production overhead using a rate of 200% on direct wages. This rate was calculated from the following budgeted figures:

	(£)
Variable production costs	64 000
Fixed production costs	96 000
Direct labour costs	80 000

Problem 1
The normal selling price of product X is £22 and production cost for one unit is:

	(£)
Raw materials	8
Direct labour	4
Production overhead	8
	£20

There is a possibility of supplying a special order for 2000 units of product X at £16 each. If the order were accepted the normal budgeted sales would not be affected and the company has the necessary capacity to produce the additional units.

Problem 2
The cost of making component Q, which forms part of product Y, is stated below:

	(£)
Raw materials	4
Direct labour	8
Production overhead	16
	£28

Component Q could be bought from an outside supplier for £20. You are required, assuming that fixed production costs will not change, to:
(a) State whether the company should:
    (i) accept the special order in problem 1;

(ii) continue making component Q or buy it from outside in Problem 2;
(Both your statements must be supported by details of cost.)
(b) Comment on the principle you have followed in your cost analysis to arrive at your answers to the two problems.

CIMA Cost Accounting 1

6 Due to a national wage agreement, you find that wage rates for skilled workers are to increase by 50% over the budget figures. There is a shortage of such skilled workers and it takes over a year to train new recruits adequately. The managing director has asked you for advice as to which order of priority on the product range would give best use of the skilled labour resources available. The cost of unskilled labour, of which there is no shortage, will go up by 20% over budget.

The original budget figures for the next period before allowing for the increase in labour cost detailed above, were:

Product	V	W	X	Y	Z
Maximum production in units	3000	4000	6000	7000	9000
Selling price per unit	£16	£15	£18	£15	£30
Variable costs per unit					
Material	3	5	4	7	6
Skilled labour £4 per hour	4	4	6	2	8
Unskilled labour £2 per hour	2	2	1	1	4

Variable overheads are recovered at the rate of £1 per labour hour. The skilled labour available amounts to 30 000 hours in the period and there are fixed costs of £22 800.
You are required to:
(a) calculate the product mix which would result in the maximum profit;   (*12 marks*)
(b) comment on the results of the revised budget.   (*6 marks*)

(*Total 18 marks*)

AAT

7 The production manager of your organization has approached you for some costing advice on project X, a one-off order from overseas that he intends to tender for. The costs associated with the project are as follows:

	(£)
Material A	4 000
Material B	8 000

Direct labour	6 000
Supervision	2 000
Overheads	12 000
	32 000

You ascertain the following:

(i) Material A is in stock and the above was the cost. There is now no other use for material A, other than the above project, within the factory and it would cost £1750 to dispose of. Material B would have to be ordered at the cost shown above.

(ii) Direct labour costs of £6000 relate to workers that will be transferred to this project from another project. Extra labour will need to be recruited to the other project at a cost of £7000.

(iii) Supervision costs have been charged to the project on the basis of $33\frac{1}{3}$% of labour costs and will be carried out by existing staff within their normal duties.

(iv) Overheads have been charged to the project at the rate of 200% on direct labour.

(v) The company is currently operating at a point above break-even.

(vi) The project will need the utilization of machinery that will have no other use to the company after the project has finished. The machinery will have to be purchased at a cost of £10 000 and then disposed of for £5250 at the end of the project.

The production manager tells you that the overseas customer is prepared to pay up to a maximum of £30 000 for the project and a competitor is prepared to accept the order at that price. He also informs you the minimum that he can charge is £40 000 as the above costs show £32 000, and this does not take into consideration the cost of the machine and profit to be taken on the project.

Required:

(a) Cost the project for the production manager, clearly stating how you have arrived at your figures and giving reasons for the exclusion of other figures. *(12 marks)*

(b) Write a report to the production manager stating whether the organization should go ahead with the tender for the project, the reasons why and the price, bearing in mind that the competitor is prepared to undertake the project for £30 000. *(8 marks)*

Note: The project should only be undertaken if it shows a profit.

(c) State four non-monetary factors that should be taken into account before tendering for this project. *(2 marks)*

(d) What would be your advice if you were told that the organization was operating below break-even point? Give reasons for your advice. *(3 marks)*

(Total 25 marks)
AAT Cost Accounting and Budgeting

8 A company in the civil engineering industry with headquarters located 22 miles from London undertakes contracts anywhere in the United Kingdom.

The company has had its tender for a job in north-east England accepted at £288 000 and work is due to begin in March. However, the company has also been asked to undertake a contract on the south coast of England. The price offered for this contract is £352 000. Both of the contracts cannot be taken simultaneously because of constraints on staff site management personnel and on plant available. An escape clause enables the company to withdraw from the contract in the north-east, provided notice is given before the end of November and an agreed penalty of £28 000 is paid.

The following estimates have been submitted by the company's quantity surveyor:

Cost estimates	North-east (£)	South coast (£)
Materials:		
In stock at original cost, Material X	21 600	
In stock at original cost, Material Y		24 800
Firm orders placed at original cost, Material X	30 400	
Not yet ordered – current cost, Material X	60 000	
Not yet ordered – current cost, Material Z		71 200
Labour – hired locally	86 000	110 000
Site management	34 000	34 000

Staff accommodation and travel for site management	6 800	5 600
Plant on site – depreciation	9 600	12 800
Interest on capital, 8%	5 120	6 400
Total local contract costs	253 520	264 800
Headquarters costs allocated at rate of 5% on total contract costs	12 676	13 240
	266 196	278 040
Contract price	288 000	352 000
Estimated profit	21 804	73 960

Notes:

1. X, Y and Z are three building materials. Material X is not in common use and would not realize much money if re-sold; however, it could be used on other contracts but only as a substitute for another material currently quoted at 10% less than the original cost of X. The price of Y, a material in common use, has doubled since it was purchased; its net realizable value if re-sold would be its new price less 15% to cover disposal costs. Alternatively it could be kept for use on other contracts in the following financial year.

2. With the construction industry not yet recovered from the recent recession, the company is confident that manual labour, both skilled and unskilled, could be hired locally on a subcontracting basis to meet the needs of each of the contracts.

3. The plant which would be needed for the south coast contract has been owned for some years and £12 800 is the year's depreciation on a straight-line basis. If the north-east contract is undertaken, less plant will be required but the surplus plant will be hired out for the period of the contract at a rental of £6000.

4. It is the company's policy to charge all contracts with notional interest at 8% on estimated working capital involved in contracts. Progress payments would be receivable from the contractee.

5. Salaries and general costs of operating the small headquarters amount to about £108 000 each year. There are usually ten contracts being supervised at the same time.

6. Each of the two contracts is expected to last from March to February which, coincidentally, is the company's financial year.

7. Site management is treated as a fixed cost.

You are required, as the management accountant to the company,

(a) to present comparative statements to show the net benefit to the company of undertaking the more advantageous of the two contracts;   *(12 marks)*

(b) to explain the reasoning behind the inclusion in (or omission from) your comparative financial statements, of each item given in the cost estimates and the notes relating thereto.   *(13 marks)*

(Total 25 marks)

CIMA Stage 2 Cost Accounting

9 Blackarm Ltd makes three products and is reviewing the profitability of its product line. You are given the following budgeted data about the firm for the coming year.

Product Sales (in units)	A 100 000 (£)	B 120 000 (£)	C 80 000 (£)
Revenue	1 500 000	1 440 000	880 000
Costs:			
Material	500 000	480 000	240 000
Labour	400 000	320 000	160 000
Overhead	650 000	600 000	360 000
	1 550 000	1 400 000	760 000
Profit/(Loss)	(50 000)	40 000	120 000

The company is concerned about the loss on product A. It is considering ceasing production of it and switching the spare capacity of 100 000 units to Product C.

You are told:

(i) All production is sold.

(ii) 25% of the labour cost for each product is fixed in nature.

(iii) Fixed administration overheads of £900 000 in total have been apportioned to each product on the basis of units sold and are included in the overhead costs above. All other overhead costs are variable in nature.

(iv) Ceasing production of product A would eliminate the fixed labour charge associated with it and one-sixth of the fixed administration overhead apportioned to product A.

(v) Increasing the production of product C by 100 000 units would mean that the fixed labour cost associated with product C would double, the variable labour cost would rise by 20% and its selling price would have to be decreased by £1.50 in order to achieve the increased sales.

Required:
(a) Prepare a marginal cost statement for a unit of each product on the basis of:
   (i) the original budget;
   (ii) if product A is deleted. *(12 marks)*
(b) Prepare a statement showing the total contribution and profit for each product group on the basis of:

(i) the original budget;
(ii) if product A is deleted. *(8 marks)*
(c) Using your results from (a) and (b) advise whether product A should be deleted from the product range, giving reasons for your decision. *(5 marks)*
(Total 25 marks)
AAT Cost Accounting and Budgeting

Solutions to Review Problems

SOLUTION 1

	X	Y	Z
Contribution per unit	£41	£54	£50
Kg used (Limiting factor)	2 (£10/5)	1	3
Contribution per kg	£20.5	£54	£16.67
Ranking	2	1	3

Answer $= B$

SOLUTION 2

The material is in regular use and if used will have to be replaced at a cost of £1950 (600 × £3.25). The cash flow consequences are £1950.

Answer $= D$

SOLUTION 3

Assuming that fixed costs will remain unchanged whether or not the company makes or buys the components the relevant cost of manufacture will be the variable cost. Under these circumstances the company should only purchase components if the purchase price is less than the variable cost. Therefore the company should only purchase component T.

Answer $= D$

SOLUTION 4

Incremental cost of new employees $=$ £40 000 × 4 $=$ £160 000

Supervision is not an incremental cost.
Incremental costs of retraining $=$ £15 000 + £100 000 replacement cost $=$ £115 000
Retraining is the cheaper alternative and therefore the relevant cost of the contract is £115 000.

Answer $= B$

SOLUTION 5

(a) Direct wages percentage overhead rate
$$= \frac{£64\,000 \text{ (Variable)} + £96\,000 \text{ (Fixed)}}{\text{Direct labour costs (£80\,000)}}$$
$$= 200\% \text{ of direct wages}$$

Variable overhead rate
$$= \frac{£64\,000 \text{ Variable}}{£80\,000 \text{ Direct labour costs}}$$
$$= 80\% \text{ of direct wages}$$

Problem 1:

	(£)	Per unit	2 000 units
Additional revenue		16.00	32 000
Additional costs:			
Raw materials	8.00		
Direct labour	4.00		
Variable overhead (80% × £4)	3.20	15.20	30 400
		£0.80	£1 600

The order should be accepted because it provides a contribution to fixed costs and profits. It is assumed that direct labour is a variable cost.

Problem 2:

Relevant manufacturing costs of the component:

	(£)
Raw material	4.00
Direct labour	8.00
Variable overhead (80% × £8)	6.40
	18.40

The additional costs of manufacturing are lower than the costs of purchasing. Therefore the company should manufacture the component. It is assumed that spare capacity exists.

(b) Relevant cost and revenue principles have been followed. See Chapter 10 for an explanation.

SOLUTION 6

(a)

	V (£)	W (£)	X (£)	Y (£)	Z (£)
Selling price	16	15	18	15	30
Material	3	5	4	7	6
Skilled labour	6	6	9	3	12
Unskilled labour	2.4	2.4	1.2	1.2	4.8
Variable overhead	2	2	2	1	4
Total variable cost	13.4	15.4	16.2	12.2	26.8
Contribution	2.6	(0.4)	1.8	2.8	3.2
Number of skilled hours	1	1	1.5	0.5	2
Contribution per skilled hour	2.6	(0.4)	1.2	5.6	1.6
Ranking	2	Drop	4	1	3
Skilled hours allocated (W1)	3000		5500	3500	18 000
			(Balance)		

The product mix will be:

	(£)
Y (7000 units × £2.80 contribution)	19 600
V (3000 units × £2.60 contribution)	7 800
Z (9000 units × £3.20 contribution)	28 800
X (5500 hours × £1.80 contribution)	6 600
1.5 hours	
Total contribution	62 800
Less fixed costs	22 800
Maximum profit	40 000

Workings:

(W1) Maximum units demanded X skilled hours per unit.

(b) If the labour hours constraint is removed the output of product X should be increased to the maximum demand of 6000 units. At present

the constraint on skilled labour hours results in a lost contribution of £4201 (6000 units less 3666 units allocated in (a) × £1.80 unit contribution). Therefore the company should consider ways of removing this constraint. As long as the costs of removing the constraint are less than £4201, total profit will increase. Product W should be dropped from the range provided it does not affect the sales of other products.

SOLUTION 7

(a)

	Relevant costs of the project
Material A	(1 750)
Material B	8 000
Direct labour	7 000
Net cost of machinery	4 750
Relevant cost	18 000
Contract price	30 000
Contribution	12 000

Notes:

(1) There is a saving in material costs of £1750 if material A is not used.

(2) The actual cost of material B represents the incremental cost.

(3) The hiring of the labour on the other contract represents the additional cash flows of undertaking this contract.

(4) The net cost of purchasing the machinery represents the additional cash flows associated with the contract.

(5) Supervision and overheads will still continue even if the contract is not accepted and are therefore irrelevant.

(b) The report should indicate that the costs given in the question do not represent incremental cash flows arising from undertaking the contract. As the company is operating at an activity level in excess of break-even point any sales revenue in excess of £18 000 incremental costs will provide an additional contribution which will result in an increase in profits. Assuming that the company has spare capacity, and that a competitor is prepared to accept the order at £30 000, then a tender price slightly below £30 000 would be appropriate.

(c) Before accepting the contract the following non-monetary factors should be considered.

    (i) Is there sufficient spare capacity to undertake the project?

    (ii) Is the overseas customer credit worthy?

    (iii) Has the workforce the necessary skills to undertake the project?

    (iv) Is the contract likely to result in repeat business with the customer?

(d) If the company were operating below the break-even point, acceptance of the order would provide a further contribution towards fixed costs and reduce the existing loss. In the short term it is better to accept the order and reduce the total loss but if, in the long run, there are not enough orders to generate sufficient contributions to cover total fixed costs, then the company will not survive.

SOLUTION 8

(a)

	North East (£)	South coast (£)
Material X from stock (i)	19 440	
Material Y from stock (ii)		49 600
Firm orders of material X (iii)	27 360	
Material X not yet ordered (iv)	60 000	
Material Z not yet ordered (v)		71 200
Labour (vi)	86 000	110 000
Site management (vii)	—	—
Staff accommodation and travel for site management (viii)	6 800	5 600
Plant rental received (ix)	(6 000)	—
Penalty clause (x)		28 000
	193 600	264 400
Contract price	288 000	352 000
Net benefit	94 400	87 600

(b) (i) If material X is not used on the North East contract the most beneficial use is to use it as a substitute material thus avoiding future purchases of £19 440 (0.9 × 21 600). Therefore by using the stock quantity of material X the company will have to spend £19 440 on the other materials.

    (ii) Material Y is in common use and the company should not dispose of it. Using the materials on the South coast contract will mean that they will have to be replaced at a cost of £49 600 (£24 800 × 2). Therefore the future cash flow impact of taking on the contract is £49 600.

    (iii) It is assumed that with firm orders for materials it is not possible to cancel the purchase. Therefore the cost will occur whatever future alternative is selected. The materials will be used as a substitute material if they are not used on the contract and therefore, based on the same reasoning as note (i) above, the relevant cost is the purchase price of the substitute material (0.9 × £30 400).

    (iv) The material has not been ordered and the cost will only be incurred if the contract is undertaken. Therefore additional cash flows of £60 000 will be incurred if the company takes on the North East contract.

    (v) The same principles apply here as were explained in note (iv) and additional cash flows of £71 200 will be incurred only if the company takes on the South coast contract.

    (vi) It is assumed that labour is an incremental cost and therefore relevant.

    (vii) The site management function is performed by staff at central headquarters. It is assumed that the total company costs in respect of site management will remain unchanged in the short term whatever contracts are taken on. Site management costs are therefore irrelevant.

    (viii) The costs would be undertaken only if the contracts are undertaken. Therefore they are relevant costs.

    (ix) If the North East contract is undertaken the company will be able to hire out surplus plant and obtain a £6000 cash inflow.

    (x) If the South coast contract is undertaken the company will have to withdraw from the North East contract and incur a penalty cost of £28 000.

    (xi) The headquarter costs will continue whichever alternative is selected and they are not relevant costs.

    (xii) It is assumed that there will be no differential cash flows relating to notional interest. However, if the interest costs associated with the contract differ then they would be relevant and should be included in the analysis.

(xiii) Depreciation is a sunk cost and irrelevant for decision-making.

SOLUTION 9

(a) (i)

Product	A (£)	B (£)	C (£)
Selling price	15	12	11
Less variable costs:			
Materials	(5)	(4)	(3)
Labour	(3)	(2)	(1.5)
Variable overhead (1)	(3.50)	(2)	(1.5)
Contribution	3.50	4	5

Note:

(1) Fixed overheads are apportioned to products on the basis of sales volume and the remaining overheads are variable with output.

(ii)

Product	B (£)	C (£)
Selling price	12	9.50
Less variable costs:		
Materials	(4)	(3)
Labour	(2)	(1.80)
Variable overhead	(2)	(1.50)
Contribution	4	3.20

(b) (i)

Product	A	B	C	Total
Total contribution	350 000	480 000	400 000	1 230 000
Less fixed costs:				
Labour				(220 000)
Fixed administration				(900 000)
Profit				110 000

(ii)

Product	B	C	Total
Total contribution[a]	480 000	576 000	1 056 000
Less fixed costs:			
Labour[b]			(160 000)
Fixed administration[c]			(850 000)
Profit			46 000

Notes:

[a] B = 120 000 units × £4 contribution, C = 18 000 units × £3.20 contribution.

[b] (25% × £320 000 for B) plus (25% × £160 000 × 2 for C).

[c] Fixed administration costs will decline by $\frac{1}{6}$ of the amount apportioned to Product A (100/300 × £900 000). Therefore fixed overheads will decline from £900 000 to £850 000.

(c) Product A should not be eliminated even though a loss is reported for this product. If Product A is eliminated the majority of fixed costs allocated to it will still continue and will be borne by the remaining products. Product A generates a contribution of £350 000 towards fixed costs but the capacity released can be used to obtain an additional contribution from Product C of £176 000 (£576 000 − £400 000). This will result in a net loss in contribution of £174 000. However, fixed cost savings of £110 000 (£50 000 administration apportioned to Product A plus £100 000 labour for A less an extra £40 000 labour for Product C) can be obtained if Product A is abandoned. Therefore there will be a net loss in contribution of £64 000 (£174 000 − £110 000) and profits will decline from £110 000 to £64 000.

Activity-based costing

The aim of the previous chapter was to provide you with an understanding of the principles that should be used to identify relevant costs and revenues for various types of decisions. It was assumed that relevant costs could easily be measured but, in reality, it was pointed out that the indirect relevant costs can be difficult to identify and measure. The measurement of indirect relevant costs for decision-making using activity-based costing (ABC) techniques will be examined in this chapter. The aims of this chapter are to provide you with a conceptual understanding of ABC and explain how an ABC system operates.

Unless otherwise stated we shall assume that products are the cost objects but the techniques used, and the principles established, can also be applied to other cost objects such as customers, services and locations. We begin with an examination of the role that a cost accumulation system plays in generating relevant cost information for decision-making.

You should note that this chapter extends the material covered in Chapter 4. To understand the content of this chapter it is essential that you thoroughly understand the content of Chapter 4. You are therefore recommended to refresh your memory of the material covered in Chapter 4 and read pages 74–85 prior to reading this chapter. Finally, ABC is an advanced topic and may not be included as part of your course curriculum. You should check your course content to ascertain if you will need to read this chapter.

Learning objectives

After studying this chapter you should be able to:

- explain the role of a cost accumulation system for generating relevant cost information for decision-making;

- describe the differences between activity-based and traditional costing systems;

- illustrate how traditional costing systems can provide misleading information for decision-making;

- compute product costs for an activity-based costing system;

- explain each of the four stages involved in designing ABC systems;

- describe the ABC cost hierarchy.

The role of a cost accumulation system in generating relevant cost information for decision-making

There are three main reasons why a cost accumulation system is required to generate relevant cost information for decision-making. They are:

1. many indirect costs are relevant for decision-making;
2. an attention-directing information system is required to identify those potentially unprofitable products that require more detailed special studies;
3. product decisions are not independent.

There is a danger that only those incremental costs that are uniquely attributable to individual products will be classified as relevant for decision-making. Direct costs are transparent and how they will be affected by decisions is clearly observable. In contrast, how indirect costs will be affected by decisions is not clearly observable. There has been a tendency in the past to assume that these costs are fixed and irrelevant for decision-making. In many organizations, however, these are costs that have escalated over the years. The message is clear – they cannot be assumed to be fixed and irrelevant for decision-making.

The costs of many joint resources fluctuate in the long term according to the demand for them. The cost of support functions fall within this category. They include activities such as materials procurement, materials handling, production scheduling, warehousing, expediting and customer order processing. The costs of these activities are either not directly traceable to products, or would involve such detailed tracing, the costs of doing so would far exceed their benefits. Product introduction, discontinuation, redesign and mix decisions determine the demand for support function resources. For example, if a decision results in a 10% reduction in the demand for the resources of a support activity then we would expect, in the long term, for some of the costs of that support activity to decline by 10%. Therefore, to estimate the impact that decisions will have on the support activities (and their future costs) a cost accumulation system is required that assigns indirect costs, using cause-and-effect allocations, to products.

For decision-making it could be argued that relevant incremental costs need only be ascertained when the need arises. For example, why not undertake special studies involving incremental cost/revenue analysis at periodic intervals to make sure that each product is still profitable? Estimates could be made only when undertaking a special study of those relevant costs that would be avoided if a product was discontinued. This approach is fine for highly simplified situations where an organization only produces a few products and where all relevant costs are uniquely attributable to individual products. However, most organizations produce hundreds of products and the range of potential decisions to explore undertaking special studies is enormous and unmanageable. For example, Kaplan (1990) considers a situation where a company has 100 products and outlines the difficulties of determining which product, or product combinations, should be selected for undertaking special studies. Kaplan states:

> First how do you think about which product you should even think about making a decision on? There are 100 different products to consider. But think about all the combinations of these products: which two products, three products or groupings of 10 or 20 products should be analyzed? It's a simple exercise to calculate that there are 2^{100} different combinations of the 100 products ... so there is no way to do an incremental revenue/incremental analysis on all relevant combinations (p. 13).

To cope with the vast number of potential product combinations organizations need attention-directing information to highlight those specific products, or combination of products, that appear to be questionable and which require further detailed special studies to ascertain their viability. Periodic product profitability analysis meets this requirement. A cost accumulation system is therefore required to assign costs to products for periodic profitability analysis.

The third reason for using a cost accumulation system is that many product related decisions are not independent. Consider again those joint resources shared by most products and that fluctuate in the longer term according to the demand for them. If we focus only on individual products and assume that they are independent, decisions will be taken in isolation of decisions made on other products. For joint resources the incremental/avoidable costs relating to a decision to add or drop a single product may be zero. Assuming that 20 products are viewed in this manner then the sum of the incremental costs will be zero. However, if the 20 products are viewed as a whole there may be a significant change in resource usage and incremental costs for those joint resources that fluctuate according to the demand for them.

Cooper (1990b) also argues that decisions should not be viewed independently. He states:

> The decision to drop one product will typically not change 'fixed' overhead spending. In contrast, dropping 50 products might allow considerable changes to be made. Stated somewhat tritely, the sum of the parts (the decision to drop individual products) is not equal to the sum of the whole (the realisable savings from having dropped 50 products). To help them make effective decisions, managers require cost systems that provide insights into the whole, not just isolated individual parts (p. 58).

Thus, where product decisions are not independent the multiplication of product costs, that include the cost of joint resources, by the units lost from ceasing production (or additional units from introducing a new product) may provide an approximation of the change in the long term of total company costs arising from the decisions. The rationale for this is that the change in resource consumption will ultimately be followed by a change in the cash flow pattern of the organization because organizations make product introduction or abandonment decisions for many products rather than just a single product.

Types of cost systems

Costing systems can vary in terms of which costs are assigned to cost objects and their level of sophistication. Typically cost systems are classified as follows:

1. direct costing systems;
2. traditional absorption costing systems;
3. activity-based costing systems.

Direct costing systems only assign direct costs to cost objects. Hence they report contributions to indirect costs. They are appropriate for decision-making where the cost of those joint resources that fluctuate according to the demand for them are insignificant. Negative or low contribution items should then be highlighted for special studies. An estimate of those indirect costs that are relevant to the decision should be incorporated within the analysis at the special study stage. The disadvantage of direct costing systems is that systems are not in place to measure and assign indirect costs to cost objects. Thus any attempt to incorporate indirect costs into the analysis at the special studies stage must be based on guesswork and arbitrary estimates. Direct costing systems can therefore only be recommended where indirect costs are a low proportion of an organization's total costs.

Both traditional and ABC systems assign indirect costs to cost objects. The major features of traditional systems were described in Chapter 4. In this chapter we shall concentrate on ABC.

A comparison of traditional and ABC systems

Figure 11.1 illustrates the major differences between traditional costing and ABC systems. The upper panel of this diagram is identical to Figure 4.3 that was used in Chapter 4 to describe a traditional costing system. It is apparent from Figure 11.1 that both systems involve the two-stage allocation process. In the first stage a traditional system allocates overheads to production and service departments and then reallocates service department costs to the production departments. An ABC system assigns overheads to each major activity (rather than departments). With ABC systems, many activity-based cost centres (alternatively known as activity cost pools) are established, whereas with traditional systems overheads tend to be pooled by departments, although they are normally described as cost centres.

Activities consist of the aggregation of many different tasks and are described by verbs associated with objects. Typical support activities include: schedule production, set-up machines, move materials, purchase materials, inspect items, process supplier records, expedite and process customer orders. Production process activities include machine products and assemble products. Within the production process, activity cost centres are often identical to the cost centres used by traditional cost systems. Support activities are also sometimes identical to cost centres used by traditional systems, such as when the purchasing department and activity are both treated as cost centres. Overall, however, ABC systems will normally have a greater number of cost centres.

The second stage of the two-stage allocation process allocates costs from cost centres (pools) to products or other chosen cost objects. Traditional costing systems trace overheads to products using a small number of second stage allocation bases (normally described as overhead allocation rates), which vary directly with the volume produced. Instead of using the terms 'allocation bases' or 'overhead allocation rates' the term '**cost driver**' is used by ABC systems. Direct labour and machine hours are the allocation bases that are normally used by traditional costing systems. In contrast, ABC systems use many different second-stage cost drivers, including non-volume-based drivers, such as the number of production runs for production scheduling and the number of purchase orders for the purchasing activity. A further distinguishing feature is that traditional systems normally allocate service/support costs to production centres. Their costs are merged with the production cost centre costs and thus included within the production centre overhead rates. In contrast, ABC systems tend to establish separate cost driver rates for support centres, and assign the cost of support activities directly to cost objects without any reallocation to production centres.

Therefore the major distinguishing features of ABC systems are that within the two-stage allocation process they rely on:

1. a greater number of cost centres, and

2. a greater number and variety of second stage cost drivers.

By using a greater number of cost centres and cost drivers that cause activity resource consumption, and assigning activity costs to cost objects on the basis of cost driver usage, ABC systems can more accurately measure the resources consumed by cost objects. Traditional cost systems report less accurate costs because they use cost drivers where no cause-and-effect relationships exist to assign support costs to cost objects.

FIGURE 11.1 *An illustration of the two-stage allocation process for traditional and activity-based costing systems.*

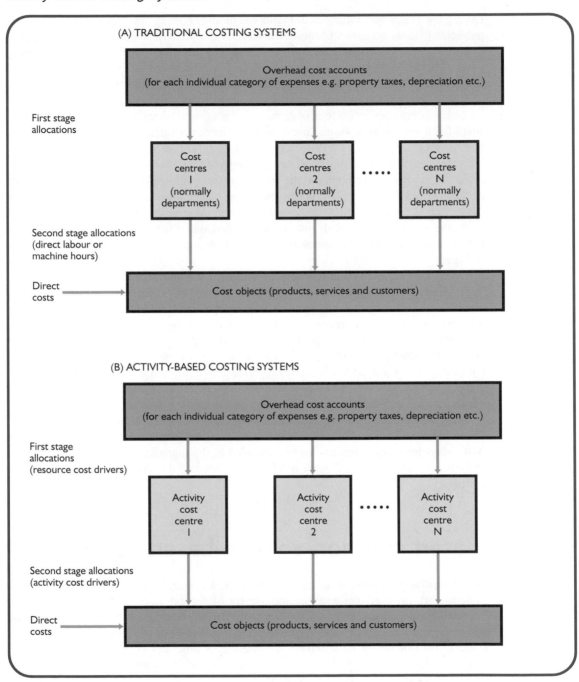

The emergence of ABC systems

During the 1980s the limitations of traditional product costing systems began to be widely publicized. These systems were designed decades ago when most companies manufactured a narrow range of products, and direct labour and materials were the dominant factory costs. Overhead costs were relatively small, and the distortions arising from inappropriate overhead allocations were not significant. Information processing costs were high, and it was therefore difficult to justify more sophisticated overhead allocation methods.

Today companies produce a wide range of products; direct labour represents only a small fraction of total costs, and overhead costs are of considerable importance. Simplistic overhead allocations using a declining direct labour base cannot be justified, particularly when information processing costs are no longer a barrier to introducing more sophisticated cost systems. Furthermore, the intense global competition of the 1980s has made decision errors due to poor cost information more probable and more costly. Over the years the increased opportunity cost of having poor cost information, and the decreased cost of operating more sophisticated cost systems, increased the demand for more accurate product costs (Holzer and Norreklit, 1991). It is against this background that ABC has emerged.

Decreasing information processing costs resulted in a few firms in the USA and Europe implementing ABC type systems during the 1980s. In a series of articles based on observations of innovative ABC type systems Cooper and Kaplan conceptualized the ideas underpinning these systems and coined the term ABC. These articles were first published in 1988. They generated a considerable amount of publicity and consultants began to market and implement ABC systems before the end of the decade. In a survey of UK companies Innes and Mitchell (1991) reported that approximately 10% of the surveyed companies had implemented, or were in the process of implementing ABC. Based on their experience of working with early US adopters, Cooper and Kaplan articulated their ideas and reported further theoretical advances in articles published between 1990 and 1992. These ideas and the theoretical advances are described in the remainder of this chapter. ABC ideas have now become firmly embedded in the management accounting literature and educational courses and many practitioners have attended courses and conferences on the topic.

Volume-based and non-volume-based cost drivers

Our comparison of ABC systems with traditional costing systems indicated that ABC systems rely on a greater number and variety of second stage cost drivers. The term 'variety of cost drivers' refers to the fact that ABC systems use both volume-based and non-volume-based cost drivers. In contrast, traditional systems use only volume-based cost drivers. **Volume-based cost drivers** assume that a product's consumption of overhead resources is directly related to units produced. In other words, they assume that the overhead consumed by products is highly correlated with the number of units produced. Typical volume-based cost drivers used by traditional systems are units of output, direct labour hours and machine hours. These cost drivers are appropriate for measuring the consumption of expenses such as machine energy costs, depreciation related to machine usage, indirect labour employed in production centres and inspection costs where each item produced is subject to final inspection. For example, machine hours are an appropriate cost driver for energy costs since if volume is increased by 10%, machine hours are likely to increase by 10%, thus causing 10% more energy costs to be consumed. Similarly, an increase in volume of 10% is likely to increase the consumption of direct labour hours by 10% and, assuming that indirect labour hours are correlated with direct labour hours, 10% more indirect labour costs will be consumed.

Volume-based drivers are appropriate in the above circumstances because activities are performed each time a unit of the product or service is produced. In contrast, non-volume related activities are not performed each time a unit of the product or service is produced. Consider, for example, two activities – setting up a machine and re-engineering products. Set-up resources are consumed each time a machine is changed from one product to another. It costs the same to set-up a machine for 10 or 5000 items. As more set-ups are done more set-up resources are consumed. The number of set-ups, rather than the number of units produced, is a more appropriate measure of the consumption of the set-up activity. Similarly, product re-engineering costs may depend upon the number of different engineering works orders and not the number of units produced. For both of these activities, **non-volume-based cost drivers** such as number of set-ups and engineering orders are needed for the accurate assignment of the costs of these activities.

Using only volume-based cost drivers to assign non-volume related overhead costs can result in the reporting of distorted product costs. The extent of distortion depends on what proportion of total overhead costs the non-volume based overheads represent and the level of product diversity. If a large proportion of an organization's costs are unrelated to volume there is danger that inaccurate product costs will be reported. Conversely, if non-volume related overhead costs are only a small proportion of total overhead costs, the distortion of product costs will not be significant. In these circumstances traditional product costing systems are likely to be acceptable.

Product diversity applies when products consume different overhead activities in dissimilar proportions. Differences in product size, product complexity, sizes of batches and set-up times cause product diversity. If all products consume overhead resources in similar proportions product diversity will be low and products will consume non-volume related activities in the same proportion as volume-related activities. Hence, product cost distortion will not occur with traditional product costing systems. Two conditions are therefore necessary for product cost distortion – non-volume-related overhead costs are a large proportion of total overhead costs and product diversity applies. Where these two conditions exist traditional product costing systems can result in the overcosting of high volume products and undercosting of low volume products. Consider the information presented in Example 11.1.

The reported product costs and profits for the two products are as follows:

	Traditional system		ABC system	
	Product HV (£)	**Product LV** (£)	**Product HV** (£)	**Product LV** (£)
Direct costs	310 000	40 000	310 000	40 000
Overheads allocated[a]	300 000 (30%)	50 000 (5%)	150 000 (15%)	150 000 (15%)
Reported profits/(losses)	(10 000)	60 000	140 000	(40 000)
Sales revenues	600 000	150 000	600 000	150 000

Note
[a] Allocation of £1 million overheads using direct labour hours as the allocation base for the traditional system and number of batches processed as the cost driver for the ABC system.

Because product HV is a high volume product that consumes 30% of the direct labour hours whereas product LV, the low volume product consumes only 5%, the traditional system that uses direct labour hours as the allocation base allocates six times more

EXAMPLE 11.1

Assume that the Balearic company has only one overhead cost centre or cost pool. It currently operates a traditional costing system using direct labour hours to allocate overheads to products. The company produces several products, two of which are products HV and LV. Product HV is made in high volumes whereas product LV is made in low volumes. Product HV consumes 30% of the direct labour hours and product LV consumes only 5%. Because of the high volume production product HV can be made in large production batches but the irregular and low level of demand for product LV requires it to be made in small batches. A detailed investigation indicates that the number of batches processed causes the demand for overhead resources. The traditional system is therefore replaced with an ABC system using the number of batches processed as the cost driver. You ascertain that each product accounts for 15% of the batches processed during the period and the overheads assigned to the cost centre that fluctuate in the long term according to the demand for them amount to £1 million. The direct costs and sales revenues assigned to the products are as follows:

	Product HV (£)	Product LV (£)
Direct costs	310 000	40 000
Sales revenues	600 000	150 000

Show the product profitability analysis for products HV and LV using the traditional and ABC systems.

overheads to product HV. However, ABC systems recognize that overheads are caused by other factors, besides volume. In our example, all of the overheads are assumed to be volume unrelated. They are caused by the number of batches processed and the ABC system establishes a cause-and-effect allocation relationship by using the number of batches processed as the cost driver. Both products require 15% of the total number of batches so they are allocated with an equal amount of overheads.

It is apparent from the consumption ratios of the two products that the traditional system based on direct labour hours will overcost high volume products. **Consumption ratios** represent the proportion of each activity consumed by a product. The consumption ratios if direct labour hours are used as the cost driver are 0.30 for product HV and 0.05 for product LV so that six times more overheads will be assigned to product HV. When the number of batches processed are used as the cost driver the consumption ratios are 0.15 for each product and an equal amount of overhead will be assigned to each product. Distorted product costs are reported with the traditional costing system that uses the volume-based cost driver because the two conditions specified above apply. First, non-volume related overheads are a large proportion of total overheads, being 100% in our example. Second, product diversity exists because the product consumption ratios for the two identified cost drivers are significantly different. Our illustration shows that if the consumption ratios for batches processed had been the same as the ratios for direct labour the traditional and ABC systems would report identical product costs.

With the traditional costing system misleading information is reported. A small loss is reported for product HV and if it were discontinued the costing system mistakenly gives the impression that overheads will decline in the longer term by £300 000. Furthermore, the message from the costing system is to concentrate on the more profitable speciality products like product LV. In reality this strategy would be disastrous because low volume products like product LV are made in small batches and require more people for scheduling production, performing set-ups, inspection of the batches and handling a large number of customer requests for small orders. The long-term effect would be escalating overhead costs.

In contrast, the ABC system allocates overheads on a cause-and-effect basis and more accurately measures the relatively high level of overhead resources consumed by product LV. The message from the profitability analysis is the opposite from the traditional system; that is, product HV is profitable and product LV is unprofitable. If product LV is discontinued, and assuming that the cost driver is the cause of all the overheads then a decision to discontinue product LV should result in the reduction in resource spending on overheads by £150 000.

Example 11.1 is very simplistic. It is assumed that the organization has established only a single cost centre or cost pool, when in reality many will be established with a traditional system, and even more with an ABC system. Furthermore, the data have been deliberately biased to show the superiority of ABC. The aim of the illustration has been to highlight the potential cost of errors that can occur when information extracted from simplistic and inaccurate cost systems is used for decision-making.

An illustration of the two-stage process for an ABC system

We shall now use the data presented in Example 4.1 (the Enterprise Company) from Chapter 4 to illustrate ABC in more detail. This example was used to provide the relevant information to compute the overhead rates shown in Exhibit 4.2 (see Chapter 4) for a traditional costing system. To refresh your memory, and to enable you to compare traditional and ABC systems, you should now refer back to Chapter 4 and read pages 78–84 relating to the two-stage allocation process for a traditional costing system. Example 4.1 and Exhibit 4.2 are now repeated so that you do not have to be constantly referring back to Chapter 4.

With the ABC system it is assumed that the activity cost centres for machining and assembling products are identical to the production cost centres used by the traditional costing system. We shall also assume that three activity cost centres have been established for each of the support functions. They are purchasing components, receiving components and disbursing materials for the materials procurement function and production scheduling, setting-up machines and a quality inspection of the completed products for the general factory support function. Exhibit 11.1 provides the additional information required for an ABC system and also shows the activity-based product cost calculations.

If you refer to column 2 in the upper section of Exhibit 11.1 you will see that the costs assigned to the production activities have been extracted from row 1 in the overhead analysis sheet shown in Exhibit 4.2, that was used for the traditional costing system. In the overhead analysis sheet we only assigned support costs with the traditional costing system to the materials procurement and the general factory support functions, and not to the activities within these support functions. However, the costs for the activities within these functions would be derived adopting the same approach as that used in Exhibit 4.2, but to simplify the presentation the cost assignments to the individual activity cost centres within the material procurement and general factory support functions are not shown.

EXAMPLE 4.1

(from Chapter 4)

The annual overhead costs for the Enterprise Company which has three production centres (two machine centres and one assembly centre) and two service centres (materials procurement and general factory support) are as follows:

	(£)	(£)
Indirect wages and supervision		
Machine centres: X	1 000 000	
Y	1 000 000	
Assembly	1 500 000	
Materials procurement	1 100 000	
General factory support	1 480 000	6 080 000
Indirect materials		
Machine centres: X	500 000	
Y	805 000	
Assembly	105 000	
Materials procurement	0	
General factory support	10 000	1 420 000
Lighting and heating	500 000	
Property taxes	1 000 000	
Insurance of machinery	150 000	
Depreciation of machinery	1 500 000	
Insurance of buildings	250 000	
Salaries of works management	800 000	4 200 000
		11 700 000

The following information is also available:

	Book value of machinery (£)	Area occupied (sq. metres)	Number of employees	Direct labour hours	Machine hours
Machine shop: X	8 000 000	10 000	300	1 000 000	2 000 000
Y	5 000 000	5 000	200	1 000 000	1 000 000
Assembly	1 000 000	15 000	300	2 000 000	
Stores	500 000	15 000	100		
Maintenance	500 000	5 000	100		
	15 000 000	50 000	1000		

Details of total materials issues (i.e. direct and indirect materials) to the production centres are as follows:

	(£)
Machine shop X	4 000 000
Machine shop Y	3 000 000
Assembly	1 000 000
	8 000 000

<table>
<tr><td>**EXHIBIT 4.2**

Overhead analysis sheet (from Chapter 4)</td><td>Note from the second column in the upper section of Exhibit 11.1 that the costs assigned to the purchasing, receiving and disbursement of materials activities total £1 760 000, the same as the total allocated to the materials procurement function by the traditional system in Exhibit 4.2. Similarly, the total costs</td></tr>
</table>

			Production centres			Service centres	
Item of expenditure	Basis of allocation	Total (£)	Machine centre X (£)	Machine centre Y (£)	Assembly (£)	Materials procurement (£)	General factory support (£)
Indirect wage and supervision	Direct	6 080 000	1 000 000	1 000 000	1 500 000	1 100 000	1 480 000
Indirect materials	Direct	1 420 000	500 000	805 000	105 000		10 000
Lighting and heating	Area	500 000	100 000	50 000	150 000	150 000	50 000
Property taxes	Area	1 000 000	200 000	100 000	300 000	300 000	100 000
Insurance of machinery	Book value of machinery	150 000	80 000	50 000	10 000	5 000	5 000
Depreciation of machinery	Book value of machinery	1 500 000	800 000	500 000	100 000	50 000	50 000
Insurance of buildings	Area	250 000	50 000	25 000	75 000	75 000	25 000
Salaries of works management	Number of employees	800 000	240 000	160 000	240 000	80 000	80 000
(1)		11 700 000	2 970 000	2 690 000	2 480 000	1 760 000	1 800 000
Reallocation of service centre costs							
Materials procurement	Value of materials issued	—	880 000	660 000	220 000	1 760 000	
General factory support	Direct labour hours	—	450 000	450 000	900 000		1 800 000
(2)		11 700 000	4 300 000	3 800 000	3 600 000	—	—
Machine hours and direct labour hours			2 000 000	1 000 000	2 000 000		
Machine hour overhead rate			£2.15	£3.80			

assigned to the production scheduling, set-up and quality inspection activities in the upper section of Exhibit 11.1 total £1 800 000, the same as the total costs allocated to the general factory support function in Exhibit 4.2.

Now look at columns 1 and 3 in the upper section of Exhibit 11.1. You will see that with the ABC system the Enterprise Company has established nine activity cost centres and seven different second-stage cost drivers. Note also that the cost drivers for the production activities are volume-based and are the same as those used for the traditional costing system. Based on their observations of ABC systems Kaplan and Cooper (1998) suggest that relatively simple ABC systems having 30–50 activity cost centres and many cost drivers ought to report reasonably accurate costs.

Cost drivers should be significant determinants of the cost of activities. For example, if the cost of processing purchase orders is determined by the number of purchase orders that each product generates, then the number of purchase orders would represent the cost driver for the cost of processing purchase orders. Other cost drivers used by the Enterprise Company are shown in column 3 of the upper section of Exhibit 11.1. They are the number

EXHIBIT 11.1

An illustration of cost assignment with an ABC system

of receipts for receiving components, number of production runs for disbursing materials and scheduling production, number of set-up hours for setting up the machines and the number of first item inspections for quality inspection of a batch of completed products. You will see from column 5 in the first section of Exhibit 11.1 that cost driver rates are computed by dividing the activity centre cost by the quantity of the cost driver used.

(1) Activity	(2) Activity cost (£)	(3) Activity cost driver	(4) Quantity of activity cost driver	(5) Activity cost driver rate (Col. 2 / Col. 4)
Production activities:				
Machining: activity centre A	2 970 000	Number of machine hours	2 000 000 machine hours	£1.485 per hour
Machining: activity centre B	2 690 000	Number of machine hours	1 000 000 machine hours	£2.69 per hour
Assembly	2 480 000	Number of direct labour hours	2 000 000 direct lab. hours	£1.24 per hour
	8 140 000			
Materials procurement activities:				
Purchasing components	960 000	Number of purchase orders	10 000 purchase orders	£96 per order
Receiving components	600 000	Number of material receipts	5 000 receipts	£120 per receipt
Disburse materials	200 000	Number of production runs	2 000 production runs	£100 per production run
	1 760 000			
General factory support activities:				
Production scheduling	1 000 000	Number of production runs	2 000 production runs	£500 per production run
Set-up machines	600 000	Number of set-up hours	12 000 set-up hours	£50 per set-up hour
Quality inspection	200 000	Number of first item inspections	1 000 inspections	£200 per inspection
	1 800 000			
Total cost of all manufacturing activities	11 700 000			

Computation of product costs

(1) Activity	(2) Activity cost driver rate	(3) Quantity of cost driver used by 100 units of product A	(4) Quantity of cost driver used by 200 units of product B	(5) Activity cost assigned to product A (Col. 2 × Col. 3)	(6) Activity cost assigned to product B (Col. 2 × Col. 4)
Machining: activity centre A	£1.485 per hour	500 hours	2 000 hours	742.50	2 970.00
Machining: activity centre B	£2.69 per hour	1 000 hours	4 000 hours	2 690.00	10 760.00
Assembly	£1.24 per hour	1 000 hours	4 000 hours	1 240.00	4 960.00
Purchasing components	£96 per order	1 component	1 component	96.00	96.00
Receiving components	£120 per receipt	1 component	1 component	120.00	120.00
Disburse materials	£100 per production run	5 production runs[a]	1 production run	500.00	100.00
Production scheduling	£500 per production run	5 production runs[a]	1 production run	2 500.00	500.00
Set-up machines	£50 per set-up hour	50 set-up hours	10 set-up hours	2 500.00	500.00
Quality inspection	£200 per inspection	1 inspection	1 inspection	200.00	200.00
Total overhead cost				10 588.50	20 206.00
Units produced				100 units	200 units
Overhead cost *per unit*				£105.88	£101.03
Direct costs *per unit*				100.00	200.00
Total cost *per unit* of output				205.88	301.03

Note
[a]Five production runs are required to machine several unique components before they can be assembled into a final product.

Activity centre costs are assigned to products by multiplying the cost driver rate by the quantity of the cost driver used by products. These calculations are shown in the second section of Exhibit 11.1. You will see from the first section in Exhibit 11.1 that the costs assigned to the purchasing activity are £960 000 for processing 10 000 purchasing orders resulting in a cost driver rate of £96 per purchasing order. The second section shows that a batch of 100 units of product A, and 200 units of product B, each require one purchased component and thus one purchase order. Therefore purchase order costs of £96 are allocated to each batch. The same approach is used to allocate the costs of the remaining activities shown in Exhibit 11.1. You should now work through Exhibit 11.1 and study the product cost calculations.

The costs assigned to products using each costing system are as follows:

	Traditional costing system (£)	**ABC system** (£)
Product A	166.75	205.88
Product B	333.50	301.03

Compared with the ABC system the traditional system undercosts product A and overcosts product B. By reallocating the service centre costs to the production centres and allocating the costs to products on the basis of either machine hours or direct labour hours the traditional system incorrectly assumes that these volume-based allocation bases are the cause of the costs of the support activities. Compared with product A, product B consumes twice as many machine and direct labour hours per unit of output. Therefore, relative to product A, the traditional costing system allocates twice the amount of support costs to product B.

In contrast, ABC systems create separate cost centres for each major support activity and allocates costs to products using cost drivers that are the significant determinants of the cost of the activities. The ABC system recognizes that a batch of both products consume the same quantity of purchasing, receiving and inspection activities and, for these activities, allocates the same costs to both products. Because product B is manufactured in batches of 200 units, and product A in batches of 100 units, the cost per unit of output for product B is half the amount of product A for these activities. Product A also has five unique machined components, whereas product B has only one, resulting in a batch of product A requiring five production runs whereas a batch of product B only requires one. Therefore, relative to product B, the ABC system assigns five times more costs to product A for the production scheduling and disbursement of materials activities (see columns 5 and 6 in the lower part of Exhibit 11.1). Because product A is a more complex product it requires relatively more support activity resources and the cost of this complexity is captured by the ABC system.

The unit costs derived from traditional and ABC systems must be used with care. For example, if a customer requested a batch of 400 units of product B the cost would not be twice the amount of a batch of 200 units. Assuming that for a batch of 400 units the number of purchase orders, material receipts, production runs, set-up hours and inspections remained the same as that required for a batch of 200 units the cost of the support activities would remain unchanged, but the direct costs would increase by a factor of two to reflect the fact that twice the amount of resources would be required.

Designing ABC systems

The discussion so far has provided a broad overview of ABC. We shall now examine ABC in more detail by looking at the design of ABC systems. Four steps are involved. They are:

1. identifying the major activities that take place in an organization;
2. assigning costs to cost pools/cost centres for each activity;

3. determining the cost driver for each major activity;

4. assigning the cost of activities to products according to the product's demand for activities.

The first two steps relate to the first stage, and the final two steps to the second stage, of the two-stage allocation process shown in Figure 11.1. Let us now consider each of these stages in more detail.

STEP 1: IDENTIFYING ACTIVITIES

Activities are composed of the aggregation of units of work or tasks and are described by verbs associated with tasks. For example, purchasing of materials might be identified as a separate activity. This activity consists of the aggregation of many different tasks, such as receiving a purchase request, identifying suppliers, preparing purchase orders, mailing purchase orders and performing follow-ups.

Activities are identified by carrying out an activity analysis. Innes and Mitchell (1995b) suggest that a useful starting point is to examine a physical plan of the workplace (to identify how all work space is being used) and the payroll listings (to ensure all relevant personnel have been taken into account). This examination normally has to be supplemented by a series of interviews with the staff involved, or having staff complete a time sheet for a specific time period explaining how their time is spent. Interviewers will ask managers and employees questions such as what staff work at the location and what tasks are performed by the persons employed at the location.

Many detailed tasks are likely to be identified in the first instance, but after further interviews, the main activities will emerge. The activities chosen should be at a reasonable level of aggregation based on costs versus benefits criteria. For example, rather than classifying purchasing of materials as an activity, each of its constituent tasks could be classified as separate activities. However, this level of decomposition would involve the collection of a vast amount of data and is likely to be too costly for product costing purposes. Alternatively, the purchasing activity might be merged with the materials receiving, storage and issuing activities to form a single materials procurement and handling activity. This is likely to represent too high a level of aggregation because a single cost driver is unlikely to provide a satisfactory determinant of the cost of the activity. For example, selecting the number of purchase orders as a cost driver may provide a good explanation of purchasing costs but may be entirely inappropriate for explaining costs relating to receiving and issuing. Therefore, instead of establishing materials procurement and handling as a single activity it may be preferable to decompose it into three separate activities; namely purchasing, receiving and issuing activities, and establish separate cost drivers for each activity.

In some of the early ABC systems hundreds of separate activity cost centres were established but recent studies suggest that between twenty and thirty activity centres tend to be the norm. The final choice of activities must be a matter of judgement but it is likely to be influenced by factors such as the total cost of the activity centre (it must be of significance to justify separate treatment) and the ability of a single driver to provide a satisfactory determinant of the cost of the activity. Activities with the same product consumption ratios can use the same cost driver to assign costs to products. Thus, all activities that have the same cost driver can be merged to form a single activity cost centre. However, if there are significant differences in activity product consumption ratios products will consume activities in dissimilar proportions and the activities should not be aggregated.

STEP 2: ASSIGNING COSTS TO ACTIVITY COST CENTRES

After the activities have been identified the cost of resources consumed over a specified period must be assigned to each activity. The aim is to determine how much the organization is spending on each of its activities. Many of the resources will be directly attributable to specific activity centres but others (such as labour and lighting and heating costs) may be indirect and jointly shared by several activities. These costs should be assigned to activities on the basis of cause-and-effect cost drivers, or interviews with staff who can provide reasonable estimates of the resources consumed by different activities. Arbitrary allocations should not be used. The greater the amount of costs traced to activity centres by cost apportionments at this stage the more arbitrary and less reliable will be the product cost information generated by ABC systems. Cause-and-effect cost drivers used at this stage to allocate shared resources to individual activities are called **resource cost drivers**

STEP 3: SELECTING APPROPRIATE COST DRIVERS FOR ASSIGNING THE COST OF ACTIVITIES TO COST OBJECTS

In order to assign the costs attached to each activity cost centre to products a cost driver must be selected for each activity centre. Cost drivers used at this stage are called **activity cost drivers**. Several factors must be borne in mind when selecting a suitable cost driver. First, it should provide a good explanation of costs in each activity cost pool. Second, a cost driver should be easily measurable, the data should be relatively easy to obtain and be identifiable with products. The costs of measurement should therefore be taken into account.

Activity cost drivers consist of transaction and duration drivers. **Transaction drivers**, such as the number of purchase orders processed, number of customer orders processed, number of inspections performed and the number of set-ups undertaken, all count the number of times an activity is performed. Transaction drivers are the least expensive type of cost driver but they are also likely to be the least accurate because they assume that the same quantity of resources is required every time an activity is performed. However, if the variation in the amount of resources required by individual cost objects is not great transaction drivers will provide a reasonably accurate measurement of activity resources consumed. If this condition does not apply then duration cost drivers should be used.

Duration drivers represent the amount of time required to perform an activity. Examples of duration drivers include set-up hours and inspection hours. For example, if one product requires a short set-up time and another requires a long time then using set-up hours as the cost driver will more accurately measure activity resource consumption than the transaction driver (number of set-ups) which assumes that an equal amount of activity resources are consumed by both products. Using the number of set-ups will result in the product that requires a long set-up time being undercosted whereas the product that requires a short set-up will be overcosted. This problem can be overcome by using set-up hours as the cost driver, but this will increase the measurement costs.

In most situations data will not initially be available relating to the past costs of activities or potential cost driver volumes. To ascertain potential cost drivers interviews will be required with the personnel involved with the specific activities. The interviews will seek to ascertain what causes the particular activity to consume resources and incur costs. The final choice of a cost driver is likely to be based on managerial judgement after taking into account the factors outlined above.

STEP 4: ASSIGNING THE COST OF THE ACTIVITIES TO PRODUCTS

The final stage involves applying the cost driver rates to products. Therefore the cost driver must be measurable in a way that enables it to be identified with individual products. Thus, if set-up hours are selected as a cost driver, there must be a mechanism for measuring the set-up hours consumed by each product. Alternatively, if the number of set-ups is selected as the cost driver measurements by products are not required since all products that require a set-up are charged with a constant set-up cost. The ease and cost of obtaining data on cost driver consumption by products is therefore a factor that must be considered during the third stage when an appropriate cost driver is being selected.

Activity hierarchies

ABC systems classify manufacturing activities along a cost hierarchy dimension consisting of:

1. unit-level activities;
2. batch-level activities;
3. product-sustaining activities;
4. facility-sustaining activities.

Unit-level activities (also known as **volume-related activities**) are performed each time a unit of the product or service is produced. Expenses in this category include direct labour, direct materials, energy costs and expenses that are consumed in proportion to machine processing time (such as maintenance). Unit-level activities consume resources in proportion to the number of units of production and sales volume. For example, if a firm produces 10% more units it will consume 10% more labour cost, 10% more machine hours and 10% more energy costs. Typical cost drivers for unit level activities include labour hours, machine hours and the quantity of materials processed. These cost drivers are also used by traditional costing systems. Traditional systems are therefore also appropriate for assigning the costs of unit-level activities to cost objects.

Batch-related activities, such as setting up a machine or processing a purchase order, are performed each time a batch of goods is produced. The cost of batch-related activities varies with the number of batches made, but is common (or fixed) for all units within the batch. For example, set-up resources are consumed when a machine is changed from one product to another. As more batches are produced, more set-up resources are consumed. It costs the same to set-up a machine for 10 or 5000 items. Thus the demands for the set-up resources are independent of the number of units produced after completing the set-up. Similarly, purchasing resources are consumed each time a purchasing order is processed, but the resources consumed are independent of the number of units included in the purchase order. Other examples of batch-related costs include resources devoted to production scheduling, first-item inspection and materials movement. Traditional costing systems treat batch-related expenses as fixed costs, whereas ABC systems assume that they vary with the number of batches processed.

Product-sustaining activities or **service-sustaining activities** are performed to enable the production and sale of individual products (or services). Examples of product-sustaining activities provided by Kaplan and Cooper (1998) include maintaining and updating product specifications and the technical support provided for individual products and services. Other examples are the resources to prepare and implement engineering change notices (ECNs), to design processes and test routines for individual products, and to perform product enhancements. The costs of product-sustaining activities are incurred irrespective of the number of units of output or the number of batches processed and their expenses will tend to increase as the number of products manufactured is increased. ABC uses product-level bases such as number of active part numbers and number of ECNs to assign these costs to products. Kaplan and Cooper (1998) have extended their ideas to situations where customers are the cost objects with the equivalent term for product-sustaining being **customer-sustaining activities**. Customer market research and support for an individual customer, or groups of customers if they represent the cost object, are examples of customer-sustaining activities.

The final activity category is **facility-sustaining** (or **business-sustaining**), **activities**. They are performed to support the facility's general manufacturing process and include general administrative staff, plant management and property costs. They are incurred to support the organization as a whole and are common and joint to all products manufactured in the plant. There would have to be a dramatic change in activity, resulting in an expansion or contraction in the size of the plant, for facility-sustaining costs to change. Such events are most unlikely in most organizations. Therefore the ABC literature advocates that these costs should not be assigned to products since they are unavoidable and irrelevant for most decisions. Instead, they are regarded as common costs to *all* products made in the plant and deducted as a lump sum from the total of the operating margins from *all* products.

Cost versus benefits considerations

In Chapter 4 it was pointed out that the design of a cost system should be based on cost versus benefit considerations. A sophisticated ABC system will clearly generate the most accurate product costs. However, the cost of implementing and operating an ABC system is significantly more expensive than operating a direct costing or a traditional costing system. The partial costs reported by direct costing systems, and the distorted costs reported by traditional systems, may result in significant mistakes in decisions (such as selling unprofitable products or dropping profitable products) arising from the use of this information. If the cost of errors arising from using partial or distorted information generated from using these systems exceeds the additional costs of implementing and operating an ABC system then an ABC system ought to be implemented. In other words ABC must meet the cost/benefit criterion and improvements should be made in the level of sophistication of the costing system up to the point where the marginal cost of improvement equals the marginal benefit from improvement.

The optimal costing system is different for different organizations. A simplistic traditional costing system may report reasonably accurate product costs in organizations that have the following characteristics:

1. low levels of competition;
2. non-volume-related indirect costs that are a low proportion of total indirect costs;
3. a fairly standardized product range all consuming organizational resources in similar proportions (i.e. low product diversity).

In contrast, a sophisticated ABC system may be optimal for organizations having the following characteristics:

1. intensive competition;
2. non-volume related indirect costs that are a high proportion of total indirect costs;

3. a diverse range of products, all consuming organizational resources in signicantly different proportions (i.e. high product diversity).

Single product firms and multiple-product firms that have entire facilities dedicated to the production of a single product have few problems with costing accuracy. With the former all costs will be directly attributable to the single product and with the latter only the costs of central facilities, such as central headquarter costs, will be indirect. All of the costs of the dedicated facilities will be directly attributable to products and therefore indirect costs will be a low proportion of total costs.

In Chapter 3 the major features of a just-in-time (JIT) manufacturing system were described. JIT manufacturing systems result in the establishment of production cells that are dedicated to the manufacturing of a single product or a family of similar products. With JIT firms many of the support activities can be directly traced to the product dedicated cells. Thus, a high proportion of costs can be directly assigned to products. We can conclude that the benefits from implementing ABC product costing will be lower for single products or firms that have facilities dedicated to single products.

Periodic review of an ABC data base

The detailed tracking of costs is unnecessary when ABC information is used for decision-making. A data base should be maintained that is reviewed periodically, say once or twice a year. In addition periodic cost and profitability audits should be undertaken to provide a strategic review of the costs and profitability of a firm's products, customers and sales outlets. The data base and periodic cost and profitability review can be based on either past or future costs. Early adopters, and firms starting off with ABC initially analysed past costs. However, rather than focusing on the past it is preferable to concentrate on the future profitability of products and customers using estimated activity-based costs. It is therefore recommended that an activity-cost data base is maintained at estimated standard costs that are updated on an annual or semi-annual basis.

ABC in service organizations

Kaplan and Cooper (1998) suggest that service companies are ideal candidates for ABC, even more than manufacturing companies. Their justification for this statement is that most of the costs in service organizations are indirect. In contrast, manufacturing companies can trace important components (such as direct materials and direct labour) of costs to individual products. Therefore indirect costs are likely to be a much smaller proportion of total costs. Service organizations must also supply most of their resources in advance and fluctuations in the usage of activity resources by individual services and customers does not influence short-term spending to supply the resources. Such costs are treated by traditional costing systems as fixed and irrelevant for most decisions. This resulted in a situation where profitability analysis was not considered helpful for decision-making. Furthermore, until recently many service organizations were either government owned monopolies or operated in a highly regulated, protected and non-competitive environment. These organizations were not subject to any great pressures to improve profitability by identifying and eliminating non-profit making activities. Cost increases could also be absorbed by increasing the prices of services to customers. Little attention was therefore given to developing cost systems that accurately measured the costs and profitability of individual services.

Privatization of government owned monopolies, deregulation, intensive competition and an expanding product range created the need for service organizations to develop management accounting systems that enabled them to understand their cost base and determine the sources of profitability for their products/services, customers and markets. Many service organizations have therefore only recently implemented management accounting systems. They have had the advantage of not having to meet some of the constraints imposed on manufacturing organizations, such as having to meet financial accounting stock valuation requirements or the reluctance to scrap or change existing cost systems that might have become embedded in organizations. Furthermore, service organizations have been implementing new costing systems at the same time as the deficiencies of traditional systems were being widely publicized.

A UK survey by Drury and Tayles (2000) suggests that service organizations are more likely to implement ABC systems. They reported that 51% of the financial and service organizations surveyed, compared with 15% of manufacturing organizations, had implemented ABC. Kaplan and Cooper (1998) illustrate how ABC was applied in The Co-operative Bank, a medium sized UK bank. ABC was used for product and customer profitability analysis. The following are some of the activities and cost drivers that were identified:

Activity	Cost driver
Provide ATM services	Number of ATM transactions
Clear debit items	Number of debits processed
Clear credit items	Number of credits processed
Issue chequebooks	Number of chequebooks issued
Computer processing	Number of computer transactions
Prepare statements of account transactions	Number of statements issued
Administer mortgages	Number of mortgages maintained

Activity costs were allocated to the different savings and loans products based on their demand for the activities using the cost drivers as a measure of resource consumption. Some expenses, such as finance and human resource management, were not assigned to products because they were considered to be for the benefit of the organization as a whole and not attributable to individual products. These business sustaining costs represented approximately 15% of total operating expenses. Profitability analysis was extended to customer segments within product groups. The study revealed that approximately half of the current accounts, particularly those with low balances and high transactions were unprofitable. By identifying the profitable customer segments the marketing function was able to direct its effort to attracting more new customers, and enhancing relationships with those existing customers, whose behaviour would be profitable to the bank.

ABC cost management applications

Our aim in this chapter has been to look at how ABC can be used to provide information for decision-making by more accurately assigning costs to cost objects, such as products, customers and locations. In addition, ABC can be used for a range of cost management

FIGURE 11.2 *Product costing and cost management applications of ABC.*

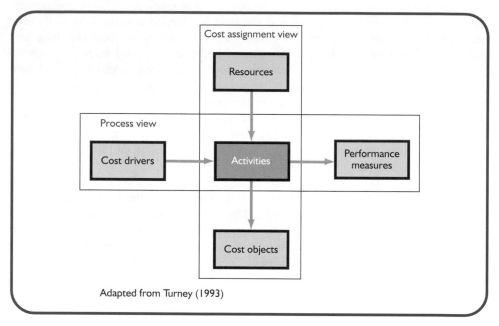

Adapted from Turney (1993)

applications. They include cost reduction, activity-based budgeting, performance measurement, benchmarking of activities, process management and business process re-engineering. Figure 11.2 illustrates the product costing and cost management applications of ABC. The vertical box relates to product costing where costs are first assigned to activities and then to cost objects. The horizontal box relates to cost management. Here a process approach is adopted and costs are assigned to activities which then represent the basis for cost management applications. Thus, ABC can be adopted for both product costing and cost management or applied only to product costing or cost management. If ABC is only applied to cost management the second stage of assigning costs from activities to cost objects is omitted.

The decision to implement ABC should not, therefore, be based only on its ability to produce more accurate and relevant decision-making information. Indeed, a survey by Innes and Mitchell (1995a) on ABC applications suggests that the cost management applications tend to outweigh the product costing applications which were central to ABC's initial development. We shall examine ABC applications to cost management in more detail in Chapter 14.

EXHIBIT 11.2

*Surveys of
company
practice*

Significant variations in the usage of ABC both within the same country and across different countries have been reported. These differences may arise from the difficulty in precisely defining the difference between traditional costing systems and ABC systems and the specific time period when the surveys were actually undertaken.

Survey evidence suggests that over the last decade there has been an increasing interest in ABC. In the UK, surveys in the early 1990s reported adoption rates around 10% (Innes and Mitchell, 1991; Nicholls, 1992; Drury *et al.*, 1993). Similar adoption rates of 10% were found in Ireland (Clarke, 1992) and 14% in Canada (Armitage and Nicholson, 1993). In the USA Green and Amenkhienan (1992) claimed that 45% of firms used ABC to some extent. More recent surveys suggest higher ABC adoption rates. In the UK reported usage was 20% (Innes and Mitchell, 1995a), 22% (Banerjee and Kane, 1996), 21% (Evans and Ashworth, 1996) and 23% (Drury and Tayles, 2000). In the USA Shim and Stagliano (1997) reported a usage rate of 27%.

Reported usage rates for mainland Europe are 19% in Belgium (Bruggeman *et al.*, 1996) and 6% in Finland in 1992, 11% in 1993 and 24% in 1995 (Virtanen *et al.*, 1996). Low usage rates have been reported in Denmark (Israelsen *et al.*, 1996), Sweden (Ask *et al.*, 1996) and Germany (Scherrer, 1996). Activity-based techniques do not appear to have been adopted in Greece (Ballas and Venieris, 1996), Italy (Barbato *et al.*, 1996) or Spain (Saez-Torrecilla *et al.*, 1996).

Other studies have examined the applications of ABC. Innes and Mitchell (1995a) found that cost reduction was the most widely used application. Other widely used applications included product/service pricing, cost modelling and performance measurement/improvement. ABC was used for stock valuation by 29% of ABC adopters thus suggesting that the majority of ABC users have separate systems for stock valuation and management accounting applications.

According to Bjornenak (1997a) there has been little research on who adopts ABC and for what reasons. His survey indicated that 40% of the responding Norwegian companies had adopted ABC as an idea (i.e. they had implemented ABC or planned to do so). Different variables relating to cost structure, competition, existing cost systems, size and product diversity were tested as explanatory factors for the adoption of ABC but only cost structure and size were found to be statistically significant. The UK study by Drury and Tayles (2000) indicated that company size and business sector had a significant impact on ABC adoption rates. The adoption rates were 45% for the largest organizations and 51% for financial and service organizations. Although the ABC adopters used significantly more cost pools and cost drivers than the non-adopters most adopters used fewer cost pools and drivers compared with what is recommended in the literature. Approximately, 50% of the ABC adopters used less than 50 cost centres and less than 10 separate types of cost driver rates.

Friedman and Lyne's (1995) case study research of 12 UK companies cited top management support as a significant factor influencing the success or failure of ABC systems. Implementation problems identified by the various studies included the amount of work in setting up the system and data collection, difficulties in identifying activities and selecting cost drivers, lack of resources and inadequate computer software. The benefits reported by the studies included more accurate cost information for product pricing, more accurate profitability analysis, improved cost control and a better understanding of cost causation.

Summary

Indirect relevant costs can be difficult to identify and measure. This chapter has shown how ABC systems can identify and measure relevant costs. ABC systems do not report relevant costs for all possible situations but they do provide a superior way of determining relevant costs. The major distinguishing features between ABC and traditional costing systems were compared. ABC systems rely on a greater number of cost centres and second stage cause-and-effect cost drivers. An ABC system involves the following four stages:

1. identify the major activities which take place in an organization;
2. create a cost centre/cost pool for each major activity;
3. determine the cost driver for each major activity;
4. trace the cost of activities to products according to a product's demand (using cost drivers as a measure of demand) for activities.

ABC systems provide more meaningful decision-making information because they recognize that many of the so-called fixed overhead costs vary in proportion to changes other than production volume. By identifying the costs drivers that cause costs to change and assigning costs to products on the basis of cost driver usage, costs can be more accurately traced to products. Thus, cause-and-effect relationships provide a superior way of determining relevant costs. ABC systems classify manufacturing activities along a cost hierarchy dimension consisting of unit-level, batch-level, product-sustaining and facility-sustaining activities. The implementation of an ABC system should be dependent upon meeting the cost/benefit criterion and improvements should be made in the level of sophistication of the costing system up to the point where the marginal cost of improvement equals the marginal benefit from improvement. Sophisticated ABC systems are likely to be optimal in organizations having the following characteristics – intensive competition, a high proportion of indirect costs and a diverse product range.

Finally, you should refer to Exhibit 11.2 which presents a summary of the surveys undertaken in various countries relating to ABC adoption rates, the applications of ABC and the factors influencing the adoption of ABC systems.

Key Terms and Concepts

activities (p. 260)
activity cost drivers (p. 271)
batch-related activities (p. 272)
business-sustaining activities (p. 273)
consumption ratios (p. 264)
cost drivers (p. 260)
customer-sustaining activities (p. 273)
duration drivers (p. 271)
facility-sustaining activities (p. 273)

non-volume-based cost drivers (p. 263)
product-sustaining activities (p. 272)
resource cost drivers (p. 271)
service-sustaining activities (p. 272)
transaction drivers (p. 271)
unit-level activities (p. 272)
volume-related activities (p. 272)
volume-based cost drivers (p. 262)

Key Examination Points

ABC did not emerge until the late 1980s, and therefore fewer questions have been set on this topic. As a result, this chapter includes only a small number of review problems and end-of-chapter questions. It is likely that most questions will require you to compute product costs for a traditional system and an activity-based system and explain the difference between the product costs. It is also likely that examiners will require you to outline the circumstances where ABC systems are likely to prove most beneficial. Finally, note that ABC may not be included as part of your course curriculum so do check your course content prior to reading the chapter.

Review Problems

(For additional problems without answers relating to the content of this chapter you should refer to pages 498–502.)

1 Having attended a CIMA course on activity-based costing (ABC) you decide to experiment by applying the principles of ABC to the four products currently made and sold by your company. Details of the four products and relevant information are given below for one period:

Product	A	B	C	D
Output in units	120	100	80	120
Costs per unit:	(£)	(£)	(£)	(£)
Direct material	40	50	30	60
Direct labour	28	21	14	21
Machine hours (per unit)	4	3	2	3

The four products are similar and are usually produced in production runs of 20 units and sold in batches of 10 units.

The production overhead is currently absorbed by using a machine hour rate, and the total of the production overhead for the period has been analysed as follows:

	(£)
Machine department costs (rent, business rates, depreciation and supervision)	10 430
Set-up costs	5 250
Stores receiving	3 600
Inspection/Quality control	2 100
Materials handling and despatch	4 620

You have ascertained that the 'cost drivers' to be used are as listed below for the overhead costs shown:

Cost	Cost Driver
Set up costs	Number of production runs
Stores receiving	Requisitions raised
Inspection/Quality control	Number of production runs
Materials handling and despatch	Orders executed

The number of requisitions raised on the stores was 20 for each product and the number of orders executed was 42, each order being for a batch of 10 of a product. You are required

(a) to calculate the total costs for each product if all overhead costs are absorbed on a machine hour basis; (*4 marks*)

(b) to calculate the total costs for each product, using activity-based costing; (*7 marks*)

(c) to calculate and list the unit product costs from your figures in (a) and (b) above, to show the differences and to comment briefly on any conclusions which may be drawn which could have pricing and profit implications.

(*4 marks*)
(*Total 15 marks*)
CIMA Stage 2 Cost Accounting

2 The following information provides details of the costs, volume and cost drivers for a particular period in respect of ABC plc, a hypothetical company:

	Product X	Product Y	Product Z	Total
1. Production and sales (units)	30 000	20 000	8000	
2. Raw material usage (units)	5	5	11	
3. Direct material cost	£25	£20	£11	£1 238 000
4. Direct labour hours	$1\frac{1}{3}$	2	1	88 000
5. Machine hours	$1\frac{1}{3}$	1	2	76 000
6. Direct labour cost	£8	£12	£6	
7. Number of production runs	3	7	20	30
8. Number of deliveries	9	3	20	32
9. Number of receipts $(2 \times 7)^a$	15	35	220	270
10. Number of production orders	15	10	25	50
11. Overhead costs:				
Set-up	30 000			
Machines	760 000			
Receiving	435 000			
Packing	250 000			
Engineering	373 000			
	£1 848 000			

^{a}The company operates a just-in-time inventory policy, and receives each component once per production run.

In the past the company has allocated overheads to products on the basis of direct labour hours.

However, the majority of overheads are more closely related to machine hours than direct labour hours.

The company has recently redesigned its cost system by recovering overheads using two volume-related bases: machine hours and a

SOLUTIONS TO REVIEW PROBLEMS **281**

materials handling overhead rate for recovering overheads of the receiving department. Both the current and the previous cost system reported low profit margins for product X, which is the company's highest-selling product. The management accountant has recently attended a conference on activity-based costing, and the overhead costs for the last period have been analysed by the major activities in order to compute activity-based costs.

From the above information you are required to:

(a) Compute the product costs using a traditional volume-related costing system based on the assumptions that:

(i) all overheads are recovered on the basis of direct labour hours (i.e. the company's past product costing system);

(ii) the overheads of the receiving department are recovered by a materials handling overhead rate and the remaining overheads are recovered using a machine hour rate (i.e. the company's current costing system).

(b) Compute product costs using an activity-based costing system.

(c) Briefly explain the differences between the product cost computations in (a) and (b).

Solutions to Review Problems

SOLUTION 1

(a) Total machine hours = (120 × 4 hrs) + (100 × 3 hrs) + (80 × 2 hrs) + (120 × 3 hrs) = 1300 hrs

Machine hour overhead rate

$$= \frac{£10\,430 + £5250 + £3600 + £2100 + £4620}{1300 \text{ hrs}}$$

= £20 per machine hour

Product	A (£)	B (£)	C (£)	D (£)
Direct material	40	50	30	60
Direct labour	28	21	14	21
Overheads at £20 per machine hour	80	60	40	60
	148	131	84	141
Units of output	120	100	80	120
Total cost	£17 760	£13 100	£6720	£16 920

(b)

Costs	(£)	Cost driver	Cost driver transactions	Cost per unit (£)
Machine department	10 430	Machine hours	1300 hours	8.02
Set-up costs	5 250	Production runs	21	250
Stores receiving	3 600	Requisitions raised	80 (4 × 20)	45
Inspection/quality control	2 100	Production runs	21	100
Materials handling	4 620	Number of orders executed	42	110

Note
Number of production runs = Total output (420 units)/20 units per set-up.

Number of orders executed = Total output (420 units)/10 units per order.

The total costs for each product are computed by multiplying the cost driver rate per unit by the quantity of the cost driver consumed by each product.

	A	B	C	D
Prime costs	8 160 (£68 × 120)	7 100	3 520	9 720
Set ups	1 500 (£250 × 6)	1 250 (£250 × 5)	1 000	1 500
Stores/receiving	900 (£45 × 20)	900	900	900
Inspection/quality	600 (£100 × 6)	500	400	600
Handling despatch	1 320 (£110 × 12)	1 100 (£110 × 10)	880	1 320
Machine dept cost[a]	3 851	2 407	1 284	2 888
Total costs	16 331	13 257	7 984	16 928

Note
[a] A = 120 units × 4 hrs × £8.02;
B = 100 units × 3 hrs × £8.02

(c) Cost per unit

Costs from (a)	148.00	131.00	84.00	141.00
Costs from (b)	136.00	132.57	99.80	141.07
Difference	(11.91)	1.57	15.80	0.07

Product A is over-costed with the traditional system. Products B and C are undercosted and similar costs are reported with product D. It is claimed that ABC more accurately measures resources consumed by products (see 'Volume-based and non-volume-based cost drivers' in Chapter 11). Where cost-plus pricing is used, the transfer to an ABC system will result in different product prices. If activity-based costs are used for stock valuations then stock valuations and reported profits will differ.

SOLUTION 2

(a) (i)

Direct labour overhead rate

$$= \frac{\text{total overheads (£1 848 000)}}{\text{total direct labour hours (88 000)}}$$

$$= £21 \text{ per direct labour hour}$$

Product costs

Product	X (£)	Y (£)	Z (£)
Direct labour	8	12	6
Direct materials	25	20	11
Overhead[a]	28	42	21
Total cost	61	74	38

Note
[a] X = $1\frac{1}{3}$ hours × £21
Y = 2 hours × £21
Z = 1 hour × £21

(ii) Materials handling

Overhead rate

$$= \frac{\text{receiving department overheads (£435 000)}}{\text{direct material cost (£1 238 000)}}$$
$$\times 100$$

$$= 35.14\% \text{ of direct material cost}$$

Machine hour overhead rate

$$= \frac{\text{other overheads (£1 413 000)}}{76 000 \text{ machine hours}}$$

$$= £18.59 \text{ per machine hour}$$

Product costs

Product	X (£)	Y (£)	Z (£)
Direct labour	8.00	12.00	6.00
Direct materials	25.00	20.00	11.00
Materials handling overhead	8.78 (£25 × 35.14%)	7.03 (£20 × 35.14%)	3.87 (£11 × 35.14%)
Other overheads[a] (machine hour basis)	24.79	18.59	37.18
Total cost	66.57	57.62	58.05

Note
[a] X = $1\frac{1}{3}$ × £18.59
Y = 1 × £18.59
Z = 2 × £18.59

(b) The cost per transaction or activity for each of the cost centres is as follows:

Set-up cost

Cost per setup

$$= \frac{\text{setup cost (£30 000)}}{\text{number of production runs (30)}} = £1000$$

Receiving

Cost per receiving order

$$= \frac{\text{receiving cost (£435 000)}}{\text{number of orders (270)}} = £1611$$

Packing

Cost per packing order

$$= \frac{\text{packing cost (£250 000)}}{\text{number of orders (32)}} = £7812$$

Engineering

Cost per production order

$$= \frac{\text{engineering cost (£373 000)}}{\text{number of production orders (50)}} = £7460$$

The total set-up cost for the period was £30 000 and the cost per transaction or activity for the period is £1000 per set-up. Product X required three production runs, and thus £3000 of the set-up cost is traced to the production of product X for the period. Thus the cost per set-up per unit produced for product X is £0.10 (£3000/30 000 units).

Similarly, product Z required 20 set-ups, and so £20 000 is traced to product Z. Hence the cost per set-up for product Z is £2.50 (£20 000/8000 units).

The share of a support department's cost that is traced to each unit of output for each product is therefore calculated as follows:

cost per transaction

$$\times \frac{\text{number of transactions per product}}{\text{number of units produced}}$$

The unit standard costs for products X, Y and Z using an activity-based costing system are

	X	Y	Z
Direct labour	£8.00	£12.00	£6.00
Direct materials	25.00	20.00	11.00
Machine overhead[a]	13.33	10.00	20.00
Set-up costs	0.10	0.35	2.50
Receiving[b]	0.81	2.82	44.30
Packing[c]	2.34	1.17	19.53
Engineering[d]	3.73	3.73	23.31
Total manufacturing cost	53.31	50.07	126.64

Notes
[a]Machine hours × machine overhead rate (£760 000/76 000 hrs)

[b]X = (£1611 × 15)/30 000
 Y = (£1611 × 35)/20 000
 Z = (£1611 × 220)/8 000
[c]X = (£7812 × 9)/30 000
 Y = (£7812 × 3)/20 000
 Z = (£7812 × 20)/8 000
[d]X = (£7460 × 15)/30 000
 Y = (£7460 × 10)/20 000
 Z = (£7460 × 25)/8 000

(c) The traditional product costing system assumes that products consume resources in relation to volume measures such as direct labour, direct materials or machine hours. The activity-based system recognizes that some overheads are unrelated to production volume, and uses cost drivers that are independent of production volume. For example, the activity-based system assigns the following percentage of costs to product Z, the low volume product:

  Set-up-related costs   66.67%
                 (20 out of 30 set-ups)
  Delivery-related costs   62.5%
                 (20 out of 32 deliveries)
  Receiving costs   81.5%
                 (220 out of 270 receiving orders)
  Engineering-related costs   50%
                 (25 out of 50 production orders)

In contrast, the current costing system assigns the cost of the above activities according to production volume, measured in machine hours. The total machine hours are

  Product X 40 000 (30 000 × $1\frac{1}{3}$)
  Product Y 20 000 (20 000 × 1)
  Product Z <u>16 000</u> (8 000 × 2)
         <u>76 000</u>

Therefore 21% (16 000/76 000) of the non-volume-related costs are assigned to product Z if machine hours are used as the allocation base. Hence the traditional system undercosts the low-volume product, and, on applying the above approach, it can be shown that the high-volume product (product X) is overcosted. For example, 53% of the costs (40 000/76 000) are traced to product X with the current system, whereas the activity-based system assigns a much lower proportion of non-volume-related costs to this product.

Capital investment decisions

12

Capital investment decisions are those decisions that involve current outlays in return for a stream of benefits in future years. It is true to say that all of the firm's expenditures are made in expectation of realizing future benefits. The distinguishing feature between short-term decisions and capital investment (long-term) decisions is time. Generally, we can classify short-term decisions as those that involve a relatively short time horizon, say one year, from the commitment of funds to the receipt of the benefits. On the other hand, capital investment decisions are those decisions where a significant period of time elapses between the outlay and the recoupment of the investment. We shall see that this commitment of funds for a significant period of time involves an interest cost, which must be brought into the analysis. With short-term decisions, funds are committed only for short periods of time, and the interest cost is normally so small that it can be ignored.

Capital investment decisions normally represent the most important decisions that an organization makes, since they commit a substantial proportion of a firm's resources to actions that are likely to be irreversible. Such decisions are applicable to all sectors of society. Business firms' investment decisions include investments in plant and machinery, research and development, advertising and warehouse facilities. Investment decisions in the public sector include new roads, schools and airports. Individuals' investment decisions include house-buying and the purchase of consumer durables. In this chapter we shall examine the economic evaluation of the desirability of investment proposals. We shall concentrate on the investment decisions of business firms, but the same principles, with modifications, apply to individuals, and the public sector.

Learning objectives

After studying this chapter, you should be able to:

- explain the opportunity cost of an investment;
- distinguish between compounding and discounting;
- explain the concept of net present value (NPV) and internal rate of return (IRR);
- calculate NPV, IRR, payback period and accounting rate of return;
- explain the limitations of payback and the accounting rate of return methods;
- calculate the incremental taxation payments arising from a proposed investment.

The opportunity cost of an investment

You will recall that in Chapter 1 we adopted the view that, broadly, firms seek to maximize the present value of future net cash inflows. It is therefore important that you acquire an intuitive understanding of the term 'present value'.

Investors can invest in securities traded in financial markets. If you prefer to avoid risk, you can invest in government securities, which will yield a *fixed* return. On the other hand, you may prefer to invest in *risky* securities such as the ordinary shares of companies quoted on the stock exchange. If you invest in the ordinary shares of a company, you will find that the return will vary from year to year, depending on the performance of the company and its future expectations. Investors normally prefer to avoid risk if possible, and will generally invest in risky securities only if they believe that they will obtain a greater return for the increased risk. Suppose that **risk-free gilt-edged securities** issued by the government yield a return of 10%. You will therefore be prepared to invest in ordinary shares only if you expect the return to be greater than 10%; let us assume that you require an *expected* return of 15% to induce you to invest in ordinary shares in preference to a risk-free security.

Suppose you invest in company X ordinary shares. Would you want company X to invest your money in a capital project that gives less than 15%? Surely not, assuming the project has the same risk as the alternative investments in shares of other companies that are yielding a return of 15%. You would prefer company X to invest in other companies' ordinary shares at 15% or, alternatively, to repay your investment so that you could invest yourself at 15%.

The rates of return that are available from investments in securities in financial markets such as ordinary shares and government gilt-edged securities represent the **opportunity cost of an investment** in capital projects; that is, if cash is invested in the capital project, it cannot be invested elsewhere to earn a return. A firm should therefore invest in capital projects only if they yield a return in excess of the opportunity cost of the investment. The opportunity cost of the investment is also known as the **minimum required rate of return, cost of capital, discount rate** or **interest rate**.

The return on securities traded in financial markets provides us with the opportunity costs, that is the required rates of return available on securities. The expected returns that investors require from the ordinary shares of different companies vary because some companies' shares are more risky than others. The greater the risk, the greater the expected returns. Consider Figure 12.1. You can see that as the risk of a security increases the return that investors require to compensate for the extra risk increases. Consequently, investors will expect to receive a return in excess of 15% if they invest in securities that have a higher risk than company X ordinary shares. If this return was not forthcoming, investors would not purchase high-risk securities. It is therefore important that companies investing in high-risk capital projects earn higher returns to compensate investors for this risk. You can also see that a risk-free security such as a gilt-edged government security yields the lowest return, i.e. 10%. Consequently, if a firm invests in a project with zero risk, it should earn a return in excess of 10%. If the project does not yield this return and no other projects are available then the funds earmarked for the project should be repaid to the shareholders as dividends. The shareholders could then invest the funds themselves at 10%.

Compounding and discounting

Our objective is to calculate and compare returns on an investment in a capital project with an alternative equal risk investment in securities traded in the financial markets. This comparison is made using a technique called **discounted cash flow (DCF)** analysis.

FIGURE 12.1 *Risk–return trade-off.*

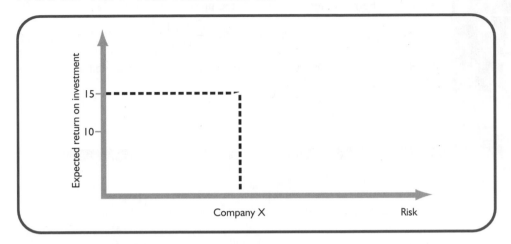

Because a DCF analysis is the opposite of the concept of **compounding interest**, we shall initially focus on compound interest calculations.

Suppose you are investing £100 000 in a risk-free security yielding a return of 10% payable at the end of each year. Exhibit 12.1 shows that if the interest is reinvested, your investment will accumulate to £146 410 by the end of year 4. Period 0 in the first column of Exhibit 12.1 means that no time has elapsed or the time is *now*, period 1 means one year later, and so on. The values in Exhibit 12.1 can also be obtained by using the formula:

$$FV_n = V_0(1 + K)^n \tag{12.1}$$

where FV_n denotes the future value of an investment in n years, V_0 denotes the amount invested at the beginning of the period (year 0), K denotes the rate of return on the investment and n denotes the number of years for which the money is invested. The calculation for £100 000 invested at 10% for two years is

$$FV_2 = £100\,000\,(1 + 0.10)^2 = £121\,000$$

In Exhibit 12.1 all of the year-end values are equal as far as the time value of money is concerned. For example, £121 000 received at the end of year 2 is equivalent to £100 000 received today and invested at 10%. Similarly, £133 100 received at the end of year 3 is equivalent to £121 000 received at the end of year 2, since £121 000 can be invested at the end of year 2 to accumulate to £133 100. Unfortunately, none of the amounts are directly comparable at any single moment in time, because each amount is expressed at a different point in time.

When making capital investment decisions, we must convert cash inflows and outflows for different years into a common value. This is achieved by converting the cash flows into their respective values at the same point in time. Mathematically, any point in time can be chosen, since all four figures in Exhibit 12.1 are equal to £100 000 at year 0, £110 000 at year 1, £121 000 at year 2, and so on. However, it is preferable to choose the point in time at which the decision is taken, and this is the present time or year 0. All of the values in Exhibit 12.1 can therefore be expressed in values at the present time (i.e. '**present value**') of £100 000.

The process of converting cash to be received in the future into a value at the present time by the use of an interest rate is termed **discounting** and the resulting present value is the **discounted present value**. Compounding is the opposite of discounting, since it is the

EXHIBIT 12.1

The value of £100 000 invested at 10%, compounded annually, for four years

future value of present value cash flows. Equation (12.1) for calculating future values can be rearranged to produce the present value formula:

$$V_0 \text{ (present value)} = \frac{FV_n}{(1+K)^n} \tag{12.2}$$

By applying this equation, the calculation for £121 000 received at the end of year 2 can be expressed as

$$\text{present value} = \frac{£121\,000}{(1+0.10)^2} = £100\,000$$

End of year	Interest earned (£)	Total investment (£)
0		100 000
	0.10 × 100 000	10 000
1		110 000
	0.10 × 110 000	11 000
2		121 000
	0.10 × 121 000	12 100
3		133 100
	0.10 × 133 100	13 310
4		146 410

You should now be aware that £1 received today is not equal to £1 received one year from today. No rational person will be equally satisfied with receiving £1 a year from now as opposed to receiving it today, because money received today can be used to earn interest over the ensuing year. Thus one year from now an investor can have the original £1 plus one year's interest on it. For example, if the interest rate is 10% each £1 invested now will yield £1.10 one year from now. That is, £1 received today is equal to £1.10 one year from today at 10% interest. Alternatively, £1 one year from today is equal to £0.9091 today, its present value because £0.9091, plus 10% interest for one year amounts to £1. The concept that £1 received in the future is not equal to £1 received today is known as the **time value of money**

We shall now consider four different methods of appraising capital investments: the net present value, internal rate of return, accounting rate of return and payback methods. We shall see that the first two methods take into account the time value of money whereas the accounting rate of return and payback methods ignore this factor.

The concept of net present value

By using discounted cash flow techniques and calculating present values, we can compare the return on an investment in capital projects with an alternative equal risk investment in securities traded in the financial market. Suppose a firm is considering four projects (all of which are risk-free) shown in Exhibit 12.2. You can see that each of the projects is identical with the investment in the risk-free security shown in Exhibit 12.1 because you can cash in this investment for £110 000 in year 1, £121 000 in year 2, £133 100 in year 3 and £146 410 in year 4. In other words your potential cash receipts from the risk-free security are identical to the net cash flows for projects A, B, C and D shown in Exhibit 12.2. Consequently, the firm should be indifferent as to whether it uses the funds to invest in the projects or invests the funds in securities of identical risk traded in the financial markets.

The most straightforward way of determining whether a project yields a return in excess of the alternative equal risk investment in traded securities is to calculate the **net present value (NPV)**. This is the present value of the net cash inflows less the project's initial investment outlay. If the rate of return from the project is greater than the return from an equivalent risk investment in securities traded in the financial market, the NPV will be positive. Alternatively, if the rate of return is lower, the NPV will be negative. A positive NPV therefore indicates that an investment should be accepted, while a negative value indicates that it should be rejected. A zero NPV calculation indicates that the firm should be indifferent to whether the project is accepted or rejected.

You can see that the present value of each of the projects shown in Exhibit 12.2 is £100 000. You should now deduct the investment cost of £100 000 to calculate the project's NPV. The NPV for each project is zero. The firm should therefore be indifferent to whether it accepts any of the projects or invests the funds in an equivalent risk-free security. This was our conclusion when we compared the cash flows of the projects with the investments in a risk-free security shown in Exhibit 12.1.

You can see that it is better for the firm to invest in any of the projects shown in Exhibit 12.2 if their initial investment outlays are less than £100 000. This is because we have to pay £100 000 to obtain an equivalent stream of cash flows from a security traded in the financial markets. Conversely, we should reject the investment in the projects if their initial investment outlays are greater than £100 000. You should now see that the NPV rule leads to a direct comparison of a project with an equivalent risk security traded in the financial market. Given that the present value of the net cash inflows for each project is £100 000, their NPVs will be positive (thus signifying acceptance) if the initial investment outlay is less than £100 000 and negative (thus signifying rejection) if the initial outlay is greater than £100 000.

EXHIBIT 12.2

Evaluation of four risk-free projects

	A (£)	B (£)	C (£)	D (£)
Project investment outlay	100 000	100 000	100 000	100 000
End of year cash flows:				
Year 1	110 000	0	0	0
2	0	121 000	0	0
3	0	0	133 100	0
4	0	0	0	146 410
present value =	$\dfrac{110\,000}{1.10}$	$\dfrac{121\,000}{(1.10)^2}$	$\dfrac{133\,100}{(1.10)^3}$	$\dfrac{146\,410}{(1.10)^4}$
	= 100 000	= 100 000	= 100 000	= 100 000

Calculating net present values

You should now have an intuitive understanding of the NPV rule. We shall now learn how to calculate NPVs. The NPV can be expressed as:

$$NPV = \frac{FV_1}{1+K} + \frac{FV_2}{(1+K)^2} + \frac{FV_3}{(1+K)^3} + \cdots + \frac{FV_n}{(1+K)^n} - I_0 \qquad (12.3)$$

where I_0 represents the investment outlay and FV represents the future values received in years 1 to n. The rate of return K used is the return available on an equivalent risk security in the financial market. Consider the situation in Example 12.1.

EXAMPLE 12.1

The Bothnia Company is evaluating two projects with an expected life of three years and an investment outlay of £1 million. The estimated net cash inflows for each project are as follows:

	Project A (£)	Project B (£)
Year 1	300 000	600 000
Year 2	1 000 000	600 000
Year 3	400 000	600 000

The opportunity cost of capital for both projects is 10%. You are required to calculate the net present value for each project.

The net present value calculation for Project A is:

$$NPV = \frac{£300\,000}{(1.10)} + \frac{£1\,000\,000}{(1.10)^2} + \frac{£400\,000}{(1.10)^3} - £1\,000\,000 = +£399\,700$$

Alternatively, the net present value can be calculated by referring to a published table of present values. You will find examples of such a table if you refer to Appendix A (see page 546). To use the table, simply find the discount factors by referring to each year of the cash flows and the appropriate interest rate.

For example, if you refer to year 1 in Appendix A, and the 10% column, this will show a discount factor of 0.9091. For years 2 and 3 the discount factors are 0.8264 and 0.7513. You then multiply the cash flows by the discount factors to find the present value of the cash flows. The calculation is as follows:

Year	Amount (£)	Discount factor	Present value (£)
1	300	0.9091	272 730
2	1000	0.8264	826 400
3	400	0.7513	300 520
			1 399 650
		Less initial outlay	1 000 000
		Net present value	399 650

The difference between the two calculations is due to rounding differences.

Note that the discount factors in the present value table are based on £1 received in n years time calculated according to the present value formula (equation 12.2). For example, £1 received in years 1, 2 and 3 when the interest rate is 10% is calculated as follows:

$$\text{Year } 1 = £1/1.10 = 0.9091$$
$$\text{Year } 2 = £1(1.10)^2 = 0.8264$$
$$\text{Year } 3 = £1(1.10)^3 = 0.7513$$

The positive net present value from the investment indicates the increase in the market value of the shareholders' funds which should occur once the stock market becomes aware of the acceptance of the project. The net present value also represents the potential increase in present consumption that the project makes available to the ordinary shareholders, after any funds used have been repaid with interest. For example, assume that the firm finances the investment of £1 million in Example 12.1 by borrowing £1 399 700 at 10% and repays the loan and interest out of the project's proceeds as they occur. You can see from the repayment schedule in Exhibit 12.3 that £399 700 received from the loan is available for current consumption, and the remaining £1 000 000 can be invested in the project. The cash flows from the project are just sufficient to repay the loan. Therefore acceptance of the project enables the ordinary shareholders' present consumption to be increased by the net present value of £399 700. Hence the acceptance of all available projects with a positive net present value should lead to the maximization of shareholders' wealth.

Let us now calculate the net present value for Project B shown in Example 12.1. When the annual cash flows are constant, the calculation of the net present value is simplified. The discount factors when the cash flows are the same each year (that is, an annuity) are set out in Appendix B (see page 547). We need to find the discount factor for 10% for three years. If you refer to Appendix B, you will see that it is 2.487. The NPV is calculated as follows:

Annual cash inflow	Discount factor	Present value (£)
£600 000	2.487	1 492 200
	Less investment cost	1 000 000
	Net present value	492 200

You will see that the total present value for the period is calculated by multiplying the cash inflow by the discount factor. It is important to note that the annuity tables shown in Appendix B can only be applied when the annual cash flows are the same each year.

The internal rate of return

The **internal rate of return (IRR)** is an alternative technique for use in making capital investment decisions that also takes into account the time value of money. The internal rate of return represents the true interest rate earned on an investment over the course of its economic life. This measure is sometimes referred to as the **discounted rate of return**. The internal rate of return is the interest rate K that when used to discount all cash flows resulting from an investment, will equate the present value of the cash receipts to the present value of the cash outlays. In other words, it is the discount rate that will cause the net present value of an investment to be zero. Alternatively, the internal rate of return can be described as the maximum cost of capital that can be applied to finance a project without causing harm to the shareholders. The internal rate of return is found by solving for the value of K from the following formula:

$$I_0 = \frac{FV_1}{1+K} + \frac{FV_2}{(1+K)^2} + \frac{FV_3}{(1+K)^3} + \cdots + \frac{FV_n}{(1+K)^n} \tag{12.4}$$

EXHIBIT 12.3

The pattern of cash flows assuming that the loan is repaid out of the proceeds of the project

It is easier, however, to use the discount tables. Let us now calculate the internal rate of return for Project A in Example 12.1.

The IRR can be found by trial and error by using a number of discount factors until the NPV equals zero. For example, if we use a 25% discount factor, we get a positive NPV of £84 800. We must therefore try a higher figure. Applying 35% gives a negative NPV of £66 530. We know then that the NPV will be zero somewhere between 25% and 35%. In fact, the IRR is

Year	Loan outstanding at start of year (1) (£)	Interest at 10% (2) (£)	Total amount owed before repayment (3) = (1)+(2) (£)	Proceeds from project (4) (£)	Loan outstanding at year end (5) = (3)−(4) (£)
1	1 399 700	139 970	1 539 670	300 000	1 239 670
2	1 239 670	123 967	1 363 637	1 000 000	363 637
3	363 637	36 363	400 000	400 000	0

approximately 30%, as indicated in the following calculation:

Year	Net cash flow (£)	Discount factor (30%)	Present value of cash flow (£)
1	300 000	0.7692	230 760
2	1 000 000	0.5917	591 700
3	400 000	0.4552	182 080
		Net present value	1 004 540
		Less initial outlay	1 000 000
		Net present value	4 540

It is claimed that the calculation of the IRR does not require the prior specification of the cost of capital. The decision rule is that if the IRR is greater than the opportunity cost of capital, the investment is profitable and will yield a positive NPV. Alternatively, if the IRR is less than the cost of capital, the investment is unprofitable and will result in a negative NPV. Therefore any interpretation of the significance of the IRR will still require that we estimate the cost of capital. The calculation of the IRR is illustrated in Figure 12.2.

The dots in the graph represent the NPV at different discount rates. The point where the line joining the dots cuts the horizontal axis indicates the IRR (the point at which the NPV is zero). Figure 12.2 indicates that the IRR is 30%, and you can see from this diagram that the interpolation method can be used to calculate the IRR without carrying out trial and error calculations. When we use interpolation, we infer the missing term (in this case the discount rate at which NPV is zero) from a known series of numbers. For example, at a discount rate of 25% the NPV is +£84 800 and for a discount rate of 35% the NPV is

− £66 530. The total distance between these points is £151 330 (+£84 800 and − £66 530). The calculation for the approximate IRR is therefore

$$25\% + \frac{84\,800}{151\,330} \times (35\% - 25\%) = 30.60\%$$

In other words, if you move down line A in Figure 12.2 from a discount rate of 25% by £84 800, you will reach the point at which NPV is zero. The distance between the two points on line A is £151 330, and we are given the discount rates of 25% and 35% for these points. Therefore 84 800/151 330 represents the distance that we must move between these two points for the NPV to be zero. This distance in terms of the discount rate is 5.60% [(84 800/151 330) × 10%] which, when added to the starting point of 25%, produces an IRR of 30.60%. The formula using the interpolation method is as follows:

$$A + \frac{C}{C - D}(B - A) \tag{12.5}$$

where A is the discount rate of the low trial, B is the discount rate of the high trial, C is the NPV of cash inflow of the low trial and D is the NPV of cash inflow of the high trial. Thus

$$25\% + \left[\frac{84\,800}{84\,800 - (-66\,530)} \times 10\% \right]$$

$$= 25\% + \left[\frac{84\,800}{151\,330} \times 10\% \right]$$

$$= 30.60\%$$

Note that the interpolation method only gives an approximation of the IRR. The greater the distance between any two points that have a positive and a negative NPV, the less accurate is the IRR calculation. Consider using interpolation based on the two points marked on line B in Figure 12.2. The point where it cuts the horizontal axis is approximately 33%, whereas the actual IRR is 30.60%.

The calculation of the IRR is easier when the cash flows are of a constant amount each year. Let us now calculate the internal rate of return for project B in Example 12.1. Because the cash flows are equal each year, we can use the annuity table in Appendix B. When the cash flows are discounted at the IRR, the NPV will be zero. The IRR will therefore be at the point where

$$[\text{annual cash flow}] \times \left[\begin{array}{c} \text{discount factor for number of years} \\ \text{for which cash flow is received} \end{array} \right] - \left[\begin{array}{c} \text{investment} \\ \text{cost} \end{array} \right] = 0$$

Rearranging this formula, the internal rate of return will be at the point where

$$\text{discount factor} = \frac{\text{investment cost}}{\text{annual cash flow}}$$

Substituting the figures for project B in Example 12.1,

$$\text{discount factor} = \frac{£1\,000\,000}{£600\,000} = 1.666$$

We now examine the entries for the year 3 row in Appendix B to find the figures closest to 1.666. They are 1.673 (entered in the 36% column) and 1.652 (entered in the 37% column). We can therefore conclude that the IRR is between 36% and 37%. However, because the cost of capital is 10%, an accurate calculation is unnecessary; the IRR is far in excess of the cost of capital.

The calculation of the IRR can be rather tedious (as the cited examples show), but the trial-and-error approach can be programmed for fast and accurate solution by a computer or calculator. The calculation problems are no longer a justification for preferring the NPV

FIGURE 12.2 *Interpretation of the internal rate of return.*

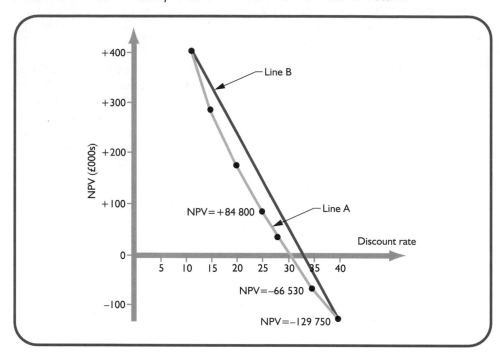

method of investment appraisal. Nevertheless, there are theoretical justifications, that support the NPV method.

Relevant cash flows

Investment decisions, like all other decisions, should be analysed in terms of the cash flows that can be directly attributable to them. These cash flows should include the incremental cash flows that will occur in the future following acceptance of the investment. The cash flows will include cash inflows and outflows, or the inflows may be represented by savings in cash outflows. For example, a decision to purchase new machinery may generate cash savings in the form of reduced out-of-pocket operating costs. For all practical purposes such cost savings are equivalent to cash receipts.

It is important to note that depreciation is not included in the cash flow estimates for capital investment decisions, since it is a non-cash expense. This is because the capital investment cost of the asset to be depreciated is included as a cash outflow at the start of the project, and depreciation is merely a financial accounting method for allocating past capital costs to future accounting periods. Any inclusion of depreciation will lead to double counting.

Timing of cash flows

Our calculations have been based on the assumption that any cash flows in future years will occur in one lump sum at the year end. Obviously, this is an unrealistic assumption, since cash flows are likely to occur at various times throughout the year, and a more accurate method is to assume monthly cash flows and the monthly discount rates or continuous compounding. However, the use of annual cash flows enables all cash flows which occur in a single year to be combined and discounted in one computation. Even though the calculated results that are obtained are not strictly accurate, they are normally accurate enough for most decisions.

Techniques that ignore the time value of money

In addition to those methods that take into account the time value of money two other methods that ignore this factor are frequently used in practice. These are the payback method and the accounting rate of return method. Methods that ignore the time value of money are theoretically weak, and they will not necessarily lead to the maximization of the market value of ordinary shares. Nevertheless, the fact that they are frequently used in practice means that we should be aware of these techniques and their limitations.

Payback method

The **payback method** is one of the simplest and most frequently used methods of capital investment appraisal. It is defined as the length of time that is required for a stream of cash proceeds from an investment to recover the original cash outlay required by the investment. If the stream of cash flows from the investment is constant each year, the payback period can be calculated by dividing the total initial cash outlay by the amount of the expected annual cash proceeds. Therefore if an investment requires an initial outlay of £60 000 and is expected to produce annual cash inflows of £20 000 per year for five years, the payback period will be £60 000 divided by £20 000, or three years. If the stream of expected proceeds is not constant from year to year, the payback period is determined by adding up the cash inflows expected in successive years until the total is equal to the original outlay. Example 12.2 illustrates two projects, A and B, that require the same initial outlay of £50 000 but that display different time profiles of benefits.

In Example 12.2 project A pays back its initial investment cost in three years, whereas project B pays back its initial cost in four years so that project A would be ranked in preference to project B. However, project B has a higher NPV, and the payback method incorrectly ranks project A in preference to project B. Two obvious deficiencies are apparent from these calculations. First, the payback method does not take into account cash flows that are earned after the payback date and, secondly, it fails to take into account the differences in the timing of the proceeds which are earned before the payback date. Payback computations ignore the important fact that future cash receipts cannot be validly compared with an initial outlay until they are discounted to their present values.

Not only does the payback period incorrectly rank project A in preference to project B, but the method can also result in the acceptance of projects that have a negative NPV. Consider the cash flows for project C in Example 12.3.

The payback period for project C is three years, and if this was within the time limit set by management, the project would be accepted in spite of its negative NPV. Note also that the payback method would rank project C in preference to project B in Example 12.3, despite the fact that B would yield a positive NPV.

The payback period can only be a valid indicator of the time that an investment requires to pay for itself, if all cash flows are first discounted to their present values and the discounted values are then used to calculate the payback period. This adjustment gives rise to what is known as the adjusted or **discounted payback method**. Even when such an adjustment is made, the adjusted payback method cannot be a complete measure of an

EXAMPLE 12.2

The cash flows and NPV calculations for two projects are as follows:

	Project A		Project B	
	(£)	(£)	(£)	(£)
Initial cost		50 000		50 000
Net cash inflows				
Year 1	10 000		10 000	
Year 2	20 000		10 000	
Year 3	20 000		10 000	
Year 4	20 000		20 000	
Year 5	10 000		30 000	
Year 6	—		30 000	
Year 7	—	80 000	30 000	140 000
NPV at a 10% cost capital		10 500		39 460

investment's profitability. It can estimate whether an investment is likely to be profitable, but it cannot estimate how profitable the investment will be.

Despite the theoretical limitations of the payback method it is the method most widely used in practice (see Exhibit 12.4). Why, then, is payback the most widely applied formal investment appraisal technique? It is a particularly useful approach for ranking projects where a firm faces liquidity constraints and requires a fast repayment of investments. The payback method may also be appropriate in situations where risky investments are made in uncertain markets that are subject to fast design and product changes or where future cash flows are extremely difficult to predict. The payback method assumes that risk is time-related: the longer the period, the greater the chance of failure. By concentrating on the early cash flows, payback uses data in which managers have greater confidence. Thus, the payback period can be used as a rough measure of risk, based on the assumption that the longer it takes for a project to pay for itself, the riskier it is. Managers may also choose projects with quick payback periods because of self-interest. If a manager's performance is

EXAMPLE 12.3

The cash flows and NPV calculation for project C are as follows:

	(£)	(£)
Initial cost		50 000
Net cash outflows		
Year 1	10 000	
Year 2	20 000	
Year 3	20 000	
Year 4	3 500	
Year 5	3 500	
Year 6	3 500	
Year 7	3 500	64 000
NPV (at 10% cost of capital)		(−1036)

EXHIBIT 12.4

Surveys of practice

Surveys conducted by Pike (1996) relating to the investment appraisal techniques by 100 large UK companies between 1975 and 1992 provide an indication of the changing trends in practice in large UK companies. Pike's findings relating to the percentage of firms using different appraisal methods are as follows:

	1975 %	1981 %	1986 %	1992 %
Payback	73	81	92	94
Accounting rate of return	51	49	56	50
DCF methods (IRR or NPV)	58	68	84	88
Internal rate of return (IRR)	44	57	75	81
Net present value (NPV)	32	39	68	74

Source: Pike (1996)

A study of 300 UK manufacturing organizations by Drury *et al.* (1993) sought to ascertain the extent to which particular techniques were used. The figures below indicate the percentage of firms that often or always used a particular technique:

	All organizations %	Smallest organizations %	Largest organizations %
Payback (unadjusted)	63	56	55
Discounted payback	42	30	48
Accounting rate of return	41	35	53
Internal rate of return	57	30	85
Net present value	43	23	80

Few studies have been undertaken in mainland Europe. The following usage rates relate to surveys undertaken in the USA and Belgium. For comparative purposes Pike's UK study is also listed :

	UK[a] %	USA[b] %	Belgium[c] %
Payback	94	72	50
Accounting rate of return	50	65	65
Internal rate of return	81	91	77
Net present value	74	88	60
Discounted payback		65	68

[a]Pike (1996)
[b]Trahan and Gitman (1995)
[c]Dardenne (1998)

It is apparent from the above surveys that firms use a combination of appraisal methods. The studies by Pike indicate a trend in the increasing usage of discount rates. The Drury *et al.* study suggests that larger organizations use net present value and internal rate of return to a greater extent than the smaller organizations. The Drury *et al.* study also asked the respondents to rank the appraisal methods in order of importance for evaluating major projects. The larger organizations ranked internal rate of return first, followed by payback and net present value whereas the smaller organizations ranked payback first, internal rate of return second and intuitive management judgement third.

The use of the accounting rate of return probably reflects the fact that it is a widely used external financial accounting measure by financial markets and managers therefore wish to assess what impact a project will have on the external reporting of this measure. Also it is a widely used measure for evaluating managerial performance.

measured using short-term criteria, such as net profits, there is a danger that he or she may choose projects with quick paybacks to show improved net profits as soon as possible. The payback method is also frequently used in conjunction with the NPV or IRR methods. It serves as a simple first-level screening device that identifies those projects that should be subject to more rigorous investigation. A further attraction of payback is that it is easily understood by all levels of management and provides an important summary measure: how quickly will the project recover its initial outlay? Ideally, the payback method should be used in conjunction with the NPV method, and the cash flows discounted before the payback period is calculated.

Accounting rate of return

The **accounting rate of return** (also known as the **return on investment** and **return on capital employed**) is calculated by dividing the average annual profits from a project into the average investment cost. It differs from other methods in that profits rather than cash flows are used. Note that profits are not equal to cash flows because financial accounting profit measurement is based on the accruals concept. Assuming that depreciation represents the only non-cash expense, profit is equivalent to cash flows less depreciation. The use of accounting rate of return can be attributed to the wide use of the return on investment measure in financial statement analysis.

When the average annual net profits are calculated, only additional revenues and costs that follow from the investment are included in the calculation. The average annual net profit is therefore calculated by dividing the difference between incremental revenues and costs by the estimated life of the investment. The incremental costs include either the *net* investment cost or the total depreciation charges, these figures being identical. The average investment figure that is used in the calculation depends on the method employed to calculate depreciation. If straight-line depreciation is used, it is presumed that investment will decline in a linear fashion as the asset ages. The average investment under this assumption is one-half of the amount of the initial investment plus one-half of the scrap value at the end of the project's life.[1]

For example, the three projects described in Examples 12.2 and 12.3 for which the payback period was computed required an initial outlay of £50 000. If we assume that the projects have no scrap values and that straight-line depreciation is used, the average investment for each project will be £25 000. The calculation of the accounting rate of return for each of these projects is as follows:

$$\text{accounting rate of return} = \frac{\text{average annual profits}}{\text{average investment}}$$

$$\text{project A} = \frac{6\,000}{25\,000} = 24\%$$

$$\text{project B} = \frac{12\,857}{25\,000} = 51\%$$

$$\text{project C} = \frac{2\,000}{25\,000} = 8\%$$

For project A the total profit over its five-year life is £30 000 (£80 000 − £50 000), giving an average annual profit of £6000. The average annual profits for projects B and C are calculated in a similar manner.

It follows that the accounting rate of return is superior to the payback method in one respect; that is, it allows for differences in the useful lives of the assets being compared. For example, the calculations set out above reflect the high earnings of project B over the whole life of the project, and consequently it is ranked in preference to project A. Also, projects A and C have the same payback periods, but the accounting rate of return correctly indicates that project A is preferable to project C.

However, the accounting rate of return suffers from the serious defect that it ignores the time value of money. When the method is used in relation to a project where the cash inflows do not occur until near the end of its life, it will show the same accounting rate of return as it would for a project where the cash inflows occur early in its life, providing that the average cash inflows are the same. For this reason the accounting rate of return cannot be recommended. Nevertheless, the accounting rate of return is widely used in practice (see Exhibit 12.4). This is probably due to the fact that the annual accounting rate of return is widely used to measure the managerial performance of different business units within a company. Therefore, managers are likely to be interested in how any new investment contributes to the business unit's overall accounting rate of return.

Qualitative factors

Not all investment projects can be described completely in terms of monetary costs and benefits (e.g. a new cafeteria for the employees or the installation of safety equipment). Nevertheless, the procedures described in this chapter may be useful by making the value placed by management on quantitative factors explicit. For example, if the present value of the cash outlays for a project is £100 000 and the benefits from the project are difficult to quantify, management must make a value judgement as to whether or not the benefits are in excess of £100 000. In the case of capital expenditure on facilities for employees, or expenditure to avoid unpleasant environmental effects from the company's manufacturing process, one can take the view that the present value of the cash outlays represents the cost to shareholders of the pursuit of goals other than the maximization of shareholders' funds. In other words, ordinary shareholders, as a group in the bargaining coalition, should know how much the pursuit of other goals is costing them.

Summary

In this chapter we have noted that capital investment decisions are of vital importance, since they involve the commitment of large sums of money and they affect the whole conduct of the business for many future years. The commitment of funds for long periods of time entails a large interest cost, which must be incorporated into the analysis. We have seen that the rate of return that is required by investors can be incorporated by converting future cash flows to their present values. For business firms the rate of return includes a risk-free interest rate plus a risk premium to compensate for uncertainty. For certain cash flows, which we have assumed in this chapter, the required rate of return is the risk-free rate.

The assumed objective of capital investment appraisal is to maximize shareholders wealth, and this is achieved by the acceptance of all projects that yield positive net present values. Two alternative methods of evaluating capital investment decisions that take into account the time value of money have been examined: the net present value and the internal rate of return. We also considered the payback and accounting rate of return methods for evaluating capital investment decisions, since these are frequently used in practice, but because neither incorporates the time value of money, we must conclude that they are theoretically unsound.

In order to simplify the presentation of capital investment appraisal the impact of taxation has been omitted. For an explanation of how taxation should be incorporated into the appraisal you should refer to Appendix 12.1. Before reading the Appendix you should check your course curriculum since the impact of taxation is often not included in first year management accounting courses.

Appendix 12.1: Taxation and investment decisions

In our discussions so far we have ignored the impact of taxation. Taxation rules differ between countries but in most countries similar principles tend to apply relating to the taxation allowances available on capital investment expenditure. Companies rarely pay taxes on the profits that are disclosed in their annual published accounts, since certain expenses that are deducted in the published accounts are not allowable deductions for taxation purposes. For example, depreciation is not an allowable deduction; instead, taxation legislation enables **capital allowances** (also known as **writing-down allowances** or **depreciation tax shields**) to be claimed on capital expenditure that is incurred on plant and machinery and other fixed assets. Capital allowances represent standardized depreciation allowances granted by the tax authorities. These allowances vary from country to country but their common aim is to enable the *net* cost of assets to be deducted as an allowable expense, either throughout their economic life or on an accelerated basis which is shorter than an asset's economic life.

Taxation laws in different countries typically specify the amount of capital expenditure that is allowable (sometimes this exceeds the cost of the asset where a government wishes to stimulate investment), the time period over which the capital allowances can be claimed and the depreciation method to be employed. Currently in the UK, companies can claim annual capital allowances of 25% on the written-down value of plant and equipment based on the reducing balance method of depreciation. Different percentage capital allowances are also available on other assets such as industrial buildings where an allowance of 4% per annum based on straight line depreciation can be claimed.[2]

Let us now consider how taxation affects the NPV calculations. You will see that the calculation must include the incremental tax cash flows arising from the investment. Consider the information presented in Example 12A.1.

EXAMPLE 12A.1

The Sentosa Company operates in Ruratania where investments in plant and machinery are eligible for 25% annual writing-down allowances on the written-down value using the reducing balance method of depreciation. The corporate tax rate is 35%. The company is considering whether to purchase some machinery which will cost £1 million and which is expected to result in additional net cash inflows and profits of £500 000 per annum for four years. It is anticipated that the machinery will be sold at the end of year 4 for its written-down value for taxation purposes. Assume a one year lag in the payment of taxes. Calculate the net present value.

The first stage is to calculate the annual writing down allowances (i.e. the capital allowances). The calculations are as follows:

End of year	Annual writing-down allowance (£)	Written-down value (£)
0	0	1 000 000
1	250 000 (25% × £1 000 000)	750 000
2	187 500 (25% × £750 000)	562 500
3	140 630 (25% × £562 500)	421 870
4	105 470 (25% × £421 870)	316 400
	683 600	

Next we calculate the additional taxable profits arising from the project. The calculations are as follows:

	Year 1 (£)	Year 2 (£)	Year 3 (£)	Year 4 (£)
Incremental annual profits	500 000	500 000	500 000	500 000
Less annual writing-down allowance	250 000	187 500	140 630	105 470
Incremental taxable profits	250 000	312 500	359 370	394 530
Incremental tax at 35%	87 500	109 370	125 780	138 090

You can see that for each year the incremental tax payment is calculated as follows:

corporate tax rate × (incremental profits − capital allowance)

Note that depreciation charges should not be included in the calculation of incremental cash flows or taxable profits. We must now consider the timing of the taxation payments. In the UK taxation payments vary depending on the end of the accounting year, but they are generally paid approximately one year after the end of the company's accounting year. We shall apply this rule to our example. This means that the tax payment of £87 500 for year 1 will be paid at the end of year 2, £109 370 tax will be paid at the end of year 3 and so on.

The incremental tax payments are now included in the NPV calculation:

Year	Cash flow (£)	Taxation	Net cash flow (£)	Discount factor	Present value (£)
0	−1 000 000	0	−1 000 000	1.0000	− 1 000 000
1	+500 000	0	+500 000	0.9091	+ 454 550
2	+500 000	−87 500	+412 500	0.8264	+348 090
3	+500 000	−109 370	+390 630	0.7513	+293 480
4	+500 000 ⎱ +316 400[a] ⎰	−125 780	+690 620	0.6830	+471 690
5	0	− 138 090	− 138 090	0.6209	− 85 740

Net present value + 482 070

[a]Sale of machinery for written down value of £316 400.

The taxation rules in most countries allow capital allowances to be claimed on the *net* cost of the asset. In our example the machine will be purchased for £1 million and the estimated realizable value at the end of its life is its written-down value of £316 400. Therefore the estimated net cost of the machine is £683 600. You will see from the calculation of the writing-down allowances on page 302 that the total of the writing-down allowances amount to the net cost. How would the analysis change if the estimated realizable value for the machine was different from its written-down value, say £450 000? The company will have claimed allowances of £683 600 but the estimated net cost of the machine is £550 000 (£1 million − £450 000 estimated net realizable value). Therefore excess allowances of £133 600 (£683 600 − £550 000) will have been claimed and an adjustment must be made at the end of year 4 so that the tax authorities can claim back the excess allowance. This adjustment is called a **balancing charge**.

Note that the above calculation of taxable profits for year 4 will now be as follows:

Incremental annual profits	500 000
Less annual writing-down allowance	(105 470)
Add balancing charge	133 600
Incremental taxable profits	528 130
Incremental taxation at 35%	184 845

Let us now assume that the estimated disposal value is less than the written-down value for tax purposes, say £250 000. The net investment cost is £750 000 (£1 000 000 − £250 000), but you will see that our calculations at the start of this section indicate that estimated taxation capital allowances of £683 600 will have been claimed by the end of year 4. Therefore an adjustment of £66 400 (£750 000 − £683 600) must be made at the end of year 4 to reflect the fact that insufficient capital allowances have been claimed. This adjustment is called a **balancing allowance**.

Thus in year 4 the total capital allowance will consist of an annual writing-down allowance of £105 470 plus a balancing allowance of £66 400, giving a total of £171 870. Taxable profits for year 4 are now £328 130 (£500 000 − £171 870), and tax at the rate of 35% on these profits will be paid at the end of year 5.

Notes

1 Consider a project that costs £10 000 and has a life of four years and an estimated scrap value of £2000. The diagram shown below illustrates why the project's scrap value is added to the initial outlay to calculate the average capital employed. You can see that at the mid-point of the project's life the capital employed is equal to £6000 (i.e. $\frac{1}{2}$ (10 000+£2000)).

2 In 2002 the profits of UK companies were subject to a corporate tax rate of 30%. For small companies with annual profits of less than £300 000 the corporate tax rate was 19%.

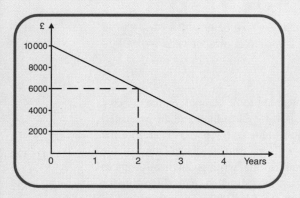

Key Terms and Concepts

accounting rate of return (p. 298)
balancing allowance (p. 303)
balancing charge (p. 303)
capital allowance (p. 301)
compounding interest (p. 287)
cost of capital (p. 286)
depreciation tax shields (p. 301)
discount rate (p. 286)
discounted cash flow (p. 286)
discounted payback method (p. 295)
discounted present value (p. 287)
discounted rate of return (p. 291)
discounting (p. 287)

interest rate (p. 286)
internal rate of return (p. 291)
minimum required rate of return (p. 286)
net present value (p. 289)
opportunity cost of an investment (p. 286)
payback method (p. 295)
present value (p. 287)
return on capital employed (p. 298)
return on investment (p. 298)
risk-free gilt-edged securities (p. 286)
time value of money (p. 288)
writing down allowance (p. 301)

Key Examination Points

A common mistake is a failure to distinguish between relevant and irrelevant cash flows. Remember to include only incremental cash flows in a DCF analysis. Depreciation and reapportionments of overheads should not be included.

Another common error is to use the wrong present-value table. With unequal annual cash flows, use Appendix A (the discount factors will be less than 1), and if the cash flows are the same each year, use Appendix B (the discount factors will be greater than 1 from year 2 onwards). Where IRR calculations are required, very accurate calculations of the IRR will not be required, and an approximate answer using the interpolation method should be appropriate.

Review Problems

(For additional problems without answers relating to the content of this chapter you should refer to pages 502–507.)

1 The May Company is preparing its capital budget for the year. A question has arisen as to whether or not to replace a machine with a new and more efficient machine. An analysis of the situation reveals the following, based on operations at a normal level of activity:

	Old machine	New machine
Cost new	£40 000	£80 000
Book value	£30 000	—
Estimated physical life remaining	10 years	10 years
Depreciation per year	£4 000	£8 000
Labour cost per year	£15 000	£5 000
Material cost per year	£350 000	£345 000
Power per year	£2 000	£4 500
Maintenance per year	£5 000	£7 500

The expected scrap value of both the new and the old machine in 10 years' time is estimated to be zero. The old machine could be sold now for £20 000.

The cost of capital and the investment cut-off rate for the May company is 10%. Advise the Company.

(20 marks)
JMB 'A' Level

2 The following data are supplied relating to two investment projects, only one of which may be selected:

	Project A (£)	Project B (£)
Initial capital expenditure	50 000	50 000
Profit (loss) year 1	25 000	10 000
2	20 000	10 000
3	15 000	14 000
4	10 000	26 000

Estimated resale value at end of year 4	10 000	10 000

Notes:
1. Profit is calculated after deducting straight-line depreciation.
2. The cost of capital is 10%.

Required:
(a) Calculate for each project:
  (i) average annual rate of return on average capital invested;
  (ii) payback period;
  (iii) net present value. *(12 marks)*
(b) Briefly discuss the relative merits of the three methods of evaluation mentioned in (a) above. *(10 marks)*
(c) Explain which project you would recommend for acceptance. *(3 marks)*
(Total 25 marks)
AAT Pilot Paper

3 A machine with a purchase price of £14 000 is estimated to eliminate manual operations costing £4000 per year. The machine will last five years and have no residual value at the end of its life.
  You are required to calculate:
(a) the discounted cash flow (DCF) rate of return;
(b) the level of annual saving necessary to achieve a 12% DCF return;
(c) the net present value if the cost of capital is 10%.

4 Sound Equipment Ltd was formed five years ago to manufacture parts for hi-fi equipment. Most of its customers were individuals wanting to assemble their own systems. Recently, however, the company has embarked on a policy of expansion and has been approached by JBZ plc, a multinational manufacturer of consumer electronics. JBZ has offered Sound Equipment Ltd a contract to build an amplifier for its latest consumer product. If accepted, the contract will increase Sound Equipment's turnover by 20%.

  JBZ's offer is a fixed price contract over three years, although it is possible for Sound Equipment to apply for subsequent contracts. The contract will involve Sound Equipment purchasing a specialist machine for £150 000. Although the machine has a 10-year life, it would be written off over the three years of the initial contract as it can only be used in the manufacture of the amplifier for JBZ.

The production director of Sound Equipment has already prepared a financial appraisal of the proposal. This is reproduced below. With a capital cost of £150 000 and total profits of £60 300, the production director has calculated the return on capital employed as 40.2%. As this is greater than Sound Equipment's cost of capital of 18%, the production director is recommending that the board accepts the contract.

	Year 1 (£)	Year 2 (£)	Year 3 (£)	Total
Turnover	180 000	180 000	180 000	540 000
Materials	60 000	60 000	60 000	180 000
Labour	40 000	40 000	40 000	120 000
Depreciation	50 000	50 000	50 000	150 000
Pre-tax profit	30 000	30 000	30 000	90 000
Corporation tax at 33%	9 900	9 900	9 900	29 700
After-tax profit	20 100	20 100	20 100	60 300

You are employed as the assistant accountant to Sound Equipment Ltd and report to John Green, the financial director, who asks you to carry out a full financial appraisal of the proposed contract. He feels that the production director's presentation is inappropriate. He provides you with the following additional information:

- Sound Equipment pays corporation tax at the rate of 33%;
- the machine will qualify for a 25% writing-down allowance on the reducing balance;
- the machine will have no further use other than in manufacturing the amplifier for JBZ;

- on ending the contract with JBZ, any outstanding capital allowances can be claimed as a balancing allowance;
- the company's cost of capital is 18%;
- the cost of materials and labour is forecast to increase by 5% per annum for years 2 and 3.

John Green reminds you that Sound Equipment operates a just-in-time stock policy and that production will be delivered immediately to JBZ, who will, under the terms of the contract, immediately pay for the deliveries. He also reminds you that suppliers are paid immediately on receipt of goods and that employees are also paid immediately.

Write a report to the financial director. Your report should:

(a) use the net present value technique to identify whether or not the initial three-year contract is worthwhile;

(b) explain your approach to taxation in your appraisal;

(c) identify *one* other factor to be considered before making a final decision.

Notes:
For the purpose of this task, you may assume the following:

- the machine would be purchased at the beginning of the accounting year;
- there is a one-year delay in paying corporation tax;
- all cashflows other than the purchase of the machine occur at the end of each year;
- Sound Equipment has no other assets on which to claim capital allowances.

AAT Technicians Stage

Solutions to Review Problems

SOLUTION 1

The analysis should be based on a comparison of the PV of the future cash outflows. The original cost of the old machine, the book value and the depreciation cost per year do not represent future cash outflows and should not therefore be included in the analysis. The additional annual cash outflows for each machine are as follows:

	Old machine (£)	New machine (£)
Labour costs	15 000	5 000
Material costs	350 000	345 000
Power	2 000	4 500
Maintenance	5 000	7 500
	372 000	362 000

Because the cash outflows are identical, each year the PV of an annuity can be used. The above cash outflows are therefore multiplied by a discount factor of 6.145:

	Old machine (£)	New machine (£)
Operating costs	2 285 940 (372 000 × 6.145)	2 224 490 (362 000 × 6.145)
Purchase cost of new machine		80 000
Sale of old machine		(20 000)
	2 285 940	2 284 490

The PV of the cash outflows is £1450 lower for the new machine. The new machine should therefore be purchased. Note that operating sales revenue is the same for both machines. Hence it is not relevant to the decision.

An alternative approach would be to compare the PV of the annual cost savings from the new machine $(10\,000 \times 6.145 = £61\,450)$ with the net investment cost $(80\,000 - £20\,000)$. The new machine yields a positive NPV of £1450 and should be purchased.

SOLUTION 2

(a) (i)

$$\text{Average capital invested} = \frac{£50\,000 + £10\,000}{2} = £30\,000$$

For an explanation of why the project's scrap value is added to the initial cost to calculate the average capital employed, you should refer to note 1 following Appendix 12.1.

Note that the mid-point of the project's life is two years and the written down value

at the end of year 2 is £30 000.

Average annual profit (Project A)

$$= \frac{£25\,000 + £20\,000 + £15\,000 + £10\,000}{4}$$

$$= £17\,500$$

Average annual profit (Project B)

$$= \frac{£10\,000 + £10\,000 + £14\,000 + £26\,000}{4}$$

$$= £15\,000$$

Average annual return:

$$\text{A} \quad 58.33\% \quad \left(\frac{£17\,500}{£30\,000} \times 100\right)$$

$$\text{B} \quad 50\% \quad \left(\frac{£15\,000}{£30\,000} \times 100\right)$$

(ii) Payback period:

$$\text{Project A} \quad 1.5 \text{ years} \quad \left(1 + \frac{£15\,000}{£30\,000}\right)$$

$$\text{Project B} \quad 2.4 \text{ years} \quad \left(2 + \frac{£10\,000}{£24\,000}\right)$$

(iii)

Year	Project A Cash inflows (W1) (£)	Project B Cash inflows (W1) (£)	Discount factor	Project A PV (£)	Project B PV (£)
1	35 000	20 000	0.909	31 815	18 180
2	30 000	20 000	0.826	24 780	16 520
3	25 000	24 000	0.751	18 775	18 024
4	20 000	36 000	0.683	13 660	24 588
4	10 000	10 000	0.683	6 830	6 830
				95 860	84 142
		Investment cost		(50 000)	(50 000)
		NPV		45 860	34 142

Workings:
(W1) Cash flows = Profit + depreciation. Note that the estimated resale value is included as a year 4 cash inflow.

(b) See Chapter 12 for the answer to this section of the problem.

(c) Project A is recommended because it has the highest NPV and also the shortest payback period.

SOLUTION 3

(a) The IRR is where:

annual cash inflows × discount factor = investment cost
i.e. £4000 × discount factor = £14 000
Therefore discount factor = $\frac{£14\,000}{£4\,000}$
= 3.5

We now work along the five-row table of the cumulative discount tables to find the discount rate with a discount factor closest to 3.5. This is 13%. Therefore the IRR is 13%.

(b) The annual saving necessary to achieve a 12% internal rate of return is where:

annual savings × 12% discount factor = investment cost
i.e. annual savings × 3.605 = £14 000
Therefore annual savings = $\frac{£14\,000}{3.605}$
= £3 883

(c) NPV is calculated as follows:

	(£)
£4000 received annually from years 1–5:	
£4000 × 3.791 discount factor	15 164
Less investment cost	14 000
NPV	1 164

SOLUTION 4

The report should include the information contained in items (a) to (c) below:

(a) Depreciation is not a cash flow. The operating net cash inflows (before tax) therefore consist of sales less materials and labour costs. The NPV calculation is as follows:

Year	0 (£)	1 (£)	2 (£)	3 (£)	4 (£)
Net cash inflows before tax		80 000	75 000	69 750	
Tax^a			(14 025)	(15 469)	4 826
Investment outlay	(150 000)				
Net cash flow	(150 000)	80 000	60 975	54 281	4 826
Discount factor (18%)	1.000	0.847	0.718	0.609	0.516
Present value	(150 000)	67 760	43 780	33 057	2 490

NPV = −£2 913

Note:
^{a}The tax computation is as follows:

Year	1 (£)	2 (£)	3 (£)
Net cash inflows before tax	80 000	75 000	69 750
Writing down allowances	37 500	28 125	84 375
Taxable profit	42 500	46 875	(14 625)
Tax at 33%	14 025	15 469	(4 826)
Writing down allowances:			
Opening WDV	150 000	112 500	84 375
Writing down allowances (25%)	37 500	28 125	
Closing WDV	112 500	84 375	Nil
Balancing allowance			84 375

(b) Because corporation taxes are payable on taxable profits and not accounting profits depreciation has been replaced by the Inland Revenue's allowable depreciation (known as written-down allowances). The net cost of the asset is £150 000 and written-down allowances received amounted to £65 625 (£37 500 + £28 125). Therefore a balancing allowance is available at the end of the asset's life of £84 375 (£150 000 − £65 625). The Inland Revenue allows the net cost of the asset to be claimed over its life with a balancing adjustment in the final year. Because taxation is normally payable nine months after the company's accounting year end the taxation cash flows are shown to be delayed by one year. This is a simplification of the actual situation but is normally sufficiently accurate for appraising investments.

(c) Other factors to be considered include:
  (i) The probability of obtaining a subsequent contract. There would be no need to purchase a further machine and the project would therefore yield a positive NPV.
  (ii) The negative NPV is very small and if the company has other profitable activities it may be worthwhile accepting in order to have the chance of obtaining a second contract and establishing long-term relationships with a large multinational customer.
  (iii) Capacity that is available. If other profitable opportunities have to be forgone to undertake the contract because of shortage of capacity then the opportunity cost should be included in the financial analysis.

Information for Planning, Control and Performance Measurement

The objective in this section is to consider the implementation of decisions through the planning and control process. Planning involves systematically looking at the future, so that decisions can be made today which will bring the company its desired results. Control can be defined as the process of measuring and correcting actual performance to ensure that plans for implementing the chosen course of action are carried out.

Part Four contains three chapters. Chapter 13 considers the role of budgeting within the planning process and the relationship between the long-range plan and the budgeting process. Chapters 14 and 15 are concerned with the control process. To fully understand the role that management accounting control systems play in the control process, it is necessary to be aware of how they relate to the entire array of control mechanisms used by organizations. Chapter 14 describes the different types of controls that are used by companies. The elements of management accounting control systems are described within the context of the overall control process. Chapter 15 focuses on the technical aspects of accounting control systems. It describes the major features of a standard costing system: a system that enables the differences between the planned and actual outcomes to be analysed in detail.

13

The budgeting process

In the previous four chapters we have considered how management accounting can assist managers in making decisions. The actions that follow managerial decisions normally involve several aspects of the business, such as the marketing, production, purchasing and finance functions, and it is important that management should coordinate these various interrelated aspects of decision-making. If they fail to do this, there is a danger that managers may each make decisions that they believe are in the best interests of the organization when, in fact, taken together they are not; for example, the marketing department may introduce a promotional campaign that is designed to increase sales demand to a level beyond that which the production department can handle. The various activities within a company should be coordinated by the preparation of plans of actions for future periods. These detailed plans are usually referred to as **budgets**.

Our objective in this chapter is to focus on the planning process within a business organization and to consider the role of budgeting within this process. What do we mean by planning? Planning is the design of a desired future and of effective ways of bringing it about (Ackoff, 1981). A distinction is normally made between short-term planning (budgeting) and **long-range planning**, alternatively known as **strategic** or **corporate planning**. How is long-range planning distinguished from other forms of planning? Sizer (1989) defines long-range planning as a systematic and formalized process for purposely directing and controlling future operations towards desired objectives for periods extending beyond one year. Short-term planning or budgeting, on the other hand, must accept the environment of today, and the physical, human and financial resources at present available to the firm. These are to a considerable extent determined by the quality of the firm's long-range planning efforts.

Learning objectives

After studying this chapter, you should be able to:

- distinguish between long-term planning and budgeting
- describe the six different purposes of budgets;
- describe the various stages in the budget process;
- prepare functional and master budgets.

Relationship between budgeting and long-term planning

The annual budget should be set within the context of longer-term plans, which are likely to exist even if they have not been made explicit. Long-term planning involves strategic planning over several years and the identification of the basic strategy of the firm (i.e. the future direction the organization will take) and the gaps which exist between the future needs and present capabilities. A long-term plan is a statement of the preliminary targets and activities required by an organization to achieve its strategic plans together with a broad estimate for each year of the resources required. Because long-term planning involves 'looking into the future' for several years the plans tend to be uncertain, general in nature, imprecise and subject to change.

Budgeting is concerned with the implementation of the long-term plan for the year ahead. Because of the shorter planning horizon budgets are more precise and detailed. Budgets are a clear indication of what is expected to be achieved during the budget period whereas long-term plans represent the broad directions that top management intend to follow.

The budget is not something that originates 'from nothing' each year – it is developed within the context of ongoing business and is ruled by previous decisions that have been taken within the long-term planning process. When the activities are initially approved for inclusion in the long-term plan, they are based on uncertain estimates that are projected for several years. These proposals must be reviewed and revised in the light of more recent information. This review and revision process frequently takes place as part of the annual budgeting process, and it may result in important decisions being taken on possible activity adjustments within the current budget period. The budgeting process cannot therefore be viewed as being purely concerned with the current year – it must be considered as an integrated part of the long-term planning process.

The multiple functions of budgets

Budgets serve a number of useful purposes. They include:

1. *planning* annual operations;
2. *coordinating* the activities of the various parts of the organization and ensuring that the parts are in harmony with each other;
3. *communicating* plans to the various responsibility centre managers;
4. *motivating* managers to strive to achieve the organizational goals;
5. *controlling* activities;
6. *evaluating* the performance of managers.

Let us now examine each of these six factors.

PLANNING

The major planning decisions will already have been made as part of the long-term planning process. However, the annual budgeting process leads to the refinement of those plans, since managers must produce detailed plans for the implementation of the long-range plan. Without the annual budgeting process, the pressures of day-to-day operating problems may tempt managers not to plan for future operations. The budgeting process ensures that managers do plan for future operations, and that they consider how conditions in the next year might change and what steps they should take now to respond to these changed conditions. This process encourages managers to anticipate problems before they arise, and hasty decisions that are made on the spur of the moment, based on expediency rather than reasoned judgement, will be minimized.

COORDINATION

The budget serves as a vehicle through which the actions of the different parts of an organization can be brought together and reconciled into a common plan. Without any guidance, managers may each make their own decisions, believing that they are working in the best interests of the organization. For example, the purchasing manager may prefer to place large orders so as to obtain large discounts; the production manager will be concerned with avoiding high stock levels; and the accountant will be concerned with the impact of the decision on the cash resources of the business. It is the aim of budgeting to reconcile these differences for the good of the organization as a whole, rather than for the benefit of any individual area. Budgeting therefore compels managers to examine the relationship between their own operations and those of other departments, and, in the process, to identify and resolve conflicts.

COMMUNICATION

If an organization is to function effectively, there must be definite lines of communication so that all the parts will be kept fully informed of the plans and the policies, and constraints, to which the organization is expected to conform. Everyone in the organization should have a clear understanding of the part they are expected to play in achieving the annual budget. This process will ensure that the appropriate individuals are made accountable for implementing the budget. Through the budget, top management communicates its expectations to lower level management, so that all members of the organization may understand these expectations and can coordinate their activities to attain them. It is not just the budget itself that facilitates communication – much vital information is communicated in the actual act of preparing it.

MOTIVATION

The budget can be a useful device for influencing managerial behaviour and motivating managers to perform in line with the organizational objectives. A budget provides a standard that under certain circumstances, a manager may be motivated to strive to achieve. However, budgets can also encourage inefficiency and conflict between managers. If individuals have actively participated in preparing the budget, and it is used as a tool to assist managers in managing their departments, it can act as a strong motivational device by providing a challenge. Alternatively, if the budget is dictated from above, and imposes a threat rather than a challenge, it may be resisted and do more harm than good.

CONTROL

A budget assists managers in managing and controlling the activities for which they are responsible. By comparing the actual results with the budgeted amounts for different categories of expenses, managers can ascertain which costs do not conform to the original plan and thus require their attention. This process enables management to operate a system of **management by exception** which means that a manager's attention and effort can be concentrated on significant deviations from the expected results. By investigating the reasons for the deviations, managers may be able to identify inefficiencies such as the purchase of inferior quality materials. When the reasons for the inefficiencies have been found, appropriate control action should be taken to remedy the situation.

PERFORMANCE EVALUATION

A manager's performance is often evaluated by measuring his or her success in meeting the budgets. In some companies bonuses are awarded on the basis of an employee's ability to achieve the targets specified in the periodic budgets, or promotion may be partly dependent upon a manager's budget record. In addition, the manager may wish to evaluate his or her own performance. The budget thus provides a useful means of informing managers of how well they are performing in meeting targets that they have previously helped to set.

Conflicting roles of budgets

Because a single budget system is normally used to serve several purposes there is a danger that they may conflict with each other. For instance the planning and motivation roles may be in conflict with each other. Demanding budgets that may not be achieved may be appropriate to motivate maximum performance, but they are unsuitable for planning purposes. For these a budget should be set based on easier targets that are expected to be met.

There is also a conflict between the planning and performance evaluation roles. For planning purposes budgets are set in advance of the budget period based on an anticipated set of circumstances or environment. Performance evaluation should be based on a comparison of actual performance with an adjusted budget to reflect the circumstances under which managers actually operated. In practice, many firms compare actual performance with the original budget (adjusted to the actual level of activity, i.e. a flexible budget), but if the circumstances envisaged when the original budget was set have changed then there will be a planning and evaluation conflict.

The budget period

The conventional approach is that once per year the manager of each budget centre prepares a detailed budget for one year. The budget is divided into either twelve monthly or thirteen four-weekly periods for control purposes.

An alternative approach is for the annual budget to be broken down by months for the first three months, and by quarters for the remaining nine months. The quarterly budgets are then developed on a monthly basis as the year proceeds. For example, during the first quarter, the monthly budgets for the second quarter will be prepared; and during the second quarter, the monthly budgets for the third quarter will be prepared. The quarterly budgets may also be reviewed as the year unfolds. For example, during the first quarter, the budget for the next three quarters may be changed as new information becomes available. A new budget for a fifth quarter will also be prepared. This process is known as **continuous** or **rolling budgeting**, and ensures that a twelve month budget is always available by adding a quarter in the future as the quarter just ended is dropped. Contrast this with a budget prepared once per year. As the year goes by, the period for which a budget is available will shorten until the budget for next year is prepared. Rolling budgets also ensure that planning is not something that takes place once a year when the budget is being formulated. Instead, budgeting is a continuous process, and managers are encouraged to constantly look ahead and review future plans. Furthermore, it is likely that actual performance will be compared with a more realistic target, because budgets are being constantly reviewed and updated.

Irrespective of whether the budget is prepared on an annual or a continuous basis, it is important that monthly or four-weekly budgets be used for *control* purposes.

Administration of the budgeting process

It is important that suitable administration procedures be introduced to ensure that the budget process works effectively. In practice, the procedures should be tailor-made to the requirements of the organization, but as a general rule a firm should ensure that procedures are established for approving the budgets and that the appropriate staff support is available for assisting managers in preparing their budgets.

THE BUDGET COMMITTEE

The budget committee should consist of high-level executives who represent the major segments of the business. Its major task is to ensure that budgets are realistically established and that they are coordinated satisfactorily. The normal procedure is for the functional heads to present their budget to the committee for approval. If the budget does not reflect a reasonable level of performance, it will not be approved and the functional head will be required to adjust the budget and re-submit it for approval. It is important that the person whose performance is being measured should agree that the revised budget can be achieved; otherwise, if it is considered to be impossible to achieve, it will not act as a motivational device. If budget revisions are made, the budgetees should at least feel that they were given a fair hearing by the committee. We shall discuss budget negotiation in more detail later in this chapter.

The budget committee should appoint a budget officer, who will normally be the accountant. The role of the budget officer is to coordinate the individual budgets into a budget for the whole organization, so that the budget committee and the budgetee can see the impact of an individual budget on the organization as a whole.

ACCOUNTING STAFF

The accounting staff will normally assist managers in the preparation of their budgets; they will, for example, circulate and advise on the instructions about budget preparation, provide past information that may be useful for preparing the present budget, and ensure that managers submit their budgets on time. The accounting staff do not determine the content of the various budgets, but they do provide a valuable advisory and clerical service for the line managers.

BUDGET MANUAL

A budget manual should be prepared by the accountant. It will describe the objectives and procedures involved in the budgeting process and will provide a useful reference source for managers responsible for budget preparation. In addition, the manual may include a timetable specifying the order in which the budgets should be prepared and the dates when they should be presented to the budget committee. The manual should be circulated to all individuals who are responsible for preparing budgets.

Stages in the budgeting process

The important stages are as follows:

1. communicating details of budget policy and guidelines to those people responsible for the preparation of budgets;
2. determining the factor that restricts output;
3. preparation of the sales budget;
4. initial preparation of various budgets;
5. negotiation of budgets with superiors;
6. coordination and review of budgets;
7. final acceptance of budgets;
8. ongoing review of budgets.

Let us now consider each of these stages in more detail.

COMMUNICATING DETAILS OF THE BUDGET POLICY

Many decisions affecting the budget year will have been taken previously as part of the long-term planning process. The long-range plan is therefore the starting point for the preparation of the annual budget. Thus top management must communicate the policy effects of the long-term plan to those responsible for preparing the current year's budgets. Policy effects might include planned changes in sales mix, or the expansion or contraction of certain activities. In addition, other important guidelines that are to govern the preparation of the budget should be specified – for example the allowances that are to be made for price and wage increases, and the expected changes in productivity. Also, any expected changes in industry demand and output should be communicated by top management to the managers responsible for budget preparation. It is essential that all managers be made aware of the policy of top management for implementing the long-term plan in the current year's budget so that common guidelines can be established. The process also indicates to the managers responsible for preparing the budgets how they should respond to any expected environmental changes.

DETERMINING THE FACTOR THAT RESTRICTS PERFORMANCE

In every organization there is some factor that restricts performance for a given period. In the majority of organizations this factor is sales demand. However, it is possible for production capacity to restrict performance when sales demand is in excess of available capacity. Prior to the preparation of the budgets, it is necessary for top management to determine the factor that restricts performance, since this factor determines the point at which the annual budgeting process should begin.

PREPARATION OF THE SALES BUDGET

The volume of sales and the sales mix determine the level of a company's operations, when sales demand is the factor that restricts output. For this reason, the sales budget is the most important plan in the annual budgeting process. This budget is also the most difficult plan to produce, because total sales revenue depends on the actions of customers. In addition, sales demand may be influenced by the state of the economy or the actions of competitors.

INITIAL PREPARATION OF BUDGETS

The managers who are responsible for meeting the budgeted performance should prepare the budget for those areas for which they are responsible. The preparation of the budget should be a 'bottom-up' process. This means that the budget should originate at the lowest levels of management and be refined and coordinated at higher levels. The justification for this approach is that it enables managers to participate in the preparation of their budgets and increases the probability that they will accept the budget and strive to achieve the budget targets.

There is no single way in which the appropriate quantity for a particular budget item is determined. Past data may be used as the starting point for producing the budgets, but this does not mean that budgeting is based on the assumption that what has happened in the past will occur in the future. Changes in future conditions must be taken into account, but past information may provide useful guidance for the future. In addition, managers may look to the guidelines provided by top management for determining the content of their budgets. For example, the guidelines may provide specific instructions as to the content of their budgets and the permitted changes that can be made in the prices of purchases of materials and services. For production activities standard costs may be used as the basis for costing activity volumes which are planned in the budget.

NEGOTIATION OF BUDGETS

To implement a participative approach to budgeting, the budget should be originated at the lowest level of management. The managers at this level should submit their budget to their superiors for approval. The superior should then incorporate this budget with other budgets for which he or she is responsible and then submit this budget for approval to his or her superior. The manager who is the superior then becomes the budgetee at the next higher level. The process is illustrated in Figure 13.1. Sizer (1989) describes this approach as a two-way process of a top-down statement of objectives and strategies, bottom-up budget preparation and top-down approval by senior management.

The lower-level managers are represented by boxes 1–8. Managers 1 and 2 will prepare their budgets in accordance with the budget policy and the guidelines laid down by top

FIGURE 13.1 *An illustration of budgets moving up the organization hierarchy.*

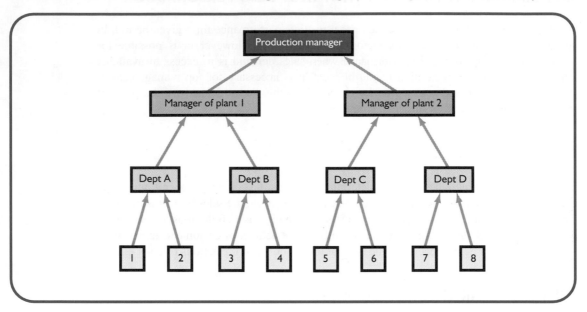

management. The managers will submit their budget to their supervisor, who is in charge of the whole department (department A). Once these budgets have been agreed by the manager of department A, they will be combined by the departmental manager, who will then present this budget to his or her superior (manager of plant 1) for approval. The manager of plant 1 is also responsible for department B, and will combine the agreed budgets for departments A and B before presenting the combined budget to his or her supervisor (the production manager). The production manager will merge the budget for plants 1 and 2, and this final budget will represent the production budget that will be presented to the budget committee for approval.

At each of these stages the budgets will be negotiated between the budgetees and their superiors, and eventually they will be agreed by both parties. Hence the figures that are included in the budget are the result of a bargaining process between a manager and his or her superior. It is important that the budgetees should participate in arriving at the final budget and that the superior does not revise the budget without giving full consideration to the subordinates' arguments for including any of the budgeted items. Otherwise, real participation will not be taking place, and it is unlikely that the subordinate will be motivated to achieve a budget that he or she did not accept.

It is also necessary to be watchful that budgetees do not deliberately attempt to obtain approval for easily attainable budgets, or attempt to deliberately understate budgets in the hope that the budget that is finally agreed will represent an easily attainable target. It is equally unsatisfactory for a superior to impose difficult targets in the hope that an authoritarian approach will produce the desired results. The desired results may be achieved in the short term, but only at the cost of a loss of morale and increased labour turnover in the future.

The negotiation process is of vital importance in the budgeting process, and can determine whether the budget becomes a really effective management tool or just a clerical device. If managers are successful in establishing a position of trust and confidence with their subordinates, the negotiation process will produce a meaningful improvement in the budgetary process and outcomes for the period.

COORDINATION AND REVIEW OF BUDGETS

As the individual budgets move up the organizational hierarchy in the negotiation process, they must be examined in relation to each other. This examination may indicate that some budgets are out of balance with other budgets and need modifying so that they will be compatible with other conditions, constraints and plans that are beyond a manager's knowledge or control. For example, a plant manager may include equipment replacement in his or her budget when funds are simply not available. The accountant must identify such inconsistencies and bring them to the attention of the appropriate manager. Any changes in the budgets should be made by the responsible managers, and this may require that the budgets be recycled from the bottom to the top for a second or even a third time until all the budgets are coordinated and are acceptable to all the parties involved. During the coordination process, a budgeted profit and loss account, a balance sheet and a cash flow statement should be prepared to ensure that all the parts combine to produce an acceptable whole. Otherwise, further adjustments and budget recycling will be necessary until the budgeted profit and loss account, the balance sheet and the cash flow statement prove to be acceptable.

FINAL ACCEPTANCE OF THE BUDGETS

When all the budgets are in harmony with each other, they are summarized into a **master budget** consisting of a budgeted profit and loss account, a balance sheet and a cash flow statement. After the master budget has been approved, the budgets are then passed down through the organization to the appropriate responsibility centres. The approval of the master budget is the authority for the manager of each responsibility centre to carry out the plans contained in each budget.

BUDGET REVIEW

The budget process should not stop when the budgets have been agreed. Periodically, the actual results should be compared with the budgeted results. These comparisons should normally be made on a monthly basis and a report sent to the appropriate budgetees in the first week of the following month, so that it has the maximum motivational impact. This will enable management to identify the items that are not proceeding according to plan and to investigate the reasons for the differences. If these differences are within the control of management, corrective action can be taken to avoid similar inefficiencies occurring again in the future. However, the differences may be due to the fact that the budget was unrealistic to begin with, or that the actual conditions during the budget year were different from those anticipated; the budget for the remainder of the year would than be invalid.

During the budget year, the budget committee should periodically evaluate the actual performance and reappraise the company's future plans. If there are any changes in the actual conditions from those originally expected, this will normally mean that the budget plans should be adjusted. This revised budget then represents a revised statement of formal operating plans for the remaining portion of the budget period. The important point to note is that the budgetary process does not end for the current year once the budget has begun; budgeting should be seen as a continuous and dynamic process.

A detailed illustration

Let us now look at an illustration of the procedure for constructing budgets in a manufacturing company, using the information contained in Example 13.1. Note that the level of detail included here is much less than that which would be presented in practice. A truly realistic illustration would fill many pages, with detailed budgets being analysed in various ways. We shall consider an annual budget, whereas a realistic illustration would analyse the annual budget into twelve monthly periods. Monthly analysis would considerably increase the size of the illustration, but would not give any further insight into the basic concepts or procedures. In addition, we shall assume in this example that the budgets are prepared for only two responsibility centres (namely departments 1 and 2). In practice, many responsibility centres are likely to exist.

Sales budget

The sales budget shows the quantities of each product that the company plans to sell and the intended selling price. It provides the predictions of total revenue from which cash receipts from customers will be estimated, and it also supplies the basic data for constructing budgets for production costs, and for selling, distribution and administrative expenses. The sales budget is therefore the foundation of all other budgets, since all expenditure is ultimately dependent on the volume of sales. If the sales budget is not accurate, the other budget estimates will be unreliable. We will assume that the Enterprise Company has completed a marketing analysis and that the following annual sales budget is based on the result:

Schedule 1 – Sales budget for year ending 200X

Product	Units sold	Selling price (£)	Total revenue (£)
Alpha	8500	400	3 400 000
Sigma	1600	560	896 000
			4 296 000

Schedule 1 represents the *total* sales budget for the year. In practice, the *total* sales budget will be supported by detailed *subsidiary* sales budgets where sales are analysed by areas of responsibility, such as sales territories, and into monthly periods analysed by products. The detailed *subsidiary* sales budget could be set out as shown on page 323.

Note that with the detailed subsidiary monthly budgets the total budgeted sales of £4 296 000 is analysed by each sales territory for each month of the budget period. The detailed analysis assumes that sales are divided among the four sales territories as follows:

	Alpha	Sigma
North	3000 units	500 units
South	2500 units	600 units
East	1000 units	200 units
West	2000 units	300 units
	8500 units	1600 units

EXAMPLE 13.1

The Enterprise Company manufactures two products, known as alpha and sigma. Alpha is produced in department 1 and sigma in department 2. The following information is available for 200X.

Standard material and labour costs:

	(£)
Material X	7.20 per unit
Material Y	16.00 per unit
Direct labour	12.00 per hour

Overhead is recovered on a direct labour hour basis.

The standard material and labour usage for each product is as follows:

	Model alpha	Model sigma
Material X	10 units	8 units
Material Y	5 units	9 units
Direct labour	10 hours	15 hours

The balance sheet for the previous year end 200X was as follows:

	(£)	(£)	(£)
Fixed assets:			
Land		170 000	
Buildings and equipment	1 292 000		
Less depreciation	255 000	1 037 000	1 207 000
Current assets:			
Stocks, finished goods	99 076		
raw materials	189 200		
Debtors	289 000		
Cash	34 000		
	611 276		
Less current liabilities			
Creditors	248 800		362 476
Net assets			1 569 476
Represented by shareholder's interest:			
120 000 ordinary shares of £1 each		1 200 000	
Reserves		369 476	
			1 569 476

Other relevant data is as follows for the year 200X:

	Finished product	
	Model alpha	Model sigma
Forecast sales (units)	8500	1600
Selling price per unit	£400	£560
Ending inventory required (units)	1870	90
Beginning inventory (units)	170	85

	Direct material	
	Material X	**Material Y**
Beginning inventory (units)	8 500	8000
Ending inventory required (units)	10 200	1700

	Department 1 **(£)**	**Department 2** **(£)**
Budgeted variable overhead rates (per direct labour hour):		
Indirect materials	1.20	0.80
Indirect labour	1.20	1.20
Power (variable portion)	0.60	0.40
Maintenance (variable portion)	0.20	0.40
Budgeted fixed overheads		
Depreciation	100 000	80 000
Supervision	100 000	40 000
Power (fixed portion)	40 000	2 000
Maintenance (fixed portion)	45 600	3 196

	(£)
Estimated non-manufacturing overheads:	
Stationery etc. (Administration)	4 000
Salaries	
Sales	74 000
Office	28 000
Commissions	60 000
Car expenses (Sales)	22 000
Advertising	80 000
Miscellaneous (Office)	8 000
	276 000

Budgeted cash flows are as follows:

	Quarter 1 **(£)**	**Quarter 2** **(£)**	**Quarter 3** **(£)**	**Quarter 4** **(£)**
Receipts from customers	1 000 000	1 200 000	1 120 000	985 000
Payments:				
Materials	400 000	480 000	440 000	547 984
Payments for wages	400 000	440 000	480 000	646 188
Other costs and expenses	120 000	100 000	72 016	13 642

You are required to prepare a master budget for the year 200X and the following budgets:

1. sales budget;
2. production budget;
3. direct materials usage budget;

4. direct materials purchase budget;
5. direct labour budget;
6. factory overhead budget;
7. selling and administration budget;
8. cash budget.

Detailed monthly budgets for North, South, East and West sales territories

		North		South		East		West		Total	
		Units	Value (£)	Units	Value (£)	Units	Value (£)	Units	Value (£)	Units	Value (£)
Month 1	Alpha										
	Sigma		———		———		———		———		———
	Total		———		———		———		———		———
Month 2											
Month 3											
Month 4											
Month 5											
Month 6											
Month 7											
Month 8											
Month 9											
Month 10											
Month 11											
Month 12											
Total months 1–12											
	Alpha	3000	1 200 000	2500	1 000 000	1000	400 000	2000	800 000	8500	3 400 000
	Sigma	500	280 000	600	336 000	200	112 000	300	168 000	1600	896 000
			1 480 000		1 336 000		512 000		968 000		4 296 000

Production budget and budgeted stock levels

When the sales budget has been completed, the next stage is to prepare the production budget. This budget is expressed in *quantities only* and is the responsibility of the production manager. The objective is to ensure that production is sufficient to meet sales demand and that economic stock levels are maintained. The production budget (schedule 2) for the year will be as follows:

Schedule 2 – Annual production budget

	Department 1 (alpha)	Department 2 (sigma)
Units to be sold	8 500	1600
Planned closing stock	1 870	90
Total units required for sales and stocks	10 370	1690
Less planned opening stocks	170	85
Units to be produced	10 200	1605

The total production for each department should also be analysed on a monthly basis.

Direct materials usage budget

The supervisors of departments 1 and 2 will prepare estimates of the materials which are required to meet the production budget. The materials usage budget for the year will be as follows:

Schedule 3 – Annual direct material usage budget

	Department 1			Department 2					
	Units	Unit price (£)	Total (£)	Units	Unit price (£)	Total (£)	Total units	Total unit price (£)	Total (£)
Material X	102 000[a]	7.20	734 400	12 840[c]	7.20	92 448	114 840	7.20	826 848
Material Y	51 000[b]	16.00	816 000	14 445[d]	16.00	231 120	65 445	16.00	1 047 120
			1 550 400			323 568			1 873 968

[a] 10 200 units production at 10 units per unit of production.
[b] 10 200 units production at 5 units per unit of production.
[c] 1605 units production at 8 units per unit of production.
[d] 1605 units production at 9 units per unit of production.

Direct materials purchase budget

The direct materials purchase budget is the responsibility of the purchasing manager, since it will be he or she who is responsible for obtaining the planned quantities of raw materials to meet the production requirements. The objective is to purchase these materials at the right time at the planned purchase price. In addition, it is necessary to take into account the planned raw material stock levels. The annual materials purchase budget for the year will be as follows:

Schedule 4 – Direct materials purchase budget

	Material X (units)	Material Y (units)
Quantity necessary to meet production requirements as per material usage budget	114 840	65 445
Planned closing stock	10 200	1 700
	125 040	67 145
Less planned opening stock	8 500	8 000
Total units to be purchased	116 540	59 145
Planned unit purchase price	£7.20	£16
Total purchases	£839 088	£946 320

Note that this budget is a summary budget for the year, but for detailed planning and control it will be necessary to analyse the annual budget on a monthly basis.

Direct labour budget

The direct labour budget is the responsibility of the respective managers of departments 1 and 2. They will prepare estimates of the departments' labour hours required to meet the planned production. Where different grades of labour exist, these should be specified separately in the budget. The budget rate per hour should be determined by the industrial relations department. The direct labour budget will be as follows:

Schedule 5 – Annual direct labour budget

	Department 1	Department 2	Total
Budgeted production (units)	10 200	1 605	
Hours per unit	10	15	
Total budgeted hours	102 000	24 075	126 075
Budgeted wage rate per hour	£12	£12	
Total wages	£1 224 000	£288 900	£1 512 900

Factory overhead budget

The factory overhead budget is also the responsibility of the respective production department managers. The total of the overhead budget will depend on the behaviour of the costs of the individual overhead items in relation to the anticipated level of production. The overheads must also be analysed according to whether they are controllable or non-controllable for the purpose of cost control. The factory overhead budget will be as follows:

Schedule 6 – Annual factory overhead budget
Anticipated activity – 102 000 direct labour hours (department 1)
24 075 direct labour hours (department 2)

	Variable overhead rate per direct labour hour		Overheads		Total
	Department 1 (£)	Department 2 (£)	Department 1 (£)	Department 2 (£)	(£)
Controllable overheads:					
Indirect material	1.20	0.80	122 400	19 260	
Indirect labour	1.20	1.20	122 400	28 890	
Power (variable portion)	0.60	0.40	61 200	9 630	
Maintenance (variable portion)	0.20	0.40	20 400	9 630	
			326 400	67 410	393 810
Non-controllable overheads:					
Depreciation			100 000	80 000	
Supervision			100 000	40 000	
Power (fixed portion)			40 000	2 000	
Maintenance (fixed portion)			45 600	3 196	
			285 600	125 196	410 796
Total overhead			612 000	192 606	804 606
Budgeted departmental overhead rate			£6.00[a]	8.00[b]	

[a]£612 000 total overheads divided by 102 000 direct labour hours.
[b]£192 606 total overheads divided by 24 075 direct labour hours.

The budgeted expenditure for the variable overhead items is determined by multiplying the budgeted direct labour hours for each department by the budgeted variable overhead rate per hour. It is assumed that all variable overheads vary in relation to direct labour hours.

Selling and administration budget

The selling and administration budgets have been combined here to simplify the presentation. In practice, separate budgets should be prepared: the sales manager will be responsible for the selling budget, the distribution manager will be responsible for the distribution expenses and the chief administrative officer will be responsible for the administration budget.

Schedule 7 – Annual selling and administration budget

	(£)	(£)
Selling:		
Salaries	74 000	
Commission	60 000	
Car expenses	22 000	
Advertising	80 000	236 000

Administration:		
Stationery	4 000	
Salaries	28 000	
Miscellaneous	8 000	40 000
		276 000

Departmental budgets

For cost control the direct labour budget, materials usage budget and factory overhead budget are combined into separate departmental budgets. These budgets are normally broken down into twelve separate monthly budgets, and the actual monthly expenditure is compared with the budgeted amounts for each of the items concerned. This comparison is used for judging how effective managers are in controlling the expenditure for which they are responsible. The departmental budget for department 1 will be as follows:

Department 1 – Annual departmental operating budget

	(£)	Budget (£)	Actual (£)
Direct labour (from schedule 5):			
102 000 hours at £12		1 224 000	
Direct materials (from schedule 3):			
102 000 units of material X at £7.20 per unit	734 400		
51 000 units of material Y at £16 per unit	816 000	1 550 400	
Controllable overheads (from schedule 6):			
Indirect materials	122 400		
Indirect labour	122 400		
Power (variable portion)	61 200		
Maintenance (variable portion)	20 400	326 400	
Uncontrollable overheads (from schedule 6):			
Depreciation	100 000		
Supervision	100 000		
Power (fixed portion)	40 000		
Maintenance (fixed portion)	45 600	285 600	
		3 386 400	

Master budget

When all the budgets have been prepared, the budgeted profit and loss account and balance sheet provide the overall picture of the planned performance for the budget period.

Budgeted profit and loss account for the year ending 200X

	(£)	(£)
Sales (schedule 1)		4 296 000
Opening stock of raw materials (from opening balance sheet)	189 200	
Purchases (schedule 4)	1 785 408[a]	
	1 974 608	

Less closing stock of raw materials (schedule 4)		100 640[b]
Cost of raw materials consumed		1 873 968
Direct labour (schedule 5)		1 512 900
Factory overheads (schedule 6)		804 606
Total manufacturing cost		4 191 474
Add opening stock of finished goods (from opening balance sheet)	99 076	
Less closing stock of finished goods	665 984[c]	
		(566 908)
Cost of sales		3 624 566
Gross profit		671 434
Selling and administration expenses (schedule 7)		276 000
Budgeted operating profit for the year		395 434

[a]£839 088 (X) + £946 320 (Y) from schedule 4.
[b]10 200 units at £7.20 plus 1700 units at £16 from schedule 4.
[c]1870 units of alpha valued at £332 per unit, 90 units of sigma valued at £501.60 per unit. The product unit costs are calculated as follows:

	Alpha		Sigma	
	Units	**(£)**	**Units**	**(£)**
Direct materials				
X	10	72.00	8	57.60
Y	5	80.00	9	144.00
Direct labour	10	120.00	15	180.00
Factory overheads:				
Department 1	10	60.00	—	—
Department 2	—	—	15	120.00
		332.00		501.60

Budgeted balance sheet as at 31 December

	(£)	**(£)**
Fixed assets:		
Land		170 000
Building and equipment	1 292 000	
Less depreciation[a]	435 000	857 000
		1 027 000
Current assets:		
Raw material stock	100 640	
Finished good stock	665 984	
Debtors[b]	280 000	
Cash[c]	199 170	
	1 245 794	
Current liabilities:		
Creditors[d]	307 884	937 910
		1 964 910

Represented by shareholders' interest:		
300 000 ordinary shares of £1 each	1 200 000	
Reserves	369 476	
Profit and loss account	395 434	1 964 910

[a]£255 000 + £180 000 (schedule 6) = £435 000.
[b]£289 000 opening balance + £4 296 000 sales − £4 305 000 cash.
[c]Closing balance as per cash budget.
[d]£248 800 opening balance + £1 785 408 purchases + £141 660 indirect materials − £1 867 984 cash.

Cash budgets

The objective of the **cash budget** is to ensure that sufficient cash is available at all times to meet the level of operations that are outlined in the various budgets. The cash budget for Example 13.1 is presented below and is analysed by quarters, but in practice monthly or weekly budgets will be necessary. Because cash budgeting is subject to uncertainty, it is necessary to provide for more than the minimum amount required, to allow for some margin of error in planning. Cash budgets can help a firm to avoid cash balances that are surplus to its requirements by enabling management to take steps in advance to invest the surplus cash in short-term investments. Alternatively, cash deficiencies can be identified in advance, and steps can be taken to ensure that bank loans will be available to meet any temporary cash deficiencies. For example, by looking at the cash budget for the Enterprise Company, management may consider that the cash balances are higher than necessary in the second and third quarters of the year, and they may invest part of the cash balance in short-term investments.

The overall aim should be to manage the cash of the firm to attain maximum cash availability and maximum interest income on any idle funds.

Cash budget for year ending 200X

	Quarter 1 (£)	Quarter 2 (£)	Quarter 3 (£)	Quarter 4 (£)	Total (£)
Opening balance	34 000	114 000	294 000	421 984	34 000
Receipts from debtors	1 000 000	1 200 000	1 120 000	985 000	4 305 000
	1 034 000	1 314 000	1 414 000	1 406 984	4 339 000
Payments:					
Purchase of materials	400 000	480 000	440 000	547 984	1 867 984
Payment of wages	400 000	440 000	480 000	646 188	1 966 188
Other costs and expenses	120 000	100 000	72 016	13 642	305 658
	920 000	1 020 000	992 016	1 207 814	4 139 830
Closing balance	114 000	294 000	421 984	199 170	199 170

Final review

The budgeted profit and loss account, the balance sheet and the cash budget will be submitted by the accountant to the budget committee, together with a number of budgeted financial ratios such as the return on capital employed, working capital, liquidity and gearing ratios. If these ratios prove to be acceptable, the budgets will be approved. In Example 13.1 the return on capital employed is approximately 20%, but the working capital ratio (current assets : current liabilities) is excessive, being over 4 : 1, so management should consider alternative ways of reducing investment in working capital before finally approving the budgets.

Computerized budgeting

In the past, budgeting was a task dreaded by many management accountants. You will have noted from Example 13.1 that many numerical manipulations are necessary to prepare the budget. In the real world the process is far more complex, and, as the budget is being formulated, it is altered many times since some budgets are found to be out of balance with each other or the master budget proves to be unacceptable.

In today's world, the budgeting process is computerized instead of being primarily concerned with numerical manipulations, the accounting staff can now become more involved in the real planning process. Computer-based financial models normally consist of mathematical statements of inputs and outputs. By simply altering the mathematical statements budgets can be quickly revised with little effort. However, the major advantage of computerized budgeting is that management can evaluate many different options before the budget is finally agreed. Establishing a model enables 'What-if?' analysis to be employed. For example, answers to the following questions can be displayed in the form of a master budget: What if sales increase or decrease by 10%? What if unit costs increase or decrease by 5%? What if the credit terms for sales were reduced from 30 to 20 days?

In addition, computerized models can incorporate actual results, period by period, and carry out the necessary calculations to produce budgetary *control* reports. It is also possible to adjust the budgets for the remainder of the year when it is clear that the circumstances on which the budget was originally set have changed.

Summary

Every organization needs to plan and consider how to confront future potential risks and opportunities. In most organizations this process is formalized by preparing annual budgets and monitoring performance against the budgets. Budgets are merely a collection of plans and forecasts. They reflect the financial implications of business plans, identifying the amount, quantity and timing of resources needed.

The annual budget should be set within the context of longer-term plans, which are likely to exist even if they have not been made explicit. Long-term planning involves strategic planning over several years and the identification of the basic strategy of the firm (i.e. the future direction the organization will take) and the gaps which exist between the future needs and present capabilities. A long-term plan is a statement of the preliminary targets and activities required by an organization to achieve its strategic plans together with a broad estimate for each year of the resources required. Because long-term planning involves 'looking into the future' for several years ahead, the plans tend to be uncertain, general in nature, imprecise and subject to change.

Annual budgeting is concerned with the implementation of the long-term plan for the year ahead. Before the annual budgeting process is begun, top management must communicate the policy effects of the long-term plan to those responsible for preparing the current year's budgets. Normally, the sales budget is the first to be prepared, and this supplies the basic data for producing the remaining budgets. The managers responsible for meeting budgeted performance should prepare the budgets for those areas for which they are responsible and submit them to their superiors for approval. As the budgets move up the organizational hierarchy, they must be examined in relation to each other to ensure that all the parts combine to produce an acceptable whole. When all the budgets are in mutual harmony, they will be summarized into a master budget consisting of a budgeted profit and loss account, a balance sheet and a cash flow statement. The approval of the master budget will constitute authority for the managers of each responsibility centre to carry out the plans contained in each budget. The process should not stop when all the budgets have been agreed; periodically, the actual results should be compared with the budget and remedial action taken to ensure that the results conform to plan. Budgeting is a continuous and dynamic process, and should not end once the annual budget has been prepared.

Budgets are required to achieve many different aims within an organization. Not only are they an aid to planning, coordinating and communicating the activities of a business, but they are also used as a control and motivating device. In addition, budgets are also used as a basis for evaluating a manager's performance.

Key Terms and Concepts

budgeting (p. 312)
budgets (p. 311)
cash budgets (p. 329)
continuous budgeting (p. 315)
corporate planning (p. 311)

long-range planning (p. 311)
management by exception (p. 314)
master budget (p. 319)
rolling budgeting (p. 315)
strategic planning (p. 311)

Key Examination Points

First year management accounting courses typically involve budgeting questions that require the preparation of functional or cash budgets. A common mistake is to incorrectly deduct closing stocks and add opening stocks when preparing production and material purchase budgets. Occasionally essay questions are set and you should regard Questions 13.2–13.3 as representing typical essay questions.

Review Problems

(For additional problems without answers relating to the content of this chapter you should refer to pages 508–516.)

1 When preparing a production budget, the quantity to be produced equals

A sales quantity + opening stock + closing stock

B sales quantity − opening stock + closing stock

C sales quantity − opening stock − closing stock

D sales quantity + opening stock − closing stock

E sales quantity *CIMA Stage 2*

2 BDL plc is current preparing its cash budget for the year to 31 March 2003. An extract from its sales budget for the same year shows the following sales values:

	(£)
March	60 000
April	70 000
May	55 000
June	65 000

40% of its sales are expected to be for cash. Of its credit sales, 70% are expected to pay in the month after sale and take a 2% discount; 27% are expected to pay in the second month after the sale, and the remaining 3% are expected to be bad debts.

The value of sales receipts to be shown in the cash budget for May 2002 is:

A £38 532

B £39 120

C £60 532

D £64 220

E £65 200 *CIMA Stage 2*

3 A master budget comprises:

A the budgeted profit and loss account;

B the budgeted cash flow, budgeted profit and loss account and budgeted balance sheet;

C the budgeted cash flow;

D the capital expenditure budget;

E the entire set of budgets prepared.

CIMA Stage 2

4 R Limited manufactures three products A, B and C.

You are required:

(a) Using the information given below, to prepare budgets for the month of January for

  (i) sales in quantity and value, including total value;

  (ii) production quantities;

  (iii) material usage in quantities;

  (iv) material purchases in quantity and value, including total value;

  (Note that particular attention should be paid to your layout of the budgets.)

(b) To explain the term 'principal budget factor' and state what it was assumed to be in (a).

Product		Quantity (units)	Price each (£)
Sales:	A	1000	100
	B	2000	120
	C	1500	140

Materials used in the company's products:			
Material	M1	M2	M3
Unit cost	£4	£6	£9

Quantities used in:	M1 (units)	M2 (units)	M3 (units)
Product A	4	2	–
Product B	3	3	2
Product C	2	1	1

Finished stocks:	Product A (units)	Product B (units)	Product C (units)
Quantities			
1st January	1000	1500	500
31st January	1100	1650	550

Material stocks:	M1 (units)	M2 (units)	M3 (units)
1st January	26 000	20 000	12 000
31st January	31 200	24 000	14 400

(20 marks)
CIMA Cost Accounting 1

5 The management of Beck plc have been informed that the union representing the direct production workers at one of their factories, where a standard product is produced, intends to call a strike. The accountant has been asked to advise the management of the effect the strike will have on cash flow.

The following data has been made available:

	Week 1	Week 2	Week 3
Budgeted sales	400 units	500 units	400 units
Budgeted production	600 units	400 units	Nil

The strike will commence at the beginning of week 3 and it should be assumed that it will continue for at least four weeks. Sales at 400 units per week will continue to be made during the period of the strike until stocks of finished goods are exhausted. Production will stop at the end of week 2. The current stock level of finished goods is 600 units. Stocks of work in progress are not carried.

The selling price of the product is £60 and the budgeted manufacturing cost is made up as follows:

	(£)
Direct materials	15
Direct wages	7
Variable overheads	8
Fixed overheads	18
Total	£48

Direct wages are regarded as a variable cost. The company operates a full absorption costing system and the fixed overhead absorption rate is based upon a budgeted fixed overhead of £9000 per week. Included in the total fixed overheads is £700 per week for depreciation of equipment. During the period of the strike direct wages and variable overheads would not be incurred and the cash expended on fixed overheads would be reduced by £1500 per week.

The current stock of raw materials are worth £7500; it is intended that these stocks should increase to £11 000 by the end of week 1 and then remain at this level during the period of the strike. *All direct materials are paid for one week after they have been received. Direct wages are paid one week in arrears. It should be assumed that all relevant overheads are paid for immediately the expense is incurred.* All sales are on credit, 70% of the sales value is received in cash from the debtors at the end of the first week after the sales have been made and the balance at the end of the second week.

The current amount outstanding to material suppliers is £8000 and direct wage accruals amount to £3200. Both of these will be paid in week 1. The current balance owing from debtors is £31 200, of which £24 000 will be received during week 1 and the remainder during week 2. The current balance of cash at bank and in hand is £1000.

Required:

(a) (i) Prepare a cash budget for weeks 1 to 6 showing the balance of cash at the end of each week together with a suitable analysis of the receipts and payments during each week. *(13 marks)*

(ii) Comment upon any matters arising from the cash budget which you consider should be brought to management's attention. *(4 marks)*

(b) Explain why the reported profit figure for a period does not normally represent the amount of cash generated in that period.
(5 marks)
(Total 22 marks)
ACCA Level 1 Costing

6 The budgeted balance sheet data of Kwan Tong Umbago Ltd is as follows:

1 March	Cost (£)	Depreciation to date (£)	Net (£)
Fixed assets			
Land and buildings	500 000	—	500 000
Machinery and equipment	124 000	84 500	39 500
Motor vehicles	42 000	16 400	25 600
	666 000	100 900	565 100
Working capital:			
Current assets			
Stock of raw materials (100 units)		4320	
Stock of finished goods (110 units)[a]		10 450	
Debtors (January £7680 February £10 400)		18 080	
Cash and bank		6 790	
		39 640	
Less current liabilities			
Creditors (raw materials)		3 900	35 740
			600 840
Represented by:			
Ordinary share capital (fully paid) £1 shares			500 000
Share premium			60 000
Profit and loss account			40 840
			600 840

[a]The stock of finished goods was valued at marginal cost

The estimates for the next four-month period are as follows:

	March	April	May	June
Sales (units)	80	84	96	94
Production (units)	70	75	90	90
Purchases of raw materials (units)	80	80	85	85
Wages and variable overheads at £65 per unit	£4550	£4875	£5850	£5850
Fixed overheads	£1200	£1200	£1200	£1200

The company intends to sell each unit for £219 and has estimated that it will have to pay £45 per unit for raw materials. One unit of raw material is needed for each unit of finished product.

All sales and purchases of raw materials are on credit. Debtors are allowed two months' credit and suppliers of raw materials are paid after one month's credit. The wages, variable overheads and fixed overheads are paid in the month in which they are incurred.

Cash from a loan secured on the land and buildings of £120 000 at an interest rate of 7.5% is due to be received on 1 May. Machinery costing £112 000 will be received in May and paid for in June.

The loan interest is payable half yearly from September onwards. An interim dividend to 31 March of £12 500 will be paid in June.

Depreciation for the four months, including that on the new machinery is:

Machinery and equipment	£15 733
Motor vehicles	£3 500

The company uses the FIFO method of stock valuation. Ignore taxation.

Required:
(a) Calculate and present the raw materials budget and finished goods budget in terms of units, for each month from March to June inclusive. *(5 marks)*
(b) Calculate the corresponding sales budgets, the production cost budgets and the budgeted closing debtors, creditors and stocks in terms of value. *(5 marks)*
(c) Prepare and present a cash budget for each of the four months. *(6 marks)*
(d) Prepare a master budget, i.e. a budgeted trading and profit and loss account, for the four months to 30 June, and budgeted balance sheet as at 30 June. *(10 marks)*
(e) Advise the company about possible ways in which it can improve its cash management. *(9 marks)*
(Total 35 marks)
ACCA Paper 8 Managerial Finance

Solutions to Review Problems

SOLUTION 1

Answer = B

SOLUTION 2

	(£)	(£)
Cash sales		22 000
Credit sales		
April		
(70% × 0.6 × 0.98 × £70 000)	28 812	
March (27% × 0.6 × £60 000)	9 720	38 532
		60 532

SOLUTION 3

Answer = B

SOLUTION 4

(a) (i)

	Sales quantity and value budget Products			
	A	B	C	Total
Sales quantities	1 000	2 000	1 500	
Selling prices	£100	£120	£140	
Sales value	£100 000	£250 000	£210 000	£550 000

(ii)

Production quantities budget

	Products		
Sales quantities	1000	2000	1500
Add closing stock	1100	1650	550
	2100	3650	2050
Deduct opening stock	1000	1500	500
Units to be produced	1100	2150	1550

(iii)

Material usage budget (quantities)

Production quantities		Materials				
	M1		M2		M3	
	Units per product	Total	Units per product	Total	Units per product	Total
A 1100	4	4 400	2	2 200	—	—
B 2150	3	6 450	3	6 450	2	4 300
C 1550	2	3 100	1	1 550	1	1 550
Usage in quantities		13 950		10 200		5 850

(iv)

Material purchases budget (quantities and value)

	M1	M2	M3	Total
Materials usage budget	13 950	10 200	5 850	
Add closing stock	31 200	24 000	14 400	
	45 150	34 200	20 250	
Deduct opening stock	26 000	20 000	12 000	
Purchases in quantities	19 150	14 200	8 250	
Price per unit	£4	£6	£9	
Value of purchases	£76 600	£85 200	£74 250	£236 050

(b) The principal budget factor is also known as the limiting factor or key factor. The CIMA Terminology describes the principal budget factor as follows: 'The factor which, at a particular time, or over a period, will limit the activities of an undertaking. The limiting factor is usually the level of demand for the products or services of the undertaking but it could be a shortage of one of the productive resources, e.g. skilled labour, raw material, or machine capacity. In order to ensure that the functional budgets are reasonably capable of fulfillment, the extent of the influence of this factor must first be assessed.'

In the absence of any information to the contrary in the question, it is assumed that the principal budget factor is sales demand. See 'Determining the factor that restricts performance' in Chapter 13 for a discussion of the importance of the principal budget factor in the budgeting process.

SOLUTION 5

(a) (i) *Cash budget for weeks 1–6*

Week:	1 (£)	2 (£)	3 (£)	4 (£)	5 (£)	6 (£)
Receipts from debtors[a]	24 000	24 000	28 200	25 800	19 800	5 400
Payments:						
To material suppliers[b]	8 000	12 500	6 000	nil	nil	nil
To direct workers[c]	3 200	4 200	2 800	nil	nil	nil
For variable overheads[d]	4 800	3 200	nil	nil	nil	nil
For fixed overhead[e]	8 300	8 300	6 800	6 800	6 800	6 800
Total payments	24 300	28 200	15 600	6 800	6 800	6 800
Net movement	(300)	(4 200)	12 600	19 000	13 000	(1 400)
Opening balance (week 1 given)	1 000	700	(3 500)	9 100	28 100	41 100
Closing balance	700	(3 500)	9 100	28 100	41 100	39 700

Notes

[a] Debtors:

Week:	1	2	3	4	5	6
Units sold*	400	500	400	300	—	—
Sales (£)	24 000	30 000	24 000	18 000	—	—
Cash received (70%)		16 800	21 000	16 800	12 600	
(30%)			7 200	9 000	7 200	5 400
Given	24 000	7 200				
Total receipts (£)	24 000	24 000	28 200	25 800	19 800	5 400

* Sales in week 4 = opening stock (600 units) + production in weeks 1 and 2 (1000 units) less sales in weeks 1–3 (1300 units) = 300 units.

[b] Creditors:

Week:	1 (£)	2 (£)	3 (£)	4	5	6
Materials consumed at £15	9 000	6 000	—	—	—	—
Increase in stocks	3 500	—				
Materials purchased	12 500	6 000				
Payment to suppliers	8 000 (given)	12 500	6 000	nil	nil	nil

[c] Wages:

Week:	1 (£)	2 (£)	3 (£)	4	5	6
Wages consumed at £7	4 200	2 800	nil	nil	nil	nil
Wages paid	3 200 (given)	4 200	2 800	—	—	—

[d] Variable overhead payment = budgeted production × budgeted cost per unit.
[e] Fixed overhead payments for weeks 1–2 = fixed overhead per week (£9000) less weekly depreciation (£700).
Fixed overhead payments for weeks 3–6 = £8300 normal payment less £1500 per week.

(ii) *Comments*

1. Finance will be required to meet the cash deficit in week 2, but a lowering of the budgeted material stocks at the end of week 1 would reduce the amount of cash to be borrowed at the end of week 2.

2. The surplus cash after the end of week 2 should be invested on a short-term basis.

3. After week 6, there will be no cash receipts, but cash outflows will be £6800 per week. The closing balance of £39 700 at the end of week 6 will be sufficient to finance outflows for a further 5 or 6 weeks (£39 700/£6800 per week).

(b) The answer should include a discussion of the matching concept, emphasizing that revenues and expenses may not be attributed to the period when the associated cash inflows and outflows occur. Also, some items of expense do not affect cash outflow (e.g. depreciation).

SOLUTION 6

(a) *Raw materials:*

(Units)	March	April	May	June
Opening stock	100	110	115	110
Add: Purchases	80	80	85	85
	180	190	200	195
Less: Used in production	70	75	90	90
Closing stock	110	115	110	105

(Units) *Finished production:*				
Opening stock	110	100	91	85
Add: Production	70	75	90	90
	180	175	181	175
Less: Sales	80	84	96	94
Closing stock	100	91	85	81

(b) *Sales:*

					Total
(at £219 per unit)	£17 520	£18 396	£21 024	£20 586	£77 526

Production cost:					
Raw materials (using FIFO)	3 024 (1)	3 321 (2)	4 050	4 050	14 445
Wages and variable costs	4 550	4 875	5 850	5 850	21 125
	£7 574	£8 196	£9 900	£9 900	£35 570

Debtors:
Closing debtors = May + June sales = £41 610
Creditors:
June purchases 85 units × £45 = £3825
Notes:
(1)   70 units × £4320/100 units = £3024.
(2)   (30 units × £4320/100 units + (45 units × £45) = £3321.

Closing stocks:
Raw materials 105 units × £45 = £4725
Finished goods 81 units × £110$^{(1)}$ = £8910
Note:
$^{(1)}$ Materials (£45) + Labour and Variable Overhead (£65). It is assumed that stocks are valued on a variable costing basis.

(c) *Cash budget:*

		March (£)	April (£)	May (£)	June (£)
Balance b/fwd		6 790	4 820	5 545	132 415
Add: Receipts					
Debtors (two months' credit)		7 680	10 400	17 520	18 396
Loan		—	—	120 000	—
	(A)	14 470	15 220	143 065	150 811
Payments:					
Creditors (one month's credit)		3 900	3 600	3 600	3 825
			(80 × £45)		
Wages and variable overheads		4 550	4 875	5 850	5 850
Fixed overheads		1 200	1 200	1 200	1 200
Machinery		—	—	—	112 000
Interim dividend		—	—	—	12 500
	(B)	9 650	9 675	10 650	135 375
Balance c/fwd	(A) − (B)	4 820	5 545	132 415	£15 436

(d) *Master budget:*

Budgeted trading and profit and loss account for the four months to 30 June

	(£)	(£)
Sales		77 526
Cost of sales: Opening stock finished goods	10 450	
Add: Production cost	35 570	
	46 020	
Less: Closing stock finished goods	8 910	37 110
		40 416
Less: Expenses		
Fixed overheads (4 × £1200)	4 800	
Depreciation		
Machinery and equipment	15 733	
Motor vehicles	3 500	
Loan interest (2/12 × 7$\frac{1}{2}$% of £120 000)	1 500	25 533
		14 883
Less: Interim dividends		12 500
		2 383
Add: Profit and loss account balance b/fwd		40 840
		£43 223

Budgeted balance sheet as at 30 June

Fixed assets	Cost (£)	Depreciation to date (£)	Net (£)
Land and buildings	500 000	—	500 000
Machinery and equipment	236 000	100 233	135 767
Motor vehicles	42 000	19 900	22 100
	778 000	120 133	657 867

Current assets			
Stock of raw materials		4 725	
Stock of finished goods		8 910	
Debtors		41 610	
Cash and bank balances		15 436	
		70 681	
Less: Current liabilities			
Creditors	3 825		
Loan interest owing	1 500	5 325	65 356
			£723 223

Capital employed	(£)
Ordinary share capital £1 shares (fully paid)	500 000
Share premium	60 000
Profit and loss account	43 233
	603 223
Secured loan ($7\frac{1}{2}$%)	120 000
	£723 223

Management control systems

Control is the process of ensuring that a firm's activities conform to its plan and that its objectives are achieved. There can be no control without objectives and plans, since these predetermine and specify the desirable behaviour and set out the procedures that should be followed by members of the organization to ensure that a firm is operated in a desired manner.

Drucker (1964) distinguishes between 'controls' and 'control'. **Controls** are measurement and information, whereas control means direction. In other words, 'controls' are purely a means to an end; the end is control. '**Control**' is the function that makes sure that actual work is done to fulfil the original intention, and 'controls' are used to provide information to assist in determining the control action to be taken. For example, material costs may be greater than budget. 'Controls' will indicate that costs exceed budget and that this may be because the purchase of inferior quality materials causes excessive wastage. 'Control' is the action that is taken to purchase the correct quality materials in the future to reduce excessive wastage.

'Controls' encompasses all the methods and procedures that direct employees towards achieving the organization objectives. Many different control mechanisms are used in organizations and the management accounting control system represents only one aspect of the various control mechanisms that companies use to control their managers and employees. To fully understand the role that management accounting control systems play in the control process, it is necessary to be aware of how they relate to the entire array of control mechanisms used by organizations.

This chapter begins by describing the different types of controls that are used by companies. The elements of management accounting control systems will then be described within the context of the overall control process.

Learning objectives:

After studying this chapter you should be able to:

- describe the three different types of controls used in organizations;
- describe a cybernetic control system;
- distinguish between feedback and feed-forward controls;
- define the four different types of responsibility centres;
- explain the different elements of management accounting control systems;
- describe the controllability principle and the methods of implementing it;
- describe the different types of financial performance targets and the effects of their level of difficulty on motivation and performance;
- describe the influence of participation in the budgeting process;
- explain why a performance measurement system should also emphasize non-financial measures;

- describe activity-based cost management.

Different types of controls

Companies use many different control mechanisms to cope with the problem of organizational control. To make sense of the vast number of controls that are used we shall classify them into three categories using approaches that have been adopted by Ouchi (1979) and Merchant (1998). They are:

1. action (or behavioural) controls;
2. personnel and cultural (or clan and social) controls;
3. results (or output) controls.

The terms in parentheses refer to the classification used by Ouchi whereas the other terms refer to the categories specified by Merchant. Because the classifications used by both authors are compatible we shall use the terms interchangeably.

ACTION OR BEHAVIOURAL CONTROLS

Behavioural controls involve observing the actions of individuals as they go about their work. They are appropriate where cause and effect relationships are well understood, so that if the correct means are followed, the desired outcomes will occur. Under these circumstances effective control can be achieved by having superiors watch and guide the actions of subordinates. For example, if the foreman watches the workers on the assembly line and ensures that the work is done exactly as prescribed then the expected quality and quantity of work should ensue.

Instead of using the term behavioural controls Merchant uses the term action controls. He defines **action controls** as applying to those situations where the actions themselves are the focus of controls. They are usable and effective only when managers know what actions are desirable (or undesirable) and have the ability to make sure that the desirable actions occur (or that the undesirable actions do not occur). Forms of action controls described by Merchant include behavioural constraints, preaction reviews and action accountability.

The aim of *behavioural constraints* is to prevent people from doing things that should not be done. They include physical constraints, such as computer passwords that restrict accessing or updating information sources to authorized personnel, and administrative constraints. Imposing ceilings on the amount of capital expenditure that managers may authorize is an example of an administrative constraint. For example, managers at lower levels may be able to authorize capital expenditure below £10 000 within a total annual budget of, say, £100 000. The aim is to ensure that only those personnel with the necessary expertise and authority can authorize major expenditure and that such expenditure remains under their control.

Preaction reviews involve the scrutiny and approval of action plans of the individuals being controlled before they can undertake a course of action. Examples include the approval by municipal authorities of plans for the construction of properties prior to building commencing or the approval by a tutor of a dissertation plan prior to the student being authorized to embark on the dissertation.

Action accountability involves defining actions that are acceptable or unacceptable, observing the actions and rewarding acceptable or punishing unacceptable actions. Examples of action accountability include establishing work rules and procedures and company codes of conduct that employees must follow.

Action controls that focus on *preventing* undesirable behaviour are the ideal form of control because their aim is to prevent the behaviour from occurring. They are preferable to *detection* controls that are applied after the occurrence of the actions because they avoid the costs of undesirable behaviour. Nevertheless, detection controls can still be useful if they are applied in a timely manner so that they can lead to the early cessation of undesirable actions. Their existence also discourages individuals from engaging in such actions.

PERSONNEL, CULTURAL AND SOCIAL CONTROLS

Clan and social controls are the second types of controls described by Ouchi. **Clan controls** are based on the belief that by fostering a strong sense of solidarity and commitment towards organizational goals people can become immersed in the interests of the organization.

The main feature of clan controls is the high degree of employee discipline attained through the dedication of each individual to the interests of the whole. At a less extreme level clan controls can be viewed as corporate cultures or a special form of **social control** such as the selection of people who have already been socialized into adopting particular norms and patterns of behaviour to perform particular tasks. For example, if the only staff promoted to managerial level are those who display a high commitment to the firm's objectives then the need for other forms of controls can be reduced, provided that the managers are committed to achieving the 'right' objectives.

Merchant adopts a similar approach to Ouchi and classifies personnel and cultural controls as a second form of control. He defines **personnel controls** as helping employees do a good job by building on employees' natural tendencies to control themselves. In particular, they ensure that the employees have the capabilities (in terms of intelligence, qualifications and experience) and the resources needed to do a good job. Merchant identifies three major methods of implementing personnel controls. They are selection and placement, training and job design and the provision of the necessary resources. Selection and placement involves finding the right people to do a specified job. Training can be used to ensure that employees know how to perform the assigned tasks and to make them fully aware of the results and actions that are expected from them. Job design entails designing jobs in such a way that enable employees to undertake their tasks with a high degree of success. This requires that jobs are not made too complex, onerous or badly defined so that employees do not know what is expected of them.

Cultural controls represent a set of values, social norms and beliefs that are shared by members of the organization and that influence their actions. Cultural controls are exercised by individuals over one another – for example, procedures used by groups within an organization to regulate performance of their own members and to bring them into line when they deviate from group norms. It is apparent from the above description that cultural controls are virtually the same as social controls.

RESULTS OR OUTPUT CONTROLS

Output or **results controls** involve collecting and reporting information about the outcomes of work effort. The major advantage of results controls is that senior managers do not have to be knowledgeable about the means required to achieve the desired results or be involved in directly observing the actions of subordinates. They merely rely on output reports to ascertain whether or not the desired outcomes have been achieved. Accounting control systems can be described as a form of output controls. They are mostly defined in monetary terms such as revenues, costs, profits and ratios such as return on investment. Results measures also include non-accounting measures such as the number of units of defective production, the number of loan applications processed or ratio measures such as the number of customer deliveries on time as a percentage of total deliveries.

Results controls involve the following stages:

1. establishing results (i.e. performance) measures that minimize undesirable behaviour;
2. establishing performance targets;
3. measuring performance;
4. providing rewards or punishment.

Ideally desirable behaviour should improve the performance measure and undesirable behaviour should have a detrimental effect on the measure. Without a pre-set performance target individuals do not know what to aim for. Various research studies suggest that the existence of a clearly defined quantitative target is likely to motivate higher performance than vague statements such as 'do your best'. It is also difficult for employees or their superiors to interpret performance unless actual performance can be compared against predetermined standards.

The third stage specified above relates to measuring performance. Ability to measure some outputs effectively constrains the use of results measures. For example, it can be extremely difficult to measure the outputs of support departments. Consider a personnel department. The accomplishment of the department can be difficult to measure and other forms of control might be preferable. Merchant suggests that to evoke the right behaviours results measures should be precise, objective, timely and understandable.

Whilst 100% accuracy is not essential, measurements should be sufficiently accurate for the purpose required. If measures are not sufficiently precise they will have little information value and may lead to managers misevaluating performance. Measures should also be objective and free from bias. Where performance is self-measured and reported there is a danger that measures will be biased. Objectivity can be increased by performance being measured by people who are independent of the process being measured. Timeliness relates to the time lag between actual performance and the reporting of the results. Significant delays in reporting will result in the measures losing most of their motivational impact and a lengthy delay in taking remedial action when outcomes deviate from target. Finally, measures should be understandable by the individuals whose behaviours are being controlled. If measures are not understandable it is unlikely that managers will know how their actions will affect the measure and there is a danger that the measures will lose their motivational impact.

The final stage of results controls involves encouraging employees to achieve organizational goals by having rewards (or punishments) linked to their success (or failure) in achieving the results measures. Organizational rewards include salary increases, bonuses, promotions and recognition. Employees can also derive intrinsic rewards through a sense of accomplishment and achievement. Punishments include demotions, failure to obtain the rewards and possibly the loss of one's job.

Cybernetic control systems

The traditional approach in the management control literature has been to view results controls as a simple **cybernetic system**. In describing this process authors often use a mechanical model such as a thermostat that controls a central heating system as a resemblance. This process is illustrated in Figure 14.1. You will see that the control system consists of the following elements:

1. The process (the room's temperature) is continually monitored by an automatic regulator (the thermostat).
2. Deviations from a predetermined level (the desired temperature) are identified by the automatic regulator.
3. Corrective actions are started if the output is not equal to the predetermined level. The automatic regulator causes the input to be adjusted by turning the heater on if the temperature falls below a predetermined level. The heater is turned off when the output (temperature) corresponds with the predetermined level.

The output of the process is monitored, and whenever it varies from the predetermined level, the input is automatically adjusted. Emmanuel *et al.* (1990) state that four conditions must be satisfied before any process can be said to be controlled. First, objectives for the process being controlled must exist. Without an aim or purpose control has no meaning. Secondly, the output of the process must be measurable in terms of the dimensions defined by the objectives. In other words, there must be some mechanism for ascertaining whether the process is attaining its objectives. Thirdly, a predictive model of the process being controlled is required so that causes for the non-attainment can be identified and proposed corrective actions evaluated. Finally, there must be a capability for taking action so that deviations from objectives can be reduced. Emmanuel *et al.* stress that if any of these conditions are not met the process cannot be considered to be 'in control'.

Result controls resemble the thermostat control model. Standards of performance are determined, measurement systems monitor performance, comparisons are made between the standard and actual performance and feedback provides information on the variances. Note that the term **variance** is used to describe the difference between the standard and actual performance of the actions that are being measured.

Feedback and feed-forward controls

The cybernetic system of control described in Figure 14.1 is that of feedback control. **Feedback control** involves monitoring outputs achieved against desired outputs and taking whatever corrective action is necessary if a deviation exists. In **feed-forward control** instead of actual outputs being compared against desired outputs, predictions are made of what outputs are expected to be at some future time. If these expectations differ from what is desired, control actions are taken that will minimize these differences. The objective is for control to be achieved before any deviations from desired outputs actually occur. In other words, with feed-forward controls likely errors can be anticipated and steps taken to avoid them, whereas with feedback controls actual errors are identified after the event and corrective action is taken to implement future actions to achieve the desired outputs.

Feed-forward control requires the use of a predictive model that is sufficiently accurate to ensure that control action will improve the situation and not cause it to deteriorate

FIGURE 14.1 *A cybernetic control system.*

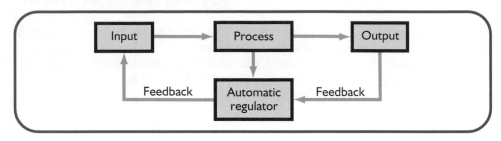

further. A major limitation of feedback control is that errors are allowed to occur. This is not a significant problem when there is a short time lag between the occurrence of an error and the identification and implementation of corrective action. Feed-forward control is therefore preferable when a significant time lag occurs. The budgeting process is a feed-forward control system. To the extent that outcomes fall short of what is desired, alternatives are considered until a budget is produced that is expected to achieve what is desired. The comparison of actual results with budget, in identifying variances and taking remedial action to ensure that future outcomes will conform with budgeted outcomes is an illustration of a feedback control system. Thus accounting control systems consist of both feedback and feed-forward controls.

Management accounting control systems

To enable you to understand the role that management accounting control systems play within the overall control process this chapter has initially adopted a broad approach to describing management control systems. We shall now concentrate on management accounting control systems which represent the predominant controls in most organizations.

Why are accounting controls the predominant controls? There are several reasons. First, all organizations need to express and aggregate the results of a wide range of dissimilar activities using a common measure. The monetary measure meets this requirement. Second, profitability and liquidity are essential to the success of all organizations and financial measures relating to these and other areas are closely monitored by stakeholders. It is therefore natural that managers will wish to monitor performance in monetary terms. Third, financial measures also enable a common decision rule to be applied by all managers when considering alternative courses of action. That is, a course of action will normally benefit a firm only if it results in an improvement in its financial performance. Fourth, measuring results in financial terms enables managers to be given more autonomy. Focusing on the outcomes of managerial actions, summarized in financial terms, gives managers the freedom to take whatever actions they consider to be appropriate to achieve the desired results. Finally, outputs expressed in financial terms continue to be effective in uncertain environments even when it is unclear what course of action should be taken. Financial results provide a mechanism to indicate whether the actions benefited the organization.

Responsibility centres

The complex environment in which most businesses operate today makes it virtually impossible for most firms to be controlled centrally. This is because it is not possible for central management to have all the relevant information and time to determine the detailed plans for all the organization. Some degree of decentralization is essential for all but the smallest firms. Organizations decentralize by creating responsibility centres. A responsibility centre may be defined as a unit of a firm where an individual manager is held responsible for the unit's performance. There are four types of responsibility centres. They are:

1. cost or expense centres;
2. revenue centres;
3. profit centres;
4. investment centres.

The creation of responsibility centres is a fundamental part of management accounting control systems. It is therefore important that you can distinguish between the various forms of responsibility centres.

COST OR EXPENSE CENTRES

Cost or **expense centres** are responsibility centres whose managers are normally accountable for only those costs that are under their control. We can distinguish between two types of cost centres – standard cost centres and discretionary cost centres. The main features of **standard cost centres** are that output can be measured and the input required to produce each unit of output can be specified. Control is exercised by comparing the standard cost (that is, the cost of the inputs that *should* have been consumed in producing the output) with the cost that was *actually* incurred. The difference between the actual cost and the standard cost is described as the **variance**. Standard cost centres and variance analysis will be discussed extensively in the next chapter.

Standard cost centres are best suited to units within manufacturing firms but they can also be established in service industries such as units within banks, where output can be measured in terms of the number of cheques or the number of loan applications processed, and there are also well defined input–output relationships. Although cost centre managers are not accountable for sales revenues they can affect the amount of sales revenue generated if quality standards are not met and outputs are not produced according to schedule. Therefore quality and timeliness performance measures are also required besides financial measures.

Discretionary expense centres are those responsibility cost centres where output cannot be measured in financial terms and there are no clearly observable relationships between inputs (the resources consumed) and the outputs (the results achieved). Control normally takes the form of ensuring that actual expenditure adheres to budgeted expenditure for each expense category and also ensuring that the tasks assigned to each centre have been successfully accomplished. Examples of discretionary centres include advertising and publicity and research and development departments. You should note that in discretionary centres underspending against budget may not necessarily be a good thing since this may result in a lower level of service than that originally planned by management. For example, underspending on research and development may indicate that the amount to be spent on research and development has not been followed. One of the major problems arising in discretionary expense centres is measuring the effectiveness of expenditures. For example, the marketing support department may not have exceeded an advertising budget but this does not mean that the advertising expenditure has been effective. The advertising may have been incorrectly timed, it may have been directed to the wrong audience, or it may have contained the wrong message. Determining the effectiveness and efficiency of discretionary expense centres is one of the most difficult areas of management control.

REVENUE CENTRES

Revenue centres are responsibility centres where managers are accountable only for financial outputs in the form of generating sales revenues. Typical examples of revenue centres are where regional sales managers are accountable for sales within their regions. Revenue centre managers may also be held accountable for selling expenses, such as salesperson salaries, commissions and order-getting costs. They are not, however, made accountable for the cost of the goods and services that they sell.

PROFIT CENTRES

Both cost and revenue centre managers have limited decision-making authority. Cost centre managers are accountable only for managing inputs of their centres and decisions relating to outputs are made by other units within the firm. Revenue centres are accountable for selling the products or services but they have no control over their manufacture. A significant increase in managerial autonomy occurs when unit managers are given responsibility for both production and sales. In this situation managers are normally free to set selling prices, choose which markets to sell in, make product-mix and output decisions and select suppliers. Units within an organization whose managers are accountable for both revenues and costs are called **profit centres**

INVESTMENT CENTRES

Investment centres are responsibility centres whose managers are responsible for both sales revenues and costs and, in addition, have responsibility and authority to make working capital and capital investment decisions. Typical investment centre performance measures include return on investment and economic value added. These measures are influenced by revenues, costs and assets employed and thus reflect the responsibility that managers have for both generating profits and managing the investment base. Investment centres represent the highest level of managerial autonomy. They include the company as a whole, operating subsidiaries, operating groups and divisions.

The nature of management accounting control systems

Management accounting control systems have two core elements. The first is the formal planning processes such as budgeting and long-term planning that were described in the previous chapter. These processes are used for establishing performance expectations for evaluating performance. The second is responsibility accounting which involves the creation of responsibility centres. Responsibility centres enable accountability for financial results and outcomes to be allocated to individuals throughout the organization. The objective of **responsibility accounting** is to accumulate costs and revenues for each individual responsibility centre so that the deviations from a performance target (typically the budget) can be attributed to the individual who is accountable for the responsibility centre. For each responsibility centre the process involves setting a performance target, measuring performance, comparing performance against the target, analysing the variances and taking action where significant variances exist between actual and target performance. Financial performance targets for profit or investment centres are typically in terms of profits, return on investment or economic value added whereas performance targets for cost centres are defined in terms of costs.

Responsibility accounting is implemented by issuing performance reports at frequent intervals (normally monthly) that inform responsibility centre managers of the deviations from budgets for which they are accountable and are required to take action. An example of a performance report issued to a cost centre manager is presented in the lower section of Exhibit 14.1. You should note that at successively higher levels of management less detailed information is reported. You can see from the upper sections of Exhibit 14.1 that the information is condensed and summarized as the results relating to the responsibility centre are reported at higher levels. Exhibit 14.1 only includes financial information. In addition non-financial measures such as those relating to quality and timeliness may be reported. We shall look at non-financial measures in more detail at the end of this chapter.

Responsibility accounting involves:

- distinguishing between those items which managers can control and for which they should be held accountable and those items over which they have no control and for which they are not held accountable;
- determining how challenging the financial targets should be;
- determining how much influence managers should have in the setting of financial targets.

We shall now examine each of these items in detail.

The controllability principle

Responsibility accounting is based on the application of the **controllability principle** which means that it is appropriate to charge to an area of responsibility only those costs that are significantly influenced by the manager of that responsibility centre. The controllability principle can be implemented by either eliminating the uncontrollable items from the areas for which managers are held accountable or calculating their effects so that the reports distinguish between controllable and uncontrollable items.

Applying the controllability principle is difficult in practice because many areas do not fit neatly into either controllable and uncontrollable categories. Instead, they are partially controllable. For example, even when outcomes may be affected by occurrences outside a manager's control; such as competitors' actions, price changes and supply shortages, managers can take action to reduce their adverse effects. They can substitute alternative materials where the prices of raw materials change or they can monitor and respond to competitors' actions. If these factors are categorized as uncontrollables managers will be motivated not to try and influence them. A further problem is that even when a factor is clearly uncontrollable, it is difficult to measure in order to highlight its impact on the reported outcomes.

DEALING WITH THE DISTORTING EFFECTS OF UNCONTROLLABLE FACTORS BEFORE THE MEASUREMENT PERIOD

Management can attempt to deal with the distorting effects of uncontrollables by making adjustments either before or after the measurement period. Uncontrollable and controllable factors can be determined prior to the measurement period by specifying which budget line

EXHIBIT 14.1

Responsibility accounting monthly performance reports

items are to be regarded as controllable and uncontrollable. Uncontrollable items can either be excluded from performance reports or shown in a separate section within the performance report so that they are clearly distinguishable from controllable items. The latter approach has the advantage of drawing managerial attention to those costs that a company incurs to support their

Performance report to managing director

| | | Budget | | Variance[a] F (A) | |
		Current month (£)	Year to date (£)	This month (£)	Year to date (£)
Managing director	→ Factory A	453 900	6 386 640	80 000(A)	98 000(A)
	Factory B	X	X	X	X
	Factory C	X	X	X	X
	Administration costs	X	X	X	X
	Selling costs	X	X	X	X
	Distribution costs	X	X	X	X
		2 500 000	30 000 000	400 000(A)	600 000(A)

Performance report to production manager of factory A

| | | Budget | | Variance F (A) | |
		Current month	Year to date	This month	Year to date
Production manager	Works manager's office	X	X	X	X
	▷ Machining department 1	165 600	717 600	32 760(A)	89 180(A)
	Machining department 2	X	X	X	X
	Assembly department	X	X	X	X
	Finishing department	X	X	X	X
		453 900	6 386 640	80 000(A)	98 000(A)

Performance report to head of responsibility centre

| | | Budget | | Variance F (A) | |
		Current month	Year to date	This month	Year to date
Head of responsibility centre	Direct materials	X	X	X	X
	Direct labour	X	X	X	X
	Indirect labour	X	X	X	X
	Indirect materials	X	X	X	X
	Power	X	X	X	X
	Maintenance	X	X	X	X
	Idle time	X	X	X	X
	Other	X	X	X	X
		165 600	717 600	32 760(A)	89 180(A)

[a]F indicates a favourable variance (actual cost less than budgeted cost) and (A) indicates an adverse budget (actual cost greater than budget cost). Note that, at the lowest level of reporting, the responsibility centre head's performance report contains detailed information on operating costs. At successively higher levels of management less detail is reported. For example, the managing director's information on the control of activities consists of examining those variances that represent significant departures from the budget for each factory and functional area of the business and requesting explanations from the appropriate managers.

activities. Managers may be able to indirectly influence these costs if they are made aware of the sums involved.

How do we distinguish between controllable and uncontrollable items? Merchant (1989) suggests that the following general rule should be applied to all employees – 'Hold employees accountable for the performance areas you want them to pay attention to.' Applying this rule explains why some organizations assign the costs of shared resource pools, such as administrative costs relating to personnel and data processing departments, to responsibility centres. Assigning these costs authorizes managers of the user responsibility centres to question the amount of the costs and the quantity and quality of services supplied. In addition, responsibility centres are discouraged from making unnecessary requests for the use of these services when they are aware that increases in costs will be assigned to the users of the services.

DEALING WITH THE DISTORTING EFFECTS OF UNCONTROLLABLE FACTORS AFTER THE MEASUREMENT PERIOD

Variance analysis and flexible performance standards can be used to remove the effects of uncontrollable factors from the results measures after the measurement period. **Variance analysis** seeks to analyse the factors that cause the actual results to differ from pre-determined budgeted targets. In particular, variance analysis helps to distinguish between controllable and uncontrollable items and identify those individuals who are accountable for the variances. For example, variances analysed by each type of cost, and by their price and quantity effects, enables variances to be traced to accountable individuals and also to isolate those variances that are due to uncontrollable factors. Variance analysis will be discussed extensively in the next chapter.

Flexible performance standards apply when targets are adjusted to reflect variations in uncontrollable factors arising from the circumstances not envisaged when the targets were set. The most widely used flexible performance standard is to use **flexible budgets** whereby the uncontrollable volume effects on cost behaviour are removed from the manager's performance reports. Because some costs vary with changes in the level of activity, it is essential when applying the controllability principle to take into account the variability of costs. For example, if the actual level of activity is greater than the budgeted level of activity then those costs that vary with activity will be greater than the budgeted costs purely because of changes in activity. Let us consider the simplified situation presented in Example 14.1.

Assuming that the increase in activity was due to an increase in sales volume greater than that anticipated when the budget was set then the increases in costs arising from the volume change are beyond the control of the responsibility centre manager. It is clearly

EXAMPLE 14.1

An item of expense that is included in the budget for a responsibility centre varies directly in relation to activity at an estimated cost of £5 per unit of output. The budgeted monthly level of activity was 20 000 units and the actual level of activity was 24 000 units at a cost of £105 000.

inappropriate to compare actual *variable* costs of £105 000 from an activity level of 24 000 units with budgeted *variable* costs of £100 000 from an activity level of 20 000 units. This would incorrectly suggest an overspending of £5000. If managers are to be made responsible for their costs, it is essential that they are responsible for performance under the conditions in which they worked, and not for a performance based on conditions when the budget was drawn up. In other words, it is misleading to compare actual costs at one level of activity with budgeted costs at another level of activity. At the end of the period the original budget must be adjusted to the actual level of activity to take into account the impact of the uncontrollable volume change on costs. This procedure is called flexible budgeting. In Example 14.1 the performance report should be as follows:

Budgeted expenditure	Actual expenditure
(flexed to 24 000 units)	(24 000 units)
£120 000	£105 000

The budget is adjusted to reflect what the costs should have been for an actual activity of 24 000 units. This indicates that the manager has incurred £15 000 less expenditure than would have been expected for the actual level of activity, and a favourable variance of £15 000 should be recorded on the performance report, not an adverse variance of £5000, which would have been recorded if the original budget had not been adjusted.

In Example 14.1 it was assumed that there was only one variable item of expense, but in practice the budget will include many different expenses including fixed, semi-variable and variable expenses. You should note that fixed expenses do not vary in the short-term with activity and therefore the budget should remain unchanged for these expenses. The budget should be flexed only for variable and semi-variable expenses.

GUIDELINES FOR APPLYING THE CONTROLLABILITY PRINCIPLE

Dealing with uncontrollables represents one of the most difficult areas for the design and operation of management accounting control systems. The following guidelines published by the Report of the Committee of Cost Concepts and Standards in the United States in 1956 still continues to provide useful guidance:

1. If a manager *can significantly influence the quantity and price paid* for a service then the manager is responsible for all the expenditure incurred for the service.
2. If the manager *can significantly influence the quantity of the service but not the price paid* for the service then only that amount of difference between actual and budgeted expenditure that is due to usage should be identified with the manager.
3. If the manager *cannot significantly influence either the quantity or the price paid* for the service then the expenditure is uncontrollable and should not be identified with the manager.

An example of the latter situation is when the costs of an industrial relations department are apportioned to a department on some arbitrary basis; such arbitrary apportionments are likely to result in an allocation of expenses that the managers of responsibility centres may not be able to influence. In addition to the above guidelines Merchant's general rule should also be used as a guide – 'Hold employees accountable for the performance areas you want them to pay attention to.'

Setting financial performance targets

There is substantial evidence from a large number of studies that the existence of a defined, quantitative goal or target is likely to motivate higher levels of performance than when no such target is stated. People perform better when they have a clearly defined goal to aim for and are aware of the standards that will be used to interpret their performance. There are three approaches that can be used to set financial targets. They are targets derived from engineering studies of input–output relationships, targets derived from historical data and targets derived from negotiations between superiors and subordinates.

Engineered targets can be used when there are clearly defined and stable input–output relationships such that the inputs required can be estimated directly from product specifications. For example, in a fast-food restaurant for a given output of hamburgers it is possible to estimate the inputs required because there is a physical relationship between the ingredients such as meats, buns, condiments and packaging and the number of hamburgers made. Input–output relationships can also be established for labour by closely observing the processes to determine the quantity of labour that will be required for a given output.

Where clearly defined input–output relationships do not exist other approaches must be used to set financial targets. One approach is to use **historical targets** derived directly from the results of previous periods. Previous results plus an increase for expected price changes may form the basis for setting the targets or an improvement factor may be incorporated into the estimate, such as previous period costs less a reduction of 10%. The disadvantage of using historical targets is that they may include past inefficiencies or may encourage employees to underperform if the outcome of efficient performance in a previous period is used as a basis for setting a more demanding target in the next period.

Negotiated targets are set based on negotiations between superiors and subordinates. The major advantage of negotiated targets is that they address the information asymmetry gap that can exist between superior and subordinate. This gap arises because subordinates have more information than their superiors on the relationships between outputs and inputs and the constraints that exist at the operating level, whereas superiors have a broader view of the organization as a whole and the resource constraints that apply. Negotiated targets enable the information asymmetry gap to be reduced so that the targets set incorporate the constraints applying at both the operational level and the firm as a whole. You should refer back to the previous chapter for a more detailed discussion of the negotiation process.

Targets vary in their level of difficulty and the chosen level has a significant effect on motivation and performance. Targets are considered to be moderately difficult (or highly achievable) when they are set at the average level of performance for a given task. According to Merchant (1990) most companies set their annual profit budgets targets at levels that are highly achievable. Their budgets are set to be challenging but achievable 80–90 per cent of the time by an effective management team working at a consistently high level of effort. Targets set at levels above average are labelled as difficult, tight or high, and those set below average are classed as easy, loose or low (Chow, 1983).

THE EFFECT OF THE LEVEL OF BUDGET DIFFICULTY ON MOTIVATION AND PERFORMANCE

The fact that a financial target represents a specific quantitative goal gives it a strong motivational potential, but the targets set must be accepted if managers are to be motivated to achieve higher levels of performance. Unfortunately, it is not possible to specify exactly the optimal degree of difficulty for financial targets, since task uncertainty and cultural, organizational and personality factors all affect an individual manager's reaction to a financial target.

Figure 14.2 derived from Otley (1987) shows the theoretical relationship between budget difficulty, aspiration levels and performance. In Figure 14.2 it is assumed that performance and aspiration levels are identical. Note that the **aspiration level** relates to the personal goal of the budgetee (that is, the person who is responsible for the budget). In other words, it is the level of performance that they hope to attain. You will see from Figure 14.2 that as the level of budget difficulty is increased both the budgetees' aspiration level and performance increases. However, there becomes a point where the budget is perceived as impossible to achieve and the aspiration level and performance decline dramatically. It can be seen from Figure 14.2 that the budget level that motivates the best level of performance may not be achievable. In contrast, the budget that is expected to be achieved (that is, the expectations budget in Figure 14.2) motivates a lower level of performance.

Therefore if budgets are to be set at a level that will motivate individuals to achieve maximum performance, adverse budget variances are to be expected. In such a situation it is essential that adverse budget variances are not used by management as a punitive device, since this is likely to encourage budgetees to attempt to obtain looser budgets by either underperforming or deliberately negotiating easily attainable budgets. This may lead to fewer adverse variances, but also to poorer overall performance.

To motivate the best level of actual performance, demanding budgets should be set and small adverse variances should be regarded as a healthy sign and not as something to be avoided. If budgets are always achieved with no adverse variances, this indicates that the standards are too loose to motivate the best possible results.

Participation in the budgeting and target setting process

Participation relates to the extent that subordinates or budgetees are able to influence the figures that are incorporated in their budgets or targets. Participation is sometimes referred to as **bottom-up budget setting** whereas a non-participatory approach whereby subordinates have little influence on the target setting process is sometimes called **top-down budget setting**

Allowing individuals to participate in the setting of performance targets has several advantages. First, individuals are more likely to accept the targets and be committed to achieving them if they have been involved in the target setting process. Second, participation can reduce the information asymmetry gap that applies when standards are imposed from above. Subordinates have more information than their superiors on the relationships between outputs and inputs and the constraints that exist at the operating level whereas the superiors have a broader view of the organization as a whole and the resource constraints that apply. This information sharing process enables more effective targets to be set that attempt to deal with both operational and organizational constraints. Finally, imposed standards can encourage negative attitudes and result in demotivation and alienation. This in turn can lead to a rejection of the targets and poor performance.

Participation has been advocated by many writers as a means of making tasks more challenging and giving individuals a greater sense of responsibility. For many years participation in decision-making was thought to be a panacea for effective organizational effort but this school of thought was later challenged. The debate has never been resolved. The believers have never been able to demonstrate that participation really does have a

FIGURE 14.2 *The effect of budget difficulty on performance. Source: Otley (1987).*

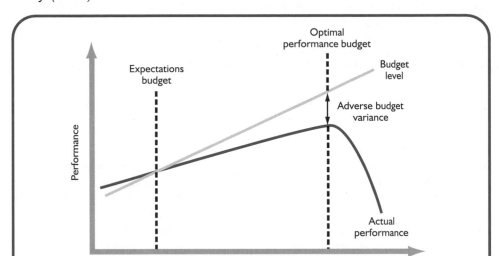

positive effect on productivity and the sceptics have never been able to prove the opposite (Macintosh, 1985). The empirical studies have presented conflicting evidence on the usefulness of participation in the management process. For every study indicating that participation leads to better attitudes and improved performance, an alternative frequently exists suggesting the opposite.

Because of the conflicting findings relating to the effectiveness of participation research has tended to concentrate on studying how various factors influence the effectiveness of participation. Hopwood (1978) identified the importance of the work situation in determining the appropriateness of participation. He states:

> In highly programmed, environmentally and technologically constrained areas, where speed and detailed control are essential for efficiency, participative approaches may have much less to offer from the point of view of the more economic aspects of organizational effectiveness... In contrast, in areas where flexibility, innovation and the capacity to deal with unanticipated problems are important, participation in decision-making may offer a more immediate and more narrowly economic payoff than more authoritarian styles.

The evidence from the various studies suggests that participative styles of management will not necessarily be more effective than other styles, and that participative methods should be used with care. It is therefore necessary to identify those situations where there is evidence that participative methods are effective, rather than to introduce universal application into organizations. Participation must be used selectively; but if it is used in the right circumstances, it has an enormous potential for encouraging the commitment to organizational goals, improving attitudes towards the budgeting system, and increasing subsequent performance. Note, however, at this stage that participation does suffer from the limitation that performance is measured by precisely the same standard that the budgetee has been involved in setting. This gives the budgetee the opportunity to negotiate lower targets that increase the probability of target achievement and the accompanying rewards. Therefore an improvement in performance – in terms of comparison with the budget – may result merely from a lowering of the standard. Ideally external reference points should be available, since this can provide an indication as to whether the participation process leads to low performance because of loose standards.

Non-financial performance measures

Earlier in this chapter it was pointed out that performance reports (such as the one illustrated in Exhibit 14.1) should not include only financial measures. In addition, non-financial measures should also be reported. There is a danger that if performance reports include only those items which can be expressed in monetary terms, managers will concentrate on only these variables and ignore other important variables that cannot easily be quantified in monetary terms. It is always possible to obtain short-term improvements in cost control by hierarchical pressure to cut costs and raise productivity, but this will eventually have negative effects on managerial performance in the form of adverse motivational changes, increased labour turnover and reduced product quality. The problem is that reductions in costs are measured and included in performance reports, but the state of the morale of a department cannot easily be measured. Performance reports should therefore be broadened to incorporate other variables besides costs and revenues. Unfortunately, performance reports based only on costs and revenues do not give a sufficient indication of the future results that can be expected from present actions.

Financial summaries of performance provide only a limited view of the efficiency and effectiveness of actual operations. Consider a situation where a purchasing department regularly achieved the budget for all expense items. The message from a responsibility performance reporting system that incorporates only financial measures suggests that the department was well managed. However, the department provided a poor service to the production departments. Low-cost suppliers were selected who provide poor-quality materials and frequently failed to meet delivery dates. This caused much wasted effort in chasing up orders and prejudiced the company's ability to deliver to its customers on time. To evaluate the performance of the department there is clearly a need to incorporate non-financial measures that provide information on the quality of the service provided by the department.

In recent years there has been a shift from treating financial figures as the foundation for performance measurement and control to treating them as one among a broader set of measures. In today's worldwide competitive environment companies are competing in terms of product quality, delivery, reliability, after-sales service and customer satisfaction. None of these variables is directly measured by responsibility performance reporting systems that rely solely on financial measures, despite the fact that they represent major goals of world-class manufacturing companies. Companies are also adopting new manufacturing techniques and technologies that focus on minimizing throughput times, stock levels and set-up times. By focusing mainly on measuring costs, there is a danger that the performance reporting system will motivate managers to focus exclusively on cost reduction and ignore other important strategic manufacturing goals.

The changes described above have resulted in much greater emphasis being placed on non-financial performance measures that provide feedback on the key variables required to compete successfully in today's competitive environment. These non-financial measures focus on such factors as quality, reliability, flexibility and delivery performance. Such factors are seen as increasingly crucial in today's competitive environment. Typical non-financial measures include defects as a percentage of good production, frequency of machine breakdowns, percentage of deliveries not on time, customer surveys and market shares for each major product.

EXHIBIT 14.2

Customer order processing activity

	(£000s)
Traditional analysis	
Salaries	320
Stationery	40
Travel	140
Telephone	40
Depreciation of equipment	40
	580
ABM analysis	
Preparing quotations	120
Receiving customer orders	190
Assessing the creditworthiness of customers	100
Expediting	80
Resolving customer problems	90
	580

Activity-based cost management

So far in this chapter the major features of traditional management accounting control systems and the mechanisms that can be used to control costs have been described. Traditional management accounting control systems focus mainly on comparing actual results against a pre-set standard (typically the budget), identifying and analysing variances and taking remedial action to ensure that future outcomes conform with budgeted outcomes. Traditional systems have been criticized because they tend to be based on the preservation of the *status-quo* and the ways of performing existing activities are not reviewed. The emphasis is on cost containment rather than cost reduction.

During the 1990s increasing emphasis has been given to **cost management** where the focus is on cost reduction and continuous improvement and change rather than cost containment. Whereas traditional cost control systems are routinely applied on a continuous basis, cost management tends to be applied on an *ad hoc* basis when an opportunity for cost reduction is identified. Cost management consists of those actions that are taken by managers to reduce costs, some of which are prioritized on the basis of information extracted from an ABC system.

The early adopters of activity-based costing (ABC) used it to produce more accurate product (or service) costs but it soon became apparent to the users that it could be extended beyond purely product costing to a range of cost management applications. The terms **activity-based management (ABM)** or **activity-based cost management (ABCM)** are used to describe the cost management applications of ABC. To implement an ABM system only the first three of the four stages described in Chapter 11 for designing an activity-based product costing system are required. They are:

1. identifying the major activities that take place in an organization;
2. assigning costs to cost pools/cost centres for each activity;
3. determining the cost driver for each major activity.

Thus, firms can omit the final stage of assigning activity costs to products and adopt ABC solely for cost management without activity-based product costing. Alternatively, organizations can design an activity-based system that incorporates both ABM and activity-based product costing but note that only the first three stages are required for ABM.

ABM views the business as a set of linked activities that ultimately add value to the customer. It focuses on managing the business on the basis of the activities that make up the organization. ABM is based on the premise that activities consume costs. Therefore by managing activities costs will be managed in the long term. The goal of ABM is to enable customer needs to be satisfied while making fewer demands on organizational resources. Besides providing information on what activities are performed, ABM provides information on the cost of activities, why the activities are undertaken, and how well they are performed.

Traditional budget and control reports analyse costs by types of expense for each responsibility centre. In contrast, ABM analyses costs by activities and thus provides management with information on why costs are incurred and the output from the activity (in terms of cost drivers). Exhibit 14.2 illustrates the difference between the conventional analysis and the activity-based analysis in respect of customer order processing. The major differences are that the ABM approach reports by *activities* whereas the traditional analysis is by *departments*. Also ABM reporting is by sub-activities but traditional reporting is by expense categories. Another distinguishing feature of ABM reporting is that it often reports information on activities that cross departmental boundaries. For example, different production departments and the distribution department might undertake customer processing activities. They may resolve customer problems by expediting late deliveries. The finance department may assess customer credit worthiness and the remaining customer processing activities might be undertaken by the customer service department. Therefore the total cost of the customer processing activity could be considerably in excess of the costs that are assigned to the customer service department. However, to simplify the presentation it is assumed in Exhibit 14.2 that the departmental and activity costs are identical but if the cost of the customer order processing activity was found to be, say, three times the amount assigned to the customer service department, this would be important information because it may change the way in which the managers view the activity. For example, the managers may give more attention to reducing the costs of the customer processing activity.

It is apparent from an examination of Exhibit 14.2 that the ABM approach provides more meaningful information. It gives more visibility to the cost of undertaking the activities that make up the organization and may raise issues for management action that are not highlighted by the traditional analysis. For example, why is £90 000 spent on resolving customer problems? Attention-directing information such as this is important for managing the cost of the activities.

Johnson (1990) suggests that knowing costs by activities is a catalyst that eventually triggers the action necessary to become competitive. Consider a situation where salespersons, as a result of costing activities, are informed that it costs £50 to process a customer's order. They therefore become aware that it is questionable to pursue orders with a low sales value. By eliminating many small orders, and concentrating on larger value orders, the demand for customer-processing activities should decrease, and future spending on this activity should be reduced.

Prior to the introduction of ABM most organizations have been unaware of the cost of undertaking the activities that make up the organization. Knowing the cost of activities enables those activities with the highest cost to be highlighted so that they can be prioritized for detailed studies to ascertain whether they can be eliminated or performed more efficiently. To identify and prioritize the potential for cost reduction many organizations have found it useful to classity activities as either value added or non-value added. Definitions of what constitutes value added and non-value added activities vary. A common definition is that a **value added activity** is an activity that customers perceive as adding usefulness to the product or service they purchase. For example, painting a car would be a value added activity in an organization that manufactures cars. Other definitions are an activity that is being performed as efficiently as possible or an activity that supports the primary objective of producing outputs.

In contrast, a **non-value added activity** is an activity where there is an opportunity for cost reduction without reducing the product's service potential to the customer. Examples of non-value added activities include inspecting, storing and moving raw materials. The cost of these activities can be reduced without reducing the value of the products to the customers. Non-value added activities are essentially those activities that customers should not be expected to pay for. Reporting the cost of non-value added activities draw management's attention to the vast amount of waste that has been tolerated by the organization. This should prioritize those activities with the greatest potential for cost reduction by eliminating or carrying them out more effectively, such as reducing material movements, improving production flows and taking actions to reduce stock levels. Taking action to reduce or eliminate non-value added activities is given top priority because by doing so the organization permanently reduces the cost it incurs without reducing the value of the product to the customer.

A survey of activity-based costing applications by Innes and Mitchell (1995a) indicated that many organizations use cost driver rates as a measure of cost efficiency and performance for the activity concerned. The cost driver rate is computed by dividing the activity costs by the cost driver volume. For example, if the number of purchase orders is the cost driver and the cost of processing 10 000 purchase orders is £100 000, the cost per purchasing order is £10. Assume now that improvements in procedures in the purchasing activity enable costs to be reduced to £80 000. If the same number of orders can be processed with fewer resources the cost of processing an order will be reduced to £8. Reporting and focusing on cost driver rates can thus be used to motivate managers to reduce the cost of performing activities.

Summary

The aim of management control systems is to influence employee behaviours in desirable ways in order to increase the probability that an organization's objectives will be achieved. Companies use many different control mechanisms to cope with the problem of organizational control. To fully understand the role that management accounting control systems play in the control process, it is necessary to be aware of how they relate to the entire array of control mechanisms used by firms.

We therefore initially examined the different types of controls that are used by firms. Three different categories were identified – action/behavioural controls, personnel and cultural controls and results/output controls. With action controls the actions themselves are the focus of controls. They are usable and effective only when managers know what actions are desirable (or undesirable) and have the ability to make sure that the desirable actions occur (or that the undesirable actions do not occur). Personnel controls help employees do a good job by building on employees' natural tendencies to control themselves. They include selection and placement, training and job design. Cultural controls represent a set of values, social norms and beliefs that are shared by members of the organization and that influence their actions. Output or results controls involve collecting and reporting information about the outcomes of work effort. They involve the following stages – establishing results and performance targets, measuring performance and providing rewards or punishments based on an employee's ability to achieve the performance target.

The creation of responsibility centres is a fundamental part of management accounting control systems. Four different types of responsibility centres were described. They were cost (or expense) centres, revenue centres, profit centres and investment centres. Management accounting control systems have two core elements. The first, is the formal planning processes such as budgeting and long-term planning. These processes are used for establishing performance expectations for evaluating performance. The second is responsibility accounting which involves the creation of responsibility centres. Responsibility centres enable accountability for financial results/outcomes to be allocated to individuals throughout the firm. The objective of responsibility accounting is to accumulate costs and revenues for each individual responsibility centre so that the deviations from a performance target can be attributed to the individual who is accountable. For each responsibility centre the process involves setting a performance target, measuring performance, comparing performance against the target, analysing the variances and taking action where significant variances exist between actual and target performance.

Responsibility accounting involves:

1. distinguishing between those items which managers can control and for which they should be held accountable and those items over which they have no control and for which they are not held accountable;
2. determining how challenging the financial targets should be;
3. determining how much influence managers should have in the setting of financial targets.

The controllability principle states that it is appropriate to charge to an area of responsibility only those costs that are significantly influenced by the manager of that responsibility centre. The general rule that should be applied is to hold employees accountable for the performance area you want them to pay attention to.

Different types of financial performance targets have been described and the impact of their level of difficulty on motivation and performance examined.

Participation or bottom-up budget setting was compared with top-down budget setting. The benefits arising from participation in the budget process were outlined. It was concluded that participation must be used selectively; but if it is used in the right circumstances, it has an enormous potential for encouraging commitment to organizational goals, improving attitudes towards the budgeting system, and increasing subsequent performance.

It was emphasized that the performance reporting system should not include only financial measures. The key non-financial measures should also be reported for each responsibility centre that are necessary to compute effectively in today's global competitive environment. Finally, it was explained how ABC can be extended to cost management in the form of activity-based cost management.

Key Terms and Concepts

action controls (p. 340)
activity-based cost management (ABCM) (p. 355)
activity-based management (ABM) (p. 355)
aspiration level (p. 352)
behavioural controls (p. 340)
bottom-up budget setting (p. 352)
clan controls (p. 341)
control (p. 339)
controllability principle (p. 347)
controls (p. 339)
cost centres (p. 345)
cost management (p. 355)
cultural controls (p. 341)
cybernetic system (p. 343)
discretionary expense centres (p. 345)
engineered targets (p. 351)
expense centres (p. 345)
feedback control (p. 343)
feed-forward control (p. 343)

flexible budgets (p. 349)
historical targets (p. 351)
investment centres (p. 346)
negotiated targets (p. 351)
non-value added activity (p. 357)
output controls (p. 342)
participation (p. 352)
personnel controls (p. 341)
profit centres (p. 346)
responsibility accounting (p. 346)
results controls (p. 342)
revenue centres (p. 346)
social control (p. 341)
standard cost centres (p. 345)
top-down budget setting (p. 352)
value-added activity (p. 357)
variance (pp. 343, 345)
variance analysis (p. 349)

Key Examination Points

Essay questions are the most appropriate mechanism for testing students' understanding of the content of this chapter. However, they tend not to be frequently used on first-year courses but they are widely used on courses beyond the introductory level. The most frequently examined topic on first year courses is to prepare flexible budgets (e.g. Review problem 3). Also questions requiring you to comment on, or redraft performance reports are frequently set (e.g. Review problems 4 and 6). A common error is to compare actual performance with an unflexed budget. If you are required to prepare flexible budgets remember to flex the budget on the basis of targeted costs for actual output rather than input measures, such as direct labour or input hours.

Review Problems

(For additional problems without answers relating to the content of this chapter you should refer to pages 516–525.)

1. A fixed budget is:
   A a budget for a single level of activity;
   B used when the mix of products is fixed in advance of the budget period;
   C a budget which ignores inflation;
   D used only for fixed costs;
   E an overhead cost budget.   *CIMA Stage 2*

2. A flexible budget is:
   A a budget of variable production costs only;
   B a budget which is updated with actual costs and revenues as they occur during the budget period;
   C a budget which shows the costs and revenues at different levels of activity;
   D a budget which is prepared using a computer spreadsheet model;
   E a budget which is prepared for a period of six months and reviewed monthly; following

such review a further one month's budget is prepared. *CIMA Stage 2*

3. (a) Explain what is meant by the terms 'fixed budget' and 'flexible budget', and state the main objective of preparing flexible budgets. *(5 marks)*

(b) (i) Prepare a flexible budget for 20X5 for the overhead expenses of a production department at the activity levels of 80%, 90% and 100%, using the information listed below. *(12 marks)*

1. The direct labour hourly rate is expected to be £3.75.

2. 100% activity represents 60 000 direct labour hours.

3. Variable costs:
   Indirect labour
   £0.75 per direct labour hour
   Consumable supplies
   £0.375 per direct labour hour
   Canteen and other welfare services
   6% of direct *and* indirect labour costs

4. Semi-variable costs are expected to correlate with the direct labour hours in the same manner as for the last five years, which was:

Year	Direct labour hours	Semi-variable costs (£)
20X0	64 000	20 800
20X1	59 000	19 800
20X2	53 000	18 600
20X3	49 000	17 800
20X4	40 000 (estimate)	16 000 (estimate)

5. Fixed costs:

	(£)
Depreciation	18 000
Maintenance	10 000
Insurance	4 000
Rates	15 000
Management salaries	25 000

6. Inflation is to be ignored.

(ii) Calculate the budget cost allowance for 20X5 assuming that 57 000 direct labour hours are worked. *(3 marks)*
(Total 20 marks)
CIMA Cost Accounting 1

4. The Victorial Hospital is located in a holiday resort that attracts visitors to such an extent that the population of the area is trebled for the summer months of June, July and August. From past experience, this influx of visitors doubles the activity of the hospital during these months. The annual budget for the hospital's laundry department is broken down into four quarters, namely April–June, July–September, October–December and January–March, by dividing the annual budgeted figures by four. The budgeting work has been done for the current year by the secretary of the hospital using the previous year's figures and adding 16%. It is realized by the Hospital Authority that management information for control purposes needs to be improved, and you have been recruited to help to introduce a system of responsibility accounting.

You are required, from the information given, to:

(a) comment on the way in which the quarterly budgets have been prepared and to suggest improvements that could be introduced when preparing the budgets for 2001/2002;

(b) state what information you would like to flow from the actual against budget comparison (note that calculated figures are *not* required);

(c) state the amendments that would be needed to the current practice of budgeting and reporting to enable the report shown below to be used as a measure of the efficiency of the laundry manager.

Victorial Hospital – Laundry department
Report for quarter ended 30 September 2000

	Budget	Actual
Patients days	9 000	12 000
Weight processed (kgs)	180 000	240 000
	(£)	(£)
Costs:		
Wages	8 800	12 320
Overtime premium	1 400	2 100
Detergents and other supplies	1 800	2 700

Water, water softening and heating	2 000	2 500
Maintenance	1 000	1 500
Depreciation of plant	2 000	2 000
Manager's salary	1 250	1 500
Overhead, apportioned:		
for occupancy	4 000	4 250
for administration	5 000	5 750

(15 marks)
CIMA Cost Accounting 1

5. Club Atlantic is an all-weather holiday complex providing holidays throughout the year. The fee charged to guests is fully inclusive of accommodation and all meals. However, because the holiday industry is so competitive, Club Atlantic is only able to generate profits by maintaining strict financial control of all activities.

The club's restaurant is one area where there is a constant need to monitor costs. Susan Green is the manager of the restaurant. At the beginning of each year she is given an annual budget which is then broken down into months. Each month she receives a statement monitoring actual costs against the annual budget and highlighting any variances. The statement for the month ended 31 October is reproduced below along with a list of assumptions:

**Club Atlantic Restaurant Performance
Statement
Month to 31 October**

	Actual	Budget	Variance (over)/ under
Number of guest days	11 160	9 600	(1560)
	(£)	(£)	(£)
Food	20 500	20 160	(340)
Cleaning materials	2 232	1 920	(312)
Heat, light and power	2 050	2 400	350
Catering wages	8 400	7 200	(1200)
Rent rates, insurance and depreciation	1 860	1 800	(60)
	35 042	33 480	(1562)

Assumptions:
(a) The budget has been calculated on the basis of a 30-day calendar month with the cost of rents, insurance and depreciation being an apportionment of the fixed annual charge.
(b) The budgeted catering wages assume that:
  (i) there is 1 member of the catering staff for every 40 guests staying at the complex;
  (ii) the daily cost of a member of the catering staff is £30.
(c) All other budgeted costs are variable costs based on the number of guest days.

Task 1
Using the data above, prepare a revised performance statement using flexible budgeting. Your statement should show both the revised budget and the revised variances. Club Atlantic uses the existing budgets and performance statements to motivate its managers as well as for financial control. If managers keep expenses below budget they receive a bonus in addition to their salaries. A colleague of Susan is Brian Hilton. Brian is in charge of the swimming pool and golf course, both of which have high levels of fixed costs. Each month he manages to keep expenses below budget and in return enjoys regular bonuses. Under the current reporting system, Susan Green only rarely receives a bonus.

At a recent meeting with Club Atlantic's directors Susan Green expressed concern that the performance statement was not a valid reflection of her management of the restaurant. You are currently employed by Hall and Co., the club's auditors, and the directors of Club Atlantic have asked you to advice them whether there is any justification for Susan Green's concern.

At the meeting with the Club's directors, you were asked the following questions:
(a) Do budgets motivate managers to achieve objectives?
(b) Does motivating managers lead to improved performance?
(c) Does the current method of reporting performance motivate Susan Green and Brian Hilton to be more efficient?

Task 2
Write a *brief* letter to the directors of Club Atlantic addressing their question and justifying your answers.
Note: You should make use of the data given in this task plus your findings in Task 1.
AAT Technicians Stage

6. (a) The following report has been prepared, relating to one product for March. This has been sent to the appropriate product manager as part of PDC Limited's monitoring procedures.

Monthly variance report – March 1

	Actual	Budget	Variance	%
Production volume (units)	9 905	10 000	95 A	0.95 A
Sales volume (units)	9 500	10 000	500 A	5.00 A
Sales revenue (£)	27 700	30 000	2300 A	7.67 A
Direct material (kg)	9 800	10 000	200 F	2.00 F
Direct material (£)	9 600	10 000	400 F	4.00 F
Direct labour (hours)	2 500	2 400	100 A	4.17 A
Direct labour (£)	8 500	8 400	100 A	1.19 A
Contribution (£)	9 600	11 600	2000 A	17.24 A

The product manager has complained that the report ignores the principle of flexible budgeting and is unfair.

Required:
Prepare a report addressed to the management team which comments critically on the monthly variance report. Include as an appendix to your report the layout of a revised monthly variance report which will be more useful to the product manager. Include row and column headings, but do *not* calculate the contents of the report.

(*15 marks*)

(b) Explain the differences between budgetary control and standard costing/variance analysis. In what circumstances would an organization find it beneficial to operate both of these cost control systems? (*5 marks*)

(*Total 20 marks*)
CIMA Operational Cost Accounting Stage 2

Solutions to Review Problems

SOLUTION 1
Answer = A

SOLUTION 2
Answer = C

SOLUTION 3
(a) A fixed budget refers to a budget which is designed to remain unchanged irrespective of the level of activity, whereas a flexible budget is a budget which adjusts the expense items for different levels of activity. See 'Flexible budgets' in Chapter 14 for an explanation of the objectives of flexible budgeting.

(b) (i)

Direct labour	£180 000	£202 500	£225 000
Direct labour hours	48 000	54 000	60 000

Flexible budget (overhead expenditure):			
Activity levels	80%	90%	100%
Direct labour hours	48 000	54 000	60 000
Variable costs	(£)	(£)	(£)
Indirect labour at £0.75 per direct labour hour	36 000	40 500	45 000
Consumable supplies at £0.375 per direct labour hour	18 000	20 250	22 500
Canteen and other welfare services at 6% of direct plus indirect wages	12 960	14 580	16 200
Semi-variable: variable (W1)	9 600	10 800	12 000
	76 560	86 130	95 700
Semi-variable: fixed (W1)	8 000	8 000	8 000
Fixed costs:			
Depreciation	18 000	18 000	18 000
Maintenance	10 000	10 000	10 000
Insurance	4 000	4 000	4 000
Rates	15 000	15 000	15 000
Management salaries	25 000	25 000	25 000
	156 560	166 130	175 700

Workings:
(W1) Obtained by using High and Low points method:

			(£)
High	64 000	Direct labour hours	20 800
Low	40 000	Direct labour hours	16 000
	24 000		4 800

$\frac{£4 800}{24 000} = £0.20$ per direct labour hour

$64 000 \times £0.20 = £12 800$ variable costs

Total costs £20 800
∴ Fixed costs £8 000

(ii) Variable cost
$(57 000/60 000 \times £95 700)$ 90 915
Fixed costs 80 000
Budgeted cost allowance 170 915

SOLUTION 4

(a) (i) Activity varies from month to month, but quarterly budgets are set by dividing total annual expenditure by 4.

(ii) The budget ought to be analysed by shorter intervals (e.g. monthly) and costs estimated in relation to monthly activity.

(iii) For control purposes monthly comparisons and cumulative monthly comparisons of planned and actual expenditure to date should be made.

(iv) The budget holder does not participate in the setting of budgets.

(v) An incremental budget approach is adopted. A zero-based approach would be more appropriate.

(vi) The budget should distinguish between controllable and uncontrollable expenditure.

(b) The information that should flow from a comparison of the actual and budgeted expenditure would consist of the variances for the month and year to date analysed into the following categories:

(i) controllable and uncontrollable items;

(ii) price and quantity variances with price variance analysed by inflationary and non-inflationary effects.

(c) (i) Flexible budgets should be prepared on a monthly basis. Possible measures of activity are number of patient days or expected laundry weight.

(ii) The laundry manager should participate in the budgetary process.

(iii) Costs should be classified into controllable and non-controllable items.

(iv) Variances should be reported and analysed by price and quantity on a monthly and cumulative basis.

(v) Comments should be added explaining possible reasons for the variances.

SOLUTION 5

Task 1:
Performance Statement – Month to 31 October
Number of guest days = Original budget   9 600
                              Flexed budget   11 160

Controllable expenses	Flexed budget (£)	Actual (£)	Variance (£)
Food (1)	23 436	20 500	2936F
Cleaning materials (2)	2 232	2 232	0
Heat, light and power (3)	2 790	2 050	740F
Catering staff wages (4)	8 370	8 400	30A
	36 828	33 182	3646F
Non-controllable expenses			
Rent, rates, insurance and depreciation (5)	1 860	1 860	0

Notes:
(1) £20 160/9600 × 11 160.
(2) £1920/9600 × 11 160.
(3) £2400/9600 × 11 160.
(4) 11 160/40 × £30.
(5) Original fixed budget based on 30 days but October is a 31-day month (£1800/30 × 31).

Task 2:
(a) See the sections on the multiple functions of budgets (motivation) in Chapter 13 and 'Setting financial performance targets' in Chapter 14 for the answers to this question.

(b) Motivating managers ought to result in improved performance. However, besides motivation, improved performance is also dependent on managerial ability, training, education and the existence of a favourable environment. Therefore motivating managers is not guaranteed to lead to improved performance.

(c) The use of a fixed budget is unlikely to encourage managers to become more efficient where budgeted expenses are variable with activity. In the original performance report actual expenditure for 11.160 guest days is compared with budgeted expenditure for 9600 days. It is misleading to compare actual costs at one level of activity with budgeted costs at another level of activity. Where the actual level of activity is above the budgeted level adverse variances are likely to be reported for variable cost items. Managers will therefore be motivated to reduce activity so that favourable variances will be reported. Therefore it is not surprising that Susan Green has expressed concern that the performance statement does not reflect a valid reflection of her performance. In contrast, most of Brian Hilton's expenses are fixed and costs will not increase when volume increases. A failure to flex the budget will therefore not distort his performance.

To motivate, challenging budgets should be set and small adverse variances should normally be regarded as a healthy sign and not something to be avoided. If budgets are always achieved with no adverse variances this may indicate that undemanding budgets may have been set which are unlikely to motivate best possible performance. This situation could apply to Brian Hilton who always appears to report favourable variances.

SOLUTION 6

(a) The report should include the following points:

   (i) Actuals are compared with a fixed budget which results in a comparison of actual and budgeted expenses for different output levels. Flexible budgeting should be adopted for performance reporting.

   (ii) Variances should be analysed into their price and quantity elements (see Chapter 15) since different managers are likely to be accountable for different categories of variances.

   (iii) The report is confusing with both physical volumes and values being presented for each budgeted item. They should be reported separately to avoid confusion.

   (iv) The report should be split into two separate sections – a section for controllable expenses and another for uncontrollable expenses. It is possible that all the expenses are controllable but if this is the case it should be clearly indicated in the report. No controllable fixed costs are included in the report. If such expenses do exist they should be reported separately.

   (v) No indication is given of the output which should have been attained from the actual level of activity.

Revised monthly variance report:

Original budget : Sales volume
                   : Production volume
Actuals   : Sales volume
                   : Production volume

	Flexed budget (£)	Actuals (£)	Quantity variance (£)	Price variance (£)	Total variance (£)	Cumulative variances for the year (£)
Sales (based on original budget)						
Less controllable expenses:						
Direct materials						
Direct labour						
Controllable contribution						
Less controllable fixed costs						
Controllable profit						

(b) This question requires an understanding of material covered in Chapter 15. Standard costing is most suited to controlling those activities that involve repetitive operations. Standard costing procedures cannot easily be applied to non-manufacturing activities where the operations are of a non-repetitive nature, since there is no basis for observing repetitive operations and consequently standards cannot easily be set.

Where standards cannot easily be applied budgets are used to control costs. A budget relates to an entire activity or operations where standards can be applied to the units of output and thus provide a basis for the detailed analysis of variances.

A single organization might use standard costing to control the costs relating to manufacturing activities and budgetary control to control the costs of support departments and non-manufacturing activities.

15

Standard costing and variance analysis

In the previous chapter the major features of management accounting control systems were examined. The different types of controls used by companies were described so that the elements of management accounting control systems could be considered within the context of the overall control process. A broad approach to control was adopted and the detailed procedures of financial controls were not examined. In this chapter we shall focus on one of the detailed financial controls that are used by organizations.

We shall consider a financial control system that enables the deviations from budget to be analysed in detail, thus enabling costs to be controlled more effectively. This system of control is called standard costing. In particular, we shall examine how a standard costing system operates and how the variances are calculated and recorded. Standard costing systems are applied in standard cost centres which were described in the previous chapter. You will recall that the main features of standard cost centres are that output can be measured and the input required to produce each unit of output can be specified. In addition, the sales variances that are described in this chapter can also be applied in the revenue centres.

Standard costs are predetermined costs; they are target costs that should be incurred under efficient operating conditions. They are not the same as **budgeted costs**. A budget relates to an entire activity or operation; a standard presents the same information on a per unit basis. A standard therefore provides cost expectations per unit of activity and a budget provides the cost expectation for the total activity. If the budget output for a product is for 10 000 units and the standard cost is £3 per unit, budgeted cost will be £30 000. We shall see that establishing standard costs for each unit produced enables a detailed analysis to be made of the difference between the budgeted cost and the actual cost so that costs can be controlled more effectively.

In the first part of the chapter (pages 368–389) we shall concentrate on those variances that are likely to be useful for cost control purposes. The final part describes those variances that are required for financial accounting purposes but that are not particularly useful for cost control. If your course does not relate

Learning objectives

After studying this chapter, you should be able to:

- explain how standard costs are set;
- explain the meaning of standard hours produced;
- define basic, ideal and currently attainable standards;
- explain how a standard costing system operates;
- calculate labour, material, overhead and sales margin variances and reconcile actual profit with budgeted profit;
- identify the causes of labour, material, overhead and sales margin variances;
- construct a departmental performance report;
- distinguish between standard variable costing and standard absorption costing;
- prepare a set of accounts for a standard costing system.

to the disposition of variances for financial accounting purposes or the recording of standard costs in the accounts, you can omit pages 389–395

Operation of a standard costing system

Standard costing is most suited to an organization whose activities consist of a series of *common* or *repetitive* operations and the input required to produce each unit of output can be specified. It is therefore relevant in manufacturing companies, since the processes involved are often of a repetitive nature. Standard costing procedures can also be applied in service industries such as units within banks, where output can be measured in terms of the number of cheques or the number of loan applications processed, and there are also well-defined input–output relationships. Standard costing cannot, however, be applied to activities of a non-repetitive nature, since there is no basis for observing repetitive operations and consequently standards cannot be set.

A standard costing system can be applied to organizations that produce many different products, as long as production consists of a series of common operations. For example, if the output from a factory is the result of five common operations, it is possible to produce many different product variations from these operations. It is therefore possible that a large product range may result from a small number of common operations. Thus standard costs should be developed for repetitive operations and product standard costs are derived simply by combining the standard costs from the operations which are necessary to make the product. This process is illustrated in Exhibit 15.1.

It is assumed that the standard costs are £20, £30, £40 and £50 for each of the operations 1 to 4. The standard cost for *product* 100 is therefore £110, which consists of £20 for operation 1, plus £40 and £50 for operations 3 and 4. The standard costs for each of the other products are calculated in a similar manner. In addition, the total standard cost for the total output of each operation for the period has been calculated. For example, six items of operation number 1 have been completed, giving a total standard cost of £120 for this operation (six items at £20 each). Three items of operation 2 have been completed, giving a total standard cost of £90, and so on.

VARIANCES ALLOCATED TO RESPONSIBILITY CENTRES

You can see from Exhibit 15.1 that different responsibility centres are responsible for each operation. For example, responsibility centre A is responsible for operation 1, responsibility centre B for operation 2, and so on. Consequently, there is no point in comparing the actual cost of *product* 100 with the standard cost of £110 for the purposes of control, since responsibility centres A, C and D are responsible for the variance. None of the responsibility centres is solely answerable for the variance. Cost control requires that responsibility centres be identified with the standard cost for the output achieved. Therefore if the actual costs for responsibility centre A are compared with the standard cost of £120 for the production of the six items (see first row in Exhibit 15.1), the manager

EXHIBIT 15.1

Standard costs analysed by operations and products

of this responsibility centre will be answerable for the full amount of the variance. Only by comparing total actual costs with total standard costs *for each operation or responsibility centre* for a period can control be effectively achieved. A

Responsibility centre	Operation no. and standard cost		Products							Total standard cost	Actual cost
	No.	(£)	100	101	102	103	104	105	106	(£)	
A	1	20	✓	✓		✓	✓	✓	✓	120	
B	2	30		✓		✓		✓		90	
C	3	40	✓		✓		✓			120	
D	4	50	✓	✓	✓				✓	200	
Standard product cost			£110	£100	£90	£50	£60	£50	£70	530	

comparison of standard *product* costs (i.e. the columns in Exhibit 15.1) with actual costs that involves several different responsibility centres is clearly inappropriate.

Figure 15.1 provides an overview of the operation of a standard costing system. You will see that the standard costs for the actual output for a particular period are traced to the managers of responsibility centres who are responsible for the various operations. The actual costs for the same period are also charged to the responsibility centres. Standard and actual costs are compared and the variance is reported. For example, if the actual cost for the output of the six items produced in responsibility centre A during the period is £220 and the standard cost is £120 (Exhibit 15.1), a variance of £100 will be reported.

DETAILED ANALYSIS OF VARIANCES

Figure 15.1 provides an overview of a standard costing system. You can see from the box below the first arrow in Figure 15.1 that the operation of a standard costing system also enables a detailed analysis of the variances to be reported. For example, variances for each responsibility centre can be identified by each element of cost and analysed according to the price and quantity content. The accountant assists managers by pinpointing where the variances have arisen and the responsibility managers can undertake to carry out the appropriate investigations to identify the reasons for the variance. For example, the accountant might identify the reason for a direct materials variance as being excessive usage of a certain material in a particular process, but the responsibility centre manager must investigate this process and identify the reasons for the excessive usage. Such an investigation should result in appropriate remedial action being taken or, if it is found that the variance is due to a permanent change in the standard, the standard should be changed.

FIGURE 15.1 *An overview of a standard costing sytem.*

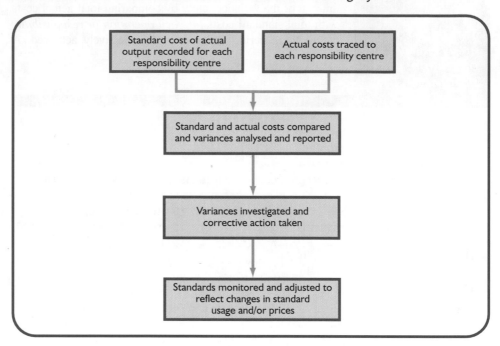

ACTUAL PRODUCT COSTS ARE NOT REQUIRED

It is questionable whether the allocation of actual costs to products serves any useful purpose. Because standard costs represent *future* target costs, they are preferable to actual *past* costs for decision-making. Also, the external financial accounting regulations in most countries specify that if standard product costs provide a reasonable approximation of actual product costs, they are acceptable for inventory valuation calculations for external reporting.

There are therefore strong arguments for not producing actual *product* costs when a standard costing system exists, since this will lead to large clerical savings. However, it must be stressed that actual costs must be accumulated periodically for each operation or responsibility centre, so that comparisons can be made with standard costs. Nevertheless, there will be considerably fewer responsibility centres than products, and the accumulation of actual costs is therefore much less time consuming.

COMPARISONS AFTER THE EVENT

It may be argued that there is little point in comparing actual performance with standard performance, because such comparisons can only be made after the event. Nevertheless, if people know in advance that their performance is going to be judged, they are likely to act differently from the way they would have done if they were aware that their performance was not going to be measured. Furthermore, even though it is not possible for a manager to change his or her performance after the event, an analysis of how well a person has performed in the past may indicate – both to the person concerned and his or her superior – ways of obtaining better performance in the future.

Establishing cost standards

Control over costs is best effected through action at the point where the costs are incurred. Hence the standards should be set for the quantities of material, labour and services to be consumed in performing an *operation*, rather than the complete *product* cost standards. Variances from these standards should be reported to show causes and responsibilities for deviations from standard. Product cost standards are derived by listing and adding the standard costs of operations required to produce a particular product. For example, if you refer to Exhibit 15.1 you will see that the standard cost of product 100 is £110 and is derived from the sum of the standard costs of operations 1, 3 and 4.

There are two approaches that can be used to set standard costs. First, past historical records can be used to estimate labour and material usage. Secondly, standards can be set based on **engineering studies**. With engineering studies a detailed study of each operation is undertaken based on careful specifications of materials, labour and equipment and on controlled observations of operations. If historical records are used to set standards, there is a danger that the latter will include past inefficiencies. With this approach, standards are set based on average past performance for the same or similar operations. Known excess usage of labour or materials should be eliminated or the standards may be tightened by an arbitrary percentage reduction in the quantity of resources required. The disadvantage of this method is that, unlike the engineering method, it does not focus attention on finding the best combination of resources, production methods and product quality. Nevertheless, standards derived from average historical usage do appear to be widely used in practice. (See Exhibit 15.3 on page 376.)

Let us now consider how standards are established for each operation for direct materials, direct labour and overheads using the engineering studies approach. Note that the standard cost for each operation is derived from multiplying the quantity of input that should be used per unit of output (i.e. the quantity standard) by the amount that should be paid for each unit of input (i.e. the price standard).

DIRECT MATERIAL STANDARDS

These are based on product specifications derived from an intensive study of the input *quantity* necessary for each operation. This study should establish the most suitable materials for each product, based on product design and quality policy, and also the optimal quantity that should be used after taking into account any wastage or loss that is considered inevitable in the production process. Material quantity standards are usually recorded on a **bill of materials**. This describes and states the required quantity of materials for each operation to complete the product. A separate bill of materials is maintained for each product. The standard material product cost is then found by multiplying the standard quantities by the appropriate standard prices.

The standard *prices* are obtained from the purchasing department. The standard material prices are based on the assumption that the purchasing department has carried out a suitable search of alternative suppliers and has selected suppliers who can provide the required quantity of sound quality materials at the most competitive price. Normally, price standards take into account the advantages to be obtained by determining the most economical order quantity and quantity discounts, best method of delivery and the most favourable credit terms. However, consideration should also be given to vendor reliability with respect to material quality and meeting scheduled delivery dates. Standard prices then provide a suitable base against which actual prices paid for materials can be evaluated.

DIRECT LABOUR STANDARDS

To set labour standards, activities should be analysed by the different operations. Each operation is studied and an allowed time computed, usually after carrying out a time and motion study. The normal procedure for such a study is to analyse each operation to eliminate any unnecessary elements and to determine the most efficient production method. The most efficient methods of production, equipment and operating conditions are then standardized. This is followed by time measurements that are made to determine the number of standard hours required by an average worker to complete the job. Unavoidable delays such as machine breakdowns and routine maintenance are included in the standard time. Wage rate standards are normally either a matter of company policy or the result of negotiations between management and unions. The agreed wage rates are applied to the standard time allowed to determine the standard labour cost for each operation.

OVERHEAD STANDARDS

The procedure for establishing standard manufacturing overhead rates for a standard costing system is the same as that which is used for establishing predetermined overhead rates as described in Chapter 4. Separate rates for fixed and variable overheads are essential for planning and control. Normally the standard overhead rate will be based on a rate per direct labour hour or machine hour of input.

Fixed overheads are largely independent of changes in activity, and remain constant over wide ranges of activity in the short term. It is therefore inappropriate for short-term cost control purposes to unitize fixed overheads to derive a fixed overhead rate per unit of activity. However, in order to meet the external financial reporting stock valuation requirements, fixed manufacturing overheads must be traced to products. It is therefore necessary to unitize fixed overheads for stock valuation purposes.

The main difference with the treatment of overheads under a standard costing system as opposed to a non-standard costing system is that the product overhead cost is based on the hourly overhead rates multiplied by the *standard hours* (that is, hours which should have been used) rather than the *actual hours* used.

At this stage it is appropriate to summarize the approach that should be used to establish cost standards. Control over costs is best effected through action at the point where they are incurred. Hence standards should be set for labour, materials and variable overheads consumed in performing an *operation*. For stock valuation purposes it is necessary to establish *product cost* standards. Standard manufacturing product costs consist of the total of the standard costs of operations required to produce the product plus the product's standard fixed overhead cost. A standard cost card should be maintained for each product and operation. It reveals the quantity of each unit of input that should be used to produce one unit of output. A typical product standard cost card is illustrated in Exhibit 15.2. In most organizations standard cost cards are now stored on a computer. Standards should be continuously reviewed, and, where significant changes in production methods or input prices occur, they should be changed in order to ensure that standards reflect current targets.

STANDARD HOURS PRODUCED

It is not possible to measure *output* in terms of units produced for a department making several different products or operations. For example, if a department produces 100 units

EXHIBIT 15.2

An illustration of a standard cost card

Date standard set ....   Product: Sigma

Direct materials

Operation no.	Item code	Quantity (kg)	Standard price (£)	A	B	C	D	Totals (£)
					Department			
1	5.001	5	3		£15			
2	7.003	4	4			£16		
								31

Direct labour

Operation no.	Standard hours	Standard rate (£)				
1	7	9	£63			
2	8	9		£72		
						135

Factory overhead

Department	Standard hours	Standard rate (£)				
B	7	3	£21			
C	8	4		£32		
						53
Total manufacturing cost per unit (£)						219

of product X, 200 units of product Y and 300 units of product Z, it is not possible to add the production of these items together, since they are not homogeneous. This problem can be overcome by ascertaining the amount of time, working under efficient conditions, it should take to make each product. This time calculation is called **standard hours produced**. In other words, **standard hours** are an *output* measure that can act as a common denominator for adding together the production of unlike items.

Let us assume that the following standard times are established for the production of one unit of each product:

> Product X   5 standard hours
> Product Y   2 standard hours
> Product Z   3 standard hours

This means that it should take five hours to produce one unit of product X under efficient production conditions. Similar comments apply to products Y and Z. The production for the department will be calculated in standard hours as follows:

Product	Standard time per unit produced (hours)	Actual output (units)	Standard hours produced
X	5	100	500
Y	2	200	400
Z	3	300	900
			1800

Remember that standard hours produced is an output measure, and flexible budget allowances should be based on this. In the illustration we should expect the *output* of 1800 standard hours to take 1800 direct labour hours of *input* if the department works at the prescribed level of efficiency. The department will be inefficient if 1800 standard hours of output are produced using, say, 2000 direct labour hours of input. The flexible budget allowance should therefore be based on 1800 standard hours produced to ensure that no extra allowance is given for the 200 excess hours of input. Otherwise, a manager will obtain a higher budget allowance through being inefficient.

Types of cost standards

The determination of standard costs raises the problem of how demanding the standards should be. Should they represent ideal or faultless performance or should they represent easily attainable performance? Standards are normally classified into three broad categories:

1. basic cost standards;
2. ideal standards;
3. currently attainable standards.

BASIC COST STANDARDS

Basic cost standards represent constant standards that are left unchanged over long periods. The main advantage of basic standards is that a base is provided for a comparison with actual costs through a period of years with the same standard, and efficiency trends can be established over time. When changes occur in methods of production, price levels or other relevant factors, basic standards are not very useful, since they do not represent *current* target costs. For this reason basic cost standards are seldom used.

IDEAL STANDARDS

Ideal standards represent perfect performance. Ideal standard costs are the minimum costs that are possible under the most efficient operating conditions. Ideal standards are unlikely to be used in practice because they may have an adverse impact on employee motivation. Such standards constitute goals to be aimed for rather than performance that can currently be achieved.

CURRENTLY ATTAINABLE STANDARD COSTS

These standards represent those costs that should be incurred under efficient operating conditions. They are standards that are difficult, but not impossible, to achieve. **Attainable standards** are easier to achieve than ideal standards because allowances are made for normal spoilage, machine breakdowns and lost time. The fact that these standards represent a target that can be achieved under efficient conditions, but which is also viewed as being neither too easy to achieve nor impossible to achieve, provides the best norm to which actual costs should be compared. Attainable standards can vary in terms of the level of difficulty. For example, if tight attainable standards are set over a given time period, there might only be a 70% probability that the standard will be attained. On the other hand, looser attainable standards might be set with a probability of 90% attainment. Attainable standards are equivalent to highly achievable standards described in Chapter 14.

Attainable standards that are likely to be achieved are preferable for planning and budgeting. It is preferable to prepare the master budget and cash budget using these standards. Clearly, it is inappropriate to use standards that may not be achieved for planning purposes. Hence attainable standards that are likely to be achieved lead to economies, since they can be used for both *planning* and *control*. However, easily attainable standards are unlikely to provide a challenging target that will motivate higher levels of efficiency.

For an indication of the types of cost standards that companies actually use you should refer to Exhibit 15.3.

PURPOSES OF STANDARD COSTING

Standard costing systems are widely used because they provide cost information for many different purposes such as the following.

- Providing a prediction of future costs that can be used for *decision-making purposes*. Standard costs can be derived from either traditional or activity-based costing systems. Because standard costs represent *future* target costs based on the elimination of avoidable inefficiencies they are preferable to estimates based on adjusted past costs which may incorporate inefficiencies. For example, in markets where competitive prices do not exist products may be priced on a bid basis. In these situations standard costs provide more appropriate information because efficient competitors will seek to eliminate avoidable costs. It is therefore unwise to assume that inefficiencies are recoverable within the bid price.

- Providing a *challenging target* which individuals are motivated to achieve. For example research evidence suggests that the existence of a defined quantitative goal or target is likely to motivate higher levels of performance than would be achieved if no such target was set.

- Assisting in *setting budgets* and evaluating managerial performance. Standard costs are particularly valuable for budgeting because a reliable and convenient source of data is provided for converting budgeted production into physical and monetary resource requirements. Budgetary preparation time is considerably reduced if standard costs are available because the standard costs of operations and products can be readily built up into total costs of any budgeted volume and product mix.

- Acting as a *control device* by highlighting those activities which do not conform to plan and thus alerting managers to those situations that may be 'out of control' and in need of corrective action. With a standard costing system variances are analysed in great detail such as by element of cost, and price and quantity elements. Useful feedback is therefore provided in pinpointing the areas where variances have arisen.

EXHIBIT 15.3

Surveys of company practice

• Simplifying the task of tracing costs to products for *profit measurement and inventory valuation* purposes. Besides preparing annual financial accounting profit statements most organizations also prepare monthly internal profit statements. If actual costs are used a considerable amount

Since its introduction in the early 1900s standard costing has flourished and is now one of the most widely used management accounting techniques. Three independently conducted surveys of USA practice indicate highly consistent figures in terms of adopting standard costing systems. Cress and Pettijohn (1985) and Schwarzbach (1985) report an 85% adoption rate, while Cornick *et al.* (1988), found that 86% of the surveyed firms used a standard costing system. A Japanese survey by Scarborough *et al.* (1991) reported a 65% adoption rate. Surveys of UK companies by Drury *et al.* (1993) and New Zealand companies by Guilding *et al.* (1998) report adoption rates of 76% and 73% respectively.

In relation to the methods to set labour and material standards Drury *et al.* reported the following usage rates:

	Extent of use (%)				
	Never	**Rarely**	**Sometimes**	**Often**	**Always**
Standards based on design/ engineering studies	18	11	19	31	21
Observations based on trial runs	18	16	36	25	5
Work study techniques	21	18	19	21	21
Average of historic usage	22	11	23	35	9

In the USA Lauderman and Schaeberle (1983) reported that 43% of the respondents used average historic usage, 67% used engineering studies, 11% used trial runs under controlled conditions and 15% used other methods. The results add up to more than 100% because some companies used more than one method.

Drury *et al.* also reported that the following types of standards were employed:

Maximum efficiency standards	5%
Achievable but difficult to attain standards	44%
Average past performance standards	46%
Other	5%

of time is required in tracking costs so that monthly costs can be allocated between cost of sales and inventories. A data processing system is required which can track monthly costs in a resource efficient manner. Standard costing systems meet this requirement. You will see from Figure 15.2 that product costs are maintained at standard cost. Inventories and cost of goods sold are recorded at standard cost and a conversion to actual cost is made by writing off all variances arising during the period as a period cost. Note that the variances from standard cost are extracted by comparing actual with standard costs at the responsibility centre level, and not at the product level, so that actual costs are not assigned to individual products.

FIGURE 15.2 *Standard costs for inventory valuation and profit measurement.*

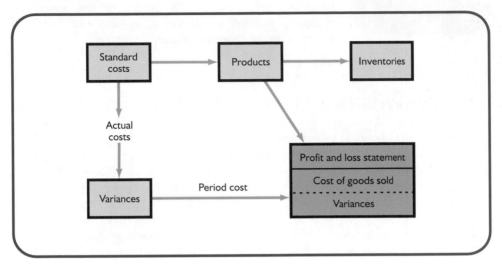

Variance analysis

It is possible to compute variances simply by committing to memory a series of variance formulae. If you adopt this approach, however, it will not help you to understand what a variance is intended to depict and what the relevant variables represent. In our discussion of each variance we shall therefore concentrate on the fundamental meaning of the variance, so that you can logically deduce the variance formulae as we go along.

All of the variances presented in this chapter are illustrated from the information contained in Example 15.1 on page 378. Note that the level of detail presented is highly simplified. A truly realistic situation would involve many products, operations and responsibility centres but would not give any further insights into the basic concepts or procedures.

Figure 15.3 shows the breakdown of the profit variance (the difference between budgeted and actual profit) into the component cost and revenue variances that can be calculated for a standard variable costing system. We shall now calculate the variances set out in Figure 15.3 using the data presented in Example 15.1.

Material variances

The costs of the materials which are used in a manufactured product are determined by two basic factors: the price paid for the materials, and the quantity of materials used in production. This gives rise to the possibility that the actual cost will differ from the standard cost because the *actual quantity* of materials used will be different from the *standard quantity* and/or that the *actual price* paid will be different from the *standard price*. We can therefore calculate a material usage and a material price variance.

EXAMPLE 15.1

Alpha manufacturing company produces a single product, which is known as sigma. The product requires a single operation, and the standard cost for this operation is presented in the following standard cost card:

Standard cost card for product sigma	**(£)**
Direct materials:	
2 kg of A at £10 per kg	20.00
1 kg of B at £15 per kg	15.00
Direct labour (3 hours at £9 per hour)	27.00
Variable overhead (3 hours at £2 per direct labour hour)	6.00
Total standard variable cost	68.00
Standard contribution margin	20.00
Standard selling price	88.00

Alpha Ltd plan to produce 10 000 units of sigma in the month of April, and the budgeted costs based on the information contained in the standard cost card are as follows:

Budget based on the above standard costs and an output of 10 000 units	**(£)**	**(£)**	**(£)**
Sales (10 000 units of sigma at £88 per unit)			880 000
Direct materials:			
A: 20 000 kg at £10 per kg	200 000		
B: 10 000 kg at £15 per kg	150 000	350 000	
Direct labour (30 000 hours at £9 per hour)		270 000	
Variable overheads (30 000 hours at £2 per direct labour hour)		60 000	680 000
Budgeted contribution			200 000
Fixed overheads			120 000
Budgeted profit			80 000

Annual budgeted fixed overheads are £1 440 000 and are assumed to be incurred evenly throughout the year. The company uses a variable costing system for internal profit measurement purposes.

The actual results for April are:

	(£)	**(£)**
Sales (9000 units at £90)		810 000
Direct materials:		
A: 19 000 kg at £11 per kg	209 000	
B: 10 100 kg at £14 per kg	141 400	
Direct labour (28 500 hours at £9.60 per hour)	273 600	
Variable overheads	52 000	676 000
Contribution		134 000
Fixed overheads		116 000
Profit		18 000

Manufacturing overheads are charged to production on the basis of direct labour hours. Actual production and sales for the period were 9000 units.

FIGURE 15.3 *Variance analysis for a variable costing system.*

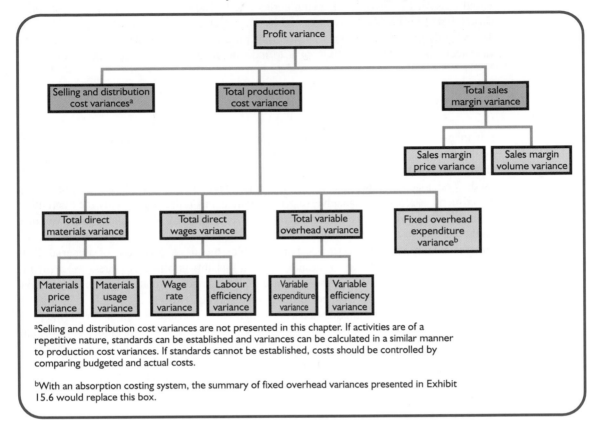

^aSelling and distribution cost variances are not presented in this chapter. If activities are of a repetitive nature, standards can be established and variances can be calculated in a similar manner to production cost variances. If standards cannot be established, costs should be controlled by comparing budgeted and actual costs.

^bWith an absorption costing system, the summary of fixed overhead variances presented in Exhibit 15.6 would replace this box.

Material price variances

The starting point for calculating this variance is simply to compare the standard price per unit of materials with the actual price per unit. You should now read Example 15.1. You will see that the standard price for material A is £10 per kg, but the actual price paid was £11 per kg. The price variance is £1 per kg. This is of little consequence if the excess purchase price has been paid only for a small number of units or purchases. But the consequences are important if the excess purchase price has been paid for a large number of units, since the effect of the variance will be greater.

The difference between the standard material price and the actual price per unit should therefore be multiplied by the quantity of materials purchased. For material A the price variance is £1 per unit; but since 19 000 kg were purchased, the excess price was paid out 19 000 times. Hence the total material price variance is £19 000 adverse. The formula for the material price variance now follows logically:

the **material price variance** is equal to the difference between the standard price (SP) and the actual price (AP) per unit of materials multiplied by the quantity of materials purchased (QP):

$$(SP - AP) \times QP$$

Now refer to material B in Example 15.1. The standard price is £15, compared with an actual price of £14 giving a £1 saving per kg. As 10 100 kg were purchased, the total price variance will be £10 100 (10 100 kg at £1). The variance for material B is favourable and that for material A is adverse. The normal procedure is to present the amount of the variances followed by symbols A or F to indicate either adverse or favourable variances.

POSSIBLE CAUSES

It is incorrect to assume that the material price variance will always indicate the efficiency of the purchasing department. Actual prices may exceed standard prices because of a change in market conditions that causes a general price increase for the type of materials used. The price variance might therefore be beyond the control of the purchasing department. Alternatively, an adverse price variance may reflect a failure by the purchasing department to seek the most advantageous sources of supply. A favourable price variance might be due to the purchase of inferior quality materials, which may lead to inferior product quality or more wastage. For example, the price variance for material B is favourable, but we shall see in the next section that this is offset by excess usage. If the reason for this excess usage is the purchase of inferior quality materials then the material usage variance should be charged to the purchasing department.

It is also possible that another department may be responsible for all or part of the price variance. For example, a shortage of materials resulting from bad inventory control may necessitate an emergency purchase being made at short notice. The supplier may incur additional handling and freight charges on special rush orders, and may therefore charge a higher price for the materials. In this situation the price variance will be the responsibility of the stores department and not the purchasing department.

CALCULATION ON QUANTITY PURCHASED OR QUANTITY USED

We have noted that the price variance may be due to a variety of causes, some of which will be beyond a company's control, but others of which may be due to inefficiencies. It is therefore important that variances be reported as quickly as possible so that any inefficiencies can be identified and remedial action taken. A problem occurs, however, with material purchases in that the time of purchase and the time of usage may not be the same: materials may be purchased in one period and used in a subsequent period. For example, if 10 000 units of a material are purchased in period 1 at a price of £1 per unit over standard and 2000 units are used in each of periods 1 to 5, the following alternatives are available for calculating the price variance:

1. The full amount of the price variance of £10 000 is reported in *period 1* with quantity being defined as the *quantity purchased*.
2. The price variance is calculated with quantity being defined as the *quantity used*. The unit price variance of £1 is multiplied by the quantity used (i.e. 2000 units), which means that a price variance of £2000 will be reported for each of *periods 1 to 5*.

Method 1 is recommended, because the price variance can be reported in the period in which it is incurred, and reporting of the total variance is not delayed until months later when the materials are used. Also adopting this approach enables corrective action to be taken earlier. For the sake of simplicity we shall assume in Example 15.1 that the actual purchases are identical with the actual usage.

Material usage variance

The starting point for calculating this quantity variance is simply to compare the standard quantity that should have been used with the actual quantity which has been used. Refer again to Example 15.1. You will see that the standard usage for the production of one unit of sigma is 2 kg for material A. As 9000 units of sigma are produced, 18 000 kg of material A should have been used; however, 19 000 kg are actually used, which means there has been an excess usage of 1000 kg.

The importance of this excess usage depends on the price of the materials. For example, if the price is £0.01 per kg then an excess usage of 1000 kg will not be very significant, but if the price is £10 per unit then an excess usage of 1000 kg will be very significant. It follows that to assess the importance of the excess usage, the variance should be expressed in monetary terms.

CALCULATION BASED ON STANDARD PRICE OR ACTUAL PRICE

Should the standard material price per kg or the actual material price per kg be used to calculate the variance? The answer is the standard price. If the *actual* material price is used, the usage variance will be affected by the efficiency of the purchasing department, since any excess purchase price will be assigned to the excess usage. It is therefore necessary to remove the price effects from the usage variance calculation, and this is achieved by valuing the variance at the standard price. Hence the 1000 kg excess usage of material A is multiplied by the standard price of £10 per unit, which gives an adverse usage variance of £10 000. The formula for the variance is

the **material usage variance** is equal to the difference between the standard quantity (SQ) required for actual production and the actual quantity (AQ) used multiplied by the standard material price (SP):

$$(SQ - AQ) \times SP$$

For material B you will see from Example 15.1 that the standard quantity is 9000 kg (9000 units × 1 kg) but 10 100 kg have been used. The excess usage of 1100 kg is multiplied by the standard price of £15 per kg, which gives an adverse variance of £16 500. Note that the principles of flexible budgeting described in the previous chapter also apply here, with *standard quantity being based on actual production and not budgeted production*. This ensures that a manager is evaluated under the conditions in which he or she actually worked and not those envisaged at the time the budget was prepared.

POSSIBLE CAUSES

The material usage variance is normally controllable by the manager of the appropriate production responsibility centre. Common causes of material usage variances include the careless handling of materials by production personnel, the purchase of inferior quality materials, pilferage, changes in quality control requirements, or changes in methods of production. Separate material usage variances should be calculated for each type of material used and allocated to each responsibility centre.

Total material variance

From Figure 15.3 you will see that this variance is the total variance before it is analysed into the price and usage elements. The formula for the variance is

the **total material variance** is the difference between the standard material cost (SC) for the actual production and the actual cost (AC):

$$SC - AC$$

For material A the standard material cost is £20 per unit (see Example 15.1) giving a total standard material cost of £180 000 (9000 units × £20). The actual cost is £209 000, and therefore the variance is £29 000 adverse. The price variance of £19 000 plus the usage variance of £10 000 agrees with the total material variance. Similarly, the total material variance for material B is £6400, consisting of a favourable price variance of £10 100 and an adverse usage variance of £16 500.

Note that if the price variance is calculated on the actual quantity *purchased* instead of the actual quantity *used*, the price variance plus the usage variance will agree with the total variance only when the quantity purchased is equal to the quantity which is used in the particular accounting period. Reconciling the price and usage variance with the total variance is merely a reconciliation exercise, and you should not be concerned if reconciliation of the sub-variances with the total variance is not possible.

Labour variances

The cost of labour is determined by the price paid for labour and the quantity of labour used. Thus a price and quantity variance will also arise for labour. Unlike materials, labour cannot be stored, because the purchase and usage of labour normally takes place at the same time. Hence the actual quantity of hours *purchased* will be equal to the actual quantity of hours *used* for each period. For this reason the price variance plus the quantity variance should agree with the total labour variance.

Wage rate variance

This variance is calculated by comparing the standard price per hour with the actual price paid per hour. In Example 15.1 the standard wage rate per hour is £9 and the actual wage rate is £9.60 per hour, giving a wage rate variance of £0.60 per hour. To determine the importance of the variance, it is necessary to ascertain how many times the excess payment of £0.60 per hour is paid. As 28 500 labour hours are used (see Example 15.1), we multiply 28 500 hours by £0.60. This gives an adverse wage rate variance of £17 100. The formula for the wage rate variance is

the **wage rate variance** is equal to the difference between the standard wage rate per hour (SR) and the actual wage rate (AR) multiplied by the actual number of hours worked (AH):

$$(SR - AR) \times AH$$

Note the similarity between this variance and the material price variance. Both variances multiply the difference between the standard price and the actual price paid for a unit of a resource by the actual quantity of resources used.

POSSIBLE CAUSES

The wage rate variance may be due to a negotiated increase in wage rates not yet having been reflected in the standard wage rate. In a situation such as this the variance cannot be regarded as controllable. Unexpected overtime can also be the cause of the variance. Labour rate variances may also occur because a standard is used that represents a single average rate for a given operation performed by workers who are paid at several different rates. In this situation part or all of the variance may be due to the assignment of skilled labour to work that is normally performed by unskilled labour. The variance may then be regarded as the responsibility of the foreman, because he should have matched the appropriate grade of labour to the task at hand. However, the wage rate variance is probably the one that is least subject to control by management. In most cases the variance is due to wage rate standards not being kept in line with changes in actual wage rates, and for this reason it is not normally controllable by departmental managers.

Labour efficiency variance

The labour efficiency variance represents the quantity variance for direct labour. The quantity of labour that should be used for the actual output is expressed in terms of *standard hours produced*. In Example 15.1 the standard time for the production of one unit of sigma is three hours. Thus a production level of 9000 units results in an output of 27 000 standard hours. In other words, working at the prescribed level of efficiency, it should take 27 000 hours to produce 9000 units. However, 28 500 direct labour hours are actually required to produce this output, which means that 1500 excess direct labour hours are used. We multiply the excess direct labour hours by the *standard* wage rate to calculate the variance. This gives an adverse variance of £13 500. The formula for calculating the labour efficiency variance is

the **labour efficiency variance** is equal to the difference between the standard labour hours for actual production (SH) and the actual labour hours worked (AH) during the period multiplied by the standard wage rate per hour (SR):

$$(SH - AH) \times SR$$

This variance is similar to the material usage variance. Both variances multiply the difference between the standard quantity and actual quantity of resources consumed by the standard price.

POSSIBLE CAUSES

The labour efficiency variance is normally controllable by the manager of the appropriate production responsibility centre and may be due to a variety of reasons. For example, the use of inferior quality materials, different grades of labour, failure to maintain machinery in proper condition, the introduction of new equipment or tools and changes in the production processes will all affect the efficiency of labour. An efficiency variance may not always be controllable by the production foreman; it may be due, for example, to poor production scheduling by the planning department, or to a change in quality control standards.

Total labour variance

From Figure 15.3 you will see that this variance represents the total variance before analysis into the price and quantity elements. The formula for the variance is

> the **total labour variance** is the difference between the standard labour cost (SC) for the actual production and the actual labour cost (AC):

$$SC - AC$$

In Example 15.1 the actual production was 9000 units, and, with a standard labour cost of £27 per unit, the standard cost is £243 000. The actual cost is £273 600, which gives an adverse variance of £30 600. This consists of a wage rate variance of £17 100 and a labour efficiency variance of £13 500.

Variable overhead variances

A *total* variable overhead variance is calculated in the same way as the total direct labour and material variances. In Example 15.1 the output is 9000 units and the standard variable overhead cost is £6 *per unit* produced. The standard cost of production for variable overheads is thus £54 000. The actual variable overheads incurred are £52 000, giving a favourable variance of £2000. The formula for the variance is

> the **total variable overhead variance** is the difference between the standard variable overheads charged to production (SC) and the actual variable overheads incurred (AC):

$$SC - AC$$

Where variable overheads vary with direct labour or machine hours of *input* the total variable overhead variance will be due to one or both of the following:

1. A *price* variance arising from actual expenditure being different from budgeted expenditure.
2. A *quantity* variance arising from actual direct labour or machine hours of input being different from the hours of input, which *should* have been used.

These reasons give rise to the two sub-variances, which are shown in Figure 15.3: the variable overhead expenditure variance and the variable overhead efficiency variance.

Variable overhead expenditure variance

To compare the actual overhead expenditure with the budgeted expenditure, it is necessary to flex the budget. Because it is assumed in Example 15.1 that variable overheads will vary with direct labour hours of *input* the budget is flexed on this basis. Actual variable overhead expenditure is £52 000, resulting from 28 500 direct labour hours of input. For this level of activity variable overheads of £57 000, which consist of 28 500 input hours at £2 per hour, should have been spent. Spending was £5000 less than it should have been, and the result is a favourable variance.

Comparing budgeted and the actual overhead costs for 28 500 direct labour hours of input ensures that any efficiency content is removed from the variance. This means that any difference must be due to actual variable overhead spending being different from the budgeted variable overhead spending. The formula for the variance is

> the **variable overhead expenditure variance** is equal to the difference between the budgeted flexed variable overheads (BFVO) for the actual direct labour hours of input and the actual variable overhead costs incurred (AVO):

$$\text{BFVO} - \text{AVO}$$

POSSIBLE CAUSES

Variable overhead represents the aggregation of a large number of individual items, such as indirect labour, indirect materials, electricity, maintenance and so on. The variable overhead can arise because the prices of individual items have changed. Alternatively, the variance can also be affected by how efficiently the individual variable overhead items are used. Waste or inefficiency, such as using more kilowatt-hours of power than should have been used will increase the cost of power and, thus, the total cost of variable overhead. The variable overhead expenditure on its own is therefore not very informative. Any meaningful analysis of this variance requires a comparison of the actual expenditure for each individual item of variable overhead expenditure against the budget. If you refer to the performance report presented in Exhibit 15.8 on pages 396–397, you can see how the £5000 variable overhead expenditure variance can be analysed by individual items of expenditure. Control should be exercised by focusing on the individual line items of the expenditure variances and not the total variance.

Variable overhead efficiency variance

In Example 15.1 it is assumed that variable overheads vary with direct labour hours of input. The variable overhead efficiency variance arises because 28 500 direct labour hours of input were required to produce 9000 units. Working at the prescribed level of efficiency, it should take 27 000 hours to produce 9000 units of output. Therefore an extra 1500 direct labour hours of input were required. Because variable overheads are assumed to vary with direct labour hours of input, an additional £3000 (1500 hours at £2) variable overheads will be incurred. The formula for the variance is

> the **variable overhead efficiency variance** is the difference between the standard hours of output (SH) and the actual hours of input (AH) for the period multiplied by the standard variable overhead rate (SR):

$$(\text{SH} - \text{AH}) \times \text{SR}$$

You should note that if it is assumed that variable overheads vary with direct labour hours of input, this variance is identical to the labour efficiency variance. Consequently, the reasons for the variance are the same as those described previously for the labour efficiency variance. If you refer again to Figure 15.3, you will see that the variable overhead expenditure variance (£5000 favourable) plus the variable efficiency variance (£3000 adverse) add up to the total variable overhead variance of £2000 favourable.

Similarities between materials, labour and overhead variances

So far, we have calculated price and quantity variances for different material, direct labour and variable overheads. You will have noted the similarities between the computations of the three quantity and price variances. For example, we calculated the quantity variances (i.e. material usage, labour efficiency and variable overhead efficiency variances) by multiplying the difference between the standard quantity (SQ) of resources consumed for the actual production and the actual quantity (AQ) of resources consumed by the standard price (SP) per unit of the resource. Thus, the three quantity variances can be formulated as

$$(SQ - AQ) \times SP$$

Note that the standard quantity is derived from determining the quantity that should be used *for the actual production* for the period so that the principles of flexible budgeting are applied. The price variances (i.e. material price, wage rate and variable overhead expenditure variances) were calculated by multiplying the difference between the standard price (SP) and the actual price (AP) per unit of a resource by the actual quantity (AQ) of resources acquired/used. The price variances can be formulated as

$$(SP - AP) \times AQ$$

This can be re-expressed as

$$(AQ \times SP) - (AQ \times AP)$$

Note that the first term in this formula (with AQ representing actual hours) is equivalent to the budgeted flexed variable overheads that we used to calculate the variable overhead expenditure variance. The last term represents the actual cost of the resources consumed.

We can therefore calculate all the price and quantity variances illustrated so far in this chapter by applying the formulae outlined above.

Fixed overhead expenditure or spending variance

The final cost variance shown in Figure 15.3 is the fixed overhead expenditure variance. With a variable costing system, fixed manufacturing overheads are not unitized and allocated to products. Instead, the total fixed overheads for the period are charged as an expense to the period in which they are incurred. Fixed overheads are assumed to remain unchanged in the short term in response to changes in the level of activity, but they may change in response to other factors. For example, price increases may cause expenditure on fixed overheads to increase. The fixed overhead expenditure variance therefore explains the difference between budgeted fixed overheads and the actual fixed overheads incurred. The formula for the variance is called the **fixed overhead expenditure variance** and is the difference between the budgeted fixed overheads (BFO) and the actual fixed overhead (AFO) spending:

$$BFO - AFO$$

In Example 15.1 budgeted fixed overhead expenditure is £120 000 and actual fixed overhead spending £116 000. Therefore the fixed overhead expenditure variance is £4000. Whenever the actual fixed overheads are less than the budgeted fixed overheads, the variance will be favourable. The total of the fixed overhead expenditure variance on its own is not particularly informative. Any meaningful analysis of this variance requires a comparison of the actual expenditure for each individual item of fixed overhead expenditure against the budget. The difference may be due to a variety of causes, such as changes in salaries paid to supervisors, or the appointment of additional supervisors. Only by comparing individual items of expenditure and ascertaining the reasons for the variances, can one determine whether the variance is controllable or uncontrollable. Generally, this variance is likely to be uncontrollable in the short term.

Sales variances

Sales variances can be used to analyse the performance of the sales function or revenue centres on broadly similar terms to those for manufacturing costs. The most significant feature of sales variance calculations is that they are calculated in terms of profit or contribution margins rather than sales values. Consider Example 15.2.

You will see that when the variances are calculated on the basis of sales *value*, it is necessary to compare the budgeted sales *value* of £110 000 with the actual sales of £120 000. This gives a favourable variance of £10 000. This calculation, however, ignores the impact of the sales effort on profit. The budgeted profit contribution is £40 000, which consists of 10 000 units at £4 per unit, but the actual impact of the sales effort in terms of profit margins indicates a profit contribution of £36 000, which consists of 12 000 units at £3 per unit, indicating an adverse variance of £4000. If we examine Example 15.2, we can see that the selling prices have been reduced, and that this has led not only to an increase in the total sales revenue but also to a reduction in total profits. The objective of the selling function is to influence favourably total profits. Thus a more meaningful performance measure will be obtained by comparing the results of the sales function in terms of profit or contribution margins rather than sales revenues.

Note that with a standard absorption costing system, *profit* margins are used (selling price less total unit manufacturing cost), whereas with a standard variable costing system, *contribution* margins (selling price less unit manufacturing variable cost) are used to calculate the variances.

Let us now calculate the sales variances for a standard variable costing system from the information contained in Example 15.1.

Total sales margin variance

Where a variable costing approach is adopted, the total sales *margin* variance seeks to identify the influence of the sales function on the difference between budget and actual profit contribution. In Example 15.1 the budgeted profit contribution is £200 000, which consists of budgeted sales of 10 000 units at a contribution of £20 per unit. This is compared with the contribution from the actual sales volume of 9000 units. Because the sales function is responsible for the sales volume and the unit selling price, but not the unit manufacturing costs, the standard cost of sales and not the actual cost of sales is deducted from the actual sales revenue. The calculation of *actual* contribution for ascertaining the total sales margin variance will therefore be as follows:

The budgeted sales for a company are £110 000 consisting of 10 000 units at £11 per unit. The standard cost per unit is £7. Actual sales are £120 000 (12 000 units at £10 per unit) and the actual cost per unit is £7.

	(£)
Actual sales revenue (9000 units at £90)	810 000
Standard variable cost of sales for actual sales volume (9000 units at £68)	612 000
Actual profit contribution margin	198 000

To calculate the total sales margin variance, we compare the budgeted contribution of £200 000 with the actual contribution of £198 000. This gives an adverse variance of £2000 because the actual contribution is less that the budgeted profit contribution.

The formula for calculating the variance is as follows:

the **total sales margin variance** is the difference between the actual contribution (AC) and the budgeted contribution (BC) (both based on standard unit costs):

$$AC - BC$$

Using the standard cost to calculate both the budgeted and the actual contribution ensures that the production variances do not distort the calculation of the sales variances. The effect of using standard costs throughout the contribution margin calculations means that the sales variances arise because of changes in those variables controlled by the sales function (i.e. selling prices and sales quantity). Consequently, Figure 15.3 indicates that it is possible to analyse the total sales margin variance into two sub-variances – a sales margin price variance and a sales margin volume variance.

Sales margin price variance

In Example 15.1 the actual selling price is £90 but the budgeted selling price is £88. With a standard unit variable cost of £68, the change in selling price has led to an increase in the contribution margin from £20 per unit to £22 per unit. Because the actual sales volume is 9000 units, the increase in the selling price means that an increased contribution margin is obtained 9000 times, giving a favourable sales margin price variance of £18 000. The formula for calculating the variance is

the **sales margin price variance** is the difference between the actual contribution margin (AM) and the standard margin (SM) (both based on standard unit costs) multiplied by the actual sales volume (AV):

$$(AM - SM) \times AV$$

Sales margin volume variance

To ascertain the effect of changes in the sales volume on the difference between the budgeted and the actual contribution, we must compare the budgeted sales volume with the actual sales volume. You will see from Example 15.1 that the budgeted sales are 10 000 units but the actual sales are 9000 units, and to enable us to determine the impact of this reduction in sales volume on profit, we must multiply the 1000 units by the standard contribution margin of £20. This gives an adverse variance of £20 000.

The use of the standard margin (standard selling price less standard cost) ensures that the standard selling price is used in the calculation, and the volume variance will not be affected by any *changes* in the actual selling prices. The formula for calculating the variance is

the **sales margin volume variance** is the difference between the actual sales volume (AV) and the budgeted volume (BV) multiplied by the standard contribution margin (SM):

$$(AV - BV) \times SM$$

Reconciling budgeted profit and actual profit

Top management will be interested in the reason for the actual profit being different from the budgeted profit. By adding the favourable production and sales variances to the budgeted profit and deducting the adverse variances, the reconciliation of budgeted and actual profit shown in Exhibit 15.4 can be presented in respect of Example 15.1.

Example 15.1 assumes that Alpha Ltd produces a single product consisting of a single operation and that the activities are performed by one responsibility centre. In practice, most companies make many products, which require operations to be carried out in different responsibility centres. A reconciliation statement such as that presented in Exhibit 15.4 will therefore normally represent a summary of the variances for many responsibility centres. The reconciliation statement thus represents a broad picture to top management that explains the major reasons for any difference between the budgeted and actual profits.

Standard absorption costing

The external financial accounting regulations in most countries require that companies should value inventories at full absorption manufacturing cost. The effect of this is that fixed overheads should be allocated to products and included in the closing inventory valuations. With the variable costing system, fixed overheads are not allocated to products. Instead, the total fixed costs are charged as an expense to the period in which they are incurred. (For a discussion of the differences between variable and absorption costing systems you should refer back to Chapter 8.) With an absorption costing system, an additional fixed overhead variance is calculated. This variance is called a **volume variance**. In addition, the sales margin variances must be expressed in unit *profit* margins instead of *contribution* margins. These variances are not particularly useful for control purposes. If your course does not relate to the disposition of variances to meet financial accounting requirements, you can omit pages 389–395.

With a standard absorption costing system, predetermined fixed overhead rates are established by dividing annual budgeted fixed overheads by the budgeted annual level of activity. We shall assume that in respect of Example 15.1, budgeted annual fixed overheads are £1 440 000 (£120 000 per month) and budgeted annual activity is 120 000 units (10 000 units per month). The fixed overhead rate per *unit* of output is calculated as follows:

$$\frac{\text{budgeted fixed overheads (£1 440 000)}}{\text{budgeted activity (120 000 units)}} = £12 \text{ per unit of sigma produced}$$

We have noted earlier in this chapter that in most situations more than one product will be produced. Where different products are produced, units of output should be converted to standard hours. In Example 15.1 the output of one unit of sigma requires three direct labour hours. Therefore, the budgeted output in standard hours is 360 000 hours (120 000 × 3 hours). The fixed overhead rate per standard hour of output is

$$\frac{\text{budgeted fixed overheads (£1 440 000)}}{\text{budgeted standard hours (360 000)}} = £4 \text{ per standard hour}$$

By multiplying the number of hours required to produce one unit of Sigma by £4 per hour, we also get a fixed overhead allocation of £12 for one unit of Sigma (3 hours × £4). For the remainder of this chapter output will be measured in terms of standard hours produced.

We shall assume that production is expected to occur evenly throughout the year. Monthly budgeted production *output* is therefore 10 000 units, or 30 000 standard direct labour hours. At the planning stage an input of 30 000 direct labour hours (10 000 × 3 hours) will also be planned as the company will budget at the level of efficiency specified in the calculation of the product standard cost. Thus the **budgeted hours of input** and the **budgeted hours of output** (i.e. the standard hours produced) will be the same at the planning stage. In contrast, the *actual* hours of input may differ from the *actual* standard hours of output. In Example 15.1 the actual direct labour hours of input are 28 500, and 27 000 standard hours were actually produced.

With an absorption costing system, fixed overheads of £108 000 (27 000 standard hours of output at a standard rate of £4 per hour) will have been charged to products for the month of April. Actual fixed overhead expenditure was £116 000. Therefore, £8000 has not been allocated to products. In other words, there has been an under-recovery of fixed overheads. Where the fixed overheads allocated to products exceeds the overhead incurred, there will be an over-recovery of fixed overheads. The under- or over-recovery of fixed overheads represents the total fixed overhead variance for the period. The total fixed overhead variance is calculated using a formula similar to those for the total direct labour and total direct materials variances:

the **total fixed overhead variance** is the difference between the standard fixed overhead charged to production (SC) and the actual fixed overhead incurred (AC):

$$\text{SC(£108 000)} - \text{AC(£116 000)} = £8000\text{A}$$

Note that the standard cost for the actual production can be calculated by measuring production in standard hours of output (27 000 hours × £4 per hour) or units of output (9000 units × £12 per unit).

The under- or over-recovery of fixed overheads (i.e. the fixed overhead variance) arises because the fixed overhead rate is calculated by dividing *budgeted* fixed overheads by *budgeted* output. If actual output or fixed overhead expenditure differs from budget, an under- or over-recovery of fixed overheads will arise. In other words, the under- or over-recovery may be due to the following:

1. A fixed overhead expenditure variance of £4000 arising from actual *expenditure* (£116 000) being different from budgeted *expenditure* (£120 000).

2. A fixed overhead volume variance arising from actual *production* differing from budgeted production.

The fixed overhead expenditure variance also occurs with a variable costing system. The favourable variance of £4000

	(£)	(£)	(£)
Budgeted net profit			80 000
Sales variances:			
Sales margin price	18 000F		
Sales margin volume	20 000A	2 000A	
Direct cost variances:			
Material: Price	8 900A		
Usage	26 500A	35 400A	
Labour: Rate	17 100A		
Efficiency	13 500A	30 600A	
Manufacturing overhead variances:			
Fixed overhead expenditure	4 000F		
Variable overhead expenditure	5 000F		
Variable overhead efficiency	3 000A	6 000F	62 000A
Actual profit			18 000

was explained earlier in this chapter. The volume variance arises only when inventories are valued on an absorption costing basis.

Volume variance

This variance seeks to identify the portion of the total fixed overhead variance that is due to actual production being different from budgeted production. In Example 15.1 the standard fixed overhead rate of £4 per hour is calculated on the basis of a normal activity of 30 000 standard hours per month. Only when actual standard hours produced are 30 000 will the budgeted monthly fixed overheads of £120 000 be exactly recovered. Actual output, however, is only 27 000 standard hours. The fact that the actual production is 3000 standard hours less than the budgeted output hours will lead to a failure to recover £12 000 fixed overhead (3000 hours at £4 fixed overhead rate per hour). The formula for the variance is

the **volume variance** is the difference between actual production (AP) and budgeted production (BP) for a period multiplied by the standard fixed overhead rate (SR):

$$(AP - BP) \times SR$$

The volume variance reflects the fact that fixed overheads do not fluctuate in relation to output in the short term. Whenever actual production is less than budgeted production, the fixed overhead charged to production will be less than the budgeted cost, and the volume variance will be adverse. Conversely, if the actual production is greater than the budgeted production, the volume variance will be favourable.

POSSIBLE CAUSES

Changes in production volume from the amount budgeted may be caused by shifts in demand for products, labour disputes, material shortages, poor production scheduling, machine breakdowns, labour efficiency and poor production quality. Some of these factors may be controllable by production or sales management, while others may not.

When the adverse volume variance of £12 000 is netted with the favourable expenditure variance of £4000, the result is equal to the total fixed overhead adverse variance of £8000. It is also possible to analyse the volume variance into two further sub-variances – the volume efficiency variance and the capacity variance.

Volume efficiency variance

If we wish to identify the reasons for the volume variance, we may ask why the actual production was different from the budgeted production. One possible reason may be that the labour force worked at a different level of efficiency from that anticipated in the budget.

The actual number of direct labour hours of input was 28 500. Hence one would have expected 28 500 hours of output (i.e. standard hours produced) from this input, but only 27 000 standard hours were actually produced. Thus one reason for the failure to meet the budgeted output was that output in standard hours was 1500 hours less than it should have been. If the labour force had worked at the prescribed level of efficiency, an additional 1500 standard hours would have been produced, and this would have led to a total of £6000 (£1500 hours at £4 per standard hour) fixed overheads being absorbed. The inefficiency of labour is therefore one of the reasons why the actual production was less than the budgeted production, and this gives an adverse variance of £6000. The formula for the variance is

> the **volume efficiency variance** is the difference between the standard hours of output (SH) and the actual hours of input (AH) for the period multiplied by the standard fixed overhead rate (SR):

$$(SH - AH) \times SR$$

You may have noted that the physical content of this variance is a measure of labour efficiency and is identical with the labour efficiency variance. Consequently, the reasons for this variance will be identical with those previously described for the labour efficiency variance.

Volume capacity variance

This variance indicates the second reason why the actual production might be different from the budgeted production. The budget is based on the assumption that the direct labour hours of input will be 30 000 hours, but the actual hours of input are 28 500 hours. The difference of 1500 hours reflects the fact that the company has failed to utilize the planned capacity. If we assume that the 1500 hours would have been worked at the prescribed level of efficiency, an additional 1500 standard hours could have been produced and an additional £6000 fixed overhead could have been absorbed. Hence the capacity variance is £6000 adverse.

Whereas the volume efficiency variance indicated a failure to utilize capacity *efficiently*, the volume capacity variance indicates a failure to utilize capacity *at all*. The formula is

the **volume capacity variance** is the difference between the actual hours of input (AH) and the budgeted hours of input (BH) for the period multiplied by the standard fixed overhead rate (SR):

$$(AH - BH) \times SR$$

A failure to achieve the budgeted capacity may be for a variety of reasons. Machine breakdowns, material shortages, poor production scheduling, labour disputes and a reduction in sales demand are all possible causes of an adverse volume capacity variance.

Summary of fixed overhead variances

The volume efficiency variance is £6000 adverse, and the volume capacity variance is also £6000 adverse. When these two variances are added together, they agree with the fixed overhead volume variance of £12 000. Exhibit 15.5 summarizes how the volume variance is analysed according to capacity and efficiency.

The actual *output* was 3000 hours less than the budget, giving an adverse volume variance. The capacity variance indicates that one reason for failing to meet the budgeted output was that 1500 hours of *capacity* were not utilized. In addition, those 28 500 hours that were utilized only led to 27 000 hours of output. An inefficient use of 1500 hours capacity therefore provides a second explanation as to why the budgeted output was not achieved. A fixed overhead rate of £4 per hour is applied to the physical quantity of the variances, so that fixed overhead variances may be presented in monetary terms. Exhibit 15.6 summarizes the variances we have calculated in this section.

Reconciliation of budgeted and actual profit for a standard absorption costing system

The reconciliation of the budgeted and actual profits is shown in Exhibit 15.7. You will see that the reconciliation statement is identical with the variable costing reconciliation

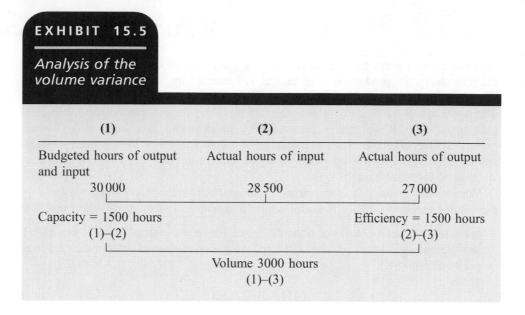

EXHIBIT 15.5

Analysis of the volume variance

	(1)	(2)	(3)
	Budgeted hours of output and input	Actual hours of input	Actual hours of output
	30 000	28 500	27 000

Capacity = 1500 hours (1)–(2)

Efficiency = 1500 hours (2)–(3)

Volume 3000 hours (1)–(3)

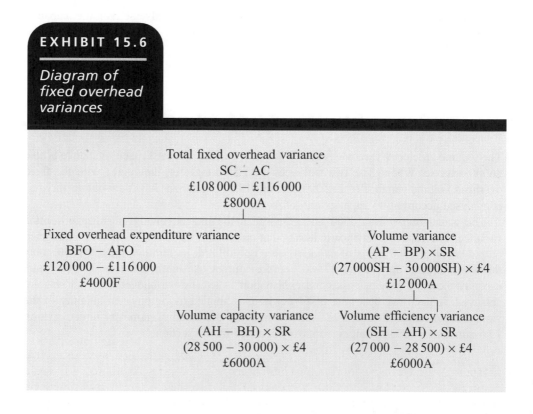

EXHIBIT 15.6

Diagram of fixed overhead variances

Total fixed overhead variance
SC – AC
£108 000 – £116 000
£8000A

Fixed overhead expenditure variance
BFO – AFO
£120 000 – £116 000
£4000F

Volume variance
(AP – BP) × SR
(27 000SH – 30 000SH) × £4
£12 000A

Volume capacity variance
(AH – BH) × SR
(28 500 – 30 000) × £4
£6000A

Volume efficiency variance
(SH – AH) × SR
(27 000 – 28 500) × £4
£6000A

statement, apart from the fact that the absorption costing statement includes the fixed overhead volume variance and values the sales margin volume variance at the standard profit margin per unit instead of the contribution per unit. If you refer back to page 389, you will see that the contribution margin for Sigma is £20 per unit sold whereas the profit margin per unit after deducting fixed overhead cost (£12 per unit) is £8. Multiplying the

	(£)	(£)	(£)	(£)
Budgeted net profit				80 000
Sales variances:				
Sales margin price		18 000F		
Sales margin volume		8 000A	10 000F	
Direct cost variances:				
Material – Price: Material A	19 000A			
Material B	10 100F	8 900A		
– Usage: Material A	10 000A			
Material B	16 500A	26 500A	35 400A	
Labour – Rate		17 100A		
Efficiency		13 500A	30 600A	
Manufacturing overhead variances:				
Fixed – Expenditure	4 000F			
Volume	12 000A	8 000A		
Variable – Expenditure	5 000F			
Efficiency	3 000A	2 000F	6 000A	62 000A
Actual profit				18 000

difference in budgeted and actual sales volumes of 1000 units by the standard profit margin gives a sales volume margin variance of £8000. Note that the sales margin price variance is identical for both systems.

Performance reports

The managers of responsibility centres will require a more detailed analysis of the variances to enable them to exercise control, and detailed performance reports should be prepared at monthly or weekly intervals to bring to their attention any significant variances. A typical performance report based on the information contained in Example 15.1 is presented in Exhibit 15.8. A departmental performance report should include only those items that the responsibility manager can control or influence. The material price and wage rate variances and the monetary amount of the volume variance are *not* presented, since these are not considered to be within the control of the manager of the responsibility centre. However, the volume variance and the two sub-variances (capacity and efficiency) are restated in non-monetary terms in Exhibit 15.8. You can see that these variances have

EXHIBIT 15.8

A typical departmental performance report

DEPARTMENTAL PERFORMANCE REPORT

Department..............................
Period............. April 20XX ....

Control ratios: Efficiency 94.7%   Capacity 95%   Volume 90%

Actual production — 27 000 standard hours
Actual working hours — 28 500 hours
Budgeted hours — 30 000 hours

DIRECT MATERIALS

Type	Standard quantity	Actual quantity	Difference	Standard price	Usage variance	Reason
A	18 000 kg	19 000	1000	£10.00	£10 000A	
B	9 000 kg	10 100	1100	£15.00	£16 500A	

DIRECT LABOUR

Grade	Standard hours	Actual hours	Difference	Standard cost	Actual cost	Total variance	Analysis Efficiency	Rate	Reason
	27 000	28 500	1500	£243 000	£273 600	£30 600	£13 500A	£17 100A	

OVERHEADS

	Allowed cost	Actual cost	Expenditure variance	Reason	Variable overhead efficiency variance (hours)	(£)
Controllable costs (variable):						
Indirect labour				Difference		
Power				between	1500	3000A
Maintenance				standard		
Indirect materials				hours and actual hours at £2 per hour		
Total	£57 000	£52 000	£5000F		1500	3000A
Uncontrollable costs (fixed):						
Lighting and heating						
Depreciation						
Supervision						
	£120 000	116 000	4000F			

	SUMMARY Variances (£)		Variances as a % of a standard cost	
	This month (£)	Cumulative (£)	This month (%)	Cumulative (%)
Direct materials usage	26 500A			
Direct labour:				
Efficiency	13 500A			
Wage rate	17 100A			
Controllable overheads:				
Expenditure	5 000F			
Variable overhead	3 000A			
Total	55 100A			
Comments:				

been replaced by the following three control ratios:

$$\textbf{production volume ratio} = \frac{\text{standard hours of actual output (27 000)}}{\text{budgeted hours of output (30 000)}} \times 100$$

$$= 90\%$$

$$\textbf{production efficiency ratio} = \frac{\text{standard hours of actual output (27 000)}}{\text{actual hours worked (28 500)}} \times 100$$

$$= 94.7\%$$

$$\textbf{capacity usage ratio} = \frac{\text{actual hours worked (28 500)}}{\text{budgeted hours of input (30 000)}} \times 100$$

$$= 95\%$$

You can interpret these ratios in the same way as was described for the equivalent monetary variances. The ratios merely represent the replacement of an *absolute* monetary measure with a *relative* performance measure.

A comparison of current variances with those of previous periods and/or with those of the year to date is presented in the summary of the performance report. This information is often useful in establishing a framework within which current variances can be evaluated. In addition to weekly or monthly performance reports, the manager of a responsibility centre should receive daily reports on those variances that are controllable on a daily basis. This normally applies to material usage and labour efficiency. For these variances the weekly or monthly performance reports will provide a summary of the information that has previously been reported on a daily basis.

Recording standard costs in the accounts

If you are not studying for a specialist accounting qualification it is possible that your curriculum may not include the recording of standard costs. You should therefore check whether or not this topic is included in your curriculum to ascertain if you need to read this section. Standard costs can be used for planning, control, motivation and decision-making purposes without being entered into the books. However, the incorporation of standard costs into the cost accounting system greatly simplifies the task of tracing costs for inventory valuation and saves a considerable amount of data processing time. For example. if raw material stocks are valued at standard cost, the stock records may be maintained in terms of physical quantities only. The value of raw materials stock may be obtained simply by multiplying the physical quantity of raw materials in stock by the standard cost per unit. This avoids the need to record stocks on a first-in, first-out or average cost basis. The financial accounting regulations in most countries specify, that inventory valuations based on standard costs may be included in externally published financial statements, provided the standard costs used are current and attainable. Most companies that have established standard costs therefore incorporate them into their cost accounting recording system.

Variations exist in the data accumulation methods adopted for recording standard costs, but these variations are merely procedural and the actual inventory valuations and profit calculations will be the same whichever method is adopted. In this chapter we shall illustrate a standard absorption costing system that values all inventories at standard cost, and all entries that are recorded in the inventory accounts will therefore be at *standard prices*. Any differences between standard costs and actual costs are debited or credited to variance accounts. Adverse variances will appear as debit balances, since they are additional costs in excess of standard. Conversely, favourable variances will appear as credit balances. Only production variances are recorded, and sales variances are not entered in the accounts.

Let us now consider the cost accounting records, for Example 15.1, which was presented earlier in this chapter. We shall assume that the company operates an integrated cost accounting system. The variances recorded in the accounts are for an absorption costing system summarized in the reconciliation statement presented in Exhibit 15.7. The appropriate ledger entries are presented in Exhibit 15.9. Each ledger entry and journal entry has been labelled with numbers from 1 to 13 to try to give you a clear understanding of each accounting entry.

PURCHASE OF MATERIALS

19 000 kg of raw material A at £11 per kg and 10 100 kg of raw material B at £14 per kg were purchased. This gives a total purchase cost of £209 000 for A and £141 400 for B. The standard prices were £10 per kg for A and £5 per kg for B. The accounting entries for material A are

	(£)	(£)
1. Dr Stores ledger control account (AQ × SP)	190 000	
1. Dr Material price variance account	19 000	
1. Cr Creditors control account (AQ × AP)		209 000

You will see that the stores ledger control account is debited with the standard price (SP) for the actual quantity purchased (AQ), and the actual price (AP) to be paid is credited to the creditors control account. The difference is the material price variance. The accounting entries for material B are

	(£)	(£)
2. Dr Stores ledger control account (AQ × SP)	151 500	
2. Cr Material price variance account		10 100
2. Cr Creditors (AQ × AP)		141 400

USAGE OF MATERIALS

19 000 kg of A and 10 100 kg of B were actually issued, and the standard usage (SQ) was 18 000 and 9000 kg at standard prices of £10 and £15. The accounting entries for material A are

	(£)	(£)
3. Dr Work in progress (SQ × SP)	180 000	
3. Dr Material usage variance	10 000	
3. Cr Stores ledger control account (AQ × SP)		190 000

Work in progress is debited with the standard quantity of materials at the standard price and the stores ledger account is credited with the actual quantity issued at the standard price. The difference is the material usage variance. The accounting entries for material B are

	(£)	(£)
4. Dr Work in progress (SQ × SP)	135 000	
4. Dr Material usage variance	16 500	
4. Cr Stores ledger control account (AQ × SP)		151 500

DIRECT WAGES

The actual hours worked were 28 500 hours for the month. The standard hours produced were 27 000. The actual wage rate paid was £9.60 per hour, compared with a standard rate of £9 per hour. The actual wages cost is recorded in the same way in a standard costing system as an actual costing system. The accounting entry for the actual wages paid is

	(£)	(£)
5. Dr Wages control account	273 600	
5. Cr Wages accrued account		273 600

The wages control account is then cleared as follows:

	(£)	(£)
6. Dr Work in progress (SQ × SP)	243 000	
6. Cr Wages control account		243 000
6. Dr Wage rate variance	17 100	
6. Dr Labour efficiency variance	13 500	
6. Cr Wages control account		30 600

The wages control account is credited and the work in progress account is debited with the standard cost (i.e. standard hours produced times the standard wage rate). The wage rate and labour efficiency variance accounts are debited, since they are both adverse variances and account for the difference between the actual wages cost (recorded as a debit in the wages control account) and the standard wages cost (recorded as a credit in the wages control account).

MANUFACTURING OVERHEAD COSTS INCURRED

The actual manufacturing overhead incurred is £52 000 for variable overheads and £116 000 for fixed overheads. The accounting entries for actual overhead *incurred* are recorded in the same way in a standard costing system as in an actual costing system. That is,

	(£)	(£)
7. Dr Factory variable overhead control account	52 000	
7. Dr Factory fixed overhead control account	116 000	
7. Cr Expense creditors		168 000

ABSORPTION OF MANUFACTURING OVERHEADS AND RECORDING THE VARIANCES

Work in progress is debited with the standard manufacturing overhead cost for the output produced. The standard overhead rates were £4 per standard hour for fixed overhead and £2 per standard hour for variable overheads. The actual output was 27 000 standard hours. The standard fixed overhead cost is therefore £108 000 (27 000 standard hours at £4 per hour) and the variable overhead cost is £54 000. The accounting entries for fixed overheads are

	(£)	(£)
8. Dr Work in progress (SQ × SP)	108 000	
8. Dr Volume variance	12 000	
8. Cr Factory fixed overhead control account		120 000
8. Dr Factory fixed overhead control account	4 000	
8. Cr Fixed overhead expenditure variance		4 000

You will see that the debit of £108 000 to the work in progress account and the corresponding credit to the factory fixed overhead control account represents the standard fixed overhead cost of production. The difference between the debit entry of £116 000 in the factory fixed overhead control account in Exhibit 15.9 for the *actual* fixed overheads incurred, and the credit entry of £108 000 for the *standard* fixed overhead cost of production is the total fixed overhead variance, which consists of an adverse volume variance of £12 000 and a favourable expenditure variance of £4000. This is recorded as a debit to the volume variance account and a credit to the expenditure variance account. The accounting entries for variable overheads are

	(£)	(£)
9. Dr Work in progress account (SQ × SP)	54 000	
9. Dr Variable overhead efficiency variance	3 000	
9. Cr Factory variable overhead control account		57 000
9. Dr Factory variable overhead control account	5 000	
9. Cr Variable overhead expenditure variance account		5 000

The same principles apply with variable overheads. The debit to work in progress account and the corresponding credit to the factory variable overhead control account of £54 000 is the standard variable overhead cost of production. The difference between the debit entry of £52 000 in the factory variable overhead account in Exhibit 15.9 for the *actual* variable overheads incurred and the credit entry of £54 000 for the *standard* variable overhead cost of production is the total variable overhead variance, which consists of an adverse efficiency variance of £3000 and a favourable expenditure variance of £5000.

COMPLETION OF PRODUCTION

In Exhibit 15.9 the total amount recorded on the debit side of the work in progress account is £720 000. As there are no opening or closing stocks, this represents the total standard cost of production for the period, which consists of 9000 units at £80 per unit. When the completed production is transferred from work in progress to finished goods stock, the accounting entries will be as follows:

	(£)	(£)
10. Dr Finished stock account	720 000	
10. Cr Work in progress account		720 000

Because there are no opening or closing stocks, both the work in progress account and the stores ledger account will show a nil balance.

SALES

Sales variances are not recorded in the accounts, so actual sales of £810 000 for 9000 units will be recorded as

	(£)	(£)
11. Dr Debtors	810 000	
11. Cr Sales		810 000

EXHIBIT 15.9

Accounting entries for a standard costing system

Stores ledger control account

1. Creditors (material A)	190 000	3. Work in progress (material A)	180 000
2. Creditors (material B)	151 500		
		3. Material usage variance (material A)	10 000
		4. Work in progress (material B)	135 000
		4. Material usage variance (material B)	16 500
	341 500		341 500

Creditors control account

2. Material price variance (material B)	10 100	1. Stores ledger control (material A)	190 000
		1. Material price variance (material A)	19 000
		2. Stores ledger control (material B)	151 500

Variance accounts

1. Creditors (material A)	19 000	2. Creditors (material price B)	10 100
3. Stores ledger control (material A usage)	10 000	8. Fixed factory overhead (expenditure)	4 000
4. Stores ledger control (material B usage)	16 500	9. Variable factory overhead (expenditure)	5 000
6. Wages control (wage rate)	17 100		19 100
6. Wages control (lab. effic'y)	13 500	13. Costing P + L a/c (balance)	72 000
8. Fixed factory overhead (volume)	12 000		
9. Variable factory overhead (effic'y)	3 000		
	91 100		91 100

Work in progress control account

3. Stores ledger (material A)	180 000	10. Finished goods stock account	720 000
4. Stores ledger (material B)	135 000		
6. Wages control	243 000		
8. Fixed factory overhead	108 000		
9. Variable factory overhead	54 000		
	720 000		720 000

Wages control account

5. Wages accrued account	273 600	6. WIP	243 000
		6. Wage rate variance	17 100
		6. Labour efficiency variance	13 500
	273 600		273 600

Fixed factory overhead control account

7. Expense creditors	116 000	8. WIP	108 000
8. Expenditure variance	4 000	8. Volume variance	12 000
	120 000		120 000

Variable factory overhead control account

7. Expense creditors	52 000	9. WIP	54 000
9. Expenditure	5 000	9. Efficiency variance	3 000
	57 000		57 000

Finished goods stock control account

| 10. WIP | 720 000 | 12. Cost of sales | 720 000 |

Cost of sales account

| 12. Finish goods stock | 720 000 | 13. Costing P + L a/c | 720 000 |

Costing P + L Account

12. Cost of sales at standard cost	720 000	11. Sales	810 000
13. Variance account (net variances)	72 000		
Profit for period	18 000		
	810 000		810 000

As all the production for the period has been sold, there will be no closing stock of finished goods, and the standard cost of production for the 9000 units will be transferred from the finished goods account to the cost of sales account:

	(£)	(£)
12. Dr Cost of sales account	288 000	
12. Cr Finished goods account		288 000

Finally, the cost of sales account and the variance accounts will be closed by a transfer to the costing profit and loss account (the item labelled 13 in Exhibit 15.9). The balance of the costing profit and loss account will be the *actual* profit for the period.

CALCULATION OF PROFIT

To calculate the profit, we must add the adverse variances and deduct the favourable variances from the standard cost of sales, which is obtained from the cost of sales account.

This calculation gives the actual cost of sales for the period, which is then deducted from the actual sales to produce the actual profit for the period. The calculations are as follows:

	(£)	(£)	(£)
Sales			810 000
Less standard cost of sales		720 000	
Plus adverse variances:			
Material A price variance	19 000		
Material usage variance	26 500		
Wage rate variance	17 100		
Labour efficiency variance	13 500		
Volume variance	12 000		
Variable overhead efficiency variance	3 000	91 100	
		811 100	
Less favourable variances:			
Material B price variance	10 100		
Fixed overhead expenditure variance	4 000		
Variable overhead expenditure variance	5 000	19 100	
Actual cost of sales			792 000
Actual profit			18 000

Summary

In this chapter we have explained the variance computations for a standard variable and a standard absorption costing system. With a standard variable costing system, fixed overheads are not allocated to products. Sales margin variances are therefore reported in terms of contribution margins and a single fixed overhead variance, that is, the fixed overhead expenditure variance is reported. With a standard absorption costing system, fixed overheads are allocated to products, and this process leads to the creation of a fixed overhead volume variance and the reporting of sales margin variances measured in terms of profit margins. The fixed overhead volume variance is not particularly helpful for cost control purposes, but this variance is required for financial accounting purposes.

To enable you to review your understanding of variance calculations, the formulae for the variances that we have considered in this chapter are summarized below. In each case the formula is arranged so that a positive variance is favourable and a negative variance unfavourable. The following variances are reported for both variable and absorption standard costing systems.

Materials and labour

1. Material price variance = (standard price per unit of material – actual price) × quantity of materials purchased

2. Material usage variance = (standard quantity of materials for actual production – actual quantity used) × standard price per unit

3. Total materials cost variance = (actual production × standard material cost per unit of production) – actual materials cost

4. Wage rate variance = (standard wage rate per hour – actual wage rate) × actual labour hours worked

5. Labour efficiency variance = (standard quantity of labour hours for actual production – actual labour hours) × standard wage rate

6. Total labour cost variance = (actual production × standard labour cost per unit of production) – actual labour cost

Fixed production overhead

7. Fixed overhead expenditure = budgeted fixed overheads – actual fixed overheads

Variable production overhead

8. Variable overhead expenditure variance = (budgeted variable overheads for actual input volume – actual variable overhead cost)

9. Variable overhead efficiency variance = (standard quantity of input hours for actual production – actual input hours) × variable overhead rate

10. Total variable overhead variance = (actual production × standard variable overhead rate per unit) – actual variable overhead cost

Sales margins

11. Sales margin price variance = (actual unit contribution margin* – standard unit contribution margin) × actual sales volume

(*Contribution margins are used with a variable standard costing system whereas profit margins are used with an absorption costing system. With both systems, actual margins are calculated by deducting *standard* costs from actual selling price.)

12. Sales margin volume variance = (actual sales volume – budgeted sales volume) × standard contribution margin

13. Total sales margin variance = total actual contribution – total budgeted contribution

With a standard absorption costing system the following additional variances can be reported:

14. Fixed overhead volume variance = (actual production – budgeted production) × standard fixed overhead rate

15. Volume efficiency variance = (standard quantity of input hours for actual production – actual input hours) × standard fixed overhead rate

16. Volume capacity variance = (actual hours of input – budgeted hours of input) × standard fixed overhead rate

17. Total fixed overhead variance = (actual production × standard fixed overhead rate per unit) – actual fixed overhead cost

Key Terms and Concepts

attainable standards (p. 375)
basic cost standards (p. 374)
bill of materials (p. 371)
budgeted costs (p. 367)
budgeted hours of input (p. 390)
budgeted hours of output (p. 390)
capacity usage ratio (p. 397)
engineering studies (p. 371)
fixed overhead expenditure variance (p. 386)
ideal standards (p. 374)
labour efficiency variance (p. 383)
material price variance (p. 379)
material usage variance (p. 381)
production efficiency ratio (p. 397)
production volume ratio (p. 397)
sales margin price variance (p. 388)

sales margin volume variance (p. 389)
standard costs (p. 367)
standard hours (p. 373)
standard hours produced (p. 373)
total fixed overhead variance (p. 390)
total labour variance (p. 384)
total material variance (p. 382)
total sales margin variance (p. 388)
total variable overhead variance (p. 384)
variable overhead efficiency variance (p. 385)
variable overhead expenditure variance (p. 385)
volume capacity variance (p. 393)
volume efficiency variance (p. 392)
volume variance (pp. 389, 391)
wage rate variance (p. 382).

Key Examination Points

A common error that students make it to calculate quantity variances based on the original fixed budget. Remember to flex the budget. Therefore the starting point when answering a standard costing question should be to calculate actual production. If more than one product is produced, output should be expressed in standard hours. If standard overhead rates are not given, you can calculate the rates by dividing budgeted fixed and variable overheads by the budgeted output. Remember that output can be measured by units produced or standard hours produced. Make sure you are consistent and use overhead rates per standard hours if production is measured in standard

hours, or overhead rates per unit produced if output is measured in terms of units produced. You should always express output in standard hours if the question requires the calculation of overhead efficiency variances. If the question does not specify whether you should calculate the variances on an absorption or variable costing basis choose your preferred method and state the approach you have selected in your answer.

Frequently questions are set that give you the variances but require calculations of actual costs and inputs (see review problems 9 and 10 and Questions 15.24–15.27). Students who calculate variances simply by committing to memory a series of variance formulae experience difficulties in answering these questions. Make sure you understand how the variances are calculated, and check your answers with the solutions to the review problems.

Review Problems

(For additional problems without answers relating to the content of this chapter you should refer to pages 525–540.)

1. During a period, 17500 labour hours were worked at a standard cost of £6.50 per hour. The labour efficiency variance was £7800 favourable.

    How many standard hours were produced?

A	1 200
B	16 300
C	17 500
D	18 700

2. T plc uses a standard costing system, which is material stock account being maintained at standard costs. The following details have been extracted from the standard cost card in respect of direct materials:

    8 kg at £0.80/kg = £6.40 per unit
    Budgeted production in April was 850 units.

    The following details relate to actual materials purchased and issued to production during April, when actual production was 870 units:

Materials purchased	8200 kg costing £6888
Materials issued to production	7150 kg

    Which of the following correctly states the material price and usage variance to be reported?

	Price	Usage
A	£286 (A)	£152 (A)
B	£286 (A)	£280 (A)
C	£286 (A)	£294 (A)
D	£328 (A)	£152 (A)
E	£328 (A)	£280 (A)

    CIMA Stage 2

3. PQ Limited operates a standard costing system for its only product. The standard cost card is as follows:

Direct material (4 kg at £2/kg)	£8.00
Direct labour (4 hours at £4/hour)	£16.00
Variable overhead (4 hours at £3/hour)	£12.00
Fixed overhead (4 hours at £5/hour)	£20.00

    Fixed overheads are absorbed on the basis of labour hours. Fixed overhead costs are budgeted at £12 000 per annum, arising at a constant rate during the year.

    Activity in period 3 is budgeted to be 10% of total activity for the year. Actual production during period 3 was 500 units, with actual fixed overhead costs incurred being £9800 and actual hours worked being 1970.

    The fixed overhead expenditure variance for period 3 was:

A	£2200 (F)
B	£200 (F)
C	£50 (F)
D	£200 (A)
E	£2200 (A)

    CIMA Stage 2

4. QR Limited uses a standard absorption costing system. The following details have been extracted from its budget for April:

Fixed production overhead cost	£48 000
Production (units)	4 800

    In April the fixed production overhead cost was under-absorbed by £8000 and the fixed production overhead expenditure variance was £2000 adverse.

    The actual number of units produced was:

A	3800
B	4000
C	4200
D	5400
E	5800

    CIMA Stage 2

5. F Limited has the following budget and actual data:

Budget fixed overhead cost	£100 000
Budget production (units)	20 000
Actual fixed overhead cost	£110 000
Actual production (units)	19 500

The fixed overhead volume variance:

A   is £500 adverse;
B   is £2500 adverse;
C   is £10 000 adverse;
D   is £17 500 adverse;
E   cannot be calculated from the data given.

CIMA Stage 2 Specimen Paper

6. J Limited operates a standard cost accounting system. The following information has been extracted from its standard cost card and budgets:

Budgeted sales volume	5000 units
Budgeted selling price	£10.00 per unit
Standard variable cost	£5.60 per unit
Standard total cost	£7.50 per unit

If it used a standard marginal cost accounting system and its actual sales were 4500 units at a selling price of £12.00, its sales volume variance would be:

A   £1250 adverse
B   £2200 adverse
C   £2250 adverse
D   £3200 adverse
E   £5000 adverse

CIMA Stage 2 Specimen Paper

7. BS Limited manufactures one standard product and operates a system of variance accounting. As assistant management accountant, you are responsible for preparing the monthly operating statements. Data from the budget, the standard product cost and actual data for the month ended 31 October are given below.

Using the data given, you are required to prepare the operating statement for the month ended 31 October to show the budgeted profit;

the variances for direct materials, direct wages, overhead and sales, each analysed into causes; and actual profit.

Budgeted and standard cost data:

Budgeted sales and production for the month: 10 000 units

Standard cost for each unit of product:
Direct material: X: 10 kg at £1 per kg
                    Y: 5 kg at £5 per kg
Direct wages: 5 hours at £3 per hour
Fixed production overhead is absorbed at 200% of direct wages
Budgeted sales price has been calculated to give a profit of 20% of sales price

Actual data for month ended 31 October:

Production: 9500 units sold at a price of 10% higher than that budgeted
Direct materials consumed:
    X: 96 000 kg at £1.20 per kg
    Y: 48 000 kg at £4.70 per kg
Direct wages incurred 46 000 hours at £3.20 per hour
Fixed production overhead incurred £290 000

(30 marks)
CIMA Cost Accounting 2

8. Bronte Ltd manufactures a single product, a laminated kitchen unit with a standard cost of £80 made up as follows:

	(£)
Direct materials (15 sq. metres at £3 per sq. metre)	45
Direct labour (5 hours at £4 per hour)	20
Variable overheads (5 hours at £2 per hour)	10
Fixed overheads (5 hours at £1 per hour)	5
	80

The standard selling price of the kitchen unit is £100. The monthly budget projects production and sales of 1000 units. Actual figures for the month of April are as follows:
Sales 1200 units at £102
Production 1400 units
Direct materials 22 000 sq. metres at £4 per sq. metre
Direct wages 6800 hours at £5

Variable overheads £11 000

Fixed overheads £6000

You are required to prepare:

(a) a trading account reconciling actual and budgeted profit and showing all the appropriate variances; (*13 marks*)

(b) ledger accounts in respect of the above transactions.

ICAEW Accounting Techniques*

(* The original examination question did not include part (b).)

9. The following data relate to actual output, costs and variances for the four-weekly accounting period number 4 of a company that makes only one product. Opening and closing work in progress figures were the same.

	(£000)
Actual production of product XY	18 000 units
Actual costs incurred:	
Direct materials purchased and used (150 000 kg)	210
Direct wages for 32 000 hours	136
Variable production overhead	38

	(£000)
Variances:	
Direct materials price	15 F
Direct materials usage	9 A
Direct labour rate	8 A
Direct labour efficiency	16 F
Variable production overhead expenditure	6 A
Variable production overhead efficiency	4 F

Variable production overhead varies with labour hours worked.

A standard marginal costing system is operated.

You are required to:

(a) present a standard product cost sheet for one unit of product XY, (*16 marks*)

(b) describe briefly *three* types of standard that can be used for a standard costing system, stating which is usually preferred in practice and why. (*9 marks*)

(*Total 25 marks*)

CIMA Cost Accounting Stage 2

10. The following data have been collected for the month of April by a company which operates a standard absorption costing system:

Actual production of product EM	600 units
Actual costs incurred:	(£)
Direct material E 660 metres	6 270
Direct material M 200 metres	650
Direct wages 3200 hours	23 200
Variable production overhead (which varied with hours worked)	6 720
Fixed production overhead	27 000
Variances	(£)
Direct material price:	
Material E	330 F
Material M	50 A
Direct material usage:	
Material E	600 A
Material M	nil
Direct labour rate	800 A
Direct labour efficiency	1400 A
Variable production overhead:	
expenditure	320 A
efficiency	400 A
Fixed production overhead:	
expenditure	500 F
volume	2500 F

Opening and closing work in progress figures were identical, so can be ignored.

You are required to:

(a) prepare for the month of April a statement of total standard costs for product EM; (*3 marks*)

(b) prepare a standard product cost sheet for one unit of product EM; (*7 marks*)

(c) calculate the number of units of product EM which were budgeted for April; (*2 marks*)

(d) state how the material and labour cost standards for product EM would originally have been determined. (*3 marks*)

(*Total 15 marks*)

CIMA Stage 2 Cost Accounting

Solutions to Review Problems

SOLUTION 1

A favourable labour efficiency variance indicates that actual hours used were less than the standard hours produced. The favourable variance was £7800. Therefore the standard hours produced were 18 700 (17 500 + £7800/£6.50).

Answer = D

SOLUTION 2

Materials price variance
$$= \text{(Standard price} - \text{Actual price)} \times \text{Actual quantity}$$
$$= \text{(Actual quantity} \times \text{Standard price)} - \text{Actual cost}$$
$$= (8200 \times £0.80) - £6888$$
$$= £328 \text{ Adverse}$$
Material usage variance
$$= \text{(Standard quantity} - \text{Actual quantity)} \times \text{Standard price}$$
$$= (870 \times 8 \text{ kg} = 6960 - 7150) \times £0.80$$
$$= £152 \text{ Adverse}$$

Answer = D

SOLUTION 3

Fixed overhead variance
$$= \text{Budgeted cost (not flexed)} - \text{Actual cost}$$
$$= £10 000 \text{ per month} - £9800$$
$$= £200 \text{ Favourable}$$

Answer = B

SOLUTION 4

Standard fixed overhead rate
$$= \frac{\text{Budgeted cost (£48 000)}}{\text{Budgeted output (4800 units)}} = £10$$
Overheads incurred
$$= \text{Budgeted cost} + \text{Expenditure variance} (£2 000) = £50 000$$
Overheads absorbed
$$= £50 000 - \text{Under-absorption (£8000)} = £42 000$$
Actual number of units produced
$$= £42 000/£10 = £4200$$

Answer = C

SOLUTION 5

Volume variance
$$= \text{(Actual production} - \text{Budgeted production)} \times \text{Fixed overhead rate}$$
$$= (19 500 - 20 000) \times (£100 000/20 000)$$
$$= £2500A$$

Answer = B

SOLUTION 6

Sales volume variance
$$= \text{(Actual sales volume} - \text{Budgeted sales volume)} \times \text{Standard contribution margin}$$
$$= (4500 - 5000) £4.40$$
$$= £2200 \text{ Adverse}$$

Answer = B

SOLUTION 7

1. *Preliminary calculations*
The standard product cost and selling price are calculated as follows:

	(£)
Direct materials	
X (10 kg at £1)	10
Y (5 kg at £5)	25
Direct wages (5 hours × £3)	15
Fixed overhead (5 hours × 200% of £3)	30
Standard cost	80
Profit (20/(100 − 20)) × £80	20
Selling price	100

The actual profit for the period is calculated as follows:

	(£)	(£)
Sales (9500 at £110)		1 045 000
Direct materials: X	115 200	
Y	225 600	
Direct wages (46 000 × £3.20)	147 200	
Fixed overhead	290 000	778 000
Actual profit		267 000

	(£)	(£)

Material price variance:
  (standard price − actual price)
    × actual quantity
  X: (£1 − £1.20) × 96 000   19 200 A
  Y: (£5 − £4.70) × 48 000   14 400 F   4800 A
Material usage variance:
  (standard quantity − actual
    quantity) × standard price
  X: (9500 × 10 = 95 000 − 96 000) × £1   1000 A
  Y: (9500 × 5 = 47 500 − 48 000) × £5   2500 A   3500 A

The actual materials used are in standard proportions. Therefore there is no mix variance.

Wage rate variance:
  (standard rate − actual rate) × actual hours
  (£3 − £3.20) × 46 000   9200 A
Labour efficiency variance:
  (standard hours − actual hours) × standard rate
  (9500 × 5 = 47 500 − 46 000) × £3   4 500 F   4 700 A
Fixed overhead expenditure:
  budgeted fixed overheads − actual fixed overheads
  (10 000 × £30 = £300 000 − £290 000)   10 000 F
Volume efficiency variance:
  (standard hours − actual hours) × fixed overhead rate
  (47 500 − 46 000) × £6   9 000 F
Volume capacity variance:
  (actual hours − budgeted hours) × fixed overhead rate
  (46 000 − 50 000) × £6   24 000 A   15 000 A
Sales margin price variance:
  (actual margin − standard margin) × actual sales volume
  (£30 − £20) × 9500   95 000 F
Sales margin volume variance:
  (actual sales volume − budgeted sales volume)
    × standard margin
  (9500 − 10 000) × £20   10 000 A   85 000 F
Total variance   67 000 F

	(£)
Budgeted profit (10 000 units at £20)	200 000
Add favourable variances (see above)	67 000
Actual profit	267 000

Note
The above calculations assume that variances are computed based on an absorption costing system. An alternative answer is to compute the variances based on a variable costing system. Adopting this approach would result in the sales margin volume variance being valued at the unit contribution of £50. The revised variance would be £25 000A (500 × £50) and no variances would be reported for the volume capacity and efficiency variances.

SOLUTION 8

(a) Material price:
  (standard price − actual price) × actual
  quantity (£3 − £4) × 22 000 = £22 000 A

Material usage:
  (standard quantity − actual quantity)
    × standard price
  ((1400 × 15 = 21 000) − 22 000) × £3
    = £3000 A
Wage rate:
  (standard rate − actual rate)
    × actual hours (£4 − £5) × 6800
    = £6800 A
Labour efficiency:
  ((1400 × 5 = 7000) − 6800) × £4 = £800 F
Fixed overhead expenditure:
  (budgeted fixed overheads
    − actual fixed overheads)
    (1000 × £5 = £5000 − £6000) = £1000 A
Volume efficiency:
  (standard hrs − actual hrs) × FOAR
  (1400 × 5 = 7000 − 6800) × £1 = £200 F
Volume capacity:
  (actual hrs − budgeted hrs) × FOAR
    (6800 − 5000) × £1 = £1800 F
Variable overhead efficiency:
  (standard hrs − actual hrs) × VOAR
    (7000 − 6800) × £2 = £400 F
Variable overhead expenditure:
  (flexed budgeted variable overheads
    − actual variable overheads)
    (6800 × £2 − £11 000) = £2600 F
Sales margin price:
  (actual margin − standard margin) × actual
  sales volume
  (£102 − £80 = £22 − £20) × 1200
    = £2400 F
Sales margin volume:
  (actual sales − budgeted sales)
    × standard margin
    (1200 − 1000) × £20 = £4000 F

Reconciliation of budgeted and actual profit

		(£)
Budgeted profit (1000 units at £20)		20 000

	Adverse (£)	Favourable (£)
Sales margin price		2 400
Sales margin volume		4 000
Material price	22 000	
Material usage	3 000	
Wage rate	6 800	
Labour efficiency		800
Fixed overhead expenditure	1 000	
Fixed overhead efficiency		200

Fixed overhead capacity		1 800
Variable overhead expenditure		2 600
Variable overhead efficiency		400
	32 800	12 200
Net adverse variance		20 600
Actual profit/(loss)		(600)

Note

It is assumed that the company operates a standard absorption costing system for stock valuation and profit measurement purposes and that there are no opening stocks. The actual profit is calculated as follows:

	(£)	(£)
Sales (1200 units × £102)		122 400
Less cost of sales		
Direct materials	88 000	
Direct wages	34 000	
Overheads	17 000	
Closing stocks (200 units at £80)	(16 000)	123 000
Profit/(Loss)		(600)

(b)

Stores ledger control account

Creditors	66 000	WIP	63 000
		Material usage variance	3 000
	66 000		66 000

Variance accounts

Creditors	22 000	Wages control	
Stores ledger		(labour efficiency)	800
(material usage)	3 000	Fixed overhead (volume)	2 000
Wages control (wage rate)	6 800	Variable overhead	
Fixed overhead		(expenditure)	2 600
(expenditure)	1 000	Variable overhead	
		(efficiency)	400
		Costing P + L a/c (balance)	27 000
	32 800		32 800

Costing P + L account

Cost of sales	96 000	Sales	122 400
Variance account		Loss for period	600
(net variances)	27 000		
	123 000		123 000

WIP control account

Stores ledger	63 000	Finished goods stock	112 000
Wages control	28 000		
Fixed factory overhead	7 000		
Variable factory overhead	14 000		
	112 000		112 000

Wages control account

Wages accrued account	34 000	WIP	28 000
Labour efficiency variance	800	Wage rate variance	6 800
	34 800		34 800

Fixed factory overhead account

Expense creditors	6 000	WIP	7 000
Volume variance	2 000	Expenditure variance	1 000
	8 000		8 000

Variable factory overhead account

Expense creditors	11 000	WIP	14 000
Expenditure variance	2 600		
Efficiency variance	400		
	14 000		14 000

Finished goods stock

WIP	112 000	Cost of sales	96 000
		Closing stock c/fwd	16 000
	112 000		112 000

Cost of sales account

Finished goods stock	96 000	Cost P + L a/c	96 000

SOLUTION 9

(a) *Standard product cost for one unit of product XY*

	(£)
Direct materials (8 kg (W2) at £1.50 (W1) per kg)	12.00
Direct wages (2 hours (W4) at £4 (W3) per hour)	8.00
Variable overhead (2 hours (W4) at £1 (W5) per hour)	2.00
	22.00

Workings

(W1) Actual quantity of materials purchased at standard price is £225 000 (actual cost plus favourable material price variance). Therefore standard price = £1.50 (£225 000/150 000 kg).

(W2) Material usage variance = 6000 kg (£9000/£1.50 standard price). Therefore standard quantity for actual production = 144 000 kg (150 000 − 6000 kg). Therefore standard quantity per unit = 8 kg (144 000 kg/18 000 units).

(W3) Actual hours worked at standard rate = £128 000 (£136 000 − £8000). Therefore standard rate per hour = £4 (£128 000/32 000 hours).

(W4) Labour efficiency variance = 4000 hours (£16 000/£4). Therefore standard hours for actual production = 36 000 hours (32 000 + 4000). Therefore standard hours per unit = 2 hours (36 000 hours/18 000 units).

(W5) Actual hours worked at the standard variable overhead rate is £32 000 (£38 000 actual variable overheads less £6000 favourable expenditure variance). Therefore, standard variable overhead rate = £1 (£32 000/32 000 hours).

(b) See 'Types of cost standards' in Chapter 15 for the answer to this question.

SOLUTION 10

(a) *Statement of total standard costs for product EM*

	Actual cost (£)	Total variance (£)	Standard cost (£)
Direct material: E	6 270	270A	6 000
M	650	50A	600
Direct labour	23 200	2 200A	21 000
Variable overhead	6 720	720A	6 000
Fixed overhead	27 000	3 000F	30 000

(b) *Standard product cost*

	(£)
Direct material E (1 metre at £10 per metre)	10.00[a]
Direct material M (0.333 metres at £3)	1.00[b]
Direct labour (5 hours at £7)	35.00[c]
Variable overhead (5 hours at £2)	10.00[d]
Fixed overhead (5 hours at £10)	50.00[e]
	106.00

Notes

[a] Standard direct material cost per unit = £6000/600 units = £10.
Actual quantity × standard price = £6600 (£6270 + £330).
Standard price per metre = £10 (£6600/660 metres).
Standard quantity = 1 metre (£10 standard cost/£10 per metre standard price).

[b] Standard direct material cost per unit = £1 (£600/600 units).
Actual quantity × standard price = £600 (£650 − £50).
Standard price = £3 (£600/200 metres).
Standard quantity = 0.333 metres (£1/£3 metres).

[c] Standard direct labour cost per unit = £35 (£21 000/600 units).
Actual hours × standard price = £22 400 (£23 200 − £800).
Standard rate = £7 (£22 400/3200 hours).
Standard quantity = 5 hours (£35/£7 per hour).

[d] Standard variable overhead rate per unit = £10 (£6000/600 units).
Standard hours calculated in note c = 5 hours.
Standard rate = £2 (£10/5 hours).

[e] Standard fixed overhead rate per unit = £50 (£30 000/600 units).
Standard hours calculated in note c = 5 hours.
Standard fixed overhead rate = £10 (£50/5 hours).

(c) Actual fixed overheads + expenditure variance = budgeted fixed overheads
Budgeted fixed overheads = £27 000 + £500 = £27 500
Budgeted production = budgeted fixed overheads/standard cost = £27 500/50 = 550 units

(d) See 'Establishing cost standards' in Chapter 15 for the answer to this question.

Questions

Chapter 2

* Indicates that a suggested solution is to be found in the *Students' Manual*.

2.1*
Fixed costs are conventionally deemed to be:
A constant per unit of output;
B constant in total when production volume changes;
C outside the control of management;
D those unaffected by inflation.

CIMA Stage 1 Cost Accounting

2.2*
Prepare a report for the Managing Director of your company explaining how costs may be classified by their behaviour, with particular reference to the effects both on total and on unit costs. Your report should
(i) say why it is necessary to classify costs by their behaviour, and
(ii) be illustrated by sketch graphs within the body of the report.   (*15 marks*)

CIMA Stage 1 Accounting

2.3*
Describe three different methods of cost classification and explain the utility of each method.

(*11 marks*)
ACCA Level 1 Costing

2.4*
Cost classification used in costing include:
(i)   period costs
(ii) product costs
(iii) variable costs
(iv) opportunity costs

Required:
Explain each of these classifications, with examples of the types of costs that may be included.

(*17 marks*)
ACCA Level 1 Costing

2.5*
(a) Describe the role of the cost accountant in a manufacturing organization.   (*8 marks*)
(b) Explain whether you agree with each of the following statements:
   (i)   'All direct costs are variable.'

   (ii) 'Variable costs are controllable and fixed costs are not.'
   (iii) 'Sunk costs are irrelevant when providing decision making information.'

(*9 marks*)
(*Total 17 marks*)
ACCA Level 1 Costing

2.6*
'Costs may be classified in a variety of ways according to their nature and the information needs of management.' Explain and discuss this statement, illustrating with examples of the classifications required for different purposes.

(*22 marks*)
ICSA Management Accounting

2.7*
It is commonly suggested that a management accounting system should be capable of supplying different measures of cost for different purposes. You are required to set out the main types of purpose for which cost information may be required in a business organization, and to discuss the alternative measures of cost which might be appropriate for each purpose.

ICAEW Management Accounting

2.8*
Opportunity cost and *sunk cost* are among the concepts of cost commonly discussed.

You are required:
(i)   to define these terms precisely;   (*4 marks*)
(ii) to suggest for each of them situations in which the concept might be applied;   (*4 marks*)
(iii) to assess briefly the significance of each of the concepts.   (*4 marks*)

ICAEW P2 Management Accounting

2.9*
Distinguish between, and provide an illustration of:
(i) 'avoidable' and 'unavoidable' costs;
(ii) 'cost centres' and 'cost units'.

(*8 marks*)
ACCA Foundation Paper 3

2.10
For the relevant cost data in items (1)–(7), indicate which of the following is the best classification.
(a) sunk cost   (b) incremental cost
(c) variable cost   (d) fixed cost

(e) semi-variable cost   (f) semi-fixed cost
(g) controllable cost   (h) non-controllable cost
(i) opportunity cost

(1) A company is considering selling an old machine. The machine has a book value of £20 000. In evaluating the decision to sell the machine, the £20 000 is a . . .
(2) As an alternative to the old machine, the company can rent a new one. It will cost £3000 a year. In analysing the cost–volume behaviour the rental is a . . .
(3) To run the firm's machines, here are two alternative courses of action. One is to pay the operator a base salary plus a small amount per unit produced. This makes the total cost of the operators a . . .
(4) As an alternative, the firm can pay the operators a flat salary. It would then use one machine when volume is low, two when it expands, and three during peak periods. This means that the total operator cost would now be a . . .
(5) The machine mentioned in (1) could be sold for £8000. If the firm considers retaining and using it, the £8000 is a . . .
(6) If the firm wishes to use the machine any longer, it must be repaired. For the decision to retain the machine, the repair cost is a . . .
(7) The machine is charged to the foreman of each department at a rate of £3000 a year. In evaluating the foreman, the charge is a . . .

2.11

A company manufactures and retails clothing. You are required to group the costs which are listed below and numbered (1)–(20) into the following classifications (each cost is intended to belong to only one classification):
(i)   direct materials
(ii)   direct labour
(iii)   direct expenses
(iv)   indirect production overhead
(v)   research and development costs
(vi)   selling and distribution costs
(vii)   administration costs
(viii) finance costs

(1) Lubricant for sewing machines
(2) Floppy disks for general office computer
(3) Maintenance contract for general office photocopying machine
(4) Telephone rental plus metered calls
(5) Interest on bank overdraft
(6) Performing Rights Society charge for music broadcast throughout the factory
(7) Market research undertaken prior to a new product launch
(8) Wages of security guards for factory
(9) Carriage on purchase of basic raw material
(10) Royalty payable on number of units of product XY produced
(11) Road fund licences for delivery vehicles
(12) Parcels sent to customers
(13) Cost of advertising products on television
(14) Audit fees
(15) Chief accountant's salary
(16) Wages of operatives in the cutting department
(17) Cost of painting advertising slogans on delivery vans
(18) Wages of storekeepers in materials store
(19) Wages of forklift truck drivers who handle raw materials
(20) Developing a new product in the laboratory
(10 marks)
CIMA Cost Accounting 1

2.12*

(a) 'Discretionary costs are troublesome because managers usually find it difficult to separate and quantify the results of their use in the business, as compared with variable and other fixed costs.'

You are required to discuss the above statement and include in your answer the meaning of discretionary costs, variable costs and fixed costs; give two illustrations of each of these three named costs. *(12 marks)*

(b) A drug company has initiated a research project which is intended to develop a new product. Expenditures to date on this particular research total £500 000 but it is now estimated that a further £200 000 will need to be spent before the product can be marketed. Over the estimated life of the product the profit potential has a net present value of £350 000.

You are required to advise management whether they should continue or abandon the project. Support your conclusion with a numerate statement and state what kind of cost is the £500 000. *(5 marks)*

(c) Opportunity costs and notional costs are not recognized by financial accounting systems but need to be considered in many decisions taken by management.

You are required to explain briefly the meanings of opportunity costs and notional costs; give two examples of each to illustrate the meanings you have attached to them.

(8 marks)
(Total 25 marks)
CIMA Stage 2 Cost Accounting

2.13 Analysis of costs by behaviour for decision-making

The Northshire Hospital Trust operates two types of specialist X-ray scanning machines, XR1 and XR50. Details for the next period are estimated as follows:

Machine	XR1	XR50
Running hours	1 100	2 000
	(£)	(£)
Variable running costs (excluding plates)	27 500	64 000
Fixed costs	20 000	97 500

A brain scan is normally carried out on machine type XR1: this task uses special X-ray plates costing £40 each and takes four hours of machine time. Because of the nature of the process, around 10% of the scans produce blurred and therefore useless results.

Required:
(a) Calculate the cost of a satisfactory brain scan on machine type XR1. *(7 marks)*
(b) Brain scans can also be done on machine type XR50 and would take only 1.8 hours per scan with a reduced reject rate of 6%. However, the cost of the X-ray plates would be £55 per scan.

Required:
Advise which type should be used, assuming sufficient capacity is available on both types of machine. *(8 marks)*
(Total 15 marks)
CIMA Stage 1 Cost Accounting

2.14* Sunk and opportunity costs for decision-making

Mrs Johnston has taken out a lease on a shop for a down payment of £5000. Additionally, the rent under the lease amounts to £5000 per annum. If the lease is cancelled, the initial payment of £5000

is forfeit. Mrs Johnston plans to use the shop for the sale of clothing, and has estimated operations for the next twelve months as follows:

	(£)	(£)
Sales	115 000	
Less Value-added tax (VAT)	15 000	
Sales Less VAT		100 000
Cost of goods sold	50 000	
Wages and wage related costs	12 000	
Rent including the down payment	10 000	
Rates, heating, lighting and insurance	13 000	
Audit, legal and general expenses	2 000	
		87 000
Net profit before tax		13 000

In the figures no provision has been made for the cost of Mrs Johnston but it is estimated that one half of her time will be devoted to the business. She is undecided whether to continue with her plans, because she knows that she can sublet the shop to a friend for a monthly rent of £550 if she does not use the shop herself.

You are required to:
(a) (i) explain and identify the 'sunk' and 'opportunity' costs in the situation depicted above;
(ii) state what decision Mrs Johnston should make according to the information given, supporting your conclusion with a financial statement; *(11 marks)*
(b) explain the meaning and use of 'notional' (or 'imputed') costs and quote *two* supporting examples. *(4 marks)*
(Total 15 marks)
CIMA Foundation Cost Accounting 1

2.15* Relevant costs and cost behaviour

(a) Distinguish between 'opportunity cost' and 'out of pocket cost' giving a numerical example of each using your own figures to support your answer. *(6 marks)*
(b) Jason travels to work by train to his 5-day week job. Instead of buying daily tickets he finds it cheaper to buy a quarterly season ticket which costs £188 for 13 weeks.

Debbie, an acquaintance, who also makes the same journey, suggests that they both travel in Jason's car and offers to give him £120 each quarter towards his car expenses. Except for weekend travelling and using it for local college attendance near his home on three evenings each week to study for his CIMA Stage 2, the car remains in Jason's garage.

Jason estimates that using his car for work would involve him, each quarter, in the following expenses:

	(£)
Depreciation (proportion of annual figure)	200
Petrol and oil	128
Tyres and miscellaneous	52

You are required to state whether Jason should accept Debbie's offer and to draft a statement to show clearly the monetary effect of your conclusion. *(5 marks)*

(c) A company with a financial year 1 September to 31 August prepared a sales budget which resulted in the following cost structure:

		% of sales
Direct materials		32
Direct wages		18
Production overhead:	variable	6
	fixed	24
Administrative and selling costs:	variable	3
	fixed	7
Profit		10

After ten weeks, however, it became obvious that the sales budget was too optimistic and it has now been estimated that because of a reduction in sales volume, for the full year, sales will total £2 560 000 which is only 80% of the previously budgeted figure.

You are required to present a statement for management showing the amended sales and cost structure in £s and percentages, in a marginal costing format.

(4 marks)
(Total 15 marks)
CIMA Stage 2 Cost Accounting

Chapter 3

* Indicates that a suggested solution is to be found in the *Students' Manual*.

3.1
Describe the essential requirements of an effective material stock control system. *(17 marks)*
ACCA Level 1 Costing

3.2
You have been given full responsibility for stock-taking of your company's inventory and its subsequent valuation. There are approximately 4000 different categories of stock, ranging from small components to finished products.
(a) Detail the factors required in order to achieve an efficient stocktake and inventory valuation. *(8 marks)*
(b) How would you recognize and deal with obsolescent stock and slow-moving stock? *(7 marks)*
(c) What is a perpetual inventory system? What benefits would accrue from its installation? *(7 marks)*
AAT

3.3*
The managing director of a company manufacturing and selling a range of goods has been looking through the previous period's accounts, and has noted that the cost of direct materials purchased, expressed as a percentage of sales, is higher than the budgeted material cost of sales, expressed as a percentage of sales. He concludes from this comparison that the company has been wasting or losing significant amounts of material.

Required:
(a) Provide *four* reasons why the managing director's conclusions regarding material waste/ losses could be incorrect. *(6 marks)*
(b) Assuming that the managing director is correct, identify *three* points where material waste/losses could have occurred, and for each point you have identified, outline a control procedure which could assist in reducing the material waste or losses. *(11 marks)*
ACCA Level 1 Costing

3.4

The management of a company manufacturing electrical components is considering introducing an historic batch costing system into its factory.

Required:
(a) Outline the information and procedures required in order to obtain the actual direct material cost of each batch of components manufactured. (*7 marks*)
(b) Identify the elements which could make up a direct operative's gross wage and for each element explain, with supporting reasons, whether it should be regarded as part of the prime cost of the components manufactured.
(*10 marks*)
ACCA Level 1 Costing

3.5* Stores pricing

Z Ltd had the following transactions in one of its raw materials during April

Opening stock		40 units	@ £10 each
April 4	Bought	140 units	@ £11 each
10	Used	90 units	
12	Bought	60 units	@ £12 each
13	Used	100 units	
16	Bought	200 units	@ £10 each
21	Used	70 units	
23	Used	80 units	
26	Bought	50 units	@ £12 each
29	Used	60 units	

You are required to:
(a) write up the stores ledger card using
  (i) FIFO and
  (ii) LIFO
  methods of stock valuation; (*8 marks*)
(b) state the cost of material used for each system during April; (*2 marks*)
(c) describe the weighted-average method of valuing stocks and explain how the use of this method would affect the cost of materials used and the balance sheet of Z Ltd compared to FIFO and LIFO in times of consistently rising prces. (Do NOT restate the stores ledger card for the above transactions using this method.)
(*5 marks*)
(*Total 15 marks*)
CIMA Stage 1 Accounting

3.6* Stores pricing and preparation of the stores control account

A company operates an historic batch costing system, which is not integrated with the financial accounts, and uses the weighted average method of pricing raw material issues. A weighted average price (to three decimal places of a pound £) is calculated after each purchase of material.

Receipts and issues of Material X for a week were as follows:

Receipts into stock			Issues to production	
Day	kg	£	Day	kg
1	1400	1092.00	2	1700
4	1630	1268.14	5	1250

At the beginning of the week, stock of material X was 3040 kg at a cost of £0.765 per kg. Of the issues of material on day 2, 60 kg were returned to stock on day 3. Of the receipts of material on day 1, 220 kg were returned to the supplier on day 4. Invoices for the material receipts during the week remained unpaid at the end of the week.

Required:
(a) Prepare a tabulation of the movement of stock during the week, showing the changes in the level of stock, its valuation per kilogram, and the total value of stock held.
(b) Record the week's transactions in the material X stock account in the cost ledger, indicating clearly in each case the account in which the corresponding entry should be posted.
(*9 marks*)
ACCA Foundation Paper 3

3.7 Stores pricing and calculation of EOQ

(a) Atlas Limited Is having difficulty costing material X to the various jobs that it is used on. The material is bought in bulk and recent receipts and issues have been:

1/6/03	Balance b/f	1000 kilos at £4 per kilo
3/6/03	Receipts	2000 kilos at £5 per kilo
6/6/03	Receipts	1500 kilos at £5.5 per kilo
9/6/03	Issues	2500 kilos

| 12/6/03 | Receipts | 3000 kilos at £4.5 per kilo |
| 14/6/03 | Issues | 3500 kilos |

Required:

Cost the issue of material X for June and calculate the value of the closing stock on the following bases:

(i)   FIFO;

(ii) LIFO;

(iii) weighted average.   (*10 marks*)

(b) Atlas is reviewing its stock control policy with regard to material X. You are told that the cost of making one order is £100, the cost of holding 1 kilo for one year is £0.25 and the annual demand for material X is 80 000. There is no lead time or buffer stock.

Required:

Determine the following for material X:

(i)   the economic order quantity, briefly explaining what this figure represents;

(ii) the average stock;

(iii) the number of orders to be made per year.   (*8 marks*)

(c) Explain what you understand by the terms 'buffer stock' and 'lead time', and briefly consider any stock policy that would minimize or eliminate such stock costs.   (*7 marks*)

(*Total 25 marks*)

AAT Cost Accounting and Budgeting

3.8* Stores pricing and calculation of EOQ and max./min. stock levels

You have been appointed as inventory accountant to a company where material is a major element of cost. The chief accountant wants to instal an efficient material control and pricing system within the company and seeks your advice upon a number of issues:

(a) Material XY has fluctuated in price over period 11 November 2003 and the chief accountant is unsure what price to cost the issues to job 124. You are given the following information:

Material XY		Kilos	Cost
November 1	Opening Balance	20 000	£60 000
November 3	Receipts	5 000	£4 per kilo
November 10	Receipts	12 000	£5 per kilo
November 17	Issues	24 000	
November 20	Receipts	17 000	£4.50 per kilo
November 27	Issues	20 000	

Required:

(i)   Cost the issues on 17 November and 27 November to job 124 using two different methods of pricing.   (*6 marks*)

(ii) On the assumption that the direct labour for job 124 is £50 000 and overhead is recovered on the basis of 110% of direct material, calculate the selling price for job 124 if profit is 10% of selling price on the basis of the two methods that you selected in (i).   (*4 marks*)

(iii) Comment critically upon the results that you have arrived at on the two methods used in (i) and (ii).   (*2 marks*)

(b) At the moment there are a number of stores spread throughout the factory, each duplicating the holding of stock. Stocktaking is carried out once a year, which requires the suspension of production for one week with overtime rates being paid to the stock checkers. The chief accountant maintains that the cost levels associated with the present system are too high and, with the planned growth of the company taken into consideration, a more efficient cost-effective system is required.

Required:

Evaluate

(i)   continuous stocktaking;

(ii) centralized store keeping, as methods whereby the chief accountant's objectives can be met.   (*7 marks*)

(c) The ordering of material KL has caused concern in the past, according to the chief accountant. There have been occasions when an excessive amount of stock has been carried beyond any possible demand, and when the problem has been addressed and the stock level cut, orders have been unfulfilled and sales lost because the company has run out of material KL. The chief accountant has now said he wants a policy that achieves:

(i)   adequate stock of material KL, thus minimizing the risk of shortage and production dislocation, balanced with,

(ii) avoidance of excessive stack levels of material KL and the consequent tying up of scarce funds.

You are given the following information:

(i)   Budgeted average demand for material KL is 400 kilos per week and production is maintained for 50 weeks in the year.

(ii) The order cost is £150 per order.

(iii) The standard material cost of KL is £6 per kilo and carrying costs are $33\frac{1}{3}$% of that figure per annum for each kilo.

(iv) The maximum usage in any one week is 600 kilos and the minimum 400.

On average, the orders take anything from one to three weeks to be delivered after they have been placed.

Required:

In order to meet the chief accountant's objectives, what is:

(i) the optimum order quantity that should be placed?

(ii) the re-order level for stock of KL?

(iii) the minimum level of stock that should be held?

(iv) the maximum level of stock that should be held? (*6 marks*)

(*Total 25 marks*)

AAT Cost Accounting and Budgeting

3.9* Stores pricing and labour cost accounting

S. Poynter Public Limited Company, an engineering company constructing special-purpose equipment to customer specification, employs a system of job costing to determine the actual cost of products manufactured. Shown below is the incomplete stores account, for month 11, of one component used in the construction of the equipment.

Stores account – Component XYZ

Date	Quantity (units)	Price (£)	Value (£)	Date	Quantity (units)	Price (£)	Value (£)
1/11/02				2/11/02			
Opening stock	35	2.00	70	Job 123	25		
5/11/02				10/11/02			
Creditors	40	2.25	90	Job 147	38		
13/11/02				24/11/02			
Creditors	30	2.50	75	Job 151	48		
23/11/02				30/11/02			
Creditors	50	2.80	140	Closing stock	44		
	155		375		155		

Ten of the components issued on 24 November to job 151 were to replace units which had been previously issued to that job but had been damaged and scrapped as a result of incorrect installation.

Required:

(a) Calculate the value of the closing stock of component XYZ using the following methods of pricing material issues:

(i) first in, first out;

(ii) last in, first out. (*6 marks*)

(b) Using the weighted average method of pricing, calculate the value of the components issued on 24 November. Explain how the ten components issued to replace those previously damaged should be treated in the cost accounts and briefly outline the reasons for your recommended treatment. (Calculations should be to two decimal places only.) (*8 marks*)

(c) During month 11 the total wages earned by the direct operatives in one department were made up as follows:

	(£)
Basic pay (£6 per hour)	9 600
Overtime earnings (basic time rate plus overtime premium)	2 880
Shift premium	720
Total wages	13 200

Overtime, which is paid at basic time rate plus one-half, is worked as a means of generally increasing the output of the factory. Analysis of the direct workers' returned work tickets reveals that 280 hours was non-productive time, 60 hours were spent producing capital equipment for the company, and the remainder of the time was spent on jobs.

Required:

Using appropriate journal entries, show how the above wages should be recorded in the cost accounting system, which is not integrated with the financial accounts. (*8 marks*)

(*Total 22 marks*)

ACCA Foundation Costing

3.10 Evaluation of an incentive scheme

XYZ Ltd is considering introducing an incentive scheme. Current production for the period is 100 units, and total wages paid are £600 for this production. Material costs are £5 per unit. Fixed overheads are £1000 for the period and the current selling price is £25.

Management decides to introduce a piecework system, paying £9 for each unit produced, based on an estimate that production for the period will double to 200 units.

Your managing director asks you to provide a financial evaluation of the scheme and to indicate any other factors which cannot be quantified but which may be affected by the introduction of the scheme.

3.11 Calculation of earnings
The following information is available:

Normal working day:	8 hours
Guaranteed rate of pay (on time basis)	£5.50 per hour
Standard time allowed to produce 1 unit:	3 minutes
Piecework price:	£0.10 per standard minute
Premium bonus:	75% of time saved, in addition to hourly pay

Required:
For the following levels of output produced in one day:

80 units
120 units
210 units

calculate earnings based on:
(i) piecework, where earnings are guaranteed at 80% of time-based pay;
(ii) premium bonus system. (*12 marks*)
AAT Cost Accounting and Budgeting

3.12* Calculation earnings
A company currently remunerates its factory workers on a time basis and is now considering the introduction of alternative methods of remuneration. The following information relates to two employees for one week:

	Y	Z
Hours worked	44	40
Rate of pay per hour	£3.50	£4.50
Units of output achieved	480	390

The time allowed for each unit of output is seven standard minutes. For purposes of piecework calculations each minute is valued at £0.05.

Required:
(a) Calculate the earnings of each employee where earnings are based on:

(i) piecework rates with earnings guaranteed at 80% of pay calculated on an hourly basis; (*4 marks*)
(ii) premium bonus scheme in which bonus (based on 75% of time saved) is added to pay calculated on an hourly basis. (*3 marks*)
(b) Describe *two* situations in which the time basis of remuneration is likely to be more appropriate than piecework schemes. (*4 marks*)
(*Total 11 marks*)
AAT Cost Accounting and Budgeting

3.13* Calculation of earnings and a discussion of time-based and individual performance-based remuneration systems
(a) Describe the characteristics of factory direct and indirect labour cost and explain the treatment of factory overtime wages and holiday pay in cost accounting systems. (*9 marks*)
(b) A Ltd makes engineering components. The company has been manufacturing 6000 components per week, with six direct employees working a 40-hour week, at a basic wage of £4.00 per hour. Each worker operates independently.

A new remuneration scheme is being introduced. Each employee will receive payment on the following basis:

first 800 components per week	16 pence per unit
next 200	17
all additional	18

There will be a guaranteed minimum wage of £140 per week. It is expected that output will increase to 6600 components per week with the new scheme.

Required:
Describe the general features of time-based and individual-performance-based remuneration systems, and outline the relative merits of each type of system. (Use the above figures to illustrate your discussion, making whatever additional assumptions that you feel are necessary.)
(*16 marks*)
(*Total 25 marks*)
ACCA Level 1 Costing

3.14* Calculation of labour turnover and efficiency ratio
X Ltd has an average of 42 workers employed in one of its factories in a period during which 7 workers left and were replaced.

The company pays a basic rate of £4.60 per hour to all its direct personnel. This is used as the standard rate. In addition, a factory-wide bonus scheme is in operation. A bonus of half of the efficiency ratio in excess of 100% is added as a percentage to the basic hourly rate, e.g. if the efficiency ratio is 110% then the hourly rate is £4.83 (i.e. £4.60 + (£4.60 × 5%)).

During the period 114 268 units of the company's single product were manufactured in 4900 hours. The standard hour is 22 units.

Required:
(a) Calculate the labour turnover percentage for the period. *(3 marks)*
(b) Identify the reasons for, and costs of, labour turnover, and discuss how it may be reduced. *(12 marks)*
(c) Calculate the hourly wage rate paid for the period, and the total labour variance. *(10 marks)*
(Total 25 marks)
ACAA Cost and Management Accounting 1

3.15* Computation of earnings and analysis by direct and indirect categories
(a) Explain how the following cost items, relating to direct personnel, would be processed in a manufacturing business's cost accounts:
  (i) idle time; *(3 marks)*
  (ii) overtime. *(3 marks)*
(b) The following information is available regarding the labour costs in a factory department for a week:

	Direct personnel	Indirect personnel
Payroll hours:		
Production	432	117
Training	24	—
Idle time	32	4
Total	488	121
Rate per hour:		
Basic	£7.50	£6.00
Overtime premium	£2.50	£2.00

The following additional information is provided:
(i) There are 12 direct personnel and 3 indirect personnel in the department.

(ii) Group bonuses for the week, shared by all workers in the department, total £520.
(iii) The basic wage rates apply to a normal working week of 37 hours.
(iv) Overtime is worked in order to meet the general requirements of production.
(v) The idle time and the time spent training during the week are regarded as normal.
(vi) The expected number of payroll hours of direct personnel in the week (excluding time spent training), required to produce the output achieved, is 470.

Required:
(i) Calculate the total amounts paid in the week (before share of group bonus) to direct personnel and indirect personnel respectively. *(4 marks)*
(ii) Determine the total amounts to be charged as direct wages and indirect wages respectively. *(5 marks)*
(iii) Complete the Wages Control Account in the company's separate cost accounting system, clearly indicating the account in which each corresponding entry woud be made. *(3 marks)*
(iv) Calculate the efficiency ratio relating to the direct personnel (expressed as a percentage to one decimal place). *(2 marks)*
(Total 20 marks)
ACCA Management Information – Paper 3

3.16 Effect of incentive scheme on company costs
(a) Shown below is a summary of the previous week's payroll data for the moulding department in Peal Public Limited Company, a company manufacturing two different types of telephone receiver.

	Direct workers	Indirect workers
Hours worked:		
Ordinary time	3600 hours	800 hours
Overtime	630 hours	80 hours
Basic hourly rate of pay	£3.60	£2.10
Net wages paid	£12 864	£1 420
Analysis of direct workers' time		
Productive time:		
Type-1 receiver – 4800 units	2400 hours	
Type-2 receiver – 1500 units	1125 hours	
Non-productive down time	705 hours	

The moulding department employs 90 direct and 20 indirect operatives. All operatives are paid at hourly time rates; overtime, which is regularly worked to meet budgeted production targets, is paid at time rate plus one-third. The company operates a batch costing system, using actual costs, which is fully integrated with the financial accounts.

Construct the moulding department's wages control account for the previous week, *clearly* indicating the accounts into which the corresponding entries would be posted. (*9 marks*)

(b) The works manager of Peal plc is considering introducing a piecework incentive scheme for the direct workers in the moulding department. Work study services have examined the manufacturing process in the moulding department, and consider that the operation to produce Type-1 receivers should be performed under normal conditions, by one operative in 24 minutes; for a Type- 2 receiver the corresponding time is 36 minutes. Unavoidable non-productive downtime is expected to remain at approximately 20% of productive time.

Having considered the above times, the works manager suggests that direct operatives should be paid a piece rate of £1.90 for each Type-1 receiver produced, £2.85 for each Type-2 receiver produced; and non-productive downtime should be paid at £2.50 per hour.

As the accountant of Peal plc you have been asked to appraise the above scheme. It should be assumed that the previous week's payroll data shown in (a) above represents an average week in the moulding department, although the weekly volume of production and consequent wages do fluctuate around this mean figure. No further information has been provided.

Required:
(i) Examine the effect of the proposed scheme on the labour costs in the moulding department. Any assumptions you consider necessary should be clearly stated.
(*7 marks*)
(ii) Briefly discuss any additional considerations which would need to be thoroughly examined, before the feasibility of the proposed incentive scheme could be finally assessed. (*6 marks*)
(*Total 22 marks*)
ACCA Level 1 Costing

3.17*
A domestic appliance retailer with multiple outlets stocks a popular toaster known as the Autocrisp 2000, for which the following information is available:

Average sales	75 per day
Maximum sales	95 per day
Minimum sales	50 per day
Lead time	12–18 days
Re-order quantity	1750

(i) Based on the data above, at what level of stocks would a replenishment order be issued?
A 1050. B 1330. C 1710.
D 1750.
(ii) Based on the data above, what is the maximum level of stocks possible?
A 1750. B 2860. C 3460.
D 5210.
CIMA Stage 1 Cost Accounting

3.18 Calculation of EOQ and frequency at ordering
A company is planning to purchase 90 800 units of a particular item in the year ahead. The item is purchased in boxes, each containing 10 units of the item, at a price of £200 per box. A safety stock of 250 boxes is kept.

The cost of holding an item in stock for a year (including insurance, interest and space costs) is 15% of the purchase area. The cost of placing and receiving orders is to be estimated from cost data collected relating to similar orders, where costs of £5910 were incurred on 30 orders. It should be assumed that ordering costs change in proportion to the number of orders placed. 2% should be added to the above ordering costs to allow for inflation.

Required:
Calculate the order quantity that would minimize the cost of the above item, and determine the required frequency of placing orders, assuming that usage of the item will beeven over the year.
(*8 marks*)
ACCA Foundation Stage Paper 3

3.19*
(a) Write short notes to explain each of the following in the context of materials control:
(i) Continuous stocktaking.
(ii) Perpetual inventory system.
(iii) ABC inventory analysis. (*9 marks*)

(b) State the factors that should influence the decision regarding economic order quantities of raw materials. (*7 marks*)

(c) Calculate three normal control levels, which maybe used in stock control systems, from the following information for a particular raw material:

Economic order quantity, 12 000 kilos
Lead time, 10 to 14 working days
Average usage, 600 kilos per day
Minimum usage, 400 kilos per day
Maximum usage, 800 kilos per day

(*9 marks*)
(*Total 25 marks*)
ACCA Level 1 Costing

3.20* Calculation of EOQ

XYZ Ltd produces a product which has a constant monthly demand of 4000 units. The product requires a component which XYZ Ltd purchases from a supplier at £10 per unit. The component requires a three-day lead time from the date of order to the date of delivery. The ordering cost is £0.60 per order and the holding cost is 10% per annum.

(a) You are required to calculate:
(i) The economic order quantity.
(ii) The number of orders required per year.
(iii) The total cost of ordering and holding the components for the year.

(b) Assuming that there is no safety stock and that the present stock level is 400 components, when should the next order be placed? (Assume a 360-day year.)

(c) Discuss the problems which most firms would have in attempting to apply the EOQ formula.

3.21 Calculation of EOQ

Most textbooks consider that the optimal re-order quantity for materials occurs when 'the cost of storage is equated with the cost of ordering'. If one assumes that this statement is acceptable and also, in attempting to construct a simple formula for an optimal re-order quantity, that a number of basic assumptions must be made, then a recognized formula can be produced using the following

symbols:

C_o = cost of placing an order

C_h = cost of storage per annum, expressed as a percentage of stock value

D = demand in units for a material, per annum

Q = re-order quantity, in units

$Q/2$ = average stock level, in units

p = price per unit

You are required:

(a) to present formulae, using the symbols given above, representing:
(i) total cost of ordering,
(ii) total cost of storage,
(iii) total cost of ordering and storage,
(iv) optimal re-order quantity; (*4 marks*)

(b) to state the limitations experienced in practice which affect the user of the formula for optimal re-order quantity as expressed in (a) (iv) above; (*4 marks*)

(c) to calculate the optimal re-order quantity from the following data:

Cost of storage is 20% per annum of stock value
Cost of placing an order is £30 each
Demand for material is 2000 units per annum
Price of material is £70 per unit; (*3 marks*)

(d) to explain a system of stock usage which renders economic order quantity re-ordering obsolete. (*4 marks*)
(*Total 15 marks*)
CIMA Stage 2 Accounting

3.22* Calculation of EOQ and average stocks

A company uses Material Z (cost £3.50 per kg) in the manufacture of Products A and B. The following forecast information is provided for the year ahead:

	Product A	Product B
Sales (units)	24 600	9 720
Finished goods stock increase by year end (units)	447	178
Post-production rejection rate (%)	1	2
Material Z usage (kg per completed unit, net of wastage)	1.8	3.0
Material Z wastage (%)	5	11

Additional information:

Average purchasing lead time for Material Z is two weeks.

Usage of Material Z is expected to be even over the year.

Annual stock holding costs are 18% of the material cost.

The cost of placing orders is £30 per order.

The re-order level for Material Z is set at the average usage in average lead time, plus 1000 kg of safety (buffer) stock.

Required:
(a) State two items that would be regarded as 'stock holding costs' and explain how they may be controlled effectively. (*5 marks*)
(b) Calculate for the year ahead:
   (i)   the required production of Products A and B (in units), (*3 marks*)
   (ii) the total requirement for Material Z (in kgs), (*3 marks*)
   (iii) the Economic Order Quantity for Material Z (in kgs). (*5 marks*)
(c) Calculate the average stock investment (£) and the annual stock holding costs (£) for Material Z. (*4 marks*)
                                  (*Total 20 marks*)
   ACCA Management Information – Paper 3

3.23 Calculation of EOQ
Sandy Lands Ltd carries an item of inventory in respect of which the following data apply:

fixed cost of ordering per batch	£10
expected steady quarterly volume of sales	3125 units
cost of holding one unit in stock for one year	£1

You are required to:
(i)   calculate the minimum annual cost of ordering and stocking the item; (*4 marks*)
(ii) calculate to the nearest whole number of units the optimal batch size if the expected steady quarterly volume of sales
      first falls to 781 units and
      second rises to 6250 units
      and to state the relationship between the rates of change of sales and the optimal batch size; (*4 marks*)
(iii) explain the basis of the derivation of the formula for the optimal batch size which is given in the table of formulae. (*4 marks*)
   ICAEW Management Accounting

3.24* Calculation of re-order and maximum stock levels
A retail company has been reviewing the adequacy of its stock control systems and has identified three products for investigation. Relevant details for the three products are set out below:

Item code	EOQ	Stock (warehouse and stores)			Weekly sales (£000)			Gross* margin
	(000 units)	(000 units)	(£/unit at cost)		mini- mum	nor- mal	maxi- mum	(% of sales)
14/363	25	32.5	2.25		26	28	30	42
11/175	500	422.7	0.36		130	143	160	46
14/243	250	190	0.87		60	96	128	37

* Gross margin = sales − purchase cost of product.

Outstanding order: Item code 14/243 – order for 250 000 units placed two trading days ago.

There are six trading days per week.

All orders are delivered by suppliers into the retailer's central warehouse. The lead time is one week from placement of order. A further week is required by the retailer in order to transfer stock from central warehouse to stores. Both of these lead times can be relied upon.

Required:
(a) Calculate for each product:
   (i)   the minimum and maximum weekly sales units
   (ii) the stock re-order level
   (iii) the maximum stock control level. (*9 marks*)
(b) Comment upon the adequacy of the existing stock control of the three products. (*5 marks*)
                                  (*Total 14 marks*)
   ACCA Foundation Stage Paper 3

3.25 Calculation of minimum purchase cost when cost per unit is not constant
A company is reviewing the purchasing policy for one of its raw materials as a result of a reduction in production requirement. The material, which is used evenly throughout the year, is used in only one of the company's products, the production of which is currently 12 000 units per annum. Each finished unit of the product contains 0.4 kg of the material. 20% of the material is lost in the production process. Purchases can be made in multiples of 500 kg, with a minimum purchase order quantity of 1000 kg.

The cost of the raw material depends upon the purchase order quantity as follows:

Order quantity (kg)	Cost per kg (£)
1000	1.00
1500	0.98
2000	0.965
2500	0.95
3000 and above	0.94

Costs of placing and handling each order are £90, of which £40 is an apportionment of costs which are not expected to be affected in the short term by the number of orders placed. Annual holding costs of stock are £0.90 per unit of average stock, of which only £0.40 is expected to be affected in the short term by the amount of stock held.

The lead time for the raw materials is one month, and a safety stock of 250 kg is required.

Required:
(a) Explain, and illustrate from the situation described above, the meaning of the terms 'variable', 'semivariable' and 'fixed' costs.

(8 marks)

(b) Calculate the annual cost of pursuing alternative purchase order policies and thus advise the company regarding the purchase order quantity for the material that will minimize cost.

(14 marks)
(Total 22 marks)
ACCA Level 1 Costing

Chapter 4

* Indicates that a suggested solution is to be found in the *Students' Manual*.

4.1*

A firm makes special assemblies to customers' orders and uses job costing. The data for a period are:

	Job no. AA10 (£)	Job no. BB15 (£)	Job no. CC20 (£)
Opening WIP	26 800	42 790	—
Material added in period	17 275	—	18 500
Labour for period	14 500	3 500	24 600

The budgeted overheads for the period were £126 000.

(i) What overhead should be added to job number CC20 for the period?
A £24 600
B £65 157
C £72 761
D £126 000

(ii) Job no. BB15 was completed and delivered during the period and the firm wishes to earn $33\frac{1}{3}$% profit on sales.

What is the selling price of job number BB15?
A £69 435
B £75 521
C £84 963
D £138 870

(iii) What was the approximate value of closing work in progress at the end of the period?
A £58 575
B £101 675
C £147 965
D £217 323

CIMA Stage 1

4.2*

A company absorbs overheads on machine hours. In a period, actual machine hours were 17 285, actual overheads were £496 500 and there was under-absorption of £12 520.

What was the budgeted level of overheads?
A £483 980
B £496 500
C £509 020
D It cannot be calculated from the information provided.

CIMA Stage 1 Cost Accounting

4.3*

The following information is to be used for sub-questions (i) and (ii) below:

Budgeted labour hours	48 500
Actual labour hours	49 775
Budgeted overheads	£691 125
Actual overheads	£746 625

(i) Based on the data above, what is the labour hour absorption rate (to 2 decimal places) as conventionally calculated?
A £13.88 B £14.25 C £15.00 D £15.39

(ii) Based on the data above, what is the amount (to the nearest whole number) of overhead under-/over-absorbed?

A NIL
B £19 412 over-absorbed
C £37 331 under-absorbed
D £55 500 under-absorbed

CIMA Stage 1 – Cost Accounting and Quantitative Methods

4.4*

The following data are to be used for questions (i) and (ii) below:

Budgeted overheads	£373 750
Budgeted absorption rate per machine hour	£32 50
Actual overheads	£370 450
Actual machine hours	11 950

(i) Based on the data above, how many machine hours (to the nearest hour) were budgeted?
   A 11 398   B 11 500   C 11 825
   D 11 950

(ii) Based on the data above, what was the amount of overhead (to the nearest £) under-absorbed/over-absorbed?
   A £10 774 under-absorbed
   B £13 300 over-absorbed
   C £14 625 under-absorbed
   D £17 925 over-absorbed

CIMA Stage 1 – Cost Accounting and Quantitative Methods

4.5

(a) Explain why predetermined overhead absorption rates are preferred to overhead absorption rates calculated from factual information after the end of a financial period.

(b) The production overhead absorption rates of factories X and Y are calculated using similar methods. However, the rate used by factory X is lower than that used by factory Y. Both factories produce the same type of product. You are required to discuss whether or not this can be taken to be a sign that factory X is more efficient than factory Y.   (*20 marks*)
CIMA Cost Accounting 1

4.6

Critically consider the purpose of calculating production overhead absorption rates.

4.7

(a) Specify and explain the factors to be considered in determining whether to utilize a single factory-wide recovery rate for all production overheads or a separate rate for each cost centre, production or service department.
     (*12 marks*)

(b) Describe three methods of determining fixed overhead recovery rates and specify the circumstances under which each method is superior to the other methods mentioned.
     (*8 marks*)
     (*Total 20 marks*)
ACCA P2 Management Accounting

4.8 Overhead analysis, calculation of overhead rate and overhead charged to a unit of output

A company makes a range of products with total budgeted manufacturing overheads of £973 560 incurred in three production departments (A, B and C) and one service department.

Department A has 10 direct employees, who each work 37 hours per week.

Department B has five machines, each of which is operated for 24 hours per week.

Department C is expected to produce 148 000 units of final product in the budget period.

The company will operate for 48 weeks in the budget period.

Budgeted overheads incurred directly by each department are:

Production department A	£261 745
Production department B	£226 120
Production department C	£93 890
Service department	£53 305

The balance of budgeted overheads are apportioned to departments as follows:

Production department A	40%
Production department B	35%
Production department C	20%
Service department	5%

Service department overheads are apportioned equally to each production department.

You are required to:

(a) Calculate an appropriate predetermined overhead absorption rate in each production department.   (*9 marks*)

(b) Calculate the manufacturing overhead cost per unit of finished product in a batch of 100 units which take nine direct labour hours in department A and three machine hours in department B to produce.   (*3 marks*)
     (*Total 12 marks*)
ACCA Foundation Paper 3

4.9 Overhead analysis sheet and calculation of overhead absorption rates

PTS Limited is a manufacturing company which uses three production departments to make its product. It has the following factory costs which are expected to be incurred in the year to 31 December:

		(£)
Direct wages	Machining	234 980
	Assembly	345 900
	Finishing	134 525

		(£)
Indirect wages and salaries	Machining	120 354
	Assembly	238 970
	Finishing	89 700

	(£)
Factory rent	12 685 500
Business rates	3 450 900
Heat and lighting	985 350
Machinery power	2 890 600
Depreciation	600 000
Canteen subsidy	256 000

Other information is available as follows:

	Machining	Assembly	Finishing
Number of employees	50	60	18
Floor space occupied (m²)	1 800	1 400	800
Horse power of machinery	13 000	500	6 500
Value of machinery (£000)	250	30	120
Number of labour hours	100 000	140 000	35 000
Number of machine hours	200 000	36 000	90 000

You are required
(a) to prepare the company's overhead analysis sheet for the year to 31 December; (9 marks)
(b) to calculate appropriate overhead absorption rates (to two decimal places) for each department. (6 marks)
(Total 15 marks)
CIMA Stage 1 Accounting

4.10* Overhead analysis, calculation of overhead rates and a product cost

Knowing that you are studying for the CIMA qualification, a friend who manages a small business has sought your advice about how to produce quotations in response to the enquiries which her business receives. Her business is sheet metal fabrication – supplying ducting for dust extraction and airconditioning installations. She believes that she has lost orders recently through the use of a job cost estimating system which was introduced, on the advice of her auditors, seven years ago. You are invited to review this system.

Upon investigation, you find that a plant-wide percentage of 125% is added to prime costs in order to arrive at a selling price. The percentage added is intended to cover all overheads for the three production departments (Departments P, Q and R), all the selling, distribution and administration costs, and the profit.

You also discover that the selling, distribution and administration costs equate to roughly 20% of total production costs, and that to achieve the desired return on capital employed, a margin of 20% of sales value is necessary.

You recommend an analysis of overhead cost items be undertaken with the objective of determining a direct labour hour rate of overhead absorption for each of the three departments work passes through. (You think about activity-based costing but feel this would be too sophisticated and difficult to introduce at the present time.)

There are 50 direct workers in the business plus 5 indirect production people.

From the books, records and some measuring, you ascertain the following information which will enable you to compile an overhead analysis spreadsheet, and to determine overhead absorption rates per direct labour hour for departmental overhead purposes:

Cost/expense	Annual amount (£)	Basis for apportionment where allocation not given
Repairs and maintenance	62 000	Technical assessment: P £42 000, Q £10 000, R £10 000
Depreciation	40 000	Cost of plant and equipment
Consumable supplies	9 000	Direct labour hours
Wage-related costs	87 000	12½% of direct wages costs
Indirect labour	90 000	Direct labour hours
Canteen/rest/smoke room	30 000	Number of direct workers
Business rates and insurance	26 000	Floor area

Other estimates/information

	Department P	Department Q	Department R
Estimated direct labour hours	50 000	30 000	20 000
Direct wages costs	£386 000	£210 000	£100 000
Number of direct workers	25	15	10
Floor area in square metres	5 000	4 000	1 000
Plant and equipment, at cost	£170 000	£140 000	£90 000

Required:

(a) Calculate the overhead absorption rates for each department, based on direct labour hours.
(*9 marks*)

(b) Prepare a sample quotation for Job 976, utilizing information given in the question, your answer to (a) above, and the following additional information:

Estimated direct material cost: £800

Estimated direct labour hours:
30 in Department P
10 in Department Q
5 in Department R
(*3 marks*)

(c) Calculate what would have been quoted for Job 976 under the 'auditors' system' and comment on whether your friend's suspicions about lost business could be correct (*3 marks*)
(*Total 15 marks*)
CIMA Stage 2 Cost Accounting

4.11* Overhead analyis and calculation of product costs

A furniture-making business manufactures quality furniture to customers' orders. It has three production departments and two service departments. Budgeted overhead costs for the coming year are as follows:

	Total (£)
Rent and Rates	12 800
Machine insurance	6 000
Telephone charges	3 200
Depreciation	18 000
Production Supervisor's salaries	24 000
Heating & Lighting	6 400
	70 400

The three production departments – A, B and C, and the two service departments – X and Y, are housed in the new premises, the details of which, together with other statistics and information, are given below.

	Departments				
	A	B	C	X	Y
Floor area occupied (sq. metres)	3000	1800	600	600	400
Machine value (£000)	24	10	8	4	2
Direct labour hrs budgeted	3200	1800	1000		
Labour rates per hour	£3.80	£3.50	£3.40	£3.00	£3.00
Allocated Overheads: Specific to each department (£000)	2.8	1.7	1.2	0.8	0.6
Service Department X's costs apportioned	50%	25%	25%		
Service Department Y's costs apportioned	20%	30%	50%		

Required:

(a) Prepare a statement showing the overhead cost budgeted for each department, showing the basis of apportionment used. Also calculate suitable overhead absorption rates. (*9 marks*)

(b) Two pieces of furniture are to be manufactured for customers. Direct costs are as follows:

	Job 123	Job 124
Direct Material	£154	£108
Direct Labour	20 hours Dept A	16 hours Dept A
	12 hours Dept B	10 hours Dept B
	10 hours Dept C	14 hours Dept C

Calculate the total costs of each job.
(*5 marks*)

(c) If the firm quotes prices to customers that reflect a required profit of 25% on selling price, calculate the quoted selling price for each job. (*2 marks*)

(d) If material costs are asignificant part of total costs in a manufacturing company, describe a system of material control that might be used in order to effectively control costs, paying particular attention to the stock control aspect.
(*9 marks*)
(*Total 25 marks*)
AAT Stage 3 Cost Accounting and Budgeting

4.12 Overhead analysis sheet and calculation of overhead rates

Dunstan Ltd manufactures tents and sleeping bags in three separate production departments. The principal manufacturing processes consist of cutting material in the pattern cutting room, and sewing the material in either the tent or the sleeping bag departments. For the year to 31 July cost centre expenses and other relevant information are budgeted as follows:

	Total (£)	Cutting room (£)	Tents (£)	Sleeping bags (£)	Raw material stores (£)	Canteen (£)	Maintenance (£)
Indirect wages	147 200	6 400	19 500	20 100	41 200	15 000	45 000
Consumable materials	54 600	5 300	4 100	2 300	—	18 700	24 200
Plant depreciation	84 200	31 200	17 500	24 600	2 500	3 400	5 000
Power	31 700						
Heat and light	13 800						
Rent and rates	14 400						
Building insurance	13 500						
Floor area (sq. ft)	30 000	8 000	10 000	7 000	1 500	2 500	1 000
Estimated power usage (%)	100	17	38	32	3	8	2
Direct labour (hours)	112 000	7 000	48 000	57 000	—	—	—
Machine usage (hours)	87 000	2 000	40 000	45 000	—	—	—
Value of raw material issues (%)	100	62.5	12.5	12.5	—	—	12.5

Requirements:
(a) Prepare in columnar form a statement calculating the overhead absorption rates for each machine hour and each direct labour hour for each of the three production units. You should use bases of apportionment and absorption which you consider most appropriate, and the bases used should be clearly indicated in your statement. *(16 marks)*
(b) 'The use of pre-determined overhead absorption rates based on budgets is preferable to the use of absorption rates calculated from historical data available after the end of a financial period.'

Discuss this statement insofar as it relates to the financial management of a business.
(5 marks)
(Total 21 marks)
ICAEW PI A/C Techniques

4.13* Calculation of overhead rates and a product cost
DC Limited is an engineering company which uses job costing to attribute costs to individual products

and services provided to its customers. It has commenced the preparation of its fixed production overhead cost budget for 2001 and has identified the following costs:

	(£000)
Machining	600
Assembly	250
Finishing	150
Stores	100
Maintenance	80
	1180

The stores and maintenance departments are production service departments. An analysis of the services they provide indicates that their costs should be apportioned accordingly:

	Machining	Assembly	Finishing	Stores	Maintenance
Stores	40%	30%	20%	—	10%
Maintenance	55%	20%	20%	5%	—

The number of machine and labour hours budgeted for 2001 is:

	Machining	**Assembly**	**Finishing**
Machine hours	50 000	4 000	5 000
Labour hours	10 000	30 000	20 000

Requirements:
(a) Calculate appropriate overhead absorption rates for each production department for 2001. *(9 marks)*
(b) Prepare a quotation for job number XX34, which is to be commenced early in 2001, assuming that it has:
  Direct materials   costing £2400
  Direct labour   costing £1500
and requires:

	Machine hours	**Labour hours**
Machining department	45	10
Assembly department	5	15
Finishing department	4	12

and that profit is 20% of selling price.
(5 marks)
(c) Assume that in 2001 the actual fixed overhead cost of the assembly department totals

£300 000 and that the actual machine hours were 4200 and actual labour hours were 30 700.

Prepare the fixed production overhead control account for the assembly department, showing clearly the causes of any over/under-absorption. (*5 marks*)

(d) Explain how activity based costing would be used in organizations like DC Limited.

(*6 marks*)
(*Total marks 25*)
CIMA Stage 2 Operational Cost Accounting

4.14* Job cost calculation

A printing and publishing company has been asked to provide an estimate for the production of 100 000 catalogues, of 64 pages (32 sheets of paper) each, for a potential customer.

Four operations are involved in the production process: photography, set-up, printing and binding.

Each page of the catalogue requires a separate photographic session. Each session costs £150.

Set-up would require a plate to be made for each page of the catalogue. Each plate requires four hours of labour at £7 per hour and £35 of materials. Overheads are absorbed on the basis of labour hours at an hourly rate of £9.50.

In printing, paper costs £12 per thousand sheets. Material losses are expected to be 2% of input. Other printing materials will cost £7 per 500 catalogues. 1000 catalogues are printed per hour of machine time. Labour and overhead costs incurred in printing are absorbed at a rate of £62 per machine hour.

Binding costs are recovered at a rate per machine hour. The rate is £43 per hour and 2500 catalogues are bound per hour of machine time.

A profit margin of 10% of selling price is required.

You are required to:
(a) determine the total amount that should be quoted for the catalogue job by the printing and publishing company. (*11 marks*)
(b) calculate the additional costs that would be charged to the job if the labour efficiency ratio achieved versus estimate in set-up is 90%.

(*4 marks*)
(*Total 15 marks*)
ACCA Foundation Stage Paper 3

4.15 Computation of three different overhead absorption rates and a cost-plus selling price

A manufacturing company has prepared the following budgeted information for the forth-coming year:

	(£)
Direct material	800 000
Direct labour	200 000
Direct expenses	40 000
Production overhead	600 000
Administrative overhead	328 000
Budgeted activity levels include:	
Budgeted production units	600 000
Machine hours	50 000
Labour hours	40 000

It has recently spent heavily upon advanced technological machinery and reduced its workforce. As a consequence it is thinking about changing its basis for overhead absorption from a percentage of direct labour cost to either a machine hour or labour hour basis. The administrative overhead is to be absorbed as a percentage of factory cost.

Required:
(a) Prepare pre-determined overhead absorption rates for production overheads based upon the three different bases for absorption mentioned above. (*6 marks*)
(b) Outline the reasons for calculating a predetermined overhead absorption rate. (*2 marks*)
(c) Select the overhead absorption rate that you think the organization should use giving reasons for your decision. (*3 marks*)
(d) The company has been asked to price job AX, this job requires the following:

Direct material	£3788
Direct labour	£1100
Direct expenses	£422
Machine hours	£120
Labour hours	£220

Compute the price for this job using the absorption rate selected in (c) above, given that the company profit margin is equal to 10% of the price. (*6 marks*)
(e) The company previously paid its direct labour workers upon a time basis but is now contemplating moving over to an incentive scheme.

Required:
Draft a memo to the Chief Accountant outlining the general characteristics and advantages of employing a successful incentive scheme.

(8 marks)
(Total 25 marks)
AAT Cost Accounting and Budgeting

4.16* Various overhead absorption rates and under-/over-recovery

The following data relate to a manufacturing department for a period:

	Budget data (£)	Actual data (£)
Direct material cost	100 000	150 000
Direct labour cost	250 000	275 000
Production overhead	250 000	350 000
Direct labour hours	50 000 hours	55 000 hours

Job ZX was one of the jobs worked on during the period. Direct material costing £7000 and direct labour (800 hours) costing £4000 were incurred.

Required:
(i) Calculate the production overhead absorption rate predetermined for the period based on:
  (a) percentage of direct material cost;
  (b) direct labour hours. *(3 marks)*
(ii) Calculate the production overhead cost to be charged to Job ZX based on the rates calculated in answer to (i) above. *(2 marks)*
(iii) Assume that the direct labour hour rate of absorption is used. Calculate the under- or over-absorption of production overheads for the period and state an appropriate treatment in the accounts. *(4 marks)*
(iv) Comment briefly on the relative merits of the two methods of overhead absorption used in (i) above. *(6 marks)*
(Total 15 marks)
AAT Cost Accounting and Budgeting

4.17 Calculation of overhead absorption rates and under-/over-recovery of overheads

BEC Limited operates an absorption costing system. Its budget for the year ended 31 December shows that it expects its production overhead expenditure to be as follows:

	Fixed (£)	Variable (£)
Machining department	600 000	480 000
Hand finishing department	360 000	400 000

During the year it expects to make 200 000 units of its product. This is expected to take 80 000 machine hours in the machining department and 120 000 labour hours in the hand finishing department.

The costs and activity are expected to arise evenly throughout the year, and the budget has been used as the basis of calculating the company's absorption rates.

During March the monthly profit statement reported
(i) that the actual hours worked in each department were
  Machining   6000 hours
  Hand finishing   9600 hours
(ii) that the actual overhead costs incurred were

	Fixed (£)	Variable (£)
Machining	48 500	36 000
Hand finishing	33 600	33 500

(iii) that the actual production was 15 000 units.

Required:
(a) Calculate appropriate predetermined absorption rates for the year ended 31 December; *(4 marks)*
(b) (i) Calculate the under/over absorption of overhead for each department of the company for March; *(4 marks)*
  (ii) Comment on the problems of using predetermined absorption rates based on the arbitrary apportionment of overhead costs, with regard to comparisons of actual/target performance; *(4 marks)*
(c) State the reasons why absorption costing is used by companies. *(3 marks)*
(Total 15 marks)
CIMA Stage 1 Accounting

4.18* Calculation of overhead absorption rates and under-/over-recovery of overheads

A manufacturing company has two production cost centres (Departments A and B) and one service cost centre (Department C) in its factory.

A predetermined overhead absorption rate (to two decimal places of £) is established for each of the production cost centres on the basis of budgeted overheads and budgeted machine hours.

The overheads of each production cost centre comprise directly allocated costs and a share of the costs of the service cost centre.

Budgeted production overhead data for a period is as follows:

	Department A	Department B	Department C
Allocated costs	£217 860	£374 450	£103 970
Apportioned costs	£45 150	£58 820	(£103 970)
Machine hours	13 730	16 110	
Direct labour hours	16 360	27 390	

Actual production overhead costs and activity for the same period are:

	Department A	Department B	Department C
Allocated costs	£219 917	£387 181	£103 254
Machine hours	13 672	16 953	
Direct labour hours	16 402	27 568	

70% of the actual costs of Department C are to be apportioned to production cost centres on the basis of actual machine hours worked and the remainder on the basis of actual direct labour hours.

Required:
(a) Establish the production overhead absorption rates for the period. (*3 marks*)
(b) Determine the under- or over-absorption of production overhead for the period in each production cost centre. (Show workings clearly.) (*12 marks*)
(c) Explain when, and how, the repeated distribution method may be applied in the overhead apportionment process. (*5 marks*)
(*Total 20 marks*)
ACCA Management Information – Paper 3

4.19* Analysis of under-/over-recovery of overheads and a discussion of blanket versus department overheads
(a) One of the factories in the XYZ Group of companies absorbs fixed production overheads into product cost using a predetermined machine hour rate.

In Year 1, machine hours budgeted were 132 500 and the absorption rate for fixed production overheads was £18.20 per machine hour. Overheads absorbed and incurred were £2 442 440 and £2 317 461 respectively.

In Year 2, machine hours were budgeted to be 5% higher than those actually worked in Year 1. Budgeted and actual fixed production overhead expenditure were £2 620 926 and £2 695 721 respectively, and actual machine hours were 139 260.

Required:
Analyse, in as much detail as possible, the under-/over-absorption of fixed production overhead occurring in Years 1 and 2, and the change in absorption rate between the two years. (*15 marks*)
(b) Contrast the use of
(i) blanket as opposed to departmental overhead absorption rates;
(ii) predetermined overhead absorption rates as opposed to rates calculated from actual activity and expenditure.
(*10 marks*)
(*Total 25 marks*)
ACCA Cost and Management Accounting 1

4.20 Various overhead absorption rates
AC Limited is a small company which undertakes a variety of jobs for its customers.

	Budgeted profit and loss statement for the year ending 31 December	
	(£)	(£)
Sales		750 000
Cost:		
Direct materials	100 000	
Direct wages	50 000	
Prime cost	150 000	
Fixed production overhead	300 000	
Production cost	450 000	
Selling, distribution and administration cost	160 000	
		610 000
Profit		£140 000
Budgeted data:		
Labour hours for the year	25 000	
Machine hours for the year	15 000	
Number of jobs for the year	300	

An enquiry has been received, and the production department has produced estimates of the prime cost involved and of the hours required to complete job A57.

	(£)
Direct materials	250
Direct wages	200
Prime cost	£450
Labour hours required	80
Machine hours required	50

You are required to:
(a) calculate by different methods *six* overhead absorption rates; (*6 marks*)
(b) comment briefly on the suitability of each method calculated in (a); (*8 marks*)
(c) calculate cost estimates for job A57 using in turn each of the six overhead absorption rates calculated in (a). (*6 marks*)
(*Total 20 marks*)
CIMA Foundation Cost Accounting 1

4.21 Calculation of under-/over-recovery of overheads

A company produces several products which pass through the two production departments in its factory. These two departments are concerned with filling and sealing operations. There are two service departments, maintenance and canteen, in the factory.

Predetermined overhead absorption rates, based on direct labour hours, are established for the two production departments. The budgeted expenditure for these departments for the period just ended, including the apportionment of service department overheads, was £110 040 for filling, and £53 300 for sealing. Budgeted direct labour hours were 13 100 for filling and 10 250 for sealing.

Service department overheads are apportioned as follows:

Maintenance	– Filling	70%
Maintenance	– Sealing	27%
Maintenance	– Canteen	3%
Canteen	– Filling	60%
	– Sealing	32%
	– Maintenance	8%

During the period just ended, actual overhead costs and activity were as follows:

	(£)	Direct labour hours
Filling	74 260	12 820
Sealing	38 115	10 075
Maintenance	25 050	
Canteen	24 375	

Required:
(a) Calculate the overheads absorbed in the period and the extent of the under-/over-absorption in each of the two production departments.
(*14 marks*)
(b) State, and critically assess, the objectives of overhead apportionment and absorption.
(*11 marks*)
(*Total 25 marks*)
ACCA Level 1 Cost and Management Accounting 1

4.22* Calculation of fixed and variable overhead rates, normal activity level and under-/over-recovery of overheads

(a) C Ltd is a manufacturing company. In one of the production departments in its main factory a machine hour rate is used for absorbing production overhead. This is established as a predetermined rate, based on normal activity. The rate that will be used for the period which is just commencing is £15.00 per machine hour. Overhead expenditure anticipated, at a range of activity levels, is as follows:

Activity level (machine hours)	(£)
1500	25 650
1650	26 325
2000	27 900

Required:
Calculate:
(i) the variable overhead rate per machine hour;
(ii) the total budgeted fixed overhead;
(iii) the normal activity level of the department; and
(iv) the extent of over-/under-absorption if actual machine hours are 1700 and expenditure is as budgeted. (*10 marks*)
(b) In another of its factories, C Ltd carries out jobs to customers' specifications. A particular

job requires the following machine hours and direct labour hours in the two production departments:

	Machining Department	Finishing Department
Direct labour hours	25	28
Machine hours	46	8

Direct labour in both departments is paid at a basic rate of £4.00 per hour. 10% of the direct labour hours in the finishing department are overtime hours, paid at 125% of basic rate. Overtime premiums are charged to production overhead.

The job requires the manufacture of 189 components. Each component requires 1.1 kilos of prepared material. Loss on preparation is 10% of unprepared material, which costs £2.35 per kilo.

Overhead absorption rates are to be established from the following data:

	Machining Department	Finishing Department
Production overhead	£35 280	£12 480
Direct labour hours	3 500	7 800
Machine hours	11 200	2 100

Required:
(i) Calculate the overhead absorption rate for each department and justify the absorption method used.
(ii) Calculate the cost of the job. (*15 marks*)
(*Total 25 marks*)
ACCA Level 1

4.23 Under- and over-absorption of overheads and calculation of budgeted expenditure and activity
A large firm of solicitors uses a job costing system to identify costs with individual clients. Hours worked by professional staff are used as the basis for charging overhead costs to client services. A predetermined rate is used, derived from budgets drawn up at the beginning of each year commencing on 1 April.

In the year to 31 March 2000 the overheads of the solicitors' practice, which were absorbed at a rate of £7.50 per hour of professional staff, were over-absorbed by £4760. Actual overheads

incurred were £742 600. Professional hours worked were 1360 over budget.

The solicitors' practice has decided to refine its overhead charging system by differentiating between the hours of senior and junior professional staff, respectively. A premium of 40% is to be applied to the hourly overhead rate for senior staff compared with junior staff.

Budgets for the year to 31 March 2001 are as follows:

Senior professional staff hours	21 600
Junior professional staff hours	79 300
Practice overheads	£784 000

Required:
(a) Calculate for the year ended 31 March 2000:
  (i) budgeted professional staff hours;
  (ii) budgeted overhead expenditure. (*5 marks*)
(b) Calculate, for the year ended 31 March 2001, the overhead absorption rates (to three decimal places of a £) to be applied to:
  (i) senior professional staff hours;
  (ii) junior professional staff hours. (*4 marks*)
(c) How is the change in method of charging overheads likely to improve the firm's job costing system? (*3 marks*)
(d) Explain briefly why overhead absorbed using predetermined rates may differ from actual overhead incurred for the same period. (*2 marks*)
(*Total 14 marks*)
ACCA Foundation Paper 3

4.24* Calculation of overhead absorption rates and product costs
Bookdon Public Limited Company manufactures three products in two production departments, a machine shop and a fitting section; it also has two service departments, a canteen and a machine maintenance section. Shown below are next year's budgeted production data and manufacturing costs for the company.

	Product X	Product Y	Product Z
Production	4200 units	6900 units	1700 units
Prime cost:			
Direct materials	£11 per unit	£14 per unit	£17 per unit
Direct labour:			
Machine shop	£6 per unit	£4 per unit	£2 per unit
Fitting section	£12 per unit	£3 per unit	£21 per unit
Machine hours per unit	6 hours per unit	3 hours per unit	4 hours per unit

	Machine shop	Fitting section	Canteen	Machine maintenance section	Total
Budgeted overheads (£):					
Allocated overheads	27 660	19 470	16 600	26 650	90 380
Rent, rates, heat and light					17 000
Depreciation and insurance of equipment					25 000
Additional data:					
Gross book value of equipment (£)	150 000	75 000	30 000	45 000	
Number of employees	18	14	4	4	
Floor space occupied (square metres)	3 600	1 400	1 000	800	

It has been estimated that approximately 70% of the machine maintenance section's costs are incurred servicing the machine shop and the remainder incurred servicing the fitting section.

Required:

(a) (i) Calculate the following budgeted overhead absorption rates:

A machine hour rate for the machine shop.

A rate expressed as a percentage of direct wages for the fitting section.

All workings and assumptions should be clearly shown. (*12 marks*)

(ii) Calculate the budgeted manufacturing overhead cost per unit of product X.

(*2 marks*)

(b) The production director of Bookdon PLC has suggested that 'as the actual overheads incurred and units produced are usually different from the budgeted and as a consequence profits of each month end are distorted by over-/under-absorbed overheads, it would be more accurate to calculate the actual overhead cost per unit each month end by dividing the total number of all units actually produced during the month into the actual overheads incurred.'

Critically examine the production director's suggestion. (*8 marks*)

(*Total 22 marks*)

ACCA Level 1 costing

4.25* Reapportionment of service department overheads and a calculation of under-/over-recovery of overheads

An organization has budgeted for the following production overheads for its production and service cost centres for the coming year:

Cost centre	(£)
Machining	180 000
Assembly	160 000
Paint shop	130 000
Engineering shop	84 000
Stores	52 000
Canteen	75 000

The product passes through the machining, assembly and paint shop cost centres and the following data relates to the cost centres:

	M/c	Ass	Paint shop	Eng shop	Stores
No. of employees	81	51	39	30	24
Eng Shop–service hrs	18 000	12 000	10 000		
Stores (orders)	180	135	90	45	

The following budgeted data relates to the production cost centres:

	M/c	Assembly	Paint shop
M/c hours	9 200	8 100	6 600
Lab hours	8 300	11 250	9 000
Lab cost	£40 000	£88 000	£45 000

Required:

(a) Apportion the production overhead costs of the service cost centres to the production cost centres and determine predetermined overhead absorption rates for the three production cost centres on the following basis:

Machining–Machine hours.

Assembly–Labour hours.

Paint shop–Labour costs. (*11 marks*)

(b) Actual results for the production cost centres were:

	M/c	Assembly	Paint shop
M/c hours	10 000	8 200	6 600
Lab hours	4 500	7 800	6 900
Lab cost	£25 000	£42 000	£35 000
Actual O/h	£290 000	£167 000	£155 000

Prepare a statement showing the under-/over-absorption per cost centre for the period under review. (*7 marks*)

(c) Explain why overheads need to be absorbed upon pre-determined bases such as the above. Consider whether these bases for absorption are appropriate in the light of changing technology, suggesting any alternative basis that you consider appropriate. (*7 marks*)

(*Total 25 marks*)

AAT Cost Accounting and Budgeting

4.26* Reapportionment of service department costs and a product cost calculation

Shown below is an extract from next year's budget for a company manufacturing three different products in three production departments:

	Product A	Product B	Product C
Production (units)	4000	3000	6000
Direct material cost (£ per unit)	7	4	9
Direct labour requirements (hours per unit):			
Cutting department:			
Skilled operatives	3	5	2
Unskilled operatives	6	1	3
Machining department	$\frac{1}{2}$	$\frac{1}{4}$	$\frac{1}{3}$
Pressing department	2	3	4
Machine hour requirements (hours per unit):			
Machining department	2	$1\frac{1}{2}$	$2\frac{1}{2}$

The skilled operatives employed in the cutting department are paid £4 per hour and the unskilled operatives are paid £2.50 per hour. All the operatives in the machining and pressing departments are paid £3 per hour.

	Production departments			Service departments	
	Cutting	Machining	Pressing	Engineering	Personnel
Budgeted total overheads (£)	154 482	64 316	58 452	56 000	34 000
Service department costs are incurred for the benefit of other departments as follows:					
Engineering services	20%	45%	25%	—	10%
Personnel services	55%	10%	20%	15%	—

The company operates a full absorption costing system.

Required:

(a) Calculate, as equitably as possible, the total budgeted manufacturing cost of:

(i) one completed unit of Product A, and

(ii) one incomplete unit of Product B which

has been processed by the cutting and machining departments but which has not yet been passed into the pressing department. (*15 marks*)

(b) At the end of the first month of the year for which the above budget was prepared the production overhead control account for the machining department showed a credit balance. Explain the possible reasons for that credit balance. (*7 marks*)

(*Total 22 marks*)

ACCA Level 1 Costing

4.27 Reapportionment of service department costs

JR Co. Ltd's budgeted overheads for the forthcoming period applicable to its production departments, are as follows:

	(£000)
1	870
2	690

The budgeted total costs for the forthcoming period for the service departments, are as follows:

	(£000)
G	160
H	82

The use made up each of the services has been estimated as follows:

	Production department		Service department	
	1	2	G	H
G (%)	60	30	—	10
H (%)	50	30	20	—

Required:

Apportion the service department costs to production departments:

(i) using the step-wise ('elimination') method, starting with G;

(ii) using the reciprocal (simultaneous equation) method;

(iii) commenting briefly on your figures.

(*8 marks*)

(*Total 20 marks*)

ACCA Paper 8 Managerial Finance

Chapter 5

*Indicates that a suggested solution is to be found in the *Students' Manual*.

5.1*
A company operates an integrated cost and financial accounting system.

The accounting entries for the return of unused direct materials from production would be:

A DR Work-in-progress account; CR Stores control account.
B DR Stores control account; CR Work-in-progress account.
C DR Stores control account; CR Finished goods account.
D DR Cost of sales account; CR Work-in-progress account.

CIMA Stage 1—Cost Accounting and Quantitative Methods

5.2*
At the end of a period, in an integrated cost and financial accounting system, the accounting entries for overhead over-absorbed would be:

A DR Profit and loss account CR Work-in-progress control account
B DR Profit and loss account CR Overhead control account
C DR Work-in-progress control account CR Overhead control account
D DR Overhead control account CR Profit and loss account

CIMA Stage 1—Cost Accounting and Quantitative Methods

5.3*
In an interlocking accounting system, the profit shown in the financial accounts was £79 252 but the cost accounts showed £74 294 profit.

The following stock valuations were the only differences between the two sets of accounts:

Stock valuations:	Cost accounts	Financial accounts
Opening stock	£10 116	£9217
Closing stock	£24 053	X

What was the value of X?
A £18 196   B £23 154   C £24 952
D £28 112

CIMA Stage 1—Cost Accounting and Quantitative Methods

5.4*
The following data have been taken from the books of CB plc, which uses a non-integrated accounting system:

	Financial accounts (£)	Cost accounts (£)
Opening stock of materials	5000	6400
Closing stock of materials	4000	5200
Opening stock of finished goods	9800	9600
Closing stock of finished goods	7900	7600

The effect of these stock valuation differences on the profit reported by the financial and cost accounting ledgers is that

A the financial accounting profit is £300 greater than the cost accounting profit.
B the financial accounting profit is £2100 greater than the cost accounting profit.
C the cost accounting profit is £300 greater than the financial accounting profit.
D the cost accounting profit is £900 greater than the financial accounting profit.
E the cost accounting profit is £2100 greater than the financial accounting profit.

CIMA Stage 2—Operational Cost Accounting

5.5* Integrated accounts and computation of the net profit
Set out below are incomplete cost accounts for a period for a manufacturing business:

Stores Ledger Control Account

Opening Balance	£60 140		
Cost Ledger Control A/c	£93 106		
	£153 246		£153 246

Production Wages Control Account

Cost Ledger Control A/c		Finished Goods A/c	£87 480
		Production O'hd Control A/c	
	___		___

Production Overhead Control Account

Cost Ledger Control A/c	£116 202		
Prod. Wages Control A/c			
	___		___

Finished Goods Control Account

Opening Balance	£147 890	Prod. Cost of Sales (variable)	
		Closing Balance	£150 187
	___		___

Notes:
1. *Raw materials:*
   Issues of materials from stores for the period:

   Material Y: 1164 kg (issued at a periodic weighted average price, calculated to two decimal places of £).
   Other materials: £78 520.

No indirect materials are held on the Stores ledger.

Transactions for Material Y in the period:

> Opening stock: 540 kg, £7663
> Purchases: 1100 kg purchased at £14·40 per kg.

2. *Payroll:*

	Direct workers	Indirect workers
Hours worked:		
Basic time	11 140	4250
Overtime	1 075	405
Productive time—direct workers	11 664	
Basic hourly rate (£)	7·50	5·70

Overtime, which is paid at basic rate plus one third, is regularly worked to meet production targets.

3. *Production overheads:*

The business uses a marginal costing system. 60% of production overheads are fixed costs. Variable production overhead costs are absorbed at a rate of 70% of actual direct labour.

4. *Finished goods:*

There is no work in progress at the beginning or end of the period, and a Work in Progress Account is not kept. Direct materials issued, direct labour and production overheads absorbed are transferred to the Finished Goods Control Account.

Required:

(a) Complete the above four accounts for the periods, by listing the missing amounts and descriptions. *(13 marks)*

(b) Provide an analysis of the indirect labour for the period. *(3 marks)*

(c) Calculate the contribution and the net profit for the period, based on the cost accounts prepared in (a) and using the following additional information:

Sales £479 462

Selling and administration overheads:
variable £38 575
fixed £74 360

(4 marks)
(Total 20 marks)
ACCA Management Information—Paper 3

5.6 Intermediate: Integrated cost accounting

XY Limited commenced trading on 1 February with fully paid issued share capital of £500 000, Fixed Assets of £275 000 and Cash at Bank of £225 000. By the end of April, the following transactions had taken place:

1. Purchases on credit from suppliers amounted to £572 500 of which £525 000 was raw materials and £47 500 was for items classified as production overhead.

2. Wages incurred for all staff were £675 000, represented by cash paid £500 000 and wage deductions of £175 000 in respect of income tax etc.

3. Payments were made by cheque for the following overhead costs:

	£
Production	20 000
Selling	40 000
Administration	25 000

4. Issues of raw materials were £180 000 to Department A, £192 500 to Department B and £65 000 for production overhead items.

5. Wages incurred were analysed to functions as follows:

	£
Work in progress — Department A	300 000
Work in progress — Department B	260 000
Production overhead	42 500
Selling overhead	47 500
Administration overhead	25 000
	675 000

6. Production overhead absorbed in the period by Department A was £110 000 and by Department B £120 000.

7. The production facilities, when not in use, were patrolled by guards from a security firm and £26 000 was owing for this service. £39 000 was also owed to a firm of management consultants which advises on production procedures; invoices for these two services are to be entered into the accounts.

8. The cost of finished goods completed was

	Department A (£)	Department B (£)
Direct labour	290 000	255 000
Direct materials	175 000	185 000
Production overhead	105 000	115 000
	570 000	555 000

9. Sales on credit were £870 000 and the cost of those sales was £700 000.
10. Depreciation of productive plant and equipment was £15 000.
11. Cash received from debtors totalled £520 000.
12. Payments to creditors were £150 000.

You are required
(a) to open the ledger accounts at the commencement of the trading period;
(b) using integrated accounting, to record the transactions for the three months ended 30 April;
(c) to prepare, in vertical format, for presentation to management,
    (i) a profit statement for the period;
    (ii) the balance sheet at 30 April.
        (20 marks)
        CIMA Stage 2 Cost Accounting

5.7 Interlocking accounts
AZ Limited has separate cost and financial accounting systems interlocked by control accounts in the two ledgers. From the cost accounts, the following information was available for the period:

	(£)
Cost of finished goods produced	512 050
Cost of goods sold	493 460
Direct materials issued	197 750
Direct wages	85 480
Production overheads (as per the financial accounts)	208 220
Direct material purchases	216 590

In the cost accounts, additional depreciation of £12 500 per period is charged and production overheads are absorbed at 250% of wages.

The various account balances at the beginning of the period were:

	(£)
Stores control	54 250
Work in progress control	89 100
Finished goods control	42 075

Required:
(a) Prepare the following control accounts in the cost ledger, showing clearly the double entries between the accounts, and the closing balances:
    Stores control
    Work in progress control
    Finished goods control
    Production overhead control   (10 marks)
(b) Explain the meaning of the balance on the production overhead control account.
        (2 marks)
(c) When separate ledgers are maintained, the differing treatment of certain items may cause variations to arise between costing and financial profits. Examples of such items include stock valuations, notional expenses, and non-costing items charged in the financial accounts. Briefly explain the above three examples and state why they may give rise to profit differences.   (3 marks)
        (Total 15 marks)
        CIMA Stage 1 Cost Accounting

5.8 Preparation of interlocking accounts from incomplete information
(a) Describe briefly three major differences between:
    (i) financial accounting, and
    (ii) cost and management accounting.
        (6 marks)
(b) Below are incomplete cost accounts for a period:

Stores ledger control account (£000)	
Opening balance	176.0
Financial ledger control a/c	224.2

Production wages control account (£000)	
Financial ledger control a/c	196.0

Production overhead control account (£000)

Financial ledger control a/c	119.3

Job ledger control account (£000)

Opening balance	114.9

The balances at the end of the period were:

	(£000)
Stores ledger	169.5
Jobs ledger	153.0

During the period 64 500 kilos of direct material were issued from stores at a weighted average price of £3.20 per kilo. The balance of materials issued from stores represented indirect materials.

75% of the production wages are classified as 'direct'. Average gross wages of direct workers was £5.00 per hour. Production overheads are absorbed at a predetermined rate of £6.50 per direct labour hour.

Required:
Complete the cost accounts for the period.

(8 marks)
(Total 14 marks)
ACCA Foundation Paper 3

5.9* Preparation of cost accounts from reconciliation statement

(a) The cost accountant and the financial accountant of C Limited had each completed their final accounts for the year. Shown below are the manufacturing, trading and profit and loss accounts, together with a statement reconciling the cost and financial profits. You are required to show the following accounts in the cost ledger:
(i) raw materials;
(ii) work in progress;
(iii) finished goods;
(iv) profit and loss.

Manufacturing, Trading and Profit and Loss Account for the year ended 31 December

	(£000)	(£000)		(£000)	(£000)
Raw material			Trading account,		
Opening stock	110		cost of goods		
Purchases	640		manufactured		1000
	750				
Less: Returns	20				
	730				
Closing stock	130	600			

Direct wages

Paid	220	
Accrued	20	240
Prime cost		840
Production expenses		162
Work in progress:		
Opening stock	25	
Closing stock	27	(2)
		1000

				1000
Finished goods:			Sales	1530
Opening stock	82		Less: Returns	30
Manufactured	1000			1500
	1082			
Closing stock	72			
	1010			
Gross profit	490			
	1500			1500
Administration expenses	200		Gross Profit	490
Sales expenses	70		Discount received	10
Discount allowed	20			
Debenture interest	10			
Net profit	200			
	500			500

[Reconciliation Statement]

	(£000)	(£000)	(£000)
Profit shown in the financial accounts			200
Items not shown in the cost accounts:			
Discount allowed		20	
Debenture interest		10	
Sales expenses		70	
Discount received		(10)	90
			290
Difference in stock valuation:			
Opening stock, raw materials	7		
Opening stock, finished goods	9		
Closing stock, raw materials	15		
		31	
Closing stock, work in progress	(5)		
Opening stock, work in progress	(3)		
Closing stock, finished goods	(4)		
		(12)	
			19
Profit shown in the cost accounts			309

Notes:
Production overhead is absorbed at a rate of $66\frac{2}{3}\%$ of wages.
Administration overhead is written off in the period in which it incurred.

(b) Discuss briefly the reasons for including in a cost accounting system notional interest on capital locked up in stock and its treatment in preparing a reconciliation of cost and financial profits.

(*25 marks*)
CIMA Cost Accounting 2

5.10 Integrated accounts and stores pricing

On 30 October 2002 the following were among the balances in the cost ledger of a company manufacturing a single product (Product X) in a single process operation:

	Dr	Cr
Raw Material Control Account	£87 460	
Manufacturing Overhead Control Account		£5 123
Finished Goods Account	£148 352	

The raw material ledger comprised the following balances at 30 October 2002:

Direct materials:		
Material A:	18 760 kg	£52 715
Material B:	4 242 kg	£29 994
Indirect materials:		£4 751

12 160 kg of Product X were in finished goods stock on 30 October 2002.

During November 1999 the following occurred:

(i) Raw materials purchased on credit:
Material A: 34 220 kg at £2·85/kg
Material B: 34 520 kg at £7·10/kg
Indirect: £7221

(ii) Raw materials issued from stock:
Material A: 35 176 kg
Material B: 13 364 kg
Indirect: £6917

Direct materials are issued at weighted average prices (calculated at the end of each month to three decimal places of £).

(iii) Wages incurred:
Direct: £186 743 (23 900 hours)
Indirect: £74 887

(iv) Other manufacturing overhead costs totalled £112 194. Manufacturing overheads are absorbed at a predetermined rate of £8·00 per direct labour hour. Any over/under absorbed overhead at the end of November should be left as a balance on the manufacturing overhead control account.

(v) 45 937 kg of Product X were manufactured. There was no work-in-progress at the beginning or end of the period. A normal loss of 5% of input is expected.

(vi) 43 210 kg of Product X were sold. A monthly weighted average cost per kg (to three decimal places of £) is used to determine the production cost of sales.

Required:
(a) Prepare the following cost accounts for the month of November 2002:
Raw Material Control Account
Manufacturing Overhead Control Account
Work-in-Progress Account
Finished Goods Account.
All entries to the accounts should be rounded to the nearest whole £. Clearly show any workings supporting your answer. (*16 marks*)
(b) Explain the concept of equivalent units and its relevance in a process costing system.

(*4 marks*)
(*Total 20 marks*)
ACCA Management Information—Paper 3

5.11* Stores pricing and preparation of relevant ledger accounts

V Ltd operates interlocking financial and cost accounts. The following balances were in the cost ledger at the beginning of a month, the last month (Month 12) of the financial year:

	Dr	Cr
Raw material stock control a/c	£28 944	
Finished goods stock control a/c	£77 168	
Financial ledger control a/c		£106 112

There is no work in progress at the end of each month.

21 600 kilos of the single raw material were in stock at the beginning of Month 12. Purchases and issues during the month were as follows:

Purchases:

7th, 17 400 kilos at £1.35 per kilo

29th, 19 800 kilos at £1.35 per kilo

Issues:

1st, 7270 kilos

8th, 8120 kilos

15th, 8080 kilos

22nd, 9115 kilos

A weighted average price per kilo (to four decimal places of a £) is used to value issues of raw material to production. A new average price is determined after each material purchase, and issues are charged out in total to the nearest £.

Costs of labour and overhead incurred during Month 12 were £35 407. Production of the company's single product was 17 150 units.

Stocks of finished goods were:

Beginning of Month 12,   16 960 units.

End of Month 12,   17 080 units.

Transfers from finished goods stocks on sale of the product are made on a FIFO basis.

Required:

(a) Prepare the raw material stock control account, and the finished goods stock control account, for Month 12. (Show detailed workings to justify the summary entries made in the accounts.)   (*12 marks*)

(b) Explain the purpose of the financial ledger control account.   (*4 marks*)

(c) Prepare the raw material usage and the raw material purchases budgets for the year ahead (in kilos) using the following information where relevant:

Sales budget, 206 000 units.

Closing stock of finished goods at the end of the budget year should be sufficient to meet 20 days sales demand in the year following that, when sales are expected to be 10% higher in volume than in the budget year.

Closing stock of raw materials should be sufficient to produce 11 700 units.

(NB You should assume that production efficiency will be maintained at the same level, and that there are 250 working days in each year.)

(*9 marks*)
(*Total 25 marks*)
ACCA Level 1 Costing

5.12* Integrated accounts, profits computation and reconciliation relating to absorption and marginal costing

A company manufactures two products (A and B). In the period just ended production and sales of the two products were:

	Product A (000 units)	Product B (000 units)
Production	41	27
Sales	38	28

The selling prices of the products were £35 and £39 per unit for A and B respectively.

Opening stocks were:

Raw materials	£72 460	
Finished goods:		
Product A	£80 640	(3200 units)
Product B	£102 920	(3100 units)

Raw material purchases (on credit) during the period totalled £631 220. Raw material costs per unit are £7.20 for Product A and £11.60 for Product B.

Direct labour hours worked during the period totalled 73,400 (1 hour per unit of Product A and 1.2 hours per unit of Product B), paid at a basic rate of £8.00 per hour.

3250 overtime hours were worked by direct workers, paid at a premium of 25% over the basic rate. Overtime premiums are treated as indirect production costs. Other indirect labour costs during the period totalled £186 470 and production overhead costs (other than indirect labour) were £549 630. Production overheads are absorbed at a rate of £10.00 per direct labour hour (including £6.80 per hour for fixed production overheads). Any over/under-absorbed balances are transferred to the Profit and Loss Account in the period in which they arise. Non-production overheads totalled £394 700 in the period.

Required:

(a) Prepare the following accounts for the period in the company's integrated accounting system:

(i) Raw material stock control;

(ii) Production overhead control;

(iii) Finished goods stock control (showing the details of the valuation of closing stocks as a note).   (*12 marks*)

(b) Prepare the Profit and Loss Account for the period, clearly showing sales, production cost of sales and gross profit for each product.

(4 marks)

(c) Calculate, and explain, the difference in the net profit (loss) for the period if the marginal costing method is employed. *(4 marks)*

(Total 20 marks)

ACCA Management Information—Paper 3

5.13* Labour cost accounting

(a) Describe briefly the purpose of the 'wages control account'. *(3 marks)*

(b) A manufacturing company has approximately 600 weekly paid direct and indirect production workers. It incurred the following costs and deductions relating to the payroll for the week ended 2 May:

	(£)	(£)
Gross wages		180 460
Deductions:		
Employees' National Insurance	14 120	
Employees' pension fund contributions	7 200	
Income tax (PAYE)	27 800	
Court order retentions	1 840	
Trade union subscriptions	1 200	
Private health care contributions	6 000	
Total deductions		58 160
Net wages paid		122 300

The employer's National Insurance contribution for the week was £18 770.

From the wages analysis the following information was extracted:

	Direct workers (£)	Indirect workers (£)
Paid for ordinary time	77 460	38 400
Overtime wages at normal hourly rates	16 800	10 200
Overtime premium (treat as overhead)	5 600	3 400
Shift premiums/ allowances	8 500	4 500

Capital work in progress expenditure*	—	2 300*
Statutory sick pay	5 700	3 300
Paid for idle time	4 300	—
	118 360	62 100

*Work done by building maintenance workers concreting floor area for a warehouse extension.

You are required to show journal entries to indicate clearly how each item should be posted into the accounts

(i) from the payroll, and

(ii) from the Wages Control Account to other accounts, based on the wages analysis.

Note: Narrations for the journal entries are not required. *(12 marks)*

(Total 15 marks)

CIMA Stage 2 Cost Accounting

5.14 Labour cost accounting and recording of journal entries

(a) Identify the costs to a business arising from labour turnover. *(5 marks)*

(b) A company operates a factory which employed 40 direct workers throughout the four-week period just ended. Direct employees were paid at a basic rate of £4.00 per hour for a 38-hour week. Total hours of the direct workers in the four-week period were 6528. Overtime, which is paid at a premium of 35%, is worked in order to meet general production requirements. Employee deductions total 30% of gross wages. 188 hours of direct workers' time were registered as idle.

Required:

Prepare journal entries to account for the labour costs of direct workers for the period. *(7 marks)*

(Total 12 marks)

ACCA Foundation Stage Paper 3

5.15* Calculation as analysis of gross wages and preparation of wages and overhead control accounts

The finishing department in a factory has the following payroll data for the month just ended:

	Direct workers	Indirect workers
Total attendance time (including overtime)	2640 hours	940 hours
Productive time	2515 hours	—

Non-productive time:

Machine breakdown	85 hours	—
Waiting for work	40 hours	—
Overtime	180 hours	75 hours
Basic hourly rate	£5.00	£4.00
Group bonuses	£2840	£710
Employers' National Insurance contributions	£1460	£405

Overtime, which is paid at 140% of basic rate, is usually worked in order to meet the factory's general requirements. However, 40% of the overtime hours of both direct and indirect workers in the month were worked to meet the urgent request of a particular customer.

Required:
(a) Calculate the gross wages paid to direct workers and to indirect workers in the month.
(4 marks)
(b) Using the above information, record the relevant entries for the month in the finishing department's wages control account and production overhead control account. (You should clearly indicate the account in which the corresponding entry would be made in the company's separate cost accounting system. Workings must be shown.) (10 marks)
(Total 14 marks)
ACCA Foundation Paper 3

5.16 Preparation of the wages control account plus an evaluation of the impact of a proposed piecework system

One of the production departments in A Ltd's factory employs 52 direct operatives and 9 indirect operatives. Basic hourly rates of pay are £4.80 and £3.90 respectively. Overtime, which is worked regularly to meet general production requirements, is paid at a premium of 30% over basic rate.

The following further information is provided for the period just ended:

Hours worked:

Direct operatives:	
Total hours worked	25 520 hours
Overtime hours worked	2 120 hours
Indirect operatives:	
Total hours worked	4 430 hours
Overtime hours worked	380 hours

Production:
Product 1, 36 000 units in 7200 hours
Product 2, 116 000 units in 11 600 hours
Product 3, 52 800 units in 4400 hours

Non-productive time:	2 320 hours
Wages paid (net of tax and employees' National Insurance):	
Direct operatives	£97 955
Indirect operatives	£13 859

The senior management of A Ltd are considering the introduction of a piecework payment scheme into the factory. Following work study analysis, expected productivities and proposed piecework rates for the direct operatives, in the production department referred to above, have been determined as follows:

	Productivity (output per hour)	Piecework rate (per unit)
Product 1	6 units	£1.00
Product 2	12 units	£0.50
Product 3	14.4 units	£0.40

Non-productive time is expected to remain at 10% of productive time, and would be paid at £3.50 per hour.

Required:
(a) Prepare the production department's wages control account for the period in A Ltd's integrated accounting system. (Ignore employers' National Insurance.) (9 marks)
(b) Examine the effect of the proposed piecework payment scheme on direct labour and overhead costs. (11 marks)
(Total 20 marks)
ACCA Cost and Management Accounting 1

5.17* Computation of contract profit
A company has been carrying out work on a number of building contracts (including Contract ABC) over the six-month period ended 31 May 2002. The following information is available:

	All Contracts (including ABC)	Contract ABC
Number of contracts worked on in the six months to 31.5.02	10	—
Value	£76.2 m	£6.4 m
Duration	8–22 months (average 13 months)	11 months
Contract months	53[1]	6
Direct labour costs in the period	£9.762 m	£1.017 m
Raw material costs in the period	£10.817 m	£1.456 m
Distance from base	16 kilometres (average)	23 kilometres
Value of work certified at 31.5.02	—	£5.180 m

Note:
[1]Contract months for 'All Contracts' are the sum of the number of months' work on each individual contact during the six-month period.

Contract ABC commenced on 1 September 2001. As at 30 November 2001 cumulative costs on the contract, held in work-in-progress, totalled £1.063 m (including overheads).

The company confidently predicts that further cost after 31 May 2002 to complete Contract ABC on time (including overheads) will not exceed £0.937 m. Overheads incurred over the six-month period to 31 May 2002, which are to be apportioned to individual contracts are:

	£m
Stores operations	1.56
Contract general management	1.22
Transport	1.37
General administration	4.25

The bases of apportionment are:

Stores operations
—contract value × contract months
Contract general management
—direct labour costs
Transport
—distance from base × contract months
General administration
—contract months

Required:
(a) (i) Apportion overheads to Contract ABC for the six-month period to 31 May 2002 (to the nearest £000 for each overhead item).
    (*6 marks*)
    (ii) Determine the expected profit/loss on Contract ABC, and the amount of profit/loss on the contract that you recommend be included in the accounts of the company for the six-month period to 31 May 2002. (*7 marks*)

(b) The company is introducing a service costing system into its stores operations department. Outline the key factors to consider when introducing the service costing system. (*7 marks*)
(*Total 20 marks*)
ACCA Management Informatioin—Paper 3

5.18* Contract costing
A construction company is currently undertaking three separate contracts and information relating to these contracts for the previous year, together with other relevant data, is shown below.

	Contract MNO (£000)	Contract PQR (£000)	Contract STU (£000)	Construction services dept overhead (£000s)
Contract price	800	675	1100	
Balances brought forward at beginning of year:				
Cost of work completed	—	190	370	—
Material on site	—	—	25	—
Written-down value of plant and machinery	—	35	170	12
Wages accrued	—	2	—	—
Profit previously transferred to profit/loss a/c	—	—	15	—
Transactions during year:				
Material delivered to site	40	99	180	—
Wages paid	20	47	110	8
Payments to subcontractors	—	—	35	—
Salaries and other costs	6	20	25	21
Written down value of plant:				
issued to sites	90	15	—	—
transferred from sites	—	8	—	—
Balances carried forward at the end of year:				
Material on site	8	—	—	—
Written-down value of plant and machinery	70	—	110	5
Wages accrued	—	5	—	—
Pre-payments to subcontractors	—	—	15	—
Value of work certified at end of year	90	390	950	—
Cost of work not certified at end of year	—	—	26	—

The cost of operating the construction services department, which provides technical advice to each of the contracts, is apportioned over the contracts in proportion to wages incurred. Contract STU is scheduled for handing over to the contractee in the near future and the site engineer estimates that the extra costs required to complete the contract in addition to those tabulated above, will total £138 000. This amount includes an allowance for plant depreciation, construction services and for contingencies.

Required:
(a) Construct a cost account for each of the three contracts for the previous year and show the cost of the work completed at the year end.
(9 marks)
(b) (i) Recommend how much profit or loss should be taken, for each contract, for the previous year. *(7 marks)*
   (ii) Explain the reasons for each of your recommendations in (b) (i) above.
(6 marks)
(Total 22 marks)
ACCA Level 1 Costing

5.19 Contract costing
Thornfield Ltd is a building contractor. During its financial year to 30 June 2000, it commenced three major contracts. Information relating to these contracts as at 30 June 2000 was as follows:

	Contract 1	Contract 2	Contract 3
Date contract commenced	1 July 1999	1 January 2000	1 April 2000
	(£)	(£)	(£)
Contract price	210 000	215 000	190 000
Expenditure to 30 June 2000:			
Materials and subcontract work	44 000	41 000	15 000
Direct wages	80 000	74 500	12 000
General expenses	3 000	1 800	700
Position at 30 June 2000:			
Materials on hand at cost	3 000	3 000	1 500
Accrued expenses	700	600	600
Value of work certified	150 000	110 000	20 000
Estimated cost of work completed but not certified	4 000	6 000	9 000
Plant and machinery allocated to contracts	16 000	12 000	8 000

The plant and machinery allocated to the contracts was installed on the dates the contracts commenced. The plant and machinery is expected to have a working life of four years in the case of

contracts 1 and 3 and three years in the case of contract 2, and is to be depreciated on a straight line basis assuming nil residual values.

Since the last certificate of work was certified on contract number 1, faulty work has been discovered which is expected to cost £10 000 to rectify. No rectification work has been commenced prior to 30 June 2000.

In addition to expending directly attributable to contracts, recoverable central overheads are estimated to amount to 2% of the cost of direct wages.

Thornfield Ltd has an accounting policy of taking two thirds of the profit attributable to the value of work certified on a contract, once the contract is one third completed. Anticipated losses on contracts are provided in full.

Progress claims equal to 80% of the value of work certified have been invoiced to customers.

You are required to:
(a) prepare contract accounts for each contract for the year to 30 June 2000, calculating any attributable profit or loss on each contract;
(12 marks)
(b) calculate the amount to be included in the balance sheet of Thornfield Ltd as on 30 June 2000 in respect of these contracts. *(4 marks)*
(Total 16 marks)
ICAEW Accounting Techniques

5.20 Contract costing
(a) PZ plc undertakes work to repair, maintain and construct roads. When a customer requests the company to do work PZ plc supplies a fixed price to the customer and allocates a works order number to the customer's request. This works order number is used as a reference number on material requisitions and timesheets to enable the costs of doing the work to be collected.

PZ plc's financial year ends on 30 April. At the end of April 2000 the data shown against four of PZ plc's works orders were:

Works order number	488	517	518	519
Date started	1/3/99	1/2/00	14/3/00	18/3/00
Estimated completion date	31/5/00	30/7/00	31/5/00	15/5/00

	(£000)	(£000)	(£000)	(£000)
Direct labour costs	105	10	5	2
Direct material costs	86	7	4	2
Selling price	450	135	18	9
Estimated direct costs to complete orders:				
Direct labour	40	60	2	2
Direct materials	10	15	1	1
Independent valuation of work done up to 30 April 2000	350	30	15	5

Overhead costs are allocated to works orders at the rate of 40% of direct labour costs.

It is company policy not to recognize profit on long-term contracts until they are at least 50% complete.

Required:

(i) State, with reasons, whether the above works orders should be accounted for using contract costing or job costing.

(4 marks)

(ii) Based on your classification at (i) above, prepare a statement showing *clearly* the profit to be recognized and balance sheet work in progress valuation of *each* of the above works orders in respect of the financial year ended 30 April 2000.

(10 marks)

(iii) Comment critically on the policy of attributing overhead costs to works orders on the basis of direct labour cost.

(6 marks)

(b) Explain the main features of process costing. Describe what determines the choice between using process costing or specific order costing in a manufacturing organization.

(10 marks)
(Total 30 marks)
CIMA Operational Cost Accounting Stage 2

Chapter 6

*Indicates that a suggested solution is to be found in the Students' Manual.

6.1*

In a process account, abnormal gains are valued at
A the same unit rate as good production.

B the cost of raw materials.
C their scrap value.
D the cost of good production less scrap value.
CIMA Stage 1—Cost Accounting and Quantitative Methods

6.2*

In process costing, where losses have a positive scrap value, when an abnormal gain arises, the abnormal gain account is
A debited with the normal production cost of the abnormal gain units.
B credited with the normal production cost of the abnormal gain units and credited with the scrap value of the abnormal gain units.
C debited with the scrap value of the abnormal gain units and credited with the normal production cost of the abnormal gain units.
D debited with the normal production cost of the abnormal gain units and credited with the scrap value of the abnormal gain units.
E credited with the normal production cost of the abnormal gain units.
CIMA Stage 2—Operational Cost Accounting

6.3*

Process B had no opening stock. 13 500 units of raw material were transferred in at £4.50 per unit. Additional material at £1.25 per unit was added in process. Labour and overheads were £6.25 per completed unit and £2.50 per unit incomplete.

If 11 750 completed units were transferred out, what was the closing stock in process B?
A £ 77 625.00
B £ 14 437.50
C £141 000.00
D £ 21 000.00
CIMA Stage 1

6.4*

A chemical process has a normal wastage of 10% of input. In a period, 2500 kgs of material were input and there was an abnormal loss of 75 kgs.

What quantity of good production was achieved?
A 2175 kg
B 2250 kg
C 2325 kg
D 2475 kg
CIMA Stage 1 Cost Accounting

6.5* Intermediate

KL Processing operates the FIFO method of accounting for opening work in process in its mixing process. The following data relates to April:

Opening work in process	1 000 litres valued at	£1 500
Input	30 000 litres costing	£15 000
Conversion costs		£10 000
Output	24 000 litres	
Closing work in process	3 500 litres	

Losses in processes are expected to be 10% of period input. They are complete as to input material costs but are discovered after 60% conversion. Losses have a scrap value of £0.20 per litre.

Opening work in process was 100% complete as to input materials, and 70% complete as to conversion. Closing work in process is complete as to input materials and 80% complete as to conversion.

A   The number of material-equivalent units was
   (i)   26 300 litres
   (ii)   26 600 litres
   (iii)   27 000 litres
   (iv)   28 000 litres
   (v)   29 000 litres

B   The number of conversion-equivalent units was
   (i)   26 400 litres
   (ii)   26 600 litres
   (iii)   26 800 litres
   (iv)   27 000 litres
   (v)   27 400 litres

(Total 20 marks)
CIMA Stage 1 Operational Cost Accounting

6.6*

The following details relate to the main process of Z Limited, a paint manufacturer:

Opening work in process	2 400 litres	fully complete as to materials and 30% complete as to conversion
Material input	58 000 litres	
Normal loss is 5% of input		
Output to next process	52 500 litres	
Closing work in process	3 000 litres	fully complete as to materials and 50% complete as to conversion

All losses occur at the end of the process.

The numbers of equivalent units to be included in Z Limited's calculation of the cost per equivalent unit, using a *weighted average basis* of valuation, are

	Materials	Conversion
A	53 100	51 600
B	55 500	54 000
C	55 500	53 300
D	57 500	56 000
E	57 500	55 300

CIMA Stage 2—Operational Cost Accounting

6.7

(a) Describe the distinguishing characteristics of production systems where
   (i)   job costing techniques would be used, and
   (ii)   process costing techniques would be used. *(3 marks)*

(b) Job costing produces more accurate product costs than process costing. Critically examine the above statement by contrasting the information requirements, procedures and problems associated with each costing method.
(14 marks)
(Total 17 marks)
ACCA Level 1 Costing

6.8 Preparation of process accounts with all output fully completed

A product is manufactured by passing through three processes: A, B and C. In process C a by-product is also produced which is then transferred to process D where it is completed. For the first week in October, actual data included:

	Process A	Process B	Process C	Process D
Normal loss of input (%)	5	10	5	10
Scrap value (£ per unit)	1.50	2.00	4.00	2.00
Estimated sales value of by-product (£ per unit)	—	—	8.00	—
Output (units)	5760	5100	4370	—
Output of by-product (units)	—	—	510	450
	(£)	**(£)**	**(£)**	**(£)**
Direct materials (6000 units)	12 000	—	—	—
Direct materials added in process	5 000	9 000	4 000	220
Direct wages	4 000	6 000	2 000	200
Direct expenses	800	1 680	2 260	151

Budgeted production overhead for the week is £30 500.

Budgeted direct wages for the week are £12 200.

You are required to prepare:
(a) accounts for process A, B, C and D.
                                                    (20 marks)
(b) abnormal loss account and abnormal gain account.   *(5 marks)*
                                          (Total 25 marks)
                        CIMA P1 Cost Accounting 2

6.9 Discussion question on methods of apportioning joint costs and the preparation of process accounts with all output fully completed

(a) 'Whilst the ascertainment of product costs could be said to be one of the objectives of cost accounting, where joint products are produced and joint costs incurred, the total cost computed for the product may depend upon the method selected for the apportionment of joint costs, thus making it difficult for management to make decisions about the future of products.'

You are required to discuss the above statement and to state *two* different methods of apportioning joint costs to joint products.
                                                    (8 marks)

(b) A company using process costing manufactures a single product which passes through two processes, the output of process 1 becoming the input to process 2. Normal losses and abnormal losses are defective units having a scrap value and cash is received at the end of the period for all such units.

The following information relates to the four-week period of accounting period number 7.

Raw material issued to process 1 was 3000 units at a cost of £5 per unit.

There was no opening or closing work-in-progress but opening and closing stocks of finished goods were £20 000 and £23 000 respectively.

	Process 1	Process 2
Normal loss as a percentage of input	10%	5%
Output in units	2800	2600
Scrap value per unit	£2	£5
Additional components	£1000	£780

Direct wages incurred	£4000	£6000
Direct expenses incurred	£10 000	£14 000
Production overhead as a percentage of direct wages	75%	125%

You are required to present the accounts for
    Process 1
    Process 2
    Finished goods
    Normal loss
    Abnormal loss
    Abnormal gain
    Profit and loss (so far as it relates to any of the accounts listed above).   *(17 marks)*
                                          (Total 25 marks)
                        CIMA Stage 2 Cost Accounting

6.10* Preparation of process accounts with all output fully completed

A chemical compound is made by raw material being processed through two processes. The output of Process A is passed to Process B where further material is added to the mix. The details of the process costs for the financial period number 10 were as shown below:

Process A

Direct material	2000 kilograms at 5 per kg
Direct labour	£7200
Process plant time	140 hours at £60 per hour

Process B

Direct material	1400 kilograms at £12 per kg
Direct labour	£4200
Process plant time	80 hours at £72.50 per hour

The departmental overhead for Period 10 was £6840 and is absorbed into the costs of each process on direct labour cost.

	Process A	Process B
Expected output was	80% of input	90% of input
Actual output was	1400 kg	2620 kg

Assume no finished stock at the beginning of the period and no work in progress at either the beginning or the end of the period.

Normal loss is contaminated material which is sold as scrap for £0.50 per kg from Process A and £1.825 per kg from Process B, for both of which immediate payment is received.

You are required to prepare the accounts for Period 10, for
(i)   Process A,
(ii) Process B,
(iii) Normal loss/gain,
(iv) Abnormal loss/gain,
(v)   Finished goods,
(vi) Profit and loss (extract).   (*15 marks*)
CIMA Stage 2 Cost Accounting

6.11* Equivalent production and no losses
A firm operates a process, the details of which for the period were as follows. There was no opening work-in-progress. During the period 8250 units were received from the previous process at a value of £453 750, labour and overheads were £350 060 and material introduced was £24 750. At the end of the period the closing work-in-progress was 1600 units, which were 100% complete in respect of materials, and 60% complete in respect of labour and overheads. The balance of units were transferred to finished goods.

Requirements:
(a)   Calculate the number of equivalent units produced.   (*3 marks*)
(b)   Calculate the cost per equivalent unit.   (*2 marks*)
(c)   Prepare the process account.   (*7 marks*)
(d)   Distinguish between joint products and by-products, and briefly explain the difference in accounting treatment between them.   (*3 marks*)
(*Total 15 marks*)
CIMA Stage 1 Cost Accounting and Quantitative Methods

6.12 Equivalent production and losses in process
Industrial Solvents Limited mixes together three chemicals – A, B and C – in the ratio 3 : 2 : 1 to produce Allklean, a specialized anti-static fluid. The chemicals cost £8, £6 and £3.90 per litre respectively.

In a period, 12 000 litres in total were input to the mixing process. The normal process loss is 5% of input and in the period there was an abnormal loss of 100 litres whilst the completed production was 9500 litres.

There was no opening work-in-progress (WIP) and the closing WIP was 100% complete for materials and 40% complete for labour and overheads. Labour and overheads were £41 280 in total for the period. Materials lost in production are scrapped.

Required:
(a)   Calculate the volume of closing WIP.   (*3 marks*)
(b)   Prepare the mixing process account for the period, showing clearly volumes and values.   (*9 marks*)
(c)   Briefly explain what changes would be necessary in your account if an abnormal gain were achieved in a period.   (*3 marks*)
(*Total 15 marks*)
CIMA Stage 1 Cost Accounting

6.13 Losses in process (weighted average)
(a)   Outline the characteristics of industries in which a process costing system is used and give two examples of such industries.   (*5 marks*)
(b)   ATM Chemicals produces product XY by putting it through a single process. You are given the following details for November.

Input Costs

Materials costs	25 000 kilos at £2.48 per kilo
Labour costs	8 000 hours at £5.50 per hour
Overhead costs	£63 000

You are also told the following:
(i)   Normal loss is 4% of input.
(ii)   Scrap value of normal loss is £2.00 per kilo.
(iii) Finished output amounted to 15 000 units.
(iv)   Closing work in progress amounted to 6000 units and was fully complete for material $\frac{2}{3}$ complete for labour and $\frac{1}{2}$ for overheads.
(v)   There was no opening work in progress.

Required:
(i) Prepare the Process account for the month of November detailing the value of the finished units and the work in progress. *(12 marks)*
(ii) Prepare an Abnormal Loss account.
(2 marks)
(c) Distinguish between normal and abnormal losses, their costing treatment and how each loss may be controlled. *(6 marks)*
(Total 25 marks)
AAT Cost Accounting and Budgeting

6.14* Losses in process (weighted average)
A company operates expensive process plant to produce a single product from one process. At the beginning of October, 3400 completed units were still in the processing plant, awaiting transfer to finished stock. They were valued as follows:

	(£)
Direct material	25 500
Direct wages	10 200
Production overhead	20 400 (200% of direct wages)

During October, 37 000 further units were put into process and the following costs charged to the process:

	(£)
Direct materials	276 340
Direct wages	112 000
Production overhead	224 000

36 000 units were transferred to finished stock and 3200 units remained in work-in-progress at the end of October which were complete as to material and half-complete as to labour and production overhead. A loss of 1200 units, being normal, occurred during the process.
The average method of pricing is used.

You are required to
(a) prepare for the month of October, a statement (or statements) showing
(i) production cost per unit in total and by element of cost;
(ii) the total cost of production transferred to finished stock;

(iii) the valuation of closing work-in-progress in total and by element of cost;
(15 marks)
(b) describe five of the characteristics which distinguish process costing from job costing.
(10 marks)
(Total 25 marks)
CIMA Stage 2 Cost Accounting

6.15 Losses in process (weighted average)
A company manufactures a product that goes through two processes. You are given the following cost information about the processes for the month of November.

	Process 1	Process 2
Unit input	15 000	—
Finished unit input from Process 1	—	10 000
Finished unit output to Process 2	10 000	—
Finished unit output from Process 2	—	9 500
Opening WIP – Units	—	2 000
– Value	—	£26 200
Input – Materials	£26 740	
– Labour	£36 150	£40 000
– Overhead	£40 635	£59 700
Closing WIP – Units	4 400	1 800

You are told:
(1) The closing WIP in Process 1 was 80% complete for material, 50% complete for labour and 40% complete for overhead.
(2) The opening WIP in Process 2 was 40% complete for labour and 50% complete for overhead. It had a value of labour £3200, overheads £6000 for work done in Process 2.
(3) The closing WIP in Process 2 was two-thirds complete for labour and 75% complete for overhead.
(4) No further material needed to be added to the units transferred from Process 1.
(5) Normal loss is budgeted at 5% of total input in Process 1 and Process 2. Total input is to be inclusive of any opening WIP.
(6) Normal loss has no scrap value in Process 1 and can be sold for the input value from Process 1, in Process 2.
(7) Abnormal losses have no sales value.
(8) It is company policy to value opening WIP in a process by the weighted average method.

Required:
(a) Prepare accounts for:
   (i) Process 1.
   (ii) Process 2.
   (iii) Normal loss.
   (iv) Any abnormal loss/gain. *(19 marks)*
(b) Compare and contrast a joint product with a by-product. *(6 marks)*
(Total 25 marks)
AAT Cost Accounting and Budgeting

6.16 Losses in process (weighted average)

(a) A company uses a process costing system in which the following terms arise:
   conversion costs
   work-in-process
   equivalent units
   normal loss
   abnormal loss.

Required:
Provide a definition of each of these terms.
(5 marks)

(b) Explain how you would treat normal and abnormal losses in process costs accounts.
(4 marks)

(c) One of the products manufactured by the company passes through two separate processes. In each process losses, arising from rejected material, occur. In Process 1, normal losses are 20% of input. In Process 2, normal losses are 10% of input. The losses arise at the end of each of the processes. Reject material can be sold. Process 1 reject material can be sold for £1.20 per kilo, and Process 2 reject material for £1.42 per kilo.

Information for a period is as follows:
Process 1:
   Material input 9000 kilos, cost £14 964.
   Direct labour 2450 hours at £3.40 per hour.
   Production overhead £2.60 per direct labour hour.
   Material output 7300 kilos.

Process 2:
   Material input 7300 kilos.
   Direct labour 1000 hours at £3.40 per hour.
   Production overhead £2.90 per direct labour hour.
   Material output 4700 kilos.
At the end of the period 2000 kilos of material were incomplete in Process 2. These were 50% complete as regards direct labour and production overhead.

There was no opening work-in-process in either process, and no closing work-in-process in Process 1.

Required:
Prepare the relevant cost accounts for the period.
(16 marks)
(Total 25 marks)
ACCA Level 1 Costing

6.17 Losses in process and weighted averages method

ABC plc operates an integrated cost accounting system and has a financial year which ends on 30 September. It operates in a processing industry in which a single product is produced by passing inputs through two sequential processes. A normal loss of 10% of input is expected in each process.

The following account balances have been extracted from its ledger at 31 August:

	Debit (£)	Credit (£)
Process 1 (Materials £4400; Conversion costs £3744)	8144	
Process 2 (Process 1 £4431; Conversion costs £5250)	9681	
Abnormal loss	1400	
Abnormal gain		300
Overhead control account		250
Sales		585 000
Cost of sales	442 500	
Finished goods stock	65 000	

ABC plc uses the weighted average method of accounting for work in process.

During September the following transactions occurred:

Process 1

materials input	4000 kg costing £22 000	
labour cost		£12 000
transfer to process 2	2400 kg	

Process 2

transfer from process 1	2400 kg	
labour cost		£15 000
transfer to finished goods	2500 kg	

Overhead costs incurred amounted to	£54 000
Sales to customers were	£52 000

Overhead costs are absorbed into process costs on the basis of 150% of labour cost.

The losses which arise in process 1 have no scrap value: those arising in process 2 can be sold for £2 per kg.

Details of opening and closing work in process for the month of September are as follows:

	Opening	Closing
Process 1	3000 kg	3400 kg
Process 2	2250 kg	2600 kg

In both processes closing work in process is fully complete as to material cost and 40% complete as to conversion cost.

Stocks of finished goods at 30 September were valued at cost of £60 000.

Required:
Prepare the ledger accounts for September and the annual profit and loss account of ABC plc. (Commence with the balances given above, balance off and transfer any balances as appropriate.)

(25 marks)
CIMA Stage 2 Operational Cost Accounting

6.18* Losses in process (weighted average method) and decision-making based on relevant costs

ABC plc manufactures processed foods in two successive processes.

During April 2000, ABC plc produced a total output of 4570 kgs of maize-meal from its final process, which it can sell for £6.50 per kg.

Details relating to each of the two processes are as follows:

	Process 1	Process 2
Opening work in process	500 kgs	200 kgs
Valued at: Previous process cost	£ n/a	£360
Materials	£500	£ n/a
Conversion cost	£520	£105
Raw materials input	10 000 kgs	n/a
costing	£5500	
Conversion cost	£6 500	£7 400
Closing work in process	800 kgs	150 kgs
	(40% processed)	(70% processed)
Normal waste as a % of input raw materials or of previoius process transfers	30%	15%
Output	6800 kgs	4570 kgs

All materials are added at the start of processing and all losses are completely processed.

Required:
(a) Prepare: process 1 account,
process 2 account,
abnormal loss/gain account.
(15 marks)
(b) MZ Limited has offered ABC plc a temporary contract to purchase all output from process 1 at a price of £4.40 per kg.
Advise ABC plc whether it should accept the offer, assuming that costs in April 2000 are representative of future costs, and that process 2 costs are 70% variable. Include in your advice the additional factors which should be considered, and which are not included in the process account calculations you have produced in answer to part (a).*(10 marks)*
(c) Distinguish between joint products and by-products. Explain their accounting treatment.
(5 marks)
(Total marks 30)
CIMA Stage 2—Operational Cost Accounting

6.19* Losses in process (weighted average)

Chemical Processors manufacture Wonderchem using two processes, mixing and distillation. The following details relate to the distillation process for a period

No opening work in progress (WIP)	
Input from mixing	36 000 kg at a cost of £166 000
Labour for period	£43 800
Overheads for period	£29 200

Closing WIP of 8000 kg, which was 100% complete for materials and 50% complete for labour and overheads.

The normal loss in distillation is 10% of fully complete production. Actual loss in the period was 3600 kg, fully complete, which were scrapped.

Required:
(a) Calculate whether there was a normal or abnormal loss or abnormal gain for the period.
(2 marks)
(b) Prepare the distillation process account for the period, showing clearly weights and values.
(10 marks)
(c) Explain what changes would be required in the accounts if the scrapped production

had a resale value, *and* give the accounting entries. (*3 marks*)
(*Total 15 marks*)
CIMA Stage 1 Cost Accounting

6.20 Process accounts involving an abnormal gain and equivalent production

The following information relates to a manufacturing process for a period:

Materials costs	£16 445
Labour and overhead costs	£28 596

10 000 units of output were produced by the process in the period, of which 420 failed testing and were scrapped. Scrapped units normally represent 5% of total production output. Testing takes place when production units are 60% complete in terms of labour and overheads. Materials are input at the beginning of the process. All scrapped units were sold in the period for £0.40 per unit.

Required:
Prepare the process accounts for the period, including those for process scrap and abnormal losses/gains. (*12 marks*)
ACCA Foundation Stage Paper 3

6.21* Preparation of process accounts with output fully completed and a discussion of FIFO and average methods of WIP valuation

(a) Z Ltd manufactures metal cans for use in the food processing industry. The metal is introduced in sheet form at the start of the process. Normal wastage in the form of offcuts is 2% of input. The offcuts can be sold for £0.26 per kilo. Each metal sheet weighs 2 kilos and is expected to yield 80 cans. In addition to wastage through offcuts, 1% of cans manufactured are expected to be rejected. These rejects can also be sold at £0.26 per kilo.

Production, and costs incurred, in the month just completed, were as follows:

Production:	3 100 760 cans
Costs incurred:	
Direct materials:	39 300 metal sheets at £2.50 per sheet
Direct labour and overhead:	£33 087

There was no opening or closing work in process.

Required:
Prepare the process accounts for the can manufacturing operation for the month just completed.
(*15 marks*)

(b) Another of the manufacturing operations of Z Ltd involves the continuous processing of raw materials with the result that, at the end of any period, there are partly completed units of product remaining.

Required:
With reference to the general situation outlined above
(i) explain the concept of equivalent units (*3 marks*)
(ii) describe, and contrast, the FIFO and average methods of work in process valuation. (*7 marks*)
(*Total 25 marks*)
ACCA Level 1 Costing

6.22* FIFO method and losses in process

The manufacture of one of the products of A Ltd requires three separate processes. In the last of the three processes, costs, production and stock for the month just ended were:
(1) Transfers from Process 2: 180 000 units at a cost of £394 200.
(2) Process 3 costs: materials £110 520, conversion costs £76 506.
(3) Work in process at the beginning of the month: 20 000 units at a cost of £55 160 (based on FIFO pricing method). Units were 70% complete for materials, and 40% complete for conversion costs.
(4) Work in process at the end of the month: 18 000 units which were 90% complete for materials, and 70% complete for conversion costs.
(5) Product is inspected when it is complete. Normally no losses are expected but during the month 60 units were rejected and sold for £1.50 per unit.

Required:
(a) Prepare the Process 3 account for the month just ended. (*15 marks*)
(b) Explain how, and why, your calculations would be affected if the 60 units lost were treated as normal losses. (*5 marks*)

(c) Explain how your calculations would be affected by the use of weighted average pricing instead of FIFO. (*5 marks*)
(*Total 25 marks*)
ACCA Cost and Management Accounting 1

6.23 Losses in process (FIFO and weighted average methods)

A company produces a single product from one of its manufacturing processes. The following information of process inputs, outputs and work in process relates to the most recently completed period:

	kg
Opening work in process	21 700
Materials input	105 600
Output completed	92 400
Closing work in process	28 200

The opening and closing work in process are respectively 60% and 50% complete as to conversion costs. Losses occur at the beginning of the process and have a scrap value of £0.45 per kg.

The opening work in process included raw material costs of £56 420 and conversion costs of £30 597. Costs incurred during the period were:

Materials input	£276 672
Conversion costs	£226 195

Required:
(a) Calculate the unit costs of production (£ per kg to four decimal places) using:
   (i) the weighted average method of valuation and assuming that all losses are treated as normal;
   (ii) the FIFO method of valuation and assuming that normal losses are 5% of materials input. (*13 marks*)
(b) Prepare the process account for situation (a) (ii) above. (*6 marks*)
(c) Distinguish between:
   (i) joint products, and
   (ii) by-products and contrast their treatment in process accounts. (*6 marks*)
(*Total 25 marks*)
ACCA Cost and Management Accounting 1

6.24* FIFO method and losses in process

A company operates several production processes involving the mixing of ingredients to produce bulk animal feedstuffs. One such product is mixed in two separate process operations. The information below is of the costs incurred in, and output from, Process 2 during the period just completed.

Costs incurred:

	£
Transfers from Process 1	187 704
Raw materials costs	47 972
Conversion costs	63 176
Opening work in process	3 009
Production:	Units
Opening work in process (100% complete, apart from Process 2 conversion costs which were 50% complete)	1 200
Transfers from Process 1	112 000
Completed output	105 400
Closing work in process (100% complete, apart from Process 2 conversion costs which were 75% complete)	1 600

Normal wastage of materials (including product transferred from Process 1), which occurs in the early stages of Process 2 (after all materials have been added), is expected to be 5% of input. Process 2 conversion costs are all apportioned to units of good output. Wastage materials have no saleable value.

Required:
(a) Prepare the Process 2 account for the period, using FIFO principles. (*15 marks*)
(b) Explain how, and why, your calculations would have been different if wastage occurred at the end of the process. (*5 marks*)
(*Total 20 marks*)
ACCA Cost and Management Accounting

Chapter 7

*Indicates that a suggest solution is to be found in the *Students' Manual*.

7.1

(a) Explain briefly the term 'joint products' in the context of process costing.

(*2 marks*)

(b) Discuss whether, and if so how, joint process costs should be shared amongst joint products. (Assume that no further processing is required after the split-off point.)

(11 marks)

(c) Explain briefly the concept of 'equivalent units' in process costing.

(4 marks)
(Total 17 marks)
ACCA Level 1 Costing

7.2

(a) Discuss the problems which joint products and by-products pose the management accountant, especially in his attempts to produce useful product profitability reports. Outline the usual accounting treatments of joint and by-products and indicate the extent to which these treatments are effective in overcoming the problems you have discussed. In your answer clearly describe the differences between joint and by-products and provide an example of each.

(14 marks)

(b) A common process produces several joint products. After the common process has been completed each product requires further specific, and directly attributable, expenditure in order to 'finish off' the product and put it in a saleable condition. Specify the conditions under which it is rational to undertake:
   (i) the common process, and
   (ii) the final 'finishing off' of each of the products which are the output from the common process.

Illustrate your answer with a single numerical example.

(6 marks)
(Total 20 marks)
ACCA P2 Management Accounting

7.3

Explain how the apportionment of those costs incurred up to the separation point of two or more joint products could give information which is unacceptable for (i) stock valuation and (ii) decision-making. Use figures of your own choice to illustrate your answer. *(9 marks)*
ACCA Level 2 Management Accounting

7.4* Preparation of process accounts and apportionment of joint costs

A company manufactures two types of industrial sealant by passing materials through two consecu-

tive processes. The results of operating the two processes during the previous month are shown below:

Process 1

Costs incurred (£):		
Materials 7000 kg at £0.50 per kg	3 500	
Labour and overheads	4 340	
Output (kg):		
Transferred to Process 2		6430
Defective production		570

Process 2

Cost incurred (£):		
Labour and overheads	12 129	
Output (kg):		
Type E sealant		2000
Type F sealant		4000
By-product		430

It is considered normal for 10% of the total output from process 1 to be defective and all defective output is sold as scrap at £0.40 kg. Losses are not expected in process 2.

There was no work in process at the beginning or end of the month and no opening stocks of sealants.

Sales of the month's output from Process 2 were:

Type E sealant	1100 kg
Type F sealant	3200 kg
By-product	430 kg

The remainder of the output from Process 2 was in stock at the end of the month.

The selling prices of the products are: Type E sealant £7 per kg and Type F sealant £2.50 per kg. No additional costs are incurred on either of the two main products after the second process. The by-product is sold for £1.80 per kg after being sterilized, at a cost of £0.30 per kg, in a subsequent process. The operating costs of process 2 are reduced by the net income receivable from sales of the by-product.

Required:

(a) Calculate, for the previous month, the cost of the output transferred from process 1 into process 2 and the net cost or saving arising from any abnormal losses or gains in process 1. *(6 marks)*

(b) Calculate the value of the closing stock of each sealant and the profit earned by each sealant during the previous month using the following methods of apportioning costs to joint products:

(i) according to weight of output,

(ii) according to market value of output.

(12 marks)

(c) Consider whether apportioning process costs to joint products is useful. Briefly illustrate with examples from your answer to (b) above.

(4 marks)

(Total 22 marks)

ACCA Level 1 Costing

7.5 Process costing FIFO method (no losses in process) and apportionment as joint cost

(a) The following information relates to the final process in a factory for the month just ended:

Units:

Opening work-in-progress,	500
Transfers in from previous process,	6 500
Closing work-in-progress,	600

Costs (£):

Opening work-in-progress,	1 527
Transfers in:	
Previous process costs,	14 625
Materials added,	5 760
Conversion costs,	3 608

The degree of completion of work-in-progress (WIP) was:

	Opening WIP	Closing WIP
Previous process costs	100%	100%
Materials added	80%	80%
Conversion costs	40%	60%

There is no loss of units in the process. The company uses the FIFO method for charging out the costs of productioin.

Required:

Prepare the process account for the period.

(11 marks)

(b) Another process in the factory produces joint products (M and N). Each joint product is further processed to produce saleable output. The following data is available for a period:

	Total	Product M	Product N
Joint processing costs (£)	44 730		
Production (kg)		2760	6640
Selling price (£ per kg)		11·00	4·80
Further processing costs (£ per kg)		1·20	0·90

Required:

(i) Apportion the joint costs for the period using the net realizable value method.

(4 marks)

(ii) Contrast the accounting treatment of joint products with that applied to by-products.

(5 marks)

(Total 20 marks)

ACCA Management Information—Paper 3

7.6* Preparation of joint product account and a decision on further processing

PQR Limited produces two joint products – P and Q – together with a by-product R, from a single main process (process 1). Product P is sold at the point of separation for £5 per kg, whereas product Q is sold for £7 per kg after further processing into product Q2. By-product R is sold without further processing for £1.75 per kg.

Process 1 is closely monitored by a team of chemists, who planned the output per 1000 kg of input materials to be as follows:

Product P	500 kg
Product Q	350 kg
Product R	100 kg
Toxic waste	50 kg

The toxic waste is disposed of at a cost of £1.50 per kg, and arises at the end of processing.

Process 2, which is used for further processing of product Q into product Q2, has the following cost structure:

Fixed costs	£6000 per week
Variable costs	£1.50 per kg processed

The following actual data relate to the first week of accounting period 10:

Process 1

Opening work in process	Nil
Materials input	
10 000 kg costing	£15 000
Direct labour	£10 000
Variable overhead	£4 000
Fixed overhead	£6 000

Outputs:

Product P	4800 kg
Product Q	3600 kg
Product R	1000 kg
Toxic waste	600 kg
Closing work in progress	nil

Process 2

Opening work in process	nil
Input of product Q	3600 kg
Output of product Q2	3300 kg
Closing work in progress	300 kg,
	50% converted

Conversion costs were incurred in accordance with the planned cost structure.

Required:

(a) Prepare the main process account for the first week of period 10 using the final sales value method to attribute pre-separation costs to joint products. (*12 marks*)

(b) Prepare the toxic waste accounts and process 2 account for the first week of period 10. (*9 marks*)

(c) Comment on the method used by PQR Limited to attribute pre-separation costs to its joint products. (*4 marks*)

(d) Advise the management of PQR Limited whether or not, on purely financial grounds, it should continue to process product Q into product Q2:

   (i) if product Q could be sold at the point of separation for £4.30 per kg; *and*

   (ii) if 60% of the weekly fixed costs of process 2 were avoided by not processing product Q further. (*5 marks*)

(*Total 30 marks*)

CIMA Stage 2 Operational Cost Accounting

7.7* Flow chart and calculation of cost per unit for joint products

A distillation plant, which works continuously, processes 1000 tonnes of raw material each day. The raw material costs £4 per tonne and the plant operating costs per day are £2600. From the input of raw material the following output is produced:

	(%)
Distillate X	40
Distillate Y	30
Distillate Z	20
By-product B	10

From the initial distillation process, Distillate X passes through a heat process which costs £1500 per day and becomes product X which requires blending before sale.

Distillate Y goes through a second distillation process costing £3300 per day and produces 75% of product Y and 25% of product X1.

Distillate Z has a second distillation process costing £2400 per day and produces 60% of product Z and 40% of product X2. The three streams of products X, X1 and X2 are blended, at a cost of £1555 per day to become the saleable final product XXX.

There is no loss of material from any of the processes.

By-product B is sold for £3 per tonne and such proceeds are credited to the process from which the by-product is derived. Joint costs are apportioned on a physical unit basis.

You are required to:

(a) draw a flow chart, flowing from left to right, to show for one day of production the flow of material and the build up of the operating costs for each product; (*18 marks*)

(b) present a statement for management showing for *each* of the products XXX, Y and Z, the output for *one* day, the total cost and the unit cost per tonne; (*5 marks*)

(c) suggest an alternative method for the treatment of the income receivable for by-product B than that followed in this question (figures are not required). (*2 marks*)

(*Total 25 marks*)

CIMA Stage 2 Cost Accounting

7.8 Preparation of joint and by-product process accounts

XYZ plc, a paint manufacturer, operates a process costing system. The following details related to process 2 for the month of October:

Opening work in progress	5000 litres fully complete as to transfers from process 1 and 40% complete as to labour and overhead, valued at £60 000
Transfer from process 1	65 000 litres valued at cost of £578 500
Direct labour	£101 400
Variable overhead	£80 000
Fixed overhead	£40 000
Normal loss	5% of volume transferred from process 1, scrap value £2.00 per litre
Actual output	30 000 litres of paint X (a joint product) 25 000 litres of paint Y (a joint product) 7000 litres of by-product Z
Closing work in progress	6000 litres fully complete as to transfers from process 1 and 60% complete as to labour and overhead.

The final selling price of products X, Y and Z are:

Paint X	£15.00 per litre
Paint Y	£18.00 per litre
Product Z	£4.00 per litre

There are no further processing costs associated with either paint X or the by-product, but paint Y requires further processing at a cost of £1.50 per litre.

All three products incur packaging costs of £0.50 per litre before they can be sold.

Required:
(a) Prepare the process 2 account for the month of October, apportioning the common costs between the joint products, based upon their values at the point of separation *(20 marks)*
(b) Prepare the abnormal loss/gain account, showing clearly the amount to be transferred to the profit and loss account. *(4 marks)*
(c) Describe one other method of apportioning the common costs between the joint products, *and* explain why it is necessary to make such apportionments, and their usefulness when measuring product profitability. *(6 marks)*
(Total 30 marks)
CIMA Stage 2 Operational Cost Accounting

7.9* Joint cost apportionment and decision on further processing

(a) Polimur Ltd operates a process that produces three joint products, all in an unrefined condition. The operating results of the process for October 2000 are shown below.
Output from process:

Product A	100 tonnes
Product B	80 tonnes
Product C	80 tonnes

The month's operating costs were £1 300 000. The closing stocks were 20 tonnes of A, 15 tonnes of B and 5 tonnes of C. The value of the closing stock is calculated by apportioning costs according to weight of output. There were no opening stocks and the balance of the output was sold to a refining company at the following prices:

Product A	£5 per kg
Product B	£4 per kg
Product C	£9 per kg

Required:
Prepare an operating statement showing the relevant trading results for October 2000.
(6 marks)

(b) The management of Polimur Ltd have been considering a proposal to establish their own refining operations.

The current market prices of the refined products are:

Product A	£17 per kg
Product B	£14 per kg
Product C	£20.50 per kg

The estimated unit costs of the refining operation are:

	Product A (£ per kg)	Product B (£ per kg)	Product C (£ per kg)
Direct materials	0.50	0.75	2.50
Direct labour	2.00	3.00	4.00
Variable overheads	1.50	2.25	5.50

Prime costs would be variable. Fixed overheads, which would be £700 000 monthly, would be direct to the refining operation. Special equipment is required for refining product B and this would be rented at a cost, not included in the above figures, of £360 000 per month.

It may be assumed that there would be no weight loss in the refining process and that the quantity refined each month would be similar to October's output shown in (a) above.

Required:
Prepare a statement that will assist management to evaluate the proposal to commence refining operations. Include any further comments or observations you consider relevant. *(16 marks)*
(Total 22 marks)
(ACCA Foundation Costing)

7.10* Joint cost apportionment and decision on further processing

BK Chemicals produces three joint products in one common process but each product is capable of being further processed separately after the split-off point. The estimated data given below relate to June:

	Product B	Product K	Product C
Selling price at split-off point (per litre)	£6	£8	£9
Selling price after further processing (per litre)	£10	£20	£30
Post-separation point costs	£20 000	£10 000	£22 500
Output in litres	3 500	2 500	2 000

Pre-separation point joint costs are estimated to be £40 000 and it is current practice to apportion these to the three products according to litres produced.

You are required:
(i)   to prepare a statement of estimated profit or loss for each product and in total for June if all three products are processed further, and
(ii) to advise how profits could be maximized if one or more products are sold at the split-off point. Your advice should be supported by a profit statement. *(11 marks)*
CIMA Stage 2 Cost Accounting

7.11 Joint cost apportionment, decision on further processing and allocation of scarce capacity

Three products are produced from a single process. During one period in which the process costs are

expected to be £200 000, the following outputs are expected:

	Output	Selling price
Product A	8 000 tonnes	£5 per tonne
Product B	20 000 tonnes	£5 per tonne
Product C	25 000 litres	£10 per litre

Each product can be modified after the initial process by using inputs of skilled labour, costing £8 per hour, to create superior products: Max A, Max B and Max C, respectively. Labour requirements and selling prices are as follows:

	Skilled labour	Selling price
Max A	1 hour per tonne	£20 per tonne
Max B	1.5 hours per tonne	£23 per tonne
Max C	2 hours per litre	£22 per litre

Any modification work leads to a rejection rate of 10% of the input.

Required:
(a) Calculate the apportionment to each product of the joint process costs in the period if the sales value of production basis of apportionment is used. *(3 marks)*
(b) Show which, if any, of the products should be modified into superior products. *(5 marks)*
(c) Assume that the total available skilled labour hours for the period amounted to 6000 hours. Show, giving reasons, which if any of the products should be modified. *(4 marks)*
(Total 12 marks)
AAT Cost Accounting and Budgeting

7.12 Joint cost apportionment and a decision on further processing

QR Limited operates a chemical process which produces four different products Q, R, S and T from the input of one raw material plus water. Budget information for the forthcoming financial year is as follows:

	(£000)
Raw materials cost	268
Initial processing cost	464

Product	Output in litres	Sales (£1000)	Additional processing cost (£000)
Q	400 000	768	160
R	90 000	232	128
S	5 000	32	—
T	9 000	240	8

The company policy is to apportion the costs prior to the split-off point on a method based on net sales value.

Currently, the intention is to sell product S without further processing but to process the other three products after the split-off point. However, it has been proposed that an alternative strategy would be to sell all four products at the split-off point without further processing. If this were done the selling prices obtainable would be as follows:

	Per litre (£)
Q	1.28
R	1.60
S	6.40
T	20.00

You are required:
(a) to prepare a budgeted profit statement showing the profit or loss for each product, and in total, if the current intention is proceeded with; *(10 marks)*
(b) to show the profit or loss by product, and in total, if the alternative strategy were to be adopted; *(6 marks)*
(c) to recommend what should be done and why, assuming that there is no more profitable alternative use for the plant.
(4 marks)
(Total 20 marks)
CIMA Stage 2 Cost Accounting

7.13 Joint cost apportionment and decision on further processing

A company manufactures four products from an input of a raw material to process 1. Following this process, product A is processed in process 2, product B in process 3, product C in process 4 and product D in process 5.

The normal loss in process 1 is 10% of input, and there are no expected losses in the other processes. Scrap value in process 1 is £0.50 per litre. The costs incurred in process 1 are apportioned to each product according to the volume of output of each product. Production overhead is absorbed as a percentage of direct wages.

Data in respect of the month of October:

	Process 1 (£000)	2 (£000)	3 (£000)	4 (£000)	5 (£000)	Total (£000)
Direct materials at £1.25 per litre	100					100
Direct wages	48	12	8	4	16	88
Production overhead						66

	Product A	B	C	D
Output (litres)	22 000	20 000	10 000	18 000
Selling price (£)	4.00	3.00	2.00	5.00
Estimated sales value at end of Process 1 (£)	2.50	2.80	1.20	3.00

You are required to:
(a) calculate the profit or loss for each product for the month, assuming all output is sold at the normal selling price; *(4 marks)*
(b) suggest and evaluate an alternative production strategy which would optimize profit for the month. It should not be assumed that the output of process 1 can be changed; *(12 marks)*
(c) suggest to what management should devote its attention, if it is to achieve the potential benefit indicated in (b).
(4 marks)
(Total 20 marks)
CIMA P1 Cost Accounting 2

7.14* Calculation of cost per unit and decision on further processing

A chemical company carries on production operations in two processes. Materials first pass through process I, where a compound is produced. A loss in weight takes place at the start of processing. The following data, which can be assumed to be representative, relates to the month just ended:

Quantities (kg):

Material input	200 000
Opening work in process (half processed)	40 000
Work completed	160 000
Closing work in process (two-thirds processed)	30 000

Costs (£):

Material input	75 000
Processing costs	96 000
Opening work in process:	
Materials	20 000
Processing costs	12 000

Any quantity of the compound can be sold for £1.60 per kg. Alternatively, it can be transferred to process II for further processing and packing to be sold as Starcomp for £2.00 per kg. Further materials are added in process II such that for every kg of compound used, 2 kg of Starcomp result.

Of the 160 000 kg per month of work completed in process I, 40 000 kg are sold as compound and 120 000 kg are passed through process II for sale as Starcomp. Process II has facilities to handle up to 160 000 kg of compound per month if required. The monthly costs incurred in process II (other than the cost of the compound) are:

	120 000 kg of compound input	160 000 kg of compound input
Materials (£)	120 000	160 000
Processing costs (£)	120 000	140 000

Required:
(a) Determine, using the average method, the cost per kg of compound in process I, and the value of both work completed and closing work in process for the month just ended.
(11 marks)
(b) Demonstrate that it is worth while further processing 120 000 kg of compound.
(5 marks)
(c) Calculate the minimum acceptable selling price per kg, if a potential buyer could be found for the additional output of Starcomp that could be produced with the remaining compound. *(6 marks)*
(Total 22 marks)
ACCA Level 1 Costing

7.15* Profitability analysis and a decision on further processing
C Ltd operates a process which produces three joint products. In the period just ended costs of production totalled £509 640. Output from the process during the period was:

Product W	276 000 kilos
Product X	334 000 kilos
Product Y	134 000 kilos

There were no opening stocks of the three products. Products W and X are sold in this state. Product Y is subjected to further processing. Sales of Products W and X during the period were:

Product W	255 000 kilos at £0.945 per kilo
Product X	312 000 kilos at £0.890 per kilo

128 000 kilos of Product Y were further processed during the period. The balance of the period production of the three products W, X and Y remained in stock at the end of the period. The value of closing stock of individual products is calculated by apportioning costs according to weight of output.

The additional costs in the period of further processing Product Y, which is converted into Product Z, were:

Direct labour	£10 850
Production overhead	£7 070

96 000 kilos of Product Z were produced from the 128 000 kilos of Product Y. A by-product BP is also produced which can be sold for £0.12 per kilo. 8000 kilos of BP were produced and sold in the period.

Sales of Product Z during the period were 94 000 kilos, with a total revenue of £100 110. Opening stock of Product Z was 8000 kilos, valued at £8640. The FIFO method is used for pricing transfers of Product Z to cost of sales.

Selling and administration costs are charged to all main products when sold, at 10% of revenue.

Required:
(a) Prepare a profit and loss account for the period, identifying separately the profitability of each of the three main products.
(14 marks)

(b) C Ltd has now received an offer from another company to purchase the total output of Product Y (i.e. before further processing) for £0.62 per kilo. Calculate the viability of this alternative. (*5 marks*)

(c) Discuss briefly the methods of, and rationale for, joint cost apportionment. (*6 marks*)
(*Total 25 marks*)
ACCA Level 1 Cost and Management Accounting 1

Chapter 8

* Indicates that a suggested solution is to be found in the *Students' Manual*.

8.1*

When comparing the profits reported under marginal and absorption costing during a period when the level of stocks increased,

A absorption costing profits will be higher and closing stock valuations lower than those under marginal costing.

B absorption costing profits will be higher and closing stock valuations higher than those under marginal costing.

C maginal costing profits will be higher and closing stock valuations lower than those under absorption costing.

D marginal costing profits will be lower and closing stock valuations higher than those under absorption costing.

E there is no difference in the profit reported or the valuation of closing stock between the two systems.
CIMA Stage 2—Operational Cost Accounting

8.2

In product costing the costs attributed to each unit of production may be calculated by using either
(i) absorption costing, or
(ii) marginal (or direct or variable) costing.
Similarly, in departmental cost or profit reports the fixed costs of overhead or service departments may be allocated to production departments as an integral part of the production departments' costs or else segregated in some form.

Required:
Describe absorption and marginal (or direct or variable) costing and outline the strengths and weaknesses of each method. (*c. 11 marks*)
ACCA P2 Management Accounting

8.3

Discuss the arguments for and against the inclusion of fixed overheads in stock valuation for the purpose of internal profit measurement.

8.4 Preparation of variable and absorption costing statements

Solo Limited makes and sells a single product. The following data relate to periods 1 to 4.

	(£)
Variable cost per unit	30
Selling price per unit	55
Fixed costs per period	6000

Normal activity is 500 units and production and sales for the four periods are as follows:

	Period 1 units	Period 2 units	Period 3 units	Period 4 units
Sales	500	400	550	450
Production	500	500	450	500

There were no opening stocks at the start of period 1.

Required:
(a) Prepare operating statements for EACH of the periods 1 to 4, based on marginal costing principles. (*4 marks*)

(b) Prepare operating statements for EACH of the periods 1 to 4, based on absorption costing principles. (*6 marks*)

(c) Comment briefly on the results obtained in each period AND in total by the two systems.
(*5 marks*)
(*Total 15 marks*)
CIMA Stage 1 Cost Accounting

8.5* Preparation of variable and absorption costing profit statements and an explanation of the change in profits

A company sells a single product at a price of £14 per unit. Variable manufacturing costs of the product are £6.40 per unit. Fixed manufacturing overheads, which are absorbed into the cost of production at a unit rate (based on normal activity of 20 000 units per period), are £92 000 per period. Any over- or under-absorbed fixed manufacturing overhead balances are transferred to the profit and loss account at the end of each period, in order to establish the manufacturing profit.

Sales and production (in units) for two periods are as follows:

	Period 1	Period 2
Sales	15 000	22 000
Production	18 000	21 000

The manufacturing profit in Period 1 was reported as £35 800.

Required:
(a) Prepare a trading statement to identify the manufacturing profit for Period 2 using the existing absorption costing method.
(*7 marks*)
(b) Determine the manufacturing profit that would be reported in Period 2 if marginal costing was used.
(*4 marks*)
(c) Explain, with supporting calculations:
  (i) the reasons for the change in manufacturing profit between Periods 1 and 2 where absorption costing is used in each period;
(*5 marks*)
  (ii) why the manufacturing profit in (a) and (b) differs.
(*4 marks*)
(*Total 20 marks*)
ACCA Management Information—Paper 3

8.6* Preparation of variable and absorption costing profit statements and CVP analysis

R Limited is considering its plans for the year ending 31 December 2001. It makes and sells a single product, which has budgeted costs and selling price as follows:

	£ per unit
Selling price	45
Direct materials	11
Direct labour	8
Production overhead:	
variable	4
fixed	3
Selling overhead:	
variable	5
fixed	2
Administration overhead:	
fixed	3

Fixed overhead costs per unit are based on a normal annual activity level of 96 000 units. These costs are expected to be incurred at a constant rate throughout the year.

Activity levels during January and February 2001 are expected to be:

	January units	February units
Sales	7000	8750
Production	8500	7750

Assume that there will be no stocks held on 1 January 2001.

Required:
(a) Prepare, in columnar format, profit statements for each of the two months of January and February 2001 using:
  (i) absorption costing;
  (ii) marginal costing. (*12 marks*)
(b) Reconcile and explain the reasons for any differences between the marginal and absorption profits for each month which you have calculated in your answer to (a) above.
(*3 marks*)
(c) Based upon marginal costing, calculate:
  (i) the annual breakeven sales value; and
  (ii) the activity level, in units, which will yield an annual profit of £122 800. (*4 marks*)
(d) Explain three fundamental assumptions underpinning single-product breakeven analysis.
(*6 marks*)
(*Total 25 marks*)
CIMA Stage 2—Operational Cost Accounting

8.7 Preparation of variable and absorption costing systems and CVP analysis

(a) PQ Limited makes and sells a single product, X, and has budgeted the following figures for a one-year period:

Sales, in units		160 000

	(£)	(£)
Sales		6 400 000
Production costs:		
Variable	2 560 000	
Fixed	800 000	
Selling, distribution and administration costs:		
Variable	1 280 000	
Fixed	1 200 000	
Total costs		5 840 000
Net profit		560 000

Fixed costs are assumed to be incurred evenly throughout the year. At the beginning of the year, there were no stocks of finished goods. In the first quarter of the year, 55 000 units were produced and 40 000 units were sold.

You are required to prepare profit statements for the first quarter, using
(i) marginal costing, and
(ii) absorption costing. *(6 marks)*

(b) There is a difference in the profit reported when marginal costing is used compared with when absorption costing is used.

You are required to discuss the above statement and to indicate how each of the following conditions would affect the net profit reported
(i) when sales and production are in balance at standard (or expected) volume,
(ii) when sales exceed production,
(iii) when production exceeds sales.

Use the figures from your answer to (a) above to support your discussion; you should also refer to SSAP 9. *(9 marks)*

(c) WF Limited makes and sells a range of plastic garden furniture. These items are sold in sets of one table with four chairs for £80 per set.

The variable costs per set are £20 for manufacturing and £10 for variable selling, distribution and administration.

Direct labour is treated as a fixed cost and the total fixed costs of manufacturing, including depreciation of the plastic-moulding machinery, are £800 000 per annum. Budgeted profit for the forthcoming year is £400 000.

Increased competition has resulted in the management of WF Limited engaging market research consultants. The consultants have recommended three possible strategies, as follows:

	Reduce selling price per set by %	Expected increase in sales (sets) %
Strategy 1	5	10
Strategy 2	7.5	20
Strategy 3	10	25

You are required to assess the effect on profits of each of the three strategies, and to

recommend which strategy, if any, ought to be adopted. *(10 marks)*
(Total 25 marks)
CIMA Stage 2 Cost Accounting

8.8* Preparation of variable and absorption costing statements as a reconciliation of the profits
The following budgeted profit statement has been prepared using absorption costing principles:

	January to June (£000) (£000)		July to December (£000) (£000)	
Sales		540		360
Opening stock	100		160	
Production costs:				
Direct materials	108		36	
Direct labour	162		54	
Overhead	90		30	
	460		280	
Closing stock	160		80	
		300		200
GROSS PROFIT		240		160
Production overhead: (Over)/Under absorption	(12)		12	
Selling costs	50		50	
Distribution costs	45		40	
Administration costs	80		80	
		163		182
NET PROFIT/(LOSS)		77		(22)
Sales units	15 000		10 000	
Production units	18 000		6000	

The members of the management team are concerned by the significant change in profitability between the two six-month periods. As management accountant, you have analysed the data upon which the above budget statement has been produced, with the following results:
1. The production overhead cost comprises both a fixed and a variable element, the latter appears to be dependent on the number of units produced. The fixed element of the cost is expected to be incurred at a constant rate throughout the year.
2. The selling costs are fixed.
3. The distribution cost comprises both fixed and variable elements, the latter appears to be dependent on the number of units sold. The fixed element of the cost is expected to be incurred at a constant rate throughout the year.
4. The administration costs are fixed.

Required:

(a) Present the above budgeted profit statement in marginal costing format. *(10 marks)*

(b) Reconcile EACH of the six-monthly profit/ loss values reported respectively under marginal and absorption costing. *(4 marks)*

(c) Reconcile the six-monthly profit for January to June from the absorption costing statement with the six-monthly loss for July to December from the absorption costing statement. *(4 marks)*

(d) Calculate the annual number of units required to break even. *(3 marks)*

(e) Explain briefly the advantages of using marginal costing as the basis of providing managers with information for decision making. *(4 marks)*

(Total 25 marks)

CIMA Stage 2 Operational Cost Accounting

8.9 Preparation of variable and absorption costing profit statements and comments in support of a variable costing system

A manufacturer of glass bottles has been affected by competition from plastic bottles and is currently operating at between 65 and 70 per cent of maximum capacity.

The company at present reports profits on an absorption costing basis but with the high fixed costs associated with the glass container industry and a substantial difference between sales volumes and production in some months, the accountant has been criticized for reporting widely different profits from month to month. To counteract this criticism, he is proposing in future to report profits based on marginal costing and in his proposal to management lists the following reasons for wishing to change:

1. Marginal costing provides for the complete segregation of fixed costs, thus facilitating closer control of production costs.
2. It eliminates the distortion of interim profit statements which occur when there are seasonal fluctuations in sales volume although production is at a fairly constant level.
3. It results in cost information which is more helpful in determining the sales policy necessary to maximize profits.

From the accounting records the following figures were extracted: Standard cost per gross (a gross is 144 bottles and is the cost unit used within the business):

	(£)
Direct materials	8.00
Direct labour	7.20
Variable production overhead	3.36
Total variable production cost	18.56
Fixed production overhead	7.52*
Total production standard cost	26.08

*The fixed production overhead rate was based on the following computations:

Total annual fixed production overhead was budgeted at £7 584 000 or £632 000 per month.

Production volume was set at 1 008 000 gross bottles or 70 per cent of maximum capacity.

There is a slight difference in budgeted fixed production overhead at different levels of operating:

Activity level (per cent of maximum capacity)	Amount per month (£000)
50–75	632
76–90	648
91–100	656

You may assume that actual fixed production overhead incurred was as budgeted.

Additional information:

	September	October
Gross sold	87 000	101 000
Gross produced	115 000	78 000
Sales price, per gross	£32	£32
Fixed selling costs	£120 000	£120 000
Fixed administrative costs	£80 000	£80 000

There were no finished goods in stock at 1 September.

You are required

(a) to prepare monthly profit statements for September and October using
  (i) absorption costing; and
  (ii) marginal costing; *(16 marks)*

(b) to comment briefly on the accountant's three reasons which he listed to support his proposal. *(9 marks)*

(Total 25 marks)

CIMA Stage 2 Cost Accounting

8.10* Under/over-recovery of fixed overheads and preparation and reconciliation of absorption and variable costing profit statements

(a) Discuss the arguments put forward for the use of absorption and marginal costing systems respectively. (*8 marks*)

(b) The following information is available for a firm producing and selling a single product:

	(£000)
Budgeted costs (at normal activity)	
Direct materials and labour	264
Variable production overhead	48
Fixed production overhead	144
Variable selling and administration overhead	24
Fixed selling and administration overhead	96

The overhead absorption rates are based upon normal activity of 240 000 units per period.

During the period just ended 260 000 units of product were produced, and 230 000 units were sold at £3 per unit.

At the beginning of the period 40 000 units were in stock. These were valued at the budgeted costs shown above.

Actual costs incurred were as per budget.

Required:

(i) Calculate the fixed production overhead absorbed during the period, and the extent of any under-/over-absorption. For both of these calculations you should use absorption costing.

(ii) Calculate profits for the period using absorption costing and marginal costing respectively.

(iii) Reconcile the profit figures which you calculated in (ii) above.

(iv) State the situations in which the profit figures calculated under both absorption costing and marginal costing would be the same.

(*17 marks*)
(*Total 25 marks*)
ACCA Level 1 Costing

8.11* Equivalent production and preparation of variable and absorption costing profit statements

A new subsidiary of a group of companies was established for the manufacture and sale of Product X. During the first year of operations 90 000 units were sold at £20 per unit. At the end of the year, the closing stocks were 8000 units in finished goods store and 4000 units in work-in-progress which were complete as regards material content but only half complete in respect of labour and overheads. You are to assume that there were no opening stocks. The work-in-progress account had been debited during the year with the following costs:

	(£)
Direct materials	714 000
Direct labour	400 000
Variable overhead	100 000
Fixed overhead	350 000

Selling and administration costs for the year were:

	Variable cost per unit sold (£)	Fixed cost (£)
Selling	1.50	200 000
Administration	0.10	50 000

The accountant of the subsidiary company had prepared a profit statement on the absorption costing principle which showed a profit of £11 000.

The financial controller of the group, however, had prepared a profit statement on a marginal costing basis which showed a loss. Faced with these two profit statements, the director responsible for this particular subsidiary company is confused.

You are required to

(a) prepare a statement showing the equivalent units produced and the production cost of *one* unit of Product X by element of cost and in total; (*5 marks*)

(b) prepare a profit statement on the absorption costing principle which agrees with the company accountant's statement; (*9 marks*)

(c) prepare a profit statement on the marginal costing basis; (*6 marks*)

(d) explain the differences between the two statements given for (b) and (c) above to the director in such a way as to eliminate his confusion and state why both statements may be acceptable. (*5 marks*)

(*Total 25 marks*)
CIMA Stage 2 Cost Accounting

8.12* Preparation of variable and absorption costing profit statements for FIFO and AVECO methods

The following information relates to product J, for quarter 3, which has just ended:

	Production (units)	Sales (units)	Fixed overheads (£000)	Variable costs (£000)
Budget	40 000	38 000	300	1800
Actual	46 000	42 000	318	2070

The selling price of product J was £72 per unit.

The fixed oveheads were absorbed at a predetermined rate per unit.

At the beginning of quarter 3 there was an opening stock of product J of 2000 units, valued at £25 per unit variable costs and £5 per unit fixed overheads.

Required:
(a) (i) Calculate the fixed overhead absorption rate per unit for the last quarter, and present profit statements using FIFO (first in, first out) using:
(ii) absorption costing;
(iii) marginal costing; and
(iv) reconcile and explain the difference between the profits or losses.   (*12 marks*)
(b) Using the same data, present similar statements to those required in part (a). Using the AVECO (average cost) method of valuation, reconcile the profit or loss figures, and comment briefly on the variations between the profits or losses in (a) and (b). (*8 marks*)
(*Total 20 marks*)
ACCA Paper 8 Managerial Finance

8.13 Calculation of overhead absorption rates and an explanation of the differences in profits
A company manufactures a single product with the following variable costs per unit

Direct materials	£7.00
Direct labour	£5.50
Manufacturing overhead	£2.00

The selling price of the product is £36.00 per unit. Fixed manufacturing costs are expected to be £1 340 000 for a period. Fixed non-manufacturing costs are expected to be £875 000. Fixed manufacturing costs can be analysed as follows:

Production Department 1	Department 2	Service Department	General Factory
£380 000	£465 000	£265 000	£230 000

'General Factory' costs represent space costs, for example rates, lighting and heating. Space utilization is as follows:

Production department 1	40%
Production department 2	50%
Service department	10%

60% of service department costs are labour related and the remaining 40% machine related.

Normal production department activity is:

	Direct labour hours	Machine hours	Production units
Department 1	80 000	2400	120 000
Department 2	100 000	2400	120 000

Fixed manufacturing overheads are absorbed at a predetermined rate per unit of production for each production department, based upon normal activity.

Required:
(a) Prepare a profit statement for a period using the full absorption costing system described above and showing each element of cost separately. Costs for the period were as per expectation, except for additional expenditure of £20 000 on fixed manufacturing overhead in Production Department 1. Production and sales were 116 000 and 114 000 units respectively for the period.   (*14 marks*)
(b) Prepare a profit statement for the period using marginal costing principles instead.
(*5 marks*)
(c) Contrast the general effect on profit of using absorption and marginal costing systems respectively. (Use the figures calculated in (a) and (b) above to illustrate your answer.)
(*6 marks*)
(*Total 25 marks*)
ACCA Cost and Management Accounting 1

Chapter 9

* Indicates that a suggested solution is to be found in the *Students' Manual.*

9.1*

Z plc currently sells products Aye, Bee and Cee in equal quantities and at the same selling price per unit. The contribution to sales ratio for product Aye is 40%; for product Bee it is 50% and the total is 48%. If fixed costs are unaffected by mix and are currently 20% of sales, the effect of changing the product mix to:

Aye	40%
Bee	25%
Cee	35%

is that the total contribution/total sales ratio changes to:

A 27.4%
B 45.3%
C 47.4%
D 48.4%
E 68.4%

CIMA Stage 2

9.2*

E plc operates a marginal costing system. For the forthcoming year, variable costs are budgeted to be 60% of sales value and fixed costs are budgeted to be 10% of sales value.

If E plc increases its selling prices by 10%, but if fixed costs, variable costs per unit and sales volume remain unchanged, the effect on E plc's contribution would be:

A a decrease of 2%;
B an increase of 5%
C an increase of 10%
D an increase of 25%
E an increase of $66\frac{2}{3}$%.

CIMA Stage 2

9.3*

A Limited has fixed costs of £60 000 per annum. It manufactures a single product which it sells for £20 per unit. Its contribution to sales ratio is 40%.

A Limited's breakeven point in units is:

A 1200
B 1800
C 3000
D 5000
E 7500

CIMA Stage 2 Specimen Paper

9.4*

The following data relate to the overhead expenditure of a contract cleaners at two activity levels:

Square metres cleaned	12 750	15 100
Overheads	£73 950	£83 585

What is the estimate of the overheads if 16 200 square metres are to be cleaned?

A £88 095
B £89 674
C £93 960
D £98 095

CIMA Stage 1

9.5*

A company which makes a single product has a contribution to sales ratio of 30%. Each unit is sold at £8. In a period when fixed costs were £30 000 the net profit was £56 400.

What was the total of direct wages for the period if direct wages were 20% of variable costs?

A £17 280.   B £26 400.   C £40 320.
D £57 600.

CIMA Stage 1—Cost Accounting and Quantitative Methods

9.6*

The following data have been extracted from the budget working papers of BL Limited:

Production volume	1,000 units £ per unit	2,000 units £ per unit
Direct materials	8.00	8.00
Direct labour	7.00	7.00
Production overhead— department 1	12.00	8.40
Production overhead— department 2	8.00	4.00

The total fixed cost and variable cost per unit are:

	Total fixed cost (£)	Variable cost per unit (£)
A	7 200	15.00
B	7 200	19.80
C	8 000	23.40
D	15 200	15.00
E	15 200	19.80

CIMA Stage 2—Operational Cost Accounting

9.7*

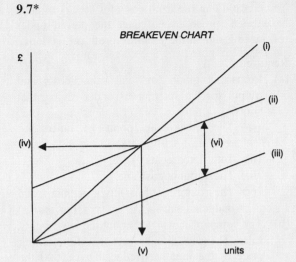

BREAKEVEN CHART

Required:
(a) Briefly describe the parts of the above break-even chart marked (i) to (vi). (*6 marks*)
(b) State and explain the assumptions of breakeven analysis. (*8 marks*)
(c) Prepare a report addressed to the Operations Manager explaining why it is important to understand the behaviour of cost when using budgetary control.
(Your report should include examples of different types of cost and an explanation of why it is useful to use fixed and flexible budgets.)
(*11 marks*)
(*Total 25 marks*)
CIMA Stage 2—Operational Cost Accounting

9.8
Figure 9.8 shows a typical cost–volume–profit chart:

Required:
(a) Explain to a colleague who is not an accountant the reasons for the change in result on this cost–volume–profit chart from a loss at point (a) to a profit at point (b). (*3 marks*)
(b) Identify and critically examine the underlying assumptions of this type of cost–volume–profit analysis and consider whether such analyses are useful to the management of an organization. (*14 marks*)
(*Total 17 marks*)
ACCA Level 1 Costing

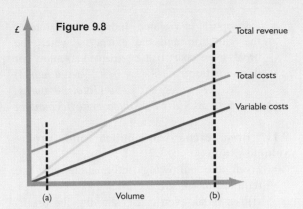

Figure 9.8

9.9
The graphs shown below show cost–volume–profit relationships as they are typically represented in (i) management accounting and (ii) economic theory. In each graph TR = total revenue, TC = total cost, and P = profit. You are required to compare these different representations of cost–volume–profit relationships, identifying, explaining and commenting on points of similarity and also differences. (*15 marks*)
ICAEW Management Accounting

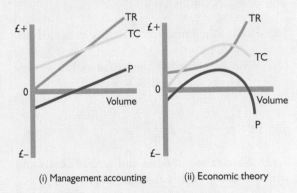

(i) Management accounting   (ii) Economic theory

9.10
'A break-even chart must be interpreted in the light of the limitations of its underlying assumptions...' (From *Cost Accounting: A Managerial Emphasis*, by C.T. Horngren.)

Required:
(a) Discuss the extent to which the above statement is valid and both describe and briefly appraise the reasons for *five* of the most important underlying assumptions of breakeven analysis. (*c. 14 marks*)
(b) For any *three* of the underlying assumptions provided in answer to (a) above, give an example of circumstances in which that

assumption is violated. Indicate the nature of the violation and the extent to which the break-even chart can be adapted to allow for this violation.   (*c. 6 marks*)
                                        (*Total 20 marks*)
                    ACCA P2 Management Accounting

9.11* Break-even, contribution and profit–volume graph

(a) From the following information you are required to construct:
  (i) a break-even chart, showing the break-even point and the margin of safety;
  (ii) a chart displaying the contribution level and the profit level;
  (iii) a profit–volume chart.

Sales	6000 units at £12 per unit = £72 000
Variable costs	6000 units at £7 per unit = £42 000
Fixed costs	= £20 000

                                          (*9 marks*)

(b) State the purposes of each of the three charts in (a) above.   (*6 marks*)
(c) Outline the limitations of break-even analysis.
                                          (*5 marks*)
(d) What are the advantages of graphical presentation of financial data to executives?
                                          (*2 marks*)
                                        (*Total 22 marks*)
                                                    AAT

9.12* Separation of fixed and variable costs and construction of a break-even graph

A building company constructs a standard unit which sells for £30 000. The company's costs can be readily identifiable between fixed and variable costs.

Budgeted data for the coming six months includes the following:

	Sales (in units)	Profit (£)
January	18	70 000
February	20	100 000
March	30	250 000
April	22	130 000
May	24	160 000
June	16	40 000

You are told that the fixed costs for the six months have been spread evenly over the period under review to arrive at the monthly profit projections.

Required:
(a) Prepare a graph for total sales, costs and output for the six months under review that shows:
  (i) The break-even point in units and revenue.
  (ii) Total fixed costs.
  (iii) The variable cost line.
  (iv) The margin of safety for the total budgeted sales.   (*14 marks*)
(b) The company is worried about the low level of sales. The sales director says that if the selling price of the unit was reduced by £5000 the company would be able to sell 10% more units. All other costs would remain the same you are told.
    Determine whether the company should reduce the selling price to attract new sales in order to maximize profit. Clearly show any workings.   (*5 marks*)
(c) Evaluate whether the assumption that costs are readily identifiable as either fixed or variable throughout a range of production is realistic. Give examples of any alternative classification.   (*6 marks*)
                                        (*Total 25 marks*)
                    AAT Cost Accounting and Budgeting

9.13* Profit–volume graph and changes in sales mix

A company produces and sells two products with the following costs:

	Product X	Product Y
Variable costs (per £ of sales)	£0.45	£0.6
Fixed costs	£1 212 000 per period	£1 212 000

Total sales revenue is currently generated by the two products in the following proportions:

Product X	70%
Product Y	30%

Required:
(a) Calculate the break-even sales revenue per period, based on the sales mix assumed above.
                                          (*6 marks*)

(b) Prepare a profit–volume chart of the above situation for sales revenue up to £4 000 000. Show on the same chart the effect of a change in the sales mix to product X 50%, product Y 50%. Clearly indicate on the chart the break-even point for each situation.   (*11 marks*)

(c) Of the fixed costs £455 000 are attributable to product X. Calculate the sales revenue required on product X in order to recover the attributable fixed costs and provide a net contribution of £700 000 towards general fixed costs and profit.   (*5 marks*)

(*Total 22 marks*)
ACCA Level 1 Costing

9.14 Multi-product profit–volume graph

JK Limited has prepared a budget for the next twelve months when it intends to make and sell four products, details of which are shown below:

Product	Sales in units (thousands)	Selling price per unit (£)	Variable cost per unit (£)
J	10	20	14.00
K	10	40	8.00
L	50	4	4.20
M	20	10	7.00

Budgeted fixed costs are £240 000 per annum and total assets employed are £570 000.

You are required

(a) to calculate the total contribution earned by each product and their combined total contributions;   (*2 marks*)

(b) to plot the data of your answer to (a) above in the form of a contribution to sales graph (sometimes referred to as a profit–volume graph) *on the graph paper provided*;

(*6 marks*)

(c) to explain your graph to management, to comment on the results shown and to state the break-even point;   (*4 marks*)

(d) to describe briefly three ways in which the overall contribution to sales ratio could be improved.   (*3 marks*)

(*Total 15 marks*)
CIMA Stage 2 Cost Accounting

9.15 Break-even chart with increases in fixed costs

(a) Identify and discuss briefly *five* assumptions underlying cost–volume–profit analysis.

(*10 marks*)

(b) A local authority, whose area includes a holiday resort situated on the east coast, operates, for 30 weeks each year, a holiday home which is let to visiting parties of children in care from other authorities. The children are accompanied by their own house mothers who supervise them throughout their holiday. From six to fifteen guests are accepted on terms of £100 per person per week. No differential charges exist for adults and children.

Weekly costs incurred by the host authority are:

	(£ per guest)
Food	25
Electricity for heating and cooking	3
Domestic (laundry, cleaning etc.) expenses	5
Use of minibus	10

Seasonal staff supervise and carry out the necessary duties at the home at a cost of £11 000 for the 30-week period. This provides staffing sufficient for six to ten guests per week but if eleven or more guests are to be accommodated, additional staff at a total cost of £200 per week are engaged for the whole of the 30-week period.

Rent, including rates for the property, is £4000 per annum and the garden of the home is maintained by the council's recreation department which charges a nominal fee of £1000 per annum.

You are required to:

(i) tabulate the appropriate figures in such a way as to show the break-even point(s) and to comment on your figures;

(*8 marks*)

(ii) draw, on the graph paper provided, a chart to illustrate your answer to (b)(i) above.   (*7 marks*)

(*Total 25 marks*)
CIMA Cost Accounting Stage 2

9.16* Break-even chart with an increase in fixed costs and incorporating expected values

A manufacturer is considering a new product which could be produced in one of two qualities – Standard or De Luxe. The following estimates have been made:

	Standard (£)	De Luxe (£)
Unit labour cost	2.00	2.50
Unit material cost	1.50	2.00
Unit packaging cost	1.00	2.00
Proposed selling price per unit	7.00	10.00
Budgeted fixed costs per period:		
0–99 999 units	200 000	250 000
100 000 and above	350 000	400 000

At the proposed selling prices, market research indicates the following demand:

Standard

Quantity	Probability
172 000	0.1
160 000	0.7
148 000	0.2

De Luxe

Quantity	Probability
195 500	0.3
156 500	0.5
109 500	0.2

You are required

(a) to draw separate break-even charts for *each* quality, showing the break-even points;
(7 marks)
(b) to comment on the position shown by the charts and what guidance they provide for management;
(3 marks)
(c) to calculate, for *each* quality, the expected unit sales, expected profits and the margin of safety;
(3 marks)
(d) using an appropriate measure of risk, to advise management which quality should be launched.
(9 marks)
(Total 22 marks)
CIMA Stage 3 Management Accounting Techniques

9.17 Analysis of costs into fixed and variable elements and break-even point calculation

(a) 'The analysis of total cost into its behavioural elements is essential for effective cost and management accounting.'

Required:
Comment on the statement above, illustrating your answer with examples of cost behaviour patterns.
(5 marks)

(b) The total costs incurred at various output levels, for a process operation in a factory, have been measured as follows:

Output (units)	Total cost (£)
11 500	102 476
12 000	104 730
12 500	106 263
13 000	108 021
13 500	110 727
14 000	113 201

Required:
Using the high–low method, analyse the costs of the process operation into fixed and variable components.
(4 marks)

(c) Calculate, and comment upon, the break-even output level of the process operation in (b) above, based upon the fixed and variable costs identified and assuming a selling price of £10.60 per unit.
(5 marks)
(Total 14 marks)
ACCA Foundation Paper 3

9.18* Non-graphical CVP analyses

A retailer with a chain of stores is planning product promotions for a future period. The following information relates to a product which is being considered for a four week promotion:

Normal weekly sales (i.e. without promotion), 2400 units at £2.80 per unit.
Normal contribution margin, 45% of normal selling price.
Promotional discount, 20% (i.e. normal selling price reduced by 20% during the promotion).
Expected promotion sales multiplier, 2.5 (i.e. weekly sales units expected during the promotion is 2.5 × 2400 = 6000 units).

Additional fixed costs incurred to run the promotion (i.e. unaffected by the level of promotional sales) are forecast to be £5400. Unit variable costs would be expected to remain at the same level as normal.

Required:

(a) Calculate the expected incremental profit/ (loss) from the promotion. (*8 marks*)

(b) Calculate the sales units multiplier that would be required during the promotion to break even compared with a no-promotion situation. (*6 marks*)

(c) Describe other factors that should be considered before making a decision regarding the promotion. (*6 marks*)

(*Total 20 marks*)
ACCA Level 1 — Cost and Management Accounting 1

9.19* Non-graphical CVP analysis and calculation of margin of safety

Z Ltd manufactures and sells three products with the following selling prices and variable costs:

	Product A (£/unit)	Product B (£/unit)	Product C (£/unit)
Selling price	3.00	2.45	4.00
Variable cost	1.20	1.67	2.60

The company is considering expenditure on advertising and promotion of Product A. It is hoped that such expenditure, together with a reduction in the selling price of the product, would increase sales. Existing annual sales volume of the three products is:

Product A	460 000 units
Product B	1 000 000 units
Product C	380 000 units

If £60 000 per annum was to be invested in advertising and sales promotion, sales of Product A at reduced selling prices would be expected to be:

590 000 units at £2.75 per unit
or 650 000 units at £2.55 per unit

Annual fixed costs are currently £1 710 000 per annum.

Required:

(a) Calculate the current break-even sales revenue of the business. (*8 marks*)

(b) Advise the management of Z Ltd as to whether the expenditure on advertising and promotion, together with selling price reduction, should be introduced on Product A. (*6 marks*)

(c) Calculate the required unit sales of Product A, at a selling price of £2.75 per unit, in order to justify the expenditure on advertising and promotion. (*5 marks*)

(d) Explain the term 'margin of safety', with particular reference to the circumstances of Z Ltd. (*6 marks*)

(*Total 25 marks*)
ACCA Level 1 Costing

9.20 Non-graphical CVP analysis and the acceptance of a special order

Video Technology Plc was established in 1987 to assemble video cassette recorders (VCRs). There is now increased competition in its markets and the company expects to find it difficult to make an acceptable profit next year. You have been appointed as an accounting technician at the company, and have been given a copy of the draft budget for the next financial year.

Draft budget for 12 months to 30 November 2001

	(£m)	(£m)
Sales income		960.0
Cost of sales:		
Variable assembly materials	374.4	
Variable labour	192.0	
Factory overheads – variable	172.8	
– fixed	43.0	(782.2)
		177.8
Gross profit		
Selling overheads – commission	38.4	
– fixed	108.0	
Administration overheads – fixed	20.0	(166.4)
Net profit		11.4

The following information is also supplied to you by the company's financial controller, Edward Davies:

1. planned sales for the draft budget in the year to 30 November 2001 are expected to be 25% less than the total of 3.2 million VCR units sold in the year to 30 November 2000;

2. the company operates a Just-In-Time stock control system, which means it holds no stocks of any kind;

3. if more than 3 million VCR units are made and sold, the unit cost of material falls by £4 per unit;

4. sales commission is based on the number of units sold and not on turnover;

5. the draft budget assumes that the factory will only be working at two-thirds of maximum capacity;

6. sales above maximum capacity are not possible.

Edward Davies explains that the Board is not happy with the profit projected in the draft budget, and that the sales director, Anne Williams, has produced three proposals to try and improve matters.

1. Proposal A involves launching an aggressive marketing campaign:
   (i) this would involve a single additional fixed cost of £14 million for advertising;
   (ii) there would be a revised commission payment of £18 per unit sold;
   (iii) sales volume would be expected to increase by 10% above the level projected in the draft budget, with no change in the unit selling price.

2. Proposal B involves a 5% reduction in the unit selling price:
   (i) this is estimated to bring the sales volume back to the level in the year to 30 November 2000.

3. Proposal C involves a 10% reduction in the unit selling price.
   (i) fixed selling overheads would also be reduced by £45 million;
   (ii) if proposal C is accepted, the sales director believes sales volume will be 3.8 million units.

Task 1
(a) For each of the three proposals, calculate the:
   (i) change in profits compared with the draft budget;
   (ii) break-even point in units and turnover.
(b) Recommend which proposal, if any, should be accepted on financial grounds.
(c) Identify *three* non-financial issues to be considered before a final decision is made.

Edward Davies now tells you that the company is considering a new export order with a proposed selling price of £3 million. He provides you with the following information:

1. The order will require two types of material:
   (i) material A is in regular use by the company.
      The amount in stock originally cost £0.85 million, but its standard cost is £0.9 million. The amount in stock is sufficient for the order. The current market price of material A to be used in the order is £0.8 million;
   (ii) material B is no longer used by the company and cannot be used elsewhere if not used on the order.
      The amount in stock originally cost £0.2 million although its current purchase price is £0.3 million. The amount of material B in stock is only half the amount required on the order. If not used on the order,
      the amount in stock could be sold for £0.1 million;

2. direct labour of £1.0 million will be charged to the order. This includes £0.2 million for idle time, as a result of insufficient orders to keep the workforce fully employed. The company has a policy of no redundancies, and spreads the resulting cost of idle time across all orders;

3. variable factory overheads are expected to be £0.9 million;

4. fixed factory overheads are apportioned against the order at the rate of 50% of variable factory overheads;

5. no sales commission will be paid.

Task 2
Prepare a memo for Edward Davies:
(a) showing whether or not the order should be accepted at the proposed selling price;
(b) identifying the technique(s) you have used in reaching this conclusion.

AAT Technicians Stage

9.21 Calculation of break-even points based on different product mix assumptions
PE Limited produces and sells two products, P and E. Budgets prepared for the next six months give the following information:

	Product P per unit £	Product E per unit £
Selling price	10.00	12.00
Variable costs: production and selling	5.00	10.00
Common fixed costs: production and selling for six months	£561 600	

(a) You are required, in respect of the forth-coming six months,

   (i) to state what the break-even point in £s will be and the number of each product this figure represents if the two products are sold in the ratio 4P to 3E; *(3 marks)*

   (ii) to state the break-even point in £s and the number of products this figure represents if the sales mix changes to 4P to 4E (ignore fractions of products); *(3 marks)*

   (iii) to advise the sales manager which product mix should be better, that in (a) (i) above or that in (a) (ii) above, and why; *(2 marks)*

   (iv) to advise the sales manager which of the two products should be concentrated on and the reason(s) for your recommendation – assume that whatever can be made can be sold, that both products go through a machining process and that there are only 32 000 machine hours available, with product P requiring 0.40 hour per unit and product E requiring 0.10 hour per unit. *(2 marks)*

(b) You are required to compare and contrast the usefulness of a conventional break-even chart with a contribution break-even chart. Your explanation should include illustrative diagrams drawn within your answer book and not on graph paper. *(5 marks)*

(Total 15 marks)
CIMA Stage 2 Cost Accounting

9.22* Calculation of break-even points based on different sales mix assumptions and a product abandonment decision

M Ltd manufactures three products which have the following revenue and costs (£ per unit).

	Product 1	2	3
Selling price	2.92	1.35	2.83
Variable costs	1.61	0.72	0.96
Fixed costs:			
Product specific	0.49	0.35	0.62
General	0.46	0.46	0.46

Unit fixed costs are based upon the following annual sales and production volumes (thousand units):

Product 1	2	3
98.2	42.1	111.8

Required:
(a) Calculate:

   (i) the break-even point sales (to the nearest £ hundred) of M Ltd based on the current product mix *(9 marks)*

   (ii) the number of units of Product 2 (to the nearest hundred) at the break-even point determined in (i) above. *(3 marks)*

(b) Comment upon the viability of Product 2. *(8 marks)*

(Total 20 marks)
ACCA Cost and Management Accounting 1

9.23* Calculation of sales by individual products to achieve a target contribution

A company manufactures and sells three products which currently have the following annual trading performance:

(£000)	Product		
	A	B	C
Sales	1794	3740	2950
Production cost of sales	1242	2860	1888
Gross profit	552	880	1062
Non-production overheads	460	770	767
Net profit	92	110	295
Sales units (000)	1150	2200	2360

For each product, units produced and sold were the same in the period.

Fixed production overheads are absorbed at a rate of £0.30 per unit for each product. Non-production overheads include certain costs which vary with activity at a rate of 10% of sales value. The remaining non-production overheads are fixed costs.

Required:
(a) Prepare a statement, in marginal costing format, showing the sales, costs, and profit contribution of each product expressed both in £ per unit (to three decimal places) and also as a % of sales (to one decimal place);

(8 marks)
(b) Calculate, based upon the current mix of sales, the sales required of each product (to the nearest £000) in order to generate a total contribution of £3.75m per annum.

(6 marks)
(Total 14 marks)
ACCA Foundation Stage Paper 3

9.24 Decision-making and non-graphical CVP analysis

York plc was formed three years ago by a group of research scientists to market a new medicine that they had invented. The technology involved in the medicine's manufacture is both complex and expensive. Because of this, the company is faced with a high level of fixed costs.

This is of particular concern to Dr Harper, the company's chief executive. She recently arranged a conference of all management staff to discuss company profitability. Dr Harper showed the managers how average unit cost fell as production volume increased and explained that this was due to the company's heavy fixed cost base. 'It is clear,' she said, 'that as we produce closer to the plant's maximum capacity of 70 000 packs the average cost per pack falls. Producing and selling as close to that limit as possible must be good for company profitability.' The data she used are reproduced below:

Production volume (packs)	40 000	50 000	60 000	70 000
Average cost per unit[a]	£430	£388	£360	£340

Current sales and production volume:	65 000 packs
Selling price per pack:	£420

[a]Defined as the total of fixed and variable costs, divided by the production volume.

You are a member of York plc's management accounting team and shortly after the conference you are called to a meeting with Ben Cooper, the company's marketing director. He is interested in knowing how profitability changes with production.

Task 1
Ben Cooper asks you to calculate:
(a) the amount of York plc's fixed costs;
(b) the profit of the company at its current sales volume of 65 000 packs;
(c) the break-even point in units;
(d) the margin of safety expressed as a percentage.

Ben Cooper now tells you of a discussion he has recently had with Dr Harper. Dr Harper had once more emphasized the need to produce as close as possible to the maximum capacity of 70 000 packs. Ben Cooper has the possibility of obtaining an export order for an extra 5000 packs but, because the competition is strong, the selling price would only be £330. Dr Harper has suggested that this order should be rejected as it is below cost and so will reduce company profitability. However, she would be prepared, on this occasion, to sell the packs on a cost basis for £340 each, provided the order was increased to 15 000 packs.

Task 2
Write a memo to Ben Cooper. Your memo should:
(a) calculate the change in profits from accepting the order for 5000 packs at £330;
(b) calculate the change in profits from accepting an order for 15 000 packs at £340;
(c) briefly explain and justify which proposal, if either, should be accepted;
(d) identify *two* non-financial factors which should be taken into account before making a final decision.

AAT Technicians Stage

9.25* Calculation of break-even points and limiting factor decision-making

You are employed as an accounting technician by Smith, Williams and Jones, a small firm of accountants and registered auditors. One of your clients is Winter plc, a large department store. Judith Howarth, the purchasing director for Winter plc, has gained considerable knowledge about bedding and soft furnishings and is considering acquiring her own business.

She has recently written to you requesting a meeting to discuss the possible purchase of Brita Beds Ltd. Brita Beds has one outlet in Mytown, a small town 100 miles from where Judith works. Enclosed with her letter was Brita Beds' latest profit and loss account. This is reproduced below.

Brita Beds Ltd
Profit and loss account – year to 31 May

Sales	(units)	(£)
Model A	1620	336 960
Model B	2160	758 160
Model C	1620	1 010 880
Turnover		2 106 000
Expenses	(£)	
Cost of beds	1 620 000	
Commission	210 600	
Transport	216 000	
Rates and insurance	8 450	
Light heat and power	10 000	
Assistants' salaries	40 000	
Manager's salary	40 000	2 145 050
Loss for year		39 050

Also included in the letter was the following information:
1. Brita Beds sells three types of bed, models A to C inclusive.
2. Selling prices are determined by adding 30% to the cost of beds.
3. Sales assistants receive a commission of 10% of the selling price for each bed sold.
4. The beds are delivered in consignments of 10 beds at a cost of £400 per delivery. This expense is shown as 'Transport' in the profit and loss account.
5. All other expenses are annual amounts.
6. The mix of models sold is likely to remain constant irrespective of overall sales volume.

Task 1
In preparation for your meeting with Judith Howarth, you are asked to calculate:
(a) the minimum number of beds to be sold if Brita Beds is to avoid making a loss;
(b) the minimum turnover required if Brita Beds is to avoid making a loss.

At the meeting, Judith Howarth provides you with further information:
1. The purchase price of the business is £300 000.

2. Judith has savings of £300 000 currently earning 5% interest per annum, which she can use to aquire Beta Beds.
3. Her current salary is £36 550.

To reduce costs, Judith suggests that she should take over the role of manager as the current one is about to retire. However, she does not want to take a reduction in income. Judith also tells you that she has been carrying out some market research. The results of this are as follows:
1. The number of households in Mytown is currently 44 880.
2. Brita Beds Ltd is the only outlet selling beds in Mytown.
3. According to a recent survey, 10% of households change their beds every 9 years, 60% every 10 years and 30% every 11 years.
4. The survey also suggested that there is an average of 2.1 beds per household.

Task 2
Write a letter to Judith Howarth. Your letter should:
(a) identify the profit required to compensate for the loss of salary and interest;
(b) show the number of beds to be sold to achieve that profit;
(c) calculate the likely maximum number of beds that Brita Beds would sell in a year;
(d) use your answers in (a) to (c) to justify whether or not Judith Howarth should purchase the company and become its manager;
(e) give *two* possible reasons why your estimate of the maximum annual sales volume may prove inaccurate.

On receiving your letter, Judith Howarth decides she would prefer to remain as the purchasing director for Winter plc rather than acquire Brita Beds Ltd. Shortly afterwards, you receive a telephone call from her. Judith explains that Winter plc is redeveloping its premises and that she is concerned about the appropriate sales policy for Winter's bed department while the redevelopment takes place. Although she has a statement of unit profitability, this had been prepared before the start of the redevelopment and had assumed that there would be in excess of 800 square metres of storage space available to the bed department. Storage space is critical as customers demand immediate delivery and are not prepared to wait until the new stock arrives.

The next day, Judith Howarth sends you a letter containing a copy of the original statement of profitability. This is reproduced below:

Model

Monthly demand (beds)	A 35 (£)	B 45 (£)	C 20 (£)
Unit selling price	240.00	448.00	672.00
Unit cost per bed	130.00	310.00	550.00
Carriage inwards	20.00	20.00	20.00
Staff costs	21.60	40.32	60.48
Department fixed overheads	20.00	20.00	20.00
General fixed overheads	25.20	25.20	25.20
Unit profit	23.20	32.48	(3.68)
Storage required per bed (square metres)	3	4	5

In her letter she asks for your help in preparing a marketing plan which will maximize the profitability of Winter's bed department while the redevelopment takes place. To help you, she has provided you with the following additional information:

1. Currently storage space available totals 300 square metres.
2. Staff costs represent the salaries of the sales staff in the bed department. Their total cost of £3780 per month is apportioned to units on the basis of planned turnover.
3. Departmental fixed overhead of £2000 per month is directly attributable to the department and is apportioned on the number of beds planned to be sold.
4. General fixed overheads of £2520 are also apportioned on the number of beds planned to be sold. The directors of Winter plc believe this to be a fair apportionment of the store's central fixed overheads.
5. The cost of carriage inwards and the cost of beds vary directly with the number of beds purchased.

Task 3

(a) Prepare a recommended monthly sales schedule in units which will maximize the profitability of Winter plc's bed department.
(b) Calculate the profit that will be reported per month if your recommendation is implemented.

AAT Technician's Stage

9.26 Marginal costing and absorption costing profit computations and calculation of break-even point for a given sales mix
A company has two products with the following unit costs for a period:

	Product A (£/unit)	Product B (£/unit)
Direct materials	1.20	2.03
Direct labour	1.40	1.50
Variable production overheads	0.70	0.80
Fixed production overheads	1.10	1.10
Variable other overheads	0.15	0.20
Fixed other overheads	0.50	0.50

Production and sales of the two products for the period were:

	Product A (000 units)	Product B (000 units)
Production	250	100
Sales	225	110

Production was at normal levels. Unit costs in opening stock were the same as those for the period listed above.

Required:
(a) State whether, and why, absorption or marginal costing would show a higher company profit for the period, and calculate the difference in profit depending upon which method is used. *(4 marks)*
(b) Calculate the break-even sales revenue for the period (to the nearest £000) based on the above mix of sales. The selling prices of products A and B were £5.70 and £6.90 per unit, respectively. *(7 marks)*
(Total 11 marks)
ACCA Foundation Stage Paper 3

9.27* Analysis of change in profit arising from changes in volume and production methods plus sales revenue required to achieve a desired profit
A company has the following summary performance over two accounting periods:

	Period 1 (£000)	Period 2 (£000)
Sales	902.0	1108.1
Variable costs	360.8	398.9
Contribution	541.2	709.2
Fixed costs	490.5	549.0
Net profit	50.7	160.2

In period 2 selling prices were 5% higher than in period 1 and cost inflation (affecting both variable and fixed costs) was also 5%.

At the start of period 2 production methods were reorganized. This was the only other factor affecting costs between the two periods (apart from inflation and volume).

Required:
(a) Calculate the percentage increase in sales volume in period 2 compared with period 1.
(*2 marks*)
(b) Calculate the increase in net profit in period 2 compared with period 1, due to:
(i) volume
(ii) reorganization of production methods. (Calculations should be done at year 1 prices.) (*6 marks*)
(c) Calculate the sales (to the nearest £000) that were required in period 2 in order to achieve the same net profit as period 1. (*3 marks*)
(d) State, and explain, the formula for the calculation of the break-even sales revenue for a period (figures are not required). (*3 marks*)
(*Total 14 marks*)
ACCA Foundation Paper 3

9.28* Decision-making and non-graphical CVP analysis

Fosterjohn Press Ltd is considering launching a new monthly magazine at a selling price of £1 per copy. Sales of the magazine are expected to be 500 000 copies per month, but it is possible that the actual sales could differ quite significantly from this estimate.

Two different methods of producing the magazine are being considered and neither would involve any additional capital expenditure. The estimated production costs for each of the two methods of manufacture, together with the additional marketing and distribution costs of selling the new magazine, are summarized below:

	Method A	Method B
Variable costs	£0.55 per copy	£0.50 per copy
Specific fixed costs	£80 000 per month	£120 000 per month
Semi-variable costs:		

The following estimates have been obtained:

350 000 copies	£55 000 per month	£47 500 per month
450 000 copies	£65 000 per month	£52 500 per month
650 000 copies	£85 000 per month	£62 500 per month

It may be assumed that the fixed cost content of the semi-variable costs will remain constant throughout the range of activity shown.

The company currently sells a magazine covering related topics to those that will be included in the new publication and consequently it is anticipated that sales of this existing magazine will be adversely affected. It is estimated that for every ten copies sold of the new publication, sales of the existing magazine will be reduced by one copy.

Sales and cost data of the existing magazine are shown below:

Sales	220 000 copies per month
Selling price	£0.85 per copy
Variable costs	£0.35 per copy
Specific fixed costs	£80 000 per month

Required:
(a) Calculate, for each production method, the net increase in company profits which will result from the introduction of the new magazine, at each of the following levels of activity:
500 000 copies per month
400 000 copies per month
600 000 copies per month
(*12 marks*)
(b) Calculate, for each production method, the amount by which sales volume of the new magazine could decline from the anticipated 500 000 copies per month, before the company makes no additional profit from the introduction of the new publication.
(*6 marks*)

(c) Briefly identify any conclusions which may be drawn from your calculations. (*4 marks*)
(*Total 22 marks*)
ACCA Foundation Costing

9.29* Decision-making and non-graphical CVP analysis

Mr Belle has recently developed a new improved video cassette and shown below is a summary of a report by a firm of management consultants on the sales potential and production costs of the new cassette.

Sales potential: The sales volume is difficult to predict and will vary with the price, but it is reasonable to assume that at a selling price of £10 per cassette, sales would be between 7500 and 10 000 units per month. Alternatively, if the selling price was reduced to £9 per cassette, sales would be between 12 000 and 18 000 units per month.

Production costs: If production is maintained at or below 10 000 units per month, then variable manufacturing costs would be approximately £8.25 per cassette and fixed costs £12 125 per month. However, if production is planned to exceed 10 000 units per month, then variable costs would be reduced to £7.75 per cassette, but the fixed costs would increase to £16 125 per month.

Mr Belle has been charged £2000 for the report by the management consultants and, in addition, he has incurred £3000 development costs on the new cassette.

If Mr Belle decides to produce and sell the new cassette it will be necessary for him to use factory premises which he owns, but are leased to a colleague for a rental of £400 per month. Also he will resign from his current post in an electronics firm where he is earning a salary of £1000 per month.

Required:
(a) Identify in the question an example of
   (i) an opportunity cost,
   (ii) a sunk cost. (*3 marks*)
(b) Making whatever calculations you consider appropriate, analyse the report from the consultants and advise Mr Belle of the potential profitability of the alternatives shown in the report.
   Any assumptions considered necessary or matters which may require further investigation or comment should be clearly stated.
(*19 marks*)
(*Total 22 marks*)
ACCA Level 1 Costing

Chapter 10

*Indicates that a suggested solution is to be found in the *Students' Manual*.

10.1*

In order to utilize some spare capacity, E Limited is preparing a quotation for a special order which requires 800 kgs of material R.

E Limited has 350 kgs of material R in stock (original cost £1.80 per kg). Material R is used in the company's main product—F. Each unit of F uses 4 kgs of material R and, based on an input cost of £1.80 per kg of R, each unit of F earns a contribution of £4.00.

The resale value of material R is £2.60 per kg. The present replacement price of material R is £3.00 per kg. Material R is readily available in the market.

The relevant cost of the 800 kgs of material R to be included in the quotation is
A £1980. B £2080. C £2400.
D £2780. E £2880.
CIMA Stage 2—Operations Cost Accounting

10.2*

Q plc makes two products–Quone and Qutwo– from the same raw material. The selling price and cost details of these products are as shown below:

	Quone (£)	Qutwo (£)
Selling price	20.00	18.00
Direct material (£2.00/kg)	6.00	5.00
Direct labour	4.00	3.00
Variable overhead unit	2.00	1.50
	12.00	9.50
Contribution per unit	8.00	8.50

The maximum demand for these products is:

Quone   500 units per week
Qutwo   unlimited number of units per week

If materials were limited to 2000 kg per week, the shadow price (opportunity cost) of these materials would be:
(a) nil;
(b) £2.00 per kg;
(c) £2.66 per kg;
(d) £3.40 per kg;
(e) none of these.
CIMA Stage 2

10.3*

M plc makes two products – M1 and M2 – budgeted details of which are as follows:

	M1 (£)	M2 (£)
Selling price	10.00	8.00
Costs per unit:		
Direct materials	2.50	3.00
Direct labour	1.50	1.00
Variable overhead	0.60	0.40
Fixed overhead	1.20	1.00
Profit per unit	4.20	2.60

Budgeted production and sales for the year ended 31 December are:

Product M1	10 000 units
Product M2	12 500 units

The fixed overhead shown above comprises both general and specific fixed overhead costs. The general fixed overhead cost has been attributed to units of M1 and M2 on the basis of direct labour cost.

The specific fixed cost totals £2500 per annum and relates to product M2 only.

(a) Both products are available from an external supplier. If M plc could purchase only one of them, the maximum price which should be paid per unit of M1 or M2 instead of internal manufacture would be:

	M1 (£)	M2 (£)
A	4.60	4.40
B	4.60	4.60
C	5.80	4.40
D	5.80	4.60
E	5.80	5.60

(b) If only product M1 were to be made, the number of units to be sold to achieve a profit of £50 000 per annum (to the nearest unit) would be

A   4074;
B   4537;
C   13 333;
D   13 796;
E   none of the above.

CIMA Stage 2

10.4* Make or buy decision

The management of Springer plc is considering next year's production and purchase budgets.

One of the components produced by the company, which is incorporated into another product before being sold, has a budgeted manufacturing cost as follows:

	(£)
Direct material	14
Direct labour	12
(4 hours at £3 per hour)	
Variable overhead	8
(4 hours at £2 per hour)	
Fixed overhead	
(4 hours at £5 per hour)	20
Total cost	54 per unit

Trigger plc has offered to supply the above component at a guaranteed price of £50 per unit.

Required:

(a) Considering cost criteria only, advise management whether the above component should be purchased from Trigger plc. Any calculations should be shown and assumptions made, or aspects which may require further investigation should be clearly stated.   (*6 marks*)

(b) Explain how your above advice would be affected by each of the two *separate* situations shown below.

   (i) As a result of recent government legislation if Springer plc continues to manufacture this component the company will incur additional inspection and testing expenses of £56 000 per annum, which are not included in the above budgeted manufacturing costs.   (*3 marks*)

   (ii) Additional labour cannot be recruited and if the above component is not manufactured by Springer plc the direct labour released will be employed in increasing the production of an existing product which is sold for £90 and which has a budgeted manufacturing cost as follows:

	(£)
Direct material	10
Direct labour	24
(8 hours at £3 per hour)	
Variable overhead	16
(8 hours at £2 per hour)	

Fixed overhead
(8 hours at £5 per hour) $\underline{\quad 40\quad}$
$\underline{\underline{90}}$ per unit

All calculations should be shown. (*4 marks*)
(c) The production director of Springer plc recently said:

'We must continue to manufacture the component as only one year ago we purchased some special grinding equipment to be used exclusively by this component. The equipment cost £100 000, it cannot be resold or used elsewhere and if we cease production of this component we will have to write off the written down book value which is £80 000.'

Draft a brief reply to the production director commenting on his statement. (*4 marks*)
(*Total 17 marks*)
ACCA Level 1 Costing

10.5 Determining minimum short-term acceptable selling price

Company A expects to have 2000 direct labour hours of manufacturing capacity (in normal time) available over the next two months after completion of current regular orders. It is considering two options in order to utilize the spare capacity. If the available hours are not utilized direct labour costs would not be incurred.

The first option involves the early manufacture of a firm future order which would as a result reduce the currently anticipated need for overtime working in a few months time. The premium for overtime working is 30% of the basic rate of £4.00 per hour, and is charged to production as a direct labour cost. Overheads are charged at £6.00 per direct labour hour. 40% of overhead costs are variable with hours worked.

Alternatively, Company A has just been asked to quote for a one-off job to be completed over the next two months and which would require the following resources:

1. *Raw materials*:
   (i) 960 kg of Material X which has a current weighted average cost in stock of £3.02 per kg and a replacement cost of £3.10 per kg. Material X is used continuously by Company A.
   (ii) 570 kg of Material Y which is in stock at £5.26 per kg. It has a current replacement cost of £5.85 per kg. If used, Material Y

would not be replaced. It has no other anticipated use, other than disposal for £2.30 per kg.
   (iii) Other materials costing £3360.
2. *Direct labour:* 2200 hours.

Required:
(a) Establish the minimum quote that could be tendered for the one-off job such that it would increase Company A's profit, compared with the alternative use of spare capacity. (Ignore the interest cost/benefit associated with the different timing of cash flows from the different options.) (*12 marks*)
(b) Explain, and provide illustrations of, the following terms:
   (i) sunk cost, (*3 marks*)
   (ii) opportunity cost, (*3 marks*)
   (iii) incremental cost. (*2 marks*)
   (*Total 20 marks*)
ACCA Level 1 Cost and Management Accounting 1

10.6 Acceptance of a contract

JB Limited is a small specialist manufacturer of electronic components and much of its output is used by the makers of aircraft for both civil and military purposes. One of the few aircraft manufacturers has offered a contract to JB Limited for the supply, over the next twelve months, of 400 identical components.

The data relating to the production of each component is as follows:
(i) Material requirements:
   3 kg material M1 – see note 1 below
   2 kg material P2 – see note 2 below
   1 Part No. 678 – see note 3 below
   Note 1. Material M1 is in continuous use by the company. 1000 kg are currently held in stock at a book value of £4.70 per kg but it is known that future purchases will cost £5.50 per kg.
   Note 2. 1200 kg of material P2 are held in stock. The original cost of this material was £4.30 per kg but as the material has not been required for the last two years it has been written down to £1.50 per kg scrap value. The only foreseeable alternative use is as a substitute for material P4 (in current use) but this would involve further processing costs of £1.60 per kg. The current cost of material P4 is £3.60 per kg.
   Note 3. It is estimated that the Part No. 678 could be bought for £50 each.

(ii) Labour requirements: Each component would require five hours of skilled labour and five hours of semi-skilled. An employee possessing the necessary skills is available and is currently paid £5 per hour. A replacement would, however, have to be obtained at a rate of £4 per hour for the work which would otherwise be done by the skilled employee. The current rate for semi-skilled work is £3 per hour and an additional employee could be appointed for this work.

(iii) Overhead: JB Limited absorbs overhead by a machine hour rate, currently £20 per hour of which £7 is for variable overhead and £13 for fixed overhead. If this contract is undertaken it is estimated that fixed costs will increase for the duration of the contract by £3200. Spare machine capacity is available and each component would require four machine hours.

A price of £145 per component has been suggested by the large company which makes aircraft.

You are required to:

(a) State whether or not the contract should be accepted and support your conclusion with appropriate figures for presentation to management;   (*16 marks*)

(b) comment briefly on *three* factors which management ought to consider and which may influence their decision.   (*9 marks*)

(*Total 25 marks*)

CIMA Cost Accounting Stage 2

10.7* Decision on which of two mutually exclusive contracts to accept

A company in the civil engineering industry with headquarters located 22 miles from London undertakes contracts anywhere in the United Kingdom.

The company has had its tender for a job in north-east England accepted at £288 000 and work is due to begin in March. However, the company has also been asked to undertake a contract on the south coast of England. The price offered for this contract is £352 000. Both of the contracts cannot be taken simultaneously because of constraints on staff site management personnel and on plant available. An escape clause enables the company to withdraw from the contract in the north-east, provided notice is given before the end of November and an agreed penalty of £28 000 is paid.

The following estimates have been submitted by the company's quantity surveyor:

Cost estimates

	North-east (£)	South coast (£)
Materials:		
In stock at original cost, Material X	21 600	
In stock at original cost, Material Y		24 800
Firm orders placed at original cost, Material X	30 400	
Not yet ordered – current cost, Material X	60 000	
Not yet ordered – current cost, Material Z		71 200
Labour – hired locally	86 000	110 000
Site management	34 000	34 000
Staff accommodation and travel for site management	6 800	5 600
Plant on site – depreciation	9 600	12 800
Interest on capital, 8%	5 120	6 400
Total local contract costs	253 520	264 800
Headquarters costs allocated at rate of 5% on total contract costs	12 676	13 240
	266 196	278 040
Contract price	288 000	352 000
Estimated profit	21 804	73 960

Notes:

1. X, Y and Z are three building materials. Material X is not in common use and would not realize much money if re-sold; however, it could be used on other contracts but only as a substitute for another material currently quoted at 10% less than the original cost of X. The price of Y, a material in common use, has doubled since it was purchased; its net realizable value if re-sold would be its new price less 15% to cover disposal costs. Alternatively it could be kept for use on other contracts in the following financial year.

2. With the construction industry not yet recovered from the recent recession, the company is confident that manual labour, both skilled and

unskilled, could be hired locally on a subcontracting basis to meet the needs of each of the
contracts.

3. The plant which would be needed for the south
coast contract has been owned for some years
and £12 800 is the year's depreciation on a
straight-line basis. If the north-east contract is
undertaken, less plant will be required but the
surplus plant will be hired out for the period of
the contract at a rental of £6000.

4. It is the company's policy to charge all contracts
with notional interest at 8% on estimated working capital involved in contracts. Progress
payments would be receivable from the contractee.

5. Salaries and general costs of operating the small
headquarters amount to about £108 000 each
year. There are usually ten contracts being
supervised at the same time.

6. Each of the two contracts is expected to last
from March to February which, coincidentally,
is the company's financial year.

7. Site management is treated as a fixed cost.

You are required, as the management accountant to
the company,

(a) to present comparative statements to show
the net benefit to the company of undertaking the more advantageous of the two
contracts; *(12 marks)*

(b) to explain the reasoning behind the inclusion
in (or omission from) your comparative financial statements, of each item given in the cost
estimates and the notes relating thereto.
(13 marks)
(Total 25 marks)
CIMA Stage 2 Cost Accounting

10.8 Preparation of a cost estimate involving the identification of relevant costs

You are the management accountant of a publishing and printing company which has been asked to
quote for the production of a programme for the
local village fair. The work would be carried out
in addition to the normal work of the company.
Because of existing commitments, some weekend
working would be required to complete the printing
of the programme. A trainee accountant has
produced the following cost estimate based upon
the resources as specified by the production
manager:

	(£)
Direct materials:	
paper (book value)	5 000
inks (purchase price)	2 400
Direct labour:	
skilled 250 hours at £4.00	1 000
unskilled 100 hours at £3.50	350
Variable overhead	
350 hours at £4.00	1 400
Printing press depreciation	
200 hours at £2.50	500
Fixed production costs	
350 hours at £6.00	2 100
Estimating department costs	400
	13 150

You are aware that considerable publicity could be
obtained for the company if you are able to win
this order and the price quoted must be very
competitive.

The following are relevant to the cost estimate
above:

1. The paper to be used is currently in stock at a
value of £5000. It is of an unusual colour which
has not been used for some time. The replacement price of the paper is £8000, while the scrap
value of that in stock is £2500. The production
manager does not foresee any alternative use for
the paper if it is not used for the village fair
programmes.

2. The inks required are not held in stock. They
would have to be purchased in bulk at a cost of
£3000. 80% of the ink purchased would be used
in printing the programme. No other use is
foreseen for the remainder.

3. Skilled direct labour is in short supply, and to
accommodate the printing of the programmes,
50% of the time required would be worked at
weekends, for which a premium of 25% above
the normal hourly rate is paid. The normal
hourly rate is £4.00 per hour.

4. Unskilled labour is presently under-utilized, and
at present 200 hours per week are recorded as
idle time. If the printing work is carried out at a
weekend, 25 unskilled hours would have to
occur at this time, but the employees concerned
would be given two hours' time off (for which
they would be paid) in lieu of each hour worked.

5. Variable overhead represents the cost of operating the printing press and binding machines.

6. When not being used by the company, the
printing press is hired to outside companies

for £6.00 per hour. This earns a contribution of £3.00 per hour. There is unlimited demand for this facility

7. Fixed production costs are those incurred by and absorbed into production, using an hourly rate based on budgeted activity.

8. The cost of the estimating department represents time spent in discussion with the village fair committee concerning the printing of its programme.

Required:

(a) Prepare a revised cost estimate using the opportunity cost approach, showing clearly the minimum price that the company should accept for the order. Give reasons for each resource valuation in your cost estimate.

(*16 marks*)

(b) Explain why contribution theory is used as a basis for providing information relevant to decision-making. (*4 marks*)

(c) Explain the relevance of opportunity costs in decision-making.

(*5 marks*)
(*Total 25 marks*)
CIMA Stage 2 Operational Costs Accounting

10.9* Calculation of minimum selling price

You have received a request from EXE plc to provide a quotation for the manufacture of a specialized piece of equipment. This would be a one-off order, in excess of normal budgeted production. The following cost estimate has already been prepared:

		Note	(£)
Direct materials:			
Steel	10 m² at £5.00 per sq. metre	1	50
Brass fittings		2	20
Direct labour			
Skilled	25 hours at £8.00 per hour	3	200
Semi-skilled	10 hours at £5.00 per hour	4	50
Overhead	35 hours at £10.00 per hour	5	350
Estimating time		6	100
			770
Administrative overhead			

at 20% of production cost	7	154
		924
Profit at 25% of total cost	8	231
Selling price		1155

Notes:

1. The steel is regularly used, and has a current stock value of £5.00 per sq. metre. There are currently 100 sq. metres in stock. The steel is readily available at a price of £5.50 per sq. metre.

2. The brass fittings would have to be bought specifically for this job: a supplier has quoted the price of £20 for the fittings required.

3. The skilled labour is currently employed by your company and paid at a rate of £8.00 per hour. If this job were undertaken it would be necessary either to work 25 hours overtime which would be paid at time plus one half *or* to reduce production of another product which earns a contribution of £13.00 per hour.

4. The semi-skilled labour currently has sufficient paid idle time to be able to complete this work.

5. The overhead absorption rate includes power costs which are directly related to machine usage. If this job were undertaken, it is estimated that the machine time required would be ten hours. The machines incur power costs of £0.75 per hour. There are no other overhead costs which can be specifically identified with this job.

6. The cost of the estimating time is that attributed to the four hours taken by the engineers to analyse the drawings and determine the cost estimate given above.

7. It is company policy to add 20% on to the production cost as an allowance against administration costs associated with the jobs accepted.

8. This is the standard profit added by your company as part of its pricing policy.

Required:

(a) Prepare, on a relevant cost basis, the lowest cost estimate that could be used as the basis for a quotation. Explain briefly your reasons for using *each* of the values in your estimate.

(*12 marks*)

(b) There may be a possibility of repeat orders from EXE plc which would occupy part of normal production capacity. What factors need to be considered before quoting for this order? (*7 marks*)

(c) When an organization identifies that it has a single production resource which is in short supply, but is used by more than one product, the optimum production plan is determined by ranking the products according to their contribution per unit of the scarce resource. Using a numerical example of your own, reconcile this approach with the opportunity cost approach used in (a) above. *(6 marks)*
(Total 25 marks)
CIMA Stage Operational Cost Accounting

10.10* Impact of a product abandonment decision and CVP analysis

(a) Budgeted information for A Ltd for the following period, analysed by product, is shown below:

	Product I	Product II	Product III
Sales units (000s)	225	376	190
Selling price (£ per unit)	11.00	10.50	8.00
Variable costs (£ per unit)	5.80	6.00	5.20
Attributable fixed costs (£000s)	275	337	296

General fixed costs, which are apportioned to products as a percentage of sales, are budgeted at £1 668 000.

Required:
(i) Calculate the budgeted profit of A Ltd, and of each of its products. *(5 marks)*
(ii) Recalculate the budgeted profit of A Ltd on the assumption that Product III is discontinued, with no effect on sales of the other two products. State and justify other assumptions made. *(5 marks)*
(iii) Additional advertising, to that included in the budget for Product I, is being considered.
   Calculate the minimum extra sales units required of Product I to cover additional advertising expenditure of £80 000. Assume that all other existing fixed costs would remain unchanged. *(3 marks)*

(iv) Calculate the increase in sales volume of Product II that is necessary in order to compensate for the effect on profit of a 10% reduction in the selling price of the product. State clearly any assumptions made. *(5 marks)*
(b) Discuss the factors which influence cost behaviour in response to changes in activity. *(7 marks)*
(Total 25 marks)
ACCA Cost and Management Accounting 1

10.11* Deleting a segment
A company manufactures and sells a wide range of products. The products are manufactured in various locations and sold in a number of quite separate markets. The company's operations are organized into five divisions which may supply each other as well as selling on the open market.

The following financial information is available concerning the company for the year just ended:

	(£000)
Sales	8600
Production cost of sales	5332
Gross profit	3268
Other expenses	2532
Net profit	736

An offer to purchase Division 5, which has been performing poorly, has been received by the company.

The gross profit percentage of sales, earned by Division 5 in the year, was half that earned by the company as a whole. Division 5 sales were 10% of total company sales. Of the production expenses incurred by Division 5, fixed costs were £316 000. Other expenses (i.e. other than production expenses) incurred by the division totalled £156 000, all of which can be regarded as fixed. These include £38 000 apportionment of general company expenses which would not be affected by the decision concerning the possible sale of Division 5.

In the year ahead, if Division 5 is not sold, fixed costs of the division would be expected to increase by 5% and variable costs to remain at the same percentage of sales. Sales would be expected to increase by 10%.

If the division is sold, it is expected that some sales of other divisions would be lost. These would provide a contribution to profits of £20 000 in the year ahead. Also, if the division is sold, the capital sum received could be invested so as to yield a return of £75 000 in the year ahead.

Required:
(a) Calculate whether it would be in the best interests of the company, based upon the expected situation in the year ahead, to sell Division 5. *(13 marks)*
(b) Discuss other factors that you feel should influence the decision. *(7 marks)*
(c) Calculate the percentage increase in Division 5 sales required in the year ahead (compared with the current year) for the financial viability of the two alternatives to be the same. (You are to assume that all other factors in the above situation will remain as forecast for the year ahead.) *(5 marks)*
(Total 25 marks)
ACCA Level 1 Costing

10.12 Decision on whether to launch a new product

A company is currently manufacturing at only 60% of full practical capacity, in each of its two production departments, due to a reduction in market share. The company is seeking to launch a new product which it is hoped will recover some lost sales.

The estimated direct costs of the new product, Product X, are to be established from the following information:

Direct materials:
Every 100 units of the product will require 30 kilos net of Material A. Losses of 10% of materials input are to be expected. Material A costs £5.40 per kilo before discount. A quantity discount of 5% is given on all purchases if the monthly purchase quantity exceeds 25 000 kilos. Other materials are expected to cost £1.34 per unit of Product X.

Direct labour (per hundred units):
Department 1: 40 hours at £4.00 per hour.
Department 2: 15 hours at £4.50 per hour.

Separate overhead absorption rates are established for each production department. Department 1 overheads are absorbed at 130% of direct wages, which is based upon the expected overhead costs and usage of capacity if Product X is launched. The

rate in Department 2 is to be established as a rate per direct labour hour also based on expected usage of capacity. The following annual figures for Department 2 are based on full practical capacity:

Overhead, £5 424 000:
Direct labour hours, 2 200 000.

Variable overheads in Department 1 are assessed at 40% of direct wages and in Department 2 are £1 980 000 (at full practical capacity).

Non-production overheads are estimated as follows (per unit of Product X):

Variable,   £0.70
Fixed,   £1.95

The selling price for Product X is expected to be £9.95 per unit, with annual sales of 2 400 000 units.

Required:
(a) Determine the estimated cost per unit of Product X. *(13 marks)*
(b) Comment on the viability of Product X. *(7 marks)*
(c) Market research indicates that an alternative selling price for Product X could be £9.45 per unit, at which price annual sales would be expected to be 2 900 000 units. Determine, and comment briefly upon, the optimum selling price. *(5 marks)*
(Total 25 marks)
ACCA Cost and Management Accounting 1

10.13* Contribution analysis and an outsourcing decision

AZ Transport Group plc comprises three divisions – AZ Buses; AZ Taxis; and Maintenance.

AZ Buses operates a fleet of eight vehicles on four different routes in Ceetown. Each vehicle has a capacity of 30 passengers. There are two vehicles assigned to each route, and each vehicle completes five return journeys per day, for six days each week, for 52 weeks per year.

AZ Buses is considering its plans for year ending 31 December. Data in respect of each route is as follows:

	Route W	Route X	Route Y	Route Z
Return travel distance (km)	42	36	44	38
Average number of passengers:				
Adults	15	10	25	20
Children	10	8	5	10
Return journey fares:				
Adults	£3.00	£6.00	£4.50	£2.20
Children	£1.50	£3.00	£2.25	£1.10

The following cost estimates have been made:

Fuel and repairs per kilometre	£0.1875
Drivers' wages per vehicle per work-day	£120
Vehicle fixed cost per annum	£2000
General fixed cost per annum	£300 000

Requirements:
(a) Prepare a statement showing the planned contribution of each route and the total contribution and profit of the AZ Buses division for the year ending 31 December. *(6 marks)*
(b) (i) Calculate the effect on the contribution of route W of increasing the adult fare to £3.75 per return journey if this reduces the number of adult passengers using this route by 20%, and assuming that the ratio of adult to child passengers remains the same. (Assume no change in the child fare.)
  (ii) Recommend whether or not AZ Buses should amend the adult fare on route W. *(4 marks)*
(c) The Maintenance division comprises two fitters who are each paid an annual salary of £15 808, and a transport supervisor who is paid an annual salary of £24 000.
  The work of the Maintenance division is to repair and service the buses of the AZ Buses division and the taxis of the AZ Taxis division. In total there are eight buses and six taxis which need to be maintained. Each vehicle requires routine servicing on a regular basis on completion of 4000 kilometres: every two months each vehicle is fully tested for safety. The Maintenance division is also responsible for carrying out any breakdown work, though the amount of regular servicing is only 10% of the Maintenance division's work.

The annual distance travelled by the taxi fleet is 128 000 kilometres.

The projected material costs associated with each service and safety check are £100 and £75 respectively, and the directors of AZ Transport Group plc are concerned over the efficiency and cost of its own Maintenance division. The company invited its local garage to tender for the maintenance contract for its fleet and the quotation received was for £90 000 per annum including parts and labour.

If the maintenance contract is awarded to the local garage then the Maintenance division will be closed down, and the two fitters made redundant with a redundancy payment being made of 6 months' salary to each fitter. The transport supervisor will be retained at the same salary and will be redeployed elsewhere in the Group instead of recruiting a new employee at an annual salary cost of £20 000.

Requirements:
(i) Calculate the cost of the existing maintenance function. *(6 marks)*
(ii) Advise the directors of AZ Transport Group plc whether to award the maintenance contract to the local garage on financial grounds. *(4 marks)*
(iii) State clearly the other factors which need to be considered before making such a decision, commenting on any other solutions which you consider may be appropriate. *(5 marks)*
(Total 25 marks)
CIMA Stage 2 Operational Cost Accounting

10.14* Limiting factor analysis
Triproduct Limited makes and sells three types of electronic security systems for which the following information is available.
Standard cost and selling prices per unit

Product	Day scan (£)	Night scan (£)	Omni scan (£)
Materials	70	110	155
Manufacturing labour	40	55	70
Installation labour	24	32	44
Variable overheads	16	20	28
Selling price	250	320	460

Fixed costs for the period are £450 000 and the installation labour, which is highly skilled, is available for 25 000 hours only in a period and is paid £8 per hour.

Both manufacturing and installation labour are variable costs.

The maximum demand for the products is:

Day scan	Night scan	Omni scan
2000 units	3000 units	1800 units

Requirements:

(a) Calculate the shortfall (if any) in hours of installation labour. (*2 marks*)

(b) Determine the best production plan, assuming that Triproduct Limited wishes to maximize profit. (*5 marks*)

(c) Calculate the maximum profit that could be achieved from the plan in part (b) above. (*3 marks*)

(d) Having carried out an investigation of the availability of installation labour, the firm thinks that by offering £12 per hour, additional installation labour would become available and thus overcome the labour shortage.

Requirement:
Based on the results obtained above, advise the firm whether or not to implement this proposal.

(*5 marks*)
(*Total 15 marks*)
CIMA Stage 1 Cost Accounting

10.15 Limiting key factors

PDR plc manufactures four products using the same machinery. The following details relate to its products:

	Product A £ per unit	Product B £ per unit	Product C £ per unit	Product D £ per unit
Selling price	28	30	45	42
Direct material	5	6	8	6
Direct labour	4	4	8	8
Variable overhead	3	3	6	6
Fixed overhead*	8	8	16	16
Profit	8	9	7	6
Labour hours	1	1	2	2
Machine hours	4	3	4	5
	Units	Units	Units	Units
Maximum demand per week	200	180	250	100

*Absorbed based on budgeted labour hours of 1000 per week.

There is a maximum of 2000 machine hours available per week.

Requirement:

(a) Determine the production plan which will maximize the weekly profit of PDR plc and prepare a profit statement showing the profit your plan will yield. (*10 marks*)

(b) The marketing director of PDR plc is concerned at the company's inability to meet the quantity demanded by its customers.

Two alternative strategies are being considered to overcome this:

(i) to increase the number of hours worked using the existing machinery by working overtime. Such overtime would be paid at a premium of 50% above normal labour rates, and variable overhead costs would be expected to increase in proportion to labour costs.

(ii) to buy product B from an overseas supplier at a cost of £19 per unit including carriage. This would need to be re-packaged at a cost of £1 per unit before it could be sold.

Requirement:
Evaluate each of the two alternative strategies and, as management accountant, prepare a report to the marketing director, stating your reasons (quantitative and qualitative) as to which, if either, should be adopted. (*15 marks*)

(*Total 25 marks*)
CIMA Stage 2 Operational Cost Accounting

10.16* Key/limiting factor decision-making

BVX Limited manufactures three garden furniture products – chairs, benches and tables. The budgeted unit cost and resource requirements of each of these items is detailed below:

	Chair (£)	Bench (£)	Table (£)
Timber cost	5.00	15.00	10.00
Direct labour cost	4.00	10.00	8.00
Variable overhead cost	3.00	7.50	6.00
Fixed overhead cost	4.50	11.25	9.00
	16.50	43.75	33.00
Budgeted volumes per annum	4000	2000	1500

These volumes are believed to equal the market demand for these products.

The fixed overhead costs are attributed to the three products on the basis of direct labour hours.

The labour rate is £4.00 per hour.

The cost of the timber is £2.00 per square metre.

The products are made from a specialist timber. A memo from the purchasing manager advises you that because of a problem with the supplier it is to be assumed that this specialist timber is limited in supply to 20 000 square metres per annum.

The sales director has already accepted an order for 500 chairs, 100 benches and 150 tables, which if not supplied would incur a financial penalty of £2000. These quantities are included in the market demand estimates above.

The selling prices of the three products are:

Chair	£20.00
Bench	£50.00
Table	£40.00

Required:
(a) Determine the optimum production plan *and* state the net profit that this should yield per annum. (*10 marks*)
(b) Calculate *and* explain the maximum prices which should be paid per sq. metre in order to obtain extra supplies of the timber. (*5 marks*)
(c) The management team has accused the accountant of using too much jargon.

Prepare a statement which explains the following terms in a way that a multi/disciplinary team of managers would understand. The accountant will use this statement as a briefing paper at the next management meeting. The terms to be explained are:
(i) variable costs;
(ii) relevant costs;
(iii) avoidable costs;
(iv) incremental costs;
(v) opportunity costs. (*10 marks*)
(*Total 25 marks*)
CIMA Operations Cost Accounting Stage 2

Both parts use the same metal, a titanium alloy, of which 13 000 kilos only are available, at £12.50 per kilo. The parts are made by passing each one through two fully-automatic computer-controlled machine lines – S and T – whose capacities are limited. Target prices have been set and the following data are available for the period:

Part details

	Part A	Part B
Maximum call-off (units)	7000	9000
Target price	£145	£115
	per unit	per unit
Alloy usage	1.6 kilos	1.6 kilos
Machine times		
Line S	0.6 hours	0.25 hours
Line T	0.5 hours	0.55 hours

Machine details

	Line S	Line T
Hours available	4000	4500
Variable overhead per machine hour	£80	£100

You are required:
(a) to calculate which part should be made during the next period to maximize contribution; (*9 marks*)
(b) to calculate the contribution which EX Limited will earn and whether the company will be able to meet the maximum call-off. (*3 marks*)
As an alternative to the target prices shown above, the aircraft manufacturer has offered the following alternative arrangement:

Target prices less 10% plus £60 per hour for each unused machine hour.
(c) You are required to decide whether your recommendation in (a) above will be altered and, if so, to calculate the new contribution. (*10 marks*)
(*Total 22 marks*)
CIMA Stage 3 Management Accounting Techniques

10.17* Allocation of scarce capacity
EX Limited is an established supplier of precision parts to a major aircraft manufacturer. It has been offered the choice of making either Part A or Part B for the next period, but not both.

10.18 Allocation of scarce capacity and make or buy decision where scarce capacity exists
PQR Limited is an engineering company engaged in the manufacture of components and finished products.

The company is highly mechanized and each of the components and finished products requires the use of one or more types of machine in its machining department. The following costs and revenues (where appropriate) relate to a single component or unit of the finished product:

	Components		Finished products	
	A	**B**	**C**	**D**
	(£)	**(£)**	**(£)**	**(£)**
Selling price			127	161
Direct materials	8	29	33	38
Direct wages	10	30	20	25
Variable overhead:				
Drilling	6	3	9	12
Grinding	8	16	4	12
Fixed overhead:				
Drilling	12	6	18	24
Grinding	10	20	5	15
Total cost	54	104	89	126

Notes:

1. The labour hour rate is £5 per hour.
2. Overhead absorption rates per machine hour are as follows:

	Variable (£)	Fixed (£)
Drilling (per hour)	3	6
Grinding (per hour)	4	5

3. Components A and B are NOT used in finished products C and D. They are used in the company's other products, none of which use the drilling or grinding machines. The company does not manufacture any other components.
4. The number of machine drilling hours available is limited to 1650 per week. There are 2500 machine grinding hours available per week. These numbers of hours have been used to calculate the absorption rates stated above.
5. The maximum demand in units per week for each of the finished products has been estimated by the marketing director as:

    Product C   250 units
    Product D   500 units

6. The internal demand for components A and B each week is as follows:

    Component A   50 units
    Component B   100 units

7. There is no external market for components A and B.
8. PQR Limited has a contract to supply 50 units of each of its finished products to a major customer each week. These quantities are included in the maximum units of demand given in note 5 above.

Requirement:
(a) Calculate the number of units of *each* finished product that PQR Limited should produce in order to maximize its profits, and the profit per week that this should yield. *(12 marks)*
(b) (i) The production director has now discovered that he can obtain unlimited quantities of components identical to A and B for £50 and £96 per unit respectively.

    State whether this information changes the production plan of the company if it wishes to continue to maximize its profits per week. If appropriate, state the revised production plan and the net benefit per week caused by the change to the production plan. *(7 marks)*

(ii) The solution of problems involving more than one limiting factor requires the use of linear programming.

    Explain why this technique must be used in such circumstances, and the steps used to solve such a problem when using the graphical linear programming technique. *(6 marks)*

(Total 25 marks)
CIMA Stage 2 Operational Cost Accounting

10.19 Limiting/key factors and a decision whether it is profitable to expand output by overtime

B Ltd manufactures a range of products which are sold to a limited number of wholesale outlets. Four of these products are manufactured in a particular department on common equipment. No other facilities are available for the manufacture of these products.

Owing to greater than expected increases in demand, normal single shift working is rapidly becoming insufficient to meet sales requirements.

Overtime and, in the longer term, expansion of facilities are being considered.

Selling prices and product costs, based on single shift working utilizing practical capacity to the full, are as follows:

	Product (£/unit)			
	W	**X**	**Y**	**Z**
Selling price	3.650	3.900	2.250	2.950
Product costs:				
Direct materials	0.805	0.996	0.450	0.647
Direct labour	0.604	0.651	0.405	0.509
Variable manu-facturing o'hd	0.240	0.247	0.201	0.217
Fixed manufacturing o'hd	0.855	0.950	0.475	0.760
Variable selling and admin o'hd	0.216	0.216	0.216	0.216
Fixed selling and admin o'hd	0.365	0.390	0.225	0.295

Fixed manufacturing overheads are absorbed on the basis of machine hours which, at practical capacity, are 2250 per period. Total fixed manufacturing overhead per period is £427 500. Fixed selling and administration overhead, which totals £190 000 per period, is shared amongst products at a rate of 10% of sales.

The sales forecast for the following period (in thousands of units) is:

Product W	190
Product X	125
Product Y	144
Product Z	142

Overtime could be worked to make up any production shortfall in normal time. Direct labour would be paid at a premium of 50% above basic rate. Other variable costs would be expected to remain unchanged per unit of output. Fixed costs would increase by £24 570 per period.

Required:
(a) If overtime is not worked in the following period, recommend the quantity of each product that should be manufactured in order to maximize profit. *(12 marks)*
(b) Calculate the expected profit in the following period if overtime is worked as necessary to meet sales requirements. *(7 marks)*

(c) Consider the factors which should influence the decision whether or not to work overtime in such a situation. *(6 marks)*
(Total 25 marks)
ACCA Cost and Management Accounting 1

10.20* Price/output and key factor decisions

You work as a trainee for a small management consultancy which has been asked to advise a company, Rane Limited, which manufactures and sells a single product. Rane is currently operating at full capacity producing and selling 25 000 units of its product each year. The cost and selling price structure for this level of activity is as follows:

	At 25 000 units output	
	(£ per unit)	(£ per unit)
Production costs		
Direct material	14	
Direct labour	13	
Variable production overhead	4	
Fixed production overhead	8	
Total production cost		39
Selling and distribution overhead:		
Sales commission – 10% of sales value	6	
Fixed	3	
		9
Administration overhead:		
Fixed		2
Total cost		50
Mark up – 20%		10
Selling price		60

A new managing director has recently joined the company and he has engaged your organization to advise on his company's selling price policy. The sales price of £60 has been derived as above from a cost-plus pricing policy. The price was viewed as satisfactory because the resulting demand enabled full capacity operation.

You have been asked to investigate the effect on costs and profit of an increase in the selling price. The marketing department has provided you with the following estimates of sales volumes which could be achieved at the three alternative sales prices under consideration.

Selling price per unit   £70   £80   £90
Annual sales volume (units) 20 000 16 000 11 000

You have spent some time estimating the effect that changes in output volume will have on cost behaviour patterns and you have now collected the following information.

Direct material: The loss of bulk discounts means that the direct material cost per unit will increase by 15% for all units produced in the year if activity reduces below 15 000 units per annum.

Direct labour: Savings in bonus payments will reduce labour costs by 10% for all units produced in the year if activity reduces below 20 000 units per annum.

Sales commission: This would continue to be paid at the rate of 10% of sales price.

Fixed production overhead: If annual output volume was below 20 000 units, then a machine rental cost of £10 000 per annum could be saved. This will be the only change in the total expenditure on fixed production overhead.

Fixed selling overhead: A reduction in the part-time sales force would result in a £5000 per annum saving if annual sales volume falls below 24 000 units. This will be the only change in the total expenditure on fixed selling and distribution overhead.

Variable production overhead: There would be no change in the unit cost for variable production overhead.

Administration overhead: The total expenditure on administration overhead would remain unaltered within this range of activity.

Stocks: Rane's product is highly perishable, therefore no stocks are held.

Task 1
(a) Calculate the annual profit which is earned with the current selling price of £60 per unit.
(b) Prepare a schedule to show the annual profit which would be earned with each of the three alternative selling prices.

Task 2
Prepare a brief memorandum to your boss, Chris Jones. The memorandum should cover the following points:

(a) Your recommendation as to the selling price which should be charged to maximize Rane limited's annual profits.
(b) *Two* non-financial factors which the management of Rane Limited should consider before planning to operate below full capacity.

Another of your consultancy's clients is a manufacturing company, Shortage Limited, which is experiencing problems in obtaining supplies of a major component. The component is used in all of its four products and there is a labour dispute at the supplier's factory, which is restricting the component's availability.

Supplies will be restricted to 22 400 components for the next period and the company wishes to ensure that the best use is made of the available components. This is the only component used in the four products, and there are no alternatives and no other suppliers.

The components cost £2 each and are used in varying amounts in each of the four products.

Shortage Limited's fixed costs amount to £8000 per period. No stocks are held of finished goods or work in progress.

The following information is available concerning the products.

Maximum demand per period	Product A 4000 units (£ per unit)	Product B 2500 units (£ per unit)	Product C 3600 units (£ per unit)	Product D 2750 units (£ per unit)
Selling price	14	12	16	17
Component costs	4	2	6	8
Other variable costs	7	9	6	4

Task 3
(a) Prepare a recommended production schedule for next period which will maximize Shortage Limited's profit.
(b) Calculate the profit that will be earned in the next period if your recommended production schedule is followed.

AAT Technicians Stage

10.21* Limiting factor optimum production and the use of simultaneous equations where more than one scarce factor exists
A company manufactures two products (X and Y) in one of its factories. Production capacity is limited to 85 000 machine hours per period. There is no restriction on direct labour hours.

The following information is provided concerning the two products:

	Product X	Product Y
Estimated demand (000 units)	315	135
Selling price (per unit)	£11.20	£15.70
Variable costs (per unit)	£6.30	£8.70
Fixed costs (per unit)	£4.00	£7.00
Machine hours (per 000 units)	160	280
Direct labour hours (per 000 units)	120	140

Fixed costs are absorbed into unit costs at a rate per machine hour based upon full capacity.

Required:
(a) Calculate the production quantities of Products X and Y which are required per period in order to maximize profit in the situation described above. *(5 marks)*
(b) Prepare a marginal costing statement in order to establish the total contribution of each product, and the net profit per period, based on selling the quantities calculated in (a) above. *(4 marks)*
(c) Calculate the production quantities of Products X and Y per period which would fully utilize both machine capacity and direct labour hours, where the available direct labour hours are restricted to 55 000 per period. (The limit of 85 000 machine hours remains.)
(5 marks)
(Total 14 marks)
ACCA Foundation Paper 3

Chapter 11

* Indicates that a suggested solution is to be found in the *Students' Manual*.

11.1

The traditional methods of cost allocation, cost apportionment and absorption into products are being challenged by some writers who claim that much information given to management is misleading when these methods of dealing with fixed overheads are used to determine product costs.

You are required to explain what is meant by *cost allocation*, cost apportionment and *absorption* and to describe briefly the alternative approach of *activity-based coasting* in order to ascertain total product costs. *(15 marks)*
CIMA Stage 2 Cost Accounting

11.2*

'It is now fairly widely accepted that conventional cost accounting distorts management's view of business through unrepresentative overhead allocation and inappropriate product costing.

This is because the traditional approach usually absorbs overhead costs across products and orders soley on the basis of the direct labour involved in their manufacture. And as direct labour as a proportion of total manufacturing cost continues to fall, this leads to more and more distortion and misrepresentation of the impact of particular products on total overhead costs.'

(From an article in *The Financial Times*)
You are required to discuss the above and to suggest what approaches are being adopted by management accountants to overcome such criticism. *(15 marks)*
CIMA Stage 2 Cost Accounting

11.3

'Attributing direct costs and absorbing overhead costs to the product/service through an activity-based costing approach will result in a better understanding of the true cost of the final output.'
(*Source:* a recent CIMA publication on costing in a service environment.)
You are required to explain and comment on the above statement. *(15 marks)*
CIMA Stage 2 Cost Accounting

11.4

In a marginal costing system only variable costs would be assigned to products or services, in which case management may rely on a *contribution approach to decisions*.

Required:
(a) Explain and discuss the contribution approach to decisions giving brief examples and drawing attention to any limitations. *(6 marks)*
A full absorption costing system would involve the assignment of both variable and fixed overhead costs to products. A traditional full absorption costing system typically uses a *single volume related allocation base* (or *cost driver*) to assign overheads to products. An activity based costing (ABC) system would use *multiple allocation bases* or (*cost drivers*), taking account of *different categories of activities and related overhead costs* such

as unit, batch, product sustaining and facility sustaining.

Required:

(b) Describe the likely stages involved in the design and operatioin of an ABC system.

(*4 marks*)

(c) Explain and discuss volume related allocation bases (or cost drivers), giving an example of one within a traditional costing system. Contrast this with the multipole allocation bases (or cost drivers) of an ABC system.

(*6 marks*)

(d) Briefly elaborate on the different categories of activities and related overhead costs, such as unit, batch, product sustaining and facility sustaining, which may be used in an ABC system.

(*4 marks*)

(*Total 20 marks*)

ACCA Paper 8 Managerial Finance

11.5 Calculation of ABC product costs and a discussion of the usefulness of ABC

Trimake Limited makes three main products, using broadly the same production methods and equipment for each. A conventional product costing system is used at present, although an activity-based costing (ABC) system is being considered. Details of the three products for a typical period are:

	Hours per unit		Materials per unit (£)	Volumes Units
	Labour hours	Machine hours		
Product X	$\frac{1}{2}$	$1\frac{1}{2}$	20	750
Product Y	$1\frac{1}{2}$	1	12	1250
Product Z	1	3	25	7000

Direct labour costs £6 per hour and production overheads are absorbed on a machine hour basis. The rate for the period is £28 per machine hour.

(a) You are required to calculate the cost per unit for each product using conventional methods.

(*4 marks*)

Further analysis shows that the total of production overheads can be divided as follows:

	(%)
Costs relating to set-ups	35
Costs relating to machinery	20
Costs relating to materials handling	15
Costs relating to inspection	30
Total production overhead	100%

The following activity volumes are associated with the product line for the period as a whole.

Total activities for the period:

	Number of set-ups	Number of movements of materials	Number of inspections
Product X	75	12	150
Product Y	115	21	180
Product Z	480	87	670
	670	120	1000

You are required

(b) to calculate the cost per unit for each product using ABC principles; (*15 marks*)

(c) to comment on the reasons for any differences in the costs in your answers to (a) and (b).

(*3 marks*)

(*Total 22 marks*)

CIMA Stage 3 Management Accounting Techniques

11.6* Preparation of conventional costing and ABC profit statements

The following budgeted information relates to Brunti plc for the forthcoming period:

	Products		
	XYI (000)	YZT (000)	ABW (000)
Sales and production (units)	50	40	30
	(£)	(£)	(£)
Selling price (per unit)	45	95	73
Prime cost (per unit)	32	84	65
	Hours	Hours	Hours
Machine department (machine hours per unit)	2	5	4
Assembly department (direct labour hours per unit)	7	3	2

Overheads allocated and apportioned to production departments (including service cost centre costs) were to be recovered in product costs as follows:

Machine department at
£1.20 per machine hour
Assembly department at
£0.825 per direct labour hour

You ascertain that the above overheads could be re-analysed into 'cost pools' as follows:

Cost pool	£000	Cost driver	Quantity for the period
Machining services	357	Machine hours	420 000
Assembly services	318	Direct labour hours	530 000
Set-up costs	26	Set-ups	520
Order processing	156	Customer orders	32 000
Purchasing	84	Suppliers' orders	11 200
	941		

You have also been provided with the following estimates for the period:

	Products		
	XYI	**YZT**	**ABW**
Number of set-ups	120	200	200
Customer orders	8 000	8 000	16 000
Suppliers' orders	3 000	4 000	4 200

Required:
(a) Prepare and present profit statements using:
  (i) conventional absorption costing;
  (5 marks)
  (ii) activity-based costing; *(10 marks)*
(b) Comment on why activity-based costing is considered to present a fairer valuation of the product cost per unit. *(5 marks)*
(Total 20 marks)
ACCA Paper 8 Managerial Finance

11.7* Computation of traditional and ABC unit costs and comments on the reported costs

BML has three product lines P1, P2 and P3. Since its creation the company has been using a single direct labour cost percentage to assign overhead costs to products.

Despite P3, a relatively new line, attracting additional business, increasing overhead costs and

a loss of market share, particularly for P2, a major product have convinced the management that the costing system is in need of some developments. A team, led by the management accountant, was established to develop an improved system of costing based on activities. The team spent several weeks collecting data (see tables below) for the different activities and products. For the accounting period in question, given in the tables below is data on BML's three product lines and overhead costs:

	P1	P2	P3
Production volume	7 500 units	12 500 units	4 000 units
Direct labour cost per unit	£4	£8	£6·4
Material cost per unit	£18	£25	£16
Selling price per unit	£47	£80	£68
Materials movements (in total)	4	25	50
Machine hours per unit	0·5	0·5	0·2
Set-ups (in total)	1	5	10
Proportion of engineering work	30%	20%	50%
Orders packed (in total)	1	7	22

Activities	Overhead cost (£)
Material receiving and handling	150 000
Machine maintenance and depreciation	390 000
Set-up labour	18 688
Engineering	100 000
Packing	60 000
	718 688

Required:
(a) Calculate the overhead rate and the product unit costs under the existing costing system.
(4 marks)
(b) Identify for each overhead activity, an appropriate cost driver from the information supplied and then calculate the product unit costs using a system that assigns overheads on the basis of the use of activities. *(9 marks)*
(c) Comment on the results of the two costing systems in (a) and (b) above. *(7 marks)*
(Total 20 marks)
ACCA Paper 8 Managerial Finance

11.8* Comparison of ABC with traditional product costing

(a) In the context of activity-based costing (ABC), it was stated in *Management Accounting – Evolution not Revolution* by Bromwich and Bhimani, that 'Cost drivers attempt to link costs to the scope of output rather than the scale of output thereby generating less arbitrary product costs for decision making.' You are required to explain the terms 'activity-based costing' and 'cost drivers'.

(13 marks)

(b) XYZ plc manufactures four products, namely A, B, C and D, using the same plant and processes. The following information relates to a production period:

Product	Volume	Material cost per unit	Direct labour per unit	Machine time per unit	Labour cost per unit
A	500	£5	$\frac{1}{2}$ hour	$\frac{1}{4}$ hour	£3
B	5000	£5	$\frac{1}{2}$ hour	$\frac{1}{4}$ hour	£3
C	600	£16	2 hours	1 hour	£12
D	7000	£17	$1\frac{1}{2}$ hours	$1\frac{1}{2}$ hours	£9

Total production overhead recorded by the cost accounting system is analysed under the following headings:

Factory overhead applicable to machine-oriented activity is £37 424
 Set-up costs are £4355

 The cost of ordering materials is £1920
 Handling materials – £7580
 Administration for spare parts – £8600.

These overhead costs are absorbed by products on a machine hour rate of £4.80 per hour, giving an overhead cost per product of:

 A = £1.20 B = £1.20 C = £4.80 D = £7.20

However, investigation into the production overhead activities for the period reveals the following totals:

Product	Number of set-ups	Number of material orders	Number of times material was handled	Number of spare parts
A	1	1	2	2
B	6	4	10	5
C	2	1	3	1
D	8	4	12	4

You are required:
(i) to compute an overhead cost per product using activity-based costing, tracing overheads to production units by means of cost drivers.

(6 marks)

(ii) to comment briefly on the differences disclosed between overheads traced by the present system and those traced by activity-based costing.

(6 marks)
(Total 25 marks)
CIMA Stage 4 Management Accounting –
Control and Audit

11.9 Comparison of traditional product costing with ABC

Duo plc produces two products A and B. Each has two components specified as sequentially numbered parts i.e. product A (parts 1 and 2) and product B (parts 3 and 4). Two production departments (machinery and fitting) are supported by five service activities (material procurement, material handling, maintenance, quality control and set up). Product A is a uniform product manufactured each year in 12 monthly high volume production runs. Product B is manufactured in low volume customised batches involving 25 separate production runs each month. Additional information is as follows:

	Product A	Product B
Production details:		
Components	Parts 1, 2	Parts 3, 4
Annual volume produced	300 000 units	300 000 units
Annual direct labour hours:		
Machinery department	500 000 DLH	600 000 DLH
Fitting department	150 000 DLH	200 000 DLH

Overhead Cost Analysis[a]

	(£000s)
Material handling	1 500
Material procurement	2 000
Set-up	1 500
Maintenance	2 500
Quality control	3 000
Machinery (machinery power, depreciation etc.)[b]	2 500
Fitting (machine, depreciation, power etc.)[b]	2 000
	15 000

[a] It may be assumed that these represent fairly homogeneous activity-based cost pools.
[b] It is assumed these costs (depreciation, power etc.) are primarily production volume driven and that direct labour hours are an appropriate surrogate measure of this.

Cost Driver Analysis

**Annual Cost Driver
Volume per Component**

Cost Driver	Part 1	Part 2	Part 3	Part 4
Material movements	180	160	1 000	1 200
Number of orders	200	300	2 000	4 000
Number of set-ups	12	12	300	300
Maintenance hours	7 000	5 000	10 000	8 000
Number of inspections	360	360	2 400	1 000
Direct labour hours	150 000	350 000	200 000	400 000
Direct labour hours	50 000	100 000	60 000	140 000

You are required to compute the unit costs for products A and B using (i) a traditional volume-based product costing system and (ii) an activity-based costing system.

(Adapted from Innes, J. and Mitchell, F., Activity Based Costing: A Review with Case Studies, *Chartered Institute of Management Accountants*, 1990.)

Chapter 12

* Indicates that a suggested solution is to be found in the *Students' Manual*

12.1* Payback and NPV calculations

A company is trying to decide which of two investment projects it should choose. The following information is provided:

	Project 1	Project 2
Capital Expenditure	£75 000	£75 000
Profit—Year 1	£30 000	£25 000
Profit—Year 2	£30 000	£15 000
Profit—Year 3	£20 000	£20 000
Profit (or loss) Year 4	(£10 000)	£20 000
(Loss)—Year 5	(£10 000)	(£15 000)

Notes:
1. Each product is expected to be operational for five years, at the end of which time there is not expected to be any scrap value.

2. Capital expenditure for both projects would be incurred immediately.
3. The profit figures are shown after including depreciation on a straight-line basis.
4. Taxation is to be ignored.
5. The company's cost of capital is 15%.

Required:
(a) Calculate for each project:
 (i) the payback period in years to one decimal place;
 (ii) The net present value. (*16 marks*)
(b) State the relative merits of the methods of evaluation mentioned in (a) above.
 (*6 marks*)
(c) Explain which project you would recommend for acceptance. (*3 marks*)
 AAT Cost Accounting and Budgeting

12.2 Calculation of accounting rate of return and NPV

A company is proposing to enter a new market and has collected the following data.

Capital expenditure on plant and machinery to product product X will total £1 500 000, to be paid immediately. During the first year, while the plant is being erected and machinery installed, no production or sales of product X is expected.

Sales of product X are expected to be 12 500 units each year from year 2 to year 5 inclusive. At the end of year 5 the plant and machinery will be sold for scrap, with cash receipts estimated at £100 000.

Data per unit of product X:

	(£)
Selling price	80
Variable cost	30
Fixed overheads	30
Profit	20

Cost and revenue data are expected to remain constant throughout the project's life.

The fixed overhead of £30 per unit is made up of depreciation (£28) and general overhead (£2). The general overheads are the company's fixed costs which are allocated to each product on the basis of an absorption rate of 6.66% of unit variable cost. There are no fixed costs which are specific to this project.

The company's cost of capital is 20% p.a.

Required:
(a) Calculate:
  (i) the average accounting rate of return on average capital employed to one decimal place; *(4 marks)*
  (ii) the net present value. *(10 marks)*
(b) Discuss the relative merits of the accounting rate of return and net present value methods of investment appraisal, and explain whether you would undertake the product. *(11 marks)*

(Total 25 marks)
AAT Cost Accounting and Budgeting

12.3* NPV and payback calculation plus a replacement decision

The management of a hotel group is deciding whether to scrap an old but still serviceable machine bought five years ago to produce fruit pies and replace it with a newer type of machine.

It is expected that the demand for the fruit pies will loast for a further five years only and will be as follows:

	Produced and sold number of pies
Year 1	40 000
Year 2	40 000
Year 3	30 000
Year 4	20 000
Year 5	20 000

The fruit pies are currently sold for £3 per pie.

Each machine is capable of meeting these requirements.

Data for the two machines are as follows:

	Existing machine (£)	New machine (£)
Capital cost	320 000	150 000
	Per unit	**Per unit**
Operating costs:		
Direct labour	£0.60	£0.40
Materials	£0.60	£0.60
Variable overheads	£0.30	£0.25
Fixed overheads:		
Depreciation	£0.80	£1.00

Allocated costs (100% direct labour costs)	£0.60	£0.40
	£2.90	£2.65

Unit operating costs, fixed overhead costs and selling price are expected to remain constant throughout the five-year period.

Required:
(a) Using data relating only to the new machine:
  (i) calculate the payback period of the new machine;
  (ii) calculate the net present value of the new machine.
  Note: The hotel group expects that its cost of capital will be 20% p.a. throughout the period. *(10 marks)*
(b) Assume that the existing machinery could be sold for £130 000 immediately, if it were replaced. Show, using present value calculations, whether the existing machine should be replaced by the new machine. *(8 marks)*
(c) Assume that no new machinery can be purchased, but that an outside caterer has offered to supply all of the hotel group's requirements for fruit pies at a price which compares favourably with the group's own cost of producing the pies. What factors other than price would need to be considered before making a decision whether to accept the offer. *(7 marks)*

(Total 25 marks)
AAT

12.4 Payback, accounting rate of return and NPV calculations plus a discussion of qualitative factors

The following information relates to three possible capital expenditure projects. Because of capital rationing only one project can be accepted.

	Project		
	A	B	C
Initial Cost	£200 000	£230 000	£180 000
Expected Life	5 years	5 years	4 years
Scrap value expected	£10 000	£15 000	£8 000
Expected Cash Inflows	(£)	(£)	(£)
End Year 1	80 000	100 000	55 000
2	70 000	70 000	65 000
3	65 000	50 000	95 000
4	60 000	50 000	100 000
5	55 000	50 000	

The company estimates its cost of capital is 18%. Calculate

(a) The pay back period for each project.
(*4 marks*)
(b) The Accounting Rate of Return for each project. (*4 marks*)
(c) The Net present value of each project.
(*8 marks*)
(d) Which project should be accepted – give reasons. (*5 marks*)
(e) Explain the factors management would need to consider: in addition to the financial factors before making a final decision on a project.
(*4 marks*)
(*Total 25 marks*)
AAT Stage 3 Cost Accounting and Budgeting

12.5* Discussion of alternative investment appraisal techniques and the calculation of payback and NPV for two mutually exclusive projects

(a) Explain why Net Present Value is considered technically superior to Payback and Accounting Rate of Return as an investment appraisal technique even though the latter are said to be easier to understand by management. Highlight the strengths of the Net Present Value method and the weaknesses of the other two methods. (*8 marks*)
(b) Your company has the option to invest in projects T and R but finance is only available to invest in one of them.

You are given the following projected data:

Project	T	R
	(£)	(£)
Initial Cost	70 000	60 000
Profits: Year 1	15 000	20 000
Year 2	18 000	25 000
Year 3	20 000	(50 000)
Year 4	32 000	10 000
Year 5	18 000	3 000
Year 6		2 000

You are told:
(1) All cash flows take place at the end of the year apart from the original investment in the project which takes place at the beginning of the project.

(2) Project T machinery is to be disposed of at the end of year 5 with a scrap value of £10 000.
(3) Project R machinery is to be disposed of at the end of year 3 with a nil scrap value and replaced with new project machinery that will cost £75 000.
(4) The cost of this additional machinery has been deducted in arriving at the profit projections for R for year 3. It is projected that it will last for three years and have a nil scrap value.
(5) The company's policy is to depreciate its assets on a straight line basis.
(6) The discount rate to be used by the company is 14%.

Required:
(i) If investment was to be made in project R determine whether the machinery should be replaced at the end of year 3.
(*4 marks*)
(ii) Calculate for projects T and R, taking into consideration your decision in (i) above:
(a) Payback period
(b) Net present value and advise which project should be invested in, stating your reasons. (*10 marks*)
(c) Explain what the discount rate of 14% represents and state two ways how it might have been arrived at. (*3 marks*)
(*Total 25 marks*)
AAT Cost Accounting and Budgeting

12.6*
An investment project has the following expected cash flows over its economic life of three years:

	(£)
Year 0	(142 700)
1	51 000
2	62 000
3	73 000

Required:
(i) Calculate the net present value (NPV) of the project at discount rates of 0%, 10% and 20% respectively.
(ii) Draw a graph of the project NPVs calculated in (i) and use the graph to estimate, and

clearly indicate, the project internal rate of return (IRR) to the nearest integer percentage.
(8 marks)
ACCA Foundation Stage Paper 3

12.7 Calculation of payback, NPV and ARR for mutually exclusive projects

Your company is considering investing in its own transport fleet. The present position is that carriage is contracted to an outside organization. The life of the transport fleet would be five years, after which time the vehicles would have to be disposed of.

The cost to your company of using the outside organization for its carriage needs is £250 000 for this year. This cost, it is projected, will rise 10% per annum over the life of the project. The initial cost of the transport fleet would be £750 000 and it is estimated that the following costs would be incurred over the next five years:

	Drivers' Costs (£)	Repairs & Maintenance (£)	Other Costs (£)
Year 1	33 000	8 000	130 000
Year 2	35 000	13 000	135 000
Year 3	36 000	15 000	140 000
Year 4	38 000	16 000	136 000
Year 5	40 000	18 000	142 000

Other costs include depreciation. It is projected that the fleet would be sold for £150 000 at the end of year 5. It has been agreed to depreciate the fleet on a straight line basis.

To raise funds for the project your company is proposing to raise a long-term loan at 12% interest rate per annum.

You are told that there is an alternative project that could be invested in using the funds raised, which has the following projected results:

> Payback = 3 years
> Accounting rate of return = 30%
> Net present value = £140 000.

As funds are limited, investment can only be made in one project.
Note: The transport fleet would be purchased at the beginning of the project and all other expenditure would be incurred at the end of each relevant year.

Required:
(a) Prepare a table showing the net cash savings to be made by the firm over the life of the transport fleet project. *(5 marks)*
(b) Calculate the following for the transport fleet project:
  (i) Payback period
  (ii) Accounting rate of return
  (iii) Net present value *(13 marks)*
(c) Write a short report to the Investment Manager in your company outlining whether investment should be committed to the transport fleet or the alternative project outlined. Clearly state the reasons for your decision.
(7 marks)
(Total 25 marks)
AAT Cost Accounting and Budgeting

12.8 NPV and payback calculations

You are employed as the assistant accountant in your company and you are currently working on an appraisal of a project to purchase a new machine. The machine will cost £55 000 and will have a useful life of three years. You have already estimated the cash flows from the project and their taxation effect, and the results of your estimates can be summarized as follows:

	Year 1	Year 2	Year 3
Post-tax cash inflow	£18 000	£29 000	£31 000

Your company uses a post-tax cost of capital of 8% to appraise all projects of this type.

Task 1
(a) Calculate the net present value of the proposal to purchase the machine. Ignore the effects of inflation and assume that all cash flows occur at the end of the year.
(b) Calculate the payback period for the investment in the machine.

Task 2
The marketing director has asked you to let her know as soon as you have completed your appraisal of the project. She has asked you to provide her with some explanation of your calculations and of how taxation affects the proposal.

Prepare a memorandum to the marketing director which answers her queries. Your memorandum should contain the following:

(a) your recommendation concerning the proposal;

(b) an explanation of the meaning of the net present value and the payback period;
(c) an explanation of the effects of taxation on the cash flows arising from capital expenditure.

AAT Technicians Stage

12.9 Present value of purchasing or renting machinery

The Portsmere Hospital operates its own laundry. Last year the laundry processed 120 000 kilograms of washing and this year the total is forecast to grow to 132 000 kilograms. This growth in laundry processed is forecast to continue at the same percentage rate for the next seven years. Because of this, the hospital must immediately replace its existing laundry equipment. Currently, it is considering two options, the purchase of machine A or the rental of machine B. Information on both options is given below:

Machine A – purchase

Annual capacity (kilograms)	£180 000
Material cost per kilogram	£2.00
Labour cost per kilogram	£3.00
Fixed costs per annum	£20 000
Life of machine	3 years
Capital cost	£60 000
Depreciation per annum	£20 000

Machine B – rent

Annual capacity (kilograms)	£170 000
Material cost per kilogram	£1.80
Labour cost per kilogram	£3.40
Fixed costs per annum	£18 000
Rental per annum	£20 000
Rental agreement	3 years
Depreciation per annum	nil

Other information:
1. The hospital is able to call on an outside laundry if there is either a breakdown or any other reason why the washing cannot be undertaken in-house. The charge would be £10 per kilogram of washing.
2. Machine A, if purchased, would have to be paid for immediately. All other cash flows can be assumed to occur at the end of the year.
3. Machine A will have no residual value at any time.

4. The existing laundry equipment could be sold for £10 000 cash.
5. The fixed costs are a direct cost of operating the laundry.
6. The hospital's discount rate for projects of this nature is 15%.

Task 1
You are an accounting technician employed by the Portsmere Hospital and you are asked to write a brief report to its chief executive. Your report should:

(a) evaluate the two options for operating the laundry, using discounted cash flow techniques;
(b) recommend the preferred option and identify *one* possible non-financial benefit;
(c) justify your treatment of the £10 000 cash value of the existing equipment;
(d) explain what is meant by discounted cashflow.

Note:
Inflation can be ignored.

AAT Technicians Stage

12.10* Calculation of payback, NPV and ARR, and recommendation of which of two mutually exclusive projects should be accepted.
(a) Essential to an understanding of the investment appraisal techniques of payback, accounting rate of return and net present value is the role of depreciation.

Required:
Explain how you would treat depreciation in a computation for each of the above appraisal techniques giving reasons for your decisions.

(*6 marks*)
(b) Company TH Ltd is considering investing in one of two mutually exclusive projects. Both projects would require an investment of £150 000 at the commencement of the project and the profile of returns is as follows:

	Project 1		Project 2	
	Profit (£)	Cash flow (£)	Profit (£)	Cash flow (£)
Year 1	40 000	60 000	30 000	54 000
Year 2	30 000	50 000	20 000	44 000
Year 3	25 000	45 000	15 000	39 000
Year 4	35 000	55 000	25 000	49 000
Year 5			50 000	74 000

You are told that the machinery associated with Project 1 will be sold for £70 000 at the end of year 4, and the machinery associated with project 2 will be sold for £30 000 at the end of year 5.

The company's cost of capital is 15%.

Required:
Determine for both projects in the:
  (i)   payback period;
  (ii) accounting rate of return;
  (iii) net present value;
and advise which project should be invested in giving your reasons. (*15 marks*)
(c) You have been asked by a manager at TH Ltd why you might need the expected disposal proceeds of the capital investment at the end of the project for any investment appraisal technique as the capital investment has already been depreciated.

Required:
Clearly answer the manager's query, identifying which investment appraisal technique, if any, utilizes the disposal proceeds of a capital investment at the end of a project. (*4 marks*)
(*Total 25 marks*)
AAT Cost Accounting and Budgeting

12.11 NPV calculation and taxation
Data
Tilsley Ltd manufactures motor vehicle components. It is considering introducing a new product. Helen Foster, the production director, has already prepared the following projections for this proposal:

| | **Year** | | | |
| | 1 | 2 | 3 | 4 |
	(£000)	(£000)	(£000)	(£000)
Sales	8 750	12 250	13 300	14 350
Direct materials	1 340	1 875	2 250	2 625
Direct labour	2 675	3 750	4 500	5 250
Direct overheads	185	250	250	250
Depreciation	2 500	2 500	2 500	2 500
Interest	1 012	1 012	1 012	1 012
Profit before tax	1 038	2 863	2 788	2 713
Corporation tax @ 30%	311	859	836	814
Profit after tax	727	2 004	1952	1 899

Helen Foster has recommended to the board that the project is not worthwhile because the cumula-tive after tax profit over the four years is less than the capital cost of the project.

As an assistant accountant at the company you have been asked by Philip Knowles, the chief accountant, to carry out a full financial appraisal of the proposal. He does not agree with Helen Foster's analysis, and provides you with the following information:

- the initial capital investment and working capital will be incurred at the beginning of the first year. All other receipts and payments will occur at the end of each year.
- the equipment will cost £10 million;
- additional working capital of £1 million;
- this additional working capital will be recovered in full as cash at the end of the four-year period;
- the equipment will qualify for a 25% per annum reducing balance writing down allowance;
- any outstanding capital allowances at the end of the project can be claimed as a balancing allowance;
- at the end of the four-year period the equipment will be scrapped, with no expected residual value;
- the additional working capital required does not qualify for capital allowances, nor is it an allowable expense in calculating taxable profit;
- Tilsley Ltd pays corporation tax at 30% of chargeable profits;
- there is a one-year delay in paying tax;
- the company's cost of capital is 17%.

Task
Write a report to Philip Knowles. Your report should:

(a) evaluate the project using net present value techniques;
(b) recommend whether the project is worth-while;
(c) explain how you have treated taxation in your appraisal;
(d) give *three* reasons why your analysis is different from that produced by Helen Foster, the production director.

Notes:
Risk and inflation can be ignored.
AAT Technicians Stage

Chapter 13

*Indicates that a suggested solution is to be found in the *Students' Manual.*

13.1*

The following details have been extracted from the debtor collection records of C Limited:

Invoices paid in the month after sale	50%
Invoices paid in the second month after sale	30%
Invoices paid in the third month after sale	15%
Bad debts	5%

Invoices are issued on the last day of each month.

Customers paying in the month after sale are entitled to deduct a 3% settlement discount.

Credit sales values for July to October 2001 are budgeted as follows:

July	August	September	October
£80 000	£60 000	£100 000	£70 000

The amount budgeted to be received in October 2001 from credit customers is

A £72 950.   B £75 000.   C £76 500.
D £78 500.   E £80 000.

CIMA Stage 2—Operational Cost Accounting

13.2 Outline:

(a) the objectives of budgetary planning and control systems;   (*7 marks*)
(b) the organization required for the preparation of a master budget.   (*10 marks*)
                                    (*Total 17 marks*)
                                    ACCA Level 1 Costing

13.3

The preparation of budgets is a lengthy process which requires great care if the ultimate master budget is to be useful for the purposes of management control within an organization.

You are required:

(a) to identify and to explain briefly the stages involved in the preparation of budgets identifying separately the roles of managers and the budget committee;   (*8 marks*)

(b) to explain how the use of spreadsheets may improve the efficiency of the budget preparation process.   (*7 marks*)
                                    (*Total 15 marks*)
                                    CIMA Stage 1 Accounting

13.4 Preparation of functional budgets

X plc manufactures Product X using three different raw materials. The product details are as follows:

Selling price per unit £250

Material A	3 kgs	material price £3.50 per kg
Material B	2 kgs	material price £5.00 per kg
Material C	4 kgs	material price £4.50 per kg
Direct labour	8 hours	labour rate £8.00 per hour

The company is considering its budgets for next year and has made the following estimates of sales demand for Product X for July to October:

July	August	September	October
400 units	300 units	600 units	450 units

It is company policy to hold stocks of finished goods at the end of each month equal to 50% of the following month's sales demand, and it is expected that the stock at the start of the budget period will meet this policy.

At the end of the production process the products are tested: it is usual for 10% of those tested to be faulty. It is not possible to rectify these faulty units.

Raw material stocks are expected to be as follows on 1 July:

Material A	1000 kgs
Material B	400 kgs
Material C	600 kgs

Stocks are to be increased by 20% in July, and then remain at their new level for the foreseeable future.

Labour is paid on an hourly rate based on attendance. In addition to the unit direct labour hours shown above, 20% of *attendance time* is spent on tasks which support production activity.

Required:

(a) Prepare the following budgets for the quarter from July to September inclusive:
   (i)   sales budget in quantity and value;
   (ii) production budget in units;
   (iii) raw material usage budget in kgs;

(iv) raw material purchases budget in kgs and value;

(v) labour requirements budget in hours and value. (*16 marks*)

(b) Explain the term '*principal budget factor*' and why its identification is an important part of the budget preparation process. (*3 marks*)

(c) Explain clearly, using data from part (a) above, how you would construct a spreadsheet to produce the labour requirements budget for August. Include a specimen cell layout diagram containing formulae which would illustrate the basis for the spreadsheet.

(*6 marks*)
(*Total 25 marks*)
CIMA Stage 2 Operational cost accounting

13.5 Preparation of functional budgets

D Limited is preparing its annual budgets for the year to 31 December 2001. It manufactures and sells one product, which has a selling price of £150. The marketing director believes that the price can be increased to £160 with effect from 1 July 2001 and that at this price the sales volume for each quarter of 2001 will be as follows:

Sales volume	
Quarter 1	40 000
Quarter 2	50 000
Quarter 3	30 000
Quarter 4	45 000

Sales for each quarter of 2002 are expected to be 40 000 units.

Each unit of the finished product which is manufactured requires four units of component R and three units of component T, together with a body shell S. These items are purchased from an outside supplier. Currently prices are:

Component R	£8.00 each
Component T	£5.00 each
Shell S	£30.00 each

The components are expected to increase in price by 10% with effect from 1 April 2001; no change is expected in the price of the shell.

Assembly of the shell and components into the finished product requires 6 labour hours: labour is currently paid £5.00 per hour. A 4% increase in

wage costs is anticipated to take effect from 1 October 2001.

Variable overhead costs are expected to be £10 per unit for the whole of 2001; fixed production overhead costs are expected to be £240 000 for the year, and are absorbed on a per unit basis. Stocks on 31 December 2000 are expected to be as follows:

Finished units	9000 units
Component R	3000 units
Component T	5500 units
Shell S	500 units

Closing stocks at the end of each quarter are to be as follows:

Finished units	10% of next quarter's sales
Component R	20% of next quarter's production requirements
Component T	15% of next quarter's production requirements
Shell S	10% of next quarter's production requirements

Required:
(a) Prepare the following budgets of D Limited for the year ending 31 December 2001, showing values for each quarter and the year in total:
(i) sales budget (in £s and units)
(ii) production budget (in units)
(iii) material usage budget (in units)
(iv) production cost budget (in £s).
(*15 marks*)

(b) Sales are often considered to be the principal budget factor of an organization.

Required:
Explain the meaning of the 'principal budget factor' and, assuming that it is sales, explain how sales may be forecast making appropriate reference to the use of statistical techniques and the use of microcomputers. (*10 marks*)
(*Total 25 marks*)
CIMA Stage 2 Operational Cost Accounting

13.6* Calculation of sales to achieve target profit and preparation of functional budgets

There is a continuing demand for three sub-assemblies – A, B and C – made and sold by MW Limited. Sales are in the ratios of A 1, B 2, C 4 and selling prices are A £215, B £250, C £300.

Each sub-assembly consists of a copper frame onto which are fixed the same components but in differing quantities as follows:

Sub-assembly	Frame	Component D	Component E	Component F
A	1	5	1	4
B	1	1	7	5
C	1	3	5	1
Buying in costs, per unit	£20	£8	£5	£3

Operation times by labour for each sub-assembly are:

Sub-assembly	Skilled hours	Unskilled hours
A	2	2
B	$1\frac{1}{2}$	2
C	$1\frac{1}{2}$	3

The skilled labour is paid £6 per hour and unskilled £4.50 per hour. The skilled labour is located in a machining department and the unskilled labour in an assembly department. A five-day week of $37\frac{1}{2}$ hours is worked and each accounting period is for four weeks.

Variable overhead per sub-assembly is A £5, B £4 and C £3.50. At the end of the current year, stocks are expected to be as shown below but because interest rates have increased and the company utilizes a bank overdraft for working capital purposes, it is planned to effect a 10% reduction in all finished sub-assemblies and bought-in stocks during Period 1 of the forthcoming year.

Forecast stocks at current year end:

Sub-assembly			
A	300	Copper frames	1 000
B	700	Component D	4 000
C	1600	Component E	10 000
		Component F	4 000

Work-in-progress stocks are to be ignored.

Overhead for the forthcoming year is budgeted to be Production £728 000, Selling and Distribution £364 000 and Administration £338 000. These costs, all fixed, are expected to be incurred evenly throughout the year and are treated as period costs.

Within Period 1 it is planned to sell one thirteenth of the annual requirements which are to be the sales necessary to achieve the company profit target of £6.5 million before tax.

You are required
(a) to prepare budgets in respect of Period 1 of the forthcoming year for
   (i) sales, in quantities and value;
   (ii) production, in quantities only;
   (iii) materials usage, in quantities;
   (iv) materials purchases, in quantities and value;
   (v) manpower budget, i.e. numbers of people needed in each of the machining department and the assembly department; *(20 marks)*
(b) to discuss the factors to be considered if the bought-in stocks were to be reduced to one week's requirements – this has been proposed by the purchasing officer but resisted by the production director. *(5 marks)*
(Total 25 marks)
CIMA Stage 2 Cost Accounting

13.7* Preparation of functional budgets
Data
Wilmslow Ltd makes two products, the Alpha and the Beta. Both products use the same material and labour but in different amounts. The company divides its year into 4 quarters, each of 12 weeks. Each week consists of 5 days and each day comprises 7 hours.

You are employed as the management accountant to Wilmslow Ltd and you originally prepared a budget for quarter 3, the 12 weeks to 17 September. The basic data for that budget is reproduced below.

Original budgetary data: quarter 3
12 weeks to 17 September

Product	Alpha	Beta
Estimated demand	1800 units	2100 units
Material per unit	8 kilograms	12 kilograms
Labour per unit	3 hours	6 hours

Since the budget was prepared, three developments have taken place.
1. The company has begun to use linear regression and seasonal variations to forecast sales demand. Because of this, the estimated demand for quarter 3 has been revised to 2000 Alphas and 2400 Betas.

2. As a result of the revised sales forecasting, you have developed more precise estimates of sales and closing stock levels.

- The sales volume of both the Alpha and Beta in quarter 4 (the 12 weeks ending 10 December) will be 20% more than in the revised budget for quarter 3 as a result of seasonal variations.
- The closing stock of finished Alphas at the end of quarter 3 should represent 5 days sales for quarter 4.
- The closing stock of finished Betas at the end of quarter 3 should represent 10 days sales for quarter 4.
- Production in quarter 4 of both Alpha and Beta is planned to be 20% more than in the revised budget for quarter 3. The closing stock of materials at the end of quarter 3 should be sufficient for 20 days production in quarter 4.

3. New equipment has been installed. The workforce is not familiar with the equipment. Because of this, for quarter 3, they will only be working at 80% of the efficiency assumed in the original budgetary data.

Other data from your original budget which has not changed is reproduced below:

- 50 production employees work a 35 hour week and are each paid £210 per week;
- overtime is paid for at £9 per hour;
- the cost of material is £10 per kilogram;
- opening stocks at the beginning of quarter 3 are as follows:
  - finished Alphas   500 units
  - finished Betas   600 units
  - material   12 000 kilograms
- there will not be any work in progress at any time.

Task 1

The production director of Wilmslow Ltd wants to schedule production for quarter 3 (the 12 weeks ending 17 September) and asks you to use the revised information to prepare the following:

(a) the revised production budget for Alphas and Betas;
(b) the material purchases budget in kilograms;
(c) a statement showing the cost of the material purchases;
(d) the labour budget in hours;
(e) a statement showing the cost of labour.

Data

Margaret Brown is the financial director of Wilmslow Ltd. She is not convinced that the use of linear regression, even when adjusted for seasonal variations, is the best way of forecasting sales volumes for Wilmslow Ltd.

The quality of sales forecasting is an agenda item for the next meeting of the Board of Directors and she asks for your advice.

Task 2

Write a *brief* memo to Margaret Brown. Your memo should:

(a) identify *two* limitations of the use of linear regression as a forecasting technique;
(b) suggest *two* other ways of sales forecasting.

AAT Contribution to the planning and allocation of resources

13.8* Budget preparation and comments on sales forecasting methods

You have recently been appointed as the management accountant to Alderley Ltd, a small company manufacturing two products, the Elgar and the Holst. Both products use the same type of material and labour but in different proportions. In the past, the company has had poor control over its working capital. To remedy this, you have recommended to the directors that a budgetary control system be introduced. This proposal has, now, been agreed.

Because Alderley Ltd's production and sales are spread evenly over the year, it was agreed that the annual budget should be broken down into four periods, each of 13 weeks, and commencing with the 13 weeks ending 4 April. To help you in this task, the sales and production directors have provided you with the following information:

1. Marketing and production data

	Elgar	**Holst**
Budgeted sales for 13 weeks (units)	845	1235
Material content per unit (kilograms)	7	8
Labour per unit (standard hours)	8	5

2. Production labour
   The 24 production employees work a 37-hour, five-day week and are paid £8 per hour. Any hours in excess of this involve Alderley in paying an overtime premium of 25%. Because of technical problems, which will continue over the next 13 weeks, employees are only able to work at 95% efficiency compared to standard.

3. Purchasing and opening stocks

The production director believes that raw material will cost £12 per kilogram over the budget period. He also plans to revise the amount of stock being kept. He estimates that the stock levels at the commencement of the budget period will be as follows:

Raw materials	Elgar	Holst
2328 kilograms	163 units	361 units

4. Closing stocks

At the end of the 13-week period closing stocks are planned to change. On the assumption that production and sales volumes for the second budget period will be similar to those in the first period:

- raw material stocks should be sufficient for 13 days' production;
- finished stocks of the Elgar should be equivalent to 6 days' sales volume;
- finished stocks of the Holst should be equivalent to 14 days' sales volume.

Task 1

Prepare in the form of a statement the following information for the 13-week period to 4 April:

(a) the production budget in units for the Elgar and Holst;
(b) the purchasing budget for Alderley Ltd in units;
(c) the cost of purchases for the period;
(d) the production labour budget for Alderley Ltd in hours;
(e) the cost of production labour for the period.

Note: Assume a five-day week for both sales and production.

The managing director of Alderley Ltd, Alan Dunn, has also only recently been appointed. He is keen to develop the company and has already agreed to two new products being developed. These will be launched in 18 months' time. While talking to you about the budget, he mentions that the quality of sales forecasting will need to improve if the company is to grow rapidly. Currently, the budgeted sales figure is found by initially adding 5% to the previous year's sales volume and then revising the figure following discussions with the marketing director. He believes this approach is increasingly inadequate and now requires a more systematic approach.

A few days later, Alan Dunn sends you a memo. In that memo, he identifies three possible strategies for increasing sales volume. They are:

- more sales to existing customers;
- the development of new markets;
- the development of new products.

He asks for your help in forecasting likely sales volumes from these sources.

Task 2

Write a brief memo to Alan Dunn. Your memo should:

(a) identify *four* ways of forecasting future sales volume;
(b) show how each of your four ways of forecasting can be applied to *one* of the sales strategies identified by Alan Dunn and justify your choice;
(c) give *two* reasons why forecasting methods might not prove to be accurate.

AAT Technicians Stage

13.9 Preparation of cash budgets

The following data and estimates are available for ABC Limited for June, July and August.

	June (£)	July (£)	August (£)
Sales	45 000	50 000	60 000
Wages	12 000	13 000	14 500
Overheads	8 500	9 500	9 000

The following information is available regarding direct materials:

	June (£)	July (£)	August (£)	September (£)
Opening stock	5000	3500	6 000	4000
Material usage	8000	9000	10 000	

Notes:

1. 10% of sales are for cash, the balance is received the following month. The amount received in June for May's sales is £29 500.
2. Wages are paid in the month they are incurred.
3. Overheads include £1500 per month for depreciation. Overheads are settled the month following. £6500 is to be paid in June for May's overheads.

4. Purchases of direct materials are paid for in the month purchased.
5. The opening cash balance in June is £11 750.
6. A tax bill of £25 000 is to be paid in July.

Required:
(a) Calculate the amount of direct material purchases in *each* of the months of June, July and August. (3 *marks*)
(b) Prepare cash budgets for June, July and August. (9 *marks*)
(c) Describe briefly the advantages of preparing cash budgets. (3 *marks*)
(*Total marks 15*)
CIMA Stage 1 Cost Accounting

13.10* Preparation of cash budgets and calculation of stock, debtor and creditor balances

In the near future a company will purchase a manufacturing business for £315 000, this price to include goodwill (£150 000), equipment and fittings (£120 000), and stock of raw materials and finished goods (£45 000). A delivery van will be purchased for £15 000 as soon as the business purchase is completed. The delivery van will be paid for in the second month of operations. The following forecasts have been made for the business following purchase:

(i) Sales (before discounts) of the business's single product, at a mark-up of 60% on production cost, will be:

Month	1	2	3	4	5	6
(£000)	96	96	92	96	100	104

25% of sales will be for cash; the remainder will be on credit, for settlement in the month following that of sale. A discount of 10% will be given to selected credit customers, who represent 25% of gross sales.

(ii) Production cost will be £5.00 per unit. The production cost will be made up of:

raw materials	£2.50
direct labour	£1.50
fixed overhead	£1.00

(iii) Production will be arranged so that closing stock at the end of any month is sufficient to meet sales requirements in the following month. A value of £30 000 is placed on the stock of finished goods which was acquired

on purchase of the business. This valuation is based on the forecast of production cost per unit given in (ii) above.

(iv) The single raw material will be purchased so that stock at the end of a month is sufficient to meet half of the following month's production requirements. Raw material stock acquired on purchase of the business (£15 000) is valued at the cost per unit which is forecast as given in (ii) above. Raw materials will be purchased on one month's credit.

(v) Costs of direct labour will be met as they are incurred in production.

(vi) The fixed production overhead rate of £1.00 per unit is based upon a forecast of the first year's production of 150 000 units. This rate includes depreciation of equipment and fittings on a straight-line basis over the next five years.

(vii) Selling and administration overheads are all fixed, and will be £208 000 in the first year. These overheads include depreciation of the delivery van at 30% per annum on a reducing balance basis. All fixed overheads will be incurred on a regular basis, with the exception of rent and rates. £25 000 is payable for the year ahead in month one for rent and rates.

Required:
(a) Prepare a monthly cash budget. You should include the business purchase and the first four months of operations following purchase. (17 *marks*)
(b) Calculate the stock, debtor, and creditor balances at the end of the four month period. Comment briefly upon the liquidity situation. (8 *marks*)
(*Total 25 marks*)
ACCA Level 1 Costing

13.11* Preparation of cash budgets

A redundant manager who received compensation of £80 000 decides to commence business on 4 January, manufacturing a product for which he knows there is a ready market. He intends to employ some of his former workers who were also made redundant but they will not all commence on 4 January. Suitable premises have been found to rent and second-hand machinery costing £60 000 has been bought out of the £80 000. This machinery has an estimated life of five years from January and no residual value.

Other data

1. Production will begin on 4 January and 25% of the following month's sales will be manufactured in January. Each month thereafter the production will consist of 75% of the current month's sales and 25% of the following month's sales.
2. Estimated sales are

	(units)	(£)
January	Nil	Nil
February	3200	80 000
March	3600	90 000
April	4000	100 000
May	4000	100 000

3. Variable production cost per unit

	(£)
Direct materials	7
Direct wages	6
Variable overhead	2
	15

4. Raw material stocks costing £10 000 have been purchased (out of the manager's £80 000) to enable production to commence and it is intended to buy, each month, 50% of the materials required for the following month's production requirements. The other 50% will be purchased in the month of production. Payment will be made 30 days after purchase.
5. Direct workers have agreed to have their wages paid into bank accounts on the seventh working day of each month in respect of the previous month's earnings.
6. Variable production overhead: 60% is to be paid in the month following the month it was incurred and 40% is to be paid one month later.
7. Fixed overheads are £4000 per month. One quarter of this is paid in the month incurred, one half in the following month, and the remainder represents depreciation on the second-hand machinery.
8. Amounts receivable: a 5% cash discount is allowed for payment in the current month and 20% of each month's sales qualify for this discount. 50% of each month's sales are received in the following month, 20% in the third month and 8% in the fourth month. The balance of 2% represents anticipated bad debts.

You are required to:

(a) (i) prepare a cash budget for each of the first four months, assuming that overdraft facilities will be available; (*17 marks*)

    (ii) state the amount receivable from customers in May; (*4 marks*)

(b) describe briefly the benefits to cash budgeting from the use of a particular type of software package. (*4 marks*)

(*Total 25 marks*)

CIMA Stage 2 Cost Accounting 2

13.12 Preparation of cash budgets

A company is to carry out a major modernization of its factory commencing in two weeks time. During the modernization, which is expected to take four weeks to complete, no production of the company's single product will be possible.

The following additional information is available:

(i) *Sales/Debtors:* Demand for the product at £100 per unit is expected to continue at 800 units per week, the level of sales achieved for the last four weeks, for one further week. It is then expected to reduce to 700 units per week for three weeks, before rising to a level of 900 units per week where it is expected to remain for several weeks. All sales are on credit, 50% being received in cash in the week following the week of sale and 50% in the week after that.

(ii) *Production/Finished goods stock:* Production will be at a level of 1200 units per week for the next two weeks. Finished goods stock is 2800 units at the beginning of week 1.

(iii) *Raw material stock:* Raw material stock is £36 000 at the beginning of week 1. This will be increased by the end of week 1 to £40 000 and reduced to £10 000 by the end of week 2.

(iv) *Costs*

	(£ per unit)
Variable:	
Raw material	35
Direct labour	20
Overhead	10
Fixed:	
Overhead	25

Fixed overheads have been apportioned to units on the basis of the normal output level of 800 units per week and include depreciation of £4000 per week.

In addition to the above unit costs, over-time premiums of £5000 per week will be incurred in weeks 1 and 2. During the modernization variable costs will be avoided, apart from direct labour which will be incurred at the level equivalent to 800 units production per week. Outlays on fixed overheads will be reduced by £4000 per week.

(v) *Payments:* Creditors for raw materials, which stand at £27 000 at the beginning of week 1, are paid in the week following purchase. All other payments are made in the week in which the liability is incurred.

(vi) *Liquidity:* The company has a bank overdraft balance of £39 000 at the beginning of week 1 and an overdraft limit of £50 000.

The company is anxious to establish the liquidity situation over the modernization period, excluding the requirements for finance for the modernization itself.

Required:

(a) Prepare a weekly cash budget covering the six-week period up to the planned completion of the modernization. (*15 marks*)

(b) Comment briefly upon any matters concerning the liquidity situation which you feel should be drawn to the attention of management. (*7 marks*)

(*Total 22 marks*)
ACCA Level 1 Costing

13.13* Preparation of cash budgets

Y plc is currently preparing its budgets for the year ending 30 September 2001.

The sales and production budgets have been completed and an extract from them is shown below:

	Production Units (000s)	Sales Units (000s)	£000
January	900	1000	50 000
February	850	800	40 000
March	1000	900	45 000
April	1200	1100	55 000
May	1250	1300	65 000
June	1175	1200	60 000
July	1100	1150	57 500
August	to be determined	1050	52 500

Budgeted production costs per unit are:

	£ per unit
Direct materials	14.00
Direct labour	12.00
Variable overhead	6.00
Fixed overhead*	8.00
Production cost	40.00

*Fixed overheads are absorbed on a unit basis assuming a normal production level of 14 000 000 units per year.

Direct materials are purchased in the month of usage and, where settlement discounts are available, Y plc's policy is to pay suppliers so as to receive these discounts. It is expected that 60% of Y plc's material costs will be received from suppliers who offer a 2% discount for payment in the month of purchase. Other material suppliers are to be paid in the month following purchase.

Direct labour costs are paid 75% in the month in which they are incurred and 25% in the following month.

Variable overhead costs are paid in the month in which they are incurred.

Fixed overhead costs include £16 000 000 depreciation. Fixed overhead expenditure accrues at a constant rate throughout the year and is paid 40% in the month in which it is incurred and 60% in the following month.

In addition to production costs, Y plc expects to incur administration overhead costs of £500 000 per month and selling overhead costs of 2% of sales value. These costs are to be paid in the month in which they are incurred.

Y plc's customers are expected to pay for items as follows:

- in the month of sale   20%
- in the month after sale   55%
- in the month two months after sale   15%
- in the month three months after sale   5%

Customers paying in the month of sale are given 1% discount. 5% of sales are expected to be bad debts.

In addition to the above, Y plc expects that:

(1) new machinery is to be acquired on 1 February 2001 costing £15 000 000. This is to be paid for in May 2001.
(2) corporation tax of £10 000 000 will be payable in June 2001.
(3) a dividend of £7 500 000 will be paid to shareholders in July 2001.
(4) bank balance at 1 April 2001 will be £14 500 000.

Required:
(a) Prepare Y plc's cash budget for the period April to July 2001, showing clearly the receipts, payments and resulting balances for each month separately. *(20 marks)*
(b) Use your answer to part (a) above to explain clearly the following:
  (i) feed-forward control;
  (ii) feed-back control. *(5 marks)*
  (Total marks 25)
  CIMA Stage 2 — Operational Cost Accounting

13.14 Direct labour budget and labour cost accounting
A company, which manufactures a range of consumer products, is preparing the direct labour budget for one of its factories. Three products are manufactured in the factory. Each product passes through two stages: filling and packing.

Direct labour efficiency standards are set for each stage. The standards are based upon the number of units expected to be manufactured per hour of direct labour. Current standards are:

	Product 1 (units/hour)	Product 2 (units/hour)	Product 3 (units/hour)
Filling	125	300	250
Packing	95	100	95

Budgeted sales of the three products are:

Product 1	850 000 units
Product 2	1 500 000 units
Product 3	510 000 units

Production will be at the same level each month, and will be sufficient to enable finished goods stocks at the end of the budget year to be:

Product 1	200 000 units
Product 2	255 000 units
Product 3	70 000 units

Stocks at the beginning of the budget year are expected to be:

Product 1	100 000 units
Product 2	210 000 units
Product 3	105 000 units

After completion of the filling stage, 5% of the output of Products 1 and 3 is expected to be rejected and destroyed. The cost of such rejects is treated as a normal loss.

A single direct labour hour rate is established for the factory as a whole. The total payroll cost of direct labour personnel is included in the direct labour rate. Hours of direct labour personnel are budgeted to be split as follows:

	% of Total time
Direct work	80
Holidays (other, than public holidays)	7
Sickness	3
Idle time	4
Cleaning	3
Training	3
	100%

All direct labour personnel are employed on a full-time basis to work a basic 35 hour, 5 day, week. Overtime is to be budgeted at an average of 3 hours per employee, per week. Overtime is paid at a premium of 25% over the basic hourly rate of £4 per hour. There will be 250 possible working days during the year. You are to assume that employees are paid for exactly 52 weeks in the year.

Required:
Calculate:
(a) The number of full-time direct employees required during the budget year. *(14 marks)*
(b) The direct labour rate (£ per hour, to 2 decimal places). *(5 marks)*
(c) The direct labour cost for each product (pence per unit to 2 decimal places). *(6 marks)*
  (Total 25 marks)
  ACCA Level 1 Costing

Chapter 14

*Indicates that a suggested solution is to be found in the *Students' Manual*.

14.1*

(a) Identify and explain the essential elements of an effective cost control system. (*13 marks*)

(b) Outline possible problems which may be encountered as a result of the introduction of a system of cost control into an organization. (*4 marks*) (*Total 17 marks*)

14.2

You have applied for the position of assistant accountant in a company manufacturing a range of products with a sales turnover of £12 million per annum and employing approximately 300 employees. As part of the selection process you are asked to spend half an hour preparing a report, to be addressed to the managing director, on the topic of 'cost control'.

You are required to write the report which should deal with what is meant by 'cost control', its purpose and the techniques which you believe would be useful within this particular company.

(*20 marks*)
CIMA Foundation Cost Accounting 1

14.3

Outline the main features of a responsibility accounting system. (*6 marks*)
ACCA Level 2 Management Accounting

14.4

Explain the meaning of each of the undernoted terms, comment on their likely impact on cash budgeting and profit planning and suggest ways in which any adverse effects of each may be reduced.

(a) Budgetary slack. (*7 marks*)
(b) Incremental budgets. (*7 marks*)
(c) Fixed budgets. (*6 marks*)

(*Total 20 marks*)
ACCA Level 2 Cost and Management Accounting II

14.5 Preparation of flexible budget, separation of fixed and variable costs and comments on variances

Secondline Ltd, aware of the uncertain nature of its market for the coming year has prepared budgeted profit forecasts based on 90%, 100% and 105% activity as follows:

	90% (£)	100% (£)	105% (£)
Revenue	1 350 000	1 500 000	1 575 000
Less:			
Material costs	337 500	375 000	393 750
Labour costs	440 000	485 000	507 500
Production overhead costs	217 500	235 000	243 750
Administration costs	120 000	130 000	135 000
Selling and distribution costs	70 000	75 000	77 500
	1 185 000	1 300 000	1 357 500
Net profit	165 000	200 000	217 500

In fact actual activity has turned out far worse than expected and only 37 500 units have been sold, with the following results:

	(£)	(£)
Revenue		1 075 000
Less expenses:		
Material costs	311 750	
Labour costs	351 500	
Production overhead costs	171 250	
Administration costs	117 500	
Selling and distribution costs	66 500	1 018 500
Net profit		56 500

You are also told that:

(i) The budgeted selling price is £30 per unit.
(ii) All production is sold.
(iii) The fixed element of the budgeted costs will remain unchanged to all levels of production.

Required:

(a) Prepare a statement for the year showing the flexed budget at the actual level of activity, the actual results and the variance of each item of revenue and cost. (*10 marks*)

(b) Examine the variances of £20 000 or greater, analysing the possible reasons for such variances and the follow-up action management can take. (*9 marks*)

(c) Secondline Ltd had seen that sales were likely to be depressed for the coming year and its sales team had secured a potential order for all the spare capacity from actual activity up to 100% activity. For this order a special selling price of £25 per unit had been agreed and budgeted variable administration costs would increase by 25%, budgeted variable production overhead costs by 20% and budgeted variable labour costs by £1 per unit. All other costs would remain the same.

Recommended whether Secondline should have maintained 100% activity for the year by accepting the order detailed above. Clearly state the reasons for your decision and show any workings. *(6 marks)*
(Total 25 marks)
AAT Cost Accounting and Budgeting

14.6 Preparation of flexible budgets
The following monthly budgeted cost values have been taken from the budget working papers of MZ Limited for the year ended 30 September 2000.

Activity level	60% (£)	70% (£)	80% (£)
Direct materials	30 000	35 000	40 000
Direct labour	40 500	47 250	54 000
Production overhead	46 000	52 000	58 000
Selling overhead	15 000	17 000	19 000
Administration overhead	28 000	28 000	28 000
	159 500	179 250	199 000

During September 2000, actual activity was 1292 units (which was equal to 68% activity) and actual costs were:

	(£)
Direct materials	33 500
Direct labour	44 000
Production overhead	46 250
Selling overhead	16 150
Administration overhead	27 800
	167 700

Required:
(a) Prepare a budgetary control statement for MZ Limited on a flexible budget basis for the month of September 2000. *(7 marks)*
(b) Explain the difference between fixed and flexible budgets, and state when each should be used to control costs. *(8 marks)*
(c) The preparation of budgets is an important task that relies on the identification of the principal budget factor.

Explain the term 'principal budget factor' and state its importance in the budget preparation process. *(5 marks)*

(d) Explain the role of the budget committee in the budget preparation process. *(5 marks)*
(Total marks 25)
CIMA Stage 2 — Operational Cost Accounting

14.7* Preparation of flexible budgets based on an analysis of past cost behaviour and an adjustment for inflation
TJ Limited is in an industry sector which is recovering from the recent recession. The directors of the company hope next year to be operating at 85% of capacity, although currently the company is operating at only 65% of capacity. 65% of capacity represents output of 10 000 units of the single product which is produced and sold. One hundred direct workers are employed on production for 200 000 hours in the current year.

The flexed budgets for the current year are:

Capacity level	55% (£)	65% (£)	75% (£)
Direct materials	846 200	1 000 000	1 153 800
Direct wages	1 480 850	1 750 000	2 019 150
Production overhead	596 170	650 000	703 830
Selling and distribution overhead	192 310	200 000	207 690
Administration overhead	120 000	120 000	120 000
Total costs	3 235 530	3 720 000	4 204 470

Profit in any year is budgeted to be $16\frac{2}{3}$% of sales.

The following percentage increases in costs are expected for next year

	Increase %
Direct materials	6
Direct wages	3
Variable production overhead	7
Variable selling and distribution overhead	7
Fixed production overhead	10
Fixed selling and distribution overhead	7.5
Administration overhead	10

You are required:
(a) to prepare for next year a flexible budget statement on the assumption that the company operates at 85% of capacity; your statement should show both contribution and profit;
(14 marks)

(b) to discuss briefly three problems which may arise from the change in capacity level;

(*6 marks*)

(c) to state who is likely to serve on a budget committee operated by TJ Limited and explain the purpose of such a committee.

(*5 marks*)

(*Total 25 marks*)

CIMA Stage 2 Cost Accounting

14.8 Preparation of flexible budgets

A manufacturing company has the following budgeted costs for one month which are based on a normal capacity level of 40 000 hours.

A departmental overhead absorption rate of £4.40 per hour has been calculated, as follows:

	Fixed (£000)	Variable per hour (£)
Overhead:		
Management and supervision	30	—
Shift premium	—	0.10
National Insurance and pension costs	6	0.22
Inspection	20	0.25
Consumable supplies	6	0.18
Power for machinery	—	0.20
Lighting and heating	4	—
Rates	9	—
Repairs and maintenance	8	0.15
Materials and handling	10	0.30
Depreciation of machinery	15	—
Production administration	12	—
	120	
Overhead rate per hour: Variable		1.40
Fixed		3.00
Total		£4.40

During the month of April, the company actually worked 36 000 hours producing 36 000 standard hours of production and incurred the following overhead costs:

	(£000)
Management and supervision	30.0
Shift premium	4.0
National Insurance and pension costs	15.0
Inspection	28.0
Consumable supplies	12.7
Power for machinery	7.8
Lighting and heating	4.2
Rates	9.0
Repairs and maintenance	15.1
Materials handling	21.4
Depreciation of machinery	15.0
Production of administration	11.5
Idle time	1.6
	175.3

You are required to:

(a) prepare a statement showing for April the flexible budget for the month, the actual costs and the variance for each overhead item;

(b) comment on each variance of £1000 or more by suggesting possible reasons for the variances reported;

(c) state, for control purposes, with reasons to support your conclusions:

   (i) whether (b) above is adequate; and

   (ii) whether the statement prepared in respect of the request in (a) above could be improved, and if so, how.

CIMA Stage 2 Cost Accounting

14.9 Preparation of flexible budgets and an explanation of variances

You have been provided with the following operating statement, which represents an attempt to compare the actual performance for the quarter which has just ended with the budget:

	Budget	Actual	Variance
Number of units sold (000s)	640	720	80
	£000	£000	£000
Sales	1024	1071	47
Cost of sales (all variable)			
Materials	168	144	
Labour	240	288	
Overheads	32	36	
	440	468	(28)
Fixed labour cost	100	94	6
Selling and distribution costs:			
Fixed	72	83	(11)
Variable	144	153	(9)
Administration costs:			
Fixed	184	176	8
Variable	48	54	(6)
	548	560	(12)
Net profit	36	43	7

Required:

(a) Using a flexible budgeting approach, re-draft the operating statement so as to provide a more realistic indication of the variances and comment briefly on the possible reasons (other than inflation) why they have occurred.
(12 marks)

(b) Explain why the original operating statement was of little use to management. *(2 marks)*

(c) Discuss the problems associated with the forecasting of figures which are to be used in flexible budgeting. *(6 marks)*
(Total 20 marks)
ACCA Paper 8 Managerial Finance

14.10* Preparation of a flexible budget performance report

The Viking Smelting Company established a division, called the reclamation division, two years ago, to extract silver from jewellers' waste materials. The waste materials are processed in a furnace, enabling silver to be recovered. The silver is then further processed into finished products by three other divisions within the company.

A performance report is prepared each month for the reclamation division which is then discussed by the management team. Sharon Houghton, the newly appointed financial controller of the reclamation division, has recently prepared her first report for the four weeks to 31 May. This is shown below:

Performance Report Reclamation Division
4 weeks to 31 May

	Actual	Budget	Variance	Comments
Production (tonnes)	200	250	50 (F)[a]	
	(£)	(£)	(£)	
Wages and social security costs	46 133	45 586	547 (A)	Overspend
Fuel	15 500	18 750	3250 (F)	
Consumables	2 100	2 500	400 (F)	
Power	1 590	1 750	160 (F)	
Divisional overheads	21 000	20 000	1 000 (A)	Overspend
Plant maintenance	6 900	5 950	950 (A)	Overspend
Central services	7 300	6 850	450 (A)	Overspend
Total	100 523	101 386	863 (F)	

[a] (A) = adverse, (F) = favourable

In preparing the budgeted figures, the following assumptions were made for May:

- the reclamation division was to employ four teams of six production employees;

- each employee was to work a basic 42-hour week and be paid £7.50 per hour for the four weeks of May;

- social security and other employment costs were estimated at 40% of basic wages;

- a bonus, shared amongst the production employees, was payable if production exceeded 150 tonnes. This varied depending on the output achieved;

1. if output was between 150 and 199 tonnes, the bonus was £3 per tonne produced;

2. if output was between 200 and 249 tonnes, the bonus was £8 per tonne produced;

3. if output exceeded 249 tonnes the bonus was £13 per tonne produced;

- the cost of fuel was £75 per tonne;
- consumables were £10 per tonne;
- power comprised a fixed charge of £500 per four weeks plus £5 per tonne for every tonne produced;
- overheads directly attributable to the division were £20 000;
- plant maintenance was to be apportioned to divisions on the basis of the capital values of each division;
- the cost of Viking's central services was to be shared equally by all four divisions.

You are the deputy financial controller of the reclamation division. After attending her first monthly meeting with the board of the reclamation division, Sharon Houghton arranges a meeting with you. She is concerned about a number of issues, one of them being that the current report does not clearly identify those expenses and variances which are the direct responsibility of the reclamation division.

Task 1

Sharon Houghton asks you to prepare a flexible budget report for the reclamation division for May in a form consistent with responsibility accounting.

On receiving your revised report. Sharon tells you about the other questions raised at the management meeting when the original report was presented. These are summarized below:

(i) Why are the budget figures based on two-year-old data taken from the proposal recommending the establishment of the reclamation division?

(ii) Should the budget data be based on what we were proposing to do or what we actually did do?

(iii) Is it true that the less we produce the more favourable our variances will be?

(iv) Why is there so much maintenance in a new division with modern equipment and why should we be charged with the actual costs of the maintenance department even when they overspend?

(v) Could the comments, explaining the variances, be improved?

(vi) Should all the variances be investigated?

(vii) Does showing the cost of central services on the divisional performance report help control these costs and motivate the divisional managers?

Task 2

Prepare a memo for the management of the reclamation division. Your memo should:

(a) answer their queries and justify your comments;

(b) highlight the main objective of your revised performance report developed in Task 1 and give two advantages of it over the original report

AAT Technicians Stage

14.11* Sales forecasting removing seasonal variations, flexible budgets and budget preparation

You work as the assistant to the management accountant for Henry Limited, a medium-sized manufacturing company. One of its products, product P, has been very successful in recent years, showing a steadily increasing trend in sales volumes. Sales volumes for the four quarters of last year were as follows:

	Quarter 1	Quarter 2	Quarter 3	Quarter 4
Actual sales volume (units)	420 000	450 000	475 000	475 000

A new assistant has recently joined the marketing department and she has asked you for help in understanding the terminology which is used in preparing sales forecasts and analysing sales trends. She has said: 'My main problem is that I do not see why my boss is so enthusiastic about the growth in product P's sales volume. It looks to me as though the rate of growth is really slowing down and has actually stopped in quarter 4. I am told that I should be looking at the deseasonalized or seasonally adjusted sales data but I do not understand what is meant by this.'

You have found that product P's sales are subject to the following seasonal variations:

	Quarter 1	Quarter 2	Quarter 3	Quarter 4
Seasonal variation (units)	+25 000	+15 000	0	−40 000

Task 1

(a) Adjust for the seasonal variations to calculate deseasonalized or seasonally adjusted sales volume (i.e. the trend figures) for each quarter of last year.

(b) Assuming that the trend and seasonal variations will continue, forecast the sales volumes for each of the four quarters of next year.

Task 2

Prepare a memorandum to the marketing assistant which explains:

(a) what is meant by seasonal variations and deseaonalized or seasonally adjusted data;

(b) how they can be useful in analysing a time series and preparing forecasts.

Use the figures for product P's sales to illustrate your explanations.

Task 3

Using the additional data below, prepare a further memorandum to the marketing assistant which explains the following:

(a) why fixed budgets are useful for planning but flexible budgets may be more useful to enable management to exercise reflective control over distribution costs,

(b) *two* possible activity indicators which could be used as a basis for flexing the budget for distribution costs,

(c) how a flexible budget cost allowance is calculated and used for control purposes. Use your own examples and figures where appropriate to illustrate your explanations.

Additional data:

The marketing assistant has now approached you for more help in understanding the company's planning and control systems. She has been talking with the distribution manager, who has tried to explain how flexible budgets are used to control distribution costs within Henry Limited. She makes the following comment. 'I thought that budgets were supposed to provide a target to plan our activities and against which to monitor our costs. How can we possibly plan and control our costs if we simply change the budgets when activity levels alter?'

Product Q is another product which is manufactured and sold by Henry Limited. In the process of preparing budgetary plans for next year the following information has been made available to you.

1. Forecast sales units of product Q for the year = 18 135 units.
2. Closing stocks of finished units of product Q at the end of next year will be increased by 15% from their opening level of 1200 units.
3. All units are subject to quality control check. The budget plans are to allow for 1% of all units checked to be rejected and scrapped at the end of the process. All closing stocks will have passed this quality control check.
4. Five direct labour hours are to be worked for each unit of product Q processed, including those which are scrapped after the quality control check. Of the total hours to be paid for, 7.5% are budgeted to be idle time.
5. The standard hourly rate of pay for direct employees is £6 per hour.
6. Material M is used in the manufacture of product Q. One finished unit of producing Q contains 9 kg of M but there is a wastage of 10% of input of material M due to evaporation and spillage during the process.
7. By the end of next year stocks of material M are to be increased by 12% from their opening level of 8000 kg. During the year a loss of 1000 kg is expected due to deterioration of the material in store.

Task 4
Prepare the following budgets for the forthcoming year:
(a) production budget for product Q, in units;
(b) direct labour budget for product Q, in hours and in £;
(c) material usage budget for material M, in kg;
(d) material purchases budget for material M, in kg.

Task 5
The supplier of material M was warned that available supplies will be below the amount indicated in your budget for Task 4 part (d) above. Explain the implications of this shortage and suggest *four* possible actions which could be taken to overcome the problem. For each suggestion, identify any problems which may arise.

AAT Technicians Stage

14.12* Preparation of flexible budgets
Data
Rivermede Ltd makes a single product called the Fasta. Last year, Steven Jones, the managing director of Rivermede Ltd, attended a course on budgetary control. As a result, he agreed to revise the way budgets were prepared in the company. Rather than imposing targets for managers, he encouraged participation by senior managers in the preparation of budgets.

An initial budget was prepared but Mike Fisher, the sales director, felt that the budgeted sales volume was set too high. He explained that setting too high a budgeted sales volume would mean his sales staff would be de-motivated because they would not be able to achieve that sales volume. Steven Jones agreed to use the revised sales volume suggested by Mike Fisher.

Both the initial and revised budgets are reproduced below complete with the actual results for the year ended 31 May.

Rivermede Ltd – budgeted and actual costs for the year ended 31 May

Fast production and sales (units)	Original budget 24 000 (£)	Revised budget 20 000 (£)	Actual results 22 000 (£)	Variances from revised budget 2000 (£)	(F)
Variable costs					
Material	216 000	180 000	206 800	26 800	(A)
Labour	288 000	240 000	255 200	15 200	(A)
Semi-variable costs					
Heat, light and power	31 000	27 000	33 400	6400	(A)
Fixed costs					
Rent, rates and depreciation	40 000	40 000	38 000	2 000	(F)
	575 000	487 000	533 400	46 400	(A)

Assumptions in the two budgets
1. No change in input prices
2. No change in the quantity of variable inputs per Fasta

As the management accountant at Rivermede Ltd, one of your tasks is to check that invoices have been properly coded. On checking the actual invoices for heat, light and power for the year to 31 May, you find that one invoice for £7520 had been incorrectly coded. The invoice should have been coded to materials.

Task 1
(a) Using the information in the original and revised budgets, identify:
  • the variable cost of material and labour per Fasta;
  • the fixed and unit variable cost within heat, light and power.
(b) Prepare a flexible budget, including variances, for Rivermede Ltd after correcting for the miscoding of the invoice.

Data
On receiving your flexible budget statement, Steven Jones states that the total adverse variance is much less than the £46 400 shown in the original statement. He also draws your attention to the actual sales volume being greater than in the revised budget. He believes these results show that a participative approach to budgeting is better for the company and wants to discuss this belief at the next board meeting. Before doing so, Steven Jones asked for your comments.

Task 2
Write a memo to Steven Jones. Your memo should:

(a) *briefly* explain why the flexible budgeting variances differ from those in the original statement given in the data to task 1;
(b) give *two* reasons why a favourable cost variance may have arisen other than through the introduction of participative budgeting;
(c) give *two* reasons why the actual sales volume compared with the revised budget's sales volume may not be a measure of improved motivation following the introduction of participative budgeting.

AAT Technicians Stage

14.13* Demand forecasts and preparation of flexible budgets
Data
Happy Holidays Ltd sells holidays to Xanadu through newspaper advertisements. Tourist are flown each week of the holiday season to Xanadu, where they take a 10 day touring holiday. In 2000, Happy Holidays began to use the least-squares regression formula to help forecast the demand for its holidays.

You are employed by Happy Holidays as an accounting technician in the financial controller's department. A colleague of yours has recently used the least-squares regression formula on a spreadsheet to estimate the demand for holidays per year. The resulting formula was:

$$y = 640 + 40x$$

where y is the annual demand and x is the year. The data started with the number of holidays sold in 1993 and was identified in the formula as year 1. In each subsequent year the value of x increases by 1 so, for example, 1998 was year 6. To obtain the *weekly* demand the result is divided by 25, the number of weeks Happy Holidays operates in Xanadu.

Task 1
(a) Use the least-squares regression formula developed by your colleague to estimate the weekly demand for holidays in Xanadu for 2001.
(b) In preparation for a budget meeting with the financial controller, draft a *brief* note. Your note should identify *three* weaknesses of the least-squares regression formula in forecasting the weekly demand for holidays in Xanadu.

Data
The budget and actual costs for holidays to Xanadu for the 10 days ended 27 November 2000 is reproduced below.

**Happy Holidays Ltd Cost Statement
10 days ended 27 November 2000**

	Fixed Budget (£)	Actual (£)	Variances (£)
Aircraft seats	18 000	18 600	600 A
Coach hire	5 000	4 700	300 F
Hotel rooms	14 000	14 200	200 A
Meals	4 800	4 600	200 F
Tour guide	1 800	1 700	100 F
Advertising	2 000	1 800	200 F
Total costs	45 600	45 600	0

Key: A = adverse, F = favourable

The financial controller gives you the following additional information:

Cost and volume information
- each holiday lasts 10 days;
- meals and hotel rooms are provided for each of the 10 days;
- the airline charges £450 per return flight per passenger for each holiday but the airline will only sell seats at this reduced price if Happy Holidays purchases seats in blocks of 20;
- the costs of coach hire, the tour guide and advertising are fixed costs;
- the cost of meals was budgeted at £12 per tourist per day;
- the cost of a single room was budgeted at £60 per day;
- the cost of a double room was budgeted at £70 per day;
- 38 tourists travelled on the holiday requiring 17 double rooms and 4 single rooms.

Sales information
- the price of a holiday is £250 more if using a single room.

Task 2
Write a memo to the financial controller. Your memo should:
(a) take account of the cost and volume information to prepare a revised cost statement using flexible budgeting and identifying any variances;
(b) state and justify which of the two cost statements is more useful for management control of costs;
(c) identify *three* factors to be taken into account in deciding whether or not to investigate individual variances.

AAT Technicians Stage

14.14 Responsibility centre performance reports
Data
Jim Smith has recently been appointed as the Head Teacher of Mayfield School in Midshire. The age of the pupils ranges from 11 years to 18 years. For many years, Midshire County Council was responsible for preparing and reporting on the school budget. From June, however, these responsibilities passed to the Head Teacher of Mayfield School.

You have recently accepted a part-time appointment as the accountant to Mayfield School, although your previous accounting experience has been gained in commercial organizations. Jim

Smith is hoping that you will be able to apply that experience to improving the financial reporting procedures at Mayfield School.

The last budget statement prepared by Midshire County Council is reproduced below. It covers the ten months to the end of May and all figures refer to cash *payments* made.

Midshire County Council Mayfield School
Statement of school expenditure against budget: 10 months ending May

	Expenditure to date	Budget to date	Under/ over spend	Total budget for year
Teachers – full-time	1 680 250	1 682 500	2250 Cr	2 019 000
Teachers – part-time	35 238	34 600	638	41 520
Other employee expenses	5 792	15 000	9 208 Cr	18 000
Administrative staff	69 137	68 450	687	82 140
Caretaker and cleaning	49 267	57 205	7 938 Cr	68 646
Resources (books, etc.)	120 673	100 000	20 673	120 000
Repairs and maintenance	458	0	458	0
Lighting and heating	59 720	66 720	7 000 Cr	80 064
Rates	23 826	19 855	3 971	23 826
Fixed assets: furniture and equipment	84 721	100 000	15 279 Cr	120 000
Stationery, postage and phone	1 945	0	1 945	0
Miscellaneous expenses	9 450	6 750	2 700	8 100
Total	2 140 477	2 151 080	10 603 Cr	2 581 296

Task 1
Write a memo to Jim Smith. Your memo should:
(a) identify *four* weaknesses of the existing statement as a management report;
(b) include an improved *outline* statement format showing revised column headings and a more meaningful classification of costs which will help Jim Smith to manage his school effectively (figures are not required);
(c) give *two* advantages of your proposed format over the existing format.

Data
The income of Mayfield School is based on the number of pupils at the school. Jim Smith provides you with the following breakdown of student numbers.

Mayfield School:
Student numbers as at 31 May

School year	Age range	Current number of pupils
1	11–12	300
2	12–13	350
3	13–14	325
4	14–15	360
5	15–16	380
6	16–17	240

7	17–18	220
Total number of students		2175

Jim also provides you with the following information relating to existing pupils:

- pupils move up one school-year at the end of July;
- for those pupils entering year 6, there is an option to leave the school. As a result only 80% of the current school-year 5 pupils go on to enter school-year 6;
- of those currently in school-year 6 only 95% continue into school-year 7;
- pupils currently in school-year 7 leave to go on to higher education or employment;
- the annual income per pupil is £1200 in years 1 to 5 and £1500 in years 6 to 7.

The new year 1 pupils come from the final year at four junior schools. Not all pupils, however, elect to go to Mayfield School. Jim has investigated this matter and derived accurate estimates of the proportion of final year pupils at each of the four junior schools who go on to attend Mayfield School.

The number of pupils in the final year at each of the four junior schools is given below along with Jim's estimate of the proportion likely to choose Mayfield School.

Junior School	Number in final year at 31 May	Proportion choosing Mayfield School
Ranmoor	60	0.9
Hallamshire	120	0.8
Broomhill	140	0.9
Endcliffe	80	0.5

Task 2
(a) Forecast the number of pupils and the income of Mayfield School for the next year from August to July.
(b) Assuming expenditure next year is 5% more than the current annual budgeted expenditure, calculate the budgeted surplus or deficit of Mayfield School for next year.

AAT Technicians Stage

Chapter 15

* Indicates that a suggested solution is to be found in the *Students' Manual*.

15.1*
During a period 25 600 labour hours were worked at a standard cost of £7.50 per hour. The direct labour efficiency variance was £8250 adverse. How many standard hours were produced?

A 1100.   B 24 500.   C 25 600.
D 26 700

CIMA Stage 1—Cost Accounting and Quantitative Methods

15.2
In a period, 11 280 kg of material were used at a total standard cost of £46 248. The material usage variance was £492 adverse.

What was the standard allowed weight of material for the period?

A	11 520 kg
B	11 280 kg
C	11 394 kg
D	11 160 kg

CIMA Stage 1 Specimen Paper

15.3*
S plc has the following fixed overhead cost data for October:

Budgeted cost	£100 000	
Actual cost	£101 400	
Budget output		10 000 standard hours
Actual output		9 000 standard hours
Actual efficiency		96%

The values of over-absorption/under-absorption caused by volume and expenditure effects are:

	Volume	Expenditure
A	£7 650 under	£1 400 under
B	£7 650 under	£7 650 under
C	£10 000 under	£1 400 under
D	£10 000 under	£7 650 under
E	£10 000 under	£11 400 under

CIMA Stage 2

15.4*
The following information relates to R plc for October:

Bought 7800 kg of material R at a total cost of £16 380

Stocks of material R increased by 440 kg

Stocks of material R are valued using standard purchase price

Material price variance was £1170 adverse

The standard price per kg for material R is:

A £1.95
B £2.10
C £2.23
D £2.25
E £2.38

CIMA Stage 2

15.5*

P Limited has the following data relating to its budgeted sales for October:

Budgeted sales	£100 000
Budgeted selling price per unit	£8.00
Budgeted contribution per unit	£4.00
Budgeted profit per unit	£2.50

During October actual sales were 11 000 units for a sales revenue of £99 000.

P Limited uses an absorption costing system.

The sales variances reported for October were:

	Price	Volume
A	£11 000 F	£3 750 A
B	£11 000 F	£6 000 A
C	£11 000 A	£6 000 A
D	£12 500 F	£12 000 A
E	£12 500 A	£12 000 A

CIMA Stage 2

15.6*

The following details have been extracted from a standard cost card of X plc:

Product X	
Direct labour:	4 hours at £5.40 per hour

During October the budgeted production was 5000 units of product X and the actual production was 4650 units of product X. Actual hours worked were 19 100 and the actual direct labour cost amounted to £98 350.

The labour variances reported were:

	Rate	Efficiency
A	£9650 F	£4860 F
B	£9650 F	£2700 A
C	£4790 F	£2575 A
D	£4790 F	£4860 F
E	£4790 F	£2700 A

CIMA Stage 2

15.7*

In a period, 5792 units were made with a standard labour allowance of 6.5 hours per unit at £5 per hour. Actual wages were £6 per hour and there was an adverse efficiency variance of £36 000.

How many labour hours were actually worked?

A 30 448
B 31 648
C 43 648
D 44 848

CIMA Stage 1

15.8*

J Limited uses a standard costing system and has the following data relating to one of its products:

	£ per unit	£ per unit
Selling price		27.00
Variable costs	12.00	
Fixed costs	9.00	
		21.00
Profit per unit		6.00

Budgeted sales for April 2000 were 800 units, but the actual sales were 850 units. The revenue earned from these sales was £22 440.

If a profit reconciliation statement were to be drawn up using marginal costing principles, the sales variances would be:

	Price	Volume
A	£480 (A)	£300 (F)
B	£480 (A)	£750 (F)
C	£510 (A)	£720 (F)
D	£510 (A)	£300 (F)
E	£510 (A)	£750 (F)

CIMA Stage 2—Operational Cost Accounting

15.9*

T plc uses a standard costing system, with its material stock account maintained at standard cost. The following details have been extracted from the standard cost card in respect of direct materials:

8 kgs@£0.40 per kg = £3.20 per unit

Budgeted production in April 2000 was 850 units.
The following details relate to actual materials purchased and issued to production during April 2000 when actual production was 870 units:

Materials purchased   8200 kg consisting £3444
Materials issued   7150 kg
  to production

Which of the following correctly states material price and usage variances to be reported?

	Price	Usage
A	£143 (A)	£76 (A)
B	£143 (A)	£140 (A)
C	£143 (A)	£147 (A)
D	£164 (A)	£76 (A)
E	£164 (A)	£140 (A)

15.10*

Z plc uses a standard costing system and has the following labour cost standard in relation to one of its products:

4 hours of skilled labour @ £12.00 per hour
  = £48.00 per unit

During April 2000, 3350 of these products were made which was 150 units fewer than budgeted. The labour cost incurred was £159 786 and the number of direct labour hours worked was 13 450.
The direct labour variances for the month were:

	Rate	Efficiency
A	£1608 (F)	£600 (A)
B	£1608 (F)	£600 (F)
C	£1614 (F)	£594 (A)
D	£1614 (F)	£600 (A)
E	£1680 (F)	£6600 (F)

CIMA Stage 2—Operational Cost Accounting

15.11 Flexible budgets and computation of labour and material variances

(a) JB plc operates a standard marginal cost accounting system. Information relating to product J, which is made in one of the company departments, is given below:

Product J	Standard marginal product cost Unit (£)
Direct material	
6 kilograms at £4 per kg	24
Direct labour	
1 hour at £7 per hour	7
Variable production overhead[a]	3
	34

[a]Variable production overhead varies with units produced

Budgeted fixed production overhead, per month: £100 000.
Budgeted production for product J: 20 000 units per month.
Actual production and costs for *month 6* were as follows:

Units of J produced	18 500
	(£)
Direct materials purchased and used: 113 500 kg	442 650
Direct labour: 17 800 hours	129 940
Variable production overhead incurred	58 800
Fixed production overhead incurred	104 000
	735 390

You are required to:
(i) prepare a columnar statement showing, by element of cost, the:
  (i) original budget;
  (ii) flexed budget;
  (iii) actual;
  (iv) total variances;   (*9 marks*)
(ii) subdivide the variances for direct material and direct labour shown in your answer to (a) (i)–(iv) above to be more informative for managerial purposes.
            (*4 marks*)
(b) Explain the meaning and use of a 'rolling forecast'.   (*2 marks*)
            (*Total 15 marks*)
            CIMA State 2 Cost Accounting

15.12* Computation of labour and material variances for a hotel

You work as the assistant to the management accountant for a major hotel chain, Stately Hotels plc. The new manager of one of the largest hotels in the chain, the Regent Hotel, is experimenting with the use of standard costing to plan and control the costs of preparing and cleaning the hotel bedrooms.

Two of the costs involved in this activity are cleaning labour and the supply of presentation soap packs.

Cleaning labour:
Part-time staff are employed to clean and prepare the bedrooms for customers. The employees are paid for the number of hours that they work, which fluctuates on a daily basis depending on how many rooms need to be prepared each day.

The employees are paid a standard hourly rate for weekday work and a higher hourly rate at the weekend. The standard cost control system is based on an average of these two rates, at £3.60 per hour.

The standard time allowed for cleaning and preparing a bedroom is fifteen minutes.

Presentation soap packs:
A presentation soap pack is left in each room every night. The packs contain soap, bubble bath, shower gel, hand lotion etc. Most customers use the packs or take them home with them, but many do not. The standard usage of packs used for planning and control purposes is one pack per room night.

The packs are purchased from a number of different suppliers and the standard price is £1.20 per pack. Stocks of packs are valued in the accounts at standard price.

Actual results for May:
During May 8400 rooms were cleaned and prepared. The following data were recorded for cleaning labour and soap packs.

Cleaning labour paid for:

Weekday labour	1850 hours at £3 per hour
Weekend labour	700 hours at £4.50 per hour
	2550

Presentation soap packs purchased and used:

6530 packs at £1.20 each	
920 packs at £1.30 each	
1130 packs at £1.40 each	
8580	

Task
(a) Using the data above, calculate the following cost variances for May:
  (i) soap pack price;
  (ii) soap pack usage;
  (iii) cleaning labour rate;
  (iv) cleaning labour utilization or efficiency.
(b) Suggest one possible cause for each of the variances which you have calculated, and outline any management action which may be necessary.

AAT Technicians Stage

15.13* Computation of labour and material variances and reconciliation statements

Malton Ltd operates a standard marginal costing system. As the recently appointed management accountant to Malton's Eastern division, you have responsibility for the preparation of that division's monthly cost reports. The standard cost report uses variances to reconcile the actual marginal cost of production to its standard cost.

The Eastern division is managed by Richard Hill. The division only makes one product, the Beta. Budgeted Beta production for May was 8000 units, although actual production was 9500 units.

In order to prepare the standard cost report for May, you have asked a member of your staff to obtain standard and actual cost details for the month of May. This information is reproduced below:

	Unit standard cost			Actual details for May		
	Quantity	Unit price	Cost per Beta (£)		Quantity	Total cost (£)
Material	8 litres	£20	160	Material	78 000 litres	1 599 000
Labour	4 hours	£6	24	Labour	39 000 hours	249 600
			184			1 848 600

Task 1
(a) Calculate the following:
  (i) the material price variance;
  (ii) the material usage variance;
  (iii) the labour rate variance;
  (iv) the labour efficiency variance (sometimes called the utilization variance);
(b) Prepare a standard costing statement reconciling the actual marginal cost of production with the standard marginal cost of production.

After Richard Hill has received your standard costing statement, you visit him to discuss the variances and their implications. Richard, however, raises a number of queries with you. He makes the following points:

- An index measuring material prices stood at 247.2 for May but at 240.0 when the standard for the material price was set.
- The Eastern division is budgeted to run at its normal capacity of 8000 units of production per month, but during May it had to manufacture an additional 1500 Betas to meet a special order agreed at short notice by Melton's sales director.
- Because of the short notice, the normal supplier of the raw material was unable to meet the extra demand and so additional materials had to be acquired from another supplier at a price per litre of £22.
- This extra material was not up to the normal specification, resulting in 20% of the special purchase being scrapped *prior* to being issued to production.
- The work force could only produce the special order on time by working overtime on the 1500 Betas at a 50% premium.

Task 2
(a) Calculate the amounts within the material price variance, the material usage variance and the labour rate variance which arise from producing the special order.
(b) (i) Estimate the revised standard price for materials based on the change in the material price index.
(ii) For the 8000 units of normal production, use your answer in (b) (i) to estimate how much of the price variance calculated in Task 1 is caused by the general change in prices.
(c) Using your answers to parts (a) and (b) of this task, prepare a revised standard costing statement. The revised statement should subdivide the variances prepared in Task 1 into those elements controllable by Richard Hill and those elements caused by factors outside his divisional control.
(d) Write a *brief* note to Richard Hill justifying your treatment of the elements you believe are outside his control and suggesting what action should be taken by the company.

AAT Technicians Stage

15.14* Reconciliation of actual and budgeted profit (including overhead variances)
A local restaurant has been examining the profitability of its set menu. At the beginning of the year the selling price was based on the following predicted costs:

		(£)
Starter	*Soup of the day*	
	100 grams of mushrooms @ £3.00 per kg	0.30
	Cream and other ingredients	0.20
Main course	*Roast beef*	
	Beef 0.10 kgs @ £15.00 per kg	1.50
	Potatoes 0.2 kgs @ £0.25 per kg	0.05
	Vegetables 0.3 kgs @ £0.90 per kg	0.27
	Other ingredients and accompaniments	0.23
Dessert	*Fresh tropical fruit salad*	
	Fresh fruit 0.15 kgs @ £3.00 per kg	0.45

The selling price was set at £7.50, which produced an overall gross profit of 60%.

During October the number of set menus sold was 860 instead of the 750 budgeted: this increase was achieved by reducing the selling price to £7.00. During the same period an analysis of the direct costs incurred showed:

	(£)
90 kgs of mushrooms	300
Cream and other ingredients	160
70 kgs of beef	1148
180 kgs of potatoes	40
270 kgs of vegetables	250
Other ingredients and accompaniments	200
140 kgs of fresh fruit	450

There was no stock of ingredients at the beginning or end of the month.

Required:
(a) Calculate the budgeted profit for the month of October. (*2 marks*)
(b) Calculate the actual profit for the month of October. (*3 marks*)
(c) Prepare a statement which reconciles your answers to (a) and (b) above, showing the variances in as much detail as possible. (*14 marks*)

(d) Prepare a report, addressed to the restaurant manager, which identifies the two most significant variances, and comments on their possible causes. *(6 marks)*
(Total 25 marks)
CIMA State 2 Operational Cost Accounting

15.15 Reconciliation of standard and actual cost for a variable costing system

Data
You are employed as the assistant management accountant in the group accountant's office of Hampstead plc. Hampstead recently acquired Finchley Ltd, a small company making a specialist product called the Alpha. Standard marginal costing is used by all the companies within the group and, from 1 August, Finchley Ltd will also be required to use standard marginal costing in its management reports. Part of your job is to manage the implementation of standard marginal costing at Finchley Ltd.

John Wade, the managing director of Finchley, is not clear how the change will help him as a manager. He has always found Finchley's existing absorption costing system sufficient. By way of example, he shows you a summary of its management accounts for the three months to 31 May. These are reproduced below.

Statement of budgeted and actual cost of Alpha Production–3 months ended 31 May

Alpha production (units)	Actual		Budget		Variance
	10 000		12 000		
	Inputs	(£)	Inputs	(£)	(£)
Materials	32 000 metres	377 600	36 000 metres	432 000	54 400
Labour	70 000 hours	422 800	72 000 hours	450 000	27 200
Fixed overhead absorbed		330 000		396 000	66 000
Fixed overhead unabsorbed		75 000		0	(75 000)
		1 205 400		1 278 000	72 600

John Wade is not convinced that standard marginal costing will help him to manage Finchley. 'My current system tells me all I need to know,' he said. 'As you can see, we are £72 600 below budget which is really excellent given that we lost production as a result of a serious machine breakdown.'

To help John Wade understand the benefits of standard marginal costing, you agree to prepare a statement for the three months ended 31 May reconciling the standard cost of production to the actual cost of production.

Task 1
(a) Use the budget data to determine:
  (i) the standard marginal cost per Alpha; and
  (ii) the standard cost of actual Alpha production for the three months to 31 May.
(b) Calculate the following variances:
  (i) material price variance;
  (ii) material usage variance;
  (iii) labour rate variance;
  (iv) labour efficiency variance;
  (v) fixed overhead expenditure variance.
(c) Write a *short* memo to John Wade. Your memo should:
  (i) include a statement reconciling the actual cost of production to the standard cost of production;
  (ii) give *two* reasons why your variances might differ from those in his original management accounting statement despite using the same basic data;
  (iii) *briefly* discuss *one* further reason why your reconciliation statement provides improved management information.

Data
On receiving your memo, John Wade informs you that:
• the machine breakdown resulted in the workforce having to be paid for 12 000 hours even though no production took place;
• an index of material prices stood at 466.70 when the budget was prepared but at 420.03 when the material was purchased.

Task 2
Using this new information, prepare a revised statement reconciling the standard cost of production to the actual cost of production. Your statement should subdivide:

• both the labour variances into those parts arising from the machine breakdown and those parts arising from normal production; and
• the material price variance into that part due to the change in the index and that part arising for other reasons.

Data
Barnet Ltd is another small company owned by Hampstead plc. Barnet operates a job costing system making a specialist, expensive piece of hospital equipment.

Existing system

Currently, employees are assigned to individual jobs and materials are requisitioned from stores as needed. The standard and actual costs of labour and material are recorded for each job. These job costs are totalled to produce the marginal cost of production. Fixed production costs – including the cost of storekeeping and inspection of deliveries and finished equipment – are then added to determine the standard and actual cost of production. Any costs of remedial work are included in the materials and labour for each job.

Proposed system

Carol Johnson, the chief executive of Barnet, has recently been to a seminar on modern manufacturing techniques. As a result, she is considering introducing Just-in-Time stock deliveries and Total Quality Management. Barnet would offer suppliers a long-term contract at a fixed price but suppliers would have to guarantee the quality of their materials.

In addition, she proposes that the workforce is organized as a single team with flexible work practices. This would mean employees helping each other as necessary, with no employee being allocated a particular job. If a job was delayed, the workforce would work overtime without payment in order for the job to be completed on time. In exchange, employees would be guaranteed a fixed weekly wage and time off when production was slack to make up for any overtime incurred.

Cost of quality

Carol has asked to meet you to discuss the implications of her proposals on the existing accounting system. She is particularly concerned to monitor the *cost of quality*. This is defined as the total of all costs incurred in preventing defects plus those costs involved in remedying defects once they have occurred. It is a single figure measuring all the explicit costs of quality – that is, those costs collected within the accounting system.

Task 3

In preparation for the meeting, produce *brief* notes. Your notes should:

(a) identify *four* general headings (or classifications) which make up the *cost of quality*;
(b) give *one* example of a type of cost likely to be found within each category;
(c) assuming Carol Johnson's proposals are accepted, state, with reasons, whether or not:

(i) a standard marginal costing system would still be of help to the managers;
(ii) it would still be meaningful to collect costs by each individual job;

(d) identify *one* cost saving in Carol Johnson's proposals which would not be recorded in the existing costing system.

AAT Technicians Stage

15.16* Variance analysis and reconciliation of budgeted and actual profit

The Perseus Co. Ltd, a medium-sized company, produces a single produce in its one overseas factory. For control purposes, a standard costing system was recently introduced and is now in operation.

The standards set for the month of May were as follows:

Production and sales	16 000 units
Selling price (per unit)	£140
Materials	
Material 007	6 kilos per unit at £12.25 per kilo
Material XL90	3 kilos per unit at £3.20 per kilo
Labour	4.5 hours per unit at £8.40 per hour

Overheads (all fixed) at £86 400 per month are not absorbed into the product costs.

The actual data for the month of May, are as follows:

Produced 15 400 units, which were sold at £138.25 each.

Materials

Used 98 560 kilos of material 007 at a total cost of £1 256 640

Used 42 350 kilos of material XL90 at a total cost of £132 979

Labour

Paid an actual rate of £8.65 per hour to the labour force. The total amount paid out amounted to £612 766

Overheads (all fixed) £96 840

Required:

(a) Prepare a standard costing profit statement, and a profit statement based on actual figures for the month of May. (*6 marks*)
(b) Prepare a statement of the variances which reconcile the actual with the standard profit or loss figure. (*9 marks*)

(c) Explain briefly the possible reasons for inter-relationships between material variances and labour variances. (*5 marks*)
(*Total 20 marks*)
ACCA Paper 8 Management Finance

15.17 Calculation of labour, material and overhead variances and reconciliation of budgeted and actual profit

You are the management accountant of T plc. The following computer printout shows details relating to April:

	Actual	Budget
Sales volume	4900 units	5000 units
Selling price per unit	£11.00	£10.00
Production volume	5400 units	5000 units
Direct materials		
kgs	10 600	10 000
price per kg	£0.60	£0.50
Direct labour		
hours per unit	0.55	0.50
rate per hour	£3.80	£4.00
Fixed overhead:		
Production	£10 300	£10 000
Administration	£3 100	£3 000

T plc uses a standard absorption costing system.

There was no opening or closing work-in-progress.

Required:
(a) Prepare a statement which reconciles the budgeted profit with the actual profit for April, showing individual variances in as much detail as the above data permit
(*20 marks*)
(b) Explain briefly the possible causes of
  (i) the material usage variance;
  (ii) the labour rate variance; and
  (iii) the sales volume profit variance.
(*6 marks*)
(c) Explain the meaning and relevance of inter-dependence of variances when reporting to managers. (*4 marks*)
(*Total 30 marks*)
CIMA Stage 2 Operational Cost Accounting

15.18 Computation of fixed overhead variances

A manufacturing company has provided you with the following data, which relate to component RYX for the period which has just ended:

	Budget	Actual
Number of labour hours	8 400	7 980
Production units	1 200	1 100
Overhead cost (all fixed)	£22 260	£25 536

Overheads are absorbed at a rate per standard labour hour.
Required:
(a) (i) Calculate the fixed production overhead cost variance and the following subsidiary variances:
     expenditure
     efficiency
     capacity
  (ii) Provide a summary statement of these four variances. (*7 marks*)
(b) Briefly discuss the possible reasons why adverse fixed production overhead expenditure, efficiency and capacity variances occur. (*10 marks*)
(c) Briefly discuss two examples of interrelationships between the fixed production overhead efficiency variances and the material and labour variances. (*3 marks*)
(*Total 20 marks*)
ACCA Paper 8 Managerial Finance

15.19 Labour and overhead variances and ex-post wage rate analysis

Data
The Eastern Division of Countryside Communications plc assembles a single product, the Beta. The Eastern Division has a fixed price contract with the supplier of the materials used in the Beta. The contract also specifies that the materials should be free of any faults. Because of these clauses in the contract, the Eastern Division has no material variances when reporting any differences between standard and actual production.

You have recently accepted the position of assistant management accountant in the Eastern Division. One of your tasks is to report variances in production costs on a four-weekly basis. Fixed overheads are absorbed on the basis of standard labour hours. A colleague provides you with the following data:

Standard costs and budgeted production – four weeks ended 27 November

	Quantity	Unit price	Standard cost per Beta
Material	30 metres	£12.00	£360.00
Labour	10 hours	£5.25	£52.50
Fixed overhead	10 hours	£15.75	£157.50
Standard cost per Beta			£570.00
Budgeted production	1200 Betas	£570.00	£684 000

Actual production – four weeks ended 27 November

	Quantity	Total cost
Actual cost of material	31 200 metres	£374 400
Actual cost of labour	11 440 hours	£59 488
Actual fixed cost overheads		£207 000
Actual cost of actual production		£640 888
Actual production	1040 Betas	

Task 1

(a) Calculate the following variances:
   (i) the labour rate variance;
   (ii) the labour efficiency variance (sometimes called the utilization variance);
   (iii) the fixed overhead expenditure variance (sometimes known as the price variance);
   (iv) the fixed overhead volume variance;
   (v) the fixed overhead capacity variance;
   (vi) the fixed overhead efficiency variance (sometimes known as the usage variance).
(b) Prepare a statement reconciling the standard cost of actual production with the actual cost of actual production.

Data

When the Eastern Division's budget for the four weeks ended 27 November was originally prepared, a national index of labour rates stood at 102.00. In preparing the budget, Eastern Division had allowed for a 5% increase in labour rates. For the actual four weeks ended 27 November, the index stood at 104.04.

Because of this, Ann Green, Eastern Division's production director, is having difficulty understanding the meaning of the labour rate variance calculated in task 1.

Task 2

Write a memo to Ann Green. Your memo should:
(a) identify the original labour rate before allowing for the 5% increase;
(b) calculate the revised standard hourly rate using the index of 104.04;
(c) subdivide the labour rate variance calculated in task 1(a) into that part due to the change in the index and that part arising for other reasons;
(d) *briefly* interpret the possible meaning of these two subdivisions of the labour rate variance;
(e) give *two* reasons why the index of labour rates might not be valid in explaining part of the labour rate variance;
(f) *briefly* explain the meaning of the following variances calculated in task 1 and for *each* variance suggest *one* reason why it may have occurred;
   (i) the fixed overhead expenditure (or price) variance;
   (ii) the fixed overhead capacity variance;
   (iii) the fixed overhead efficiency (or usage) variance.

AAT Technicians Stage

15.20 Discussion and calculation of overhead variances

(a) Explain fully how the variances between actual and standard production overhead costs may be analysed, where overhead absorption is based upon separate direct labour hour rates for variable and fixed overheads. (*12 marks*)
(b) Calculate fixed production overhead variances in as much detail as possible, in the following situation:

	Budget	Actual
Fixed overhead (£)	246 000	259 000
Direct labour (hours)	123 000	141 000
Output (units)	615 000	(see below)

The company operates a process costing system. At the beginning of the period 42 000 half completed units were in stock. During the period 680 000 units were completed and 50 000 half completed units remained in stock at the end of the period.

(13 marks)
(Total 25 marks)
ACCA Level 1 Costing

15.21* Calculation of labour, material and overhead variances

The summary production budget of a factory with a single product for a four week period is as follows:

Production quantity   240 000 units
Production costs:
   Material: 336 000 kg at £4.10 per kg
   Direct labour: 216 000 hours at
                £4.50 per hour
   Variable overheads: £475 200
   Fixed overheads: £1 521 600

Variable overheads are absorbed at a predetermined direct labour hour rate. Fixed overheads are absorbed at a predetermined rate per unit of output.

During the four week period the actual production was 220 000 units which incurred the following costs:

Material: 313 060 kg costing £1 245 980
Direct labour: 194 920 hours costing £886 886
Variable overheads: £433 700
Fixed overheads: £1 501 240

Required:
(a) Calculate the cost variances for the period.

(12 marks)
(b) Give reasons in each case why the direct labour efficiency, variable overhead efficiency and fixed overhead volume variances may have arisen.

(8 marks)
(Total 20 marks)
ACCA Level 1
Cost and Management Accounting 1

15.22* Computation of variable overhead variances

The following details have been extracted from the standard cost card for product X:

	(£/unit)
Variable overhead	
4 machine hours at £8.00/hour	32.00
2 labour hours at £4.00/hour	8.00
Fixed overhead	20.00

During October 5450 units of the product were made compared to a budgeted production target of 5500 units. The actual overhead costs incurred were:

Machine-related variable overhead	£176 000
Labour-related variable overhead	£42 000
Fixed overhead	£109 000

The actual number of machine hours was 22 000 and the actual number of labour hours was 10 800.

Required:
(a) Calculate the overhead cost variances in as much detail as possible from the data provided. *(12 marks)*
(b) Explain the meaning of, and give possible causes for, the variable overhead variances which you have calculated. *(8 marks)*
(c) Explain the benefits of using multiple activity bases for variable overhead absorption.

(5 marks)
(Total 25 marks)
CIMA Stage 2 Operational Cost Accounting

15.23* Variance analysis and reconciliation of standard with actual cost

SK Limited makes and sells a single product 'Jay' for which the standard cost is as follows:

		£ per unit
Direct materials	4 kilograms at £12.00 per kg	48.00
Direct labour	5 hours at £7.00 per hour	35.00
Variable production overhead	5 hours at £2.00 per hour	10.00
Fixed production overhead	5 hours at £10.00 per hour	50.00
		143.00

The variable production overhead is deemed to vary with the hours worked.

Overhead is absorbed into production on the basis of standard hours of production and the normal volume of production for the period just ended was 20 000 units (100 000 standard hours of production).

For the period under consideration, the actual results were:

Production of 'Jay'	**18 000 units** **(£)**
Direct material used – 76 000 kgs at a cost of	836 000
Direct labour cost incurred – for 84 000 hours worked	604 800
Variable production overhead incurred	172 000
Fixed production overhead incurred	1 030 000

You are required

(a) to calculate and show, by element of cost, the standard cost for the output for the period;
(2 marks)

(b) to calculate and list the relevant variances in a way which reconciles the standard cost with the actual cost (*Note*: Fixed production overhead sub-variances of capacity and volume efficiency (productivity) are *not* required).
(9 marks)

(c) to comment briefly on the usefulness to management of statements such as that given in your answer to (b) above. *(4 marks)*
(Total 15 marks)
CIMA Stage 2 Cost Accounting

15.24* Material price and usage variances and calculation of material price and usage working backwards from variances

AB Ltd manufactures a range of products. One of the products, Product M, requires the use of materials X and Y. Standard material costs for the manufacture of an item of product M in period 1 included:

Material X: 9 kilos at 1.20 per kilo

Total purchases of material X in period 1, for use in all products, were 142 000 kilos, costing £171 820. 16 270 kilos were used in the period in the manufacture of 1790 units of product M.

In period 2 the standard price of material X was increased by 6%, whilst the standard usage of the material in product M was left unchanged. 147 400 kilos of material X were purchased in period 2 at a

favourable price variance of £1031.80. A favourable usage variance of 0.5% of standard occurred on material X in the manufacture of product M in the period.

Required:
(a) Calculate:
(i) the total price variance on purchases of material X in period 1; *(2 marks)*
(ii) the material X usage variance arising from the manufacture of product M in period 1; *(3 marks)*
(iii) the actual cost inflation of material X from period 1 to period 2 (calculate as a percentage increase to one decimal place); *(5 marks)*
(iv) the percentage change in actual usage of material X per unit of product M from period 1 to period 2 (calculate to one decimal place). *(5 marks)*

(b) Describe, and contrast, the different types of standards that may be set for raw material usage and labour efficiency. *(10 marks)*
(Total 25 marks)
ACCA Cost and Management Accounting 1

15.25 Calculation of actual input data working back from variances

The following profit reconciliation statement has been prepared by the management accountant of ABC Limited for March:

			(£)
Budgeted profit			30 000
Sales volume profit variance			5 250A
Selling price variance			6 375F
			31 125
Cost variances:	A	F	
	(£)	(£)	
Material:			
price	1 985		
usage		400	
Labour:			
rate		9 800	
efficiency	4 000		
Variable overhead:			
expenditure		1 000	
efficiency	1 500		

Fixed overhead:

expenditure		500
volume	24 500	
	31 985	11 700
		20 285A
Actual profit		10 840

The standard cost card for the company's only product is as follows:

		(£)
Materials	5 litres at £0.20	1.00
Labour	4 hours at £4.00	16.00
Variable overhead	4 hours at £1.50	6.00
Fixed overhead	4 hours at £3.50	14.00
		37.00
Standard profit		3.00
Standard selling price		40.00

The following information is also available:
1. There was no change in the level of finished goods stock during the month.
2. Budgeted production and sales volumes for March were equal.
3. Stocks of materials, which are valued at standard price, decreased by 800 litres during the month.
4. The actual labour rate was £0.28 lower than the standard hourly rate.

Required:
(a) Calculate the following:
   (i) the actual production/sales volume;
   (4 marks)
   (ii) the actual number of hours worked;
   (4 marks)
   (iii) the actual quantity of materials purchased;
   (4 marks)
   (iv) the actual variable overhead cost incurred;
   (2 marks)
   (v) the actual fixed overhead cost incurred.
   (2 marks)
(b) ABC Limited uses a standard costing system whereas other organizations use a system of budgetary control. Explain the reasons why a system of budgetary control is often preferred to the use of standard costing in non-manufacturing environments. *(9 marks)*
(Total 25 marks)
CIMA Stage 2 — Operational Cost Accounting

15.26* Calculation of actual quantities working backwards from variances

The following profit reconciliation statement summarizes the performance of one of SEW's products for March.

	(£)
Budgeted profit	4250
Sales volume variance	850A
Standard profit on actual sales	3400
Selling price variance	4000A
	(600)

Cost variances:	Adverse (£)	Favourable (£)	
Direct material price		1000	
Direct material usage	150		
Direct labour rate	200		
Direct labour efficiency	150		
Variable overhead expenditure	600		
Variable overhead efficiency	75		
Fixed overhead efficiency		2500	
Fixed overhead volume		150	
Actual profit	1175	3650	2475F
			1875

The budget for the same period contained the following data:

Sales volume		1500 units
Sales revenue	£20 000	
Production volume		1500 units
Direct materials purchased		750 kg
Direct materials used		750 kg
Direct material cost	£4 500	
Direct labour hours		1125
Direct labour cost	£4 500	
Variable overhead cost	£2 250	
Fixed overhead cost	£4 500	

Additional information:
- Stocks of raw materials and finished goods are valued at standard cost.
- During the month the actual number of units produced was 1550.

- The actual sales revenue was £12 000.
- The direct materials purchased were 1000 kg.

Required:

(a) Calculate

(i) the actual sales volume;

(ii) the actual quantity of materials used;

(iii) the actual direct material cost;

(iv) the actual direct labour hours;

(v) the actual direct labour cost;

(vi) the actual variable overhead cost;

(vii) the actual fixed overhead cost.

(19 marks)

(b) Explain the possible causes of the direct materials usage variance, direct labour rate variance and sales volume variance.

(6 marks)

(Total 25 marks)

CIMA Operational Cost Accounting Stage 2

15.27* Calculation of labour variances and actual material inputs working backwards from variances

A company manufactures two components in one of its factories. Material A is one of several materials used in the manufacture of both components.

The standard direct labour hours per unit of production and budgeted production quantities for a 13 week period were:

	Standard direct labour hours	Budgeted production quantities
Component X	0.40 hours	36 000 units
Component Y	0.56 hours	22 000 units

The standard wage rate for all direct workers was £5.00 per hour. Throughout the 13-week period 53 direct workers were employed, working a standard 40-hour week.

The following actual information for the 13-week period is available:

Production:
  Component X, 35 000 units
  Component Y, 25 000 units
Direct wages paid, £138 500
Material A purchases, 47 000 kilos costing £85 110
Material A price variance, £430 F

Material A usage (component X), 33 426 kilos
Material A usage variance (component X), £320.32 A

Required:

(a) Calculate the direct labour variances for the period; *(5 marks)*

(b) Calculate the standard purchase price for material A for the period and the standard usage of material A per unit of production of component X. *(8 marks)*

(c) Describe the steps, and information, required to establish the material purchase quantity budget for material A for a period. *(7 marks)*

(Total 20 marks)

ACCA Cost and Management Accounting 1

15.28* Comparison of absorption and marginal costing variances

You have been provided with the following data for S plc for September:

Accounting method: Variances:	Absorption (£)	Marginal (£)
Selling price	1900 (A)	1900 (A)
Sales volume	4500 (A)	7500 (A)
Fixed overhead expenditure	2500 (F)	2500 (F)
Fixed overhead volume	1800 (A)	n/a

During September production and sales volumes were as follows:

	Sales	Production
Budget	10 000	10 000
Actual	9 500	9 700

Required:

(a) Calculate:

(i) the standard contribution per unit;

(ii) the standard profit per unit;

(iii) the actual fixed overhead cost total.

(9 marks)

(b) Using the information presented above, explain why different variances are calculated depending upon the choice of marginal or absorption costing. *(8 marks)*

(c) Explain the meaning of the fixed overhead volume variance and its usefulness to management. *(5 marks)*

(d) Fixed overhead absorption rates are often calculated using a single measure of activity. It is suggested that fixed overhead costs should be attributed to cost units using multiple measures of activity (activity-based costing).

Explain 'activity-based costing' and how it may provide useful information to managers.

(Your answer should refer to both the setting of cost driver rates and subsequent overhead cost control.) (*8 marks*)

(*Total 30 marks*)

CIMA Operational Cost Accounting Stage 2

15.29 Calculation of production ratios

NAB Limited has produced the following figures relating to production for the week ended 21 May:

	Production (in units)	
	Budgeted	**Actual**
Product A	400	400
Product B	400	300
Product C	100	140

Standard production times were:

	Standard hours per unit
Product A	5.0
Product B	2.5
Product C	1.0

During the week 2800 hours were worked on production.

You are required:

(a) (i) to calculate the production volume ratio and the efficiency ratio for the week ended 21 May; (*4 marks*)

(ii) to explain the significance of the two ratios you have calculated and to state which variances may be related to each of the ratios; (*5 marks*)

(b) to explain the three measures of capacity referred to in the following statement:

During the recent recession, increased attention was paid to 'practical capacity' and 'budgeted capacity' because few manufacturing companies could anticipate working again at 'full capacity'.

(*6 marks*)

(*Total 15 marks*)

CIMA Stage 2 Cost Accounting

15.30* Accounting entries for a standard costing system

A company uses Material Z in several of its manufacturing processes. On 1 November, 9000 kilos of the material were in stock. These materials cost £9630 when purchased. Receipts and issues of Material Z during November were:

Receipts
4 November, 10 000 kilos costing £10 530
23 November, 8000 kilos costing £8480

Issues
2 November, 2000 kilos to Process 1
7 November, 4500 kilos to Process 2
20 November, 4000 kilos to Process 1
27 November, 6000 kilos to Process 3

The company operates a standard costing system. The standard cost of Material Z during November was £1.04 per kilo.

Process 1 is exclusively concerned with the production of Product X. Production information for November is as follows:

Opening work-in-process, 6000 units
– complete as to materials; 50% complete for direct labour and overheads.
Completed units, 9970.
Closing work-in-process, 8000 units
– complete as to materials; 75% complete for direct labour and overheads.

The standard cost per unit of Product X comprises the following:
Material Z, 0.5 kilos at £1.04 per kilo
Direct labour, 0.1 hours at £4.80 per hour
Overhead, absorbed on direct labour hours at £5.00 per hour.

Costs (other than Material Z) incurred in Process 1 during November were:
Direct labour, 1340 hours at £4.80 per hour
Overheads, £6680.

Required:

(a) Prepare the stock account and material price variance account for Material Z for the month of November on the assumption that:

(i) The material price variance is identified on purchase of material.

(ii) The material price variance is identified at the time of issue of material to production (assume that the weighted average pricing method is used).

(*9 marks*)

(b) State which of the above two methods, (a) (i) or (a) (ii), you would prefer. State briefly the reasons for your preference. (*4 marks*)

(c) Prepare the account for Process 1 for the month of November. (Assume that Material Z is charged to the process at standard price.) (*12 marks*) (*Total 25 marks*) *ACCA Level 1 Costing*

15.31* Calculation of labour, material and overhead variances plus appropriate accounting entries

JC Limited produces and sells one product only, Product J, the standard cost for which is as follows for one unit.

	(£)
Direct material X – 10 kilograms at £20	200
Direct material Y – 5 litres at £6	30
Direct wages – 5 hours at £6	30
Fixed production overhead	50
Total standard cost	310
Standard gross profit	90
Standard selling price	400

The fixed production overhead is based on an expected annual output of 10 800 units produced at an even flow throughout the year; assume each calendar month is equal. Fixed production overhead is absorbed on direct labour hours.

During April, the first month of the financial year, the following were the actual results for an actual production of 800 units.

		(£)
Sales on credit:		320 000
800 units at £400		
Direct materials:		
X 7800 kilograms	159 900	
Y 4300 litres	23 650	
Direct wages: 4200 hours	24 150	
Fixed production overhead	47 000	
		254 700
Gross profit		65 300

The material price variance is extracted at the time of receipt and the raw materials stores control is maintained at standard prices. The purchases, bought on credit, during the month of April were:

X 9000 kilograms at £20.50 per kg from K Limited

Y 5000 litres at £5.50 per litre from C p.l.c.

Assume no opening stocks.

Wages owing for March brought forward were £6000.

Wages paid during April (net) £20 150.

Deductions from wages owing to the Inland Revenue for PAYE and NI were £5000 and the wages accrued for April were £5000.

The fixed production overhead of £47 000 was made up of expense creditors of £33 000, none of which was paid in April, and depreciation of £14 000.

The company operates an integrated accounting system.

You are required to

(a) (i) calculate price and usage variances for each material,

  (ii) calculate labour rate and efficiency variances,

  (iii) calculate fixed production overhead expenditure, efficiency and volume variances; (*9 marks*)

(b) show all the accounting entries in T accounts for the month of April – the work-in-progress account should be maintained at standard cost and each balance on the separate variance accounts is to be transferred to a Profit and Loss Account which you are also required to show; (*18 marks*)

(c) explain the reason for the difference between the actual gross profit given in the question and the profit shown in your profit and loss account. (*3 marks*) (*Total 30 marks*) *CIMA Stage 2 Cost Accounting*

15.32 Calculation of variances and accounting entries for an interlocking standard costing system

B Ltd manufactures a single product in one of its factories. Information relating to the month just ended is as follows:

(i) Standard cost per hundred units:

	(£)
Raw materials: 15 kilos at £7 per kilo	105
Direct labour: 10 hours at £6 per hour	60
Variable production overhead:	
10 hours at £5 per hour	50
	215

(ii) 226 000 units of the product were completed and transferred to finished goods stock.

(iii) 34 900 kilos of raw material were purchased in the month at a cost of £245 900.

(iv) Direct wages were £138 545 representing 22 900 hours' work.

(v) Variable production overheads of £113 800 were incurred.

(vi) Fixed production overheads of £196 800 were incurred.

(vii) Stocks at the beginning and end of the month were:

	Opening Stock	Closing Stock
Raw materials	16 200 kilos	16 800 kilos
Work in progress	—	4000 units, (complete as to raw materials but only 50% complete as to direct labour and overhead)
Finished goods	278 000 units	286 000 units

Raw materials, work in progress, and finished goods stocks are maintained at standard cost. You should assume that no stock discrepancies or losses occurred during the month just ended.

Required:
(a) Prepare the cost ledger accounts relating to the above information in B Ltd's interlocking accounting system. Marginal costing principles are employed in the cost ledger.
(17 marks)
(b) Explain and contrast the different types of standards that may be set as a benchmark for performance measurement. *(8 marks)*
(Total 25 marks)
ACCA Cost and Management Accounting 1

15.33 Accounting entries for a standard costing system
Fischer Ltd manufactures a range of chess sets, and operates a standard costing system. Information relating to the 'Spassky' design for the month of March is as follows:

(1) Standard costs per 100 sets

	(£)
Raw materials:	
Plaster of Paris, 20 kg at £8 per kg	160
Paint, 1/2 litre at £30 per litre	15
Direct wages, $2\frac{1}{2}$ hours at £10 per hour	25
Fixed production overheads,	
400% of direct wages	100
	300

(2) Standard selling price per set £3.80
(3) Raw materials, work in progress and finished goods stock records are maintained at standard cost.
(4) Stock levels at the beginning and end of March were as follows:

	1 March	31 March
Plaster of Paris	2800 kg	2780 kg
Paint	140 litres	170 litres
Finished sets	900 sets	1100 sets

There was no work in progress at either date.
(5) Budgeted production and sales during the month were 30 000 sets. Actual sales, all made at standard selling price, and actual production were 28 400 and 28 600 sets respectively.
(6) Raw materials purchased during the month were 5400 kg of plaster of Paris at a cost of £43 200 and 173 litres of paint at a cost of £5800.
(7) Direct wages were 730 hours at an average rate of £11 per hour.
(8) Fixed production overheads amounted to £34 120.

Required:
Prepare for the month of March:
(a) the cost ledger accounts for raw materials, work in progress and finished goods;
(10 marks)
(b) (i) budget trading statement,
(ii) standard cost trading statement,
(iii) financial trading statement, and
(iv) a reconciliation between these statements identifying all relevant variances.
(14 marks)
(Total 24 marks)
ICAEW Accounting Techniques

Bibliography

Ackoff, R.L. (1981) *Creating the Corporate Future*, Wiley.

Ahmed, M.N. and Scapens, R.W. (1991) Cost allocation theory and practice: the continuing debate, in *Issues in Management Accounting* (eds D. Ashton, T. Hopper and R.W. Scapens), Prentice-Hall, pp. 39–60.

American Accounting Association (1957) *Accounting and Reporting Standards for Corporate Financial Statements and Preceding Statements and Supplements*, p. 4.

American Accounting Association (1966) *A Statement of Basic Accounting Theory*, American Accounting Association.

Armitage, H.M. and Nicholson, R. (1993) Activity based costing: a survey of Canadian practice, Issue Paper No. 3, Society of Management Accountants of Canada.

Ask, U. and Ax, C. (1992) Trends in the Development of Product Costing Practices and Techniques – A Survey of Swedish Manufacturing Industry, Paper presented at the 15th Annual Congress of the European Accounting Association, Madrid.

Ask, U., Ax, C. and Jonsson, S. (1996) Cost management in Sweden: from modern to post-modern, in *Management Accounting: European Perspectives* (ed. A. Bhimani), Oxford, Oxford University Press, pp. 199–217.

Ballas, A. and Venieris, G. (1996) A survey of management accounting practices in Greek firms, in *Management Accounting: European Perspectives* (ed. A. Bhimani), Oxford, Oxford University Press, pp. 123–39.

Banerjee, J. and Kane, W. (1996) Report on CIMA/JBA survey, *Management Accounting*, October, **30**, 37.

Barbato, M.B., Collini, P. and Quagli, (1996) Management accounting in Italy, in *Management Accounting: European Perspectives* (ed. A. Bhimani), Oxford, Oxford University Press, pp. 140–163.

Baxter, W.T. and Oxenfeldt, A.R. (1961) Costing and pricing: the cost accountant versus the economist, *Business Horizons*, Winter, 77–90; also in *Studies in Cost Analysis*, 2nd edn (ed. D. Solomons) Sweet and Maxwell (1968), pp. 293–312.

Berliner, C. and Brimson, J.A. (1988) *Cost Management for Today's Advanced Manufacturing*, Harvard Business School Press.

Bjornenak, T. (1997a) Diffusion and accounting: the case of ABC in Norway, *Management Accounting Research*, **8**(1), 3–17.

Bjornenak, T. (1997b) Conventional wisdom and accounting practices, *Management Accounting Research*, **8**(4) 367–82.

Blayney, P. and Yokoyama, I. (1991) Comparative analysis of Japanese and Australian cost accounting and management practices, Working paper, University of Sydney, Australia.

Boons, A., Roozen, R.A. and Weerd, R.J. de (1994) Kosteninformatie in de Nederlandse Industrie, in *Relevantie methoden en ontwikkelingen* (Rotterdam: Coopers and Lybrand).

Brealey, R.A. and Myers, S.C. (1999) *Principles of Corporate Finance*, McGraw-Hill, New York.

Bruggeman, W., Slagmulder, R. and Waeytens, D. (1996) Management accounting changes; the Belgian experience, in *Management Accounting: European Perspectives* (ed. A. Bhimani), Oxford, Oxford University Press, pp. 1–30.

Chartered Institute of Management Accountants (1996) *Management Accounting: Official Terminology*, CIMA.

Chenhall, R.H. and Langfield-Smith, K. (1998) Adoption and benefits of management accounting practices: an Australian perspective, *Management Accounting Research*, **9**(1), 1–20.

Chow, C.W. (1983) The effect of job standards, tightness and compensation schemes on performance: an exploration of linkages, *The Accounting Review*, October, 667–85.

Clarke, P.J. (1992) Management Accounting Practices and Techniques in Irish Manufacturing Firms, The 15th Annual Congress of the European Accounting Association, Madrid, Spain.

Clarke, P. (1995) Management accounting practices and techniques in Irish manufacturing companies, Working paper, Trinity College, Dublin.

Cooper, R. (1990a) Cost classifications in unit–based and activity–based manufacturing cost systems, *Journal of Cost Management*, Fall, 4–14.

Cooper, R. (1990b) Explicating the logic of ABC, *Management Accounting*, November, 58–60.

Cooper, R. and Kaplan, R.S. (1987) How cost accounting systematically distorts product costs, in *Accounting and Management: Field Study Perspectives* (eds W.J. Bruns and R.S. Kaplan), Harvard Business School Press, Ch. 8.

Cooper, R. and Kaplan, R.S. (1988) Measure costs right: make the right decisions, *Harvard Business Review*, September/October, 96–103.

Cooper, R. and Kaplan, R.S. (1991) *The Design of Cost Management Systems: Text, Cases and Readings*, Prentice-Hall.

Cooper, R. and Kaplan, R.S. (1992) Activity based systems: measuring the costs of resource usage, *Accounting Horizons*, September, 1–13.

Cornick, M., Cooper, W. and Wilson, S. (1988) How do companies analyze overhead?, *Management Accounting*, June, 41–3.

Cress, W. and Pettijohn, J. (1985) A survey of budget-related planning and control policies and procedures, *Journal of Accounting Education*, **3**, Fall, 61–78.

Cyert, R.M. and March, J.G. (1969) *A Behavioural Theory of the Firm*, Prentice-Hall.

Dardenne, P. (1998) Capital budgeting practices – Procedures and techniques by large companies in Belgium, paper presented at the 21st Annual Congress of the European Accounting Association, Antwerp, Belgium.

Drucker, P.F. (1964) Controls, control and management, in *Management Controls: New Directions in Basic Research* (eds C.P. Bonini, R. Jaedicke and H. Wagner), McGraw-Hill.

Drury, C. and Tayles, M. (1994) Product costing in UK manufacturing organisations, *The European Accounting Review*, **3**(3), 443–69.

Drury, C. and Tayles, M. (2000), *Cost system design and profitability analysis in UK companies*, Chartered Institute of Management Accountants.

Drury, C., Braund, S., Osborne, P. and Tayles, M. (1993) A survey of management accounting practices in UK manufacturing companies, ACCA Research Paper, Chartered Association of Certified Accountants.

Emmanuel, C., Otley, D. and Merchant, K. (1990) *Accounting for Management Control*, International Thomson Business Press.

Emore, J.R. and Ness, J.A. (1991) The slow pace of meaningful changes in cost systems, *Journal of Cost Management for the Manufacturing Industry*, Winter, 36–45.

Evans, H. and Ashworth, G. (1996) Survey conclusions: wakeup to the competition, *Management Accounting* (UK), May, 16–18.

Fitzgerald, L. and Moon, P. (1996) *Performnce Management in Service Industries*, Chartered Institute of Management Accountants.

Friedman, A.L. and Lyne, S.R. (1995) *Activity-based Techniques: The Real Life Consequences*, Chartered Institute of Management Accountants.

Green, F.B. and Amenkhienan, F.E. (1992) Accounting innovations: A cross sectional survey of manufacturing firms, *Journal of Cost Management for the Manufacturing Industry*, Spring 58–64.

Guilding, C., Lamminmaki, D. and Drury, C. (1998) Budgeting and standard costing practices in New Zealand and the United Kingdom, *The International Journal of Accounting*, **33**(5), 41–60.

Holzer, H.P. and Norreklit, H. (1991) Some thoughts on the cost accounting developments in the United States, *Management Accounting Research*, March, 3–13.

Hopper, T., Kirkham, L., Scapens, R.W. and Turley, S. (1992) Does financial accounting dominate management accounting – A research note, *Management Accounting Research*, **3**(4), 307–11.

Hopwood, A.G. (1978) Towards an organisational perspective for the study of accounting and information systems, *Accounting, Organisations and Society*, **3**(1), 3–14.

Horngren, C.T. (1967) Process costing in perspective: forget FIFO, *Accounting Review*, July.

Innes, J. and Mitchell, F. (1991) ABC: A survey of CIMA members, *Management Accounting*, October, 28–30.

Innes, J. and Mitchell, F. (1995a) A survey of activity-based costing in the UK's largest companies, *Management Accounting Research*, June, 137–54.

Innes, J. and Mitchell, F. (1995b) Activity-based costing, in *Issues in Management Accounting* (eds D. Ashton, T. Hopper and R.W. Scapens), Prentice-Hall, pp. 115–36.

Israelsen, P., Anderson, M., Rohde, C. and Sorensen, P.E. (1996) Management accounting in Denmark: theory and practice, in *Management Accounting: European Perspectives* (ed. A. Bhimani), Oxford, Oxford University Press, pp. 31–53.

Johnson, H.T. (1990) Professors, customers and value: bringing a global perspective to management accounting education, in *Performance Excellence in Manufacturing and Services Organizations* (ed. P. Turney), American Accounting Association.

Johnson, H.T. and Kaplan, R.R. (1987) *Relevance Lost: The Rise and Fall of Management Accounting*, Harvard Business School Press.

Joshi, P.L. (1998) An explanatory study of activity-based costing practices and benefits in large size manufacturing companies in India, *Accounting and Business Review*, **5**(1), 65–93.

Joye, M.P. and Blayney, P.J. (1990) Cost and management accounting practice in Australian manufacturing companies: survey results, Monograph No 7, University of Sydney.

Joye, M.P. and Blayney, P.J. (1991) Strategic management accounting survey, Monograph No. 8, University of Sydney.

Kaplan, R.S. (1990) Contribution margin analysis: no longer relevant/strategic cost management: the new paradigm, *Journal of Management Accounting Research* (USA), Fall, 2–15.

Kaplan, R.S. and Atkinson, A.A. (1998) *Advanced Management Accounting*, Prentice-Hall, Ch.3

Kaplan, R.S. and Cooper, R. (1998) *Cost and Effect: Using Integrated Systems to Drive Profitability and Performance*, Harvard Business School Press.

Lauderman, M. and Schaeberle, F.W. (1983) The cost accounting practices of firms using standard costs, *Cost and Management* (Canada), July/August, 21–5.

Lukka, K. and Granlund, M. (1996) Cost accounting in Finland: Current practice and trends of development, *The European Accounting Review*, **5**(1), 1–28.

Macintosh, N.B. (1985) *The Social Software of Accounting and Information Systems*, Wiley.

Merchant, K.A. (1989) *Rewarding Results: Motivating Profit Center Managers*, Harvard Business School Press.

Merchant, K.A. (1990) How challenging should profit budget targets be? *Management Accounting*, November, 46–8.

Merchant, K.A. (1998) *Modern Management Control Systems: Text and Cases*, Prentice-Hall, New Jersey.

Nicholls, B. (1992) ABC in the UK – a status report, *Management Accounting*, May, 22–3.

Otley, D.T. (1987) *Accounting Control and Organizational Behaviour*, Heinemann.

Ouchi, W.G. (1979) A conceptual framework for the design of organizational control mechanisms, *Management Science*, 833–48.

Pike, R.H. (1996) A longitudinal study of capital budgeting practices, *Journal of Business Finance and Accounting*, **23**(1), 79–92.

Saez-Torrecilla, A., Fernandez-Fernandez, A., Texeira-Quiros, J. and Vaquera-Mosquero, M. (1996) Management accounting in Spain: trends in thought and practice, in *Management Accounting: European Perspective 3* (ed. A. Bhimani), Oxford, Oxford University Press, pp. 180–90.

Scarborough, P.A., Nanni, A. and Sakurai, M. (1991) Japanese management accounting practices and the effects of assembly and process automation, *Management Accounting Research*, **2**, 27–46.

Scherrer, G. (1996) Management accounting: a German perspective, in *Management Accounting: European Perspectives* (ed. A. Bhimani), Oxford, Oxford University Press, pp. 100–22.

Schwarzbach, H.R. (1985) The impact of automation on accounting for direct costs, *Management Accounting* (USA), **67**(6), 45–50.

Shim, E. and Stagliano, A. (1997) A survey of US manufacturers on implementation of ABC, *Journal of Cost Management*, March/April, 39–41.

Simon, H.A. (1959) Theories of decision making in economics and behavioural science, *The American Economic Review*, June, 233–83.

Sizer, J. (1989) *An Insight into Management Accounting*, Penguin, Chs 11, 12.

Sizer, J. and Mottram, G. (1996) Successfully evaluating and controlling investments in advanced manufacturing technology, in *Management Accounting Handbook* (ed. C. Drury), Butterworth-Heinemann.

Slater, K. and Wootton, C. (1984) *Joint and By-product Costing in the UK*, Institute of Cost and Management Accounting.

Trahan, E.A. and Gitman, L.J. (1995) Bridging the theory–practice gap in corporate finance: A survey of chief finance officers, *The Quarterly Review of Economics and Finance*, **35**(1), Spring, 73–87.

Turney, P. (1993) *Common Cents: The ABC Performance Breakthrough*, Cost Technology, Hillsboro, Oregon, USA.

Virtanen, K., Malmi, T., Vaivio, J. and Kasanen, E. (1996) Drivers of management accounting in Finland, in *Management Accounting: European Perspectives* (ed. A. Bhimani), Oxford, Oxford University Press, pp. 218–41.

Young, P.H. (1985) *Cost Allocation: Methods, Principles, Applications*, Amsterdam: North Holland.

Appendices

Appendix A: Present value of £1

Years hence	1%	2%	4%	6%	8%	10%	12%	14%	15%	16%	18%	20%	22%	24%	25%	26%	28%	30%	35%
1	0.990	0.980	0.962	0.943	0.926	0.909	0.893	0.877	0.870	0.862	0.847	0.833	0.820	0.806	0.800	0.794	0.781	0.769	0.741
2	0.980	0.961	0.925	0.890	0.857	0.826	0.797	0.769	0.756	0.743	0.718	0.694	0.672	0.650	0.640	0.630	0.610	0.592	0.549
3	0.971	0.942	0.889	0.840	0.794	0.751	0.712	0.675	0.658	0.641	0.609	0.579	0.551	0.524	0.512	0.500	0.477	0.455	0.406
4	0.961	0.924	0.855	0.792	0.735	0.683	0.636	0.592	0.572	0.552	0.516	0.482	0.451	0.423	0.410	0.397	0.373	0.350	0.301
5	0.951	0.906	0.822	0.747	0.681	0.621	0.567	0.519	0.497	0.476	0.437	0.402	0.370	0.341	0.328	0.315	0.291	0.269	0.223
6	0.942	0.888	0.790	0.705	0.630	0.564	0.507	0.456	0.432	0.410	0.370	0.335	0.303	0.275	0.262	0.250	0.227	0.207	0.165
7	0.933	0.871	0.760	0.665	0.583	0.513	0.452	0.400	0.376	0.354	0.314	0.279	0.249	0.222	0.210	0.198	0.178	0.159	0.122
8	0.923	0.853	0.731	0.627	0.540	0.467	0.404	0.351	0.327	0.305	0.266	0.233	0.204	0.179	0.168	0.157	0.139	0.123	0.091
9	0.914	0.837	0.703	0.592	0.500	0.424	0.361	0.308	0.284	0.263	0.225	0.194	0.167	0.144	0.134	0.125	0.108	0.094	0.067
10	0.905	0.820	0.676	0.558	0.463	0.386	0.322	0.270	0.247	0.227	0.191	0.162	0.137	0.116	0.107	0.099	0.085	0.073	0.050
11	0.896	0.804	0.650	0.527	0.429	0.350	0.287	0.237	0.215	0.195	0.162	0.135	0.112	0.094	0.086	0.079	0.066	0.056	0.037
12	0.887	0.788	0.625	0.497	0.397	0.319	0.257	0.208	0.187	0.168	0.137	0.112	0.092	0.076	0.069	0.062	0.052	0.043	0.027
13	0.879	0.773	0.601	0.469	0.368	0.290	0.229	0.182	0.163	0.145	0.116	0.093	0.075	0.061	0.055	0.050	0.040	0.033	0.020
14	0.870	0.758	0.577	0.442	0.340	0.263	0.205	0.160	0.141	0.125	0.099	0.078	0.062	0.049	0.044	0.039	0.032	0.025	0.015
15	0.861	0.743	0.555	0.417	0.315	0.239	0.183	0.140	0.123	0.108	0.084	0.065	0.051	0.040	0.035	0.031	0.025	0.020	0.011
16	0.853	0.728	0.534	0.394	0.292	0.218	0.163	0.123	0.107	0.093	0.071	0.054	0.042	0.032	0.028	0.025	0.019	0.015	0.008
17	0.844	0.714	0.513	0.371	0.270	0.198	0.146	0.108	0.093	0.080	0.060	0.045	0.034	0.026	0.023	0.020	0.015	0.012	0.006
18	0.836	0.700	0.494	0.350	0.250	0.180	0.130	0.095	0.081	0.069	0.051	0.038	0.028	0.021	0.018	0.016	0.012	0.009	0.005
19	0.828	0.686	0.475	0.331	0.232	0.164	0.116	0.083	0.070	0.060	0.043	0.031	0.023	0.017	0.014	0.012	0.009	0.007	0.003
20	0.820	0.673	0.456	0.312	0.215	0.149	0.104	0.073	0.061	0.051	0.037	0.026	0.019	0.014	0.012	0.010	0.007	0.005	0.002

Appendix B: Present value of £1 received annually for n years

Years hence	1%	2%	4%	6%	8%	10%	12%	14%	15%	16%	18%	20%	22%	24%	25%	26%	28%	30%	35%	36%	37%
1	0.990	0.980	0.962	0.943	0.926	0.909	0.893	0.877	0.870	0.862	0.847	0.833	0.820	0.806	0.800	0.794	0.781	0.769	0.741	0.735	0.730
2	1.970	1.942	1.886	1.833	1.783	1.736	1.690	1.647	1.626	1.605	1.566	1.528	1.492	1.457	1.440	1.424	1.392	1.361	1.289	1.276	1.263
3	2.941	2.884	2.775	2.673	2.577	2.487	2.402	2.322	2.283	2.246	2.174	2.106	2.042	1.981	1.952	1.923	1.868	1.816	1.696	1.673	1.652
4	3.902	3.808	3.630	3.465	3.312	3.170	3.037	2.914	2.855	2.798	2.690	2.589	2.494	2.404	2.362	2.320	2.241	2.166	1.997	1.966	1.935
5	4.853	4.713	4.452	4.212	3.993	3.791	3.605	3.433	3.352	3.274	3.127	2.991	2.864	2.745	2.689	2.635	2.532	2.436	2.220	2.181	2.143
6	5.795	5.601	5.242	4.917	4.623	4.355	4.111	3.889	3.784	3.685	3.498	3.326	3.167	3.020	2.951	2.885	2.759	2.643	2.385	2.339	2.294
7	6.728	6.472	6.002	5.582	5.206	4.868	4.564	4.288	4.160	4.039	3.812	3.605	3.416	3.242	3.161	3.083	2.937	2.802	2.508	2.455	2.404
8	7.652	7.325	6.733	6.210	5.747	5.335	4.968	4.639	4.487	4.344	4.078	3.837	3.619	3.421	3.329	3.241	3.076	2.925	2.598	2.540	2.485
9	8.556	8.162	7.435	6.802	6.247	5.759	5.328	4.946	4.772	4.607	4.303	4.031	3.786	3.566	3.463	3.366	3.184	3.019	2.665	2.603	2.544
10	9.471	8.983	8.111	7.360	6.710	6.145	5.650	5.216	5.019	4.833	4.494	4.192	3.923	3.682	3.571	3.465	3.269	3.092	2.715	2.649	2.587
11	10.368	9.787	8.760	7.887	7.139	6.495	5.937	5.453	5.234	5.029	4.656	4.327	4.035	3.776	3.656	3.544	3.335	3.147	2.752	2.683	2.618
12	11.255	10.575	9.385	8.384	7.536	6.814	6.194	5.660	5.421	5.197	4.793	4.439	4.127	3.851	3.725	3.606	3.387	3.190	2.779	2.708	2.641
13	12.134	11.343	9.986	8.853	7.904	7.103	6.424	5.842	5.583	5.342	4.910	4.533	4.203	3.912	3.780	3.656	3.427	3.223	2.799	2.727	2.658
14	13.004	12.106	10.563	9.295	8.244	7.367	6.628	6.002	5.724	5.468	5.008	4.611	4.265	3.962	3.824	3.695	3.459	3.249	2.814	2.740	2.670
15	13.865	12.849	11.118	9.712	8.559	7.606	6.811	6.142	5.847	5.575	5.092	4.675	4.315	4.001	3.859	3.726	3.483	3.268	2.825	2.750	2.679
16	14.718	13.578	11.652	10.106	8.851	7.824	6.974	6.265	5.954	5.669	5.162	4.730	4.357	4.033	3.887	3.751	3.503	3.283	2.834	2.757	2.685
17	15.562	14.292	12.166	10.477	9.122	8.022	7.120	6.373	6.047	5.749	5.222	4.775	4.391	4.059	3.910	3.771	3.518	3.295	2.840	2.763	2.690
18	16.398	14.992	12.659	10.828	9.372	8.201	7.250	6.467	6.128	5.818	5.273	4.812	4.419	4.080	3.928	3.786	3.529	3.304	2.844	2.767	2.693
19	17.226	15.678	13.134	11.158	9.604	8.365	7.366	6.550	6.198	5.877	5.316	4.844	4.442	4.097	3.942	3.799	3.539	3.311	2.848	2.770	2.696
20	18.046	16.351	13.590	11.470	9.818	8.514	7.469	6.623	6.259	5.929	5.353	4.870	4.460	4.110	3.954	3.808	3.546	3.316	2.850	2.772	2.698

Index

....